KNOX COUNTY SECTIONAL CHAMPIONS
—1940-41—

The 1940–41 Fighting Dutchman of Freelandville smilingly pose for their team photo with Coach Finke and Manager Mooney. If their faces show pleasure and confidence, it is probably because they have just become giant killers. They have beaten mighty Vincennes Lincoln High (from the big county seat which always wins) in the Sectional. Then they've gone on to win the Sectional tournament, to the screaming delight of the people in their little southern Indiana town, most of whom attended the game. And though they lost in the Regional, it was to the eventual state champs.

Their faces are preserved together here as a part of Indiana's magnificent and moving high school basketball team heritage. They sit frozen in time, on the brink of manhood and World War II. What destiny awaits them as individuals? We do not know. For a moment they are one, united in the triumph they always believed they might achieve, the result of hard practice and good luck. In this one defining moment, these young men are the best of all we have to offer in the Hoosier state.

Hoosiers All

Indiana High School Basketball
Team Names
Glory Seasons
Boys and Girls
Large and Small

Second Edition

Emerson Houck

Hawthorne Publishing
Carmel, Indiana

A majority of photographs in this book are from the personal collection of Emerson Houck, photographed by him on a particular site or at the Basketball Hall of Fame in New Castle, Indiana, from their collection and used with written permission. Emerson Houck's personal photos are copyrighted by the author. Hall of Fame inductees are also copyrighted by Indiana Basketball Hall of Fame and are used with permission. Team pins by Dr. James Mast, DDS, from the Hall of Fame and available through the Indiana Basketball History Society Web site, are used with Dr. Mast's permission.

Some historical photos were available using GFDL conventions through Massive Multiauthor Collaboration sites. Most of the many photos of old schools are from Bob Adams' Indiana BATA Basketball CD, also available from the Indiana Basketball History Society Web site. They are used with Adams' generous permission and were invaluable. These photos are so numerous they were not individually identified, but the book would not have been possible without them.

A special thanks to *The Herald Bulletin,* Anderson, Indiana, Scott Underwood, Editor, and for photographer John Cleary's photo of the Delaware Indian dancing for students and for Richard Sitler's photo of the Indian Chief and Maiden in the Wigwam.

A special thanks to Hugh Schaefer for providing the Freelandville Fighting Dutchmen photo for the frontispiece.

The Golden Bear logos are owned and copyrighted property of Shelbyville Central Schools and are used with the written permission of SCS.

Color section photo of Lapel vs. Frankton game is used with permission of Lapel High School.

The jump-shot photo on the cover of Jordan Simmons from Princeton High School during the 3A state championship game of 2009 is courtesy of IHSAA and Visual Sports Network. Historic basketball photo by author.

Other books by the author: Go Huskies, Beat Felix the Cat
ISBN 0-9745335-0-5 hardbound ($35)   0-9745335-1-3 softbound ($25)

Published in the United States by
Hawthorne Publishing
15601 Oak Road
Carmel, Indiana 46033
317-867-5183
www.hawthornepub.com

DEDICATION

I dedicate this book to four men, friends, sportsmen, gentlemen, whose lives have all enriched mine as well as the lives of everyone who knew them:

John DeVoe, Indianapolis Park School 1952, Princeton University 1956

Dave Gavitt, Peterborough (NH) High School 1955, Dartmouth College 1959

Bob Jewell, Indianapolis Crispus Attucks High School 1951, Indiana Central College 1955

Tom Wallace, Muncie Burris High School 1948, Ball State University 1955

And to my own special Panthers, *Liz, Joe, and Doug*

And to my wife, *Jane, without whose love and support nothing of value would be possible.*

TABLE OF CONTENTS

Acknowledgments viii

Introduction x

Chapter 1   What's in a Name? 1

Chapter 2   *Hoosiers* the Movie 8

Chapter 3   The Beginning of It All 13

Chapter 4   The Cradle of Champions................................ 18

Chapter 5   Those Wonderful Names................................ 32

Chapter 6   More Fun with Names.................................... 47

Chapter 7   Even More Fun 61

Chapter 8   The Unusual 74

Chapter 9   Hoosier Resources.. 83

Chaper 10   Indiana in the Industrial Age 95

Chapter 11   American History 101 107

Chapter 12   A Turning Point... 123

Chapter 13   Native Americans and Indiana 134

Chapter 14   Warriors... 144

Chapter 15   More Native Americans 151

Chapter 16   Native Americans in Our Now-Closed Schools..................... 163

Chapter 17   The Old Country.. 176

Chapter 18   Faraway Places 190

Chapter 19   Small Schools, Memorable Names 210

Chapter 20   Our Agricultural Heritage............................ 224

Chapter 21   Our Current and Most Popular Animals........235

Chapter 22   Bulldogs, Wildcats, and Cougars 250

Chapter 23   More Four-Legged Friends............................ 263

Chapter 24   Evansville Central 271

Chapter 25   How 'bout Them Dogs?................................ 277

Chapter 26   The Top TwoAnimals in Our Closed Schools...................... 284

Chapter 27   The Next Two Most Popular Animals in Closed Schools ...294

Chapter 28   Horses, Bears, and More 303

Chapter 29   The Birds 313

Chapter 30   Away They Flew... 328

Chapter 31   Eels . . . and Stingers... 339

Chapter 32   Trojans and Royalty... 349

Chapter 33   From Patriots to Saints.. 361

Chapter 34   We Begin with a Rebel Yell 373

Chapter 35   Pirates, Dragons.. 383

Chapter 36   Interesting Lost Names 397

Chapter 37   Aces and Devils.. 407

Chapter 38   Trojans, Pirates and 421

Chapter 39   Other Often Quirky Names.. 434

Chapter 40   The Large and the Small 447

Appendix   463

Index   476

Second Edition: What We Learned 493

ACKNOWLEDGMENTS

This compendium could not have been written without the assistance of many individuals and organizations. We extend them our thanks:

Newspaper or magazine sources and their authors whose articles are quoted in the book:

The Odon Journal for portions of 3 columns published March 6, 13, and 20, 1959.

Donna Fritz for the article on the Freetown Spartans in *The Jackson County Banner.*

The Wabash College blog "Hoops" by Bill Boone for information on Ladoga, Alamo, and Charlie Bowerman.

Max Jones, editor of *The Terre Haute Star,* for permission to use Mike Lundsford's article on preconsolidation team names.

Hugh Schaefer, author, and Harley Sheets, publisher, for the article on Freelandville in the newsletter "Box Score."

The Warsaw Times Union for Phil Smith's articles on the history of basketball in Kosciusko County.

The Indianapolis Star, Northern Bureau, for permission to use Gene Conrad's article from *The Noblesville Ledger* entitled "The Ghosts of Walnut Grove and JC are still alive," Wednesday, February 14, 1990.

Terry Householder, publisher of *The News Sun,* Kendallville, Indiana, for permission to use Bob Gagen's article on the early days of Kendallville basketball.

Bill May, whose classic book *Tourney Time* is invaluable to any researcher of Hoosier basketball history.

The Russiaville Historical Society for that organization's permission to use the painting of the school by Mary Lou Ellis, with special thanks to Marsha Berry for expediting the permission.

Bob Whelan, founder of the Montgomery County Basketball Hall of Fame, for information on the basketball history of that county.

Chris Matthews and Becky Beavers of the Indiana Basketball Hall of Fame in New Castle for their help and support throughout this project.

Tim Nonte for valuable information and help with the project.

We also acknowledge the many individual, school, and town Web sites who provided stories and facts, especially these:

John Dedman's Web site, www.wowway.com for the comprehensive facts on Winslow High School.

The Vincennes Lincoln High School Web site and Athletic Director Dave Hill, (including information from Dr. Bill Stedman's book on the Vincennes Alices). The Hillsboro High School website.

Thanks to these individuals, too:

Herb Schwomeyer whose books *Hoosier Hysteria* and *Hoosier Hersteria* are replete with historical data.

The late Tom Wallace for the story on Burris and other information and John Hollett for insights into the 1955 Shortridge season.

IHSAA Commissioners Blake Ress (retired) and Bobby Cox and that organization for much information on high school team names, past and present, as well as state tournament facts.

Evansville Central Athletic Director Paul Neidig for his assistance. Also Clarence Doninger for his input on the Central story and Ira Harris for help with the early history of that school. I'm grateful to Kim Owens at Shelbyville High for her assistance with the Golden Bears.

Everyone associated with the Blue Jeans Williams Museum.

Walnut Grove High School alumnae Betty Culp, Phoebe Averitt, and Mary Lou Waltz for providing pictures and memories of their school and county.

Dane Starbuck and the Randolph Central website.

Arthur and Nancy Baxter, the general editors and publishers of this book for their unwavering support and untiring energy as well as their consummate professionalism and dedication to getting this book out to the public.

Appreciation is also expressed to the many schools who have shared their logos for the compendium. The schools and towns listed below were most helpful with the information contained on their Web sites: Logansport, NE DuBois, Brownstown Central, Wabash, Danville, Alexandria, Kewanna, Morocco Alumni, Versailles, Hillsboro, Randolph Central, Milltown, Evansville Central, Vincennes Lincoln, Odon, Bryant, Henryville, Greens Fork, Mauckport, Porter County Conference, Rockport, and Southwestern HS (Hanover).

The many contributions of readers Niles Layman, Bill Boone, John Edgerly, Dan Carpenter, Gregg Nowling, Steve Nontell, Tom Plimpton, Dean Monroe, Tom Speaker, Roleen Pickard, Gary Armbruster, Ed Baker, Captain Cliff Pappe, Dane Starbuck, Bob Jones and others are all greatly appreciated.

INTRODUCTION: Second Edition

First, thanks to all who bought and enjoyed Hoosiers All *in numbers sufficient to warrant a second edition. This has allowed us to correct some errors that existed in the previous edition, improve some of its graphics, and add several pages which we have called, "What We Learned." Much of that has come from readers who have provided us with new information, but some has come from our own research. With some exceptions, we have not been able to update the original pages to include titles and won-lost records of existing schools. That has been done in "What We Learned."*

In my first book *Go Huskies, Beat Felix the Cat* I attempted to bring together the unique team names chosen by high schools all over the country. In the process I hoped to gain some insight into who we are as Americans based on these choices for our sports teams.

I have long thought the names we pick for our high school teams, not only here in Indiana but pretty much everywhere, tell us a lot about who we are as a people. We do not pick them lightly. We pick them because they represent something we admire or perhaps something we aspire to be. Or maybe because of what they say about the very reason our town exists where it does. At times they are clever or funny; we may wish to share our sense of humor with others through the team identity.

Whatever the reason, those names both in the past and in the present become a rallying point for a school, a community, or an entire area, and I have chosen to center this history of Indiana basketball around them. The stories of great teams, not-to-be-forgotten coaches, "that one incredible year of the big win," are told over and over again in the local town cafe or at community service club meetings. The town team was and is an icon.

The idea of putting Indiana teams, with their names, logos, and outstanding seasons, into a book came from Roger Dickinson of the Indiana Basketball Hall of Fame. It would do what my earlier effort had attempted to do for the whole country, but with a focus on Indiana schools in more depth and with particular emphasis on basketball success stories. I thought that was a great idea and this book is meant to do just that. Some of the chapters have appeared as articles in the Hall of Fame's magazine *Indiana Basketball History.*

We now have 400-plus high schools in Indiana, with 800 more that have been lost to consolidation, the ravages of time, or shifting demographics. (See Roger Dickinson's article "Small and Mighty Patriots" in the 2007 winter issue of *Indiana Basketball History.*) I've tried to cover most of these in this book; to cover all would be a near impossibility. There's also the reality that some schools seem never to have selected a team name or mascot anyway.

In addition to documenting this general chapter of history in Indiana, I am pleased to save the stories of particular schools that have closed, especially those in

Indiana towns that had only one high school. The reasons for the closings may have been valid, but it was sad nonetheless for the people who had centered so much of their interest and social lives around those very schools that were suddenly gone. Along with the schools went the team names, so no longer were there any Sprudels in West Baden Springs, or Salts in Epsom, or Peppers in Pimento. The Railroaders are gone from Monon, and the Plowboys, Haymakers, and Shockers are no more. So, saving their stories struck me as a useful thing to do.

Over the years my wife and I have traveled throughout the state, into every county, enjoying the Hoosier countryside and seeking team stories. We have been met with smiles and warmth everywhere and particularly in the smaller towns. We've experienced the townspeople's pride for the high school that once was part of their lives. Often we were regaled with tales of that one Sectional championship. I have included the stories of those "miracle seasons" wherever possible, but every one of them is significant in its own way and should be preserved.

Much work has already gone forward to record these great tournament moments, done by other passionate basketball aficionados in the state. I stand on the shoulders of many fine chroniclers of Indiana basketball history, especially Herb Schowmeyer, whose books are scholarly and inspiring. Bob Adams is also one of these devoted record-seekers and record-keepers. He has identified 172 schools who had one glorious moment winning a Sectional. Adams' BATA Publishing Company CD's extensive collection, along with the records featured on the Indiana Basketball History Society's Web site, form the basis for much of the photographic record of school buildings in this book. During this time I have also personally been in several hundred high schools. I was impressed by the dedication of those to whom we as parents have entrusted the education of our young people. I have also been gratified by the quality of those very students who are not only better educated than they are sometimes given credit for, but are also very pleasant people, eager to help and to please.

I regret that I do not have more information on the names chosen for our girls teams, which often bear the same name as the boys teams. This is true of my own high school in Illinois. Many schools add just Lady to the team name. In order to differentiate between boys and girls teams, unless I know the specific girls team names like the Columbus East Olympians and Olympi-Annes or the Bellmont Braves and Squaws, I have fallen back on using Lady before the team name for clarity.

The reader will note that in this book there are many logos, many tigers, eagles, and bulldogs, often looking like each other and sometimes repeated. Each of these is a school's special logo and deserving of the respect and affection given it by that school.

It's inevitable that there may be some errors in these tens of thousands of pieces of data. If so, please accept my apologies. Finally, I wish to enlist the reader in helping me correct any factual inaccuracies. Please contact me at emhouck@aol.com with any new information you have that should be shared with the Hall of Fame. GO HOOSIERS!

New Richmond Girls 1917

Alamo team of 1930

Chapter 1

What's in a Name?
A Hoosier by Any Other Name. . .
Is Still a Hoosier

As we begin our story, let's focus for a moment on the one word that unites as all. We are all Hoosiers. That no one can deny. What that word means, though, is open to argument, interpretation, and almost endless discussion.

So, what exactly is a Hoosier? No one seems to know precisely, but almost everyone in Indiana is proud to be one. And unless you were born here, you'd better be prepared to live here for at least 30 years, as I have, before the locals will accept you as a Hoosier and then, perhaps, only grudgingly.

Several theories do exist as to the origination of the term Hoosiers. Everyone does agree that it preceded the movie of the same name by several years. Everyone, that is, except perhaps some folks in Hollywood who believe they invented everything from night baseball to raisin bran muffins. Anyway, here are some of the theories, with thanks in part to columnist Dave Barry, whose list is generally based on previous theories:

Hoosier was the name of a contractor who worked on the Ohio River in the early 19th century.

Hoosier is a word meaning "highlander" or "hill-dweller."

Hoosier is a word referring to anything large of its kind.

Hoosier comes from when somebody would knock on the cabin door, and in Indiana people would say, "Who's there?"

Hoosier comes from that same time when Indiana people would stand on the riverbank and shout to people on boats, "Who is ya?"

Hoosier comes from when Indiana families would hold big reunions, and the mothers, referring to the children, would ask each other, "Who's yours?"

Hoosier comes from the aftermath of knife fights in Indiana taverns, when somebody would pick up a lump of flesh and say, "Whose ear?"

Hoosier may be an interpretation of a French word for "outsider."

More recently, and certainly in a more scholarly vein, Hanover College professor Jonathan Smith has discovered 2 previously unnoticed references to the word *Hoosiers* in newspapers published way back in 1831. (That was, by the way, 60 years before James Naismith—born in Canada, for heaven's sake—hung his peach baskets and thus began the glorious game of basketball in Springfield, Massachusetts.)

From his readings, Dr. Smith concludes that Hoosiers was not a pejorative in any sense, but rather referred to industrious people who worked to improve our state's early economy. Hoosiers, he states, "were boatmen who made their living on Indiana's canals and rivers…"

It will clearly be left to greater historical scholars than I to determine which of these, or some other theory, is the correct one. In a sense it really doesn't matter. We who live in Indiana are Hoosiers, the Indiana University teams are Hoosiers, and we're rightfully happy with that.

I do imagine that when the history of our great state is finally written we will realize that Hoosiers are a very special breed. Our love for each other and the state of Indiana is only matched by the love of the thump-thump-thump of a round leather ball bouncing on a hardwood floor and that special sound that a perfect jump shot makes as it swishes through the cords hung from an iron rim just 10 feet above the floor…or the ground, or the concrete, or the grass, or the asphalt.

By the way, there is only one high school in Indiana, surprisingly, with Hoosiers in their nickname. That is the Indiana School for the Deaf, in Indianapolis. Once the Orioles they are now proudly the Deaf Hoosiers.

Let us begin our discussion of big and little teams, with all that implies, by talking about a small team—the Hoosiers at ISD, selected because of their team name. Jake McCaskey coached them for 30 years. Jake's Hall of Fame citation tell a lot about the man and the school to which he devoted so much of his life.

Deaf Hoosiers mascot

Jake McCaskey
30 years at Indiana School for the Deaf Began the 'Mr. Athletics' of the Indiana School for the Deaf … coached there 1931 to 1961 with a 229-391 record … his team won national championships for schools for the deaf in 1935 and '40 … started football, baseball and track programs at ISD, serving 38 years as athletic director … first winner of Joe Boland Award for his contribution to youth … a baseball star in high school, he got a late start in basketball … began playing the sport after graduating from Indianapolis Tech. He played on Butler's national championship team in '29, played on 3 Southside Turners teams that won Indiana-Kentucky AAU championships.

The Indiana School for the Deaf's mascot is perhaps the most obvious of any in the state.

Most are more subtle. Mascots and team names generally started to emerge in this country in the 2nd and 3rd decade of the 20th century. Early on high school teams tended to be called after either a coach's name or a name related in some way to the town. Such names as "Robertson's Five" or the "Elm City Eleven" preceded the selections we are currently used to seeing. Mascots, as we know them, were few and far between. But who had the 1st modern style mascot in Indiana? Interestingly, two schools who both selected Felix the Cat as their mascot each claim to be 1st. Here are their stories, later we will learn of challenges to their claim of longevity from other schools including Vincennes Lincoln, Crawfordsville, LaPorte, and Hillsboro.

My wife attended Indianapolis Shortridge, once a highly respected college preparatory school, one of the country's finest. It has more recently been a middle school but is scheduled to return to high school status in the near future. Most schools today have both a team name and a mascot. Shortridge's development of both is illustrative of how the process often happens. It is a fun story to tell.

The concept of a mascot has been with us for centuries and refers to the selection of "a person, animal, or object adopted by a group as a symbolic figure especially to bring them good luck," says my Webster's *New Collegiate Dictionary*. According to Laura Gaus' comprehensive work, *Shortridge High School 1864–1981*, the mascot came 1st at the distinguished Indianapolis school. It happened in February of 1925, when the blue-and-white-clad Shortridge basketball team was about to play a favored Manual High team, decked out in their bright red and white uniforms.

Just before the 2nd half tip-off, with Manual in the lead, a tiny red-dyed, or perhaps red-sweatered, dog was let loose on the floor by a Manual booster. Darting out "he pitched camp nowhere other than in the large circle in the middle of the gym," to the great delight of the many Manual fans in the boisterous crowd. Rising to the occasion, a Shortridge girl raced out onto the floor with a cat in her arms that she placed alongside the dog, who found his new companion worthy of but a sniff or two before he up and wandered off the court.

The inspired Shortridge team came back to win the game, and the cat, clearly having brought the team good luck, was enthusiastically adopted as the team mascot.

A former coach and math teacher, E. Carl Watson, wrote a poem that began, with apologies to Eugene Field,

The Manual dog and the Shortridge cat
Side by side in the circle sat,

And, at a classical-based school replete with Latin scholars, the cat was promptly named Felix. Shortridge had her mascot.

The Shortridge basketball teams had been nicknamed the Battling Burtonians for their coach, but with his retirement in 1928, a new, more permanent name was desired, one for all sports and all time, and the school paper held a contest to determine what it should be. Bluebirds, Blue Jays, and Blue Aces were among the contenders, but it was the suggestion of David Burns, a student destined to become a prominent Indianapolis architect, that was to win out. He had remembered a group of French soldiers who had stayed at the Burns' home while on an American fund-raising trip during World War I. They had belonged to a regiment known as the Blue Devils, and thus it was that the Shortridge High School Blue Devils were born. Blue Devils and Felix the Cat, nickname and mascot for an excellent school whose alumni have excelled in all walks of life.

There was also a song written by Irving Berlin about a special force of intrepid French soldiers called the Chausseuers Alpins, who wore blue berets and capes. In the song Berlin described them as the Blue Devils of France, and this was the source of Duke University's famous nickname. It was probably representatives of the same group who had stayed in the Burns home.

An early version of the Shortridge Blue Devil and a more recent one, along with Felix

If Dr. Gaus is correct, the selection of Felix the Cat by Shortridge occurred in February, 1925, just after the upset of Indianapolis Manual. Interestingly, Logansport High School also came up with Felix as their own mascot at very nearly the same time. Here is the story as they tell it on their Web site:

> *Felix the Cat became the official mascot of Logansport High School in 1926 during the cat's heyday years of popularity as a comic strip and comic book character. Logansport High School's affiliation with Felix began when*

LHS basketball coach Clifford Wells purchased a stuffed Felix doll for team captain Curly Hupp.

During halftime of a game in the 1925-26 season, Hupp, searching for a way to inspire his team to victory, took the Felix doll from his locker and placed it on the edge of the playing floor during second half warm-ups. Logansport came from behind and defeated their opponent and Felix became the permanent symbol of LHS athletics. He is believed to be the first high school mascot in the state of Indiana.

I don't know if that last sentence is accurate or not. Contrary to what some may believe, I was not there at the time. Curiously enough, the two apparently oldest mascots in our state were both Felix the Cat!

Logansport, of course, was named for Captain John Logan, whom some historians have referred to as a "White Indian." He was the "brother" of both Tecumseh and the Prophet, two names of great prominence in Indiana history. Logansport High School teams are known as the Berries. The school is located on Berry Lane and their basketball games are played in the Berry Bowl.

To truly begin to understand the heritage of Indiana high school basketball, an excellent place to start is New Castle. Two of Indiana's treasures are right there, the world's largest and finest high school fieldhouse and the nation's finest state hall of fame in any sport. They are within a few hundred yards of each other and they are both well worth a visit. The Fieldhouse seats 9,314 fans with no obstructed views and has been known to accommodate over 10,000. *USA Today* has described it as "the Cathedral of high school basketball."

Fans enter at the top, where there is a running track that is used by the entire community. They can see the floor where such Hoosier stars as Kent Benson and Steve Alford played and will remember the last regular season game at the old gym between Ray Pavy and Kokomo's Jimmy Rayl. Playing in what is known as the "Church Street Shootout," Rayl scored 49 points, Pavy 51 in New Castle's victory. Championship banners fill most of the north side along with a wall of New Castle Trojan sports heroes. The south end is devoted to the logos of the storied members of the North Central Conference. Games in this setting are truly memorable experiences.

The Hall of Fame itself is another wonderful experience for any basketball fan. It is replete with memorabilia, the exhibits are constantly changing, and who could not enjoy

Trojan logo

seeing Martinsville's John Wooden giving his pre game talk, or Oscar Robertson in his Crispus Attucks Tigers uniform, or being challenged by "the final shot." New Castle, indeed, is an Indiana treasure.

The New Castle Fieldhouse

The Indiana Basketball Hall of Fame

Roger Dickinson, retired executive director of the Indiana Basketball Hall of Fame in New Castle, has his own mascot/team name story to tell:

"I graduated from Frankton High School and the nickname of the school used to be Franks. I do not know the history but the mascot was later changed to Eagles. Perhaps it was because Frankfort was the Hot Dogs and they wanted to separate themselves from another school with a similar first name. It might have been because it would have been difficult to build around the Franks theme versus the big strong Eagle. It might have been because some called them hot dogs and Frankfort was the more well know, basketball powerhouse."

There may also be another reason, a patriotic one. Eagles, of course, are our national bird, a symbol in which all Americans take great pride. The Franks were a Germanic tribe, and there were periods in the 20th century when Germanic tribes were not favorites of many Americans. Whatever the reason, those who go to the Hall of Fame and visit its lower level will see among the many other nostalgic and historic displays an old-fashioned scoreboard hung on the wall. A look at the score reveals a close win for Frankton over their arch rivals, the Lapel Bulldogs. However, after Lapel won the Class A Boys Basketball State Championship in 2005, Roger arrived at the Hall one morning to find the score reversed. He allowed it to stand, at least for a while!

Lapel Bulldogs   *Frankton Eagles*

View of main floor from mezzanine at Indiana Basketball Hall of Fame in New Castle.

Chapter 2

Hoosiers the Movie:
Some Real History

Over the years there have been well over 1,000 high schools in Indiana. In fact, Dr. James Mast of Terre Haute has identified over 1,200 and has created authentic pins for each. In the 1938 state tournament 787 schools were entered in a single-class championship, the largest entry list of any year. As recently as 1955, 752 high schools took the court in the 1st round of that year's quest for the title.

Many of these schools have been lost to consolidation, so that now, including new schools that have been added to the field, there are just over 400 teams entered in what has become a 4-class tournament. Most of the schools lost to consolidation were tiny, serving only the town that bore their name and the surrounding farms, graduating classes numbering sometimes in the single digits. Basketball was the perfect sport for these small schools, requiring only 5 players and a gym. Hoops hung on the sides of barns that covered, and still do, the Indiana countryside.

The names chosen by these communities to honor their school, its teams and, in fact, the entire town, are marvelous indicators of what was important to the people who lived there, what amused them, or even, perhaps, what their dreams were. Many of these names would have been lost were it not for the scholarly work of the Indiana High School Association, which preserved them for posterity and kindly shared them with me, and for men with an interest in the history of our state such as James Mast, Bob Adams, and all the others working for the preservation of the sport's heritge.

The wonderful movie *Hoosiers,* starring the incomparable Gene Hackman, is one of the best sports movies ever produced. Certainly my favorite. It caught the flavor of small town "Hoosier Hysteria." Superficially it was the story of Milan, the small railroading community in Ripley County, coached by Marvin Wood. In 1954 the Milan Indians actually did defeat the highly favored Muncie Central Bearcats on a last-second jump shot by Bobby Plump—after he held the ball for a heart stopping seeming eternity of time—before a capacity crowd of some 15,000 fans at the Butler Fieldhouse, since renamed in honor of longtime Butler University Bulldog coach, Paul D. "Tony" Hinkle, to win the state championship with a 28-2 record.

Bobby Plump

Scored unprecedented triple in 1954…a state championship, the Trester Award, and Mr. Basketball…2-time All-Stater…led tiny Milan to Final 4 as junior…year later hit winning shot to beat Muncie Central and forever cast Milan as a symbol of hope for small schools everywhere…4-year letterwinner at Butler…MVP in junior and senior yrs … all-conference…set Butler single-game and career scoring records… one of NCAA's all-time best free throw shooters.

The Milan Indians

Playing in Pierceville

Butler (now Hinkle) Fieldhouse

9

The Hickory High School game against South Bend Central is a re-creation of that real-life story with poetic license. As the Hickory team is preparing to take the floor for that championship game, one of the players in the locker room far beneath the court says, "Let's win this for all the small schools that never had a chance to be here." He could have meant a school like tiny New Ross, the Blue Jays, who went 21-1 in the regular season, only to be upset in the Sectionals in 1959. The Blue Jays were led by a 6′2″ sharpshooting guard, Russell Nichols, who played at Wabash College and later became the president of Hanover College. That 1959 season began an impressive 5 year run for New Ross, during which they won 109 games while losing only 13! The Blue Jays won 67 games and lost only 9 for Coach Glen Harper, winning 4 Sectional crowns, and going to the Sweet Sixteen in 1956, finishing 26-1. Keith Greve's 1961 team also won a Regional crown.

1959	21-02	Spear, Tom
1960	21-03	Greve, Keith
1961	25-02	Greve, Keith
1962	21-04	Greve, Keith
1963	21-02	Clack, Jim

5-year Blue Jay record with coaches

New Ross High School

Or Marvin Cave who led his French Lick Red Devils, coached successfully, and later rose to be a vice president of Eli Lilly and Company.

Marvin Cave

Captained French Lick to 2 consecutive 20-win seasons in '43 and '44, 3 decades before Larry Bird...twice suffered narrow regional losses (35-32 and 38-33) to powerful Jeffersonville teams... scored 15 pts and made Bill Fox's all-tourney team in regional appearance as senior...in a college career fractured by military service, played season as starting guard on 16-4 ISU team in '44, led Berea College in scoring 1 year, then played for 2 years for Tony Hinkle at Butler. In his first year of coaching in 1949, Cave guided Worthington to a 19-6 record and the school's first sectional crown. Following 3 years at Decatur Central, he took a demanding Frankfort job and led the Hotdogs to 3 sectional titles in 4 years. In 1954, beat both Milan and Muncie Central...

French Lick High School

The insight we gain from these and other similar stories is that basketball, and indeed all sports, are an important part of the educational process. Leadership is often a by-product of athletic endeavor, and lessons learned on the practice court as well as during tension-filled moments of important games are of lifelong value.

Just as the story *Hoosiers* tells can stand for all of those lost small schools, so the Knightstown gym can become emblematic of all of the local basketball palaces and the role they played in bringing communities together. Knightstown is a short drive east of Indianapolis on the old National Road, US 40. It is well worth the trip. Just north of the downtown stores and antique malls is the beautifully restored Knightstown Academy that once housed all of the grades from kindergarten through high school for the community. The old gym was on the top floor and had to be abandoned when the pounding shoes of many years of basketball players of all ages threatened to weaken the structure of the entire building to the point of danger to its occupants.

Knightstown Academy and 2 of the author's grandsons at the "New" or "Hoosiers" gym

Thus the "new" gym was built in 1922, with the current lobby added in 1935. This gym was marvelously restored for the movie *Hoosiers,* and all of the scenes involving Hickory High School's home basketball games and practices were filmed there. The Knightstown Falcons—once also known by the delightful team name "Knightengales" as well—no longer play there, the academy having been replaced by a modern scholastic and athletic plant and a new nickname, the Panthers.

But the memories remain. The memories are strong. As you walk through the new gym, you can hear the cheers, feel the pulse of the community, share in the excitement of the hundreds of games played there to packed houses and enthusiastic fans. On the wall is a large photo of "Coach" Hackman and the Hickory Huskers, Indiana state champions, 1952. There are trophies in the trophy case and there is a ticket booth in the corner. You can almost smell the popcorn, hear the pep band tuning up. You come within a whisper of believing it really happened.

The Knightstown Panther.

New Ross Blue Jay logo.

The reconstructed gym used in the movie Hoosiers

Chapter 3

The Beginning of It All:
Naismith Ignites a Fire

The first scheduled interscholastic basketball game played in Indiana took place on March 16, 1894, at the Crawfordsville YMCA between the home team and Lafayette. Crawfordsville won. The 1st intercollegiate game in the state also took place at the same YMCA with Wabash College defeating Purdue 23-18.

There were several unofficial Indiana state championships claimed in the early days of the 20th century, including Indianapolis Shortridge in 1905, which also defeated the purported champions of Illinois and Iowa. From Bob Whelan:

Where it all started: The Crawfordsville YMCA

> *Crawfordsville finished the 1909 basketball season with a 17 and 1 record. The ONLY game they lost was to the C'ville YMCA team. In addition to Rockville they defeated the following high school teams: Lebanon (2 times), Breaks, Darlington, New Richmond, Lafayette (2 times), Rochester (2 times), West Lafayette, Monticello and Hammond...They claimed the title of Indiana High School Basketball Champion for 1909. (Marion also claimed the title, but most believed Crawfordsville to be the best.)*

For information on Breaks, see the appendix.

The IHSAA was established in 1910, and the 1st officially sanctioned state tournament was held in 1911. According to the 1911 IHSAA Yearbook, there were 218 member schools at the time, but that first tournament only included 12 entrant schools. It was held at Indiana University and was won by the Crawfordsville Athenians 24-7 over the Lebanon Tigers. (Neither school was probably yet known by those names because such selections were not common anywhere in the country until the late teens or early 20s and, as we have seen, Logansport and Shortridge each claim to be the 1st to do so in Indiana around 1925). Crawfordsville's selection of Athenians as their team name was based in part on the presence of Wabash College with its erudite scholars on the west side. It was also based on the fact that the renowned Hoosier author Lew Wallace, a Wabash graduate, wrote his masterpiece about the Roman Empire, *Ben Hur*, while residing there. He died in Crawfordsville in 1905. Why Athenians instead of Romans? The best guess is that the classicists in the area simply appreciated the Athenian society more.

Crawfordsville teams have put together quite a number of outstanding seasons over the years, beginning with a 9-3 year as early as 1901. Three years later Coach Ralph Jones (a Shortridge graduate who also coached football and basketball at Wabash College, basketball at Purdue, football at Illinois, and even the Chicago Bears) and his team won 13 of their 15 games; in 1907 they were undefeated in 12 outings.

In 1909 Coach Perry Stump and his charges were 17-1 (and claimed the unofficial state title, as above noted) in his only season as their head coach, but Dave Glascock, who replaced him, led the team to 19-3 and 16-2 records the next 2 years. In 1916 the Athenians-to-be played a 30-game season, winning 24 for Coach L. C. Freeman. J. D. Blacker was the coach in 1919 when Crawfordsville reached the rare 30-games-won level (they lost only 4), and they were 29-2 the next year! Coach Nolan Craver's team had 2 stellar seasons, 21-4 in 1928 and 18-4 in 1930. The Athenians won 24 and lost only 2 in 1955 under Coach Jerry DeWitt and then had 2 fine years with Dick Baumgartner at the helm, 24-6 in 1958 and 22-4 the next year. In 1973 they won 20 of their 25 games for Coach Paul Curtis.

The 1908 team and the Athenians

Lebanon also got off to a fast start in the early days of Indiana basketball. In 1912 the Tigers won their 1st title in a serious rout of the Franklin Grizzly Cubs, 51-11, at least partially atoning for their loss in that initial championship game. However, it was in 1913 and 1914 that the possibilities for fine teams from very small schools to win it all became apparent when Wingate, soon to be known as the Spartans, and led by the marvelous Homer Stonebraker, won back-to-back titles by beating the high schools representing the much larger cities of South Bend and Anderson. The South Bend game went an incredible 5 overtimes and was finally settled 15-14. The Wingate coach was Jesse Wood and their record was 21-4.

Thirty-eight schools entered the 1913 tournament, a number which doubled to 77 in 1914.

Homer Stonebraker
Led Wingate to state basketball champion-ship in 1913 and 1914...in early format, Wingate played 2 games on Friday, then 4 on Saturday... in 1914, "Stoney" scored all of his team's points in the second of those Saturday contests, then half of his team's 36 points in the championship game...3-time All-American at Wabash College...after serving in World War I, professional career included stints with Fort Wayne Hoosiers and Chicago Bruins...called by Abe Saperstein, founder of the Harlem Globetrotters. Coached at Hartford City, then moved to Logansport and was twice elected Cass County Sheriff.

The next year came a good deal more easily for Wingate, winning 36-8. Box scores of those final games show that Stonebraker scored 9 of his team's 15 points in 1913 and 18 of their 36 the next year. Photos of those Wingate teams show what appear to be football pants worn by the players rather than the traditional shorts, and that is apparently exactly what they were.

The Wingate Spartans

The reason? Wingate had no gym and practices were held on an outdoor court covered with cinders. Football pants were a good idea on cold afternoons, and knee pads had to be much appreciated when a spill could result in a seriously skinned knee.

All of Wingate's games had to be played away, most of them in New Richmond (one of the locales featured prominently in *Hoosiers*). Today, entering Wingate from either the north or the south, you will see signs remembering these 2 championships along with the fact that the national high school championship was also won by Wingate in 1920 in Chicago. For the record, Wingate won 22 of their 25 games that year, and

Welcome TO WINGATE STATE BASKETBALL 1913 CHAMPS 1914 NATIONAL CHAMPS - 1920

their coach was Merrill Eaton.

I wondered how they could have won that title when they did not win our own state championship. The answer is that they were declared ineligible to compete in our tournament that year due to some question about the eligibility of some of their players. Another bit of interesting information available from signage outside Wingate is that the nation's first electro-mechanical scoreboard was invented by 2 local residents and installed in their gym.

That gym was actually a barn that was built for the Wingate basketball teams.

It was heated by two wood-burning stoves at either end of the somewhat abbreviated court. Players ran the risk of knocking the stoves over in the course of close games, a considerable danger in a wooden barn. Hence the term "barn burner" to describe close games was particularly relevant.

That barn is still there, just west of Route 25 at the town's main intersection. Also still remembering those wonderful years when Wingate ruled the basketball world is the Spartan Cafe on the northeast corner. At that spot you can get a good meal and some reminiscences if you're of a mind to do either.

Wingate's success swept the state. Town after town decided "if they can do it so can we." Sectionals were added in 1915 as 155 schools entered that year's tournament; Regionals were added in 1921 to accommodate the field of 394 schools; and by 1927 64 Sectionals were required to handle the 731 schools who would enter that year's tournament. It was quite an impressive growth since those first 12 schools had squared off just 16 years earlier.

In 1915 another west central Indiana small town would claim the Indiana state high school basketball title when Thorntown became the 2nd Boone County team to do so. Thorntown was built on the site of a former Indian village at the juncture of Sugar and Prairie creeks. The original Indian name translated as "Place of Thorns" due to the many thorny bushes there. One story has it that a grieving Indian maiden pierced her heart with such a thorn, killing herself when her lover was killed in combat. The Thorntown high school teams were known as the Kewasakees, and we know they fielded a team at least as early as 1906.

The Thorntown school

Nine years later they won their only state championship when they defeated an apparently outclassed Montmorenci Tiger team in the final game 33-10. The blue and white Kewasakees finished that season with a record of 22-5 under coach Chet Hill. The heritage continued when Coach Forest Stoops led the 1943 Kewasakee team to a 19-4 record. Coach Obert Piety's teams had 5 very successful years too: 1944 24-2, 1945 19-4, 1948 22-3, 1951 21-4, and 1952 18-5.

As recently as the late 50s and early 60s the Kewasakees were still playing excellent basketball, winning 79 and losing only 18 between 1958 and 1961 under coaches Art Michael and Ted Wesolek. They were also 21-2 with Coach Carl Short at the helm in 1968. But the early Thorntown teams, their star players and coaches, are the stuff of legends. Hall of Famer Alfred Smith was a critical part of that Thorntown state championship team of 1915.

Alfred DeWitt Smith
A 4-yr starter at Thorntown High School... in 1915 scored 19 points in school's 35-10 state championship victory over Montmorenci...All-State ...averaged over 20 points a game in his high school career...began his career as a guard, but at 6-2 1/2 ended up at center...shot all of team's free throws...at Purdue, started as a sophomore, shooting all foul shots...helped Boilers to second place in Big 10...World War I interrupted the program by taking away Coach 'Piggy' Lambert...said Smith, 'Basketball became of minor importance during the war years'...coached 2 years at Lebanon and 3 years in Belvedere, Ill before moving into highly successful business career.

Thorntown also produced Eugene Beesley, the first non-family member to preside over Eli Lilly and Company, as well as Charles LaFollette, Class of '16, who

rose to become the chief financial officer of the Corning Glass Company. Thorntown is now part of Western Boone High School, the Stars, but the Kewasakees are remembered in the still-existing elementary school.

Thorntown High School basketball team 1906

Chapter 4

The Cradle of Champions:
A Passion is Born

Montgomery, Boone, and Tippecanoe counties have been labeled the Cradle of Indiana Basketball or sometimes, the Cradle of Champions. We know things got started early there, of course, perhaps within a year of James Naismith's invention of the game, and we have seen the success of Crawfordsville, Wingate, Lebanon, and Thorntown. Now let's take a look at the rest of the schools in these 3 counties.

Peach baskets on garage walls . . .

These counties weren't the only ones in Indiana to start playing basketball at an early date. It's just that they were officially among the most successful. Prominent Indiana basketball historian Bob Adams has uncovered evidence that Ridgeville in Randolph County had a high school team as early as 1892, less than 6 months after James Naismith invented the game in December 1891, in Springfield, Massachusetts. Those Ridgeville teams were eventually nicknamed the Cossacks. [See Bob Adams' interesting article in the Summer 2006 issue of the *Indiana Basketball History* magazine.] Also, the Indiana Basketball Hall of Fame has a painting of a game played outside during the 1903-04 season which Freelandville won 14-10 over Edwardsport in Knox County. All of the players are shown wearing long pants. The Hall of Fame also has an old basketball used by Beaver Dam in 1910 in Kosciusko County among its extensive collection of early day Indiana basketball memorabilia.

Above is a replica of Naismith's peach basket at the Indiana Basketball Hall of Fame. The pole was used to punch the ball out of the basket after a basket was made.

The first 8 Indiana state champions came from within a 30-mile radius of Crawfordsville. It's time for us to dig further into the rich mine this area of our state and its basketball history provides. (For further details please see the Montgomery County Hall of Fame and Bob Whalen or the Indiana Basketball History Society.)

Let's start with Ladoga, a small town in Montgomery County with an interesting history. Built on former Shawnee hunting grounds, Ladoga's rather unusual name is not of Indian origin but was the result of a choice made by young people in the town who were intrigued by a lake in Russia. In 1855 the Baptists established a seminary for women in Ladoga that eventually became the Central Indiana Normal School and Business Institute. Although the building that housed these schools still stands, the Normal School was moved to Danville and eventually became Canterbury College until closing its doors in 1951.

The largest employer in Ladoga was a canning company, and the teams from the high school were called the Canners, a unique team name in America. Ladoga has since been consolidated into Southmont High School, the Mounties. But the Canners *The Ladoga Canner* logo proudly remains at Ladoga Elementary School. Preconsolidation, the Canners had several good seasons. Coach Floyd Neff led his teams to records of 19-4 in 1929, 17-4 in 1936 and 21-3 in 1937. Beginning in 1954, Coach Jack Hester's Ladoga teams enjoyed a run of 5 years when they won 83 of 112 games, beginning with a sterling 20-3 record and ending with 1958's 18-5 mark.

We also know that Ladoga was playing basketball at least one hundred years ago. Bill Boone, a onetime Ladoga Canner, wrote an interesting piece for the Wabash College blog *Hoops* about the mid-50s, Charlie Bowerman, and the Alamo Warriors (Remember the Alamo!), excerpted as follows:

1908 Ladoga Basketball Team

> *Charlie Bowerman and I went to different schools together. He was an Alamo Warrior and I was a Ladoga Canner in the late '50s when there were still ten small schools in Montgomery County...I think that Alamo always played Ladoga at Ladoga because Alamo's gym was quite small...after I graduated in 1956 I went off to Wabash to study and become a coach and Charlie finished his senior year at Alamo, losing (in the sectional) to the... Crawfordsville team that went to the final game of the State Tournament...even though [the Warriors] led late in the game. [The sportswriters] called [Charlie Bowerman] the Wizard of Alamo.*

Ladoga High School, home of the Canners

The Alamo school

That 1957 Alamo team coached by Tom Bowerman, whose tenure at the school covered 22 seasons beginning in 1940, finished 19-2. Charlie Bowerman, of course, went on to star at Wabash College and then with the Phillips 66 Oilers when National AAU championships were as significant as the NCAA Tournaments. He retired recently after a distinguished career as one of the senior executives of the Phillips Oil Company.

Charlie Bowerman
Played 3 yrs with Phillips 66ers AAU team...played on 1963 USA team in the World Games...named to AAU teams. toured Russia...Played 3 yrs at Alamo for father & coach, Tom Bowerman, avg 12.9 ppg as sophomore, 21.4 as jr and 26.3 as sr...twice county scoring leader, 45-pt game was at the time record in Montgomery County...also class salutorian...continued career at Wabash College where he was 3-time MVP... had 3 seasons averaging over 20 ppg, capped by school record 25.4 mark as sr...led Little Giants to NCAA college division regionals.

Alamo's scarlet and white Warriors had some earlier success as well, finishing 20-5 for Coach Loyal Marker in 1938 in addition to posting 17-5 and 20-3 records for Tom Bowerman in 1942 and 1946.

In Montgomery County there were once 12 small schools plus Crawfordsville. Ten of those small schools won the county tournament at least once, New Market being the leader with 7, followed by Linden with 6. Alamo, Darlington, New Ross, and Wingate had 3, while Coal Creek, Ladoga, and Waynetown had 2 each; New Richmond and Bowers each had 1. Apparently Waveland never won that title, although they did win an impressive 6 Sectionals.

We've covered Wingate, New Ross, Ladoga, and Alamo already, and we will do so for New Market a bit later. Darlington teams were the Indians, but not for any usual reason. They were so named for a popular teacher and coach whose mother was half Miami. He was generally referred to as "Indian" Ed Miller, who coached there from 1916–23, hence the Darlington Indians. In 1957 and 1958 Coach Al Niswonger led the Indians to consecutive 18-4 records. As recently as the 1969 and 1970 seasons the Indians turned in outstanding records, undefeated both years in the regular season, of 24-1 and 23-1 under Coach Dave Nicholson. The Indians captured their lone Sectional championship in 1969. Bob Whelan tells it this way:

Darlington Indian logo

> *Darlington could NEVER WIN the Crawfordsville Sectional, but they did win the 1969 Lebanon Sectional. They had been the runner up in 1968. In 69 they entered the Lebanon Sectional with a 21-0 record. In the sectional they defeated Pike 83-69, Zionsville 81-69 and in the title game Speedway 56 to 54. They advanced to the Frankfort Regional with a 24-0 record and a game with Crawfordsville. This was the first time in history that two Montgomery County schools played each other in the regional.*

Whelan goes on to point out that the game was hard fought and close, that 43 fouls were called, 5 players fouled out of the game, and that Darlington actually made 1 more basket than Crawfordsville but lost the game at the free throw line, with a final score of 70-66. He concludes:

> *One sports writer said that if they played ten times Darlington would win at least seven times. Guess he didn't know that in the Indiana high school basketball tourney, one loss and you are OUT.*

Darlington's sole defeat in 1970 came in the Lebanon Sectional, to the host Tigers, 84-70, in the second round. Following an 18-4 season with Gene Morrison coaching in 1971, Darlington was consolidated into North Montgomery.

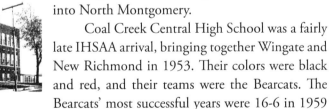

Coal Creek Central High School was a fairly late IHSAA arrival, bringing together Wingate and New Richmond in 1953. Their colors were black and red, and their teams were the Bearcats. The Bearcats' most successful years were 16-6 in 1959 under Coach Jerry Hodge and 20-6 seven years later when led by Coach Phil Miller. It was in 1966 that the Bearcats won their lone Sectional title, at Crawfordsville, with wins over the host Athenians, Ladoga, and New Ross. They also won their 1st game at the Covington Regional over Turkey Run before being eliminated by Bainbridge.

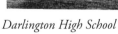

Darlington High School

The New Richmond Cardinals wore red and blue uniforms and competed in basketball as early as 1910. In 1912 they turned in a 12-1 mark for Coach H. A. Kessler. They were members of the Final Sixteen in the state tournament in 1914, losing to

Lebanon 17-9 in the semi-finals. The Cardinals won 32 games while dropping 15 in 1933 and 1934 for Coach Olin Miller, winning their only Sectional crown at Wabash College in the latter year. with wins over Linden 23-19, 28-20 over New Market, and 35-24 over Darlington. As mentioned earlier, New Richmond was used for most of the town scenes of *Hoosiers*. Their gym was also where the Wingate Spartans played most of their home games before their own barn/gym was built.

Still in the Cradle area, the Bowers Black Shirts, who wore orange and black uniforms, enjoyed an 11-5 record as early as 1916. They won the 1927 Crawfordsville Sectional, also played at Wabash College under Coach Chase (or Chayce) Cox, thus becoming the 1st school other than Crawfordsville or Wingate to win that title. They turned in a 15-5 record in 1950 led by coach Richard Bible, before consolidating with Darlington in 1955. At some time the team name was apparently changed to Blackhawks, perhaps because of the regrettable connotation of black shirts as worn by the fascists in Europe in the 30s.

New Richmond High School and Bowers High School

The gold and black Bulldogs represented Linden. Linden had many impressive seasons, beginning in 1929 when Coach Russell Hensley's Bulldogs won 19 and lost 5. In 1937 Cliff Davis coached the team to a 21-6 record, and 4 years later his team went 18-6. Alexander Cox was the coach when the 1948 and 1949 Linden teams won 17 and 18 games respectively, while losing just 3 each year. In 1952 Coach Ralph

Bunton's Bulldogs finished 19-4, and the next year Bill Springer's team won 20 of 23 starts. Their last team had a sterling record of 19-3 for coach Tom Speaker in 1971.

The red-and-white-uniformed Waveland Hornets had a great run from 1949 to 1955, winning an

Linden High School

impressive 140 games while only losing 29, including the undefeated regular season of 25-1 in 1951 for Coach Cliff Davis. That 1 loss was by a single point, 50-49, to Covington in the final game of the Clinton Regional after the Hornets had won 1 of their 6 Sectional titles, at Crawfordsville, by 2 points over the home team. Since the 1949 and 1950 Davis-led Hornets had 23-3 and 20-3 seasons, the 1951 squad's record created a 3-year mark of 68-7! Buzz, buzz! Jim Hannah's 1953 team turned in a 22-3 mark, and Jerry Holtsman's 1955 Hornets turned in another 20-win season, losing 4. Six Sectional championships were won by the Hornets between 1935 and 1953, all at Crawfordsville. Although 3 of those came in a row beginning in 1951, they never could get that coveted Regional crown, losing one to Montezuma, one to Covington, and the closest call of all, to Greencastle 39-38 in 1952. The Waveland Hornets are

 now Southmont Mounties.

Waveland High School and Waveland Hornets

The Waynetown Glad-iators also competed in red and white. Ralph Capehart coached the Gladiators to back-to-back undefeated regular season records of 24-1 in 1944 and 25-1 the next year. Both teams won the Crawfordsville Sectional, first over New Ross, 27-24, and the next year by defeating the hometown Athenians, 29-27. The 1944 squad also captured the Crawfordsville Regional, 46-45 in a double overtime thriller. Their lone defeat was suffered at the hands of Whiteland in the Anderson Semi-state. The 1945 Gladiators' only loss was to Covington in the final game of the Attica Regional. The Gladiators had earlier won 19 of 24 games for Coach J. W. Hogg in 1924 and followed that up with a 20-3 mark for Ralph Powell the next year. In 1948 they finished 18-4 for Russell Nale. The Gladiators had the nets and hardware from 3 Sectionals and that 1944 Regional in their trophy case at the time of their consolidation. Several of these schools were consolidated into North Montgomery High School, home of the Chargers, and others became Southmont Mounties.

 *The North Montgomery Chargers*

The 1st county seat for Boone County was Jamestown, but it was soon moved a few miles east to Lebanon. Jamestown High *The Southmont Mounties.* School teams were called the Little Giants, and just like their Wabash College cousins in Crawfordsville, their colors were red and white. From 1926 through 1928 the Jamestown Little Giants won 60 games and lost only 7(!) for coaches John Moore and Frank Stafford. Lucas Cevert led the 1934 Little Giants team to an 18-5 mark, followed by 15-9 the next year, 22-3 in 1936, and 19-7 in 1937. That's another 74 wins against 24 losses over that 4-year stretch. Not so little in Boone County. Jamestown was consolidated first into Jackson Township, and then into Granville Wells. Both of these schools called their teams the Rockets. The Jackson Rockets had a brief existence and their best season of the 7 they played was 17-3 for Coach Darrell Everhart in 1954. Granville Wells High School (now an elementary school) was in Jamestown, birthplace of the illustrious president (1938–1962) and chancellor of Indiana University, Dr. Herman B. Wells, who was born in Jamestown and whose banker father's name was Joseph Granville Wells. The high school fielded their Rockets from 1955 until 1974 and enjoyed a very impressive 3-season run of 24-2, 19-3, and 19-4 beginning in 1963 under Coach Vince Myer. That's 62-9! His 1963 team won the Zionsville Sectional with a hard-fought, 47-46, victory of the host Eagles. They were ousted from the tournament by Lafayette Jefferson in the Regional, but that same Jeff team was barely beaten, 73-71, in the early game of the state finals 2 weeks later by that year's State Champion Muncie Central Bearcats.

Jamestown High School, home of the Little Giants

Jackson Township High School, home of the Rockets

The Granville Wells Rocket

The Waynetown Gladiagtors logo

In Boone County, one of Jamestown's rivals was Perry Central. The Perry Central teams, wearing purple and gold, were called the Midgets. You have to wonder who fielded the bigger team when the Little Giants and the Midgets squared off! Perry Central's best record was in 1951, when they went 17-4 under Coach Ken Reeher.

Myron Dickerson is a Perry Central graduate and a Hall of Famer. His citation from the Hall of Fame follows:

Myron Dickerson
Coached at Royerton, Connersville and Muncie Northside High Schools,Four-year letter winner at Perry Central ...played baseball at Ball State...began a 26-year coaching career at Royerton (now Delta)... after 3 yrs as assistant, guided Royerton to 129-37 record in 7 seasons, including 3 county tourney championships and an undefeated season in 1961 ...in 1966 took over Connersville program, winning 93 games and 5 sectionals in 6 yrs, culminating in 1972 state championship...in that final, the Spartans won a 79-76 double-overtime game over Jeffersonville in the second afternoon game, then came back on 3 hours rest and stunned favored Gary West 80-63. He returned to Muncie where he coached Northside to a 158-68 mark over ten years, including 4 Olympic Conference titles and a 1975 semi-state appearance. He retired from coaching in 1982 with a career record of 380-158.

A 3rd small school in Boone County was in the town of Advance. The Advance teams were named for the great Seminole Indian chief, the Osceoleons. The purple-and-gold-clad Osceoleons enjoyed back-to-back 19-5 seasons in 1930 and 1931 under Coach Dick Coldwell. Advance captured Lebanon Sectional titles in 1925 and 1930.

We have previously discussed the Thorntown Kewasakees, which leaves us with 3 small schools in the Boone County portion of the Cradle area yet to cover. The blue-and-gold-uniformed Dover teams were called the Blue Devils. Their best season

Advance High School

records came in 1933, when they won 16 and lost 7 for Coach Tony Bennett; in 1940, with a 15-7 mark for Earl Overman; and in 1954, when they won 16 of 22 starts for Floyd Yegerlehner. Unfortunately the lucky 7 streak did not hold in 1961, when the Blue Devils went 2-17, but they snapped back by 1957, when Glen Fisher's Dover team won 15 of 21 games.

The Whitestown Panthers played 34 games in 1946, winning 24, with Joseph Haines coaching. That year they also captured their only Sectional, at Lebanon, with wins over Jamestown, Thorntown, Pinnell, and Zionsville. They also had a fine 23 and 2 season under Coach Lyle Neat in 1948. Robert Mills coached the Panthers to an 18-6 finish in 1962.

The Pinnell Purple Dragons had outstanding seasons in 1938, finishing 20-5 for Coach William Heath, and in 1961 and 1962, when they won 44 of 48 games while being guided by Max Price. The Dragons won their only Sectional title at Zionsville in 1962, defeating Granville Wells, Lebanon, and Whitestown.

Pinnell High School

Three larger schools remain in Boone County: Western Boone, Zionsville and Lebanon. The Zionsville Eagles won 23 of 27 as early as 1919 and went 23-2 for Paul Caldwell in 1937. They were coached for 10 years beginning in 1945 by Al Rosenstihl. During that period the Eagles won 173 games and lost only 63. One of Al's star players for a part of that stretch was a handsome young man named Jim Rosenstihl, his nephew (though raised as a son according to Jim Limp, Jim Rosenstihl's close friend for many years), who went on to become one of the most distinguished coaches in the panoply of stars that has so blessed Indiana basketball.

Jim Rosenstihl
Coached at Center Grove, Zionsville, Bluffton, and Lebanon, A 4-yr letter-winner in both basketball and baseball at Zionsville ...played for Tony Hinkle at Butler University...also played football, and captained baseball team...began his long coaching career with 3 yrs at Center Grove...spent 6 years at Zionsville, winning 103 games...2 years at Bluffton, where he won sectional both seasons...moved to Lebanon in '62 where he would spend over 2 decades with a consistent winner...his teams won over 49 championships...one semistate title...7 regionals, 21 sectionals.

Jim succeeded Al at Zionsville for 6 years while establishing the fine won-lost record of 102-44. His first 2 years he went 41-10. It was, however, when Jim moved on to Lebanon that he really put his mark on the game. Over 24 years at the helm of the Lebanon Tigers, he won 375 more games while losing only 169 against the finest competition the state could offer. He coached the legendary Rick Mount as well as the Walker brothers, Steve and Brian. Although the Tigers were not able to add to the 3 state championships they won in 1912, 1917, and 1918, they were a legitimate force in the highest echelon of the sport throughout Jim Rosenstihl's tenure. They came the closest in 1976, when they lost by 8 points in the Semi-state final to a Marion Giant team that would win it all the next week. In addition to their 3 state titles, the Lebanon Tigers won 41 Sectionals, been state runner-up twice, to the finals 12 times, and in the Sweet Sixteen 19 times, between 1911 and 1943. They racked up 18 20-win seasons, topped by Glen Curtis's 28-2 squad in 1918. The Lady Tigers have added 11 Sectional and 3 Regional nets to the school's trophy case, and Coach Tracey Hammel led her team to 3 20-win seasons including the 2006 squad's undefeated season 23-1. Western Boone has won 6 Sectional and 2 Regional titles, the latter in 1982 under Coach Howard Leedy and in 1998 (2A) with Danny Pierce at the helm. Willie Smith's 2008 Ladies finished 20-4 and captured their 5th Sectional to go with a Regional crown.

Rick Mount
The Rocket scored 2,595 points, gaining early fame by becoming the first high schooler ever featured on the cover of SPORTS ILLUSTRATED ... led Jim Rosenstihl's Tigers to final game of Lafayette semi-state ... named nation's best high school player by USA BASKETBALL YEARBOOK 1966 ... averaged 33.1 points a game last 2 years at Lebanon ... used picture-perfect jump shot to continue high scoring-ways at Purdue ...Big Ten scoring 1461 points...led ABA in 3-point shooting.

The Lebanon Tigers   *Zionsville Eagles*   *and Western Boone Stars*

The 3rd county in the Cradle area is Tippecanoe. The word *Tippecanoe* means "Don't rock the boat" in an Indian dialect—sorry, I couldn't resist. It probably is derived from the Miami Indian name for "buffalo fish." I don't know what buffalo fish are, either, but they are probably bigger than catfish and not as good.

Enough of that. Tippecanoe played an extremely important role in the history of not only our state but our country, and the town of Battle Ground is central to that history. Much has been written about the Battle of Tippecanoe and the roles played by Tecumseh's half-brother Tenskwatawa, known as The Prophet, and William Henry Harrison. Harrison was the first governor of the Northwest Territory, and he was instrumental in the creation of the Ohio and Indiana Territories from it. He then became the first territorial governor of Indiana and moved to Vincennes. In November 1811 Harrison led a collection of regulars, militia and volunteers to the area where there was an encampment of a confederation of some 600 Indians under the leadership of the Shawnee Prophet. When Harrison's troops were attacked by the Indians on November 7, the Battle of Tippecanoe ensued, the first significant encounter between Indians and whites in the Northwest Territory since the Battle of Fallen Timbers in 1794. Militarily, this battle had less significance than it did politically. Harrison was swept to the presidency of the United States. The slogan "Tippecanoe and Tyler Too" found a permanent place in American political lore. Fully 10 of our state's 92 counties are named for men who fought in the Battle of Tippecanoe.

So much for the history lesson. One of the 12 small schools once active in Tippecanoe County was located in the town of Battle Ground. Their team name? The Tomahawks. The gold-and-black Tomahawks had at least 2 exceptional seasons, going 22-4 in 1925 under Coach J. A. Coffin and 18-3 in 1965 under Coach Darrell McQuitty. And where were they consolidated? Into Harrison High School. The Harrison team names? The Raiders!

The Battle Ground Tomahawks   *Harrison Raiders*

Elsewhere, we will discuss the Klondike Nuggets and their unique and memorable team name. Of the remainder of the Tippecanoe County schools, perhaps the scariest team name belonged to the Buck Creek Cobras and the most optimistic to the Clarks Hill Hillers. Clarks Hill is nice town, with a fine restaurant and friendly people. It has many good features, but a hill does not appear to be one of them. The Cobras became East Tippecanoe Trojans before becoming Harrison Raiders, and the Hillers, after a brief sojourn at Lauramie Township Rockets were Wainwright Warriors before finally becoming McCutcheon Mavericks. Frank Alt led the Hillers to a 17-4 record in 1955.

The *Monitor* and the *Merrimac* (originally called the *Virginia*) were our nation's first iron-clad vessels. They also represented the 1st encounter of such ships at the Battle of Hampton Roads in 1862. Monitor teams remembered their naval inspiration as they were called the Commodores and their colors were navy blue and gold. They also remember their lone Sectional championship of 1943 and their wins over

Buck Creek and Clarks Hill Schools

Dayton, Lafayette Jefferson, Clarks Hill, and Battle Ground. After passing through East Tippecanoe as Trojans, they, too, are now Harrison Raiders.

Romney, though not on any body of water, nevertheless named their teams for persons generally associated with ships: they were the Pirates in purple and white. After a period as Southwestern Wildcats, they are now McCutcheon Mavericks.

Monitor High School and the USS Monitor

Montmorenci gained a significant measure of fame in 1915, when the 16-3 Tigers, coached by Charles Kutler, beat Bloomingdale Academy, Bluffton, and Fairmount to finish runner-up to Thorntown in the state's 5th official tournament. The black and gold Tigers also finished 24-1 in 1917 for coach Earl Martin. Their only loss was to Jeff in the semi-finals of the Lafayette Sectional.

Romney High School, home of the Pirates

In 1918 the Tigers gained a significant measure of revenge by upending the Bronchos in the finals of the Lafayette Sectional. They went on to defeat Muncie and Columbus in the state finals at Indiana University before they were eliminated by Bloomington in the third round, finishing 15-4 for Coach Roy Demoret. In 1923 Sylvestor Taylor's team won 22 of 25 games, followed the next year by Lynn Miller's team's 20-6 mark, a record equaled in 1936 with Richard Howell coaching. From 1951 through 1953 Cletus Hinton's Tigers won 57 games while losing only 13, the best mark being 1952's 22-2. Their final 20-win season came in 1959, 21-2 for Coach Sam Price. All told, they won 3 Sectional championships. Though located in Tippecanoe County, their consolidation was into Benton Central High School.

Shadeland was originally the name of a large farm that became a center for the breeding of Hereford cattle, first imported from England. When the town grew around the farm spot, its high school

Montmorenci High School

teams must have been kindred souls to those in Pimento. Both schools' teams were known as the Peppers. Shadeland's Peppers became Southwestern Wildcats, then McCutcheon Mavericks.

Stockwell received consideration as a potential site for Purdue University. West Lafayette, first called Chauncey and for a considerable period of time linked only to Lafayette by ferry, got the nod. Stockwell's teams were the Warriors. The school opened at least as early as 1910 and fielded basketball teams until 1955. At that time the same building became Lauramie Township High School until another merger with Wainwright's Mustangs. Eventually, they joined the others as McCutcheon Mavericks.

The Wainwright Mustang and the Stockwell and Lauramie Township School

The Wea Indians were a branch of the Miami tribe, and the Wea High School teams were understandably called the Indians. The Purple and Gold never managed to win a Sectional crown. They were Southwestern Wildcats from 1957 until 1975 and are also now McCutcheon Mavericks.

Wea Township High School and authentic Wea symbol

Jackson Township took its inspiration for their high school team name from ancient Greece. They were the Spartans. Then, later perhaps, they were also called the Rockets. Dayton, just northeast of Lafayette, fielded the Bulldogs. They, too, are both now McCutcheon Mavericks, Dayton having joined Wainwright before both became part of Southwestern en route. Neither the Bulldogs nor the Spartans ever won a Sectional title.

The Dayton Bulldogs and the   *McCutcheon Maverick Crashing Bull*

In addition to Harrison and McCutcheon there remain 3 other schools in Tippecanoe County: the Lafayette Jefferson Bronchos, about whom we will have a good deal to say later; the Central Catholic Knights; and the West Lafayette Red Devils. The Knights were 3 times Class A State Champions and once runner-up in an impressive run between 1998 and 2003. Chad Dunworthy's 1998 team won the 1st of those titles, 56-48, over Bloomfield, to finish 24-3. The next year the Knights were in the finals again, losing this one to Tecumseh 55-43, finishing 23-4. Dunworthy's 2000 squad defeated Union (Dugger) in the finals 82-70 with a 23-5 record. In 2003 they won their 3rd title, 68-64, over Southwestern (Shelbyville). Quite an impressive run, 125 wins and 36 losses over the 6 years. Earlier Albert Brown's 1973 Knights finished 25-4, winning the 1st of the school's 12 Sectionals and 8 Regional titles, and Steve Bennett's 1986 and 1987 teams won 46 of 51 games played. Geoff Salmon's Lady Knights also won a state championship, in 2006, Class A, 75-68 over South Central (Elizabeth).

The West Lafayette Red Devils have captured 7 Sectionals and 2 Regionals. Stanley Gordon's 1950 team won 20 of 25 games, and Bill Berberian's 1970 edition enjoyed a 20-3 record. His 1979 team had the same record but also won the 1st of the school's 2 Regional titles, beating Kankakee Valley and Fountain Central. In the 1st round of the Semi-states they lost to Anderson by 4 points. Anderson would finish runner-up in the state finals, also losing by 4 points, to Muncie Central. The Lady Devils have added 5 Sectional crowns to the school's trophy case as well as the 1998 Class 3A state championship, 62-45 over Franklin to finish 23-5 for Coach Steve Dietrich. His 2004 and 2005 squads also won 41 games and lost just 8.

Bronchos, Knights, and Red Devils

From this Cradle, the baby that was to mature and grow and become the passion of an entire state, rapidly did so. Places and heroes like Franklin with Fuzzy Vandivier and the Wonder Five, Martinsville with Johnny Wooden, Washington with their beloved Hatchets, and Evansville, the fabled schools of the North Central Conference came to the forefront. Fans came to know the "Region," Ft. Wayne, Terre Haute, and Indianapolis, well over 1,000 schools, small or large, from Whiting's Oilers to Madison's Cubs, from the Red Devils of Auburn to the Rappites in New Harmony. Every county caught the fever. Gyms were built that dwarfed those in any other state, tickets were often hard to come by and eventually over 41,000 fans were in attendance for the state finals games. Hoosier Hysteria had arrived!

Chapter 5

Those Wonderful Names: Whatever is a Skibo?

I came across an article in the recent past that was written by Mike Lunsford and published in the *Terre Haute TribStar*.com on January 24, 2006. It expresses very clearly my own interest in retaining the team names of all of those wonderful preconsolidation schools that are in danger of being lost. What he wrote, in part, was this:

> It's no secret that I enjoy talking about old high school nicknames; … There's something fascinating about the pre-consolidated high school era in Indiana and the unique nicknames from those old days. I don't have anything against the new but rather generic names of the latest generation of schools, but not everything that's newer is necessarily better. I think there's a good bit of history we can learn from the old names; many of the folks in the proud little towns in the old days chose nicknames and mascots that either echoed their town's name or some bit of history associated with it.
>
> It must have been pretty intimidating to know you had to square off on a Friday night in the dead of winter against the Buck Creek Cobras, the Holton Warhorses, the Kennard Leopardcats, or the Swayzee Speedkings. I don't know if I'd have enjoyed facing the Tippecanoe Police Dogs, the Waynetown Gladiators, the Banquo Ghosts, or the Redkey Wolves on the road either. Want to play against a bunch of Gorillas? That's exactly what you'd have had to do had you walked into the gym at Hartford City [sic Hartford City teams were the Airdales—the Gorillas played at Hartford Center] for a game.
>
> You could have expected to have seen Haymakers thrown around had you played in Hayden; at Summitville you'd have tipped off against the Goblins.

Holton and Kennard Houck photos of exhibits courtesy IBHOF

Cobras, Leopardcats, Police Dogs and Wolves, Ghosts and Goblins. Ghosts and Goblins? Until recently I was unaware of any unusual incidents of ghost sightings in Summitville, but we'll have more on that later. The selection of Ghosts by the citizenry of Banquo has always been one of my favorites. They knew their Shakespeare. They knew *Macbeth.* After all, wasn't their town named for one of the conspirators with Macbeth when they murdered King Duncan? Indeed it was. However, after the conspiracy falls apart, as these things seem often to do, Macbeth murders Banquo, and later in the play the ghost of Banquo comes to torment Macbeth. So the Ghosts of Banquo was a very literate choice made by the people who lived there. (It should be added that Ghosts was not the only team name used by Banquo High School. They were called the Indians from 1930 until their consolidation into Huntington North in 1956.) Although they began playing basketball as early as 1909, going 7-1 that year, Banquo's latter-day basketball history had precious few highlights as they only won 41 games while losing 216 between 1941 and 1955. The Red-and-Blue did, however, enjoy seasons of 15-1 in 1915, 18-5 in 1933, and 17-3 in 1939. It is also reported that John Haines of Banquo scored 68 points in an 87-8 win over LaFontaine in 1914. They were consolidated into Andrews (Cardinals) and Warren (Lightning Five) before all became part of the Huntington North Vikings.

The Banquo School Gym

If Banquo gets the literary prize for their selection of Ghosts—a prize, perhaps, which should be shared with the Delphi Oracles—there are 2 schools which share the prize for Literary Opportunity Missed. These are Hamlet, in Starke County, and Tennyson, in Warrick County. Both schools fielded the Tigers. I would have preferred either the Danes or the Princes for Hamlet and the Lords, or maybe even the Alfreds, for Tennyson. Oh well, whatever 'tis nobler in the mind... The Hamlet Tigers wore black and gold, which is regal at least, and they won 34 of 43 games in 1950 and 1951 for

Coach Gene Little. They have since become Oregon Davis Bobcats, a team which made some serious Indiana basketball history for itself in 2007 when both their boys and their girls teams won state championships.

The Tennyson Tigers won 3 consecutive Sectional championships for 3 different coaches beginning in 1930. Harold McRoberts led the 1930 team to the Boonville Sectional title with wins over the host team, Chandler, Yankeetown, and Rockport; Sanford Sanders took over, and his team won at Rockport, defeating Boonville, Luce Township, Gentryville, and the home team. Then Albert Haas took his Tiger team back to Boonville, where they won yet again by eliminating Rockport, Dale, Boonville, and Lynnville. The 1930 team won the 1st round of the Washington Regional over Bristow before losing the championship game to the Hatchets. How did Washington do at Indianapolis? They won the state championship. The 1931 team also won the 1st round of their Regional, defeating Tell City at Evansville before being edged by a single point, 15-14 by Evansville Central. Then, in 1932, the Tigers were back in Evansville for the Regional where this time they lost their 1st round game to Owensville. Quite an impressive record for the Hamlet Class of 1932 seniors. They have since become Boonville Pioneers.

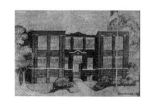

Hamlet and Tennyson High Schools

Tigers are now Bobcats and Pioneers

The southern part of Wells County in east central Indiana was once rich in oil and natural gas. I had thought that the county name was derived from the oil wells once there. I was wrong. Wells County was so designated long before oil was discovered anywhere (in 1837) and is named for William Wells. He was born in Kentucky near the Ohio River in 1770, kidnapped by a band of Indians when he was 12, and taken to the Miami tribe's campground near what is now Ft. Wayne. He was raised into young manhood by the Miamis. Wells left the Indians to join General Anthony Wayne with the hope, shared by himself and the Miami tribal leaders, that his understanding of both cultures might help bring peace between them. Unfortunately, this did not prove to be the case: Wells eventually died in the Ft. Dearborn, now Chicago, massacre of

1815. At any rate, the town of Petroleum in Wells County was so named because of the oil fields there and nearby Gas City because of the abundance of natural gas in the area.

Gas City became a manufacturing site for many glass manufacturers including the Ball Brothers, who found the abundant, low-cost natural gas advantageous to glass production. Nearby Fairmount also was a "gas city." It was later to gain fame as the birthplace of the talented young actor James Dean, who did play basketball for the Fairmount Quakers, as reported in the Winter 2007 *Indiana Basketball History* Magazine. Dean graduated from Fairmount High School in 1949, but he is not the only well-known person to have come from that school. Jim Davis, creator of "Garfield," was a member of the class of 1955, and Robert Sheets, director of the National Hurricane Center, graduated in the Quaker class of 1967. The Fairmount basketball teams enjoyed at least 6 excellent seasons in the years from 1926 until 1951 with records ranging from 18-4 to 23-2, including 4 Sectional titles. Myers Ivan's 1927 Quakers had a 20-3 record, and Keith Stroup's 1927 team finished 19-5 and won the school's 1st Sectional championship. The 2nd came in 1942 when Everett Chapman's team won 21 and lost 7. Ed Johnson's 1945 and 1946 squads went 23-2 and 21-2, the former nabbing Sectional number 3 and the Marion Regional with victories over Wabash and Kokomo. In the Muncie Semi-state Gas City won their 1st game over Portland before losing in the title game to Ft. Wayne Central who were runners-up to Anderson for the state championship the next week in Indianapolis.

From 1909 until 1923 another school called Fairmount Academy also existed in the town. The academy made it to the Final Four in 1915, losing by 3 points to Montmorenci's eventual state runner-up Tigers. Their coach was named A. Hall, and their record was 17-3. They merged into Fairmount High School in 1924. Fairmount was consolidated into Madison-Grant, the Argylls. Viewing the Argyll it is hard to imagine the Quakers would be anything like that!

Fairmount Academy, Fairmount High School, and the Madison-Grant Argyll

Petroleum teams were originally known as the Zippers, a name adopted because the basketball team, the only interscholastic team fielded by this tiny school at the outset, used uniforms with the newly invented devices known as zippers, while most other teams still used the older, more conventional fasteners. The Zippers also wanted to be known for their speed on the court. So Zippers they were for some 30-plus years until, perhaps, the novelty wore off and a new nickname, the Panthers, was selected in about 1947. Petroleum made the Sweet Sixteen for the 1913 state tournament, losing to Lafayette in the 1st round with Ira Sink coaching. They had a fine 20-3 season in 1933 for Coach Alton Meyer, and their lone Sectional title came in 1946, Eldon Carnes leading the team to a 17-6 finish. Petroleum has been consolidated with others into the new Southern Wells High School, now known as the Raiders.

Gas City teams were known as the Tigers, and they had many memorable seasons. Wilbur Cummings coached the 1939 Tigers to an 18-5 record, followed by an undefeated regular season, finishing 23-1. That sole defeat came to the Marion Giants in the final game of their Sectional, 30-22. Cummings' 1944 squad captured the school's 1st Sectional crown with a 19-4 record, followed by 20-2-1, 21-7, and 21-2 marks. He turned over the reins to John Fredenberger, whose 1948 Tigers won 23 more games while losing only 2. That added up to 104 wins and only 17 defeats–and 1 tie–for the school's final years of operation. (As an aside the Tigers had 2 earlier tie games, both in 1935. How many schools can point to 3 tie games in their basketball history, let alone 2 in 1 year?) The 1946 Gas City team not only won the school's 2nd Sectional crown and only Regional. They also defeated Portland in the 1st round of the Semi-state before being eliminated by those pesky other Tigers from Ft. Wayne Central. They are now Mississinewa Indians.

Gas City High School

The 3 present-day Wells County high school teams: Southern Wells Raiders, Norwell Knights, and Bluffton Tigers

While we're discussing the Fairmount Quakers it is also a good time to mention the Plainfield Quakers. The Society of Friends founded Plainfield in 1833. They named it in concert with their simple, straightforward philosophy of life. Plainfield became a very significant part of the Quaker organizational structure when the Western Yearly Meeting House was established there in 1858. In 1881 their Central Academy was built in Plainfield, which became Plainfield High School in 1919. Not so surprising, then, is the name given to those high school teams. The Quakers. Or, as the waitress who served us at the diner on the National Road, herself a graduate of Plainfield High, said, "The Fighting Quakers. Bit of an oxymoron, don't you think?" Those Quakers had their moments on the court, though, with a 19-4 record as early as 1916. In 1930 they won 26 of 30 games. They were 20-5 in 1983 and had back-to-back 20-6 seasons 3 years later. They went 20-4 in 1993, and only dropped 1 regular season game in 1999, closing out at 26-2 under Coach Dana Greene. The Plainfield Quakers have won 22 Sectionals, 3 Regionals, and the 1999 Washington 3A Semi-state. They went on to win the state championship with a 26-1 record, coached by Greene, defeating the Muncie Southside Rebels, 77-64. The Plainfield Lady Quakers have won 9 Sectionals themselves and one Regional.

The Plainfield Quaker

The 1923 Plainfield Quakers and young friend

Another Quaker team was at New London High School in Howard County. These Quakers did not fare quite as well as their Fairmount or Plainfield brethren, but they did manage to enjoy a few good seasons. The Blue and Gold won 11 and lost only 4 in 1914 and went 15-5 and 15-7 in 1935 and 1936. They are now a part of Western High School, the Panthers.

*New London High School
and the Western Panther*

Several schools showed not only some historical knowledge but also a good sense of humor in matching their high school team names to their town names. Let's start with Raleigh in Rush County.

Sir Walter Raleigh was responsible for establishing the first English colony in the New World at Roanoke Island in what is now North Carolina on June 4, 1584. Because the effort failed and the first settlers were never found, this has become known as "The Lost Colony." He was an active player in the many dramas that made up court life, religious strife, and relations with Ireland and Spain throughout his life in England. He is remembered in this country in many ways with the capital city of North Carolina bearing his name as well as a small town in Rush County, Indiana. The Raleigh teams: the Sir Walters. The Sir Walters best year was 1933, winning 20 while losing only 4 under Coach Kenneth Walters (Sir Kenneth?).

Sir Walter Raleigh (c.1552-1618) and the high school building. Raleigh High School was consolidated into Rushville, the Lions, also the symbol of Sir Walter's England.

Few rifles have achieved the fame of the one designed by Eliphalet Remington. The precision of its design and manufacture led to shooting accuracy unprecedented in the early 19th century, a quality sought after by several generations of Remington High School basketball players. Remington High School teams were known as the Rifles. They won 2 Sectionals, in 1943 and 1945. They are now Tri-County Cavaliers.

Remington High School and the Remington rifle

Lincolnville in Wabash County must have known a thing or two about Edgar Allan Poe. Their purple-and-gold clad teams were the Gold Bugs. They are now Southwood Knights after a waystop as Lafontaine Cossacks and/or Lagro Comets.

Lincolnville High School and the Southwood Knight

Interestingly there were also Gold Bugs at Goldsmith High School in Tipton County wearing black and gold. (Until recently there have been no schools in Indiana who were the Ravens, though. Nevermore can this be said. The recently opened Irvington Community Charter School in Indianapolis has chosen Ravens as their team's name. Since they are sponsored by Ball State, whose teams are the Cardinals, Ravens are added to their aviary along with the Burris Owls.) The Gold Bugs, however, are now Tipton Blue Devils after a brief period as Jefferson Township Yankees who, appropriately, wore red, white, and blue uniforms. Bob Fraley coached the Yankees to their lone Sectional crown in 1956 with an 18-6 record. As he reports, the school only had 74 students and was the smallest of the 12 entered at Noblesville in the host's new gym that year. Jefferson won their first game, against Noblesville, 64-55, then the Yankees ended Sheridan's 7-year run of titles by sinking 6 straight free throws in the last minute of play to nip the Blackhawks, 48-43. Saturday afternoon the Yanks had another scare, dropping the Walnut Grove Wolves by the margin of a single basket, 55-53. The championship game pitted Jefferson against Jackson, which sounds like an American history lesson or a Democratic Party convention. Jackson Central's Eagles had won 2 straight 1-point games, over Tipton's Blue Devils and Windfall's Dragons and led the Yankees by 3 at the three-quarters mark. The score was tied at 40 with just 2:46 left and the Yankees turned the tables on the Eagles, prevailing by a single point after making 1 of 2 free throws with 4 seconds left, and the celebration began in Kempton, home of the Jefferson Township Yankees. Coach Fraley points out that the school had no gym, the floor in the armory where the team practiced was only 60x30 feet and was lit by 8 150-watt bulbs. They played a few "home" games in the Tipton Armory, but most were played away, which was (probably) "an advantage to us, particularly in the tourney."

Goldsmith Goldbugs are now Tipton Blue Devils

You will note that the Tipton Blue Devil has a nicer expression than some devils that are around. Some years ago there was a movement in Tipton to change the team name from Blue Devils to something else. One suggestion was "Angels." The change was not made, but the compromise was to make the Tipton Blue Devil a bit less devilish. The Blue Devils, whatever the facial expression, have won 18 Sectional crowns and 3 Regionals. The first Regional title came in 1935, when Hall of Famer John Ward, who coached the Devils for 18 years, won the 5th of the 12 titles the school collected during his tutelage. That year they lost the first round of the Sweet Sixteen at Butler Fieldhouse to Nappanee. The next year the Blue Devils had an undefeated regular season. Ward's 1942 team also won the Regional title, defeating Huntington in the 1st round of the Semi-state before being ousted by state runner-up Muncie Burris. Larry Angle's 1988 through 1990 Devils put together 19-5, 22-4, and 22-4 seasons, annexing the 3rd Regional title in 1989. In 2008 Travis Daugherty led the team to a 21-3 season and the school's 18th Sectional title. The Lady Devils have added 7 Sectional titles as well as the 2001 Regional to the school's trophy case. Pam Taylor led the 1981 team to a 19-4 record and Kurt Ogden led the 2001 and 2002 teams to 17-9 and 19-5 finishes.

We will discuss the Beavers of Morocco in Newton County in a later chapter, when we examine our towns with an international influence in their names. For now, we will concentrate on those Beavers who played for Beaver Dam High School in Kosciusko County. Those Beaver Dam Beavers had their moments. From the *Warsaw Times Union*, Saturday March 5, 1994, Phil Smith reports:

> *At Beaver Dam, where a proud legacy was established in the 1930s, the gymnasium was cramped—to say the least. Just a few feet from the baseline was the wall, and double doors leading to the outside. "I went sliding out those doors one time on my elbow," remembers 78-year-old Gene Marshall, who played on both the 1933 and 1934 state final teams from Beaver Dam... [Marshall] the spry Beaver Dam forward hit 11-13 field goals for 22 points in the Beavers' sectional championship win over Warsaw. Marshall followed that up by nailing the game-winning free throw against Ligonier in the regional to thrust his team into its second-straight state finals.*

Beaver Dam High School and the Tippecanoe Valley Viking

That 1933 Beaver Dam team was also undefeated in the regular season and ran up an impressive 27 wins. They were coached by Hall of Famer Walter Kindy. Although the school had a student body of only 52, they won 3 straight Sectionals from 1932 through 1934 and the 1933 and 1934 Auburn Regionals. The Beavers are now Vikings, as part of Tippecanoe Valley High School.

Smithville is still a smallish town south of Bloomington, near what has now become a prosperous resort area with the creation of man-made Lake Monroe. The town was founded in 1851 by George Smith and Mansfield Bennett. When there was

a Smithville High School, the teams there were called the Skibos. I'm not sure why, but I do know that there has been a Skibo Castle in Scotland since at least the year 1275. The present building was built in 1786 and later completely renovated when purchased by Andrew Carnegie around the turn of the 19th century as a summer estate. It is

Skibo castle

now a 5-star resort hotel with a first-rate golf course. The Skibos are now part of Bloomington South. I may not be clear on exactly what a Skibo is, but I do know their mascot was a Penguin. Hall of Famer Everett Case coached the Skibos to a 28-victory season in 1922, losing 8. Cloyce Quakenbush led the 1940 team to a fine 20-4 record, as did Ken Thayer in 1951. Hall of Famer John Adams, who played on Bloomington High School's first basketball team, graduating in 1912, and later won 438 games at Vincennes, also coached at Smithville, where his 4-year mark was an impressive 86 wins and 24 losses.

Penguin, as depicted by Patty Robinson, President, Smithville Area Association

Several towns obviously had basketball on their minds when it came time to selecting nicknames. Fancy that, basketball on their minds in Indiana!

Let's start with Swayzee. When you enter Swayzee you are informed of two facts. First, it is the only Swayzee in the world. How do they know this? The answer I got, and I must say I like it, was that during World War II a sailor overseas sent a postcard with the only address being "Swayzee." No country, no state. It was correctly delivered to our Swayzee in Grant County, Indiana. Second, you are reminded that it was home to the high school that once won an incredible 9-overtime game in the state basketball tournament (1964 Regionals, 65-61 over the Liberty Center Lions). I would have loved to have seen that game, but it is certainly far from the only claim to fame that Swayzee is due. As long ago as 1913, when coached by J. A. Smith, Swayzee won 23 games while losing just 4. They were 23-3 under Coach Bayard Rouch in 1930, 19-3 in 1944 with Jay Sumpter at the helm, and 19-4 for Coach Dave Huffman in 1965. The Purple and Gold also played a rare tie game, versus the Van Buren Aces in 1951 in a game called by the referees when some things got "out of hand." Swayzee teams, before the school was consolidated into Oak Hill, were the Speed Kings. Oak Hill teams are the Golden Eagles.

1913 Swayzee Speed Kings

Liberty Center and Swayzee high schools, the welcome sign, and the Oak Hill Golden Eagles. Photo from exhibit courtesy IBHOF

Urbana High School and the Northfield Norse

There may only be one Swayzee in the world, but there were certainly 2 Speed Kings in Indiana, as the Urbana teams also answered to that name. Urbana is now a part of Northfield. These Speed Kings wore green and gold and won 17 of 23 games for Richard Reahard in 1958 and went 19 and 5 for Coach Jim Barley 3 years later.

The Rosedale Hotshots are now Riverton Parke Panthers

Rosedale, north of Terre Haute offered the Hotshots. They are now a part of the Riverton Park Panthers. In 1947 Hubert McHargue led the Black and Gold to a 19-5 season. The Hotshots captured Sectional titles at Clinton in 1926 by defeating Newport, Green Township, Bloomingdale Academy, and the home team; at South Vermillion in 1952 with wins over Montezuma, Hillsdale, Clinton, and Dana; and 1984 when they beat Clay City, Brazil, and Staunton. A. H. Hendrix coached the 1926 Hotshots, Don McNary was in charge in 1952, and James Stewart led the 1984 squad.

Speed Cats are now Patriots

Dunkirk, northeast of Marion, fielded the Speed Cats. The green-and-white-clad Dunkirk Speed Cats had several outstanding seasons in their 62 years of playing: 20-3 in 1924 under Coach Cyril Wilson, 18-3 just 10 years later when the coach was Gerald Alexander; a string of 17-6, 19-5, and 19-4 in the only 3 years Bob Primmer was their coach (1935–37); 23-2 in 1938 under Fred Fechtman; 19-4 with Paul Stuart coaching in 1943; 17-4 under Coach Fred Adams in 1946; 18-4 in 1958 followed by 19-7 the next year for Coach Bob Stephens; and a fine 22-3 in 1961 with Jack Cross at the helm. There was no retreat in our Dunkirk lads, who are now Jay County Patriots.

Both Union Township in Huntington County, near Ft. Wayne, and the town of Milton, located between Knightstown and Richmond, fielded the Sharpshooters. Milton teams wore maroon and gold and really were sharp shooters in 1953 and 1954, winning 21 of 24 games and 23 of 26 for Coach Bob Davis for a 47-6 2–year record. John Howell's 1960 squad also turned in a fine 19-5 season. They are now Cambridge City Lincoln Golden Eagles.

The Union Township Sharpshooters favored blue and white uniforms and did some fine shooting of their own. They were 11-1 as early as 1910 and were 12-3 in 1923 for Coach Burton Stevens. From 1928 through 1931 they won 58 games and lost only 13, the first 2 years under Kelro Whitman and the last, a 21-5 season, for Ray Johns. They won their 1st Sectional title in 1931 for Harold Smith by defeating Markle, Banquo, the host Vikings, and Warren. In 1951 Bob Johnson's Sharpshooters won 22 and lost only 4 and won their 2nd Sectional championship, also at Huntington, with wins over Bippus, Rock Creek Center, Lancaster Township, and Jackson Township.

Idaville, in White County, fielded basketball teams from 1909 until 1963, when they were consolidated into Twin Lakes, becoming Indians. Prior to that the green and white Idaville teams were simply called the Green Streaks. As far as I have been able to determine, they never won a Sectional championship.

Two examples of Jim Mast's pins and the Huntington North Viking

Warren, northeast of Marion, fielded the Lightning Five. Warren started play in 1910 and the blue and white Lightning Five enjoyed their best 2 seasons in 1912 when they were 20-2 and 10 years later when they were 17-4. They have joined Union Township, and others, as Huntington North Vikings.

 No story of small school success in Indiana basketball would be complete without including the remarkable run of the Muncie Burris Owls from 1939 until 1947 with the vaunted Muncie Central Bearcats always looming in their path. Hall of Famer Tom Wallace, No. 55 jumping center in the Sectional against Muncie Central's Earl Roberts in 1947 rose to an executive management position at Eli Lilly and Company and his life provides yet another example of success on the court being a precursor to success in other facets of life.

Tom Wallace
Director of Indiana Basketball Hall of Fame since 1977...chair of site-selection and building committees for Hall...former member of Ball State board of trustees...past president BSU Alumni Assoc...recd. BSU's Distinguished Alumni Award in '77...prepped at Muncie Burris High School, earning 8 letters in basketball and track...a starter for Burris' sectional and regional champions as a junior...all-regional, all-semi-state...lettered in basketball and football at Texas Western...transferred to Ball State, where he lettered in basketball and track.

Tom told the Burris story to me this way:

Burris was named for Benjamin Burris, the first president of what would become Ball State University. It opened as a Ball State lab school for student teachers K-12 and graduated its first class of 21 students in 1933. During those early years it had a regular Muncie school district on the city's west side. Total enrollment never topped 300. My graduating class included 63. Scott Fisher, Hall of Fame 1976, started the program and retired after the 1947 season. Burris never won a basketball sectional after he retired, yet Mr. Fisher won six straight sectionals against the Muncie Central Bearcats:

1. 1939 Burris lost in State Final Four to Franklin 31-25
2. 1940 Burris (22-6) lost to New Castle in Regional
3. 1941 Burris lost in Semi-state to Ft. Wayne North 46-40
4. 1942 Burris lost in final game of State Finals to the Washington Hatchets, 24-18
5. 1943 Burris, in spite of losing 2 starters from the Indiana All-Stars including Mr. Basketball from the year before, lost only one game in the regular season and were beaten in the Regional
6. 1944, lost in Semi-state to Kokomo.

During all this time there was limited enrollment and a fixed district, and year after year Burris won with new players after losing All-State players along the way. Also all of the Burris Sectional wins were against Muncie Central coaches who won state championships before and after the streak.

In 1945 and 1946 we (I played as freshman and sophomore) lost in close sectional championship games to Muncie Central. In 1947 we had 4 senior starters under 6′ and myself, a 6′3″ junior. We were ranked at times during the year, but Central was picked by some for the state title. We won for Mr. Fisher's last year before retirement and lost to Marion (whom we had beaten during the regular season) in the "final eight" night game of the Semi-state, 40-32.

Side Note: Burris won the state track meet in 1943 with four runners, all of whom had played on the basketball team as well.

The Muncie Burris Owls, the school, and Benjamin Burris

All told the Burris Owls have won 9 Sectionals, 5 Regionals, and the 1939 and 1942 Semi-states. In the 1939 Final Four Burris lost the afternoon game to the Franklin Grizzly Cubs, who would lose that night to Frankfort's Hot Dogs. In the 1942 Final Four the Owls defeated the Athenians of Crawfordsville before losing that State Final Tom mentions.

We will have much more to say about the Muncie Central Bearcats and their tremendously successful history later on!

Chapter 6

More Fun with Names: Hot Dogs and Chili—Salt and Pepper

We Hoosiers are certainly blessed with a good sense of humor. Not only did our state produce George Ade, Red Skelton, Herb Shriner, David Letterman, Phil Harris, and Carole Lombard, but we have had a great deal of fun with the selection of our high school team names and mascots. Let's have some more fun!

Frankfort was founded in 1830 by 2 brothers whose grandparents had lived near Frankfurt, Germany. It is a charming small city, the Clinton County seat, with courthouse and market square, well-kept homes, churches, a population of around 15,000, and a high school gym that seats over 6,000 spectators. The gym is round, would make all but the largest of colleges proud, and was featured in the movie *Blue Chips* starring Nick Nolte as a beleaguered basketball coach, as well as Indiana University's Bobby Knight and Matt Nover. The Frankfort Gym is named for Everett Case, who coached the Frankfort basketball team to 4 state championships between 1925 and 1939, then went on to even greater fame at North Carolina State University.

Frankfort, however, has always had fun with their town's name. Every July, during the dog days of summer, the annual Frankfort Hot Dog Festival is held, and everyone has a chance to eat his or her fill of frankfurters. The idea for this festival came from the name chosen for their high school teams: the Fighting Hot Dogs.

But, they were not always scrappy frankfurters. Tom Hall, who played quarterback for Frankfort High School in the late 40s and later was a backup to Dale Samuels at Purdue, tells me that his teams were known as the Night Hawks, because they had been among the first schools in the state to play all of their home games under the lights. The baseball teams, utilizing the school's colors, were called the Blue Sox. It was not until the early 90s that all of the Frankfort teams began to be called the Hot Dogs.

The Frankfort Hot Dog

Whatever they were called, over the years the Frankfort boys basketball teams have piled up an impressive 47 Sectional and 19 Regional championships in their trophy case to go along with those 4 state championships. From 1922 through 1931 Frankfort's Hot Dogs never won less than 20 games, with the best year being 1925's 27-2 state championship. Everett Case was the coach for all but the 1st year of that stretch, when Paul Lostutter's team finished 25-5. For that 10-year period Frankfort won an amazing 244 games and lost only 46. The 2nd state title came with 1929's 24-2 team. In 1936 another impressive string was begun, this one of 4 years duration, during which 97 games went into the victory column against only 17 on the other side of the ledger. State championships were won by the 1936 29-1 team and the 1939 26-6 team. Shortly after, Everett Case left the Midwest to take Indiana basketball to North Carolina, starting a revolution on Tobacco Road that has lasted well into the 21st century. Other 20-victory seasons were harder to come by for the Frankfort Hot Dogs, but they did arrive in 1949 when Wilbur Cummings' squad turned in a 22-6 record; in 1977, 1978, and 1982 when Hall of Famer John Millholland's squads finished 23-2, 21-7, and 23-2; and in 1995 when Marty Echelbarger's Hot Dogs turned in a 24-3 mark. Ed Niehaus has coached the girls team for 22 seasons, winning 2 Sectional titles and one Regional, and turning in a 20-5 season in 2000.

Everett Case
A non-athlete who became one of the nation's legendary coaches. A 23-year high school career, mostly at Frankfort..."Casey" posted a 726-75 record ... 4 state championships in '25, '29, '36 and '39 ... moved on to North Carolina State, where he is credited with boosting Atlantic Coast Conference basketball into the national limelight ... 377-134 record for Wolfpack ... 10 championships in old Southern Conference and ACC ... 3 time conference coach of the year ... award for outstanding player in ACC tourney is named in his honor ... State's athletics center also named in his honor. He was inducted into the National Basketball Hall of Fame.

One of the most famous towns in all the world is the west side adjacent suburb to Indianapolis, Speedway, home to Tony Hulman's (and now Tony George's) famous race-track. Everywhere in the world I have traveled, and that includes over 50 countries, when I have mentioned that I am from Indianapolis the first words I often hear are "Indy 500!" The Indianapolis 500 has for years been the most highly attended sporting event in the world, and is well known for sportscaster Tom Carnegie's famous phrase "The Greatest Spectacle in Racing." More recently it has been joined by the highly successful Nascar Allstate 400 at the Brickyard as well as, for a time, the Formula One United States Grand Prix. What would a town so surrounded by motorcars and internal combustion engines choose to call their athletic teams? None else than the Speedway Sparkplugs.

Sparkie

The 'Plugs have won 9 Sectional and 2 Regional titles. They captured their only state championship in the 2002 Class 2A Finals with a 62-48 victory over Bluffton, finishing a 22-4 season for coach Trent Lehman. Clara Caito's Lady 'Plugs won 20 of 25 games in 1984, including the first of 2 Sectional titles and their only Regional crown. Hall of Famer Morris Pollard coached the Speedway boys teams for 27 years.

Morris Pollard
4-yr varsity player at tiny Jackson...led team to '41 sectional victory over Everett Case-coached Frankfort Hot Dogs ... 3-time all-sectional...3-yr standout at Canterbury College...led team to NAIA tourney in '47... named college athlete of the yr in '49...also played football 3 yrs, baseball 2 yrs...coached 5 yrs at Amo, winning sectional in '53...2 yrs at Danville, including a sectional title...moved to Speedway where he coached 27 yrs.

Rising Sun is a town on the Ohio River, somewhat to the east of Madison. The Ohio in its twists and turns runs north to south as it flows by the riverside town. The sun, thus, actually does rise directly across the river, over the hills behind Rabbit Hash, Kentucky, with its general store over 100 years old. The river is extremely wide at this point and the view can be quite spectacular. Fortunately, the citizens of Rising Sun knew how to name their athletic teams: they are the Shiners. The Shiners have the nets from 6 Sectionals in their trophy case. Their 1st came under Coach Orville Hodson in 1930 with a very respectable 22-3 mark. Mike Wilson led the Shiners to 4 more Sectional titles, including 1989's 20-4 team. The Lady Shiners also had some very impressive seasons from 1998 through 2000 for Coach Mark Fette, first going undefeated in the regular season to finish 24-1, then going 21-3 to win their 2nd straight Regional tournament, and finally getting to the state final game in Class A only to lose a thrilling overtime contest to Triton to close out a 25-3 season. That's 70 wins and 7 losses in a 3-year span. Hard to beat that.

Shoals in Martin County is located right on US 50, one of the earliest national roads that united the country from coast to coast. The glaciers of the last great Ice Age pretty much flattened out the northern half of Indiana, but they pushed some interesting piles of earth and rock around in the southern part. One of the most interesting of these is just outside of Shoals, a mile or 2 only to the west, also on 50. It is a 60-foot-tall monolithic rock structure that, from a certain angle, resembles a huge jug. It is thus called the Jug Rock.

The Shoals High School teams are called the Jug Rox. Inside the Shoals High School gym there are no less than 4 renderings of this rock, the more enjoyable ones being 2 versions of it playing basketball! Principal David Springer, a most gracious host, also played some fine basketball himself at Indianapolis Cathedral and Nichols State.

A big rivalry in that part of the state is the one between Shoals and nearby Loogootee. Loogootee's long-time coach, Jack Butcher, 1951 grad and coach there from 1957 (after 4 years at Memphis State, interrupted by 2 in the United States Navy) until 2002, is the winning-est coach in the history of Indiana high school basketball, with over 806 notches on his belt.

Jack Butcher
Long time coach at Loogootee High School ... Graduated from Loogootee High School in 1951 as school's all-time leading scorer ... also led his team in assists and defense ...3-year starter at Memphis State in career sandwiched around a tour of duty in the Korean War ... NCAA all-regional selection as a junior .... a year later, led the Tigers to runner-up spot in NIT ... all-NIT selection ... turned down offer from Boston Celtics to return to his southern Indiana hometown to coach. He became the winningest Hoosier coach in March, 2000 with 771 victories...all at Loogootee.

There are about 240 students in Shoals High School and 300 in Loogootee. Loogootee's gym, named for Jack Butcher and also known as the Lion's Den, seats 4,500 fans in a town with a population of around 2,500 people. I am told you have to get there early to get a seat for most games the Lions play, particularly when the Jug Rox come to town!

The Lions have been playing interscholastic basketball since at least 1906. They have won 28 Sectional titles, 9 Regionals, and 3 Semi-states. They have twice been state champion runners-up, first in 1975 when Jack Butcher's charges, with a 27-2 overall record, were defeated by Bill Green's 28-1 Marion Giants, 58-46. The second time involved the State Finals, for the 2005 Class A Tournament, when Coach Steve Brett's 21-5 team was defeated by the Lapel Bulldogs under Coach Jimmie Howell, who were 25-3, by a 51-40 count. The Lions have rung up quite a number of 20-win seasons, beginning in 1939 when Leo Costello's team finished

The Loogootee Lion

23-2. His 1950 squad went 20-5 and both won Sectional titles. Jack Butcher's 3rd Lion team in 1961 won 20 games and lost 4, coming right after a 19-5 mark. That started a 4-year streak of 20-victory seasons, the next 3 being 23-3, 21-1, and 20-5, or a 4-year total of 84 wins and 13 losses. Not a bad start for a young coach! In 1967 Butcher's Lions went 20-2 and the 1970 and 1971 squads turned in 24-4 and 23-4 records. In 1974 it was 21-3, then the great 27-2 season. A 3-year streak started in 1980 with a 20-2 mark, followed by 22-4 and 23-1 seasons: 65 and 5 for that streak. Another undefeated regular season came in 1990 when the Lions lost their only game of 26 to Evansville Bosse in the 1st round of the Terre Haute Semi-state, 72-67. Jack Butcher's penultimate Loogootee team won 20 games and lost 5 in 2001, losing the Greencastle Semi-state final game in overtime, 64-61 to state-champion-to-be Attica. That's close. Not a bad finish for a great coach, either.

The Lady Lions turned in a 20-2 season for coach Sandy Siebert in 1980 and a 21-3 mark for Leslie Van Hoy in 2005. Both of those teams won Sectionals to go with the 2 others won by the girls teams and the Regional title won in 2002 by Roger Bailey's 18-7 squad.

LaPorte is a significant port on Lake Michigan. Because of extensive tree plantings in the last century, it is often referred to as "The Maple City." Although

The Slicing Machine

there were several important industries in LaPorte, one, far from the largest, so captured the imagination of the citizenry that they named their high school teams after it. What was it? Well, we've all heard the expression "the greatest thing since sliced bread" I guess. The United States Slicing Machine Company was located in LaPorte, and it would slice a lot of things, though I'm not that sure about bread. Certainly it would slice salami and bologna and turkey and would find a place in most every delicatessen and grocery store meat counter in the country.

Sure enough, the LaPorte High School teams are called the Slicers: slicing up the opposition is what they intend to do. Now, I'm sure that Slicers is an apt name for football teams, and basketball, soccer, and volleyball teams…but how about the golf team. Should they really be happy to be the LaPorte Slicers?

At any rate the Slicers on the basketball court have amassed 27 Sectional titles, 7 Regionals, and 2 Semi-states, 1944 at Hammond and 1997 at Lafayette. In 1944 the Slicers were edged by 3 points by eventual State Champion Evansville Bosse at the Coliseum in Indianapolis, 41-38, and in 1997 they lost by a single point, 57-56, to the Delta Eagles in the afternoon game at the RCA Dome. Twenty-victory seasons were accomplished in 1938, 21-6 for Coach Claron Veller; in 1940, 22-5 for Walter Blanda; in 1944 and 1948 for Norm Hubner; 22-5 and 20-4; in 1988, 1991, and 1997 for Joe Otis, 21-4, 22-4, 22-5; and in 2004, 21-4 for Tom Wells. The LaPorte girls teams have won 6 Sectional titles and one Regional, in 2000.

Two towns deserve special mention whenever you are talking about Hoosier sense of humor: Epsom, located in Daviess County, and Pimento just south of Terre Haute. Epsom has been consolidated into North Daviess High School via Montgomery or Plainville, and thus all of the former students have become Cougars after being Vikings or Midgets for a period. Pimento is now a part of the Terre Haute South Vigo Braves after a stop at Honey Creek.

North Daviess Cougars and Terre Haute South Braves

However, when these 2 schools were yet to be consolidated the sense of humor of the citizens of each was very much in evidence. They were the Epsom Salts and the Pimento Peppers. I have not been able to determine if the 2 ever played each other, but, if they did, what fun that must have been…and how savory! Regrettably, neither school ever won a Sectional insofar as I have been able to determine. Epsom, under Coach Leo O'Neill, made it to the final games of the 1932 and 1933 Washington Sectionals with wins over Elnora, 19-6, and Loogootee, 23-13, before losing to the Hatchets, 17-11, the 1st year. The next year the Salts beat Trinity, 33-11, edged Barr Township, 15-14, and took Alfordsville to task, 26-5, before losing a heartbreaker to the home team, 33-32. Pimento also had at least 2 strong seasons, 19-6 in 1931 for Coach Paul Garrigus and 17-4 for Bill Purcell in 1943. The 1931 team did manage to oust mighty Terre Haute Gerstmeyer from the

Terre Haute Sectional, 18-17, before being eliminated themselves by the Indiana State Laboratory School, 19-11. The 1943 Peppers were unable to get past the Black Cats in the 1st round of the Sectional, however.

I did discover an interesting fact about Epsom High School from the *Washington Democrat*, April 26, 1920, discussing the graduating class of that year:

> *An unusual feature in connection with the Epsom high school commencement exercises, held at the Epsom high school Saturday night, is the fact that all of the graduates, six in number, will enter the teaching profession.*

It should also be noted that the inventor of the Dictograph, K. Monroe Turner, was born in Pimento in September 1859.

Epsom and Pimento Schools, homes of the Salts and the Peppers

Pimento also produced Hall of Famer Keith Dougherty.

Keith Dougherty
Twelve students in class (at Pimento) ... 1942-43 team was 17-4; 1943-44 17-5 ... both years (Pimento Peppers) team won the Wabash Valley Preliminary tournament and advanced to the finals ... played for Hall of Famer Glen Curtis at Indiana State, left school to enter Air Force ... 21 years as a head basketball coach with 287 wins, 4 sectionals, 1 regional and 1 semi-state championship ... state runner-up in 1971 ... coached at Hymera 1950-58, Nappanee 1959-68, Elkhart 1968-72.

There's a bit more fun here. North Daviess High School is in Elnora. The original name of the town was Owl Town because of the abundance of owls in the area. The name was changed by William Griffith, who first laid out the town, to honor his wife. When a mascot and team name were needed for Elnora High School, history was remembered, and the teams were called the Owls. No Sectional titles for the red and white Owls, either, sad to say. They also had to contend with the Washington Hatchets every year. Those Owls did make it to the Sectional finals in 1937 with wins over Loogootee, 19-18, Alfordsville, 27-22, and Odon 21-19 before losing the last game to, who else, the Hatchets, 49-20. Bill Slatton's Owls turned in a 14-7 mark in the school's last year before becoming North Daviess Cougars in 1969.

Elnora High School, home of the Owls

Three other schools were incorporated into North Daviess. Plainville's sense of humor was well expressed in their choice of mascot. Since they were, after all, somewhat small, they became the Midgets. The 1936 through 1939 Midgets stood tall, running up an impressive won-lost record of 91-15(!), the first 2 under Coach Lloyd Sanders and the last 2 for Paul Johnson. They won Washington Sectionals in 1938 and 1956. The 1938 team went on to win the Washington Regional as well before losing a 31-23 decision to Martinsville's Artesians in the 1st round of that year's Sweet Sixteen. Kenneth Nelson's 1956 and 1957 teams went 25-4 and 23-2, winning the Washington Sectional in 1956 and being eliminated by one point by Loogootee St. Johns the next year, 54-53. One Plainville player who would hardly qualify as a Midget was Lloyd Bateman. Bateman stood 6´5˝ tall and weighed 230 pounds. As one of Plainville's 80 students, he became the first Hoosier high school player to score over 2,000 points in his career, totaling 2078, with a single-game high of 53. This he scored while playing only 3 quarters against Lyons in 1955, his sophomore season. During his 3 years on the Plainville varsity, Coach Nelson's teams won 88 of 100 games. They also reached the Final Four of the once potent Wabash Valley tournament that involved 120 schools from both Indiana and Illinois. Plainville Midgets? Not always, that's for sure.

Houck Photo of Exhibit
Courtesy IBHOF

Nearby Odon's teams were the Bulldogs (more on them later), and Raglesville's were the Rockets, who merged into Odon in 1940 and were joined by Plainville, Epsom, and Elnora to become the North Daviess Cougars in 1968.

Now let's turn our attention to other schools that have been consolidated into Terre Haute South. The town of Blackhawk was named in honor of the great Sauk Indian chief. Their teams were most appropriately the Chieftains. It must have been easy for them to accept the mascot of their new school, if a bit of a step down; they were the Braves. One of my all-time favorite team names came from the town of Honey Creek, whose teams were happily called the Honey Bees. And that's the boys teams! The Honey Bees won the Terre Haute Sectional in 1946, defeating Wiley, Concannon, Gerstmeyer, and the Laboratory School for Coach Lloyd Hensley, finishing 19-3. That 3rd loss came in the finals of the Martinsville Sectional, to Linton, after the Honey Bees had beaten Spencer in the 1st round.

Honey Creek High School and the Honey Bee

I also like the choice of Gophers by the town of Prairie Creek. Although the purple and white Gophers never won a Sectional, they did finish 16-4 for Harry Jarrett in 1943 and 22-3 for Dick Metz in 1959. That 3rd loss came in the final game of the Sullivan sectional by a single point to the home team, 42-41. The Prairie Creek Gophers became Honey Creek Honey Bees in 1962 before both became Terre Haute South Vigo Braves in 1971.

A bit harder for me to understand, I guess, was the team name selected by the town of Riley. Now, Riley is a good Irish name. But their teams were the Cossacks, a decidedly Russian selection. Whatever nationality, the Cossacks, who also sported purple and white uniforms, had terrific years in 1932, 21-4 for Jack Lowe; 1933, 20-4 for Ed Liston; and 20-4 in 1960 for Wayne Erwin, although they never were able to cut down the Sectional nets. In their bid for a

Gopher's pep sign. Houck photo from IBHOF.

Sectional title in 1932 they were ousted by a single point by the Honey Creek Honey Bees, 17-16. The next year it was to be by 4 points to the eventual champion Fontanet Beantowners, 16-12. As late as 1960, before they became a part of Terre Haute South in 1962, Wayne Erwin's Cossacks turned in a fine 20-win season with only 4 losses.

Riley High School, home of the Cossacks

Some of Terre Haute's original schools were split between North and South by the consolidation. These included the storied basketball programs of the Gerstmeyer Black Cats, with 11 Sectional championships, 6 Regionals, and 4 Semi-states. What a run they had in the mid-50s! In 1953 they were runner-up to the state champion South Bend Central Bears, losing the final game by a single point. The next year they were ousted by eventual state titlist Milan in the afternoon game of the finals as the Indians moved on to their memorable game with the Bearcats of Muncie Central that night. In 1956 the Black Cats again lost to the eventual champion in the afternoon game of the finals, this time to the Indianapolis Attucks Tigers. Finally, in 1957 Gerstmeyer again lost to Attucks, again in the afternoon game of the finals, only this time Attucks would not complete their try for a 3rd straight title, losing to South Bend Central that night. Gerstmeyer graduates include Bobby Leonard.

The Gerstmeyer Black Cat

Bobby Leonard
An all-around athlete at Terre Haute Gerstmeyer ... alternate on Indiana all-star team ... state tennis champion as a senior in 1950 ... 2-time All-American at Indiana University ... captain of IU's '53 national champions ... captained 2 Big 10 championship teams ... MVP as a sophomore of East-West college all-star game in Madison Square Garden ... 7 year NBA career ... coached in pro ranks 14 years ... his Indiana Pacers won the ABA 3 times...10 years as director of intramural and club sports at Stanford ... past president of World Amateur Baseball Federation ... member of executive board of U. S. Olympic Committee.

Graduates also include 6 other Hall of Famers plus baseball great Tommy John, whose pioneering arm surgery has saved many a major league pitcher's career. Other schools similarly dispersed were the Schulte Golden Bears and the Indiana State Lab School Young Sycamores.

Terre Haute Schulte Golden Bears are now North Vigo Patriots

The schools that consolidated to form North, in addition to those dispersed both ways, included the Fontanet Beantowners, who won their sole Sectional title at Terre Haute in 1933 with victories over Prairie Creek, Riley, and Wiley. Wendell Trogdon's book *Back Roads Indiana* informs us that there was an excellent restaurant in Fontanet that featured baked beans—and there is even a marker in town to remember where it was! —but that may or not be the reason for their team name. Maybe they wanted to beat the town of Boston on the other side of the state, in Wayne County. Boston, however, was content to be the Terriers.

Also in this group were the Glenn Pirates, the Otter Creek Otters (both covered elsewhere), and the Terre Haute Garfield Purple Eagles. Those Purple Eagles produced such stalwart Hall of Famers as Clyde Lovellette and Terry Dischinger, among others.

Clyde Lovellette
A dominating 6-9 center with Terre Haute Garfield ... as a junior in '47, he led his team to the state runner-up spot, scoring 25 points in a losing effort against Shelbyville ... All-State ... 3 times all-conference and all-Wabash Valley ... a 3-time All-American at Kansas ... twice led NCAA in scoring ... his Jayhawks won the national title in '52 ... that season named NCAA player of the year ... MVP in the '52 NCAA tourney ... gold medalist with the '52 U. S. Olympic team.

Terry Dischinger and the Garfield Purple Eagle
Letter-winner at Terre Haute Garfield, where he was also a champion track performer, All-State in football and also played baseball ... twice Garfield's basketball MPV ... captain and MVP of the 1958 Indiana all-star team ... Parade All-American ... went on to record-breaking career at Purdue ... 3-year All-American ... led Big 10 in scoring 3 yrs ... named to Big 10 scholastic team ... US Olympic gold medalist ... NBA rookie of the year in '63 ... all-star 3 of 9 years in league, despite career being interrupted by US Army ... MVP performer for Army all-Pacific champs...later assistant coach, then coach of all-Army basketball team...coached U.S. State Department goodwill basketball tour to Central America in '66.

Moving away from Vigo County to Miami County, how about Chili? Although it was not really much colder in Chili (and they pronounce it to rhyme with hi-fi, not chilly) than in the rest of Indiana, their teams were nonetheless the Polar Bears. The Polar Bears were hot, though, in 1954 when they posted a 21-2 record under Coach Robert Macy. Global warming?

Chili High School and the Bowdoin College polar bear

Another great choice for our clever names list was the town of Klondike just northwest of Lafayette. Combining a sense of humor with a knowledge of history of the famous gold rush of 1897, the Klondike teams were the Nuggets. That name has been retained for the town's elementary school. Their colors were blue and, appropriately, gold. Klondike High School is now part of West Lafayette High School.

Since there is another town in Indiana called Circleville, I had always assumed that Scircleville in Clinton County added the "S" to differentiate it. Wrong! Scircleville is spelled that way because it was founded in 1873 by one George Adam Scircle. Their high school teams? The Ringers, and here is the 1935 edition of The Ringers with a very respectable record of 20 wins and 6 losses, coached by Larry Hobbs, who also led the Red and White to a 20-win and 5-loss season in 1931:

The Scircleville Ringers 1935, 20-6, and their school

I'll close this round with 3 more Clinton County schools: Colfax, Kirklin and Sugar Creek. Colfax was originally called Midway, but the name was changed to honor New Carlisle resident Schuyler Colfax, who was Speaker of the United States House of Representatives before being elected vice president for Ulysses S. Grant's first term. Colfax teams were known as the Hickories, and, since eating there was a very popular thing to do after, say, Purdue football games, particularly if you liked catfish, I guessed they might be called the Hickories because of the hickory-smoked meals. But, no, most of those catfish dinners were deepfried. However, the town of Colfax had as its main employer a furniture maker whose products were made of, you guessed it, hickory. Even now the town celebrates Hickory Days every fall…and there still is at least one nice place to eat in town. Locals still remember the impressive records put up by the Hickory teams of 1941–43, winners of 62 games and losers of only 11, as well as the Frankfort Sectional championship team of 1957. That team defeated Kirklin, Scircleville, and Rossville at Frankfort and then bested Thorntown at the Lafayette Regional before being eliminated in the final game by Jefferson, who made it to the Final Four in Indianapolis themselves.

Hickory tree and leaf

Colfax High School

Kirklin is another town that I erred on originally. Their teams were the Travelers, and I, tongue in cheek of course, attributed the choice to a bit of ineptness on the basketball court. I knew that was not the case, however, as the school actually played the game very well and had its share of successful nights and seasons. So, my next guess was that they were admirers of General Robert E. Lee's horse. Another bum guess. The truth, as pointed out to me by two former Frankfort Hot Dogs, Bob and Tom Hall, was that the Kirklin teams were called the Travelers simply because they had no home court and played all of their games on the road—at least at first. There seems to be some thought that they, like the first great Wingate Spartan teams, eventually did get a home court. The black and gold Travelers are now Clinton Central Bulldogs.

Traveler, but not the Kirklin one, and Kirklin High School

Then there is the wonderfully named township of Sugar Creek. Who could not be happy living in a place so named? It is well known that we Hoosiers have some special ways of pronouncing some words. *Creek* is a good example. It often comes out more like "crick" in areas originally settled by our Scotch–Irish ancestors who used that word. Thus, it's not too surprising that the Sugar Creek teams were called the Crickets. They are also now Clinton Central Bulldogs.

Sugar Creek Consolidated School

Sugar Creek Consolidated School, home of the Crickets

Chapter 7

Even More Fun:
Oaks, Acorns, Twigs…
Immortals and Elites

In the last chapter we had a good deal of fun with some mascots that were selected by people with wonderful senses of humor. Let's do it again!

West Lebanon is located on the western edge of the state, near the town of Williamsport. Williamsport announces itself as the spot with the tallest waterfall in Indiana. My wife and I did go there to see it, and it is fairly tall, although most of the other states in the union have little to fear from it as competition for their own tallest waterfalls. Basketball is our forte, not waterfalls!

Indiana's tallest waterfall

Anyway, the West Lebanon teams were called the Pikers, which probably had nothing to do with Williamsport's waterfall, and nothing to do with the townspeople's generosity—because I am told they are as generous as any place—and more to do with the road that passed through town. I stand ready to be corrected on this, of course. They were also known as the Clippers for a time, hopefully the Yankee kind, those wonderful sailing ships made in New England. They outpaced anything the rest of the sea-going world could offer for many years, as perhaps, the West Lebanon teams hoped to do to their opposition. The purple and gold Clippers/Pikers played basketball from 1923 until 1959, never winning a Sectional crown.

West Lebanon and the Yankee Clipper Ship Lightning

Williamsport itself also had a high school. Their teams were called the Bingy Bombers. Why? You may ask, as I did. Well, the answer is that the original settlers to the area came from Bingen, Germany, and they thought the area looked a lot

 like the place they had left. So, Bingen, shortened to Bingy, Bombers it was. The Bombers name has been retained in the name of the teams of Williamsport Elementary School, updated from an airplane to a rocket! As early as 1912 Williamsport fielded a team that

won 7 games and lost only 2. The Bingy Bombers won 6 Sectional titles between 1935 and 1965, including 3 in a row for Don Andrews beginning in 1963. The 1964 red and black Bombers won 23 games and lost a heartbreaker to Crawfordsville in the Greencastle Regional, 63-62.

Both of the above schools became part of Seeger Memorial High School through consolidation. The Seeger teams, originally the Indians, are now the Patriots. The Patriots have won 2 Sectionals at Fountain Central, in 1967 and 1978.

The Lady Patriots have done better. They have won 9 Sectionals and 5 Regionals. Between 1992 and 1995 the Lady Patriots put together a record of 92 victories and only 7 losses, winning Sectional and Regional titles each year. Tom Polf's 1993 and 1995 teams were both undefeated in the regular season, 23-1 each year. This was "The Stephanie White Era" for Seeger. She was Indiana Miss Basketball in 1995 as well as National High School Player of the Year as selected by *USA Today*. She went on to lead Purdue to the national championship in 1999, winning the Wade Trophy as outstanding female basketball player in America.

The Seeger Memorial High School Patriot logo

Talk about whimsy—Horace Mann High School in Gary is named for a great American educator, born in 1796, champion of public education, Brown University graduate, lawyer, fierce advocate of freedom for slaves, and first president of Antioch College in Yellow Springs, Ohio. Their teams, in a bit of a slurry way of saying his name, are the Horace Mann Horsemen. The Horsemen won the tough Gary Sectional 5 times as well as 3 Regional crowns. Their only trip to the Final Four came in 1929 for long-time Coach Keith Crown, who held the job from 1926 through 1958. That team lost to Frankfort, 22-17, in the semi-final game at Butler

Gary Horace Mann Horsemen Shield

Fieldhouse. The Hot Dogs won the title. In 1942 the Horsemen had an outstanding 26-2 record, again losing to Frankfort, this time in the first round of the Hammond Semi-state. The Lady Horsemen garnered their only Sectional title in 1984.

Spencer is a pleasant town of about 20,000 people located on the White River northwest of Bloomington. It is the seat of what is often called "sweet" Owen County. Interestingly, both the county and the town are named for officers killed in the Battle of Tippecanoe, Captain Spier Spencer and Colonel Abraham Owen. The United States census of 1920 determined that the center of population of the country was 8 miles south-southeast of Spencer. The townspeople liked this and decided to use it for their high school nickname: the Spencer High School Cops, not of the police variety, but of the Center Of Population variety! Spencer is now home to the consolidated Owen Valley Patriots. The Cops won 9 Sectionals between 1927 and 1970. They also had an excellent 22-5 season for Glenn Rickets in 1941. (It should be noted that from 1890 until 1940 6 Indiana cities or towns had the distinction of being the nation's center of population as it gradually moved westward: Greensburg 1890, Columbus 1900, Bloomington 1910, Spencer 1920, Linton 1930, and Carlisle 1940.)

Near Princeton, in the far southwestern part of the state, is the town of Ft. Branch. You have to love a town with that name that chose to name its high school teams the Twigs! Those Twigs did extremely well under Coach Larry Holden for the 4-year stretch from 1961–64, winning 75 games while losing only 19. They also won 8 Sectionals between 1941 and 1963. Their Gibson County rivals used to have a special approach when playing Ft. Branch. They would all bring twigs to the game and at a pre-determined time would cheer "Break those twigs" while simultaneously snapping the little branches. There are more ways to have fun at an Indiana high school basketball game than most of us could ever imagine!

Ft. Branch High School, home of the Twigs

Just a bit to the east, near Jasper, the Oakland City High School teams were the Acorns. Elsewhere, the towns of Oaklandon and Oaktown were each the Oaks. I don't know whether or not either of the Oaks ever played the Acorns, or which came first! At any rate, the Oakland City Acorns enjoyed an undefeated regular season under Coach Charlie Brauser, going 23-1 in 1967, winning the Princeton Sectional by slipping past Mt. Vernon, 59-55; dropping North Posey, 57-43; and edging those very same Twigs, 67-65. Acorns over Twigs. Anyway, that lone defeat came at the hands of Evansville North in the Regional

Oaktown High School.

tournament, 71-60. That happened to be the year that the North Huskies and Bob Ford would win their state championship. The 1967 Oakland City Acorns were truly a team to remember. Brauser's teams also were 19-4 in 1966, 19-6 in 1970, and 20-3 in 1971.

For some reason unknown to me the town of Arlington, near Rushville, chose the Purple Breezes to be the name of their teams. Those Breezes did blow away much of their competition in 1934 and 1935, winning 35 of 45 games for Coach James Hyatt; in 1947 and 1948, when they won 40 and lost only 9 with Lawrence Pearl coaching; and for the 3 year period 1956–58, going 59-14, with Morris Newman in the coaching box. The Purple Breezes won Sectionals in 1942 and 1947. They are now consolidated into Rushville High School, the Lions.

Not far away, close to Knightstown, is Spiceland, first settled in the 1820s by Quakers from Virginia and the Carolinas. They established the famed Friends

Academy, precursor of Spiceland High School, now a part of the Tri High Titans. The academy's teams, called the Quakers, achieved a 17-7 record in 1920, including the New Castle Sectional crown, also won in 1919. These wins placed the Quakers in the state finals at Indiana University, where they lost a 1st round game to Logansport, 9-5, on their first trip and defeated Evansville, 31-14, before losing to Anderson, 26-4, on their second. In 1922 the academy was absorbed into Spiceland High

Spiceland Academy, home of the Quakers

School. The town of Spiceland derived its name from the abundance of wild spice bushes growing there, which often reached a height of 12 feet or more. These plants must have attracted many bumblebees, wasps, or hornets because the Spiceland teams were called the Stingers and the Yellow Jackets. The Stingers/Yellow Jackets had a great season for Virgil Schooler in 1936, finishing 23-3. They broke through and won the New Castle Sectional in 1947 for Harvey Davidson with wins over Sulphur Springs, Straughn, and Knightstown.

The Stingers of Spiceland High School

They may have once had a hat factory in Mellott, northwest of Crawfordsville, because their teams were the Derbies. The Derbies won 17 of 22 games in 1924 and captured their lone Sectional at Veedersburg in 1928. After a period as Red Devils when they were part of Richland Township, whose teams won 3 Sectionals in the 50s, they are now Mustangs at Fountain Central.

Mellott High School

Or maybe they once had a special horse race held in Mellott. If that is the case, perhaps the Montpelier Pacers came over from their town near Marion to compete. The Pacers were also called the Oil City Five and the Spartans, and they had a wonderful stretch under coaches James Barley and Jon Stroup from 1965–67, with records of 21-3, 21-3, and 21-2. They were also 18-3 in 1958. Between 1927 and 1967 Montpelier teams won 5 Sectionals. They wore black and gold and are now Blackford Bruins.

An early Montpelier High School

Blackford Bruin Tracks

Here's a natural pairing: The town of Orange, Indiana, is located near Connersville. In deference perhaps to the House of Orange, Old Nassau, and Princeton University far to the east, the Orange High School teams were the Tigers, as are those of Princeton High School in Gibson County. Byron Smith led the Orange Tigers to a 20 and 2 season in 1951. After an 8-year stint wearing the green and gold of Fayette Central's Chiefs, they are now Connersville Spartans.

Though they are the Tigers, Princeton was named after Captain William Prince, one of the original settlers, not the Ivy League school. The Tigers have enjoyed many excxellent seasons that have been carefully chronicled by former teacher and coach Tim Nonte. Princeton High School's first team was fielded in 1914 and the first of 33 Sectional titles was won for coach Charles McConnell in 1928, finishing 19-6. His 1934 and 1935 squads rang up 20-9 and 25-4 records, both years winning the Regional crown and heading for the Sweet Sixteen. In 1948 Earl Downey's Tigers went 20-5 while Dick Falls led his 1950-52 teams to 59 wins and only 13 losses. Princeton Lincoln, an all black school, consolidated with Princeton in 1949-50. Bob Lochmueller's 1956 team won the school's 3rd (of 7) Regional championships with an outstanding 25-2 mark. That year Leonard Nolcox became the first black player to play varsity ball for Princeton. In 1957 coach Bill Richeson had a 20-4 record and a Sectional title and in 1965, led by Larry Kidwell, the team rang up a 22-7 mark, losing the Final Four morning game

The Princeton Tiger

to eventual State Champion Washington Continentals and their tandem of Purdue-bound stars, Billy Keller and Ralph Taylor. In 1965-66 Princeton was joined by the White River "Rapids,"a consolidation of the Hazleton Lions and the Patoka Wrens in 1963-64, as well as the Mt. Olympus Mountaineers. Jim Jones coached the 1976 team to a 22-3 record. His 1983 Final Four team was led by Brad Fichter and had an amazingly similar experience in Indianapolis to that of their predecessors of 18 years, finishing 22-6 after losing the morning game to the eventual champion Connersville Spartans and the Heineman twins. Two years later Jones' team completed the Tigers' first undefeated season, 23-1 with the only loss to Bosse in the final game of the

Evansville Regional. Marty Echelbarger's 1989 team won 21 of 24 games, but it was the 2009 Tiger team that will never be forgotten by Gibson County fans. They won the 3A state championship in grand style, undefeated, 29-0, capturing the final game in a thrilling 2-overtime battle of the veldt over the Rochester Zebras 81-79. The Lady Tigers have added 7 Sectional nets to the Princeton trophy case and Tamara Wertman's 1996 team finished 22-4 with a Semi-state title.

From Elites to Titans in Gibson County. License plate Houck photo from exhibit courtesy IBHOF.

Here's another mascot I find compelling: Haubstadt is also in the far southwest part of the state in beautiful Gibson County. The unabashed, prideful nickname for their teams was the Elites. And elite they were in 1927, when they won 18 and lost 5; in 1930, 18-2; and in 1961, 20-3. That latter year they won their lone Sectional crown at Princeton. They did so by defeating the Ft. Branch Twigs 14-12 in 3 overtimes in the final game. They are now Titans at Gibson Southern.

Interestingly, there were also Elites at another school, at least for a time. Elberfeld's teams, in Warrick County, were known as the Elites, but also as the Hornets, and it is not clear to me if these existed at the same time or were sequential. Their teams wore red and black, and they were in pretty elite company in 1945, when Martin Blesch led the team to a 20 and 3 record. Hall of Famer Bob Lochmueller led that team. Then again, in 1958 Erwin Whitehead's team stung the opposition to the tune of 18 wins and 5 losses, and 5 years later Larry Erwin's squad won 17 of 20 games. They are now Tecumseh Braves

Bob Lochmueller
A 3-year starter at tiny Elberfield, leading team to best record in school history as a senior ... 3-year starter at University of Louisville ... led team in scoring as junior and senior ... team MVP both years, leading Louisville into the NCAA and NIT ... played 1 year for the Syracuse Nationals before career ending knee injury ... assistant coach at West Virginia ... spent 23 years as a Hoosier high school coach, with 399-150 record ...14 NCAA regional tournaments ... career capped by 5 appearances in NCAA national finals.

The Bloomingdale Academy teams in Parke County were, perhaps a bit optimistically, the Immortals. Sad to say, the academy no longer exists, but while they did they managed to win the 1915 Brazil Sectional title.

The Turkey Run Warrior

They are now a part of Turkey Run High School, the Warriors.

The following came to me via Dewey Sprunger from Monticello, from an article by Kevin Cullen that appeared in the *Lafayette Journal & Courier* on 1/27/94 titled "When a Name Meant Something." I have embellished his article with some facts and stories of my own.

1. Newton County is our youngest, becoming the 92nd when it was reconstituted in 1859. It had originally been established in 1835 but was abolished and combined with Jasper County 4 years later. Both counties were named for officers who had served under Revolutionary War hero General Francis Marion, known as "The Swamp Fox" and recently popularized in the Mel Gibson movie *The Patriot*. The area was originally well populated with beavers, and the town of

Morocco—and I don't know what any of this has to do with a country in North Africa —was in Beaver Township quite near to Beaver City and Beaver Lake. Their school teams were known as the Beavers, and before every basketball game a stuffed beaver was placed in the center circle. The Beavers won Sectional championships in 1934 and 1956. The 1934 squad also picked off the Auburn Regional, defeating Columbia City, 35-30, and Ligonier in a heart-stopping final game, 34-33.

Morocco Stuffed Beaver, pennant, and school crest; Pennant Houck photo from exhibit courtesy IBHOF

The Morocco fight song, to the tune of the University of Chicago's "Wave the Flag for Old Chicago," went like this, from their Alumni Web site:

School Fight Song Lyrics
(for those of us who have forgotten them)

We, the students of Morocco,   With the Spirit and the Courage,
Fight for our Old High,   We'll March to Victory,
Black and Gold are our Colors,   Hail to Old Morocco High School,
Floating through the Sky!   We Pledge our Loyalty!

2. Michigantown was on the Michigan Road, which ran all the way from Madison to Michigan City. Citizens of Michigan are often called Michiganders, and the Michigantown teams were quite logically called the Ganders. They actually had a live gander that they proudly displayed at their home games. Those Michigantown Ganders had a 20-3 mark for Coach Larry Farrell in 1929 and were 19-2 in 1931. He also coached the Ganders to an undefeated regular season in 1933, when they won 27 of 28 games. Joe Bell took over in 1936 and achieved an 18-4 record, followed by 16-10 and 23-3 records the next 2 years. The 1940 team had an outstanding 21-3 record, and in 1954 Wilbur Rule coached the team to a 22 and 2 mark. The Ganders, whose only Sectional title came in 1933 at Frankfort, also won the Regional at Lebanon,

beating Earl Park, 35-17, and the host Tigers, 42-30. That earned them a trip to the Sweet Sixteen where they were eliminated by Logansport 22-12.

The Clinton Central Bulldog

Gander=Male Goose!

3. Burlington had no gym. The high school first played basketball in 1912, winning 13 of 17 games, on the second floor of the general merchandise store downtown. The room was heated by a single potbellied stove. One cold night opponents asked, "Who are these guys, polar cubs?" and the name stuck: the Burlington Polar Cubs. The Cubs, who won Sectionals in 1927 and 1943 at Flora, have become Carroll County Cougars.

Burlington High School

Home of the Polar Cubs

4. I have heard a very similar story told about Winslow, which was reported to have 2 such stoves, neither one of which always did the job on chilly Indiana winter nights, resulting in the team name the Winslow Eskimos. Did they play in the igloo?

The Winslow Eskimos, and early and more recent Winslow High School buildings

The Eskimos have a proud basketball heritage that was created over many years beginning with the 1918 team's 11-4 record, and closely followed by 1919's 11-1 and 1921's 15-4. The 1922–24 seasons were outstanding with two 26-4 marks followed by a 22-4 season, a nice 3-year string of 74-12. In 1941 the Eskimos won 20 of 24 games; in 1942 they won 24 and lost only 3, following that with a 20-2 record the next year, another impressive 3-year string, this time 64 wins and only 9 losses. In 1945 Winslow won 19 and lost 3. The 1949 Eskimos were undefeated in the regular season, winning 23 of 24 games. In 1952 they went 26-2 followed by 23-1 and 18-3 seasons for Coach Kern McGlothlin. The 1949 and 1950 teams were led by Dick Farley who was to be such a significant part of Indiana University's second NCAA Championship year in 1953.

Dick Farley
Led Winslow High School to a 4 year record of 83-8...team undefeated in 1949, his junior year that group was upset in sectional by state finals bound Jasper....Named to Indiana All-Stars...3 year letterwinner at Indiana University...national champs in 53... named IU's top senior in '54...Played for the Detroit Pistons after serving in the military.

Kern McGlothlin the Wizard of Winslow.
Helped lead his Stendal Aces to 3 straight Pike County championships, 1927 through '30, despite fact team had no gymnasium and practiced outdoors ... captained Evansville College team in '34 ... played 4 years there, teaming with Hall of Famer Arad McCutchan ... a 25-year coaching career — all at small schools—, ended with a 319-134 record ... stops included Cynthiana, Stendal, Greencastle, Cannelton and Winslow ... coached Winslow to 3 appearances in Sweet 16 ... his '49 team was undefeated, but lost in sectional title game to Jasper, the eventual state champion...served as principal at Winslow and then at Fort Branch.

The 4-year stretch from 1949 through 1952 resulted in 90 wins and only 9 losses! They were also 22-4 in 1954. The Eskimos placed 7 Sectional and 3 Regional crowns in their trophy case along with many other prizes. The Sweet Sixteen teams were in 1950, 1951, and 1954. In 1950 the Eskimos beat Evansville Bosse to make the Elite Eight. They are now Chargers at Pike Central.

The 1923 and 1924 champion Eskimos

John Dedman, who supplied the above team photos, has created a wonderful Web site to preserve much of this phenomenal Winslow Eskimo basketball heritage. Among other facts he cites:

1. The colors of purple and gold were chosen by the class of 1916.

2. The name Eskimos came about in the early 30s.

3. Winslow was the first small school team to be ranked as high as third in the state (1950).

4. All games were played on the road that year and the next due to new gym construction.

5. Attica High School teams are the Red Ramblers. There are 2 theories as to why this is the case. The 1st is that their coach drove a small Nash model, which was a red Rambler. The other, generally given more credence, is that one year the team played a whole season on the road while their gym was being built. Since their school colors were red and white, they became known as the Red Ramblers. An early version of their mascot was a person dressed as a hobo with his clothes in a handkerchief tied to a stick. For various reasons this depiction fell into disfavor and was replaced by a Purdue Pete type. With the passage of more time even this version was found insufficient, and the present mascot is a ram.

The Ramblers have fielded basketball teams every year since at least 1910. Coach Floyd Coffing's teams won 20 games and lost 9 in 1926 and were 20-6 the next year. Coach E. A. Lambert's 1941 squad had a 19-4 mark, followed by 15-2 the next year and 3 fine seasons from 1948–50 when the Ramblers were 21-7, 21-5, and 18-6. Denny Blind-coached Attica teams were 21-8 in 1958 and 1959, and Ted Dunn-led teams had excellent years in 1961 and 1962, 23-4 and 25-7, followed by another strong pair in 1965 and 1966, when they went 21-5 and 19-6. The tendency to have outstanding years in pairs continued under Dan Andrews in 1968 and 1969, when the Ramblers had records of 21-5 and 20-3. They enjoyed a 22-3 season under Don Burton in 1983 and had a 3-year run for Coach Ralph Shrader beginning in 1999 with marks of 19-3, 17-6, and culminating in the 2001 Class A State Championship, 21-6. All of this has also added up to 23 Sectional titles, 6 Regionals, and one Semi-state for the very successful Attica Ramblers.

The Lady Ramblers hit their own stride in 2005, winning 3 straight Sectional titles for Coach Dave Baxter. Their 23-3 record in 2006 also brought them a Regional title.

6. Wallace teams were known as the Peppers. (They, too, should have played the Epsom Salts!) No, peppers were not grown in the area. The team was so named for the spirit of the student body, who actually helped build their own gym. That spirit helped the Peppers to the 1925 Attica Sectional championship with wins over Pine Village, Judyville, Williamsport, and Hillsboro. At the Frankfort Regional, the Peppers eliminated Wingate, 23-19, prior to being ousted by West Point.

7. Pine Village was located near a towering pine that gave its name to Pine Creek, the trading post that grew up there, and eventually to the town. When the high school team was formed it was called Pine Knots, the toughest part of the tree. Pine Knot Power! They sang:

The power of the Pine Knot makes us strong
We do our best all day long
As we read and write and calculate
Pine Knot Power makes us great!
PINE KNOT POWER!!!!

Pine Knot Power today has become Patriot Power

The Pine Knots won 6 Sectionals between 1921 and 1972. Pine Village graduate Mike Jones is a Hall of Famer:

Mike Jones
Pine Village Wonder
4 letters in baseball and 3 in basketball ... Sophomore - 12 ppg All-Sectional, set sectional scoring record of 30 points in 1953 ... Coach, Forest Martin ... 4 letters in basketball and 2 in track at Indiana State ... Senior year (18-8) Conference Champs, NAIA Regional and District Champs, All-Tourney Team ... Coach, Duane Klueh ... Coached at Roachdale 1959-61 ... Cathedral 1961-64 ... Rossville 1964-78, 4 Sectionals, 3 Regionals, 6 Holiday tourneys, 7 Conferences ... led team to 3 consecutive semi-state appearances ... District 3 Coach 3 times and Conference coach 4 times ... Wawasee 1978-81 ... Delphi 1981-92.

Wendell Trogdon, the entertaining and knowledgeable Hoosier writer, comes from Heltonville, as does Damon Bailey. Damon's performance in the 1990 state championship game for Bedford North Lawrence at the Hoosier Dome before the largest crowd ever to see a high school basketball game anywhere must rank as one of the greatest of all time. Wendell tells me that, before consolidation into Bedford North Lawrence, when Heltonville had its own high school, their teams were called the Bluejackets.

Back in the days before they had a gym, practices were outside in the cold. One of the mothers got some denim cloth and made jackets for all of the boys on the team, which they wore to practice and for pregame warm-ups. The Heltonville Bluejackets had their best season in 1954, the year Milan won the state championship for "all the small schools," winning 18 games while only losing 5 for Coach Paul Hardwick. Ira Morrison's 1955 team also did well, winning 16 of 20 games, but Heltonville never was able to capture that elusive Sectional title.

The Heltonville Bluejacket

Nearby Mitchell High School teams still are the Bluejackets, and the mascot is a bumblebee, normally called a yellowjacket, but sometimes painted blue. Astronaut Virgil I. "Gus" Grissom, the second American to fly in space, was a Mitchell native. The Bluejackets have won 12 Sectional championships, 4 Regionals, and one Semi-state. The latter came in 1940, when All-Stater Roy Ramey led Mitchell to the final game, which was lost, 33-21, to the Hammond Tech Tigers. The team finished 25-6 for Coach Henry Poison. Bill Shepherd coached the Bluejackets from 1950 through 1958, his best year being 1956, 21-4. J. R. Holmes was the coach from 1973 through 1982, his best mark being 1981's 18-4. In 1987 Stan Weber's Bluejacket team won 20 and lost only 5. The Lady Bluejackets were coached by Ross

Simpson from 1998 through 2007 with winning records every year including 2002's 20-4 mark. They captured their lone Sectional and Regional crowns in 2007.

The Mitchell Bluejacket and astronaut Gus Grissom

Tom Wallace told me the following story about Selma:

Originally the team's name was the Blue Devils, but when the star player's mother took exception to this, considering it, perhaps, a sacrilege, she informed the coach and the school that her son would not play for any team so named. A quick decision was reached to shelve the Devils and replace it with the Birds!

Selma had 3 outstanding seasons, winning 19 of 22 games in 1944 for Earl Snider and later, under John Bright, the undefeated regular season of 1964, 23-1, and the 20-5 record of 1967. That sole loss *Houck photo of exhibit courtesy IBHOF*
in 1964 came in the Muncie Sectional. After Selma defeated Burris, 55-52, they were in turn beaten by South, 64-61. The Bluebirds won their only Sectional at Winchester in 1967 with wins over Center, Monroe Central, and Union City. They are now a part of the Wapahani Raiders.

Selma School and the Wapahani Raiders' logo

Chapter 8

The Unusual:
Rappites, Jeeps, Oracles, and Alices

Although we are indeed all Hoosiers, we do have differences. We have also used considerable imagination, often our sense of humor, and many times our unique history to make the selections of our high school team names. As some of the names selected are far from obvious I think it is important that we not lose the reasons behind their selection.

The town of New Harmony, Indiana, is located in the far southwestern portion of our state, on the Wabash River near its confluence with the Ohio. A bridge across the Wabash leads to Illinois, and a short drive from there to the Shawnee National Forest and beyond that to the interesting rock formations of the Illinois version of the Garden of the Gods.

New Harmony was originally settled by the German idealist George Rapp, who had first come to Pennsylvania from Wurttemberg, Germany, to found a millenial community. He was attracted to the commercial opportunities afforded by the two rivers near his chosen Indiana site and purchased 30,000 acres in 1815 that he called Harmonie. Soon his community was prospering.

Over 150 homes were built as well as a grist mill, an oil mill, a saw mill, a grand granary, a silk factory, brick kiln, dye works, a distillery, and a brewery. There were orchards, a vineyard, and fields for a variety of crops. Unfortunately, as was true for virtually all such communes historically, this prosperity did not last, and the site was sold to a Scotsman named Robert Owen and his friend, scientist and philanthropist, William McClure.

Their vision was to create a Utopian community of scholars, educators, and scientists, and they were initially quite successful at luring many great thinkers from Europe to enjoy the fruits of a society less encumbered by the restrictions on thought they had encountered in the Old World. There was indeed freedom of thought in the town. Owen renamed the town New Harmony, and, although the Utopian ideals of a communal society failed rather rapidly, the mark of the great thinkers was indelibly left on the American scene. New Harmony became a center for scientific thought, educational innovation, and the feminist movement in the New World. Linkages were made to the Philosophical Society in Philadelphia; New Harmony became a dominant force in the fields of geology, zoology, botany, and chemistry. What was later to become the United States Geological Survey had its roots in New Harmony. Theologian Paul Tillich made retreats to New Harmony an important part of his contemplative life.

New Harmony is truly an American historic gem, well worth a visit by anyone interested in understanding and unraveling the mysteries of the past. There is, in fact, still a small high school in New Harmony. With the new class-based tournaments, they are now more often competitive in their Sectional, and once when I was there I saw spray painted in many a store window "Go Rappites." Although the Rappites have never won that elusive Sectional title, Larry Kahle coached the 1981 team to a 15-6 record, and his 1985 squad finished 16-7.

The Lady Rappites, also coached by Kahle, turned in successive seasons beginning in 2001 of 17-5, 23-2 and 20-4. I know a lot of schools that would be pleased to turn in a 3-year mark of 60 wins and 11 losses! And they did bring home the Sectional crown in 2002. Go Rappites, indeed. What a marvelous nickname for a truly marvelous place.

There are presently only 4 high schools in all of beautiful DuBois County: Jasper, Southridge, Forest Park, and Northeast Dubois. The latter is located just north of the town of Dubois, and their rather unique team name is the Jeeps. The last time I was there I met Dr. Keith Seeger, a Purdue graduate and a very pleasant, articulate man. He teaches history in the middle school in the town of Dubois. He told me his father, Ralph, was a member of the then Dubois High School basketball team before its consolidation into the county school. Ralph Seeger would also later coach basketball at his alma mater while teaching math there. It was that team who gathered behind a local church, which he pointed out to me. One afternoon some 70 years ago they came together to seek a mascot appropriate to their conception of what they wanted their team to be. They decided on Jeeps, reported their decision to their coach and principal, Dallas Ferguson, who accepted it, and Jeeps it was and is to this day. But what is a Jeep? A general-purpose vehicle for the military? No, that kind of Jeep didn't come along until World War II. I turned to the school's Web site to get the answer.

Not a vehicle but a critter

What is a Jeep?

On March 20, 1936, the comic strip "Popeye" featured an imaginary little magical character known as Eugene the Jeep, supposedly the eighth wonder of the world. Popeye once asked Professor Brainstine, "What's a Jeep?" Professor Brainstine replied with this statement:

A Jeep is an animal living in a three dimensional world—in this case our world—but really belonging to a fourth dimensional world. Here's what happened.

A number of Jeep life cells were somehow forced through the dimensional barrier into our world. They combined at a favorable time with free life cells of the African Hooey Hound. The electrical vibrations of the Hooey Hound cell and the foreign cell were the same. They were kindred cells. In fact, all things are to some extent relative, whether they be of this or some other world, now you see. The extremely favorable conditions of germination in Africa caused a fusion of these life cells. So the uniting of kindred cells caused a transmutation. The result, a mysterious strange animal.

To this, Popeye replied, "What's a Jeep?" So, the good doctor faces the same questions we face on every school road trip...

Alves J. Kreitzer, a local store owner in Dubois (who would later become the coach of the basketball team) purchased a miniature Jeep in St. Louis, and it became the team mascot. The first game played as Jeeps was played at Shoals on November 6, 1936. The Jeeps won the game 29-21 and went on to establish a 17-4 won-lost record that season. The 1937–38 season brought a mark of 18-5, and the Jeep mascot was here to stay.

Eugene the Jeep is a yellowish cat-like creature.

The only other school in the country that we know of with the JEEP as a mascot is South Wilkinson's in Ohio. [The Jeep was also the mascot of Wheatland High School in Knox County prior to its consolidation.]

When I was being interviewed at the Indiana Basketball Hall of Fame in New Castle by Dick Wolfsie for his television show, he suggested that I select several varsity letter jackets and sweaters once owned by inductees that would be demonstrative of some of our state's more uncommon mascots. One of the jackets I found in Roger Dickinson's extensive and colorful collection was from the DuBois High School Jeeps. When I looked at the name of the owner of the jacket, I was pleased to see that it had once belonged to none other than Ralph Seeger!

Ralph Seeger's letter jacket

Ralph Seeger coached the Jeeps for 12 seasons, winning 131 games. His best years as coach were 1952–54, with records of 16-5, 18-4, and 18-4. The Jeeps also went 18-5 in 1941 and 14-5 the next year. Their best record was the undefeated regular season of 1943, 16-1 under Coach Alves Kreitzer, whose overall record at DuBois was 60-17. His successor, James Jackson, coaching the Jeeps for only 3 years, won 34 and lost 12 from 1944–46.

After consolidation the now Northeast DuBois Jeeps have also had their moments, beginning in 1977 with a 20-5 season under Coach Jim Mueller. In 1987 and 1988 the Jeeps won 18 games each year, losing 5 and then 6 with Alan Matheis at the helm. (Driving the Jeep??) All told the Jeeps have won 5 Sectionals and 3 Regionals.

The Lady Jeeps have done even better, beginning with an 18 and 2 record for Coach Jerry Mills in 1985. They also had an outstanding string for Beth Neukam from 1998 through 2000, finishing 21-3, 17-7 and having an undefeated season of 23-1 in the latter year. The Lady Jeeps have cut down the nets after 10 Sectionals, 4 Regionals, and 1 Semi-state. In 2005 with Alan Matheis coaching they lost the Class 1A State Championship by a single point in a 47-46 thriller to the TriCentral Lady Trojans, finishing with a 20-6 record. His next 3 teams turned in 18-7, 19-7, and 22-4 marks for a 4-year total of 79 wins and 24 losses,

The prize for most imaginative use of history in establishing high school nicknames in Indiana could be awarded to Delphi. The town itself, with its 2,500 inhabitants, is the seat of Carroll County in the north central part of the state. It is on Deer Creek, and the Wabash River flows by just to the west. The town was laid out in 1828 and was originally called Deer Creek, then Carrollton, but that needed to be changed when it was realized there already was a town of that name in Indiana, and not too far away, either. A group of town leaders gathered to agree on a new name and a list of possibilities was submitted by War of 1812 veteran General Samuel Milroy. The name Delphi was selected in honor of the ancient Greek city, site of the most important of all Greek temples and the Oracle of Apollo, where a prophetess told visitors of their future.

Ancient Delphi was considered the center of the world by the Greeks, its location having been determined when Zeus let an eagle fly from the east of the universe and another from the west and they met over Delphi. Not a bad name for a small settlement in the relatively new state of Indiana. In the 1840s Delphi became an important port on the Wabash and Erie Canal that ran from Toledo to Evansville and later became a significant stop on the Monon Railroad line, so important to the 19th and early 20th century development of the state. Franklin Roosevelt visited Delphi once during his presidency, and it is sometimes considered the 2nd home of James Whitcomb Riley, the great Hoosier poet from Greenfield. Actor MacDonald Carey spent a good portion of his youth in Delphi. The Delphi High School teams are wonderfully called the Oracles: the Oracles of Delphi.

Two versions of the Oracle logo

The Oracles have enjoyed several outstanding seasons. In 1924 they finished 25-6 under Coach Sam Kerr, winning their 1st of the school's 20 Sectional championships. Paul Lustutter coached Delphi for 9 years beginning in 1926 during which time the Oracles won 6 straight Sectional titles as well as 3 of their 4 Regional crowns. The 1929 squad went undefeated in the regular season, finishing 23-1. The 1930 team beat the Kokomo Wildkats in the 1st round of the Sweet Sixteen before losing to Connersville at Butler Fieldhouse. In 1983 the Oracles turned in a 20-3 record with Hall of Fame Coach Mike Jones at the helm. The Delphi girls teams have won 3 Sectionals themselves, including 2 in a row for coach Jeff Gher in 1995 and 1996, finishing 18-5 and 17-7. Delphi graduates Bill Perigo and Doxie Moore are in the Hall of Fame.

Bill Perigo
3-yr standout center for Delphi High School...all-sectional, all- regional each season...twice helped his team to state finals, the second squad finishing regular season undefeated...stood only 6-1, but considered the greatest jumping center of his era...All-State...played 3 years with Western Michigan...led team to 40-13 record in that time.

Doxie Moore

A 4-year starter at Delphi High School ... a 3-time all-sectional and all-regional performer ... as a senior in 1930, his 4-minute, one-man dribbling stall gave Delphi a return trip to state tourney ... played on 2 Big 10 championship teams at Purdue University ... one of those years he unknowingly played with a broken leg ... played on 2 Big 10 football champions ... in his first intercollegiate game, he ran 78 yards for a touchdown the first time he carried the ball and scored 3 touchdowns ... AD, coach at West Lafayette ... coached and managed Sheboygan, Wis., Redskins professional basketball team ... 2 years later, in '48, became commissioner of the National Basketball League ... after merger with BAA, became manager and coach of Anderson Duffy Packers, reaching NBA championship game ... in '51, organized and was vice president and coach of Milwaukee Hawks ... Indiana Basketball Hall of Fame Foundation.

Vincennes is a fascinating city. It was founded by the French in 1732, and a number of descendents of the original settlers still live there. It soon became a hub of settlement, with its rich river valley farmland attracting settlers. When the southern part of Indiana was originally being settled, many pioneer families crossed the Ohio River at Louisville or merely stopped their barges at the Falls of the Ohio and began to make their way west from New Albany. There was no easy way to do this. Southern Indiana was densely grown with hardwood forests. Trails had to be tediously hacked out, day by day, by cutting down those trees and making a path wide enough for the wagons that would carry the homesteaders to their desired destination. Many followed an old Indian trail known as the Buffalo Trace, now roughly the route of US Highway 150. Some stopped in what are now Orange, DuBois (French for "the forest") and Martin counties, but many pressed on until they reached the banks of the Wabash River. There they developed the city of Vincennes in Knox County, in many respects Indiana's first city.

Vincennes was once the home of General George Rogers Clark, who captured the British fort there by attacking it from the west after also winning an important battle in Kaskaskia on the other side of Illinois. He is now honored by the national historic park and memorial bearing his name there. Vincennes was the first territorial capital of Indiana when William Henry Harrison, destined to become President of the United States, was the territorial governor. The capitol building, built in 1805 and called the Red House, is still there and open to the public, as is Harrison's home, Grouseland.

The Vincennes Lincoln High School teams are the Alices. This one is a little easier to understand, although there are 2 theories that seem to have equal credence as to the selection of Alices for the school's nickname. The first theory refers to the 1923 state championship Vincennes High basketball team who played, according to one sportswriter "Like Alice in Wonderland" when they defeated Muncie 27-18. (They would repeat as champions in 1981 with a 54-52 victory over Anderson.) The other, preferred by most of the locals to whom I have spoken, is that it stems from a novel, *Alice of Old Vincennes*, written by Maurice Thompson about the Revolutionary War. The book was popular in the early days of the 20th century: Alice was an orphan who fell in love with one of George Rogers Clark's soldiers. Published in 1900 it was also converted to a Broadway play. Thompson's original home was in Fairfield, but it was moved to Vincennes because it would have been inundated when the Brookville Reservoir was constructed.

At any rate, according to the school's Web site, the first time the teams were referred to as "Alices" was by the *Vincennes Commercial* newspaper as early as 1911. However, the teams were generally called the Pirates until the name Alices was officially adopted in November 1924. (Either of these dates creates a bit of an argument for those Felix the Cat fans of Indianapolis Shortridge and Logansport, though!) Either way, Alices is a unique and marvelous team name for a fine school that represents a unique and marvelous city in our unique and marvelous state.

The first basketball game played by Vincennes High School (before it became Vincennes Lincoln) was on February 25, 1905. Unfortunately, it was a loss to Freelandville. It was not until 1907 that the first win was recorded, over Princeton. In 1913 Vincennes entered the state tournament for the first time, losing to the Orleans Bulldogs. However, by 1916 (the year the school name was changed to Lincoln) the Alices (or Pirates) made it to the Final Four, losing to Crawfordsville's Athenians in the semifinals, finishing 17-4 for Coach Forest Irwin.

From that start the Alices have managed to win 68 Sectional titles, and they once won 20 in a row (here the school's Web site history departs from the IHSA *Play On* site, claiming 27 straight) before losing a 1-pointer to those pesky Freelandville FightingDutchmen in 1941. During that stretch there was a 3-year streak when the Alices were undefeated at home before finally losing one, to the Evansville Central Bears on February 2, 1923. That setback was temporary, however, as the Alices won that first state championship just over a month later. In 1969 the Alices beat the Maroons of Robinson, Illinois, to complete a 20-0 undefeated regular season, led by Hall of Famer Jerry Memering. Their only loss was at Hinkle Fieldhouse in the morning game of the State Finals to eventual State Champion Gary Roosevelt, finishing a 27-1 season. Since they had finished the previous season 24-3, Orlando "Gunner" Wyman's first 2 teams had a combined record of 51-4. Twelve years later his Alices captured the school's 2nd Indiana state championship, defeating the Anderson Indians by the margin of a single basket and finishing 26-2. That 1923 state championship had come at the old Indianapolis Coliseum, John Adams coaching the team to wins over Lyons, Franklin, Anderson, and Muncie to finish 34-1. The previous year Adams' team had accomplished a remarkable undefeated regular season 28-0. In the Sectional they defeated Graysville, 74-10, Dugger, 54-6, Freelandville, 40-24, and Sullivan, 55-4. There were 2 Regionals that year, at Purdue and Indiana universities. The Alices won their game at Bloomington, 28-8, over New Castle, earning a trip to the Sweet Sixteen in Indianapolis along with the 7 other IU winners and the 8 from West Lafayette. At the old Coliseum, Vincennes beat the Cutler Wildcats, 31-22, before losing their only game of the season to the eventual state runner-up Bloomington Panthers, 21-15. The Alices finished their season with an astonishing 38 wins and 1 loss, making the 2-year record for Vincennes Lincoln a brilliant 72 and 2! Going back 1 more year, the Alices had won 35 games and lost only 6 in 1921. I can find no record of any Indiana high school team's winning more than 38 games in 1 season or 72 in consecutive years or, hard as it is to believe, 107 games in 3 consecutive years! Dave Hill, current athletic director at Vincennes, sent the following excerpt from a book on Vincennes basketball by Dr. Bill Stedman:

> *When John L. (Adams) issued a tryout call for the 1923 team, they faced the monumental task of upholding back-to-back appearances in the State Finals and a combined won-lost record of 73-7. And the 38 straight wins without a loss by the 1922 team was also staring them in the face. To make matters even more interesting, that earlier success enabled John L. to schedule some of the toughest teams from the north central area of the state for the 1922-23 season. Those two-game home and home encounters included Anderson, Lafayette Jeff, Lebanon, Indianapolis Tech, Columbus, and Martinsville, all recognized basketball powerhouses. And, he really opened everyone's eyes when he announced his version of a "Holiday Tournament." Centralia, (the Orphans) defending Illinois Champion coached by Bruceville, IN native Arthur Trout, was scheduled for a home game the day after Christmas and Franklin, who had won three consecutive Indiana Championships, was booked for three days after that. Vincennes also agreed to play at Franklin in the regular season finale on February 23.*

A.D. Hill goes on to say:

"So, yes, we did win 38 ballgames in 1922 only to lose to Bloomington in the [state] tournament."

Gunner Wyman
Won 71 percent of his games during a 29-year coaching career...coached Vincennes to state championship in 1981...also coached 3 other teams into Final Four...Tell City in '61 and Vincennes in '68 and '69...teams also won 9 regionals, including 3 straight at Tell City, and 21 sectionals...twice named coach of the year by the Indiana Sports-writers and Broadcasters Association...coached Indiana all-stars to 2 victories over Kentucky in '81...a 3-year letterman at Florida State.

Jerry Memering
Played in state final four in 1968 and 1969 ... career scoring record at Lincoln 1650 pts, 16.5 ppg, school records ... won 4 Sectionals, 3 Regionals, 2 Semi-States; Southern Indiana Athletic Conference Champions in 1968 and 1969 ... played in 100 of 102 possible varsity games, started 97 and was 51-4 as a Junior and Senior ... leading scorer and rebounder 3 years ... Indiana All-Star ... Silver Anniversary Team 1994 ... Coaches T. L. Plain and Gunner Wyman ... 3 year varsity player for Indiana ... Big Ten All-Star team to Australia and New Zealand in 1972 ... 1973 Big Ten Champs and NCAA Final 4 ... Coaches Tom Bolyard (freshman team), Lou Watson and Bob Knight ...

Before leaving Vincennes, the Lady Alices have also been quite successful, with 12 Sectional and 4 Regional championships to add to the school's bulging trophy case. Kaye Ogle coached her 1976 Lady Alice team to an undefeated regular season, 18-1, as did Janis Hart in 2002, 21-1.

Vincennes Lincoln Alices

Alice of Old Vincennes

Alice in Wonderland? Or Alice of Old Vincennes? Take your pick!

Chapter 9

Hoosier Resources:
Teams of Stone and Sulphur

This time we'll turn to 2 of Indiana's natural resource wonders: our waters and our limestone, and also examine 3 high schools whose team name selections were derived from the colleges in the same town.

One of Indiana's glories is to be found under the earth in the form of immense oolitic limestone deposits. Ninety percent of the country's architectural grade limestone comes from Indiana. Many of America's most treasured buildings have been faced with limestone from the quarries in south central Indiana, including the Empire State Building in New York City, the United States Capitol, the National Cathedral and many state

Limestone quarry

capitols and county courthouses. Shortly after 9/11, in a large, old shed of a factory in Elletsville, workers cut and polished the stones that were used to replace those destroyed by the cowardly attack on the Pentagon. They were horrified by the deed that led to their work, but were proud to be doing it. They wrote the words of President George W. Bush on the inside of many of the stones, the words that so ably rallied the country in the dark days immediately following the attack: "We will not tire. We will not falter. We will not fail…may God bless America." These words were spoken at that very National Cathedral faced with that very Indiana limestone. Many of these men would have graduated from Ellettsville High School. They would have been Ellettsville Eagles.

The Eagles won 4 Sectionals between 1947 and 1961 and the Martinsville Regional in 1950, when they lost their lone Sweet Sixteen contest to the New Albany Bulldogs.

Four other small towns in the limestone region also provide many workers for the quarries and factories of which they are justifiably proud. St. Paul's teams in Decatur County were the Blasters, and Stinesville's in Monroe County were the Quarry Lads (and Lassies). Stinesville is generally credited with being the

The Eagles fly high

place where the Indiana limestone industry got its start, with the 1st quarry opening in 1827. The town was named for Eusebius Stein. Recently, the town has erected a monument to welcome visitors and emphasize the significance of the limestone industry to the history of the area. Carved out of Indiana limestone, the monument depicts a full-sized stonecutter from the early days of the 20th century. It also, I am pleased to report, proclaims Stinesville as home of the Quarry Lads.

The Quarry lad Statue and the gym floor at Stinesville

The Quarry Lads in their red and blue uniforms won 18 of 21 games in 1930 for coach Nelson Irwin. In 1960 they did even better with Glen Crowe in the coaching box, finishing a strong 20-3. They are now Edgewood Mustangs.

Stinesville High School

St. Paul's Blasters had a very nice string for Coach Walter Floyd from 1932 through 1936: 20-3, 19-6, 17-7, 19-4, or 75 wins and only 20 losses! They also went 19-5 in 1941 for Coach Malcolm Clay, 18-4 in 1949 for Coach Delbert Kistler, and 17-6 for Coach Bill Fisher in 1953. They won their only Sectional at Greensburg in 1956 with wins over Vernon, Jackson Township, and the home team Pirates.

Bedford and nearby Oolitic still proudly identify themselves as the "Limestone Capital of the World." Bedford's teams were the Stonecutters. Locals in Bloomington, home of the Indiana University Hoosiers, were for years known as the "cutters" as all realize who enjoyed the movie *Breaking Away*, in which the local bike team of that name carries the day at the Little 500.

St. Paul High School

Oolitic was originally named Limestone, but that name was changed when the town realized there already was a Limestone in Indiana. The quarry that contained the limestone facing for the Empire State Building is near Oolitic and is often visited by tourists. Preconsolidation Oolitic teams were the Bearcats.

The Bearcats also did quite well on several occasions. In 1924 they played a rather astonishing 39-game schedule, winning 25 with Coach Pearcy Underwood in charge. Ralph McCoy led Oolitic to a 17-4 mark in 1929, and Cletus Jenkins' team won 18 of 20 games in 1935. Knofel Fortner was the Bearcat's coach in 1946 when they were 18-3, and Bill Luse led the Bearcats to 17-4 and 18-5 marks in 1950 and

1952 respectively. His team also won the Sectional title in 1954, finishing that year at 18-7. Bob Masterson coached Oolitic to its 2nd Sectional crown in 1967 when they were 20-4. The next year his team had an undefeated regular season and finished with a 23 and 1 record. They won the Bedford Sectional with victories over Mitchell, the host Stonecutters, and Fayetteville, suffering their only loss of the season to Holland by the margin of a single basket, 61-59, at the Huntingburg Regional. The Bearcats are now Bedford North Lawrence Stars.

The consolidation that resulted in Damon Bailey's school, Bedford North Lawrence, retained the limestone association with their selection of a team name. They are the Stars, and a star refers to a particularly highly skilled stone-cutting artisan.

The Oolitic Bearcats

The Bedford Stonecutters had many seasons of glory, beginning as early as 1920, when Merle Abbott's 24-7 team won the 1st of the school's 36 Sectional titles. Two years later his 25-6 squad captured the 1st of their 20 Regional crowns. This began a 3-year string of 74 wins and only 19 defeats for the Stonecutters, culminating in a trip to the Sweet Sixteen in Indianapolis, where they made it all the way to the Final Four. Charles Ivey took over as coach in 1926 and led the Stonecutters to 3 consecutive Final Fours. All 4 of these trips were, unfortunately, thwarted by either Martinsville or Muncie. Ivey's 1927 record of 27-4 was followed by his 1929 mark of 25-4. Paul Lostutter's 1938 team gained some measure of revenge over Martinsville, beating the Artesians in a 21-20 double overtime thriller to win the Vincennes Semi-state. Ralph Holmes coached the Stonecutters from 1941 until 1955, except for 1953. His 1943 team again won the Vincennes Semi-state before losing a 36-35 nail-biter to the Lebanon Tigers in the morning game of the state finals at the new Coliseum in Indianapolis the next week. Holmes' 1942, 1947, and 1948 teams all won 20 games or more.

After consolidation Bedford North Lawrence continued to excel, winning 18 more Sectionals, 7 Regionals, 3 Semi-states, and the storied 1990 Damon Bailey-led state championship under Coach Dan Bush with a 29-2 record. That final game at the Hoosier Dome was viewed by 41,046 fans in person and by many more on television. The attendance is still a national record for a high school game.

Three other Bush-coached BNL Stars teams won over 20 games: 1987, 23-1; 1988, 26-2; and 1989, 21-3. Those 4 years resulted in 99 victories and 8 defeats! How many schools can match that? The only loss in 1987 was to Marion's state champion Giants in the 1st game of the state finals at Market Square Arena. Finally, in 1995 the Stars accomplished yet another undefeated regular season with Mark Matthews at the helm, 26-1. That single loss was to Jeffersonville, 70-69, in the final game of the

Evansville Semi-state. Dan Bush, who graduated from Oolitic, has the following Hall of Fame citation.

Dan Bush

Coached at Bedford North Lawrence...Danny was a 3 year starter and the second leading all-time school scorer with 1462 career points. He was a member of 2 sectional winning teams. He started for Indiana State University for 3 years and scored over 1,000 career points there. At the end of his senior year he was named Indiana State's Most Valuable Player and was also selected Academic All-American. At the time he was chosen to the 1993 Silver Anniversary Team he was coaching basketball at Bedford North Lawrence School.

But that's not all. How about the Lady Stars? The Austin "Pete" Pritchett Bedford North Lawrence girls teams from 1983 through 1994 never won less than 18 games, never lost more than 4, won Sectionals every year (16 in a row from 1982-1997 of the school's 20), 9 Regionals, 4 Semi-states, 2 state championships, and 2 state runner-up trophies. Over that 12-year span the Lady Stars won an astonishing 271 games while losing only 25. The crown jewel was the 29-0 mark racked up in 1991, but included were 1983's 26-1, 1989's 24-1, 1990's 25-1, and 1992's 26-1. For the 4-year period 1989 through 1992 this school's girls basketball team won 104 of 107 games played. Pat Sumitt, watch out!

One of the most beautiful and historically intriguing sections of Indiana is in the south central part of the state, where sulphur springs with supposedly curative powers were discovered in the latter part of the 18th century. This area, known as Springs Valley, attracted many visitors, first for the waters and later for the casinos that blossomed along with two fabulous hotels, one in French Lick and the other in nearby West Baden Springs. The hotel in West Baden is particularly noteworthy. Built in 1899 it was an engineering marvel because of its design. The hotel was built with over 500 rooms in two concentric circles with an access corridor between each row of rooms on the 5 floors above the ground level that housed lobby, dining rooms, a beauty salon, stock market ticker tape, and other services of interest to the hotel's well-heeled patrons. The exterior rooms overlooked the golf course, gardens, bath houses, the onsite bank, and the hills that created the valley, with the interior rooms facing a gigantic atrium. This magnificent atrium was crowned by the largest free-standing dome ever built in the world up until that time, larger even than the great dome of

St. Peter's in Rome, or the Pantheon, or St. Paul's in London. Railroad trains from the great cities of the east and west passed through Chicago, St. Louis, Cincinnati, and Louisville to bring the guests, patients, and gamblers by the hundreds to the door of the wondrous West Baden Springs Hotel, as well as to her less spectacular but equally regal neighbor in French Lick. Both the famous and the notorious: movie stars, financiers, industrialists and even gangsters came to Springs Valley in droves. Paul Dresser (from Terre Haute, brother of novelist Theodore Dreiser) wrote his Hoosier anthem "On the Banks of the Wabash" while a guest at the West Baden Springs Hotel. Prizefighters James "Gentleman Jim" Corbett and John L. Sullivan trained there. After the stock market crash in 1929, occupancy of the hotel dropped from a near capacity of over 500 rooms to less than 100 overnight as patrons rushed back to their homes to try to attend to their financial affairs. Unfortunately, the crash and ensuing Depression dealt

a near-death blow to the hotel, and the building went through several iterations as a monastery, culinary arts school, and college before passing into complete disuse and threatened demolition. Thankfully, due to the generosity of many people but primarily the Cook family of Bloomington and through the untiring efforts of the Indiana Historic Landmarks Foundation

The West Baden Springs Hotel

and the inspirational leadership of its director, Reid Williamson and its board chair, Jim Hughes, the property was saved. It has now been restored to its original splendor. It is a true Indiana gem.

When my wife and I were there on a balmy summer day we stopped in the local café for lunch and noticed several pictures of graduating classes of West Baden Springs High School, long before its consolidation. The nickname of their teams was the Sprudels. I asked our waitress if she knew why. She said she had not gone there, but she pointed out a man who appeared to be about my age at another booth who had, and said perhaps he would know. Pretty soon he and I were having coffee together and comparing notes on a wide variety of topics. After solving the world's problems, he told me that the name Sprudels derived from the waters with their supposed curative powers. But why Sprudels? He thought for a moment before replying that "Down in French Lick they had Pluto water and up here in West Baden we had Sprudel water," and he had always assumed it was because if you drank the water, known for its rather pronounced cathartic properties, you surely got the sprudels!

Of course, there's a bit more to it than that. Many of the original settlers in southern Indiana came from Germany. The word *Baden* means baths in German, and the word *Sprudeln* means to bubble up—like a bubbling spring. So, *sprudelwasser* is simply bubbly water.

At a local antique store I came across a copy of the 1926 high school yearbook called *The Blue Goose*. In the basketball section I found the following:

Due to the excellent caching of Mr. Musselman and the training of the team the quintet won 14 games out of 20 which is considered a good record.

The Sprudels were one of those 172 schools that did, in fact, win just one Sectional championship in their entire history. They did it for Coach Don Davis in 1935 at Salem by defeating the Pekin Muskateers, 21-14; the Orleans Bulldogs, 32-22; and the home team Lions, 20-17. The next week they lost a toughie at Mitchell to the Seymour Owls, 16-14.

West Baden Springs High School

Those Pluto waters from French Lick were labeled with a logo of a red devil with a pitchfork, which makes sense because Pluto was the Greek god of the underworld. It also makes sense that the French Lick High School athletic teams were called the Red Devils.

Pluto water ads

An Ad for Sprudel Salts

The consolidated Springs Valley High School teams, where the incomparable Larry Bird, generally acknowledged as one of the game's all time great players, once starred, are the Blackhawks. We'll have more to say about the Blackhawks later.

The Springs Valley Blackhawk

Larry Bird

Averaged 30.6 points per game and 20.6 rebounds as a senior at Springs Valley High School... 1974 Indiana All-Star... during his career at Indiana State he averaged 30.3 points per game and 13.3 rebounds... led the Sycamores to the 1979 NCAA tournament championship game... collegiate awards include: All-Missouri Valley Conference 1977, 1978, 1979; MVC Player of the Year, 1978, 1979; UPI third-team All-American, 1977; Consensus first-team collegiate All-American, 1978, 1979; consensus collegiate player of the year, 1979; ... as a Boston Celtic from 1979-1992 he was Rookie of the Year, All-Star MVP, NBA MVP 3 times, playoff MVP twice, NBA Champions 3 times and an NBA All-Star 12 times... 1999 Silver Anniversary Team... 3 successful years as Indiana Pacers' coach.

Trinity Springs has similar waters, but not the great hotels and exotic past of West Baden Springs or French Lick. Still, at one time as many as 6 smaller hotels did exist there to serve the needs of people wanting to bathe in and perhaps even drink the waters. The people of Trinity Springs were pretty straightforward when it came to selecting a nickname for their high school teams. Their red-and-white-clad heroes were known as the Little Sulphurs. They joined Shoals in 1943, after a relatively brief 18-year existence.

Sulphur Springs High School teams were the Blue Birds

The town of Sulphur Springs chose not to emphasize the waters, however, and were content to call their teams the Blue Birds. The blue-and-white-uniformed Sulphur Springs teams had consecutive 18-5 records for Coach Don Houston in 1956 and 1957. New Castle's Ray Pavy coached the final Blue Birds team in 1967 to a 13-9 mark.

Martinsville, the seat of Morgan County, was founded by John Martin in 1822. Even before there was a town swampy areas were drained to create fisheries. The area was famous for them, and Martinsville itself was once known as the "Goldfish Capital of the World."

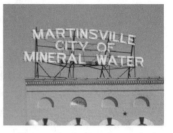

By 1888, however, artesian wells and mineral springs in the area became known for their curative powers, and from then until 1968 people from all over the world would journey to Martinsville for their health. Artesian wells occur when the local water table or aquifer is above the wellhead, and they are so named because the first ones in Europe were in the province of Artois. Martinsville thus soon became known as the Artesian City.

From the early days of the 20th century, Martinsville fell in love with, and became very good at, the game of basketball. Legendary coach Glen Curtis was so successful with his teams that in 1925 what was then the world's largest high school gym was opened with a seating capacity in excess of 5,000. Trainloads of fans came from all over Indiana and from other states as well just to see this marvel.

MARTINSVILLE vs. SHELBYVILLE, THURSDAY NIGHT, FEB. 21st
First Game in the Biggest Gym in the World.   5,000 Seats,   5,000 Tickets.
Three Bands: Masonic Home Band, Shelbyville Band, Martinsville Band.
Curtain Raiser: Masonic Home Team vs. Martinsville Second Team.
Shelbyville will bring 1500!   HOW MANY WILL WE HAVE?
Doors Open at 6:00 p. m.   First Game at 7:15.
ADMISSION: SCHOOL CHILDREN, 20 Cents; ADULTS, 50 Cents

The 1927 champion Artesians

State championships were won by Martinsville teams in 1924, 1927, and 1933. The 1927 and state tournament runner–up teams of 1926 and 1928 featured a young man whose name would become synonymous with basketball excellence, John Wooden.

Wooden as a young star

John Wooden
Played with Indianapolis Kautskys...coached at South Bend Central High School, Indiana State University, and the University of California at Los Angeles...A legend even among legends, winning 10 NCAA championships in 12-year span at UCLA...as a player at Purdue, was the first 3-time All American... set Big 10 scoring record and won Helms Foundation Award in 1932...played on Martinsville's 1927 state championship team his junior year, as well as 2 state runner-up teams, losing to Marion and Muncie Central in championship games.

Great athlete, superb coach, loyal husband, and consummate gentleman, John Wooden was always proud of his Martinsville days when he played basketball for Glen Curtis as an Artesian. And Glen Curtis was quite a man and quite a coach in his own right. His 1920 Artesians won 26 games and lost only 5, followed by 24-6 and 27-6 records for a 3-year record of 77-17. From 1924 through 1928 Curtis' squads even improved on this mark, winning 119 games and losing just 24.

Glenn Curtis
Won nearly 79 percent of his games during a career in which his teams won 663 and lost just 187 ... led Lebanon to a state title in 1918, then moved to Martinsville, where he won state championships in 1924, 1927 and 1933 ... co-coach with Tony Hinkle of the first Indiana all-star team to play Kentucky ... coached the all-star team 6 times ... never had a losing season as a coach ... in 18 years at Martinsville, won 15 sectionals and 12 regionals ... became athletic director and coach at Indiana State in 1938 ... 1946 Sycamores won the Midwest Invitational Tourney at Chicago ... coached briefly with the Indianapolis Kautskys before moving into the school administration field at Martinsville.

As early as 1917 the Artesians had a 25-7 record. Other 20-win seasons were posted by Ray Scott's 1940 team, Sam Alford's 1975 team, and Tim Wolf's 1991 and 1995 teams. All told, the Artesians have won 34 Sectional and 14 Regional titles in their illustrious history. The Lady Artesians have also enjoyed considerable success, winning 9 Sectionals and 2 Regionals, the latter in 1997 and 1998. These wins led to the Lady Artesians under coach John Conner performing the intriguing double feat of winning the last non-class state championship as well as

Martinsville's artesian well logo

the first ever Class 4A State Championship. In 1997 the Lady Artesians defeated Crown Point 65-59 to finish 26-1 and in 1998 they completed the dream with a 29-0 record, defeating previously undefeated Lake Central 71-65.

Three schools in the same small cities with colleges had some fun with their team names. Each was attentive to the selection already made by their big brothers… or sisters. Let's begin with Franklin, the home of the Franklin Wonder Five. Teams led by Robert P. "Fuzzy" Vandivier won 3 Indiana state championships in a row between 1920 and 1922. During that period the teams had winning streaks of 29 and 48 straight games while compiling a remarkable overall record of 89 wins and only 9 losses. After their final year the entire starting 5 moved across town to Franklin College, where they were again quite successful, gaining national recognition for their school. Franklin College teams are the Grizzly Bears, and Franklin High School teams are the Grizzly Cubs. In addition to those 3 state championship trophies, the Grizzly Cubs also have filled their case with 46 Sectional titles, 11 Regionals, 3 Semi-state crowns and, the 1939 Runner-up trophy. Dick Harmening's 1973–74 teams won 45 of 55 games and Tom McKinney's 1984 Cubs went 20-3. Dave Clark's 1995 and 1997 squads were 20-4 and 24-3.

Fuzzy Vandivier
Coached 18 years at Franklin High School; athletic director for another 17 years ... started at Franklin High School as a freshman...starting his sophomore year, led Grizzly Cubs to 3 straight state titles in 1920, '21 and '22...During that string, Franklin posted winning streaks of 29 and 48 games... played at Franklin College, where school gained national prominence and "Fuzzy" was named Chicago Tribune's collegiate player of the year...called by sportswriter, Fred Young, "the sweetest piece of basketball timber in the United States today."

Franklin Wonder Five and the Grizzly Cub

Grizzly Cubs

Our first Mr. Basketball, George Crowe, in 1939, was a Grizzly Cub whose Vandivier-coached squad finished 25-4.

George Crowe
Scored 13 of Franklin High School's 22 points in 1939 state championship game loss to Frankfort ... Mr. Basketball ... All State ... called by legendary Coach Fuzzy Vandivier 'the best money player I have ever seen' ... 12 letters in 3 sports at Indiana Central ... center for a nationally ranked Greyhound team ... 6-4 standout played professional basketball 7 years with Los Angeles Red Devils, New York Renaissance and Harlem Yankees ... also a standout pitcher, he played Major League baseball 10 years, with the Cincinnati Reds, Milwaukee Braves and St. Louis Cardinals. His brother is Hall of Famer Ray Crowe.

At Greencastle a Methodist school was about to go under financially when a wealthy man from New Albany named DePauw provided enough money to assure its continued success. Thus, the state of Indiana was provided with yet another outstanding liberal arts college. The name of the institution was shortly thereafter changed from Asbury Methodist School (it was also a preparatory school attended for a time by no less a Hoosier personage than Eli Lilly) to DePauw University. DePauw's teams are the Tigers, and Greencastle High School fields the Tiger Cubs. The purple-and-grey-clad Tiger Cubs have had an impressive 13 seasons with 20 or more wins, beginning with a 21-4 record under Coach William Courson in 1919. The next year they won 27 and lost 8 under the guidance of Coach Winfred Smith for a season high win total. Coach G. E. Rhea's Tiger Cubs went 21-4 in 1923. In 1930 and 1931 the Tiger Cubs were 22-6 and 25-7 for Coach William Bausman, and the next 2 years saw records of 22-9 and 26-5-1 for Coach C. N. Edmonson. Not a bad 4-year record: 95-27-1. Marion Crawley coached the Tiger Cubs of 1938 to a 22-7 season. In 1956 and 1957 Tom Goldsberry led his teams to 20-9 and 25-5 records. Dave McCracken was the coach in 1964 when Greencastle won 22 of 26 games; Hugh Miller's team won 21 games while losing only 4 as recently as 1993. All told, the Tiger Cubs have 34 Sectional and 14 Regional nets in their crowded trophy case.

Greencastle Tiger Cub

Oakland City is our 3rd entry in this "Town and Gown" section. Oakland City is home to the university of the same name, as well as Cooperstown honoree Ed Roush. Their teams, which won the National Little College Athletic Association Championship in 1981, are called the Mighty Oaks. The high school, before it was consolidated into Wood Memorial High School (the Trojans), as we have covered previously, were the Acorns.

Oakland City's logo

Chapter 10

Indiana in the Industrial Age: From Automobiles to Rockets

In this chapter we continue our investigation into the team names, mascots, and records for our present and closed schools, turning our attention to our industrial and technological heritage.

In the days following the application of the internal combustion engine to what had essentially been horse-drawn coaches, the state of Indiana played a very important part in developing the new automobiles. One of the first successful gasoline engine powered cars was designed and built by Elwood Haynes in Kokomo. Further north in South Bend the Studebaker family were adding engines to the wagons they had been building for years; soon automobile plants were springing up all over the state. In the years to come an astonishing 250 different brands of automobiles were manufactured right here in Indiana. When the Depression hit, for a variety of well-documented reasons the center of the automobile industry shifted north to Detroit. However, our heritage remains a great one.

Auburn is a good place to start—Auburn Cord Duesenberg Automobile Museum. Deluxe, imaginative and elegant cars were designed and built there: the Auburn and the Cord. Some auto buffs believe the 1936 Cord to have been the most beautiful car ever. Maybe so, maybe not, but, as someone once said about Dizzy Dean, "He may not be in a class by himself, but, whatever class he's in it sure doesn't take long to call the roll." I'm something of a classic car aficionado myself, and I do love those old Cords and Auburns. And the Stutz Bearcat. Of course let's add to the list the glorious Duesenbergs. All of those cars have something in common: along with the Marmon, the Cole, the Studebaker and several others they were made in Indiana. The marvelous car museum located in Auburn, devoted primarily to the 2 brands of cars made there and to the Duesenberg is worth a visit.

The Auburn

The Cord

The mighty Duesenberg

*Logo courtesy Auburn Cord Duesenberg
Automobile Musuem*

Collectors and car lovers from all over the world converge on Auburn annually for the auto fair. It is a unique and inspirational experience to see these mechanical marvels, most in pristine condition, lovingly maintained by their proud owners. The parade of cars and the museum are a tribute to a bygone era, historically important and preserved for future generations to behold and enjoy.

Auburn is located in DeKalb County, which was named for a German baron who fought on the side of the Colonies in the Revolutionary War. When Auburn had its own high school, their teams were called the Red Devils. The consolidated DeKalb High School team came from Ashley (Aces) High School, Waterloo (Wildcats) High School and Auburn (Red Devils) High School, now called the Barons.

*Red Devils
are now Barons*

*Barons: Houck
photo from exhibit
courtesy of IBHOF*

Both DeKalb and Auburn have had enviable success on the hardwood. The Red Devils won 21 and lost only 6 in 1931, coming right back with a 20-3 mark the next year for Coach Cecil Young. Keith Showalter-coached teams won 22 and lost

3 in 1945 and cranked that up to 26-3 in 1949. Randall Lawson-led Auburn teams enjoyed a nice 3-year run beginning in 1950, with consecutive records of 19-8, 21-7, and 26-4. Over the years the Red Devils have won 18 Sectional crowns, 6 Regionals, and the 1949 Muncie Semi-state by defeating North Central Conference powerhouses Kokomo and New Castle. At Butler Fieldhouse the Devils lost the morning game to eventual State Champion Jasper, 53-48.

Auburn's Alumni Gym

DeKalb's record is equally impressive, beginning with the undefeated regular season record of 26-1 in 1979 with Coach Jim Leix at the helm. The Barons won their own Sectional and took the only loss of the season in the final game of the Ft. Wayne Regional, to Harding. The next year the Barons again were Sectional champions and again lost in the final game of the Ft. Wayne Regional, this time to South Side by a gut-wrenching single point. Roger Hughes coached that team. His 1983 Barons turned in a 23-5 record, and Coach Cliff Hawkins' charges went 24-2 and 26-4 in 1996 and 1997.

DeKalb's trophy case includes 20 Sectional championships to go with 4 Regionals and the 2003 Lafayette Class 4A Semi-state. The Barons lost the state final game at Conseco Fieldhouse to the Indianapolis Pike Red Devils, 65-52. They were forced to be content to bring the runner-up plaque back to Waterloo.

Additionally, the Lady Barons (Baronesses?) of DeKalb have a great deal to be proud of. From 1983 to 1989, a 7-year period, the girls basketball teams won 5 of their 15 Sectional titles with records ranging from 18-5 to 23-1. Their overall record for those 7 years? A truly outstanding 140 wins and 22 losses. They were coached by Gary Daub for that entire span.

Indiana's aviation heritage is not always fully known and appreciated. Many people are unaware that although Orville Wright was born in Dayton, Ohio, Wilbur was born in Indiana on a farm near Millville, a small town just west of Hagerstown. Their pioneering flight at Kitty Hawk, North Carolina, on December 17, 1903, was in a craft inspired by the designs of Octave Chanute, a French-born civil engineer who came to America at an early age. These designs were developed by Chanute in the latter days of the 19th century on the sand dunes of northern Indiana.

The first flight

Several Indiana schools have turned to this heritage as inspiration for their nicknames. Two of these air-connected teams are the Hauser Jets, located in Hope, not far from what was once Bakalar Air Force Base, and the Adams Central Flying Jets in Monroe. Hope High School teams were the Red Devils prior to consolidation, and they enjoyed records of 23-2 in 1935 for Coach Koert McQueen and 25-2 in 1945 for Coach Lloyd Broughe, the year they not only won their only Sectional title, but also made it to the Sweet Sixteen. I had hoped that this progression would result in a good year in 1955, but alas, history is not always kind, and the Red Devils went 1-20 that year. However, Hauser's Jets had great years in 1981, 20-2, for Coach Harold Taylor, and in 2006 when they won the state Class A title with 25 wins and only 2 defeats for Coach Bob Nobbe. Hall of Famer Bill Shepherd, father of 2 outstanding basketball-playing sons and a grandson (3 generations of Indiana All Stars!), who starred at Carmel, was an important contributor to that 1945 Red Devil team.

Bill Shepherd
All-sectional, all-regional & all-semistate performer for Hope in '45, helping them to the only sectional and regional championships in its history...member of Indiana All-Star team...4-yr basketball and softball player...played 3 yrs for Tony Hinkle at Butler where he won 2 letters in baseball...followed teaching of Hinkle into successful coaching career, first at Mitchell and then Carmel (58-70)...coached Carmel to runner-up spot in the state championship in 1970...state's co-coach of the year that season...lifetime coaching record 336-145, including a 50-game home winning streak at Carmel in 1967 through 1970. He coached 2 sons who were Mr. Basketball, Billy in 1968 and Dave in 1970.

The Flying Jets enjoyed 3 excellent seasons from 1964–1966 with records of 19-8, 18-6, and 19-6, winning Sectional crowns in each year for Coach Vernon Zurcher. Sectionals were also won in 1994 and 2001. The Lady Flying Jets have also won 2 Sectionals and one Regional crown.

Hauser Jets

Adams Central Flying Jets

Other examples were the Akron and the Eden Flyers, the Brookston Bombers (covered elsewhere), and the New Market Purple Flyers. I had at first thought that the Purple Flyers referred to birds, perhaps the ubiquitous purple martins seen all over the state. However, Mrs. Patricia Nichols, First Lady Emeritus of Hanover College, assured me that their logo was an airplane. Crawfordsville Municipal Airport is, in fact, located just north of New Market. Now the New Market Elementary School retains the flyers theme, but updated to rocket status. New Market teams won Sectional crowns in 1950 and 1967. Earl "Red" Gardner is a Hall of Famer and one time Purple Flyer.

The New Market Purple Flyers

Earl "Red" Gardner
New Market Purple Flyers won the County Championship three consecutive years with Red Gardner on the team... named to the Coaches All-Sectional team in 1941...Inducted into the Indiana Basketball Hall of Fame.

EARL "RED" GARDNER

The Akron Flyers won 13 of their 17 games played as early as 1915, and in 1932 and 1933 put together consecutive seasons of 20-6 and 21-3. Coach Phil McCarter's teams did indeed fly high in 1955 and 1956, with records of 19-6 and 20-6. It seems good things do indeed come in twos for the Flyers, as they were 18-3 in 1967 and 21-3 in 1968 for Coach Floyd Henson. Henson's son Steve is still in the books as the school's all-time leading scorer. Between 1929 and 1974 the Flyers won 4 Sectional championships. In his series on the history of basketball in Kosciusko County, Phil Smith of the *Times Union* adds this relevant information:

AKRON FLYERS

> Over the years, the Akron Flyers were graced with several cagers who left indelible marks on area basketball. There was 1956's Jim Jones (1,163); 1967's Ken Weaver (1,191) and Steve Henson (1,624); 1968's Jeff McFarland (1,175); 1970's Bob Bryant (1,291) and 1975's Ron Dittman (1,461).

The Eden Flyers also had a number of fine seasons. The Black and Gold won 19 of 25 games for Coach Floyd Hines in 1930 and 19 of 22 for Coach James Clements in 1937. Max Weddle coached the Flyers to 22-2 and 23-1 in 1945 and 1946, the years Eden won their only Sectional titles, both coming at Greenfield. In 1954 Hall of Famer Orvis "Shorty" Burdsall coached the Black and Gold to a 17-4 record, and the next year, Eden's last before consolidation into Greenfield Central,

where they became the Cougars,

Paul Bradford's Flyers finished 19-5. (It should be noted that, in Indiana at least, it is not Nod that is to the east of Eden but rather Kennard, home of the Leopardcats.)

Akron and Eden schools, homes of the Flyers

Talking about our heritage in the skies reminds me of the innovative nickname selected by the students of Northwest High School in Indianapolis, opened in the 1960s.

Their teams are the Space Pioneers, combining Indiana's early history with our state's latter-day contributions to aero- and astronautics. Northwest has won 4 Sectionals. Their best record came in 2004, 20-5, for Coach Victor Bush.

One of Northwest's rivals is Broad Ripple, named for a bend in the White River where pioneers had settled as early as 1821. About 10 miles north of the center of Indianapolis, Broad Ripple's growth began in earnest with the construction of a canal there in 1837. In 1884 the Indianapolis, Delphi and Chicago Railroad—later to be a part of the Monon Line—laid its tracks through Broad Ripple Village. Two years later Broad Ripple High School was established. Today the area and the school have been absorbed into the city of Indianapolis and the Monon tracks have been taken up to provide a biking, jogging, and hiking trail that stretches from the northern suburbs to the heart of the city. The Broad Ripple High School teams are known as the Rockets and the state championship was theirs in 1980, when they defeated the New Albany Bulldogs 73-66. They have won 6 Indianapolis Sectionals and 4 Regionals.

Rippy, the Broad Ripple mascot, and (r) friends

According to Broad Ripple alumna the late Paula Gable, whose source was *Centennial Celebration*, a book about the school compiled by Ralph Bedwell in 1986, this team name was selected via a contest run by the student newspaper/yearbook, *The Riparian*, in 1929. No one seems to be quite certain why Rockets was the winning entry at that early date in the science of rocketry, but the best educated guess seems to be that it captured the sense of lofty aspirations that appealed to both students and faculty alike. Also, of course, it was alliterative, as the school is generally referred to as "Ripple."

Broad Ripple's Rockets had come oh-so-close to winning the state championship in 1945 as well, losing to Evansville Bosse's Bulldogs in 1945 by a 37-35 count in the afternoon game of the State Finals. Bosse would defeat South Bend Riley's Wildcats by a 10 point margin that night. Hall of Famer Max Allen's citation:

Max Allen

A 4-year 2-spot star at Indianapolis Broad Ripple, he captained the Rockets for 2 years under Hall of Fame coach Frank Baird. A 5´4˝ playmaker, he led the team to its first state finals in 1945. Ripple lost a memorable 37-35 afternoon game to 2-time champion Evansville Bosse in which Allen matched up with mirror image, Broc Jerrell. Considered by Baird the leader of a team which featured future collegians Ralph Chapman and Dee Baker and professional Bob Dietz. He was the first recipient of the Trester Award (previously the Gimbel Award).

For a brief period there were also Rockets representing Gill Township in Sullivan County. Gill Township was a consolidation of New Lebanon and Merom, existing from 1951 through 1957 and utilizing both school's buildings. Thus Tigers plus Beavers equaled Rockets. In 1955 the maroon and white Rockets turned in an excellent 21-4 record for Coach Carl Jones. They won their only Sectional title that year at Sullivan, defeating the home team, Farmersburg, Carlisle, and Dugger. In the first round of the Huntingburg Regional, the Rockets lost a hotly contested game to the Washington Hatchets, 65-63. They became Sullivan Golden Arrows in 1958.

Freeland Park also fielded the Rockets, in red and black. They were successively consolidated into Fowler and Benton Central, becoming Bulldogs and then Bison. The Rockets won 5 Sectionals between 1929 and 1950.

Finally, the Indiana School for the Blind and Visually Impaired in Indianapolis also calls its teams the Rockets.

Now let's talk about oil, bricks, and steel. The northwestern section of Indiana is highly industrialized. With steel mills, foundries, breweries, refineries, and a major port, it resembles Chicago, its neighboring "City of the big shoulders, husky brawling…" more than it does most of the rest of the state. It is known to residents and other Hoosiers as "The Region."

The Region begins in the east with Gary, the town built by U.S. Steel in 1906 and named for its president, Judge Elbert H. Gary. It was located to take advantage of the coal mines of Indiana, the iron ore deposits near Lake Superior, railroads that crisscrossed the area, and the water transportation available on the Great Lakes. It was designed to be a model city.

Next to Gary are East Chicago and Hammond, which nearly border Chicago. Tucked in between Hammond and East Chicago is the town of Whiting, also on the shore of Lake Michigan. Whiting was first settled in 1885, and 4 years later the Standard Oil Company built one of the world's largest refineries there. After the break-up of the Standard Oil Trust, due in part to the public sentiment aroused by Ida Tarbell and to the leadership of President Theodore Roosevelt, this portion became Standard Oil of Indiana, later known as Amoco.

It was in Whiting that chemist William Merriam Burton discovered a process for producing more gasoline per barrel of crude oil than was previously possible. It was called thermal cracking, and it revolutionized the industry. Burton rose to become president of the company, and the Whiting High School teams have always been proudly called the Oilers. In 1912, our 2nd official tournament, Whiting beat Wolf Lake and Culver at Notre Dame to qualify for the Final Four at Indiana University, where they lost to Franklin, 29-21, in the 1st game. The Oilers made it to the Sweet Sixteen again in 1922, losing to eventual runner-up Terre Haute Garfield by a 24-12 count.

Three different Whiting Oiler logos

Perhaps no industry was of greater importance to the building of America than was iron and steel. Without iron there would be no steel and without steel there would be no great railroads crisscrossing our continent, no skyscrapers reaching tall in the sky, and no automobiles. My favorite nickname in this category goes to a school in Hobart, River Forest High School. The River Forest teams are the Ingots. An ingot is defined by *Webster's New Collegiate Dictionary* as "A mass of metal cast into a convenient shape for storage or transportation to be later processed." Yay, rah, metal mass. Go Ingots.

But there's a good deal more to it than such a superficial response would imply. The ingot is a metaphor for the raw material that makes up the student body of River Forest. During the educational process there this raw material is refined, tempered, cultivated, shaped, molded, and perfected. The process insures that each student will fulfill his or her own potential, that a diploma will attest to the finished product, and that the graduate will be ready to meet the challenges of the next steps in life's complex and challenging journey. Now, to me, that's quite a statement for any mascot to make, anywhere. The *RF Ingots* Ingots under Coach Jason Quigg won their only Sectional crown, Class 2A, in 2001 and also won the Regional that year with a 47-42 victory over Winamac. Although the Lady Ingots have yet to cut down the nets at a Sectional, they did have a successful 17-6 record for Al Detterline in 1999.

Hobart itself was a center of the brick-making industry for many years. According to the school's Web site:

> *Yohan, the school's mascot, was named after a fictional student whose name appeared on the study list for days. His (full) name was Yohan Petrovich. He was a figment of George Zupko's imagination and was developed in 1942. Yohan's physique was developed by building bricks from the years he spent in the Hobart brickyards.*

The Hobart High teams are called the Brickies. Their very successful football teams play their home games in the Brickyard. The Brickies have 3 Sectional nets in their trophy case. In 1938 George Belshaw's Brickies had an excellent 21-4 record. Jim Lichtenberger's 1972 team won the school's 1st Sectional crown, finishing 22-3. In the

Gary Regional the Brickies defeated Calumet 62-53 before being eliminated by the eventual runner-up to the state championship, Gary West. The 1992 team, coached by Keith Hipskind rang up 20 wins against 5 losses, also capturing a Sectional crown. They gathered a small measure of revenge over Gary West, trimming the Cougar's claws by a 49-42 count at the East Chicago Regional. They were then ousted from the tournament by the East Chicago Central Cardinals. The Lady Brickies won their sole Sectional title in 1999 for Phil Misecko, with a 20-5 record.

I still chuckle, though, when I recall Dale Hamilton's comment *Hobart Brickie* in his book *Hoosier Hysteria Road Trip* that "Calling your basketball team the Brickies is like calling your football team the Fumblies!"

Railroads have long been important to Indiana. At one time 12 mainline railroads entered the city of Indianapolis, earning it the nickname the Crossroads of America long before the advent of interstate highways. The nation's 1st Union Station was built in Indianapolis in 1852. In the early days of Indiana's development, a railroad connecting the ports on the Ohio River with those on Lake Michigan was seen to be essential and was eventually built from New Albany to Michigan City. That line was known as the "university" line because it went through Bloomington, Greencastle, Crawfordsville, and Lafayette as it made its way north. The problem was it bypassed Indianapolis.

When a later line was constructed to connect Louisville and Indianapolis with Chicago, the 2 lines crossed at the small, unincorporated Indiana town of New Bradford. Almost at once, in 1878, the citizens of New Bradford incorporated and renamed it for 2 streams that ran through the town bearing the Potawatomi Indian names of Big and Little Monong (swiftly flowing) Creek, later shortened to Monon. The railroads led to the growth of a thriving, prosperous town.

Population rapidly expanded from about 300 to 1,200, and soon the railroad was known as the Monon Line. By 1887 there were repair shops, a roundhouse with the capacity for 18 engines, a depot that saw as many as 36 trains in every 24-hour period, and a large freight house. Not only was the town of Monon closely associated with the railroad, no railroad was ever more closely associated with Indiana: the Monon was truly the "Hoosier Line." A popular song of the time was called "Up and Down the Monon," and it went, in part,

> *Oh, up and down the Monon everything is fine,*
> *'Cause that rootin', tootin' Monon she's a Hoosier line!*

The well-known Hoosier humorist, George Ade, said it this way: "The traveler who wishes to see Indiana best must go riding on the Monon. It was the first iron trail to be pushed from one end of the state to the other…it links the Ohio with the Grand Calumet and…all its trains are 'Hoosier's." Beyond that, at one point all of the Monon line's passenger trains were painted in the cream and crimson of Indiana University and all of its freight trains in the old gold and black of Purdue University.

It was on a cold, blustery late December day that I met and enjoyed a pleasant visit with Jack Hughes, editor and publisher of the *Monon News*, a tall, erudite, engaging man in his late 60s who kindly shared this history of his town with me. We talked about the high school, now consolidated into North White along with his own high school, the Buffalo Bisons. He agreed with me that the nickname of the new school, the Vikings, because it is, after all, in the north, was not even close to being as meaningful as that of the now-closed Monon High School, which was located exactly where I thought it would be, just east of the tracks. Those early Monon High School teams were accurately and proudly called the Railroaders.

Monon teams had several memorable years on the hardwood. Coach L. H. Victor led his 1931 Railroaders to a 22-3 record. Monon also won 20 and lost only 6 in 1936, to be followed by an even better 23-5 season the next year. In 1946 the Railroaders went 19-5, with a record of 19-3 one year later. Coach Don Kennedy's 1952 team won 19 and lost 6. The Railroaders won 6 Sectional championships between 1926 and 1952.

The Garrett Railroaders

Garrett is another railroad town of some significance in Indiana. When the Baltimore & Ohio decided in 1874 to extend its line west to Chicago, a site was selected just south of Auburn where shops, a roundhouse, and yards would be constructed. The town was named Garrett in honor of the president of the railroad's western subsidiary. It was a true company town. Almost everyone who lived there was associated with the railroad. At its peak of traffic, 16 passenger trains a day stopped at the Garrett station, which was still active until just after World War II. Today the main line of CSX passes through Garrett. Garrett still has a high school, and the teams are called, as they always have been, the Railroaders, and their gym is decorated not only with the colors and mascots of their traditional athletic opponents, but with the logos of the great railroads of the country as well, such as the B&O, Union Pacific, and the Santa Fe.

The Garrett boys basketball teams have done extremely well in many years since they first took up the game in 1911. Consider the 1937 Railroaders who won 22 and lost 5, and their 1940 counterparts with an identical record, both for Coach Cameron Parks. His 1948 Railroaders finished with a 20-6 mark. Coach Ward Smith's team went 20-4 in 1956 and 20-6 the next year. Beginning in 1964 his Garrett teams had an impressive 3-year streak of 20-7, 23-2, and an undefeated regular season of 24-1. That's 67-10! That lone loss was to South Side in the final game of the Ft. Wayne Regional, 45-40, after the Railroaders had won round one over North Side by a single point, 62-61. Dennis Feagler coached Garrett to a 21-5 season in 1984. Over the years the Railroaders have won 18 Sectionals and 5 Regionals. The Lady Railroaders have added 8 Sectional and 3 Regional titles to the school's collection. In 2004 Dan Feagler's team had an outstanding 24-2 season, and his 2007 and 2008 squads turned in 21-3 and 23-4 marks. From 2003 to 2008 Feagler's Lady Railroaders have notched an impressive 120 victories and tasted defeat only 29 times.

Chapter 11

American History 101: Inspiration from Our Nation's Past

Several of our schools selected team names that have considerable historical significance. Some of these have been discussed previously, but here are some more that I hope you will find interesting.

It's been said that anyone who settled in Indiana prior to 1830 is considered a pioneer. I didn't quite make that cut, but the town of Mooresville certainly did. Named for Samuel Moore, who settled there in 1823 and tried to establish a Utopian community, Mooresville has had a long history of interest in education. There were many Quakers in the area and the Friends Academy was built at 244 N. Montgomery Street in 1861. In 1870 this building was purchased by the town to be used as a public school, grades 1-12, until 1908 when the new high school opened*.

The Mooresville teams have long been called the Pioneers. Hall of Famer Glenn Curtis once coached the Pioneers in 1917. The Pioneers have won 10 Sectional championships and 2 Regional titles, 1944 at Brazil and 1977 at Frankfort. In 1998 coach Jim Whitaker's Pioneers won 21 games and lost only 3. The Lady Pioneers have also brought considerable glory to the school, amassing 12 Sectional and 8 Regional championships as well as the 1978 Ben Davis Semi-state. That latter team won 21 games and lost only 2 for Coach Joe Johnson, who led the Mooresville girls teams for their 1st 21 years. His teams won 66 games and lost only 6 during the 3-year period beginning in 1985. Mark Hurt's 2001 through 2004 Lady Pioneers also put some "hurt" on their opponents, winning 81 games while losing just 17.

Pioneer Country

The Mooresville Pioneers and an early Mooresville school building

*See *Indiana: A New Historical Guide*, Robert M. Taylor, et al

Mooresville was also the birthplace of Paul Hadley, designer of our beautiful Indiana state flag, and an elementary school in the town is named for him.

Indiana Flag

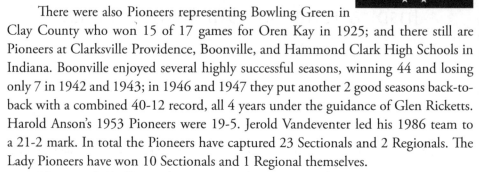

There were also Pioneers representing Bowling Green in Clay County who won 15 of 17 games for Oren Kay in 1925; and there still are Pioneers at Clarksville Providence, Boonville, and Hammond Clark High Schools in Indiana. Boonville enjoyed several highly successful seasons, winning 44 and losing only 7 in 1942 and 1943; in 1946 and 1947 they put another 2 good seasons back-to-back with a combined 40-12 record, all 4 years under the guidance of Glen Ricketts. Harold Anson's 1953 Pioneers were 19-5. Jerold Vandeventer led his 1986 team to a 21-2 mark. In total the Pioneers have captured 23 Sectionals and 2 Regionals. The Lady Pioneers have won 10 Sectionals and 1 Regional themselves.

Hammond Clark's Pioneers conquered in 5 Sectional championships, including one in 1943 for Ed Shields and a "threepeat" from 1970 through 1972 for Larry Liddle. Joe Delgado's 2007 Pioneers amassed an excellent 21-5 record, including a 3A Sectional title. The Lady Pioneers have won 2 Sectionals, in 1986 and 1987, Gary Ridgley coaching.

Clarksville Providence teams have won 5 Sectionals. They also had an undefeated season for Lou LeFevre in 2005, 19-1. His 3 teams from that year through 2007 rang up 60 wins against 11 losses. Pam Edwards' Lady Pioneers enjoyed a 17-4 season in 1997.

George Rogers Clark
High School

Clark   Pioneers

Three more versions of Hoosier Pioneers: Hammond Clark, Boonville, and Clarksville Providence

While we're discussing Colonial America, we should certainly include Plymouth. In 1620 the Pilgrims, escaping religious persecution in England, along with a significantly larger group of non-Pilgrims set sail on the Mayflower for the New World and a new life. They left Plymouth, England, and landed in the Massachusetts Colony, 1st on Cape Cod, later settling on a place they also named Plymouth. Whether or not they actually landed on a rock there, we have long commemorated their arrival at a spot designated Plymouth Rock. Plymouth, Indiana, shares that heritage. There was some question about whether a team from Plymouth should be called the Rocks, in reference to that memorialized landing spot, or should be called the Pilgrims after those hearty folk themselves. This issue was resolved with Solomonic wisdom, calling only the football teams the Rocks (sometimes Rockies) and all of the other teams the Pilgrims.

How can you mention Plymouth and not be reminded of one of the most thrilling final games in the history of our great state tournament and certainly one of the most spectacular individual efforts I have personally ever witnessed in a state championship game? The Pilgrims beat the Panthers of Gary Roosevelt in 1982 at Market Square Arena 75-74 in double overtime. That night Scott Skiles scored 39 of his team's points. (My other picks for individual effort in a winning cause? How about Damon Bailey's 30 points in Bedford North Lawrence's 63-60 victory over Concord at the Hoosier Dome. Or Oscar Robertson in 1956. Or George McGinnis in 1969. Or Glenn Robinson...well, you get the idea.)

The Pilgrims had several other impressive seasons than that 1st state championship, of course. Forrest Wood (you have to love that name) coached the 1926 team to a 20-2 mark, in the process landing the 2nd of what would be 33 Sectional crowns. The 6th came with a 23-4 mark in 1941, coached by George Belshaw. Marvin Tudor's 1967 team brought home the 11th, finishing 20-5. The Pilgrim's 1st of 12 Regional crowns came in 1970 under Steve Yoder, 23-4. Yoder's 1973 squad garnered their 2nd Regional title with a 22-2 record. Then came that wonderful 28-1 state championship season in 1982, coached by Jack Edison who held that job for a total

The Plymouth Pilgrim Rocks

of 34 years. His 1983 Pilgrims won 20 games and lost 6, and between 1994 and 1998, his teams put together an impressive string of 110 wins and only 14 losses. His 2005 team was state runner-up, losing the final Class 3A game in that heart-stopping thriller when Luke Zeller's last-second, mid-court jump shot split the net in overtime giving the Washington Hatchets a 74-72 victory and leaving Plymouth with a 22-4 final record. His next year's squad won 21 games and lost only 5, and when the 2007 Pilgrims came back to win their 2nd state championship, this at 3A, with a 25-2 record, defeating Evansville Bosse, Edison's final 3 teams had turned in a total of 68 wins and only 9 losses! Not a bad way to go out. Nor did he leave the cupboard bare, as his successor, Jake Scott, inherited a team that finished the 2008 season 22-4.

The Lady Pilgrims have added 9 Sectional nets to the school's trophy case, as well as 3 Regionals. David Cox has coached the girls since 1993. His 2001 team finished runner-up to 3A State Champion Indianapolis Cathedral, closing their season at 22 wins and 6 losses. In 2008 Cox took the Lady Pilgrims to the winner's circle at Conseco Fieldhouse, capturing the 3A State Championship by defeating Indianapolis Chatard in a thriller, 47-46, to finish 23-5.

Some 155 years after the Pilgrims arrived in the New World, things had deteriorated between the colonists and their British rulers to the extent that a serious break was clearly on the horizon. Ralph Waldo Emerson said it best:

By the rude bridge that arched the flood
Their flag to April's breeze unfurled
There the embattled farmers stood
And fired the shot heard round the world.

Lexington, Concord, the Minutemen; a Declaration of Independence, the Boston Massacre, the Battle of Bunker Hill; a Revolutionary War, George Washington and his Continental Army: a nation was born. Those early days are well represented by our Indiana high school team names. The towns of Lexington and Bunker Hill called their teams the Minutemen, as did Concord High School, state championship runners-up twice, in 1988 and 1990. Coach Jim Hahn's Minutemen had outstanding records in those years, 28-1 each season, undefeated until that final game. The 1st loss was a no-doubter, to Muncie Central by 23 points, but that 2nd one left plenty of room for what-ifs: a 3-pointer to Bedford North Lawrence and Damon Bailey, during a 6-year run in which they won a remarkable 137 games and lost just 19. Earlier they enjoyed a 24-2 season in 1949, Les McCuen's team landing the school's 1st Sectional title. Cliff Murray's 1959 team went through the regular season undefeated, finishing 24-1 with that lone defeat another heartbreaker, this time at the hands of Elkhart in the Sectional final game, 58-56. As McCuen's next 2 squads finished 22-2 and 19-5, that 3-year mark came to an impressive 85-8. As recently as 2005, Ryan Culp's team put together a 22-2 season. All of these Minutemen would have made those of 1775 proud! The Lady Minutemen (Minutewomen?) have cut down the nets at the end of 3 Sectionals.

Bunker Hill's green-and-white-clad Minutemen of 1952 and 1956 would also have made their namesakes proud, Don Long's squads finishing 18-5 and 19-3 respectively. Sectional championships were won in 1924 and 1960, both at Peru. In Scott County the red-and-white-uniformed Minutemen (also called the Panthers) of Lexington went 16-5 followed by 16-4 in 1956 and 1957 for Coach Clarence Noe. Regrettably, they never won a Sectional title. Neither did the Minutemen of Matthews, in Grant County, whose colors were purple and gold. The Matthews Minutemen had a fine 18-2 season in 1926 for Coach Dale Kelly. In 1934 they consolidated into Jefferson Township, becoming Yeomen and wearing green and white. The Yeomen also had several successful seasons as will be covered later.

Lexington High School and the Concord High Minutemen logo

The town of Onward, southwest of Peru, seemingly took the other side, calling their teams the Redcoats, although their colors were both red and blue. In 1923 the Redcoats won 18 games, losing 9, for Coach E. E. Benson.

Onward High School and some toy soldier Redcoats

They would have had their hands full with the Indianapolis Washington Continentals, whose 1969 team was led by George McGinnis and Steve Downing and coached by Bill Green. That combination may well have been the nucleus of the finest Indiana state championship five ever. We can argue that one forever, of course. Washington had won another title in 1965 with Jerry Oliver at the helm. That team saw Billy Keller score 25 points in the title game as the Continentals defeated the Ft. Wayne North Side Redskins 64-57. (Sounds more like something that would take place in the French and Indian War, though, doesn't it?) Oliver's record at Washington includes the period from 1962 through 1968 when his teams won 151 games and lost just 24. And the year he handed the reins to Bill Green resulted in that 31-0 blockbuster. In 1994 and 1995 Joe Pearson led the Continentals to 44 wins in 49 games and the 10th of the school's Sectional titles. After a period as a middle school, Washington rejoined the ranks of high schools in 2005. The Lady Continentals have yet to win a Sectional championship, but did produce our 1981 Indiana Miss Basketball, Cheryl Cook.

George Washington, Continental soldiers, and the Indianapolis Washington High School logo

Next we have the Washington, Indiana, Hatchets. Ralph Haynes, once Assistant Principal at Washington High School, pointed out to me that their teams were not always known as the Hatchets, however. From 1896 until the early 1920s they were simply known as the Old Gold and Black after their school colors, the same as Purdue's. In 1922 the star player came from a family who ran a local funeral parlor whose cars were often used to transport the team, and fans began calling them the Undertakers. This was obviously not something that was likely to last, and when a particularly strong team came along in the 1924-25 season, sportswriter Edward Brouilette wrote after one game that "The team had cut through its opponent like George Washington's hatchet had cut through the cherry tree." Fans loved it and began taking black and gold hatchets to their games. The nickname stuck. Today, the Washington Hatchets play their

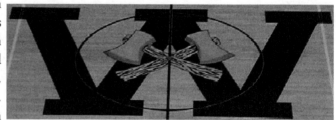

The Washington Hatchets

home basketball games in a 7,090 seat arena (not bad for a town with a population of less than 11,000) known as the Hatchet House that opened on November 23, 1966. An earlier Hatchet House, seating 4,300, had been opened in 1925 with a game against Martinsville whose team included a sophomore by the name of John Wooden.

In 2005, as mentioned to Plymouth's chagrin previously, a young man named Luke Zeller placed his name permanently among the great legends of Indiana basketball when his midcourt 3-pointer with .6 seconds on the clock gave his school their 4th state championship (their 1st in Class 3A) in as dramatic fashion as ever could be. Three years later Luke's "kid" brother (actually the middle of three), Tyler, added even more to the Washington Hatchet lore. The 7-foot-tall North Carolina Tarheel recruit's 43 points led the Hatchets to their 5th state championship, their 2nd Class 3A title, over Ft. Wayne Harding's Hawks.

The Hatchets have been playing basketball since 1905, defeating Vincennes 18-12 on December 5th of that year. Their other 3 state championships came in 1930, 1940, and 1941. They had also fielded girls teams as early as 1925. The pantheon of Washington High School stars in the Indiana Basketball Hall of Fame include players Dave DeJernett, Robert Downey, Leo Klier, Hook Mangin, Art Grove, Charles Harmon, Jim Riffey, and Sam Alford (not a bad coach, either), and coaches Burl Friddle and Marion Crawley. In total the Hatchets have amassed 43 Sectional titles and 19 Regionals. The Lady Hatchets have added 9 Sectionals, 5 Regionals, and the 1995 Seymour Semi-state titles to the school's trophy case. Dave DeJernett's Hall of Fame citation:

Dave DeJernett
A 3-year standout at Washington High School, leading team to 75-17 record ... state champions in 1930 ... 6´ 5″ center scored 11 of his team's 32 points in title game ... one of Indiana's first black high school basketball players ... All-State ... 3 appearances in state tourney ... moving to Indiana Central, became state's first dominant black collegiate player ... 4-year letterman ... 2-time All-State ... scored 506 points in days of center jump and low scores, and a dominant rebounder ... called by his high school coach, Hall of Famer Burl Friddle, "a great leader."

But those were not the only Washington Hatchets in Indiana. There were others, less notable perhaps in terms of hardwood success, but certainly important to our history as Hoosiers. These other Hatchets were found in Cass County, at Washington Township from 1922 through 1963, when they turned in their royal blue and old gold uniforms for the red, white, and blue of the Lewis Cass Kings. There was also, for a brief period, a Washington High School in Mt. Vernon, which I found interesting. I hope someone will be able to tell me what their mascot was.

Washington Township School, Cass County, also home of the Hatchets, and Mt. Vernon Washington High School

Crispus Attucks was the 1st American to be killed by the British in what is now called the Boston Massacre. He died on March 5, 1770. He was an African American, a runaway slave who, although reportedly treated well by his Framingham owner, valued freedom too highly not to escape. Due to his own deep sentiments, he sympathized with the colonists seeking freedom from Great Britain. At great personal risk, not just from the British, but also from those colonists who would return him to slavery, he joined the citizenry in a confrontation with a platoon or so of Redcoat troops on the fateful morning of his death.

Indianapolis Crispus Attucks High School was originally commissioned in 1927 as an all-African American institution. In 1986 it became a fully integrated middle school, but recently it has been returned to the status of a high school, designed now as a medical magnet school, again fielding athletic teams.

For many years the wonderful athletes who played for Attucks had limited abilities to test their skills against the best competition the state had to offer. When, in the 40s and 50s, all restrictions were lifted, fans began to realize what they had been missing. The Crispus Attucks Tigers turned out men such as Willie Gardner, Hallie Bryant, Willie Merriweather, Edgar Searcy, the incomparable Oscar Robertson, and the 1st African American Trester Award winner, Bob Jewell. Bob, who died much too young, was as fine a man as one could ever meet. His Trester Award was on his chest when he was buried.

Bob Jewell
Winner of the Trester Award as a senior at Indianapolis Crispus Attucks High School in 1951 ... 2-year varsity player for Coach Ray Crowe, and a member of the first Attucks unit to make Final Four ... member of '51 Indiana all-star team ... very active in all school activities ... among his many honors off the court was being named Student Council president ... made University of Michigan varsity as a freshman, but decided to continue his schooling in his hometown ... played 3 seasons at Indiana Central.

The 1st time I saw Oscar play was in the 1954 Indianapolis City Tournament championship game, when he made the winning basket in a sudden-death overtime against Shortridge before a packed house at the Butler Fieldhouse. Attucks went on to win the state championship that year, the 1st time an Indianapolis school had done so. They won it again in 1956. Undefeated. Something no Indiana school had ever accomplished. Their coach, who turned out men as well as basketball players, was a fine gentleman named Ray Crowe. Both are also enshrined in the Indiana Basketball Hall of Fame.

Oscar Robertson
Led Crispus Attucks to 2 straight state championships in '55 and '56...'56 team was first to win state crown with undefeated record...Mr. Basketball...2-time All-State...high school All-American...

Attucks banner
Houck photo of exhibit
courtesy IBHOF.

MVP of Indiana-Kentucky all-star game...3-time All-American at University of Cincinnati ...3-time player of the year...led nation in scoring 3 years... his 2,973 points was an NCAA record...gold medal winner on '59 Pan American team...co-captain of '60 Olympic gold medalists ... NBA's MVP in '64. All NBA 11 of 14 seasons...3-time MVP of all-star game...only NBA player ever to average a "triple-double" for an entire season.

Ray Crowe
Twice the leading scorer and captain of Whiteland team ... 4-year letter-winner ... 3 baseball letters ... 4

letters at Indiana Central ... leading scorer and captain 2 years ... captained track team, and added a baseball letter ... coached 7 years at Crispus Attucks, creating one of the great legends in high school basketball... brought Indianapolis its first state championship in '55 ... year later became state's first undefeated state champion ... runner-up next season, '57 ... state finalist in '51 ... school's athletic director 11 years...served 4 1/2 terms in the Indiana House of Representatives...assistant director with Indiana Department of Public Instruction...later, director of Indianapolis Department of Parks and Recreation.

To Ray Crowe's Hall of Fame citation I would add the following:

1. His 7-year record at Crispus Attucks was 179 wins and 20 losses.

2. His teams won 6 Sectionals, 6 Regionals, 4 Semi-states, and 3 state championships in those 7 years.

3. Two of his players were Mr. Basketball: Hallie Bryant in 1953 and Oscar Robertson in 1956.

4. In addition to Ray Crowe himself, 9 of his players plus the entire 1956 team are enshrined in the Indiana Basketball Hall of Fame, a remarkable achievement.

5. His teams set a new record that would stand for over 50 years: 45 consecutive wins.

For a more comprehensive look at the Attucks season of 1954–55 and its profound impact on Indiana basketball, see the next chapter.

John Marshall was appointed to the United States Supreme Court by President John Adams in 1801. Not only did he become the longest serving Chief Justice in our history, Marshall is generally credited with being the jurist who more than any other shaped American constitutional law. He established the principle of judicial review in which the courts have the power to strike down unconstitutional laws. Indianapolis John Marshall, recently reinstated as a high school, fields the Patriots.

Henry Clay of Kentucky was known as the "Great Compromiser." His home in Lexington, open to the public, is quite impressive. Abraham Lincoln was an admirer of Clay for that senator's abilities to resolve conflicts and bring people with disparate views to a common resolution beneficial to all. South Bend Clay High School teams were the Colonials. The Colonials have won 4 Sectionals and 1 Regional. However, they made the most of that one trip to the Sweet Sixteen. In one of the most memorable state final games ever played, the 27-2 Colonials, coached by Tom DeBaets, refused to compromise with the undefeated Valparaiso Vikings of Bob Punter, winning 93-88 in overtime.

The Clay Colonials

Michigan City Rogers (named for a local educator) teams were the Raiders, after the famous Rogers Raiders of the French and Indian War from 1754–63, with important victories at Fort Ticonderoga and Montreal. The Michigan City Raiders won some memorable victories as well, including 9 Sectional crowns and 3 Regionals in their relatively brief (1971–95) history. Bill Hahn's Raiders won 23 of 26 games in 1979. Earl Cunningham's squads put together an impressive streak from 1983 through 1987, winning 114 games while losing only19! Included was 1984's undefeated regular season, 28-1. Their only loss came in the Semi-state final, a heartbreaking thriller, 75-73, to the Warsaw Tigers, who would win the state championship in Indianapolis the next weekend defeating the Vincennes Lincoln Alices in the final game, by a 59-56 count.

Perhaps no single man has captured the imagination of the American people as has Abraham Lincoln. Besides bringing an end to the abomination that was slavery, preserving the Union, and delivering what is arguably the most familiar and eloquent speech in our history, the Gettysburg Address, he had the foresight to envision the importance of unifying the nation from Atlantic to Pacific. President Lincoln had the resolve to encourage and help finance the construction of the transcontinental railroad, which was not completed until 1869. Born in Kentucky and so often claimed by Illinois, Lincoln actually spent his formative years, from age 7 to 21, in southern Indiana. The various historical sites in our state devoted to his time here are true treasures. Lincoln's mother is buried in the family plot in Indiana, and it is no exaggeration to say that what we proudly describe as Hoosier values were well developed in this remarkable man. Lincoln High School in Cass County, which only existed from 1923 until 1933 and never managed to win a Sectional, was consolidated into Galveston, becoming Cardinals, before finally becoming Lewis Cass Kings. They called their teams "The Railsplitters."

The Railsplitter, Lincoln, Illinois, version

The Heritage Hills Patriot

The area of our state that includes the Lincoln homestead and national landmark is now served by Heritage Hills High School, the Patriots. The Patriots won 20 and lost only 4 games under Coach Dale Hein in 1980, and in 1989 his team went 21-3. The 1997 Patriots were coached by Steve Merkel to another fine 21 and 3 season. They have won 9 Sectionals. The Lady Patriots have added 4 more Sectional nets to the trophy case.

Cambridge City Lincoln calls its teams the Golden Eagles, and Vincennes Lincoln teams are, of course, the Alices, both covered elsewhere. Evansville Lincoln, an all-African American school now closed, fielded the Lions. This team won 3 Sectionals in the 50s and captured the Regional as well in 1957 before losing a double overtime thriller to Jasper in the Semi-state. Art Taylor coached that team. Lincoln High School in Randolph County unfortunately never won a Sectional title. They called their teams the Wolves.

Thomas Jonathan Jackson was perhaps the finest military tactician and the most revered commander of the Confederate Army after Robert E. Lee. Stonewall Jackson was certainly one of the bravest. He received the sobriquet "Stonewall" when under withering fire he stood erect, leading one of his compatriots to cry, "There is Jackson standing like a stone wall." Indiana could claim not one but 2 Stonewalls: Jackson Township (in Howard County) and Roanoke High School teams were both the Stonewalls.

Who can forget the immortal words of John Greenleaf Whittier about the Battle of Frederick:

> *Up from the meadows rich with corn*
> *Clear in the cool September morn*
> *The clustered spires of Frederick stand*
> *Green walled by the hills of Maryland...*

And after the horrendous battle in the poem, when the Confederate troops march into town on the way to Harper's Ferry, one of their soldiers shoots the Union flag. It is snatched up by Barbara Fritchie:

> *"Shoot if you must this old grey head*
> *But spare your country's flag" she said...*

Stonewall replies:

> *"Who touches a hair on yon grey head*
> *Dies like a dog. March on!" he said.*

The Roanoke Stonewalls are now Huntington North Vikings, and the Jackson Township Stonewalls are now Eastern (Howard) Comets. While Jackson never won

a Sectional, Roanoke got 2, in 1935 and 1936, both at Huntington. To do so each year they were forced to defeat the home team Vikings. The 1935 team lost a close one in the Huntington Regional, to Berne, 20-18.

The Roanoke High School Stonewalls Houck
photo from exhibit courtesy IBHOF

Freedom and liberty are central concepts that led to the birth of our nation, as so eloquently stated in the Declaration of Independence, generally attributed to our nation's 3rd President, Thomas Jefferson:

Roanoke High School

> *We hold these truths to be self-evident, that all men are created equal,*
> *that they are endowed by their Creator with certain unalienable Rights, that*
> *among these are Life, Liberty and the pursuit of Happiness...*

Freetown won its only Sectional title in 1925, at Seymour, with wins over Houston, Cortland, and Brownstown. They were then called only the "Freetown Five," but the next year were nicknamed the Spartans by Coach Howard Scott. Writer

Donna Fritz of the *Jackson County Banner,* herself a proud Freetown alumna, renders priceless recollections on the Brownstown Central High School web site:

> *He hoped to encourage bravery, hardiness and discipline...by using the Greeks in ancient Sparta as an example.* [This was important, as the school had no gym until 1930. The team practiced on a dirt court in the school-yard and also in an old gym] *across the street from the Wheeler Hotel...they used a room ... in the Winklepleck Funeral Home as a dressing room.*

The 1938 Spartans won 19 and lost only 2 games. That 2nd loss came at the hands of Crothersville, 20-18, in the Sectional tournament. The 1941 team had a 22-3 record, winning the invitational tourney and the county tourney. Freetown also won the 1957 Jackson County Tournament, as the sign still proclaims as you enter town 52 years later.

Fritz continues:

> *After World War II, coaches like Edgar Sprague and Ralph Scott of Clear Spring, graduates of Indiana Central (now the University of Indianapolis) induced Ray Crowe, an assistant coach, to schedule their teams with the Crispus Attucks High School team of Indianapolis...Freetown was more than willing for them to come and play their Spartans; Freetown never thought about discrimination...The gym was filled to capacity with standing room only. Following the game, the Crispus Attucks (players and coaches) were treated to a dinner provided by the Freetown restaurant, operated by Alvin Sutton. Residents remember a festive evening...the small cafe decorated for their special guests...Ray Crowe was [the] featured speaker at the FHS athletic banquet...the year that Crispus Attucks won the State Championship.*

Freetown has, of course, been consolidated. The Spartans are now Brownstown Central Braves. The gym has been nicely renovated and is used as the Freetown Community Center. The town is justifiably proud of its heritage, as should all of us Hoosiers be, and is optimistic about its future, an optimism I certainly hope will be fulfilled.

The 1925 Freetown High School Sectional champs

It has since come to my attention that towns other than Freetown also entertained the Crispus Attucks teams when they played there. One of these was Sheridan. In a letter to *The Indianapolis Star* published on December 28, 2008, Ann Leonard Quick had this to say:

> *I enjoyed Kyle Neddenriep's December 20 story on Ray and Betty Crowe. We were one of the small towns (Sheridan) that Crispus Attucks played.*
>
> *My father (Dewy Leonard) owned a drive-in restaurant and fed our basketball teams before and after the games, so when our coach, Larry Hobbs, asked my dad if he would feed their team, he said "sure."*
>
> *They were some of the nicest people we ever fed and Ray Crowe was a real gentleman.*
>
> *[For the game], the gym was filled and some even watched from the windows on the roof.*
>
> *Our local fireman had a hard time keeping people from sitting on the steps.*

Martin Luther King's inspired and inspirational speech on the Washington Mall

Freetown gym pre-renovation, the Brownstown Central Braves Arrowhead, and the Spartan logo

in 1963 has generally been referred to as his "I Have a Dream" speech. That is an apt title, of course, but I tend to think of it as his "Let Freedom Ring" speech because of those stirring words repeated before phrases such as "the prodigious hilltops of New Hampshire...the mighty mountains of New York...the heightening Alleghenies of Pennsylvania...the snow capped Rockies of Colorado...from every hill and molehill in Mississippi...from every village and hamlet...from every state and every city Let Freedom Ring!" Well, Freetown, Indiana, was a place where that did happen.

Freedom has been a fundamental precept of American life since our founding, but, unfortunately, it was not applied to all of our citizenry for another "four score and seven" years, or thereabouts due to fears of the dissolution of the 13 colonies should abolition be a requirement of union. Whether or not that was wise is debatable, but our Founding Fathers certainly got a remarkable number of things right. Still, the scourge of slavery remained and has stained our consciences ever since. But let me return to my theme. Freetown was one of several towns in Indiana to explicitly refer to freedom and liberty as important values. We have the towns of Freedom, Freeland Park, Fredonia, Free, Freeman and Freemont; we also have Liberty, 2 Liberty Centers, North Liberty, Liberty Mills and Libertyville. Not all of these were home to our high schools, however. Those that were are the Freedom Aces, the Freelandville Fighting (or Flying) Dutchmen, the Liberty Lancers/Warriors, the Liberty Center Lions in

Wells County, and the Liberty Township Lions in Porter County. These are now, respectively, Owen Valley Patriots, North Knox Warriors, Union County Patriots, Southern Wells Raiders, and Chesterton Trojans and will all be covered later. The Freeland Park Rockets were covered previously.

The scarlet and white Liberty Lancers/Warriors in Union County won 3 Sectionals, all at Connersville, between 1938 and 1967. In 1967 they also won the Regional title with victories over Morristown and Jac-Cen-Del but lost in the 1st round of the Semi-state to the New Castle Trojans in their only Sweet Sixteen appearance.

The Freedom Aces, wearing red and white uniforms, nabbed the Spencer Sectional in 1963 for Coach Bob Williams, defeating Bowling Green handily, edging Cory in overtime, and nipping the Cops 56-55. They also turned in a fine 17-3 mark under Coach Alvin Schwarz in 1959.

While addressing this subject, mention should also be made of Fountain City in Wayne County. Fountain City, it has been said, was not merely a stop on the Underground Railroad that assisted so many slaves to escape their bondage; it has been described as the Grand Central Station of such a railroad. The Levi Coffin House in Fountain City was the focal point of this activity and is now a National Historic Landmark. The Fountain City High School teams wore black and gold and were called the Little Giants. Although their lone Sectional championship came at Richmond in 1949 when they beat Milton (Paradise Lost?) and Greens Fork as well as the powerful host Red Devils, the Little Giants turned in a number of other fine seasons. In 1946 they won 23 of 25 games for Coach Buck Merritt. This was followed by a phenomenal stretch under Clyde Quakenbush for the next 6 years, leading his teams to 118 wins and 25 losses, or a 7-year string for the school of 141 wins and 27 losses. Bill Townsend's 1958 through 1961 Little Giants won 75 games and lost only 13. Little, indeed. They are now Northeastern Knights.

The Levi Coffin House in Fountain City and the logo of the Northeastern Knights

Finally, there is a significant bit of history attendant to a locale in Jefferson County that has relevance to this discussion. Lancaster is home to this important bit of Indiana history that is not as well known as perhaps it should be. On a site just east of town on Indiana Route 250 stands an impressive 3-story stone structure that was once home to an institution that was, after Oberlin College in Ohio, the nation's 2nd to provide interracial education, Eleutherian College, from the Greek word for freedom/

liberty, was founded in 1848 and supported by a Lancaster Baptist church and other abolitionists. After it was closed it was used by Lancaster as a public school. Eventually those students were enrolled in DuPont High School, home of the Hornets, later to be consolidated into Madison as the Cubs.

Eleutherian College and DuPont High School in Jefferson County

Chapter 12

A Turning Point:
The 1955 Season That Changed Everything

Many have referred to the decade of the 50s as the Golden Age of Indiana high school basketball. In many ways it certainly was. Crowds were huge at gyms all over the state. The Miracle of Milan occurred, inspiring the wonderful movie *Hoosiers*. Jimmy Rayl and Ray Pavy had their incredible encounter now known as the "Church Street Shootout." The world's largest and finest high school gym was opened in New Castle, with a capacity in excess of 9,300 fans. State tournament games began to be televised. Hoosier Hysteria was at an all-time high with close to 800 different schools competing for a single championship.

However, 1955, the middle of the decade, marked a turning point in Indiana basketball. A tournament that began in 1911, that had seen champions crowned in towns and cities across the state from places like Crawfordsville, Lebanon, Wingate, Franklin, Frankfort, Martinsville, and Thorntown, from Evansville to Ft. Wayne, from Madison to Hammond, had never seen a champion from the capitol city of Indianapolis. Not once in 44 years had a city or suburban team won the coveted prize. Forty-four different teams from every corner of the Hoosier state had cut down the nets as state champions. None of them had come from Marion County.

That all changed in 1955, when the Crispus Attucks Tigers, led by the incomparable Oscar Robertson and accompanied by an exceptionally talented supporting cast and a legendary coach, took it all. Since that memorable Attucks victory over the Gary Roosevelt Panthers, city and suburban Indianapolis schools have won 16 times: or better than once every 3 years until the last single-class Indiana tournament game was played on March 22, 1997. (Since that year, Indianapolis and suburban schools have won 8 of the 11 Class 4A titles contested.)

But that was not the only turning point represented by the Attucks team of 1955. Attucks was then an all-black school. Its team was, of course, also all black. Shortridge was an integrated school by 1955 and had black players as well as white. These two schools, located less than 5 miles apart geographically but much further apart socio-economically, were destined to meet 3 times that year: once in the regular season, once in the championship game of the city tournament, and finally in the title game of the Indianapolis Sectional.

Black players had long been successful on the Indiana high school scene. Dave DeJernetts had starred on the Washington Hatchets 1930 state championship team that won 31 games and lost only once. A 3-time All-State selection, he was inducted into the Indiana Basketball Hall of Fame in 1976 and was recently selected on Washington High School's All-Century team. John DeJernetts and teammate Garland Raney played on Marion Crawley's Washington state championship teams of 1941 and 1942. More recently Johnny Wilson had led the Anderson Indians to the state championship in 1946, as had Bill Garrett for Shelbyville's Golden Bears, who were title holders the following year. Bob Jewel had become the first African American to win the Trester Award, doing so for Attucks in 1951. These latter 3 men are also enshrined at New Castle in the Hall of Fame; their citations shown elsewhere.

But these were the exceptions, not the rule. For a variety of sociological reasons beyond the scope of this book, the limitations placed on black athletes competing in Indiana were considerable. All-black schools had not always been allowed full competition in the state, and no team with an all-black starting five had won the championship until the year 1955.

The Attucks Tigers were not the only fine team in Indianapolis that year, though. Shortridge had a team that might well have won the title had they not had the Tigers to contend with. Because of Attucks, this fine team was unable to even win the Sectional crown. This is the story of that season, told from the eyes of John Hollett, one of the starters on that Shortridge Blue Devil team. (Though, as we have seen, Shortridge teams were also known as Felix the Cat, Blue Devils was the more widely used name in 1954.)

The Crispus Attucks Tiger as recently portrayed and an earlier version

The Shortridge Blue Devil and Felix the Cat

Although it is impossible to reproduce the tension, joy, and heartbreak of the 98 seasons and hundreds of schools covered by this book, perhaps by concentrating on this one seminal season we will not only have done justice to 2 schools central to the events of that year but will have provided some insight into the universal feelings of every school in every season.

Shortridge entered the 1954-55 season with justifiably high hopes. They had height in co-captains 6′6″ center Frank Mead, 6′3″ forward Jim Loer (who would be named to the Indiana All Star team of seniors playing Kentucky's stars in June). John Hollett, 6′3″ forward, added more rebounding strength and a good shooting eye. The starting five was rounded out with a scrappy, speedy pair of guards, Herschel Turner and Bob "Biscuit" Williams. (Williams would be followed at Shortridge by brothers nicknamed "Muffin" and "Crumb"!) They had depth in subs Doug Robinson, Bob Branham, Pat McConahay, Ed Hurt, and Don Screes. They were an experienced and athletic group who well understood Coach Cleon Reynolds' disciplined offense and switching man-to-man defense. Reynolds was a Butler graduate who followed the principles of teaching the game of basketball that were developed and practiced with consummate success by the great Tony Hinkle. Everyone had worked hard over the summer to improve his game, and the team was ready for the challenge they knew would be presented by Coach Ray Crowe's impressive Attucks contingent. This group of Shortridge Blue Devils had realistic hopes of capturing the school's first Sectional crown since 1935.

The Shortridge season started well with convincing victories over the Red Devils of Brazil, the ever tough Ft. Wayne South Side Archers, and west side rival Ben Davis Giants. An overtime win over Indianapolis Tech, secured when a 15-18 foot jumper by John Hollett went through the net as time expired, was sandwiched between losses to 2 other representatives of the powerful North Central Conference, the Wildkats of Kokomo and the Anderson Indians. A 17-point thrashing of the Indianapolis Washington Continentals brought the Shortridge record to 5-2 with the Christmas break coming up, which meant city tournament time had arrived.

Things had been going on with equal intensity over on Michigan Road (now Martin Luther King, Jr. Avenue) as well. Coach Crowe had welcomed back his superbly talented group after they had spent the summer honing their skills at places like Lockefield Gardens and the Municipal Gardens, where Dust Bowl contests achieved a very high level of competition. Players whose names would be nationally recognized in a few short years, such as forwards Oscar Robertson, then just a junior, and senior Willie Merriweather, later a star on several very excellent Purdue University teams, were joined by center Sheddrick Mitchell and a pair of quick, ball-hawking guards, Bill Hampton and Bill Scott.

For several years Attucks teams had flirted with winning the state championship. The players who were greeted by Ray Crowe on that 1st day of practice in the fall of 1954 were hungry to be the ones who would cut down the nets at Butler Fieldhouse the next March. They had lost to eventual state champion Milan in the finals of the Indianapolis Semi-state the year before and instinctively knew they had the potential to go all the way this year. Shortridge was one of the major obstacles in their path.

Their season started out even more impressively than Shortridge's. The widely traveled Tigers won their first 4 games against the Ft. Wayne North Side Redskins 75-54, the Sheridan Blackhawks 80-36, the Terre Haute Gerstmeyer Black Cats 57-44, and the Wildcats of South Bend Riley 76-62, without being seriously challenged. Indianapolis Broad Ripple was dispatched rather easily (76-48) before Tech gave Ray Crowe's charges their closest test of the new season, a 10-point win for Attucks, 57-47. Thus the Tigers were 7-0 at the Christmas break and were looking forward to the city tournament with well-deserved confidence.

Back in the Shortridge gym on 34th Street, Coach Reynolds had some special training routines ready for his squad as they prepared for the city tournament and the anticipated early season match-up with the Attucks Tigers. Hollett recalls it this way:

> It was a big week whenever Attucks appeared on our schedule. The games were always played at Butler Fieldhouse and the crowds were huge, ranging from 10-15,000 per game. In preparation for Attucks Cleon Reynolds always introduced several special routines that he only used before those games. One of these involved each of us players having a rope–the same ropes we used to jump rope before practice—tied around our waists three to five times during practice. We were then told to tuck our hands through the ropes behind our backs to work on our defensive positioning by moving our feet while not being able to rely upon our hands at all. We knew how quick the Attucks players were and you simply could not defend against them unless you moved your feet.
>
> Also, Coach Reynolds had purchased smaller rims that fit inside the regulation ones. This resulted in constant work on rebounding during our scrimmages. Rebounding and defense were always particular points of emphasis especially for Attucks.
>
> Although Coach Reynolds would always remind us that "the Attucks players put on their shorts one leg at a time just like we do," some of us wondered if he really was serious.

Frank Mead recalls that Shortridge never had enough money for training meals for the team in those days, so his parents provided the players with steak dinners before big games like those with Attucks.

The stage was set for the city tournament. The draw meant that Attucks and Shortridge would meet in the championship game if both could win their 1st and 2nd round games, which they were favored to do. In those days the city tournament was a very serious, big time event. All games were played at the Butler Fieldhouse, and the title game was sure to find a capacity crowd in the neighborhood of 15,000 partisan fans and objective lovers of Indiana high school basketball filling every seat—and some standing—in one of the greatest venues ever built.

The Attucks cheerleaders would be there in their green and gold outfits and the Shortridge cheerleaders in their royal blue and white. The Attucks fans, known for their coordinated cheers, the famous "Crazy" song, and their "satisfied" chant after a victory would be matched yell for yell and cheer for cheer by the Shortridge faithful. If both schools won their first 2 games, an exciting night was in store for all.

Shortridge opened their play in the tourney with a match against another big rival, the Rockets of northside Broad Ripple High School, also about 5 miles away. In a hard-fought contest the Devils emerged the winners over their orange-and-black-clad rivals by 5 points. At almost the same time Attucks was defeating the Howe Hornets, 73-60.

In the second round Shortridge again drew a very tough Arsenal Tech team. The second match between the two was almost a duplicate of the first. In another overtime thriller Shortridge won the right to play in the finals by winning 59-53. Attucks had a much easier semi-final experience. The Tigers sent the Washington Continentals home after a 32-point drubbing, 85-53.

The week after Christmas was a cold one in Indianapolis that year, but that did nothing to discourage attendance at the Fieldhouse the night of the finals. Cars filled the parking lot early and lined Boulevard Place and the side streets for blocks and blocks. As predicted, every seat was taken in the Fieldhouse, and many people were standing, some others peeking around columns to get a view of the action. The air was filled with cheers long before the teams even came up from their locker rooms below for their pregame warm-ups.

"We've got spirit, yes we do, we've got spirit, how 'bout you?" By the time the players were introduced, the noise was deafening, and it hardly ever stopped as the game was played. Neither team was able to gain an advantage of more than a few points for any length of time. After 32 minutes the score was tied. Another overtime. "Well," Hollett recalls thinking, "we've won overtimes before. Let's get after this one."

Five tense minutes later the score was still tied. Double overtime. The players on both sides were nearly exhausted. Mead recalls that both he and Jim Loer were fighting leg cramps from the middle of the 4th quarter on.

The coaches, though they both looked cool and collected, must have been churning inside, and the crowd was spent. In those days the 2nd overtime was the last. It was sudden death. The 1st team to score would win. That rule has since been changed, as it put such a premium on winning the tip-off that would start the play.

Had that rule not been changed, the sign outside Swayzee that not only declares the town to be the only Swayzee in the world but also mentions that it is the home of the only 9 overtime state tournament game ever played in Indiana, could never have been erected!

Shortridge's John Hollett protects the ball from Bill Hampton of Crispus Attucks while Blue Devil teammates Jim Loer (3) and Herschel Turner and Tigers Sheddrick Mitchell and Oscar Robertson look on. (photo courtesy of John Hollett)

Anyway, sudden death was the rule then, and sudden death it was to be. Attucks won the tip. The ball was tossed to junior forward Oscar Robertson. Ray Crowe's players cleared the east side of the court. Oscar drove for the basket at the south end of the Fieldhouse. Fifteen thousand fans were on their feet. Perhaps for the 1st time all night the crowd was hushed. Oscar was closely guarded. He dribbled right, then left, jumped and faded, let loose a 15-footer. Swish. Half of the crowd exploded. Half were deflated. Attucks was the 1954 Indianapolis City Tournament champion. Shortridge was runner-up. Since I was fortunate enough to be home from college that Christmas break, I was there. It was one of the best high school games I have ever seen.

Before the trophies were presented, John Hollett found himself standing next to teammate and center Frank Mead. He remembers asking Frank if he realized who he jumped center with to begin the second overtime. Frank said he hadn't paid any attention to it, assuming it was their center, Sheddrich Mitchell, as it had been to open all of the periods before. John told him, "No, it wasn't. That was Oscar Robertson. He tipped it to Sheddrick who passed it back." Mead confirms that he had not realized he was jumping against Oscar. "I was so focused on getting that tip that I never even looked at the other guy in the center circle. I knew I had out-jumped Sheddrick before, and I was hoping to do so again."

Ray Crowe had known the importance of winning that tip, and he had great confidence in his junior forward, Oscar Robertson. How many times, in how many venues in how many big games was Oscar Robertson to repay that confidence to coaches at all levels!

After the city tournament, Shortridge reeled off 3 straight victories against the Artesians of Martinsville, the Warren Central Warriors, and the Howe Hornets. The victory against Howe was memorable for two reasons. First, it was yet another overtime win for Shortridge, and second, as Hollett recalls, "We all agreed that the

Howe cheerleaders were the best looking of any in town … other than our own, of course!"

Meanwhile, Attucks was defeating Sacred Heart 63-44, Ft. Wayne Central in a battle of Tigers 70-60, and Michigan City 88-69.

The season's 2nd Attucks-Shortridge meeting was next on the agenda, and this time the Devils were totally overwhelmed by the Tigers. As Hollett put it, "The team bus made it from 34th and Meridian to 49th and Boulevard, but apparently we weren't all on it. Attucks came to play, we didn't, it was as simple as that. We had worked as hard as ever for that game and Coach had brought out all of his special gimmicks. I'm not really sure what happened, but we all felt like we'd have another crack at them in the Sectionals and we meant to make the most of it."

The Blue Devils snapped back with convincing victories over the Lebanon Tigers and the Sacred Heart Spartans. Then Shortridge hit a bad patch, losing to the Crawfordsville Athenians by 11 points before dropping 2 heartbreakers, to the Manual Redskins by 3 and to the Southport Cardinals by a basket, again in overtime. Hollett's recollection of the latter game is interesting: "Their star was Tom Bennett, then a junior [and a recent inductee into the Indiana Basketball Hall of Fame]. He always shot his free throws from the extreme right side of the foul line. I later played with him for 3 years at Wabash. He shot his free throws the same way then, and continued to be very successful."

The final 2 games of the regular season were a pair of good old-fashioned barnburners. Following a hard-fought 3-point victory over Broad Ripple came a 5-point decision over Cathedral.

After the 2nd Shortridge game Attucks overwhelmed the Mishawaka Cavemen 84-59 before winning a thriller against the Hammond Noll Warriors 72-71. They then routed the Washington Continentals 75-45 before losing their chance for an undefeated season at Connersville, dropping a tough game to the Spartans 58-57. The Tigers sailed through the remainder of their regular season schedule trouncing, Cathedral 82-39, Manual 53-33, Howe 90-61, and the Bloomington University High Univees 80-36.

The stage was set for the beginning of Hoosier Hysteria with 64 Sectionals opening play all over the state of Indiana. None would be more competitive than the one at Butler. Sixteen Indianapolis teams would vie for the crown. It would require 4 wins to achieve that goal. Most of the players knew each other well by the time March rolled, around and for those teams that had experienced disappointing regular seasons, it was time for a fresh start. Everyone started even in the Indiana state tournament. School size did not matter; prior records were immaterial. A loss ended the season. It was one and done, and you had to be ready to play hard and play smart every time on the court or get upset by a hungrier 5 looking for a slice of glory.

Teams were not seeded in the Sectionals, so it was a pleasant surprise that, should Shortridge and Attucks, the 2 favorites, meet it would again be in the final game. In some ways it looked like a repeat of the stirring city tournament 10 weeks before, only now the 8 city schools were joined by the county schools, and the stakes were even higher.

Shortridge breezed by the Decatur Hawks in the 1st round while Attucks beat Washington for the 3rd time, this one by 28 points. In the 2nd round Shortridge played Ben Davis again. In a similar game to that first meeting, the Giants closed the gap by 3 points as the Blue Devils won by 8. That same day Attucks was giving the Manual Redskins a serious lesson in the game of basketball resulting, in an 87-36 final score.

There was a 3rd school in the Sectional that felt they had a right to be considered legitimate contenders for the title. That was Arsenal Technical High School, the Titans, often also called the Greenclads. Tech had a history of success in the tournament, 3 times having been a state championship finalist, the closest any Marion County team had ever come to cutting down the nets on the last Saturday of March. They had reached the semi-finals of the Sectional and were pleased to have yet a 3rd crack at Shortridge. No one in green conceded an inch to the team in blue that afternoon. Two overtime losses had simply convinced the Titans that they were due. Shortridge, however, had other thoughts. In another close game, the Blue Devils won for a 3rd time over Tech, this time extending their margin to 6 points. And they got the job done in 32 minutes!

Attucks came up against Broad Ripple in their semi-final game and the Rockets tried a slow-down game against the quick and speedy Tigers, remembering, perhaps, Milan's success with a similar tactic against the Muncie Central Bearcats in the unforgettable final game of the 1954 state championship. It would not work this time, though, and Attucks came away with a 33-19 victory. The night game would be Shortridge against Attucks once again!

Green and gold filled one side of the Butler Fieldhouse and royal blue and white the other long before the scheduled tip-off time. Partisan cheering once again filled the old barn with noise and energy. Sometime in the 1st half Hollett found himself being guarded by Oscar Robertson. He remembers Oscar saying something like, "All right, Hollett, what're you gonna do with that ball?" To which Hollett now says, "If the truth be told, I would have said, 'Not very much with you guarding me!'"

For 3 quarters the game lived up to all expectations. Shortridge, though playing without guard Bob Williams, who was too ill to even dress for the game that night, had played Attucks dead even for 24 minutes, 47-47. Everyone thought the 4th quarter would be anybody's game. Then Ray Crowe turned his team loose with a devastating full court press. The errors mounted for the Devils, and, forced to play catch up ball, shots that had earlier fallen refused to do so. The final score was Crispus Attucks 73, Shortridge 59. The slipper would not fit. Cinderella was to go home without her carriage. As Hollett recalls it, "Though we were bitterly disappointed, of course, we all knew we had lost to a great team. We wished them well. We wanted them to win it all and I'm glad, if it couldn't have been us, it was them."

Attucks, of course, did go on to win it all. In the Regionals they defeated an overmatched Wilkinson Wolves team 95-42 and the Anderson Indians 76-51. In the Semi-state it was Attucks over the Columbus Bull Dogs 80-62 and then, in a thriller, the Tigers outlasted the Muncie Central Bearcats, 71-70. Never leaving what was for them essentially a home venue, the dream came true at Butler Fieldhouse on Saturday, March 29, 1955, with a 79-67 victory over the New Albany Bulldogs, followed by a 97-74 win over the Panthers of Gary Roosevelt. Final Game Box Score:

Indianapolis Crispus Attucks (97)	FG	FT	TP	PF	Gary Roosevelt (74)	FG	FT	TP	PF
Merriweather	4	13	21	2	Williams	3	0	6	5
W. Brown	3	2	8	3	Everett	0	1	1	0
Robertson	12	6	30	4	Barnett	8	2	18	4
Burnley	0	0	0	0	Morgan	0	0	0	1
Mitchell	6	6	18	4	Elson	10	11	31	3
Milton	0	0	0	0	Guydon	0	0	0	0
Scott	3	0	6	4	McCruiston	1	1	3	1
Patton	2	0	4	0	Ligon	3	0	6	2
Hampton	3	0	6	3	Ford	3	2	8	2
Gipson	2	0	4	0	Eubanks	0	1	1	0
Totals	35	27	97	20		28	18	74	18

Officials: Charles Meade, S. T. Proffitt

The 1955 Indiana State Champion Crispus Attucks Tigers

Friendships made on the court often extend off the court, sometimes in unexpected but pleasant ways. John Hollett recalls one fondly to this day. Early in the 1954–55 season Shortridge had defeated Washington. One of their forwards remembered that he and John Hollett were about the same height. He placed a call to John sometime in the early spring and asked if John owned a tuxedo. John did. The Washington player asked if he could possibly borrow it to wear to his school's prom. John was happy to oblige him as the Shortridge prom was on a different night. Only in sports!

Both Frank Mead and John Hollett felt that Cleon Reynolds was an excellent coach, an opinion shared by the Indiana Hall of Fame selection committee. Hollett went on to play at Wabash College, while Mead played at Cornell University and then in England and Sweden. They each felt that their fundamentals were sound, and their understanding of the game sharpened by the training they received at Shortrdge. Mead also says "When you're playing in a big game with all of the emotion and excitement the crowd noise is pretty much of a dull roar in the background somewhere, but Cleon's penetrating voice always cut through and got right to you no matter what else was going on on the court at the time!"

Cleon Reynolds had an excellent assistant coach named Bob King. It was King who scouted each week's opponent and provided extensive write-ups for each player on the Shortridge team about tendencies, strengths, weaknesses, and style of play of the opposing teams and their players. These reports, according to Hollett, were extremely helpful to him and everyone else on the Blue Devil team that season. After the Sectional loss to Attucks, King offered his scouting skills to Coach Ray Crowe of Attucks, who accepted gladly. Thus King's reports may well have helped the Tigers to go all the way. Not long after, in 1960, King moved to Purdue as Assistant Coach to Ray Eddy, serving the school with distinction in a variety of positions for 33 years. Purdue recently honored King and his wife by naming the main Mackey Arena Conference room after them.

Had Attucks not been the formidable team that it clearly was in 1954–55 would Shortridge have been able to win it all? We'll never know the answer to that one, but Ray Crowe was quoted in the papers after his team's final win stating that Shortridge was the best team they had played all year. I guess you might get some argument about that from the Muncie Central fans whose beloved Bearcats dropped that heartbreaking 1-point game to the Tigers in the Indianapolis Semi-state final game, and from the Connersville faithful whose Spartans were the only team all year to notch a victory over the Tigers, or even from the Hammond Bishop Noll Warrior supporters, 1-point losers to the Tigers during the regular season.

As an encore, the next year Attucks not only defended their state championship successfully, but were undefeated, another 1st for Indiana. That entire Crispus Attucks High School team and coach Ray Crowe have been welcomed into the Indiana Basketball Hall of Fame. To date, none of the Shortridge High School players have been so honored, although both coaches Cleon Reynolds and Bob King have.

All of that having been said, there are many who will say that this Golden Age season, this turning point year, the city of Indianapolis had not just one but the two best high school basketball teams in the state of Indiana. Four yearts later the Blue Devils would again go head to head with the Tigers. Led by "Bo" Crain Shortridge beat Attucks, then coached by Bill Garrett twice during the 1959 regular season, losing a close one in the Sectional as Attucks went on to win their third state title. Nine years later, Shortridge, led by Oscar Evans, got to the finals of the State Tournament by edging an excellent Marion team in the afternoon at Hinkle only to lose by 8 points to Gary Roosevelt that night. Shortly after that Shortridge became a middle school, as did Attucks. It is a pleasure to welcome them both back to full high school status.

Another time, another place . . .

It was to be 11 years later that the colleges of America would have a similar experience to that 1955 Indiana state championship. In 1966 Texas Western University (now the University of Texas at El Paso) under Hall of Fame coach Don Haskins won the NCAA title with an all-black starting five by beating the Kentucky Wildcats. Two of those players were Hoosiers, both from Gary. Orsten Artis had been a Froebel High School Blue Devil and Harry Flournoy an Emerson High School Tornado before becoming a Miner at UTEP. The story of the Miners' season has recently been told—with considerable poetic license—in the movie *Glory Road.* The next year I attended the NCAA Final Four in Louisville. I was with the then-Dartmouth coach, Dave Gavitt (who would later himself coach Providence College to the Final Four, be our Olympic coach in 1980, and be selected as an inductee into the Naismith Basketball Hall of Fame in Springfield, MA), and thus had credentials to ride on the bus, that took the coaches from the downtown hotel where we were staying out to Freedom Hall in the Kentucky State Fairgrounds. Getting on the bus Dave and I got split up, and I ended up sitting next to a large man I somehow recognized but couldn't quite place. He asked me where I coached, and I explained that I was not a coach but a friend of Gavitt's. Then, at one of those moments when everything else seems suddenly quiet so that my query was heard by all: "Where do you coach?" Don Haskins answered politely, "At Texas Western." I was so embarrassed, and I answered "Oh, my. You're the defending champion!" Then Coach Haskins bailed me out with one of the great lines of all time: "One year you win it all, the next year you ride the bus!" Pretty true of sports in general, I think.

A depiction of Crispus Attucks as a young man

Chapter 13

Native Americans and Indiana: Many Tribes, Much Respect

The issue of using Indian names, or Indian-related ones, for teams is a contentious one. There are those who for good and sufficient reason believe that the use of such names is both demeaning and racist. I can understand their point of view, but I have yet to meet anyone who selected a team name for their school with other than respect and admiration for that name. We ought not try to forget or rewrite our history, but rather to seek greater understanding of ourselves and our futures by knowing everything we can about what came before us. Indiana means, after all, place of Indians. At least 21 tribes are known to have resided in what is now Indiana at various times. This is an important part of our history. Should we strive to understand the hardships created for the Indians of North America by the arrival of our European ancestors on this continent? By all means. Should we treat our Indian fellow citizens and neighbors as individuals, avoid stereotyping them and encourage them to reach their full potential? Absolutely. But let us keep some perspective and deal fairly with the names of our sports teams, giving all parties their due.

Some team names have been changed from those reflecting our Indian heritage, yet many still remain. This has been more pronounced in college ranks, perhaps, and in the high schools of some other states, than has been the case of our own high schools. Colleges such as Dartmouth, Stanford, Miami (Ohio), St. Johns, Marquette and others have changed their mascots to eliminate any reference to Indians. We have lost more Native American names in Indiana to consolidation, I believe, than we have to conscious decisions to move away from them. In fact, proportionately, we have a slightly greater percentage of our current 406 schools with Indian or Indian-related team names than was true of those schools we have lost. Presently there are 43 schools that use some form of Indian reference for their mascot. That's just under 11 percent. The closed schools utilized Indian-related mascots at a rate of 8 or 9 percent.

Three of our current schools have honored specific tribes with their choice of team names. Waldron's excellent basketball team caught the imagination of the entire state when Jason Delany's team went undefeated, 27-0, to win the Class A title in

2004. The Waldron teams are the Mohawks, and the team they beat in the final game was Ft. Wayne Blackhawk Christian, the Braves. One team's mascot—that of a specific tribe, the other school—named for the great Sauk chief, Blackhawk, and its teams for Indian young men.

The Waldron Mohawk

Waldron's dream season of 2004, achieving that rarity in Indiana, an undefeated season, was by no means the only good year for the Mohawks. In 1927 they won 17 and lost 4. After winning the Shelbyville Sectional, dispatching Moral, Clifford, and the host Golden Bears (then probably still Camels), the Mohawks also captured the Columbus Regional, upending Greensburg in the final game. This qualified them for the Sweet Sixteen at the Fairgrounds Exposition building in Indianapolis where Bill Webb's squad lost to Frankfort 37-31. Waldron then went to the Tri-State Invitational Tournament in Cincinnati and lost to the Logansport Berries in the final game by one point. In 1939 the Mohawks won 23 and lost just 4 for Paul Foxworthy. In 1951–52 Waldron teams won 37 games while losing only 8 with Bill Stearman at the helm. In the 3-year period beginning in 1958, Bill Doig's Mohawks won 62 of the 71 games they played. The Lady Mohawks have added 3 Sectional crowns to the school's trophy case. Waldron, by the way, was originally called Stroupville after George Stroup, but that name was not popular with the townspeople. On the way to a town meeting to discuss a new name, a man crossing a field found a scythe manufactured by the Waldron Scythe Co. of Ohio. That name was suggested and accepted.

The 2nd current school to honor a specific tribe, the Cherokees, is Morgan Township in Porter County. Interestingly, none of the 3 current schools with specific tribal names for their teams selected tribes who have a particular association with our state. They were apparently chosen not for historical reasons, but because of admirable qualities associated with those tribes or Native Americans in general.

The Morgan Township Cherokee

At any rate, the Morgan Township Cherokees have been playing basketball since at least 1924 and they had a memorable 20-4 season for Coach John Wiggins in 1935. This was followed by a 20-2 mark 5 years later for Coach Clare Dinsmore. Matt Bush took over the coaching reins in 1986 and led the 1987 and 1988 teams to 19-3 and 20-3 seasons. His teams won 4 of the school's 5 Sectionals and the 1999 Warsaw Class A Regional crown. The 2008 Cherokees won 20 of 25 games for Coach Colin McCartt. The Lady Cherokees won 24 games and lost only 4 for Coach Jeff Edwards in 1998, making it all the way to the Class A state finals where they lost the championship game to the Bloomfield Lady Cardinals.

The 3rd tribal association is in Wabash. Wabash is famous for being the first city in America to have its downtown lighted by electricity. It is also the hometown of Mark Honeywell, founder of the giant Minneapolis Honeywell Corporation. Steve

Herman of the Associated Press contacted Wabash High School, writing a piece on Indian-related mascots in Indiana in December 2005. He reported the following:

> *Wabash High School became the Apaches in 1932—even though the Apaches did not inhabit Indiana—as the result of a school contest to replace the former nickname Hill Climbers.*
>
> *"Apaches was selected mostly because of Geronimo and the image people had of Apaches as tough and strong," athletic director Matt Stone said. "Our symbol is a true-to-life head shot of an Apache Indian, and we have done everything possible to show pride in the Apaches and not degrade them."*

The Hill Climbers became the Apaches.

Although the first officially sanctioned girls state basketball tournament was not held until 1976, that certainly should not lead anyone to conclude that our Hoosier girls were not playing interscholastic basketball many years earlier. The mores and practices of the times dictated different uniforms and there were even different rules than we are accustomed to today, but the competitive spirit was always there, the lessons learned the same: striving, working to obtain results, winning and losing with equal grace, honoring your competitors and teammates alike. The Hall of Fame has photos of girls basketball teams in the 20s and even earlier. Below is the Wabash team from that era.

The 1926 county champs and the 1929 state championship plaque; photo by author from the IBHOF

You will note that Wabash claimed the girls state championship in 1929. This, of course, was not the product of a sanctioned statewide tournament, but it certainly is further evidence, if any is needed, that our young ladies were quite involved with our favorite sport from the earliest days, that they took it seriously, and that girls basketball was an important part of many communities. The Wabash girls were coached by Marcia Snow and they were affectionately called the "Snowballs."

The Fall 2008 issue of *Indiana Basketball History* includes an article by Nancy

Adams which refers to that girls mythical state championship of 1929. She points out that the Wabash girls claimed the crown after conquering the Argos Lady Dragons in a 2-game home and home series. Both schools had completed undefeated regular seasons, and the March 14, 1929, *Argos Reflector* is quoted, using language I find quite appealing, as follows:

> *Pride of Argos still our Pride*
> *Tho our girls had to bow to the*
> *"Tall Sycamores of Wabash",*
> *they remain the "Pride of Argos"–*

> *Game on local floor draws record crowd.*
> *When our undefeated high school girls were met on the hardwood last Wednesday by the equally unconquered sextet of the Wabash High School, each and all had that rare opportunity to sense "that stern joy which warriors feel in foemen worthy of their steel." Wabash had issued the challenge and the Pride of Argos was the only team in Hoosierdom qualified even to answer the defy [sic] and nothing that followed can dim the glory reflected by that outstanding fact.*

The article goes on to state that a record crowd of 800 saw the first game at Argos, won by Wabash 30-17, and that a "goodly delegation" traveled to Wabash for the second game, won by "the tall damsels" of the home team, 39-13.

Regarding the title, Roger Dickinson has discovered that having an outstanding season and beating the champions of nearby counties as well as your own often gave rise to the claim of "State Champions." Or perhaps it was a decision reached by the press, as was true of many college sports at that time as well as high school football.

Among schools now consolidated there also were several tribal names. We have previously discussed some of these, including the Thorntown Kewasakees and the Montezuma Aztecs, but here are some reminders.

Thorntown Kewasakees and Montezuma Aztecs

Others were the Owensville Kickapoos, the Hymera Shakamaks, the Fair Oaks Cherokees, the Leavenworth Wyandottes (Leavenworth teams were also called the Rivermen), the Tioga Indians of Monticello, and the Metz Mohawks. Interestingly, though Miamis, Shawnees, and Lenapes (Delawares) were closely intertwined with our state's history for decades, none of these tribal names were selected by any of our schools as far as I have been able to determine.

Hymera High School

The Hymera Shakamaks are now the Sullivan Golden Arrows and the Leavenworth Wyandottes are the Crawford County Wolfpack.

The Black and Gold Owensville Kickapoos had many fine seasons, including 1925 and 1926, when H.T. McCullough's teams won 48 games, lost only 9 and also won the first 2 of the school's 10 Sectionals. In 1931 Coach Tolvo Lahti's team went 21-7 and picked up a Sectional crown, and the next year Dave Williamson's Kickapoos won 23 of 27 games and another Sectional. Ivan Hollen's 1937 through 1939 teams all won Sectionals, the best records coming in 1938, 20-7, and the next year, 19-5.

Hymera's Shakamaks, who also wore gold and black uniforms, nabbed their lone Sectional crown in 1956, Keith Dougherty's team winning 19 and losing 7. Leavenworth's colors were yet again gold and black. Their only Sectional title came in 1967 at Tell City, when Don Denbo's team won 19 and lost 5. Monticello's red-and-white Tioga Indians turned in a 17-6 record as early as 1911. They had an excellent 27-2 season in 1938 for Coach Alva Staggs, winning the 6th of the school's impressive 16 Sectional titles, and then being edged by Royal Center in the Logansport Regional, 23-20 in overtime. John Bastin coached teams won regionals in 1955 and 1957. Though Everett Cass coached the Scarlet and White Metz Mohawks to a 15-2 season in 1940, neither Metz nor the Fair Oaks Cherokees, whose colors were blue and white, ever won a Sectional title.

The Hymera Shakamaks and the Leavenworth Wyandottes

I show these present and past depictions because they indicate to me quite clearly that the Indians selected by these schools were conceived of as dignified and historical. I have personally spoken to a full-blooded Seneca man and a young Navajo woman about their beliefs regarding the issue of Indian mascots. Their views were quite congruent: each felt that if shown with dignity and the avoidance of stereotypical images, such usage did not insult but honored a tribe. They both, however, objected to the approach taken by logos such as the one the Cleveland Indians use and of the name Redskins as used by the Washington NFL team. I fear they would also object to the use of that name by the 4 Indiana high schools who do so today. These are Ft. Wayne North Side, Indianapolis Manual, Goshen and Knox. Those schools, however, I am sure do not mean to be offensive to anyone in their usage of the word.

Knox, for example has used the name Redskin for a long time, perhaps 80 years. The title of their yearbook is *The Redskin*, even as long ago as in the late 1920s. Respect is evident in the use of the phrase "Sir Redskin," used when referring to their mascot.

Sir Redskin Departs (from an early Knox High School yearbook).

A current Knox logo

Those Knox Redskins have been playing basketball in Indiana for quite a while, boys and girls alike. The 1927 *Redskin* contains an article on the girls team's season that begins "The K.H.S. girl's basketball team was, for some reason, not very successful during the past season. But I am sure, if the matter is investigated, there are some very plausible alibis." Isn't that wonderful! What season of what team wherever they played could not benefit from such commentary? Here is the full story:

Activities of Girls' Basket Ball Team Of 1926-7

The K. H. S. girl's Basket Ball team was, for some reason, not very successful during the past season. But, I am sure, if the matter is investigated, there are some very plausible alibis.

Everyone knows that the weight of a debt upon one's back is a hindrance to progress. Our sweaters were not paid for until after the last game. Next year we will start right in without the worry of a debt, and "look the whole world in the face, for we owe not any man."

The first game was played at Hamlet; it was a "practice" game. We were not at all greedy visitors and let Hamlet defeat us by a very lopsided score. The next game with Hamlet showed us we had some "spunk" left. They were the victors by but four measly points.

We nearly won when Argos came over here but Argos almost won also; the score was a tie, which was not played off. But when we met Argos on their own floor they untied the knot and put the victory in their hands.

Games were played with Union Township, Pulaski, and Walkerton, and in all the games we met the same fate, that of being the losers; but most certainly not quitters.

The last game was played on the home floor, against Union Township. In this game we threatened to become really dangerous, as at the end of the first half they were leading by but three points. Then the La Porte County Champs pepped up and the score ended with Knox trailing behind by seven points.

It cannot be said, however, that the K. H. S. girl's Basket Ball team of 1926 27 was a total failure. We tried to show good sportsmanship and uphold the flag of Red and White. We learned the sportsmanship of other schools. This on the whole, was commendable.

And here is the team

Girls' Basket Ball Team

MISS PHILLIPS, COACH

Mary Brownstein, Guard; Marie Dunsing, Forward; Ida Engle, Forward; Ardis Loudermilk, R. Center; Margaret Lundin, J. Center; Geraldine Newby, Guard; Bonnie Rogers, Forward; Glenda Stevenson, Guard (Captain); Mrs. Abner, Manager.

The boys second team did somewhat better, winning the county championship in 1927. Here are those champs:

Second Basket Ball Team

MR. HILTY, COACH

Jesse Clabaugh, Center; Taylor Hollingsworth, Guard; Thomas Hollingsworth, Forward; John Loring, Guard; Jack Stevens, Guard; Ralph Stevenson, Forward and Center; Robert Taylor, Guard (Captain); Richard Van Deman, Forward.

The second team won the county second team championship, and were very successful in their other games.

Knox teams have done very well over the years, winning a total of 15 Sectional championships as well as the 1962 Logansport Regional and the 2000 Class 2A Regional in their own gym. The 1953 Redskins won 20 of 24 games, coached by Paul McPherson. Robert Beeson led the 1961 and 1962 squads to 21-2 and 21-5 records. In 1971 Chuck Kristen's team won 21 of 24 games played. Coach Todd Boldry's 2000 team defeated Boone Grove 62-57 to win the Regional title and finished 22-3, and his 2003 Redskins went 21-5. Brenda Whitesell's 1981 Lady Redskins won the 1st of 5 Sectionals captured by the Knox girls teams, with a 19-3 mark. Brenda Woolskin coached the Knox girls for 13 years, with her team's best records coming in 1994 and 1995, 17-4 and 18-4.

Interestingly, some schools formerly had Native American names but now have chosen other mascots to represent them. Rensselaer, now the Bombers, were formerly the Fighting Iroquois, then became simply the Indians before flying high.

Goshen has also been a staple force in Indiana high school basketball for close to a century, as this photograph of the 1914 boys team shows.

Goshen teams have been playing basketball since at least 1911, when they won 1 of the 6 games played, jumping to an 8 and 3 record the next year. The 1922 team won 19 while losing 10 for Coach R. O. Abbett. They captured the South Bend Sectional by trouncing Union Mills, 32-5; sneaking past LaPorte, 18-17; and defeating Elkhart 33-10 and Mishawaka, 19-6.

They won their Regional game at Purdue, 16-10 over Angola. This got the Redskins to the Sweet Sixteen, played that year at the Old Coliseum in Indianapolis, where they lost their 1st-round game to the Fishers Tigers, 18-9. In 1936, with Herman Byers coaching, the Redskins went 22-5. Art Cosgrove coached Goshen teams for 13

years beginning in 1960. His best records were 24-2 in 1963, 19-4 in 1967, and 21-5 in 1969. Mike Sorrell held sway for 14 years and his Redskin teams posted a 17-4 record in 1988, 21-4 in 1992, and back-to-back 17-5 seasons in his last 2 years, 1998 and 1999. The Redskins have cut down the nets after 9 Sectionals and 2 Regionals. Goshen's girls teams have added the nets from 7 Sectionals and the 1982 Elkhart Central Regional, when Dori Keyser's Lady Redskins finished 21-4.

The Goshen Redskins

The Indianapolis Manual Redskins are often remembered as one of the best teams ever that did not win the state championship. In a stirring overtime final game in 1961, the Kokomo Wildkats upset Manual, 68-66 in overtime. Or maybe it wasn't an upset: Kokomo's record for Joe Platt that year was a pretty impressive 28-1. They did beat a Redskin team that had two of the finest players in the storied history of Hoosier high school basketball, the Van Arsdale twins, Tom and Dick. Manual's record that year was 28-3. Dick Cummings was the Redskin coach and his 1960 and 1961 Redskins won 51 games and lost 7. The VanArsdales are twins in the Hall of Fame.

Dick VanArsdale
Half of most accomplished set of twins in history of competitive athletics...shared Mr. Basketball and Trester Award honors with brother, Tom...All-State at Indpls Manual HS...led Manual to Final Four...scored 26 points in afternoon game, 26 in evening loss to Kokomo...3-yr starter at Indiana University...Hoosiers' MVP...all-Big 10...All-American and academic All-American...member of U. S. team that won gold in '65 World University Games...named to NBA's all-rookie team in '66...3 seasons with New York Knicks, 9 with Phoenix Suns...named to NBA all-star team 3 times...later worked as TV and radio color commentator for the Suns.

Tom VanArsdale
12 years as a player in the National Basketball Association. . . Shared Trester Award and Mr. Basketball honors with twin brother, Dick...All-State as senior at Indianapolis Manual H. S...helped lead Manual to 2 sectional titles, and regional and semistate crowns in '61...All-Big 10 and All-American honors at Indiana University...also academic All-American...in 3 seasons he scored 1,252 points for Coach Branch McCracken, just 12 more than his twin...member of US team that won gold in '65 World University Games...drafted by Detroit Pistons.

Manual is the 2nd oldest high school in Indianapolis. They recorded a 1-6 season as early as 1901, and by 1906 the Redskins had already put 40 wins on the board, against 26 losses and 1 tie. They made it to the state finals 3 years in a row, beginning in 1913. That year Manual defeated Orleans before losing to the eventual state champions from Wingate, 16-11. Back the next year, they again beat Orleans in the 1st round and New Bethel in the next before being eliminated by the eventual state runner-up Anderson Indians, as Wingate took home their 2nd title. Alas, the 3rd time was not the charm Manual fans had hoped for. After winning the Sectional at Franklin (Indianapolis did not have a Sectional that year) by defeating Southport, the Redskins (I know they probably were not called by that name yet) were back at Indiana University for the state finals. After another 1st round win, the eventual champion again sent them home. This time it was the Thorntown Kewasakees, 30-16. Sweet Sixteen berths were earned by Manual also in 1919 and 1922. The 1919 finals were at Purdue, and Manual bested Vincennes in the 1st-round before being ousted by Bloomington, 23-12. And who won it all that year? Why, Bloomington, of course. The 1922 finals were in Indianapolis, and the Manual team again ran into Bloomington, losing in the 1st round. The Manual girls best season was in 1982, when Steve Miller's Lady Redskins won 15 of 20 games, including the only Sectional title yet won by the school's girls team.

Indianapolis Manual Redskins

Ft. Wayne North Side has had many fine seasons. Bill Mark led the 1931 Redskins to the 1st of the school's 23 Sectional titles, and 2 years later his squad also nailed down the 1st of their 13 Regional titles. Under Coach Bob Nulf they were 22-6 in 1941, again winning the Ft. Wayne Regional. Jim Hinga's 1954 Regional titlists finished 23-4, and the next year Don Bruuk's 22-7 team won the Elkhart Semi-state, defeating Sheridan 63-56 and Mishawaka 54-48. At Butler Fieldhouse the Redskins lost a thriller to Gary Roosevelt, 68-66. Hall of Famer Byard Hey, who coached the Redskins for 29 seasons, led the 1965 team to a 25-5 mark. That year they were runners-up to Jerry Oliver's 29-2 State Champion Indianapolis Washington Continentals, led by Billy Keller, 64-57. From 1975 through 1978 Hey's Redskins won an impressive 101 games and lost only 17. The high water mark was 1978's 27-2 record, the second loss coming at the hands of Elkhart Central, 65-54, in the final game of the South Bend Semi-state. Elkhart Central lost to Muncie Central the next week in Indianapolis, 89-85, in one of the most exciting Final Fours of all time. The Bearcats beat Terre Haute South, 65-64, in overtime in the final game. With Glen Heaton at the helm, the Redskins had a 21-5 record in 1995 and a 21-4 mark in 1999. All told they have won 16 Sectionals, 12 Regionals, and 2 Semi-state crowns. The North Side girls have added 2 Sectionals to the school's trophy case.

Ft. Wayne North Side Redskins

Eighteen schools top the rest of our current crop of schools with Indian-related mascots, with Warriors as their specific nickname. Not all Warriors, however, are necessarily Indian related, as we will discover in the next chapter.

Chapter 14

Warriors:
Native Peoples of the Lakes and Plains

This chapter will cover the 18 current schools with Warriors as their team name, not all of which are connected to Indians. Those that are have used respectful depictions, as you will note.

We'll begin in Bicknell, where the North Knox Warriors had a nice string of seasons starting in 1999 and ending in 2004. For the first three of those years, Mike Halliwell was coach, and his teams won 18 games each year, losing 5, then 7 and 7. The school's first (boys) Sectional was captured in 2000. Mark Dillon took over as coach in 2002, leading the team to 19-5 and 21-3 seasons and in 2004, though the won-loss record was not as strong, the Warriors did win their 2nd Sectional.

The Lady Warriors have also done very well indeed. Rick Marshall was their coach for 19 years beginning in 1988. During his tenure North Knox teams won 15 Sectionals and 5 Regionals. Twenty-win seasons occurred in 1988, 1989, 1995, 1998, 1999, 2001, 2004, 2005, and 2006. The best year was 2004, 26-2, and the 3-year period that was started then resulted in 69 wins and 13 losses. Marshall's overall record with the North Knox girls teams was 366 wins and 97 defeats.

In Denver the North Miami Warriors won their only Sectional title at Logansport in 1968 with wins over Caston, Lewis Cass, and the host Berries, 61-55. They also captured the Logansport Regional, defeating Knox and Chesterton. At the Lafayette Semi-state the Jerry Lewis-coached Warriors defeated Greencastle, 73-66, before being laid waste by Gary Roosevelt, 91-30. Still, an

The North Knox Warrior

Elite 8 season is nothing to regret, and, after all, Roosevelt did win it all at Hinkle Fieldhouse the next week. Their girls teams have captured four Sectionals, including their 1997 undefeated season under Coach Bill Fites, when they finished 20-1. This was Indiana All-Star and Notre Dame star-to-be Ruth Riley's senior year.

In Marshall Turkey Run's 1996 team, coached by Bill Chesnut, finished 19-3, although that team did not win one of the school's 4 Sectional titles, the 1st of which had come in 1964 and 1966. The Lady Warriors of Turkey Run have also captured 4 Sectional crowns and have had several impressive seasons, including 2000's 19-5 record for George Wooten and 2008's 19-6 mark for Sam Karr.

The North Miami and Turkey Run Warriors

Earl Roudebush coached the Winamac Warriors from 1926 through 1935. During his tenure Roudebush's charges won 6 of the school's 19 Sectional championships and both of its Regionals. The 1929 team lost to Rushville in the first round of the Sweet Sixteen. Three years later, however, the Warriors made it all the way to the final game, losing to New Castle by 7 points. Two Winamac players on that 1932 team were named to the *Indianapolis News* All State team. That team's record throughout the state tournament was as follows:

Sectionals at Winamac:
Winamac 28 Pulaski 11
Winamac 48 Francesville 12
Winamac 35 North Judson 12
Winamac 38 Star City 7

Regionals at Mishawaka:
Winamac 37 Nappanee 27
Winamac 23 Rochester 12

State Finals at Butler Fieldhouse:
Winamac 48 Bluffton 30
Winamac 27 Evansville Bosse 23

Winamac 34 Lebanon 31
New Castle 24 Winamac 17

Dee Baker's 1956 Warriors won 22 of 25 games, and Joe Heath's won 23 of 26 in 1965, both teams capturing Sectionals, as did Jeff Beach's 19-3 team in 1997. The Lady Warriors have had several terrific seasons as well. Since 1987 Jim Swaney has coached the girls team there, winning 8 of the school's 10 Sectional championships and their only Regional, in 1992. Between 1988

Winamac Warrior

and 1993 the Lady Warriors turned in a phenomenal 121 games won while losing only 11! This includes undefeated regular seasons from 1990 through 1992, for a regular-season winning streak of 70 games. (Though impressive, this is not the record. It is held by Ft. Wayne Northrop girls, winners of 89 consecutive regular season games and 57 consecutive games.)

Evansville Harrison Warriors had consecutive 20-2 seasons for Coach Frank Schwitz in 1965 and 1966. They also turned in a 20-6 season in 1995, 21-3 in 1999, and 22-3 records for Will Wyman. Wyman's teams won 5 Sectional titles and 3 Regionals, the latter in each of his 20-win seasons. The Lady Warriors turned in their best record at 17-5 for Coach Tom Bealmear in 2007, also capturing Sectional titles in 1992 and 1994 with John Chapman at the helm.

Scottsburg's Warriors won 21 games and lost only 3 as far back as 1920, when J. A. Mohler was the coach. Ten years later Noble Lyons led the team to a 20-6 finish that was duplicated in 1932 by P. G. Hoffner's squad. From 1944 through 1946 Ralph Feeler's teams won 57 and lost only 10, with the best year of the 3 being the 1st, 22-4. In 1955 and 1956 Charles Meyer's teams turned in 20-5 and 23-3 records. James Barley coached the Warriors to an undefeated regular season, 25-1 in 1969, and his final team enjoyed a 22-5 mark in 1978. The single 1969 loss was to Vincennes in the Semi-state. Randy Snodgrass led the 1990 team to a 22-3 record and Tony Bennett's 1995 team went 20-3. Brady Wells' Warriors turned in a 21-5 mark in 2005.

All told Scottsburg's Warriors have won 22 Sectionals and 5 Regionals. Vern Altemeyer was responsible, at least in large part, for 3 of the former and 1 of the latter. Playing for Charles Meyer, Altemeyer's 1956 Regional champions ousted Muncie Central from the Sweet Sixteen before running into the eventual State Champion Crispus Attucks Tigers in the Semi-state final game. Altemeyer rose to an executive position with Eli Lilly and Company, providing yet another example of how discipline and motivation on the court can lead to successful decision-making and assumption of responsibility later in life. He played his basketball in the Scottsburg gym, known as "The Pressure Cooker," and was well equipped for those pressures that invariably seem to accompany most careers.

Vern Altemeyer

Scottsburg's high-scoring all-star. A key to 3 straight sectional championships for Scottsburg High School before graduating in 1956. A 6'6" frontcourt player, Vern's high game was 47 points. He led his team to a regional victory as a senior, losing to eventual state champion Crispus Attucks in the semi-state final. He was a 1956 Indiana All-Star. He played at Transylvania College for Coach C. M. Newton. Named to all-Kentucky intercollegiate freshman team, he transferred to Illinois, where he earned 2 varsity letters.

The girls teams at Scottsburg are the Warriorettes. They have won 14 Sectionals themselves as well as 10 Regionals. Their 3 Semi-state titles were earned at Seymour in 1986, 1988, and 1989. The Warriorettes won the state championship for Coach Donna Cheatham in 1989 with a 26-1 record, defeating Benton Central in a thriller,

74-72 in overtime. This may have helped assuage the pain of the previous season, when her team had lost its only game of 28 in the afternoon at Market Square Arena to eventual state champion Ft. Wayne Snider by 5 points. Her 1986 team had finished runner-up to Ft. Wayne Northrop with a 24-3 record, and her 1987 team had won the Regional with a 20-3 mark. Over that 5-year period Cheatham's Warriorettes ran up a record of 119 victories and 11 losses, bringing home 5 Sectional and 5 Regional titles, 3 Semi-state crowns, and that 1 treasured state championship. Warriorette Renee Westmoreland was Indiana's Miss Basketball in 1989.

Danville's teams are also called the Warriors and they have had many an interesting season. Another version of the Warrior is also painted on their court:

The Danville Warrior

The Scottsburg Warrior

Karin Johansson discloses some interesting facts in her essay "Who Says Small Town Life is Dull?"

> *Indiana's favorite sport has always been an integral part of Danville school life. Back in 1912, Danville suffered what was probably its worst defeat at the hands of Jamestown's Skipper Skaggs. The score was 77-7 reported The Republican (Indiana's oldest continually published newspaper at 150 years old). Then there was thumbless Bill McClain of the early 1940's high school team. Bill lost his thumb in a tractor accident when he was ten, but he loved basketball so much, he refused to quit playing, even though the loss of a thumb was a considerable handicap to holding and throwing the ball. McClain perfected a new way of holding and throwing the ball which made him one of the high school team's star players. Coaches and scouts from around the state came to watch him play. In McClain's junior year, the Danville Warriors beat Indiana's stellar team, Anderson, 33-32, in the famed Wigwam. McClain got his degree from Ball State and coached at Ben Davis High School for 25 years.*

The Warriors have won 11 Sectional championships over the years and the 2000 Class 3A Sullivan Regional. One of their best seasons came in 1963. Keith Greve coached that year's team to a 22-5 record. The Danville girls have won one Sectional title, at Plainfield in 1987.

An early Danville High School building

Warren Central's Warriors have had more success on the football field than on the basketball court, but they are far from being shut out there. They have won 9 Sectional championships and two Regionals, in 1986 and 2000. The former came for Coach Gary Jacob whose team finished 23-5, and the latter for Scott Heady with a 21-6 mark. The Lady Warriors have done even better, winning 12 Sectionals, 3 Regionals, and the 1984 Ben Davis Semi-state. That year Sue Parish's team would lose a heart-breaker in the state championship game, 55-54 in overtime, to Crown Point's undefeated Lady Bulldogs to finish 27-2 themselves. From 1982 through 1986 Parish's teams won an impressive 110 games while losing only 17.

The word Wawasee means "Full Moon" and is also the name of a Miami chief who lived in the area. Several years ago Wawasee High School discontinued the use of a live mascot at their games and also replaced a warrior caricature with what is described as a "more dignified representation." School leadership is dedicated to "treating all use of a mascot with respect and honor," and they educate their students regarding potentially negative or degrading stereotyping while emphasizing the "past importance and heritage of Native Americans" to their area.

Phil Mishler's 2005 and 2006 Wawasee teams won 20 games each year, losing 7, then 6. The Warriors have placed five Sectional nets in the school's trophy case in Syracuse. The Lady Warriors have twice finished runner-up for the state championship, first in 1985 when Dale Brannon's squad finished a 23-2 season with a loss to Crown Point. Since the previous 2 years had seen records of 18-3 and 21-2, Brannon's 3-year mark was an impressive 62 and 7. Ken Zolman was coaching in 2007 when the Lady Warriors finished runner-up for the state championship a 2nd time, this to Brebeuf Jesuit, turning in a 22-4 mark. The

Lady Warriors under Zolman's guidance also enjoyed a 23-3 *The Wawasee Warrior* season the next year to go with 23-1 and 22-3 marks in 2001 and 2002. Shanna Zolman was Miss Basketball in 2002.

The Wes-Del Warriors won 21 games and lost only 3 for coach John Robbins in 1970. They have brought the nets home to Gaston from five Sectionals. The Lady Warriors had a great start, 21-10 with Sectional and Regional titles in 1976, and in 1978 and 1979 they had back-to-back undefeated regular seasons, 20-1 both years, for Kay Carmichael. They have also won 5 Sectionals in their relatively short history.

The Whiteland Warriors, previously the Wrens, finished 20-3 for Glenn Ray

in 1927. In 1944 Herman Smith led the team to a 27-3 season including the Franklin Sectional and Shelbyville Regional championships. After defeating Waynetown in the 1st round of the Semi-states, the Warriors were eliminated by Anderson. The next year they finished 21-2 for Coach Gervas Hess. Byron Gunn's 1950 squad turned in a 21-3 mark that included a 2nd Sectional crown. Gunn's 1954 through 1956 teams amassed 57 wins while losing only 11, but their 3rd Sectional title did not come until 1967 when John Milholland's (the Hall of Famer who would coach Frankfort's Hot Dogs so successfully for 19 seasons) team followed a 19-3 season with a 20-4 mark. In 1993 Kevin Smith's Warriors snagged a 4th Sectional, finishing 23-2. The final Sectional title came

in 2002 when Bob Carter's team won 18 and lost 5. Hall of Fame coach Ray Crowe graduated from Whiteland in 1934.

Woodlan's Warriors were coached by Gay Martin for 21 years during which all three of their Sectional championships were won, in 1986, 1990, and 1997. The 1986 team won 23 of 25 games losing a two-point decision to Garrett in the first round of the Ft. Wayne Regionals. Ed DeLong coached the Lady Warriors to a 19-2 record in 1984, followed by an 18-5 Sectional championship year and, in 1987, a 20-2 finish. His squads turned in a strong 4-year stint beginning in 1989 with an 18-3 record, followed by 20-4, 18-3, and 17-5 seasons: 73 wins, 15 losses including their second Sectional title in 1990. Bill Boller's 1988 and 1989 teams turned in 18-3 and 17-5 records as well.

The Woodlan Warriors

The word "calumet" means Indian pipe, often referred to as a peace pipe for its use in

The Calumet Warriors, logo, and an authentic calumet pipe

ceremonies of détente. Calumet High School in Gary also calls its teams the Warriors. Those Warriors were coached for an incredible period of at least 49 years, spanning even more, by Chris Traicoff. His 1st year of coaching at Calumet was in 1942, and he then returned at least as early as 1951 and continued every year until 1998. For the 3 years from 1964–66 the Warriors won 57 games and lost only 11, and in 1969 they recorded 18 wins in 21 games. All told, the Calumet Warriors placed five Sectional championships in their trophy case. The Lady Warriors have won two Sectional crowns, in 1976 and 2008, the latter for Dori Downing in her thirteenth year as the Calumet girls teams coach.

The Westview Warriors in LaGrange County have brought many trophies back to their home base in Topeka. In 1973 Coach Denny Foster's Warriors finished 21-3, winning the 1st of the school's 13 Sectional championships. The 2nd and 3rd came at 3-year intervals, as his 1976 team finished 19-6 and his 1979 squad ended at 21-4. Gerald Eash led the 1986 and 1987 teams to titles 4 and 5 with 21-4 and 20-5 records, and his 1994 Warriors got title number 9 with a 22-5 mark. However, the crowning achievements came in 1999 and 2000, when Coach Troy Neeley led Westview to consecutive Class 2A State Championships with 23-3 and 25-3 seasons, defeating Paoli and Winchester in the Class 2A final games. In the 1999 Tournament of Champions, the Warriors gave the Jason Gardner-led Indianapolis North Central Panthers, the 4A titlists, a strong game in the finals of that short-lived experiment. In 2008, with Robb Yoder coaching, the Warriors won their 4th Regional crown, ending at 24-2.

Randy Yoder coached the Lady Warriors to a 20-4 mark in 2005, followed by a 24-4 year that saw Westview finish runner-up to Heritage Christian in the state Class 2A championship game. All told, the Lady Warriors have also captured 5 Sectional titles.

In Lake County Hammond Bishop Noll teams have also had  many fine seasons, starting with Edgar Hudson's Warrior teams of 1955 and 1956, 20-2 followed by 21-1, with the lone loss coming to Hammond High in the Sectional. Revenge for the Warriors came the very next year when they won their first Sectional championship by defeating the Wildcats in the final game. Their 1st Regional title came in 1973, Bob Bradtke's charges finishing 17-9. Ron Luketic coached the 1981 Bishop Noll team to another undefeated regular season, 19-1, and Jack Gabor's 1984 team put together a 22-2 season. Four years later his Warriors brought the school's only Semi-state crown home to Hammond, losing the 2nd morning game to Concord's Minutemen at Market Square Arena to finish 21-6. Adam Patai coached the 2002 Warriors to a 21-5 record and the 10th of the school's 12 Sectional titles to go with their 3 Regional crowns. The Lady Warriors have added the nets from 7 Sectionals and one Regional to the school's trophy case.

Other current Warriors represent Anderson Christian Academy, Covenant Christian (Indianapolis), New Albany Christian Academy, and White's Institure, none of whom seem to use an Indian depiction. The Covenant Christian mascot is clearly not of Indian origin, more Spartan or Trojan.

The Covenant Christian Warrior

Chapter 15

More Native Americans: Braves, Squaws, and Chiefs

In the last two chapters we began our review of our current schools with Indian-related mascots and/or team names. Now we will complete that process.

Nine of our schools call their teams the Braves, with some of the girls teams called the Lady Braves. At Bellmont, however, it's the Braves and Squaws. Blackhawk Christian has already been covered.

At Brownstown Central the Indian motif is found in their arrowhead logo as well as their Brave. The Braves had a terrific season in 2004, winning 27 games and losing only 2 for Coach Dave Benter and winning the school's 7th Sectional title as well as their 1st Regional and Semi-state crowns. They were runner-up to Jimtown for the 2A state championship that year, losing the final game by 4 points.

Paula Workman coached the Lady Braves from 1991 through 2007, winning 4 Sectionals and 2 Regionals. Their best records came in 1998, 20-5, and 2001, 20-2.

The Brownstown Central Brave and Arrowhead

The Bellmont Braves have had several 20-victory seasons, beginning with Gary Miller's 1977 20-3 team. Mark Bixler's 1985 squad finished 20-4, winning the Sectional title, a feat also accomplished 2 years later by Kevin Leising's 22-4 club. Shaun Busick had consecutive 20-game seasons twice as the Braves went 20-4 in 2001 and 22-2 the next year; then 22-5 in 2004 and 25-3 the next year. Over the years the Braves have won 13 Sectional titles. The 2004 team made it all the way to the state championship game in Class 3A before finally losing to Evansville Mater Dei.

Bellmont's Brave and Squaw

The Squaws have more than held up their end of things as well, winning 10 Sectional titles and 3 Regionals. The 1st Regional title came when Claudia Mihovik's Squaws finished 18-3 in 1979; the next when Dave Miller's 1992 and 1993 teams turned in 23-2 and 18-6 marks. His 1994 team won 20 of 23 games, giving the Squaws an impressive 3-year mark of 61 wins and 11 losses. Another 20-victory season was achieved for John Cate and his girls from Decatur in 1983, 20-3.

The Indian Creek Braves won 21 games and lost only 3 in 1982 with Bob Hynds coaching. Four years later they finished 21-2 with Dave Fetheroff in charge. Seven Sectionals have been won by the Braves as well as the 1983 Columbus North Regional, after which they ran into eventual state

Indian Creek and Borden Braves

champion Connersville in the 1st round of the Sweet Sixteen. The Lady Braves had a marvelous 22-1 season in 1985 for Coach Jim Anthony as well as a 20-2 record for Dana Scott in 2003. They have brought the nets from 2 Sectionals home to Trafalgar.

Borden was originally called New Providence after the capital of Rhode Island. It was renamed after William Borden, who founded a college to train children of area farmers. The Borden Institute was closed in 1906, but the college building was used for education until the 1950s. The Borden Braves won 19 of 21 games for Coach Wes Porter in 1980 and got their 1st Sectional championship in 2008, in Class A. The Lady Braves, however, have picked off 7 Sectional titles. Their best records came in 1984, 21-2 for Coach Dan Callahan, and consecutive 19-4 seasons for Tony Rademacher, 2002 and 2003.

The Maconaquah Braves of Bunker Hill turned in excellent seasons in 1998 and 2000 for coach Rick Clark, 20-4 and 22-2. Sectional titles were won in each of those years, and, interestingly, the interim year saw the Braves finish 12-12 and still win not only the Sectional title but their only

Maconaquah and Tecumseh Braves

Regional as well. Judi Warren coached the Lady Braves to 3 Sectional crowns in a row (of the school's total of 5), the 3rd coming with a 21-2 record in 1988. Tecumseh's Braves won the Class A State Championship in 1999, Kevin Oxley's team finishing 23-5 with their final game victory over Lafayette Central Catholic. Winning their 1st Sectional ever and going all the way to the championship seemed to point the Braves in the right direction. They have won Sectionals every year but one since, as well as another Regional title in 2000, including 21-5 and 20-6 seasons in 2004 and 2007. The Lady Braves have brought one Sectional title home to Lynnville, that in 2004 with Steve O'Brien coaching.

The Terre Haute South Braves were coached by Hall of Famer Gordon Neff from 1972 through 1980. His teams went 23-3 in 1973, 25-3 in 1977, 23-7 in 1978, 25-3 in 1979, and 21-5 in 1980. For that 4-year stretch Neff's teams therefore won 94 games and lost only 18. Included in that stretch were 4 Sectional titles (out of 10 in a row), 4 Regional titles (out of 5 in a row), 3 straight Semi-state titles, and a runner-up finish to Muncie Central in the thrilling 65-64 overtime final game in

1978. Pat Rady's Braves teams of 1982 through 1984 won 65 games and lost only 11, adding 2 more Regional titles to the school's ultimate total of 11. Rady, who coached the Braves for 24 seasons, also had 20-victory seasons in 1989, 23-2, and 1991, 23-4. Mike Saylor's 2005 Braves finished 22-6, annexing the school's 17th Sectional and its 11th Regional.

Alan Maroska coached the Lady Braves from 1983 until the present—that is, 26 years (so far). His teams won 14 of the school's 15 Sectional titles, all 5 of their Regionals, and the 2002 Class 4A State Championship over South Bend Riley, finishing 25-2. Other 20-victory seasons were chalked up for the 5 years beginning in 1998—when the Lady Braves amassed an impressive 111 wins and only 17 losses!—and in 2007 and 2008, 21-2 and 20-6.

Brebeuf Jesuit, though now avoiding Indian depictions, still calls their teams the Braves. Marty Echelbarger coached the Braves to their 1st really outstanding season in 1983, when they won the Sectional and finished 22-3. They were also 19-5 the next year. Mike Miller took the reins in 1986, and his 1989 squad won 20 games while losing 5. However, it was 1991 when the Braves really made their mark, winning 27 games, losing only 2, and making it all the way to the state championship game. That game was played at the Hoosier Dome and was attended by 30,345 fans eager to see the showdown between two outstanding teams led by two great players, Alan Henderson of Brebeuf and Glenn Robinson of Gary Roosevelt. Roosevelt won that game, and fans could look forward to enjoying future Indiana-Purdue games, as the two protagonists of the state final game chose those schools for their collegiate careers. The Braves went 20-2 for Miller in 1992 and won the Class 3A State Championship, defeating Andrean's Fighting 59ers 72-56. They went 24-2 for Leo Klemm in 2000. Overall, the Braves have won 7 Sectionals, 3 Regionals, and 2 Semi-states.

The Lady Braves have also enjoyed many fine seasons. Alan Vickrey, who would later move the 3 or 4 miles east on 86th Street to successfully take the reins of the North Central Lady Panthers, started things off well with 19-3 seasons in 1980 and 1981, followed by a sterling 28-3 year. That year his Lady Braves won the Semi-state and were 41-33 losers to Valpariso's Lady Vikings in the finals early game. Another 19-5 season occurred in 1986, 20-3 in 1988, and 22-4 in 1989. Teresa Lewis took over from Vickrey in 1998, and her 2002 Lady Braves finished 25-3. Kendall Kreinhagen became the Brebeuf coach in 2004 and led the Lady Braves to their 1st state championship, defeating Ft. Wayne Bishop Luers in the 3A final game to finish 26-3. This was repeated in 2007, when Kreinhagen's team again won the 3A state championship, this time over Wawasee, 51-43, resulting in a 23-6 record.

Eight of our schools field the Raiders, but only one of these is actually Indian-related, that of Wapahani. In 1994 the Wapahani Raiders turned in a 19-3 season for Chris Benedict. Five Sectionals were won between 1983, when Ron Hecklinski was the coach, until 1999, when Terry Bales had the job. The Lady Raiders won 20 of 22 games for Tom Childs in 1988. They also have brought 5 Sectional titles home to Selma.

Cardinal Ritter in Indianapolis, for example, has a mascot showing their Raiders to be pirates, not Indians.

Cardinal Ritter Raiders

The Wapahani Raiders logo.

The Southern Wells, Northridge, and Southridge versions are certainly more of a knight.

 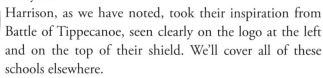

Southern Wells, Northridge and Southridge Raiders

The Raiders of West Lafayette

Harrison, as we have noted, took their inspiration from the Battle of Tippecanoe, seen clearly on the logo at the left and on the top of their shield. We'll cover all of these schools elsewhere.

Harrison's Raiders

However, there is one school whose team name would not lead us to believe that their mascot was an Indian, though their school name would. That is Shakamak in Jasonville, Greene County. Their teams are called the Lakers, but their mascot is an Indian chief. The Lakers had a fine season in 1964 for Coach Lloyd Hensley finishing 24-5 and winning the Sectional title in their first year of operation. Two years later Brian Blackmore led the Lakers to a 2nd Sectional and a 21-5 record. In 2006 the Ernie Maesch-coached Lakers finished 19-8, winning the school's 5th Sectional and 1st and only Regional title to date.

We have 4 Blackhawks, honoring the great Sauk chief. . . or do we? The Springs Valley and Sheridan Blackhawks are both birds, covered elsewhere.

The Shakamak Lakers

Two versions of the Springs Valley Blackhawks and one of Sheridan

Cowan and Westville are left, and both clearly honor the Indian chief. Though Westville has yet to win their 1st sectional, they had a fine season in 1947 for coach Charles McComas, winning 20 games and losing only 3. Three years later his Blackhawks finished 19-5, and in 1961 and 1963 Raymond Cox led his teams to

19-4 and 19-5 records. In 2007 William Berger's Blackhawks turned in an 18-4 mark. Hall of Famer John Milholland was a 1954 Westville graduate:

John Milholland

As a player for Eastern Illinois, he was All-Conference 1956, 57, 58...NAIA All-Tourney Team 1957... coaching career began at Chesterton and included Middlebury, Thorntown and Whiteland before going to Frankfort in 1967 where he coached until 1985...career record 381-214...9 sectional championships...2 regionals...7 conference championships...twice named District #3 "Coach of the Year"...27 years as high school basketball coach, 41 years in the field of education...member of Eastern Illinois Athletic Hall of Fame.

The Westville Lady Blackhawks turned in their best record in 1991, 16-3, for Coach John Erickson.

Cowan's Blackhawks won 20 games in 1935 for Coach Francis Kiger, losing 5. Steve Brunes coached the 1976 Cowan team to

Westville and two versions of Cowan, all Blackhawks

its only Sectional title at Muncie Central, defeating Burris, 64-61, and Southside, 56-54 in overtime.

The Tell City Marksmen derived their mascot from Switzerland, while the Ft. Wayne South Side Archers received their inspiration from Robin Hood and his Merrie Men in Sherwood Forest, so neither belongs in this section. Which leaves the Sullivan Golden Arrows. Is this choice Indian derived? Probably, but it is clearly muted in its usage.

Sullivan's 1938 team, coached by Paul Kelly, won 22 games and lost only 5. Larry Morin was the coach in 1976 when the Golden Arrows went 19-5, and 2 years later, when they turned in a 20-4 mark. Jeff Moore took over the reins in 1991; his 1998 squad was 19-6, followed immediately by a 22-3 record and 2 years after that by a 24-3 season. The Golden Arrows have rung up 24 Sectional titles and 4 Regionals.

The Sullivan girls teams have also done well. We know they were playing basketball there as early as 1924 because we have seen a photo and read a newspaper account indicating that the Sullivan girls team won the (mythical) state championship in 1924 by defeating the Mt. Vernon girls. Coach Gilmore's record was 12-0.

Go Sullivan Girls!

The story comes to us from scrapbooks and letters kept by Madge Wood of S.Troll Street, who, as a junior, played guard on Sullivan's girls state championship team of 1924. As we know, there were sometimes several claimants to that title. With neither a play-off to determine a winner nor very much competition from schools around the state, communities and newspapers tended to select the best from their own area and simply bestowed a title on what seemed to be the best school. It is even possible that the various sections of the state were unaware of the quality of girls basketball being played elsewhere. Communication and travel in the 20s were not what they are today. The boys teams had been made aware of each other through the medium of the state tournament itself. By the mid-20s teams from every corner of Indiana were meeting in the Sweet Sixteen and becoming well aware of the talent levels that existed everywhere else. In 1925, for example, teams from as far afield as Vincennes, Washington, and Evansville in the south, and Gary, Elkhart, and LaPorte in the north, converged on Indianapolis to find out just exactly who played the game the best that year. The girls didn't have that opportunity until some 50 years later. At any rate, it is good to know that girls teams throughout Indiana were taking the sport seriously long before we had an official, sanctioned, open-to-all tournament in 1976. There were effects beyond sports, too. Basketball in Sullivan, for instance, was a real equalizing and liberating experience for the girls who played it.

Here is the newspaper account of that state championship game played by Sullivan against Mt. Vernon in 1924:

SHS Girls Meet
Mt. Vernon in
Championship Game

The highest ambition of the Sullivan High School girls basketball team was realized Friday night when they humbled the strong Mt. Vernon sextet [In those days the game was played differently by the girls. In one set of rules, the court was divided into thirds, and 2 players from each team were confined to each section. In another, there were only 2 halves of the court, 3 players from each team in each half court.] *22-16 and thereby became the Champion High School girls team in Indiana. The Sullivan sextet in winning this game were forced to battle continuously and it was only due to snappy passing, accurate goal shooting, and superb guarding that Sullivan was victorious. The first half was played under two court rules which was a hardship to Sullivan who have been playing three court rules. Nevertheless, they outfought the speedy visitors and led [by] a 10-8 count at halftime. McGregor for Mt. Vernon led a sensational comeback in the last half and brought her team within one point of Sullivan, but coach Gilmore's protégés spurted near the end of the game and held a 6 point lead when the final whistle sounded.*

Every member of the new State Champions played gloriously and well deserves the honor which is theirs. Bland and Russell played speedy games at the forward positions and sank counters from all over the floor. Muehler and Richeson were powerful cogs, both on offense and defense, and passed with speed and accuracy. At guard, Marshall and Henderson put up the best basketball of their careers and spoiled chance after chance of their opponents to score. Wood and Kellums were subbed into the game and showed flashes of real class.

Following the state championship season of 1924, hopes were high for a repeat by Sullivan in 1925. A newspaper clipping stated the following near the end of the 1924 season:

Coach Gilmore sent in Woods, Wyatt and Smith in the last quarter and they also did good work, so we surely next year will have a peppy girls team.

Another headline and an excerpt from the article stated:

Woody's Warriors Win over Carlisle
Muehler and Richeson played an excellent game at center position while Woods and Henderson at guard spoiled many of Carlisle's chances to score.

That there was considerable excitement attendant to these girls games is apparent from the following newspaper account:

The game was patronized to the full capacity of the house "crowding" room and all by rooters of both schools.

Thirty-two (!) girls came out for practice when the coach first called for it. (Which reminds me of one of the great differences between the Hickory Huskers in the movie *Hoosiers* and the real Milan Indians: Marvin Wood had over 50 boys try out for his team, not the 8 shown in the movie!) So we know that interest was high among the Sullivan girls of the mid-20s regarding the opportunity to play interscholastic basketball. It was also high among the alumni, who came back to play the varsity girls in their 1st game on November 28. The varsity won, 25-18, not at all a bad win when you consider that the nucleus of the alumni team were from the defending state champions. Eight days later they played their 1st outside foe, edging Midland, 19-18. At least 2 more games were played in December, Sullivan losing to Dugger twice, 29-25 and 31-27. They also played Freelandville, a score that is apparently lost to us, but believed to be a win for Sullivan. The girls hit their stride, though, in January, besting Carlisle, 29-27, and routing Concannon, 51-11. In February Sullivan upended Princeton 47-11 before tying Carlisle 26-26, again giving the Princeton Lady Tigers a lesson, 35-13, and treating Coalmont with almost equal success, 35-18. Although there is some thought that this squad repeated as state champions, I have not been able

to find substantive evidence in support of that claim.

Turning to "the modern era" the Lady Arrows have also been successful, beginning with a 4-year string of 20-win seasons from 1982 through 1985, when Coach Brock Drew's charges won 80 games while losing only 7(!), including the undefeated regular season in 1984. Kathy Richter was the coach in 1992 for another 20-2 season, followed the next year by a 19-2 mark and the

Sullivan High School's state championship girls team of 1924. Madge Wood, (row 1) 3rd from left as a Sullivan champ

year after that by 17-4. In 1999 Julia Meeks led the Lady Arrows to a 20-4 record and in 2001 improved on that, finishing 24-3. All told the Lady Arrows have won an impressive 19 Sectional crowns, but only the 1982 Washington Regional. They also captured the Bedford North Lawrence Semi-state that year, losing the morning game in Indianapolis the next week to eventual state champion Heritage, 66-55.

Sullivan's Golden Arrows logo

Finally, we have 8 current schools whose team names are, plain and simply, the Indians, bringing to 43, or almost 11 percent of our current schools with some form of Indian reference in their mascot.

The Milan, Portage, Twin Lakes, Mississinewa, and Lake Central Indians

Again, it is evident that all of the portrayals utilized by Hoosier schools are dignified and have attempted to be historical. We have discussed the Milan Indians historic state championship of 1954 previously. The year before they also had a fine season, winning the Indianapolis Semi-state before losing in the morning game of the state finals to eventual state champion South Bend Central. More recently the Indians under Coach Randy Combs went 19-3 in 2000 and 20-5 the next year. All told, the Indians have won 13 Sectional crowns and 5 Regionals. Lisa Bradshaw's 1999 Milan girls team won 15 games and lost 7.

The Mississinewa Indians turned in some impressive seasons in the 50s for Coach John Fredenberger. For 5 out of 6 years from 1952 until 1957, they won at least 20 games, including a sparkling 27-1 undefeated regular season in 1954. Those 5 years saw the Indians win 113 games while losing only 9! The 1954 team won the Marion Sectional by defeating Van Buren 67-28, Swayzee 50-29, and the vaunted host team Giants 55-47. They also nailed down the Marion Regional by knocking out Hartford City, 64-49, and Bluffton, 54-36. At the Ft. Wayne Semi-state Mississinewa defeated their 2nd North Central Conference foe of the post season, Kokomo, 66-55 before suffering the only loss of their season at the hands, or claws, of the 3rd, Muncie Central, 63-48. We know the fate that was in store for the Bearcats in Indianapolis at the hands of Bobby Plump, Ray Craft, *et al*, and Marvin Woods' Milan Indians! Mississinewa also had a 20-3 season for Coach Creighton Burns in 1988. All told, they have won 11 Sectional crowns and that 1954 Regional.

The Lady Indians also put together a nice 3-year string for Coach Otis Reece: 20-2 in 1993 followed by an undefeated regular season 23-1 record the next year and a 21-2 mark in 1995. The Mississinewa girls have added 7 Sectional crowns and the 1995 Regional title to their school's trophy case in Gas City.

The Portage Indians won 21 games in 1942, losing only 3 for Coach Charles McComas, and the next year experienced an undefeated regular season, 23-1. That loss came in the semi-finals of the tough East Chicago Sectional to Hammond Tech. Greg Fisher's 1988 team won 20 and lost 6, capturing the Valparaiso Sectional by downing Chesterton, Hobart, and the host Vikings. They also snagged the Michigan City Regional with victories over Oregon Davis, 74-71, and LaPorte, slicing it almost too thin, 50-49. At the Ft. Wayne Semi-state Portage was in turn edged by Norwell, 60-57. In total the Indians have won 10 Sectionals and 2 Regionals. The Lady Indians were coached for their first 14 seasons beginning in 1974 by Bernita Adkins, whose

1976 team finished 16-1. She was succeeded by Renee Tupa, who carried on the longevity tradition, holding the reins for 17 years herself. Her charges won 19 games in 1988 and 17 2 years later, dropping only 4 each season. Three Sectional nets and the 1976 Chesterton Regional nets are in the school's trophy case.

Lake Central's Indians won 24 games and lost only 4 for Coach Jim Hammel in 1984, picking up the 4th of the school's 8 Sectional championships. That team won the Sectional title at Calumet, defeating Crown Point, 74-33, Highland, 80-66, and Merrillville, 46-45, in overtime. They also captured the school's only Regional title, at Gary, with another single-point victory, over Hammond, 67-66, and a 69-65 decision over Bishop Noll. At the Lafayette Semi-state, in a battle of Indians, Lake Central won another squeaker by a single point over Anderson. They then won that title in what for them must have been almost a laugher, 57-43 over Lebanon. In the Final Four at Market Square Arena, the Indians lost the morning game to Vincennes, 78-74.

The Lady Indians were coached by Tom Megyesi for 24 seasons, beginning in 1983. Between 1993 and 1998 the Lady Indians won a remarkable total of 138 games while losing only 13! Included in that were 6 (of 8 straight and 13 total) Sectional titles, 4 Regional titles, 3 Semi-states, and the 1994 state championship, finishing 25-1 after winning the final game over Kokomo in a thriller, 44-42. The 1998 team also was undefeated entering the state tournament, finishing 26-1, runner-up to Martinsville in the 4A state championship final game, 71-65.

At Twin Lakes, the Indians had a 17-4 season in 1968 for Jack Woodruff; they finished 22-3 under Greg Fisher in 1986 and were 20-5 in 1992 with Rick Snodgrass at the helm. They have won 7 Sectionals. It is, however, the Lady Indians in Monticello who have had astonishing success. In their relatively short existence the Twin Lakes girls have won 16 Sectional championships, 3 Regionals, and the 1980 Benton Central Semi-state. That year Coach Mary Creigh's team finished 19-5. Her team's record from 1978 through 1985 was an impressive 133 wins and only 37 losses. The Lady Indians captured 9 Sectional crowns in an 11-year period under her guidance and all 3 of the school's Regional titles. Excellent records were also turned in by Kim Bilskie's 1999 and 2000 teams, 20-4 and 21-2, and by Brad Bowman's 2005 and 2008 squads, 20-3 and 22-2. Their school building leaves no doubt they are the Indians:

Twin Lakes High School, home of the Indians and the Lady Indians

South Bend St. Joseph's uses the arrow as their logo on their football helmets and also call their teams the Indians. In 1958 they turned in a 22-2 record for Coach Angelo Turco. Bob Donewald coached the 1969 Indian squad to a 21-5 season, including Sectional and Regional titles. His 1972 team also won a Sectional title, finishing 22-3 and bringing the 4-year mark to 77 and 18. Steve Austin led the 1988 and 1989 teams to 23-2 and 29-2 records and had back-to-back excellent seasons again in 1992 and 1993, 22-5 and 25-3. Both the 1989 and 1993 teams won Semi-state championships, the former losing to ultimate champion Lawrence North at Market Square Arena, and the latter to ultimate State Champion Jeffersonville at the Hoosier Dome. The girls teams won 3 straight Sectionals for Coach Larry Shead beginning in 1985, as well as a Regional title in 1987 with records of 20-3, 21-1, and 22-3. Mike Megyese took the reins of the girls program in 1998 and by 2002 had put together a squad with a 20-5 record. That team won the 1st of 6 consecutive Sectional titles, a period during which the Lady Indians amassed 131 victories while absorbing only 24 defeats! The 2003 team was runner-up to Beech Grove, led by Purdue and WNBA star-to-be Katie Gearlds, in the State Championship, finishing 24-3.

The Union City Indians won 23 of 27 games in 1927 for coach Charles McCollough, winning the 1st of 5 Sectional titles under his tutelage. Harry Allison's 1954 team finished 22-3 and won Sectional title number 6. Tom Goldsberry's 1962 squad went 21-3, getting Sectional title 8 and his 1966 team with a less impressive record won number 9. Number 10, of the 13 now in the school's trophy case, came from Goldsberry's 21-3 team in 1969. The Union City Lady Indians have won 4 Sectional crowns and one Regional, in 2001, Class A, in their own gym. Kirk Comer led the 2002 team to an excellent 23-2 finish.

The city of Anderson is named for Chief William Anderson, whose mother was a Delaware (Lenape) Indian and whose father was of Swedish descent. Chief Anderson's Indian name was Kikthawenund meaning "making a noise" or "causing to crack" and is spelled in a variety of ways. The Anderson Indians play their home games in a beautiful arena called the Wigwam which seats just under 9,000 fans

The Union City Indian making it second only to the New Castle Field House as the largest capacity high school gym in Indiana and in America.

Every basketball fan should see at least one Anderson Indian game in the Wigwam. On the stage at one end is a complete band. Before the game the team is led on the court by an Indian chief and a maiden. He stands with her at his feet for the pre-game warmups. Then the teams leave the court for their final briefing. The national anthem is sung—if you're lucky—by Anderson native Sandi Patty. Anderson natives Carl Erskine, Ray Tolbert, or Johnny Wilson may well be in attendance.

Anderson children observe the Lenape Indian Dance

The presentation of the colors includes the American, Indiana, and POW/MIA flags. Everyone stands. The lights are dimmed. The chief and maiden perform an authentic Lenape dance, which they have learned from a Lenape Indian. The dance is lengthy and covers the entire floor and the Anderson students stand throughout, doing their chant—more of a whoop—at appropriate times. The beat of the tom-tom adds to the drama. The dance ends, the lights come up, and the chief and maiden return to center court. Soon they summon the opposing cheerleaders to join with the home cheerleaders in a large circle, sitting alternately.

The peace pipe is blessed, handed from the chief to the maiden, then to each cheerleader in turn. The teams return to the court, the chief now brandishes his tomahawk, and dances around the court. I'll have more to say about the impressive Anderson Indian teams later.

The Blessing of the Peace Pipe in the Wigwam

Chapter 16

Native Americans in Our Now-Closed Schools:
Chippewas, Blue Raiders, and Kickapoos

In the last chapters we examined our Indian heritage as expressed in the mascots selected by our current high schools. Now let's take a look at those selected by some of the 800 or so schools no longer with us.

There were 25 schools whose team names were the Indians, a smaller but significant number of Warriors, and by the time all of the Braves, Chieftains, etc., are added up there were about 70 schools whose mascots appear to be Indian-related. Of course, unless one can see their logo, or speak with someone who knows the true story, it is not possible to tell whether or not all of the Raiders and Warriors or even Blackhawks, are necessarily Indian. (As, for example, was almost certainly not the case for Alamo.) That and the fact that some names were changed leads to the probable conclusion that 70 is a high number. At any rate, it would account for about 9 percent of our now closed schools.

The Carlisle Indian School in Pennsylvania was a school attended by one of America's greatest athletes of all time, Jim Thorpe. Not only was he Olympic decathlon champion in 1912, a title that often carries with it the aphorism "World's Greatest Athlete," but he was also a fine professional football and baseball player. Perhaps in his honor, the town of Carlisle, Indiana, called their high school teams the Indians. As early as 1915 Carlisle won 9 of 12 games. The red-and-white-uniformed Indians won 18 games and lost 5 for Coach Jerry Korker in 1951 and were led to 17-5 and 27-3(!) seasons by Jim Bates in 1959 and 1960, and 20-5 by Joe Williams in 1962. There were 7 Sectional trophies and 1 Regional crown

Carlisle High School

in the Carlisle trophy case before they were consolidated into Sullivan High School, becoming the Golden Arrows. That 1960 Regional championship came via wins over traditional powerhouses Vincennes Lincoln and Washington, and the 3rd loss that year was in the first round of the Semi-state to Tell City by a mere 2 points.

The Indians of Chester Center in Keystone have since become Southern Wells Raiders. Preconsolidation, the purple-and-gold-clad Indians won 18 of 22 games for Coach David Craig (a familiar name for all Indiana Pacer fans) in 1929 and had 2 fine seasons under Albert Spandau, 21-4 in 1947 and 18-5 the next year. The Chester Center Indians won 4 Sectionals, all at Bluffton and all in the 40s.

The crest of Southern Wells

We have previously discussed the Banquo Indians/Ghosts and the Wea and Darlington Indians. The Cayuga Indians were a tribe of the Iroquois confederation located on the shores of one of the beautiful Finger Lakes of New York state, also called Cayuga, Ithaca, at the southern tip of the lake, is home to Cornell University's Big Red teams. Their memorable song has made the lake well known:

Far above Cayuga's waters
With its waves of blue
Stands our noble alma mater
Glorious to view.

Soon after the Revolutionary War many Cayuga Indians sold their land in New York and moved either to Ohio or Canada. The former joined with other Iroquois Indians and became known as the Seneca of Sandusky. The Sandusky, Indiana, High School teams were the Blackhawks, perhaps honoring the great Sauk chief. Their colors were black and white, but their mascot was clearly a bird. (They may also have been called Comets.)

1918 Sandusky Blackhawks

In 1936 the Blackhawks won 17 and lost 4 for Coach Orville Pitt. In 1940 and 1941, with Millard Sink then coaching, they finished 17-4 and 17-6. In 1955 Coach Delbert Kistler's Blackhawks won 19 and lost only 5. Their only Sectional title came in 1921 at Rushville. They also won the Regional that year before losing their lone Sweet Sixteen experience to the Vincennes Alices. Sandusky was first

Sandusky High School, home of the Blackhawks

consolidated into Clarksburg, becoming Knights and then into North Decatur, the Chargers.

Kewanna was originally called Pleasant Grove, but the name was changed to that of a Potawatomi Indian chief who lived nearby. The Kewanna High School teams were called the Indians. The Indians enjoyed a 20-6 season for Coach Hal Peck in 1954. Then, with Maurice Tolbert coaching they were 20-3 in 1956 and 20-2 in 1958. They won the Rochester Sectional in 1927 and the Winamac Sectional in 1954.

Kewanna High School in 1924, the Indian from the 1959 and 1982 year books, and an early pennant

The 1924 Kewanna boys

Girls were also playing basketball at Kewanna High School at an early date. Here is the 1924 girls team and their yearbook entry: It does seem like a rather modest write-up of a single-loss season, though!

Kewanna was dispersed among Caston, Rochester, and Winamac. Kewanna Indians are now Comets, Zebras, and Warriors

What is now northwest Indiana was home to the Potawatomi Indians under Chief Pokagon when the first white

The Girls Basketball Team

After a year of learning rules and trying hard to play basket ball without much success, the girls were encouraged by Coach Hoover and again entered the race this year.

Most of the girls will be back again next year and a good team is expected.

They are, left to right, first row: Helen Wilson, Fern Wilson, Lucille McClain, Anna Henricks, Doris Willoughby, Alice Kopp.

Second row: Helen Pensinger, Mary Lord, Mary Gould, Ruth Lebo (Captain), Sadie Carter, Mamie DeMoss, Helen Johnston, Vera DeMoss.

Schedule

Date	Winning School	Losing School	Place Played
Nov. 17	Kewanna, 17	Richland, 16	Kewanna
Nov. 23	Kewanna, 26	Argos, 3	Kewanna
Dec. 8	Kewanna, 24	Lucerne, 6	Lucerne
Dec. 15	Richland Centre, 15	Kewanna, 7	Richland Centre
Jan. 12	Kewanna, 22	Monterey, 9	Kewanna
Jan. 18	Kewanna, 12	Fulton, 0	Kewanna
Jan. 26	Kewanna, 37	Lucerne, 4	Kewanna
Feb. 8	Fulton, 8	Kewanna, 6	Fulton
Feb. 13	Kewanna, 15	Monterey, 13	Monterey

LUCILLE McCLAIN.

settlers arrived in the 1830s. Dyer, officially St. John Township High School, I am informed by proud alum Tom Plimpton, wore blue and gold uniforms. They were always in the tough Hammond Sectional and never came out on top. They were also called the Indians, and, after consolidation into Lake Central, as we have seen, they still are. All Dyer alums are proud of the fine record the Lake Central boys and girls teams have made.

Gary Dyer letter sweater

1911 Modoc basketball team

The Reelsville Indians had an undefeated regular season in 1953, finishing 26-1 for Coach Elwin McBride. In the Greencastle Sectional they handily defeated Cloverdale and Roachdale before dropping a heartbreaker, 70-67, to the home team.

Although the Modoc Indians were primarily located in northern California and the Pacific Northwest, they loaned their name to our Indiana town, whose high school teams were also called the Indians. We know they have been playing basketball there for a long time, at least since 1911. They are now a part of the Union Patriots in Randolph County.

Chippewa, Indiana, was named for another Algonquin tribe (also known as the Ojibwa) and their high school teams were the Indians as well. Our Chippewa Indians won 16 games for Coach John Emrick in 1932 and again for Wilmer Rogers in 1948, losing 6 and 5 games respectively. They have been consolidated into the Northfield Norsemen.

Modoc High School

Indians also represented DeMotte High School in Jasper County. The DeMotte Indians had a 19-4 record in 1959 for Coach Gene Bottorf and went 18-6 in 1965 with Jerry Hoover coaching, followed by an identical mark the next year, Ron Sullivan then holding the reins. They won 18 of 25 games in 1970 for Coach Rich McEwan and captured Sectional crowns at Rensselaer in 1964 and at North White in 1970. DeMotte is now part of the Kankakee Valley Kougars.

Chippewa High

The Kankakee Valley Kougar

You can get to Tunnelton by going east from Bedford on 16th Street and angling to the southeast on Tunnelton Road, which passes through Buddha. After Buddha turn south or you will miss Tunnelton entirely and find yourself heading east on the Devils Backbone Road, which can be a challenge, although the view is rewarding.

The Golden Age of Tunnelton Indian basketball was clearly the 3-year period from 1961 through 1963. Coach Hubert Fry led his teams to an 18-5 mark in 1961, followed by an undefeated regular season the next year, finishing 23-1.

George Holaday began his 8-year tour with a fine 20-3 mark the next year. He

Tunnelton High School, home of the Indians. Houck photo of license plate from exhibit courtesy of IBHOF

also concluded his tenure well, finishing at 16-6 in both 1969 and 1970, before being succeeded by J. R. Holmes, whose 1st year record with the Indians was a commendable 18-5. They are now Bedford North Lawrence Stars.

In Pike County the red-and-white-clad Petersburg teams were also called the Indians. They been consolidated into the Pike Central Chargers.

Petersburg Indians are now Pike Central Chargers The maroon and white Roann Indians finished 19-4 in 1942 for Coach Charles Beck. Five years later they turned in a 19-3 mark with David Fouts at the helm. Fouts-led teams enjoyed several other fine seasons as well: 21-5 in 1950, 18-4 in 1951, and 17-3 in 1952. That's a 3-year mark of 56 wins and only 12 losses. Interestingly, Roann had finished undefeated in 1917 in 9 starts. The Straughn Indians won 22 of 24 games in 1942, Ray Ashley coaching. They also captured the New Castle Sectional that year, defeating the powerful host Trojans 29-27, Lewisville, 35-15, and Mooreland 30-26. Roann was consolidated into Northfield, the Vikings, and Straughn is part of the Tri High Trojans.

Coesse High School teams were also

Coesse High School and Indians. Houck photo from exhibit courtesy IBHOF

called the Indians. Their best season, insofar as I have been able to ascertain it, was under Coach Arthur Lloyd in 1935, when they won 18 of 23 games played. They are now Columbia City Eagles.

The Wakarusa Indians wore purple and gold uniforms. In 1933 the Wilmer Wine-coached Indians won 24 games and lost only 4. They also won the Elkhart Sectional, defeating Jefferson Township 47-8, Bristol 33-24, and the home team, 33-23. At the Mishawaka Regional they outscored South Bend Riley, 29-23, and Winamac, 31-21. They ran into a strong Greencastle squad in the 1st round of the Sweet Sixteen, losing to the team that would finish 2nd in the state, and were themselves only 3 points shy of state champion Martinsville. The Wakarusa Indians are now Northwood Panthers.

In Owen County the Gosport Indians wore purple and white uniforms. They won back-to-back Sectional titles for Coach Tom Hodges in 1940 and 1941, as well as defeating Bloomfield in the first round of the Bloomington Regional the first year, thus making it to the Elite Eight. They are now Owen Valley Patriots.

The Walkerton Indians in St. Joseph County had a terrific year in 1956 for Coach Grover Smith, finishing 20-3 only to be defeated by South Bend Central in the 2nd round of the Sectionals. This season was preceded and followed by 18-4 and 18-5 marks, bringing the 3-year streak to a tidy 56 wins and 12 losses. They are now John Glenn Falcons.

Clay Township in Miami County chose red and black for their colors and Indians for their name. They were coached for 30 years, from 1928 through 1957, by Edward Lippold. In 1929 the Indians won 18 games and lost 6, and 2 years later they won 19, losing 7. In 1934 they had a fine year, 23-4, followed up immediately by 20-2 and 17-7 seasons. That's an impressive 60-13 record for those 3 years. The Indians had a 21-5 record in 1940, in 1947 they turned in a 19-5 mark, and in

Clay Township Indians are now Maconaquah Braves.

Coach Lippold's final season they won 19 of 22 games. Ben Bowles was the coach in 1962 when they finished 18-6. They are now a part of Maconaquah, becoming Braves.

Our other Indians were at Springfield Township (LaPorte), Glenwood, Owensburg, Wadena, and Rockfield. They are now consolidated into Michigan City, Rushville, Eastern Greene, Benton Central (via Fowler), and Delphi (via Camden) respectively. No Sectional winners, regrettably, in this group, nor can I find memorable seasons, though I am sure they exist. Hopefully, some readers will generate those memories for all of us to share.

Blackhawk teams in Vigo County were the Chieftains, which is quite appropriate. They were first consolidated into Honey Creek, becoming Honey Bees, before merging into Terre Haute South, once again regaining the Indian motif, this time as Braves. Something of a demotion, I suppose, from Chieftain to Brave.

Mt. Auburn in Shelby County also fielded the Blackhawks, although their teams were known as the Rangers as well, probably at different times. Their colors were red and black, and they are now Southwestern Spartans. I'm not sure if that's a demotion or not.

Boswell in Benton County also called their teams the Blackhawks. They had an 11-3 record as early as 1914, when P. F. Phaffman was their coach. The Blackhawks, whose logo indicates bird rather than chief, had another fine record in 1946 under the coaching direction of a man with the interesting name of Xerxes Silver. Silver's teams wore gold and black. That year the 23-2 Blackhawks won their 5th and last Sectional championship, at Ambia, with victories over Gilboa, Otterbein, and Fowler. They are now Benton Central Bison.

Boswell, home of the Blackhawks. Houck photo of pin from exhibit courtesy IBHOF

The Owensville teams were called the Kickapoos after an Algonquin tribe that lived mainly in northern Illinois and southern Wisconsin. The gold-and-black-uniformed Kickapoos won 10 Sectional championships between 1925 and 1953. The 1925 team won 24 games and lost only 5 for coach H. T. McCullough. His next year's team finished 24-4, also winning a Sectional crown. Ben Watts' 1930 Kickapoo team finished 18 and 5 and Dave Williamson's 1932 five had a 23-4 season as well as winning the Sectional title that year. In 1938 and 1939 Ivan Holen's teams finished 20-7 and 19-5, winning Sectional titles both years. The Owensville Kickpoos are now Gibson Southern Titans.

Owensville Kickapoos are now Gibson Southern Titans

Shipshewana, in the heart of the LaGrange County Amish community, is named for the Potawatomi chief who, along with many of his tribesmen, was forced to leave Indiana and move to Kansas in 1838, a sad year in American history. Their high school teams were also the Indians. Harold Coffman coached the 1961 squad to a 17-6 mark. Their lone Sectional crown came in 1944 at Kendallville where they defeated Cromwell, 35-22; Topeka, 47-32; Avila, 35-26; and Wolf Lake, 41-28. They are now consolidated into the Westview Warriors.

Shipshewana High School

Tyner, which is in Marshall County, wore uniforms of red and white. Their teams were called the Redmen. Leo Crabb's 1951 team won 15 games and lost only 6, and Hal Muncie's 1958 team won 18 of 24 starts. They are now John Glenn Falcons. Our other Redmen (also called Red Birds at one time, perhaps later) were found at Huntsville in Randolph County. They also wore red and white uniforms and had a good season in 1943 for Coach Robert Jones, winning 13 and losing 5.

There were Red Raiders at Spencerville and Ligonier and Blue Raiders represented Tolleston High School in Gary. The Ligonier teams wore red and green, and for the 3 years from 1934 through 1936 they won Sectional titles, all at Kendallville. They picked off a 4th crown in 1962 with Phil Miller coaching. His 1962 through 1964 Raiders ran up records of 16-9, 15-5, and 15-7.

Tolleston's Blue Raiders won 4 Sectionals as well as 2 East Chicago Regionals, in 1964 and 1969. Both years saw them losing to eventual state champions Lafayette Jefferson in the 1st round by a large margin in 1964, and the powerhouse Indianapolis Washington team of George McGinnis, Steve Downing, and company by a narrow 3-point margin in the state final game of 1969 at Hinkle Fieldhouse. That was only the second loss in 30 games for Coach Jim Dailey's excellent Tolleston team, a team strong enough to win the championship in many years, but not that one. Earlier, the Blue Raiders had put together a 21-2 record for Coach Vincent McGrath in 1941 and a fine string of 19-5, 18-5, 22-5, and 18-7 for Coach Joe Vance from 1962 through 1965: 77 wins and 22 losses against very tough opposition.

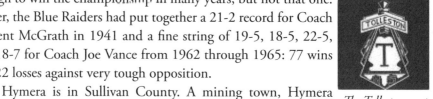

The Tolleston crest

Hymera is in Sullivan County. A mining town, Hymera was originally called Pittsburgh. Preconsolidation, the Hymera High School teams were the Shakamaks. The Hymera Shakamaks captured their sole Sectional title at Sullivan in 1956, defeating Farmerburg, 69-48; Gill Township, 63-41; and the host Golden Arrows, 60-43. At the Huntingburg Regional the Shakamaks

Hymera Shakamaks are now North Central Thunderbirds in Sullivan County.

eliminated Plainville before being sidelined by Jasper in the title game. Their overall record that year was 19 and 7, and their coach was Keith Dougherty. They are now North Central Thunderbirds.

Leavenworth High School was in Crawford County on the Ohio River. Their teams were called the Rivermen and also the Wyandottes. Wyandotte Woods is in the area, as is the Harrison–Crawford/Wyandotte complex and the town of Wyandotte.

Leavenworth Wyandottes are now in the Crawford County Wolfpack.

Coach Don Denbo led the 1967 Leavenworth squad to a 19-5 mark and the Tell City Sectional championship, their only one. At Tell City they beat English, 70-36; St.

Ferdinand, 54-47; and Perry Central, 32-30. They are now members of the Crawford County Wolfpack.

Just a few miles upstream from Leavenworth is New Amsterdam, whose teams also had dual names, the Rivermen again and the Indians. Sometimes when they played it was Rivermen against Rivermen, black and gold of Leavenworth against red and white of New Amsterdam, and sometimes it was Indians versus Wyandottes.

Fair Oaks School

Fair Oaks teams were the Cherokees, with blue and white colors. They became DeMotte Indians before becoming Kankakee Valley Kougars. Again, I cannot find evidence of that one good season for either Fair Oaks or New Amsterdam, but I am willing to bet it was there for both.

Fayette Central was a short-lived school, born in 1958, consolidated into Connersville in 1966. Their colors were green and gold and their teams were the Chiefs. Their best record was in 1960, 16-8, for Coach Robert Grove. Butler Township in Miami County fielded the blue-and-white-clad Tomahawks. Neither school ever won a Sectional. Advance teams, as covered earlier, were the Osceoleons, honoring the great Seminole Indian chief. The Battle Ground Tomahawks have also been dealt with previously.

Saratoga High School Warriors are now Winchester Golden Falcons.

Saratoga teams were the Warriors. The Warriors had a terrific 3-year run from 1940-42, winning 57 games while losing only 12. The best mark was 22-3 in 1942 under Coach Ned Bussard, after being led the first 2 years by Coach Lee Hargrave. The 1942 squad won the 1st 2 rounds of the Winchester Sectional, ousting Lynn and Parker, before losing to the home team. They are now consolidated into the Winchester Golden Falcons.

Jefferson Township High School and the South Adams Starfires

Warriors represented Jefferson Township in Adams County as well. In 1933 and 1934 Coach Olen Marsh's Warriors won 36 games while losing only 10. They are now South Adams Starfires.

Wawaka Warriors are now West Noble Chargers.

There were also Warriors at Wawaka in Noble County. The Purple and Gold won 3 Sectionals, in 1925, 1929, and 1948. They also had an 18-5 season for Coach Gene Gibson in 1963. They are now West Noble Chargers.

To get to the wonderfully named town of Clear Spring, you either have to have a pretty good map or a considerable knowledge of Jackson County. One way to do it is to take Corbetts Road west out of Freetown to Kurtz, then east a bit on Indiana 58 to Cooper Road, then south to Clear Spring. Or from Brownstown you can take 150W north to Ewing Road, then west to Indiana 135, north a few hundred yards to 200N, then west to Clear Spring Road and you've got it made. But you get the idea. However you go, folks will tell you it is well worth the effort. The Clear Spring teams were called the Warriors and the Greyhounds. In 1954 they won 19 of 23 games for Coach John Stork, Jr., and in 1961 and 1962 they went 17-6 and 18-6 for Coach Dean Zike. Clear Spring has been consolidated into Brownstown Central, keeping the Indian motif as the Braves.

Clear Spring High School

Walton in Cass County also fielded Warriors. In 1911 their undefeated regular season for Coach Crawford Cox landed Walton in the 1st official state tournament at Indiana University, where they won their first game over Morristown, 31-23, before being ousted by eventual state champion Crawfordsville, 31-12. Charles Hoover coached the 1921 Walton team to a 25-3 season and another berth in the Sweet Sixteen, earned at Purdue with a 24-21 win over Arcadia. At the old Coliseum in Indianapolis the Warriors lost their 1st round game to the Rochester Zebras. In 1928 Walton, coached by Perce Hoffner, finished 18-2, winning a 51-5 contest over Royal Center before losing a heartbreaker, 20-19, to the home team in the Logansport Sectional.

Before becoming Cass Kings, the Warriors were Washington Township Hatchets.

New Winchester's Warriors were in Hendricks County, their uniforms were red and white, and their lone Sectional crown came at Danville in 1939, where the Amos Shelton-coached team rather easily defeated Avon, Pittsboro, and Clayton. At the Anderson Regional the Warriors ousted Southport, 34-32, before losing the final game to the host Indians, 40-31.

The Westport also called Maumee Township Warriors, were consolidated into Sand Creek, becoming Indians, before becoming Greensburg Pirates. Westport did win a Sectional in 1915 for Coach O. W. Holmes. At Seymour they defeated Austin, 39-19; Crothersville, 54-29; and Hope, 36-20, to qualify for the state finals at Indiana University. In Bloomington the Warriors lost their 1st game to Bluffton, 28-18. The Sand Creek Indians had a 17-5 season for Coach Dave Porter in 1957 and a nice string for him from 1959 through 1962 of 16-7, 16-6, 15-7, and 19-2: 66 wins and 22 losses over those 4 years for the blue-and-white-uniformed

Westport High School

Sand Creek Indians. Their lone Sectional title came in 1946 for Coach Ray Hern.

The Zenas Warriors wore purple and gold. They were consolidated into Vernon,

Pulaski School

becoming Blue Devils in 1948 before eventually becoming Jennings County Panthers. Other Warriors at one time were in Pulaski (also called the Yellow Jackets). Neither of these schools ever won a Sectional title. Pulaski's colors were blue and gold, and they became Star City Stars before becoming Warriors once again at Winamac.

Woodburn Warriors were in Allen County, tucked up against the Ohio line, due east of Ft. Wayne. Coach Scott Smith's 1941 squad won 21 games, losing just 4, but were eliminated from the tough Ft. Wayne Sectional in the 2nd round by North Side. They are now a part of Woodlan (yes, that is the correct spelling) High School and are thus still the Warriors. Woodburn itself is now an elementary school, and the Warriors there are somewhat milder than they may have been before.

The Woodburn School and the Woodburn and Woodlan Warriors

Alquina High School teams were known as the Blue Arrows. They had a nice season in 1958, winning 17 and losing 6 for Coach Drake Kellas, and another 2 years later, with Gordon Ricketts coaching, the Blue Arrows achieved a 16-7 mark. They are now Connersville Spartans.

Alquina High School and the Connersville Spartan

In Monroe County the Unionville teams played as Arrows. The Unionville Arrows won the Bloomington Sectional in 1966 with a 26-2 record, coached by Ed Ellett. To win the Sectional, Unionville defeated Morgantown, 80-67; Eminence, 94-69; and the host Panthers, 69-68, in a thriller. At the Terre Haute Regional, the Arrows lost to Cloverdale, 70-62, which was certainly no disgrace, as the Clovers reached the Final Four in Indianapolis. Earlier Uniontown had completed an 18-5 record in 1942 for Coach Bart Benedetti and a fine 20-3 season in 1955 for Ed Scheinbein. They were consolidated into Bloomington North, becoming Cougars in 1973.

 *Unionville Arrows*

The Leiters Ford teams in Aubbeenaubbee Township of Fulton County were called the Braves (and also the Tigers), and they were coached for 16 seasons by John Nelson. Nelson's best teams were from 1957-59, when his Braves teams won 49 games while losing only 15, going 18-4 in the last year of that string. His 1962 squad also had a strong 18-6 mark. Leiters Ford is now consolidated into Culver, the Cavaliers.

Leiters Ford High School Braves are now Culver Cavaliers.

The Monticello teams were known as the Tioga Indians. As early as 1911 the Red and White had a 17-6 season, followed by a 15-3 mark 2 years later, but they did not go to the state finals either year, perhaps choosing not to enter the tournament. In 1932 Frank Stafford coached Monticello to an 18-7 record, but their best record came in 1938, when the Alva Staggs-led Tioga Indians won an outstanding 27 games, dropping just 2. They won the Monon Sectional by beating Brookston, 26-19; Reynolds, 34-27; Idaville, 37-19; and Morton, 33-29. That 2nd loss came in the 1st round of the Logansport Regional to Royal Center, 23-20, in overtime. Monticello won 12 Sectionals and the 1955 and 1957 Logansport Regionals. In the Semi-state in each of those years they drew Lafayette Jefferson, losing both times in the 1st round of those 2 Sweet Sixteen experiences. They are still Indians as part of Twin Lakes.

In Grant County the Sweetser teams were called the Braves, although for a period they may also simply have been the "Sweetsers" (which, when you think about it, is not at all bad). Sweetser's best season came in 1931 for Coach Myrle Rife, when they won 20 games, losing 7. Twelve years later, with J. B. Stephens coaching, the Braves won 15 and lost only 3. Hayes Taylor coached the 1957 through 1959 teams to a fine 3-year mark of 47 wins and 15 losses. Sweetser is now a part of Oak Hill, the Golden Eagles.

One of Indiana's finest all-time coaches, and an equally fine man, Jack Keefer, coached his very first victory while at Oak Hill. Since then he has been the only head boys basketball coach at Lawrence North High School, winning 4 state championships, including 3 in a row from 2004–06. On November 21, 2007, Keefer's Wildcats won his 700th game, placing him 11th on the list of all-time winningest Indiana high school coaches. . . and he has many more wins ahead in this career distinguished not just by victories but equally by the life lessons he has taught to so many young men and the quality of his own life that has been an example for them to follow.

The Oak Hill Golden Eagle

So, there you have it—the Indians as represented by our now-consolidated schools as well as those from our present schools. I am convinced that none of the schools in Indiana, past or present, has meant anything other than respect for the culture of those persons they have chosen to honor by their selection of a mascot for the teams they love.

Chapter 17

The Old Country:
We Remember Our Roots

Location has been an important component of not only the names of the towns selected by the early settlers, but of the names of the teams that represented the high schools in those towns. Many early Hoosiers came to our state from various parts of Europe. Lets start with Switzerland.

The city of Luzern, or Lucerne, Switzerland, is located on a beautiful glacier-fed lake, often referred to as Lake Luzern but also possessing a much longer German name which translates to the "Lake of the 4 forest cantons" since all 4 border on the lake. The nation of Switzerland came into being with the declaration of freedom that was signed on a meadow bordering the lake in 1291.

Luzern is a smallish city of great charm and history. It is located on both sides of the largest river draining the lake and has many medieval buildings, walls, gates, belfries, and houses of worship. There are 7 bridges over the river, 2 of wood, 1 of which is covered and is a great tourist attraction. In the winter you can buy roasted chestnuts from vendors on the bridge and watch the skaters on the frozen river below. Another of Luzern's major attractions is the magnificent sculpture near the glacier gardens called "The Lion of Lucerne." This colossal work was created out of the living rock by Bertel Thorvaldson in the early 19th century to commemorate the Swiss guards who died in defense of the Tuilleries in 1792.

Many Swiss citizens migrated to Indiana. Although the topography of their new land was not at all like that of the towering Alps they had come from, the farming was similar and they settled in quite nicely. Naturally they remembered their homeland and commemorated it in several ways.

The town of Lucerne is in Cass County and the teams that represented their town, were known as the Lions. They are now part of Pioneer High School, the Panthers.

Vevay is located in far southeastern Indiana, bordering the Ohio River. Founded in 1802 by Swiss settlers who cultivated grapes, produced wine, and established the first commercial winery in the country, Vevay is the seat of Switzerland County. The Vevay High School teams, perhaps with a recollection of the faithful Swiss guards, who are also known by any visitor to the Vatican as the protectors of the Pope, were known as the Warriors. The Warriors won 6 Sectionals between 1927 and 1958. Vevay is now consolidated into Switzerland County High School, the Pacers.

The Lion of Lucerne and Lucerne High School

(Switzerland County is also covered in What We Learned at the book's end)

Berne is the capitol of Switzerland and is also the name of one of the 4 forest cantons. The symbol of the city and canton of Berne is the bear. The town of Berne, Indiana, in Adams County near the Ohio line also chose the bear as the mascot of their high school. They are now part of South Adams High School, the Starfires. When Berne had its own school they enjoyed several years of great success. There was the undefeated regular season of 1926 finishing at 21-1 for Coach Jerome Dilts, with the only loss coming to Ft. Wayne Central in the Regional tournament; there were the years 1935-36 with 48 wins and just 7 losses for Judson Eme; and the great 4-year stretch from 1960-63 when the Bears won 87 games while losing only 18 under William Anderson in 1960 and Bruce Smith the next 3 years.

The Bears have cut down the nets at 11 Sectionals and 3 Regionals. They have twice made it to the Elite Eight: in 1935 the Bears defeated Roachdale in the 1st round of the Sweet Sixteen at Butler Fieldhouse and then lost to Shelbyville. In 1961 they defeated Elkhart before being ousted by eventual State Champion Kokomo.

Vevay High School, the famed Swiss Guard, and the Switzerland County Pacers

Two Berne Bears are enshrined in the Indiana Basketball Hall of Fame: Jerome Steiner and Bob Dro, and Hall of Famer Bob Dille coached there for a time.

Jerome Steiner

4-yr player at Berne...led team to sectional and regional titles as junior in '35...ousted from second round of state tourney by Shelbyville...All-State that year...a 3-yr starter at Butler...graduated as school's all-time leading scorer...3 straight Indiana Collegiate Conf. championships... as senior, named to Madison Square Garden's All-America team...also recognized on AP's All-America list...All-Western, all-conference and All-State...coached 2 yrs at Ladoga. Played for Kautskys and Pistons. He later refereed in the Big Ten.

Bob Dro

A 4-year athlete at tiny Berne High School ... led his team to state tourney as a sophomore in 1935 ... undefeated team the next year ... 2 more sectional titles ... a 3-year starter at Indiana University ... Hoosiers lost only 9 games in that span ... in '40, won first NCAA championship ... second-team all-Big 10 that season ... all-Big 10 as a senior ... Look All-American ... a 3-year standout for IU baseball team ... played every position but pitcher ... signed pro baseball contract with Brooklyn Dodgers organization ... injury ended his baseball career, and also hampered his brief pro basketball career ... after World War II, he coached at Pendleton and Bluffton ... named assistant athletic director at IU in '57 ... in '73, became associate athletic director, then director of community relations.

Geneva, Switzerland, is a beautiful and historic city on the southern shore of Lac Leman, often incorrectly referred to as Lake Geneva, We also have a Geneva in Adams County. Prior to consolidation into South Adams High School, the Geneva teams were the Cardinals. Although the Cardinals never captured a Sectional title, they did enjoy some memorable seasons. In 1937 Geneva won 19 of 23 games for Coach John Bauman and Harold Schultz led the Cardinals to consecutive 18-4 records in 1953 and 1954.

The Berne Bear, the South Adams Starfire, and the Geneva Cardinal

Tell City is on the banks of the Ohio and is named, of course, for the famed Swiss archer who shot an apple off of his son's head. The Tell City teams are the Marksmen. My wife and I visited Tell City and had an excellent lunch—the freshly squeezed lemonade and southern fried chicken were just right—in a charming restaurant called Capers located in a 19th-century, high-ceilinged building right across main street from the City Hall. From our table we could see the statue of William Tell with his crossbow in hand and his son at his side which is similar to the one in Altdorf, Switzerland. When we were in Altdorf on the banks of Lake Luzerne, one sunny but chilly December day, we enjoyed hot chocolate in a delightful little inn on their square with a view of that very statue. Regrettably, we parked in the wrong place and received a 30-franc ticket, on Christmas Eve, no less!

Tell City was founded by Swiss settlers from the canton of Uri where Altdorf is the principal town. Every August they celebrate a Schweizerfest complete with plenty of good beer and good food. Several years ago a delegation from Tell City visited Altdorf, and an exchange of city flags was made, according to the pleasant Treasurer's Clerk in the City Hall who told me she had been on that trip and enjoyed it immensely. The athletic contests at Tell City High often find the pep band playing the William Tell Overture to get the teams and fans fired up for their beloved cream-and-crimson Marksmen.

The Tell City Marksman

Although Tell City teams have won 34 Sectionals and 5 Regionals, the Marksmen have made it to the state finals only once, but what a memorable finals it was! The year was 1961. Tell City lost to Indianapolis Manual's Redskins in the first game setting up that thrilling overtime Kokomo vs. Indianapolis Manual final game. This alone does not begin to do justice to the illustrious history of Tell City basketball. In 1924 C. N. Dixon's Marksmen had an undefeated regular season. They won their own Sectional and suffered their lone defeat against Sullivan, 22-17 in the Regional. Again in 1950 with Ivan Hollen coaching Tell City went through the regular season undefeated. Again, they won their Sectional. In the Regional that year they beat Princeton, 61-45, before losing to Evansville Bosse, 52-46. From 1960 through 1962 Orlando "Gunner" Wyman's Marksmen teams won 81 games and lost 19, their best record being 1962's 22-2. That team also won the Tell City Sectional before dropping a close one, 67-64, to Castle in the Evansville Regional. In 1973, Bob Lochmueller's team finished 25-2. After winning the Boonville Sectional they defeated Bosse in a pulse-pounding overtime game, 69-66 and Princeton, 75-66, to gain entry into the Evansville Semi-state. In their 1st game there they upended Terre Haute South, 90-71. In the Finals they lost a heartbreaking 63-62 decision to the New Albany Bulldogs. How did New Albany do the next week in Indianapolis? They won it all. The Marksmen were within 1 point, 1 single point, half a basket, from the state championship. The Lady Marksmen have won 3 Sectional titles and 1 Regional crown, in 1977. Hall of Famers Tommy Kron and Steve Lochmueller are both Tell City Marksmen.

Tommy Kron
Star of Tell City's only final 4 team in 1961 . . . played for Hall of Famer Gunner Wyman . . . All-Conference and All-State . . . All-Star Team 1962 . . . 3-year starter for Kentucky . . . senior year was NCAA tournament runnerup . . . played professionally for St. Louis Hawk (NBA) 1966-67, Seattle Supersonics (NBA) 1967-69 and Kentucky Colonels (ABA) 1969-70

Steve Lochmueller
3-year starter at Tell City for his father Hall of Famer Bob Lochmueller. Records at Tell City include points scored single season 634, career scoring 1,333, rebounds single season 442, career rebounds 927. Team captain and MVP junior and senior years. At the University of Kentucky, won free throw award in 1973. Awarded Outstanding College Athletes of America award. Team in SEC championship 1972-1973 and NCAA Regional finals 1972-73. Member of 1996 Silver Anniversary Team.

Several towns had perhaps a somewhat more tenuous connection with the old country than those above, yet picked team names that followed through very nicely with their town names. Cadiz, for example, in Henry County called their teams the Spaniards. The Spaniards had a 14-6 season for Coach Leon Strange in 1966. Cadiz is now a part of Shenandoah High School, the Raiders.

Cadiz School and the Coat of Arms of Cadiz, Spain, and the Shenandoah High School Crest

Russiaville was almost totally destroyed by the horrendous Palm Sunday 1965 tornado. It has since bounced back, but the high school has been consolidated into Twin Lakes in Monticello. When Russiaville High School was still open their teams were the Cossacks. Oddly, the town name is neither derived from, nor indicative of people coming from Russia. It is a corruption of the French pronunciation of Richardville, a Miami/white leader whose settlement was there. We'll have more to say about Cossacks later.

   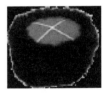

Twin Lakes Indians, the Russiaville School by Mary Ellis, and a Cossack Hat

In a sad reminder of the Russiaville storm, another devastating tornado hit the town of Moscow in early June of 2008. The town was virtually destroyed and the third longest covered bridge in Indiana was demolished. The bridge, first constructed in 1886 over the Big Flatrock River, spanned over 330 feet, was 15 feet wide and 13½ feet to the inside peak of the roof. The relevance of this to basketball is clear from the following report written by Bill McCleery and published in the June 7, 2008. *Indianapolis Star:*

> *Moscow's history and that of the Emmet L. Kennedy covered bridge are inextricably linked, said a reference librarian at Rush County Public Library.*

The Moscow High School…had no basketball team for several years said librarian Ginny Holdman. After World War I a group of male students at the school formed a team they called the River Rats. The team had no gym, no lockers and no coach. The students often held practices outdoors, she said, but when the weather was inclement they ran drills inside the bridge—moving aside if a vehicle came along needing to cross.

As the IHSAA and other records I have seen could not identify a team name for the Green and Gold Moscow High School squads I think, for now at least, River Rats will do very nicely. They are now Rushville Lions and it is hoped that the bridge will be rebuilt to its original specifications so that the annual Moscow Covered Bridge Festival may remain a fixture of southeastern Indiana.

In Parke County (home also of more covered bridges than any other county in the country) there is the historic river town of Montezuma. (For those of you reading this closely, let me assure you that I am aware that Montezuma was a person, an Aztec

The Moscow Covered Bridge

chief who met his match when Hernan Cortez and his Conquistadores appeared on the scene, and not a place. I include this here because it just seems to fit nicely.)

The Montezuma High School teams were known as the Aztecs. I have wondered if when after losing a game to an opponent and coming back to win one the 2nd time they played, they would refer to that as Montezuma's revenge. I apologize in advance for that one. The Aztecs have won 4 Sectionals In 1954 they defeated Mecca, 67-57. to win the Clinton Sectional, and defeated Fillmore 55-52 and New Ross, 70-61, to win the Greencatle Regional. In the Indianapolis Semi-state the Aztecs lost to the Milan Indians, 44-34, in Milan's famous year of glory. Montezuma is now a part of Riverton Parke High School.

Montezuma High School
where the Aztecs ruled

Also a part of Riverton Parke is the town of Mecca where the teams were called the Arabs. Originally called Maidstone, the name was changed after a settlement of Syrian Moslems was begun on the white sands and clay banks of the Big Raccoon. When groups of Arabians traveled to the larger town for provisions or entertainment, the trips became known as pilgrimages to Mecca.

Aztecs and Arabs are now Panthers

The town of Scotland in Greene County fielded the Scotties; Rome City teams in Noble County were the Romans as were the Rome teams down south in Perry County. The Trojans (also called the Panthers) represented the town of Troy in Spencer County.

Regrettably, none of these schools ever got that elusive Sectional title. Scotland did put together a nice 3-year string for Hall of Fame coach Knofel Fortner beginning in 1938, winning 45 games while losing 19 and the Rome City

Houck photo from exhibit courtesy IBHOF.

Romans finished 17-6 for coach Gene Raucht in 1961. Scotland is now consolidated into Bloomfield, Rome City into East Noble, Troy into Tell City, and Rome into Cannelton.

The Bloomfield Cardinals, the East Noble Knights, and the Cannelton Bulldogs

Holland is not only a country in northwestern Europe, it is also a town in DuBois County. Before joining Huntingburg to create Southridge, Holland teams were the Dutchmen. The Dutchmen enjoyed many highly successful seasons of basketball. From 1932-34 they won 53 games while losing only 11 for Coach Leander Smith; in 1938 and 39 they went 36-5 with Virl Spradlin at the helm; they were 31-7 for 1945 and 46 with David Eilert coaching, 21-5 in 1953, and 39-6 for 1955 and 56; in 1958 and 59 they won 36 and lost 9. Lowell McGlothlin coached all of those 50s teams. Another impressive stretch covered the 6 years from 1966 to 1971, which saw the Dutchmen win 112 games while only losing 25, the first 4 years under George Neel, the last 2 under Ray Roesner. This included their undefeated regular season of 1968 when they went 24-1, a pretty darn good mark in any league. After capturing the Huntingburg Sectional with wins over Jasper, 67-56, the host Lions, 79-50, and St. Ferdinand, 57-53, the Dutchmen moved on to the Regional where they beat an undefeated Oolitic team, 61-59, before losing to Jeffersonville by the same margin, 72-70. They won Sectional titles in 1953, 1967 and 1968. Two of those Dutchmen went on to further glory in college and the NBA. They are Gene Tormohlen, class of 1955 and Don Buse, class of 1968.

Holland High School and sign; Houck photo from exhibit courtesy IBHOF

Gene Tormohlen
Led tiny Holland High School to its first sectional championship in 1953, his sophomore year...a 3-year starter...'Bumps' moved on to University of Tennessee, where he was named all-Southeastern Conference as junior and senior...All-American as a senior...nation's second-leading rebounder...played professionally 9 seasons, the last 6 with the NBA's St. Louis Hawks...spend 12 years as NBA assistant coach and 4 years as director of college scouting for the Los Angeles Lakers.

Don Buse
Played 11 years in the ABA and the NBA...Asst Varsity coach at Southridge High School...Don led Holland High School to an undefeated season, averaging 22.5 points and 14 rebounds his senior year. He was chosen an Indiana All-Star and then went on to play for Hall of Famer Arad McCutchan at Evansville College. Led NBA in assists and steals in 1977. When named to the 1993 Silver Anniversary Team Don was living in Huntingburg and was assistant varsity coach at Southridge High School.

One of the provinces of Holland in the northwestern part of the country on the Wadden Sea is Friesland. In Knox County that became Freelandville represented by the Fighting Dutchmen. Some of those Dutchmen really did fly. Eli Myers' 1922 squad won 22 games while losing 7, and Leo Frudenberg's 1928 and 1929 teams went 20-5 and 18-6. J. G. Parker led the Royal Blue and White to a 21-6 finish in 1932; his successor Marion Small turned in a 21-4 mark the next year. In 1951 with Tom Leaman coaching the Dutchmen finished 21-5. The Fighting Dutchmen won the Vincennes Sectional in 1941, to the great chagrin of Alice fans who had become accustomed to winning that themselves. Freelandville's 35-34 victory over the host team in the 1st round snapped Lincoln's consecutive Sectional championship streak of 20 years. At the Washington Sectional Freelandville defeated the Winslow Eskimos, 47-45, before being sent home by the Hatchets, 54-43. Hugh Schaefer tells it this way in the Indiana Basketball History Society's newsletter "Box Score."

> When the (Sectional) draw was released, there was no joy in Freelandville, a northern Knox county town of about 600 people. The "Dutch" had drawn the host Vincennes Lincoln Alices. It was no small task for any team to beat Vincennes, who had not lost a sectional title since 1920. The Alices had won 76 sectional games in a row, and had never lost a sectional tourney game on their Coliseum floor. To make the odds even worse for Freelandville, Vincennes had never lost their first game in sectional play.
>
> On Friday afternoon, February 28th, 1941, the "Dutch" and the "Alices" played a whale of a ballgame. The team from Widner Township led at all of the first three quarter stops, though they held only a one point, 26-25, lead heading into the final quarter. Jimmy Ritterskamp scored seven of the "Dutch's" nine fourth quarter point as the upset to end all upsets took place. Vincennes had been beaten, 35-34. Ritterskamp ended the game with 13 points and Ronald Brown added 10 for the Dutchmen. It was the first time ever a school

from Knox county had defeated the Alices in sectional play. The tourney was not over, but the Freelandville fans were totally overjoyed. The "Dutch" had little time to rest or to enjoy their huge victory, as that same Friday night they had to return to the hardwood to play Sandborn. This game turned out to be much easier for Freelandville, as they sent Sandborn home on the short end of a 46-28 score. The next game for the "Dutch" was a date with Bruceville on Saturday afternoon. The Hilltoppers had taken two out of three contests with Freelandville, but in the game that really counted, Freelandville led by four points after three quarters, and held on to win, 23-17. The win over Bruceville advanced the "Dutch" to the championship game of the sectional, where they would be opposed by the Monroe City Bluejeans. These two teams had not met during the regular season. Freelandville led by only one point, 20-19, at half-time, but limited the Bluejeans to just eight second-half points, and won going away, 53-27, for their first and only sectional title.

After being awarded the tourney basketball and cutting down the nets, the "Dutch" returned home to a wild celebration. The team was met about two miles outside of town by the township's only fire truck, and they rode in to the center of Freelandville, where a huge bonfire burned at the intersection of two state highways.

Next up for the "Dutch" was the Washington regional, where Freelandville, the smallest school of the quartet, would take on the Winslow Eskimos in the second afternoon game. Winslow, from Pike county, had defeated traditional powers Jasper and Huntingburg in the Jasper sectional, and had a 20-3 record going into their game with Freelandville. After three quarters, things looked bad for Freelandville. They trailed by eight points, 38-30, and still trailed by that margin early in the fourth before reeling off 14 straight points, and pulled off yet another upset, 47-45. That win put the "Dutch" in the championship game of the regional, against the host and fourth-ranked Washington Hatchets. The team from Freelandville shocked the packed gym, leading 12-10 after one quarter, and midway through the third it was just a one point game. Washington pulled away late, and put an end to the Freelandville dream, 54-43. The Hatchets would go on to claim the state title.

The "Fighting Dutchmen" were coached by a Freelandville High School graduate, Oscar Finke, who would later win a regional title while coaching at Mooresville.

They are now a proud part of the North Knox Warriors.

Freelandville High School and the Friesland Flag

In DuBois County near the White River is the town of Ireland. Certainly one of the most important facets of Irish agriculture was the potato. The Potato Famine was the cause of many an Irishman's migration to America. This historical event is recognized in the team name chosen by Ireland High School: they were the Spuds. The Spuds won their only Sectional in 1963 at Huntingburg, beating Winslow, 62-46, the home team 71-55, and Springs Valley, 20-19. At the Regional, Coach Pete Gill's team again won, besting Sullivan 75-63 and the powerful Washington Hatchets, 39-37. They were eliminated by Bosse at the Evansville Semi-state, finishing their historic season 20-6. The Ireland Historical Society has these comments about their high school:

> *During Ireland High School's 61 years of existence (1909-1970), there were approximately 742 graduates. For the least graduates there were 2 in 1913 to a high of 64 graduates in 1966. Around 1092 attended Ireland at one time or another.*

Ireland is now a part of Jasper High School. Jasper is itself a town with a distinctive German heritage. Their sister city is Pfafenweiler in Baden-Wurtemburg.

Every August Jasper has a 4-day Strassenfest (Street Festival) which is well attended by locals, other Americans, and many Germans as well. Today's Jasper High School teams are indeed the Wildcats, but that was not always the case. Originally they were called the Giants, and many believe that choice was in honor of John McGraw the Cooperstown Hall of Fame manager of many successful New York National League teams. Jasper has always had a love of baseball as well as basketball, and the Indiana Baseball Hall of Fame is located there. Former St. Louis Cardinal third baseman Scott Rolen is from Jasper.

The Wildcats won the state championship in 1949. This town is one answer to the trivia question: "Who won the title with the worst record?" Their 9 losses that year ties Anderson's 1935 titlists' record; that loss record was equaled by Lafayette Central Catholic's 2003 Class A Basketball champions. Jasper residents are also pleased with their state championship. After all, from 1931 until 1935 they won over 20 games each year, including the 1934 record of 29-2, for a total of 112 wins, 23 losses, and zero state titles! An even more impressive run without a state championship came just prior to the magic year when, between 1942 and 1947 Jasper teams won 131 games and only lost 28 . . . again, without a state championship. So perhaps it was poetic justice that everything came together at just the right time for that 1949 team. Anyway, in 1960

Ireland High School in 1915

and 1961 the Wildcats again were on a tear, winning 48 and losing just 9. Overall, the Jasper teams have amassed 31 Sectional crowns and 14 Regionals.

Seven miles south of Jasper is another DuBois County city with a considerable German heritage: Huntingburg. Huntingburg also has a baseball as well as a basketball heritage: their stadium was chosen for the movie *A League of Their Own* with Tom Hanks in 1992. However, it is basketball where the rivalry between these 2 fine schools has been most pronounced. From the earlier days of the 20th century they have gone after each other with the prize being the Little Brown Jug . . . as well as bragging rights.

The Huntingburg teams were originally called the Happy Hunters; there are those who claim that this was changed to Lions because Lions would have a better shot at beating Giants than would Happy Hunters. They also believe that Giants gave way to Wildcats to counteract the Huntingburg move, Wildcats being faster than Lions and speed being an important factor in winning basketball games. Maybe so. At any rate, Huntingburg is now consolidated along with Holland into Southridge, with their teams becoming the Raiders. Although in different conferences, Jasper and Southridge still go after each other on the court and in the field with great gusto. But no state titles. I

The Jasper Wildcats

am sure they would trade a lofty record for that State Championship plaque any day.

Those Happy Hunters did have many a fine year of their own. From 1922 through 1925, the 1st 2 years for Coach Harry Apostle and the last for Coach Marlin McCoy, they won 71 games while dropping only 20. Scott Ray-coached teams went 20-4 and 20-3 in 1936 and 1937 before Paul Caldwell stepped in and led the Hunters to 23-2, 22-2, and 18-8 marks the next 3 years. In 1949 Jim Beers coached the team to a 19-4 mark. Howard Sharp-led teams turned in a 19-4 record in 1953, 18-2 in 1958, and 15-5 the next year. All told they have won 9 Sectionals, and the 1937 Regional and Semi-state titles, losing the state

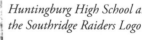

Huntingburg High School and the Southridge Raiders Logo

championship final game to the Anderson Indians, 33-23.

Another town in the area with a considerable Germanic flavor is Ferdinand, named for an Archduke of Austria. Ferdinand presents a striking view from afar as the town is approached from any direction. The area is quite flat except for a hill in Ferdinand on which are perched several impressive structures. There are church spires, the Monastery of the Immaculate Conception and the Monastery of the Sisters of St. Benedict of Ferdinand. Prior to their consolidation into Forest Park, the Ferdinand (sometimes, according to Bill May, also called St. Ferdinand) teams were the Crusaders. They are now the Forest Park Rangers and consolidation has been a good thing for this school, as has been class basketball. From 1992 through 1994 the Rangers were 58 and 11; in 2000 they won 20 while losing only 2. In 2003 and 2004 they were state Class 2A Runners-up with 23-5 and 23-2 records. They won the State Class 2A Championship in 2005 with a record of 23-4 and the next year went back-to-back with 25 wins and 3 losses.

Ferdinand High School, the Ferdinand Flag, and the Forest Park Ranger

Coach Tom Burch's charges won 113 games and lost just 17 from 2003-2007. Marty Niehaus' Lady Rangers were also state Class 2A runner-up, with a 22-5 mark in 2000, followed by an undefeated regular season 23-1 the next year.

Nearby is the town of Birdseye, named some say for the Reverend Benjamin T. "Bird" Goodman (one source says Johnson) who selected the site for the town saying "this spot suits Bird's eye." Maybe so. At any rate, the Birdseye teams were the Yellow Jackets and they joined Ferdinand to create Forest Park.

The Birdseye Yellow Jacket and Birdseye team

Chapter 18

Faraway Places:
With Strange Sounding Names Like Avilla, New Alsace, and Tangiers

Several other Indiana towns not covered elsewhere have drawn upon far away places for their names. Most of these, however, have not carried through their town name theme with their team name. Let's start with schools that are still in existence.

The ancient city of Alexandria, Egypt, is on the western part of the Nile Delta where the great river empties into the Mediterranean Sea. It was home to the most comprehensive library of its time. In Indiana Alexandria is on Route 9, just north of Anderson in Madison County, no river in sight. The Alexandria High School teams are the Tigers, and at least as early as 1922, they were fielding basketball teams. However, as the Alexandria Historical Society proudly relates it, they finally won it all in

> *1998—Class basketball comes to town and brings with it the First State Title in any sport. The sectional and regional were at home with the Tigers winning in sectional play over Frankton and Tipton then they beat Bluffton for the regional title. At the Fort Wayne semi-state the Tigers defeated Bremen in the afternoon round to move on to the night game to defeat Northwestern for the title. Alex beat Southwestern at the RCA Dome for the state Championship.*

An early Alexandria High School and the Alexandria Tiger

The 1925 Alexandria High School team

That champion-ship year the Tigers finished with a 20-7 record and were coached by Garth Cone, who held that job for 29 years from 1977 through 2005. His 1978 team won 18 of 21 games, his 1989 team went 21-4, and his 1995 and 1996 teams were 20-6 and 21-3. Earlier Julius Wysong coached the Tigers to a 21-3 mark in 1924. Henry Omer was the coach in 1932 when the team won 23 and lost 4. His teams won the school's first 2 Sectional titles. Max Bell's 1953 squad was 22-2, while Orvis Burdsall led the 1963 Tigers to a 21-4 finish. In 1995 the Tigers won 20 and lost 6, followed the next year by a 21-3 mark. In 1998 they won 20 and lost 8. In total they have won 12 Sectionals and 3 Regionals as well as that 1998 Class 2A State Championship when they defeated the Southwestern (Hanover) Wildcats 57-43.

The Alexandria Lady Tigers have won 4 Sectionals and the 2000 3A Regional crown when they finished with a 15-4 mark. They were coached by Jon Howell for 22 seasons from 1984 until 2005. In 1986 they finished 20-1, but it was the 3-year stretch beginning in 2001 that was most impressive: 21-2, 25-1, and 22-1, or a 68-4 3-year mark, though with nothing more than a single Sectional title to show for it during those 3 years. Who won the state championships then? Well, in 1986 it was Dave Riley's undefeated 29-0 Ft. Wayne Northrop Lady Bruins; in 2001 it was the Lady Irish of Indianapolis Cathedral, 29-1; in 2002 it was the Lady Knights (or is it simply the Ladies?) of Ft. Wayne Bishop Luers, 21-5; and in 2003 it was the Beech Grove Lady Hornets, led by Miss Basketball Katie Gearlds, 28-1. There is some very tough competition out there in Indiana girls high school basketball, in case you hadn't noticed.

Besides being a city in Chile, Valparaiso is also a city in Porter County. With an eye more toward their northern Indiana location perhaps than their namesake in South America, the Valparaiso High School teams are the Vikings. Indiana basketball has seen Valparaiso's Vikings create a rich history on the hardwood. The Vikings have amassed 49 Sectional crowns, 9 Regional wins and the 1994 Lafayette Jefferson Semi-state crown.

The tradition of winning teams goes a long way back. Homer Jesse's 1916 Vikings won 21 of 23 games, grabbing the Gary Sectional by a 25-15 final game score over Froebel. This qualified them for the state finals at Bloomington, where they defeated Cicero, 34-23, before being sent home by Vincennes, 22-16. From 1925 through 1935, the Vikings won Sectional titles every year, with the high-water mark occurring in 1933 as Ralph Powell's team won 25 of 28 games, including the Gary Regional, 28-26, over Brook. Again in the state finals, at Indianapolis this time, the Vikings first beat Connersville. 40-32, before losing a 3-pointer to Martinsville.

And how did the Artesians do? They simply won it all, sending Greencastle home by the identical 3-point margin. Twenty-win seasons also came in 1939, 20-7 for Powell again, and in 1952 for Bob Dille, 20-5. Virgil Sweet coached Valpo from 1955–74, turning in 20-win seasons in 1958, 20-5; 1965, 20-4; and 1966, 20-5. His teams won 14 Sectionals—11 in a row—and 2 more Regionals. Skip Collins' teams won 23 games and lost 3 in both 1980 and 1981; his 1984 team won 21 of 25 games and his 1989 team won 20 of 24 games. During his tenure 10 more Sectional nets—9 in a row—and 3 more Regional nets were cut down. Bob Punter held the coaching job from 1990 through 2007. In 1994 his Vikings won their only Semi-state before losing the state championship, in one of the most dramatic and exciting final games ever played, to South Bend Clay at Conseco Fieldhouse, 93-88, in overtime, absorbing their only loss in a 29-game season. Valpo's Bryce Drew was named 1994 Indiana Mr. Basketball. Punter's teams from 2004 through 2007 also won 88 victories and lost only 12, with Scott Martin and Robbie Hummel leading the way.

The Valparaiso Viking

The Lady Vikings were coached by Dale Ciciora in 1982 when the team won 21 games and lost 6, and in 1985 and 1986, when they had 18-3 and 18-4 finishes. Dave Kenning's 1989 Lady Viking team won 22 of 24 games, as did the next year's team, coached by Greg Kirby. Kirby's teams won 24 and 26 games the next 2 seasons, again losing only 2 each season. That's a 4-year record of 94 wins and 8 losses for the Lady Vikes in the class of 1992. Kirby's squads continued to burn the opposition for the rest of the decade, with another 4-year, 20-game streak ending in 1998, those graduates having achieved 87 wins and only 12 losses. In 1999 the team won 18 games (only) while losing 3, but 2000 saw a 25-2 mark posted for the Kelly Green and White. In their 33 seasons under the aegis of the IHSAA, the Lady Vikings have enjoyed 13 20-game-plus win seasons and have collected 20 Sectional, 11 Regional, and 5 Semi-state crowns. In 1982 they finished runner-up to Heritage for the state championship, and in 1996 they again finished runner-up, this time to Center Grove. Finally in 2000 they lost to the undefeated Ben Davis Lady Giants in the 4A state finals by the narrow margin of 56-53, earning their 3rd 2nd-place trophy. Kirby was the coach from 1990 through 2006, during which time his teams won 346 games, lost only 61, and garnered all of the aforementioned tournament titles.

While we're discussing Chile, perhaps we should devote some attention to other Latin American connections in our own town names. Elsewhere we have mentioned the Chili Polar Bears, but there are 3 other Indiana towns named for countries there: Mexico, Peru, and Brazil. In addition to Valparaiso, there are also Indiana towns named for the cities of Tampico, Monterey, Lima, Cuzco, and La Paz.

We'll start with the largest country in South America, Brazil. Brazil High School teams were called the Red Devils, and those Devils had their days. In 1923 Coach Donovan Moffet's team won 19 games while losing 11, but this was followed by 3 successive seasons of 22-7, 22-7, and 21-7. Three years, 65 wins, 21 losses. Glen Adams coached the 1928 Red Devils to a 24-3 mark, and the next year, with Raleigh Phillips at the helm, Brazil won 20 of 24 games. Babe Wheeler was the coach from 1931 until 1955. His 1934 Red Devil team won their own Sectional title, defeating Van Buren, 41-15; Clay City, 34-25; and Gosport, 26-5. At Martinsville they also won the Regional, 35-33 over Bloomington and 23-9 over Linton. In their 1st Sweet Sixteen appearance they were eliminated by Lebanon, 37-31. They won the Bloomington Regional again in 1959, only to be ousted from the Evansville Semi-state by Odon, the same Odon that would lose in double overtime by a single basket to New Albany. New Albany's fate? Also an overtime loss, to Kokomo, the state champion runners-up in Indianapolis. In Brazil's 3rd and last trip to the Sweet Sixteen in 1981, after winning the Terre Haute Regional by defeating South Vigo 66-64 and Cloverdale 58-56 in 2 squeakers, the Red Devils of Jim Buell ran into Vincennes, losing a 65-53 encounter to that year's state champions. Buehl's 1980 Red Devil team won 20 and lost only 2; and his 1983 squad went 20-4. In total Brazil teams captured 37 Sectionals and 4 Regionals before becoming a part of Northview, the Knights, in 1984. The Lady Red Devils, in their brief, 9-season life won 2 Sectionals, both for Dan Ullery, in 1979 and 1980.

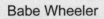

Babe Wheeler
Leading scorer of 1922 state tourney...his Terre Haute Garfield team finished second to the Franklin "Wonder Five"...only 5-10, yet All-State center...3-year starter at Purdue...twice Big 10 champions... team captain and all-conference in '28...coached high school basketball 27 years, winning 17 sectionals...411-236 record...all but 2 of those seasons at Brazil where he served as athletic director... his teams made it to Sweet 16 in '34 and '35...Wabash Valley Champs in 1943 . . . spent 30 years officiating high school and college football games . . . 28 years as a college basketball official and worked 8 years officiating in the National Basketball League.

Brazil High School and the Northview Knight

Peru still does have its high school; their teams are the Tigers, taken from the fact that Peru has been a winter headquarters for circuses for decades. Today, the Peru Circus Center is a museum that captures and preserves the excitement of the Big Top. One of Peru's most famous native sons is the incomparable Cole Porter. Porter, however, was a Yale graduate and wrote the tune "Bulldog, Bulldog, Bow Wow Wow," which drives Eli opponents crazy when the football team is doing well, because several bars of it are played after every first down, fumble recovery, pass interception or score.

I have to chuckle when I think of Cole Porter, who must indeed have loved Yale football, himself a Peru Tiger, facing 4 years in New Haven when their great rival was the Princeton Tiger.

Interestingly, Lima, the capital city of Peru, had its namesake in LaGrange County, and prior to consolidation into Lakeland High School the Lima teams were also the Tigers. The Peru Tigers have won 39 Sectionals and 3 Regionals. Their best records came in 1933, 20-3 for Coach James Loveless; 22-6 for Hall of Famer Pat

The Peru Tiger

Malaska in 1948; and 20-4 for Hall of Famer Bob Macy in 1975, the year his Hall of Fame son, who would soon star at Kentucky, was Indiana's Mr. Basketball. The 4th loss came in the Marion Regional, a hard-fought, 65-64 defeat at the hands of the Huntington Vikings. The 1943 Tigers, coached by Clare Holley, won the school's 1st Regional with wins over Logansport and Monticello. At the Hammond Semi-state they were eliminated by Gary Lew Wallace. The 2nd Regional title was earned at Logansport by Malaka's 1948 team. In a pair of white-knucklers, the Tigers edged the Oracles of Delphi 45-44, and the Berries themselves, 44-43! At the Lafayette Semi-state the drama continued with another squeaker, over South Bend Central, 45-44, before reality set in and Peru lost to Jefferson, 60-53. So did everyone else: Jeff went on to win it all the next week at Butler Fieldhouse, 54-42 over Evansville Central. That 1948 team will not soon be forgotten on the banks of the Wabash in Peru. The 3rd and final Regional title was won by Terry Hewitt's 1998 team, the 3A Bellmont title, 84-74, over Ft. Wayne Harding. In the Muncie Semi-state the Tigers were edged by Plymouth, 78-73.

Kyle Macy

Three-year starter at Peru under his Hall of Fame father, Bob, scored 2,137 points during high school career. . . Mr. Basketball in 1975. . . played freshman year at Purdue. . . during 3-year University of Kentucky career received Pan Am Gold Medal, Academic All-American 1978, All-SEC 1978, 79, 80, Mid-East Regional MVP 1978, Academic All-SEC 1978. . . Leadership Award 3 years, MVP 1979, 1980, SEC Tourney MVP 1979. . . SEC Male Athlete of the Year 1980. . . Sullivan Award, Male Student of the Year 1980. . . All-American 1979-80. . . during his career at University of Kentucky won one National Title, 2 SEC championships and 2 times SEC tourney runner-up. . . played professionally for Phoenix Suns, Chicago Bulls, Indiana Pacers, and in Italy became head coach for Morehead State University in 1997.

The Lady Tigers have won 2 Sectional titles. Their best records were 19-2 in 1995 and 18-3 the next year for Coach Mike Byron.

The Lima Tigers, appropriately garbed in orange and black, won 3 straight Sectionals from 1930 through 1932, coached by Everett Paschen. In the Regionals they were beaten by Kendallville in overtime, by Mentone, and by Auburn, respectively. They also had a 15-win season in 1962, 3 years before becoming consolidated into Lakeland and becoming Lakers. The town itself became Howe.

Cuzco, Indiana, is also named for a city in Peru. No Tigers there, however, only Bearcubs. Now they are with the Jeeps at Northeast DuBois High School.

Lima School

La Paz is the capital of Bolivia, one of the highest capitals in the world. It is also a long way from Scandinavia, but for some reason the LaPaz teams in

Cuzco High School

St. Joseph County were called the Vikings. The Vikings won 5 Sectionals between 1951 and 1958, all coached by Hugh Young. The 1949 Vikings, coached by Bob McConnell, put together an excellent 23-2 season. They are now LaVille Lancers.

Our nearest neighbors to the south also have been honored by the names we have chosen for our towns. Mexico in Miami County fielded the Bulldogs; Tampico in Jackson County the Bearcats; and Monterey in Pulaski County the Flyers. Of the 3, only Monterey ever won a Sectional, that coming when the Flyers cut down the nets at Winamac in 1961, after defeating Walkerton 77-46, San Pierre 62-34, Knox 67-57, and North Judson 51-46. At the Logansport Regional the Flyers upended Brookston before losing to the Berries, a Final Four team that year. John Lebo coached that team to a 22-6 record as well as the 20-3 team in 1960. Tampico's best season was 21-2 for Elmer Robbins in 1933. I have, regrettably, little data on Mexico, but do know that they are now North Miami Warriors. Tampico teams are now Brownstown Braves, and Monterey teams are now Culver Cavaliers.

The Mexico Bulldog and Monterey High School, home of the Flyers

Avila is a striking medieval city in Spain renowned for its impressive, well-preserved walls. Avilla in Indiana is in Noble County, and the blue and white Avilla Panthers won their first Sectional in 1941 when Wayne Strycker's squad finished 20-5. Their second and third came in 1955 and 1956 with another 20-5 mark followed by 23-3, both for Coach Bob Noel. The Panthers are now East Noble Knights.

Talking about Yale reminds me of our own Indiana town of New Haven. Like their collegiate counterparts our New Haven teams are also the Bulldogs, and they have won 4 Sectionals between 1991 and 1996. They also enjoyed 19-4 seasons in 1963 with Norm Ellenberger coaching, in 1965 under Bob Wiant, and again in 1969 with Jerry Mitchel at the helm. The Lady Bulldogs have won 3 Sectional championships themselves.

Avilla High School, home of the Panthers

The New Haven Bulldogs

Manchester is a town in England, renowned in part at least for its excellent soccer team, Manchester United, perennial contender for English and European football (soccer) honors. Manchester, Indiana, teams are the Squires. North Manchester teams prior to consolidating with Manchester were the Trojans, who were definitely factors to be reckoned with in 1924, 1947, and 1950, going 26-2, 18-3, and 19-2 respectively in those years. In the 1924 Sectional North Manchester defeated Lincolnville, 28-13; Lagro, 51-3; Laketon, 44-15 and

Chester, 57-8. In the Ft. Wayne Regional they defeated Kendallville and Marion to qualify for the state tournament in Indianapolis. At the Coliseum they defeated Logansport before losing to Bedford in the quarterfinals. They also won 9 Sectional titles.

The Squires have won 11 Sectionals as well as the 1994 Warsaw Regional. Tom Settler's 1981 and 1982 squads, 21-2 and 21-3, turned in impressive marks. Pete Smith's 1991 team enjoyed

North Manchester High School

an undefeated regular season, 22-1, the only loss being to Witco, 66-59, in the final game of the Columbia City Sectional. Mo Medley's 21-4 1994 team was followed by another spotless pre-tournament mark, 23-1. That year the Squires gained a measure of revenge over Witco, turning the tables on the Wildcats in the championship game of the Columbia City Sectional. They went on to win the Warsaw Regional, defeating Huntington, 72-64, and Plymouth 47-44. The season's sole loss was at the hands of South Bend Clay, 73-62, in the Ft. Wayne Semi-state. How did Clay's Colonials fare the next week in Indianapolis? They were crowned state champions. The 1994 season will resonate with Squire fans for years to come. The Lady Squires have captured 8 Sectional titles of their own as well as the Maconaquah Regional, in 1998, finishing 21-4 that year for Coach Judy Shewman. Beginning in 2006 the Lady Squires were coached by Mike Underwood to a 3-year mark of 60 wins and only 9 losses.

The Manchester Squire, earlier and recent versions

Nancy Alspaugh, principal of Manchester High School, also reports that their original school fight song was the school song for Hickory High in the movie *Hoosiers*.

Stratford-on-Avon is a charming English town filled with half-timber houses and stores. It is the home of William Shakespeare and his wife Anne Hathaway as well as the man for whom our country's first great university is named, John Harvard. No trip to England is complete without a visit to this historic place and a night at the theater seeing *Hamlet, King Lear, MacBeth*, or whatever wonderful play is being performed by a truly outstanding company. We have our own Avon in fast-growing Hendricks County just west of Indianapolis. Their teams are the Orioles, who have won 2 Sectional championships. In 1999 Steve Binkley's squad won 22 of 25 games. The Lady Orioles have also cut down Sectional nets twice, in 1992 and 1993, and put together

The Avon (Fightin') Oriole

197

successive 20-2 seasons for Stan Malless in 1989 and 1990 as well as winning 20 of 23 games for Steven Drabyn in 2007.

Oxford is a fascinating medieval town in west-central England, home of the famous university. It is also a small town in Benton County that produced perhaps the greatest trotter of all time, the legendary Dan Patch. The town was also home of the Oxford Blue Devils, now consolidated into the Benton Central Bison. The Blue Devils had a great year in 1945, making it to the Sweet Sixteen. They won the Fowler Sectional that year by defeating Freeland Park, Pine Township, Earl Park, and the host Bulldogs without being seriously challenged. Things were tighter at the Lafayette Regional, where the Devils ousted Zionsville 38-33 and Frankfort 33-31. They lost to Logansport in the 1st round of the Lafayette Semi-state. Dan Patch would have been proud.

Dan Patch, Oxford High School, and the Oxford Blue Devil

Still on our British theme, there were also Blue Devils wearing blue and gold at Dover High School in Boone County. Now, though I personally might have preferred Bluebirds for Dover because of my familiarity with the haunting tune played so often during World War II, Blue Devils it was. Dover never won a Sectional title, as we have said in a previous section.

Dover High School and the White Cliffs of Dover

The War of the Roses took place between the White Roses of York and the Red Roses of Lancaster. In Indiana we only had one half of that little difference of opinion, but, since we had 2 Lancasters (we actually have 3, but only 2 had their own high schools) does that equal a whole? Perhaps not. At any rate, Lancaster Township in Huntington County, now part of the Huntington North Vikings, once fielded the Lancers. In their first 4 seasons beginning in 1911, the Lancers won 24 games and lost only 3. They had undefeated seasons in 1913, 1916, and 1917, but the first of those years they were 5-0 and the latter 2 they were only 2-0 each year! Although the

Lancers never won a Sectional title, they did have a memorable undefeated season in 1951 for Coach Dale Stroud, finishing 20-1. That lone defeat came in the quarter finals of the Huntington Sectional, following wins over Huntington Catholic and the host Vikings, to Union Township.

Lancaster Township Lancers, school; Lancers Jim Mast pin at IHOF Museum

Lancaster Central's teams in Wells County, now a part of the Norwell Knights, were earlier known as the Bobcats. The Bobcats won 4 Sectionals between 1925 and 1951. That 1925 team finished a fine season 25-2 for Coach Leroy Hedges, winning that 1st Sectional at Decatur by defeating Monroe 25-8, Hartford Township 39-21, and the host Yellow Jackets 25-21. Ft. Wayne Central then ended the Bobcats' season 27-17 in the Regional. William (not Jennings) Bryan's 1949 through 1951 teams won 60 games and lost 10, with a 25-2 mark in the middle season of that streak. The 2nd loss that season was in the Sectional finals to the host Marion Giants after an opening round win over Huntington. Since Marion lost by a single point to State Champion Madison at Indianapolis 2 weeks later, Lancaster Central could look back on the season with nothing but well-deserved pride.

Lancaster Central, home of the Bobcats

We may not have had a York, but we sure did have a Little York in Washington County. Their teams were the Wildcats, and they are now part of Salem High School. We are all familiar with Salem, Massachusetts, Nathaniel Hawthorne's home, locale of the House of Seven Gables and the infamous witch trials. Well, their teams are called the Witches, which I think is pretty valid historically. Our Salem, the Washington County seat with its striking Richardson-style courthouse, fields the Lions. The Lions have 11 Sectional and 3 Regional championships in their trophy case. In 1930 Paul Schanlaub's Lions won the Bedford Regional by conquering the host Stonecutters, 12-9 and New Albany, 20-16. This led to their only trip to Indianapolis for the state finals where they lost to Connersville in the 1st round 25-18. In 1939 Tom Downey's Salem team won the New Albany Regional, ousting Mitchell, 32-28, and Seymour, 25-18. They were in turn eliminated by Vincennes at the Evansville Semi-state. In 1971 Gary Duncan's Salem team won the Huntingburg Regional by defeating Springs Valley, 58-53, and Jasper, 76-73. At the Evansville Semi-state they were upended by Floyd Central. The Lady Lions have added 5 Sectional championships of their own, with their best record 1988's 19-3 for Coach Louie Jensen. Hall of Famer Everett Dean is a Salem graduate.

The Salem courthouse and the Salem Lion

Everett Dean
A 3-sport athlete at Salem HS... all-Big 10 and Helms All-American center in 1921 at Indiana University... soon returned to IU as coach, from 1924--38 ... next stop was Stanford, from 38 through 55 ... team won NCAA national championship in 1942 ... won 17 conference titles during collegiate coaching career ...played some professional baseball and coached Stanford to 2 conference titles in that sport... as coach at IU won one Midwest Conf. basketball crown and 3 Big 10 titles, as well as 3 Big Ten baseball titles...respected author of basketball books, he has served on numerous national organizations.

North Salem is in Hendricks County and is now a part of Tri-West High School. The Blue Devils are now Bruins. The Blue Devils won Sectional crowns at Danville in 1930 and 1957 and at Brownsburg in 1960. Salem Center in Steuben County fielded the Cardinals. Although they never won a Sectional title, they did enjoy a 16-3 season for Stewart Davis in 1950. They are now Prairie Heights Panthers.

North Salem school and Blue Devil

Edinburgh is one of the most beautiful cities in the world, a true gem of a city in Scotland, with a magnificent castle on the hill at one end of the High Street where the annual Tattoo is a stirring experience. Edinburgh in Johnson County, though not as dramatic a site, is nonetheless a town with considerable pride. The Edinburgh High School was organized in 1875; basketball was played there at least as early as 1916, when the Lancers (or Maroons as they were sometimes called) won 9 of 14 games, followed the next year by a 12-3 mark. William Webb coached the 1929 team to a 21-4 season; and Don Holloway's squad won 20 of 25 games exactly 50 years later, including the school's second Sectional title. Their first had come in 1951, when Harold Hickman's squad also captured the school's only Regional. That championship was heart-racing experience for all Lancer fans as their favorites edged Madison, 52-51, and Columbus, 51-50! Whew. The slipper failed to fit against Batesville, however, in the Indianapolis Semi-state, 45-37, but it was certainly a year the people of Edinburgh remember with pride. The 3rd Sectional crown came in 1973 under Leonard Krebs, with a 17-6 record.

Edinburgh Scotland crest and the Edinburgh, Indiana, Lancer

Salisbury in southwestern England is home to one of the world's most beautiful cathedrals. Its soaring majesty and grace have inspired many an artist, poet, and worshiper for centuries. Our New Salisbury in Harrison County once fielded the Tigers. They are still feline as North Harrison Cougars.

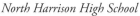

New Salisbury Tigers have become Cougars in Harrison County

North Harrison High School

Bremen, a city in north Germany, has provided Americans with such delights as St. Pauli Girl and Beck's beers. Our own Bremen has provided us with one of our most beloved governors and a premier Indiana University Hoosier fan, Otis "Doc" Bowen. The Bremen teams are the Lions. The Bremen Lions have won 9 Sectionals and 2 Regionals. The Bremen Lady Lions have added 4 Sectionals and another 2 Regionals to the school's trophy case. Coach Huber Martin's teams won 20 of 23 games in both 1982 and 1985 and were 22-3 in 1986, and Christine Kuhl's 1990 team went undefeated in the regular season, finishing 20-1.

Early Bremen High School; the Bremen, Indiana, Lion; and the Bremen, Germany, crest

North Rhine-Westphalia is a state in Germany. Westphalia is also a town in Knox County, where the high school teams were called the Wildcats. After a waystop as Sanborn Blue Jays, whose 1 Sectional crown came with a 26-3 record in 1957 under Coach Jim Hannah, they are now North Knox Warriors.

The flag of North Rhine-Westphalia and the North Knox Warrior

Not many towns in Indiana are named after countries in Africa. Angola is one, as is Morocco, the Beavers, discussed elsewhere. The Angola High School teams are the Hornets. The Hornets enjoyed a 12-3 season as early as 1916, and although they have won an impressive 15 Sectionals their only Regional title came in 1999 when Jim Speicher's team defeated the home team 59-53 in the Class 3A Regional at Plymouth. In the Semi-states the Hornets lost to eventual state runner-up Muncie South. John Hammel's 1963 Angola squad won 20 of 27 games, and Steve Grill's 1982 edition finished 20-4. The Lady Hornets have done some serious stinging of their own. Doug Curtis' charges won 20 of 25 games in 2000, 22 of 24 in 2002, and 25 of 26 the next year, also capturing the West Noble 3A Sectional crown, their first to date.

Angola Hornets

We also have the town of Tangier, very similar in name to Tangiers in northern Africa. The Tangier teams prior to consolidation into Turkey Run were the Tigers. They are now the Warriors. As Tigers Tangier won their 1st and only Sectional in 1957 at Rockville, defeating Cayuga 35-34, Newport 62-49, Montezuma 72-60, and Rockville 42-36.

We may pronounce it differently than they do in France, but our city of Versailles is nonetheless named for the glorious palace of the Sun King southeast of Paris. Versailles is in Ripley County, named for General Eleazar Wheelock Ripley, a hero of the War of 1812, graduate of Dartmouth College, and himself named for the college's founder. John DePauw was a member of the delegation chosen to find a proper locale for the seat of the new county in 1818, and that seat was then named Versailles in honor of DePauw's home in his native France. The Versailles teams, known as the Lions, went 23-2 in 1957 and 25-2 in 1959. They have 6 Sectional nets in their trophy case. Now a part of South Ripley High School, also located in Versailles, the teams are called the Raiders. The city's Web site has an interesting bit of history to relate, which may account for the appearance their mascot has of a Confederate officer on horseback:

> *The courtyard was the scene of a dramatic episode in Ripley County history in early June of 1863. General John Hunt Morgan of the Confederate Army led approximately 2,000 cavalry troops into southern Indiana in an attempt to draw Union forces north of the Ohio River.*
>
> *As he neared Versailles, a militia organized to fight but disbanded when the Confederate force came into the town from the southwest. General Morgan aimed a cannon at the newly built courthouse and threatened to fire if his troops were met with any armed resistance. Guns were confiscated and broken over a corner of the courthouse.*
>
> *The county treasury, Mason jewels, food, possessions and livestock were confiscated by Morgan's raiding cavalry. When Morgan discovered that his men had taken the Mason jewels, he ordered them returned because he was a Mason himself. They can still be seen at the Lodge Hall.*

Versailles High School and courthouse, the palace of Versailles, and the South Ripley Raider

Alsace is a portion of eastern France contested by Germany and France on and off for years, along with Lorraine. In New Alsace in Dearborn County there was once a 3-year high school, existing from 1923 until it consolidated with Guilford in 1929. One of its claims to fame is that the boys basketball team was coached by a woman, Elizabeth Dietz. She is believed to have been the 1st woman in Indiana to ever coach a boys basketball team. In 1926 Ms. Dietz stepped into the breech after there was a problem with the male coach who had been expected to lead the team. These notes come to me from Bob Chance, a friend and classmate of John Collier at Guilford:

The new Parish Hall at New Alsace had open rafters. The players would try to shoot through the rafters—like the old joke about Guilford players practicing in the covered bridge. [Author's note: as did the Moscow players.]

There was insufficient money for a concrete floor, so the team played on a dirt floor.

New Alsace won one game 54-4. Unbelievable.

New Alsace High School

[Author's note: Dietz must not have been a bad coach!]

Other sources show Dietz as coach in 1928, not 1926, and that the team's overall record under her guidance was 6-7. Either way it's a good bit of history.

The world's fascination with Napoleon Bonaparte was not lost on the early settlers of what is now Indiana, many of whom were French themselves. Napoleon, also in Ripley County, is only 11 miles from Versailles. The Napoleon teams were the Bearcats, now a part of the Jac-Cen-Del Eagles. The Bearcats won back-to-back Batesville Sectional titles in 1947 and 1948 with 23-2 and 21-2 records for Coach Millard Sink. Both of those 2nd losses were to Lawrenceburg in the Rushville Regional. In 1947 Lawrenceburg lost to eventual State Champion Shelbyville and the next year by a single point to Final Four team Anderson. Two seasons not soon to be forgotten by Napoleon fans.

Our state also commemorates 2 of Napoleon's most devastating defeats as well as one of his most significant victories. The victory was in the Piedmont region of northern Italy, over the Austrian forces near the town of Marengo. In the opera *Tosca* there is an aria commemorating the hoped-for defeat of Napoleon, but alas, that was not to be. Our Indiana Marengo is near the famous caverns of southern Indiana, and their black and gold teams were the Cavemen. The Cavemen

Jac-Cen-Del Eagle

won the 1947 Paoli Sectional and exactly 10 years later captured the New Albany Sectional for Ralph Hanger. They are now part of Crawford County, the Wolfpack.

From Cavemen to Wolfpack

Now to Napoleon's 2 famous defeats. The first was off the coast of Spain, near Trafalgar, where the British Navy under Lord Nelson once again proved that Brittania did indeed rule the waves. The other was in Belgium at a place called Waterloo, where the Iron Duke, Wellington, prevailed. Our Trafalgar is in Johnson County;

their teams were the Redbirds. The Redbirds snagged their only Sectional in 1917. This put them in the state tournament at Indiana University where they lost their 1st round game to the eventual champion Lebanon Tigers. They also had an excellent 22-win season with only 2 defeats for Coach John Hynds in 1958. That 2nd loss came in the Center Grove Sectional to Decatur Central after the Redbirds had defeated

Edinburgh and Southport. Our Waterloo is in DeKalb County. Their teams were the Wildcats. Foster Barr coached the 1937 Wildcats to a 16-4 mark, and Waterloo won 15 of 20 games in 1960, including the school's only Sectional championship, with Richard Bourquin coaching. His 1965 team also won 20 of 24 games. They are now respectively Indian Creek Braves and DeKalb Barons.

The DeKalb crest

The Waterloo Wildcat

Continuing our French motif we have New Paris in Elkhart County and Paris Crossing, quite a bit further south in Jennings County. The former fielded

the Cubs and the latter were the Lions for a time and then the Pirates. The Cubs won the Elkhart Sectional in 1927 and the Goshen Sectional in 1941. They also had a fine 20-4 season for Coach Snow Evans in 1932, and from 1962 through 1964 won 60 games while

Paris Crossing School and the Jennings County Panthers

losing only 9 under Coach Jim Hettler. New Paris is now part of Fairfield, the Falcons; and Paris Crossing, which, alas, never won a Sectional, is now consolidated into the Jennings County Panthers. The Black and Gold did have a 17-5 season for Coach M. T. Stewart in 1955, and an even better one according to alum Niles Layman, in 1954, for Coach Forest Fry. The second loss was to Madison in the Sectional semi-finals. The 1937 Lions made it to the Sectional final before losing to North Vernon.

Montpelier is a city in southern France as well as a town in Blackford County. The Montpelier teams were variously called Pacers, Oil City Five, and Spartans. Under any name they did themselves proud from 1965-67, winning 63 games and losing only 8. They also won 5 Sectionals between 1927 and 1967. They are now Bruins at Blackford High School.

New Paris High School Cubs are now Fairfield Falcons

The Blackford Bruin and Montpelier High School

In south central France Lyons is a city on the Rhone River. In Indiana Lyons is a town in Greene County where the teams were known alliteratively as the Lions. The Lyons Lions made it to the Sweet Sixteen in 1923 by beating Winslow in the Indiana University Regional. They lost their 1st-round game to Vincennes, who went on to win the state championship that year. They won 3 other Sectional crowns. Lyons eventually joined with Marco, the Bears—whose only Sectional title came in 1950—to form L&M High School. Which animal did they then choose? Neither; they were the Braves. The L&M Braves enjoyed several fine seasons, starting with a 17-3 record in 1964. Coach Jim Duffy led the 1969 and 1970 teams to 21-5 and 21-2 seasons, and in 1982 Dave Henson's charges went 20-3. Tom Oliphant took over in 1984 and led the Braves to an undefeated regular season record of 23-1, immediately followed by a 28-2 mark the next year, 51 wins and 3 losses in those 2 years. The sole loss in 1984 was to Terre Haute South in the Regional and the 2nd loss the next year was to Southridge in the final game of the Evansville Semi-state after the Braves had gained a measure of revenge over Terre Haute South by ousting them and Owen Valley from the Regional. All told, in its relatively short existence, L&M won 4 Sectional titles and that 1985 Regional at Terre Haute. Finally, L&M was consolidated into White River Valley High School. Back to the animal kingdom: the Wolverines.

Lyons High School and the White River Valley Wolverine

Orleans in France will forever be associated with a young woman named Joan of Arc, later to become St. Joan. Orleans, Indiana, was not named directly for Orleans, France, but indirectly: it was named to honor the victory of Andrew Jackson at the Battle of New Orleans. The town was founded in 1815 and refers to itself as the Dogwood Capital of Indiana. The Orleans teams, staying with the canine theme, are known as the Bulldogs, and they have enjoyed many successful seasons, winning 12 Sectional titles. They also made it to the Final Four of our 2nd state tournament in

1912, defeating Evansville 25-18 and Bicknell 26-8 before losing to eventual champion Lebanon 28-13. As recently as 2003 Orleans won the Class A Sectional on their home court, defeating Springs Valley and West Washington. They then took home the nets from the Loogootee Regional, defeating Shawe 60-50 and then, in a good old-fashioned barn burner they finally eliminated the host Lions after 3 overtimes, 40-37.

"The Maid of Orleans" statue in Paris; the Orleans, Indiana, Bulldog; and an Orleans dogwood

Carthage in northern Africa had several altercations with the mighty Roman Empire, finally coming up seriously short. Carthage High School's Blue Raiders seldom came up short in 1949 and 1950, when they won 41 games while only losing 5 for Coach Ora Clayton. They are now Knightstown High School Panthers.

Carthage High School and the Knightstown Panther

Democracy began in Greece along with many of the other values we hold dear in Western civilization. They gave us the beginnings of our philosophy: Plato, Aristotle, and Heraclitus; the genius of Euclid; the great plays of Sophocles, Aeschylus, and Euripides; the writings of Homer; and of course the Olympic games. Mt. Olympus High School in Gibson County fielded the Mountaineers. (You have to be an opimist to call your teams the Mountainers in a state where the highest point is 1,257 feet and even that is on the other side of the state.) Anyway, this team would have made any Greek Olympian proud with their undefeated regular season of 1929, going 26-1 and winning their only Sectional title, at Owensville. They are now Princeton Tigers.

Mt. Olympus High School

1929 Mt. Olympus Mountaineers Season Record

Spurgeon	18-17
Winslow	38-21
Stendal	35-23
Spurgeon	29-27
Hazleton	20-17
Huntingburg	33-25
Cynthiana	39-29
Evansville Central	20-16
Petersburg	21-15
Owensville	22-20
Princeton	29-18
Ft. Branch	46-31
Winslow	17-8
Patoka	63-31
Hazleton	32-26
Patoka	30-4
Stendal	29-20

Gibson County Tournament

Oakland City	26-13*
Princeton	12-8*
Owensville	16-11*
Tell City	26-22
Evansville Reitz	37-23

Sectional

Mount Vernon (Posey)	22-13
Hazleton	18-12
Owensville	19-12

Regional

Vincennes	12-26

Syracuse was founded by the Greeks on the Italian island of Sicily. Syracuse High School teams were the Yellow Jackets before they were consolidated into Wawasee High School, the Warriors. The blue and gold Yellow Jackets won 5 Sectionals between 1921 and 1949, as well as earning 1 of the 8 state final slots available from the 1921 Purdue Regional, 20-17 over Crawfordsville. They lost at Bloomington to Huntington, 20-16. They also won the 1926 Ft. Wayne Regional crown when they upended LaGrange, 34-13, and Columbia City, 26-17. They again lost in the 1st round of the state finals in Indianapolis, this time to North Vernon. More recently, Richard Beck's 1959 Syracuse team won 21 of 24 games.

Syracuse, Indiana, High School and the coat of arms of Syracuse, Italy

The Biblical city of Nineveh also has its namesake in Indiana, in Johnson County. Nineveh High School was the building used for the exterior and interior school shots for the movie *Hoosiers*. Regrettably, it no longer stands. When Nineveh fielded teams they were at first the Bluebirds and then the Eagles. Their colors were navy blue and gold. In 1946 they won 17 games and lost 5. The school is now a part of Indian Creek, the Braves.

Nineveh High School

Manila is the capital of the Philippines; Manilla is a town in Rush County. Although, like Nineveh, they never won a Sectional title, the Kelly green-and-white-clad Manilla Owls won 20 games and lost only 5 in 1929 for Coach Theron Dawson. The Owls have been consolidated into Rushville as the Lions.

Chapter 19

Small Schools, Memorable Names: Wampuscats, Oreos, and More

Many of our fine smaller schools have not only been consolidated but have seemingly lost some of their records. Much of the data regarding their basketball histories is difficult to find. At least we can save their mascots and team names, and with the new initiatives of the Indiana Basketball Hall of Fame, we may also rediscover some of what has been buried in obscure places for many years. Yearbooks, scrapbooks, old newspaper clippings, or local library files all may have information that will help restore the memories of the strivings, accomplishments, and enjoyable times that are such an important part of our past. Thanks also to the determined efforts of Bob Adams and others associated with the Indiana Basketball History Society, and to Bill May's tireless research into the scores of all of our state tournament games from 1911 through 2003, more and more of this fascinating part of our state's heritage is being rediscovered and preserved. Search your own closet shelves, attics, and the boxes in your garage. You may well have something worth sharing.

Many of the nicknames chosen by the towns to honor their teams just flowed off the tongue. Let's start with some of those.

Poseyville in Posey County was originally called Palestine, but that was changed to honor Brigadier General Thomas Posey. The Poseyville Posies won their lone Sectional championship at New Harmony in 1925. J. A. Duckworth's team defeated Cynthiana 14-13, the host Rappites 27-9, and Stewartsville 27-8, only to be edged 18-17 by Huntingburg in the 1st round of the Evansville Regional. Six years later the black-and-white-uniformed Posies (you might think posies would be more colorful!) won 19 of 24 games with W. L. Newton coaching. Nearby Cynthiana was named after a town in Kentucky, the town of origin of most of their early settlers. Their teams were the Annas, and their colors were black and gold or blue and gold. Both the Poseyville Posies and the Cynthiana Annas are now North Posey Vikings.

The North Posey Vikings

There were Graysville Greyhounds in Sullivan County, and there were Grandview Greyhounds in Spencer County, although the Grandview teams were also called Yellow Jackets. Graysville defeated Plainville, Sullivan, and Jackson Township to win their only Sectional title at Hymera in 1929. They were narrowly beaten by Linton, 17-16, in the 1st round of the Vincennes Regional. The goal of a Sectional crown eluded Grandview, unfortunately. The Graysville Greyhounds are now Sullivan Golden Arrows, while the Grandview Greyhounds, after a stop in Rockport as Zebras, are split between the Heritage Hills Patriots and the South Spencer Rebels. There were also Greyhounds representing Lydick in St. Joseph County who became New Carlisle Tigers and finally New Prairie Cougars.

Grandview High School, the Greyhound, and the South Spencer Rebel

The town of Twelve Mile is in Cass County; their high school teams were the Milers. Twelve Mile referred to a boundary determined by an Indian treaty. The blue-and-white-clad Milers lost only 3 of 14 games in 1921. They finished 15-5 for Coach Leonard Hawley in 1938, and 2 years later his team turned in a 19-4 mark. However, 1949 and 1950 were the glory years, 19-2 followed by an undefeated regular season record of 20-1, coached both years by Russell Brown. The Milers' only 1950 loss was to Lucerne in the Logansport Sectional. They are now Caston Comets.

Twelve Mile High School, the Caston Crest, and Comet logo

The Concannon Cannons provided the state of Indiana with one of our all-time great high school coaches, Johnny Baratto. His Hall of Fame citation, showing the variety of his achievements and his fighting spirit, is as follows:

Johnny Baratto
Posted a 468-157 career coaching record... 3 years at Fritchton, then 23 years at East Chicago Washington ... coached Senators to 1960 state championship ... state runner-up 2 years later ... 1960 state coach of the year ... 12 sectional titles amid rugged northwest Indiana competition ... 8 regional and 4 semistate crowns .. widely known as an inspirational leader who hated to lose ... played baseball at Concannon High School in West Terre Haute, then at Indiana State, ... illness kept him from playing basketball, but he became Indiana State's team manager, learning the game from Hall of Fame coach Glen Curtis

The Concannon Cannons, who wore blue and white uniforms, are now West Vigo Vikings.

Concannon High School, home of the Cannons, and the West Vigo Viking

And you also know that not all of the Wolverines were in Michigan. Wolf Lake in Noble County were not maize and blue but black and gold. They turned in an undefeated regular season in 1912, finishing 8-1 for Maynard Buckles in the school's 2nd year of basketball. That qualified them as one of what was a Final Thirteen in the second Indiana state tournament. They played the Whiting Oilers at Notre Dame in what was called a district tournament, dropping a 21-14 decision. Whiting went on to the Final Four at Indiana University after also defeating Culver's Cavaliers. Wolf Lake had another undefeated regular season in 1941, at 21-1 for Coach John Reid. Their only loss was to LaGrange in the Kendallville Sectional, a heartbreaker in overtime. The next year the 123-student school won their 1st Sectional title, defeating Albion 39-23 in the championship game at Kendallville after gaining revenge on the host team in the semi-finals. That year they also won their only Regional championship, eliminating Butler and Central at Ft. Wayne. The Wolverines then encountered Burris in the Muncie Semi-state, losing to the Owls, who would be eventual runner-up to the State Champion Washington Hatchets. In 1966 and 1967 they had back-to-back excellent seasons for Butch Wygart, 23-3 and 22-3, winning their 2nd Sectional, at Columbia City, in the latter year. They are now Central Noble Cougars.

Wolverines are now Cougars

Nor were all of the Badgers in Wisconsin. We also had Badgers in Indiana in Carroll County at Flora. Flora was actually named for the original settlers there, John and Sarah Flora, who were attracted to the locale by a spring they discovered. The town was first called Fountain City because of the spring, but that name was discarded when it was realized there already was a town of that name in Indiana. Eventually the name Flora was adopted to honor those 1st settlers, and the town now refers to itself as the "Garden Spot of Indiana."

Those Flora Badgers (I know Badgers are fauna, not flora, but, anyway, that's what their teams were called) did extremely well, too. As early as 1916 and 1917 the

Flora High School

Blue and Gold won 29 games while losing only 6. By 1925 and 1926, Ralph Pearson coaching, the Badgers put records of 25-3 and 24-6 together. In 1930 Kenneth Allee's squad won 19 and lost 5. In 1941 and 1942 Ralph Kifer coached Flora to 35 wins and 15 losses. Leonard Reid's 1945 team finished 18-7, followed by 24-5 and 20-6 records the next 2 years: 62-18 for 3 years. Les Ray's 1954 and 1955 Badgers went 19-5 followed by 18-4, and in 1959 Frank DeBruicker's team finished 17-5. Seven Sectional championships and the 1946 Logansport Regional have been won by the Flora Badgers. That year they edged Jefferson 50-48 and Culver 37-35 in the Lafayette Semi-state before losing the next week to Ft. Wayne Central, the runner-up to Anderson, in the afternoon game of the Final Four in Indianapolis.

There were also Badgers representing Union Center in Wells County. These Badgers wore black and white uniforms and had an impressive 21-5 season for Coach Oscar Naab in 1934. Two years later, with a lesser 16-8 record, the Badgers won their only Sectional, at Bluffton, defeating Lancaster 40-30 in the final game. In the Regional final the Badgers ran into Ft. Wayne Central, and, although they lost, so,

Union Center School

after all, did everyone else that year but Frankfort. The Tigers were the runners-up in the state finals that year to the Hot Dogs. In 1953 and 1955 Wendell Beck led Union Center to 18-3 and 19-4 records. In 1963 the Badgers became Norwell Knights.

The Lynnville Lindies are from Warrick County. The school is like several of the high schools in Indiana which are now elementary schools. Many proudly preserve the traditions of the old schools. Lynnville feeds Tecumseh High School.

From their Web site and Gene Raber, principal:

> *Lynnville Elementary School's mascot is Charles Lindbergh, the first solo pilot to cross the Atlantic Ocean. The Lynnville "Lindies" exemplify the spirit and bravery which carried Lindbergh through his daring voyage. Lynnville students are encouraged to share Lindbergh's qualities when pursuing academic and personal endeavors.*

When they were still a high school, the Lindies, in black and gold, won an impressive 8 Sectionals, their first in 1935 and their last in 1957. Their lone Regional championship was in 1940 when they dominated Oakland City 42-16 and edged Dale 26-25 at Evansville. The Lyndies were eliminated from the Sweet Sixteen by a Mitchell Blue Jacket team that was runner-up to Hammond Tech for the state title. Some good memories there for the Lindies.

Lynnville High School, Charles Lindbergh and the Spirit of St. Louis

Mulberry High School and the Clinton Prairie Gopher

The black and gold Mulberry Berries won 18 games and lost only 4 in 1935 for Coach Ray Hause. They are now part of Clinton Prairie.

Middlebury's Middies enjoyed several successful seasons, including a 4-year record of 70-17 culminating in an undefeated regular season of 18-1 in 1936 for Coach John Hazlitt. Their only defeat that year was dealt by Goshen in the Elkhart Sectional. Then came a 3-year span from 1943–1945 when they won 59 while losing only 9. This was accomplished in spite of having a different coach each year. A 19-3 record in 1957 was followed by 21-2 in 1958 and 18-4 in 1959, the latter two seasons under Coach Jim Roush. They are now part of the Northridge Raiders, who have also had some fine seasons, including 19-3 in 1972 and 21-4 in 1996.

Middlebury High School, home of the Middies

Yankeetown, near Evansville, was apparently named by New Englanders who were relatives of Ralph Waldo Emerson. Their teams were called the Yanks. The team name Yanks was also selected by the town with the intriguing name of Young America in Cass County. Both schools wore red, white, and blue uniforms, although Yankeetown at some point wore black and gold. Yankeetown was never able to snare a Sectional crown, but the Young America Yanks snagged 2 in a row, both at Logansport, and both at the expense of the Walton Warriors, 18-7 in 1920 and 34-24 the next year. Young America alum Joseph Platt is a Hall of Famer:

> Joseph Platt
> A 4-year performer in both basketball and baseball at Young America High School ... 3-year varsity player at Indiana University, captaining 1938 team ... Big 10 title in '36 ... 3 years as coach at Winamac High School ... coached basketball at Bunker Hill Naval Air Station, then 3 years as head coach at Carleton College in Minnesota ... returned to Indiana for a 14-year stint at Kokomo High School.

Young America High School

Both Oaktown in Knox County and Oaklandon in Marion County called their teams the Oaks. The Evansville and Crawfordsville Railroad was instrumental in determining the location of Oaktown in 1854 with the stop originally known as Oak Station before the name was changed to Oaktown. The green-and-white-clad Oaktown basketball team was 1 of 12 schools represented in the 1st official Indiana State Championship in 1911.

They lost their 1st round game to Lafayette by a score of 31 to 14. They also fielded a girls basketball team at least as early as 1924.

The 1911 State Finalists, and the Oaktown School and Oaklandon school photos

Oaklandon High School

The Oaklandon Oaks are now Lawrence Central Bears. The Oaks played in the 2nd state tournament, the Final Thirteen, in 1912, losing to Richmond at the Indianapolis YMCA. Their colors were also green and white.

Houck plate photo of exhibit courtesy IBHOF

For a time the Poling High School teams were called the Polecats. Hopefully, the Polecats were more like Flower, Bambi's friend, than most of ones I have seen. Fortunately, they changed that to the Yellow Jackets. The Purple and Gold had a 12-6 season for Coach Hal Warren in 1926 and won 16 while losing 7 under Art Habegger in 1960.

They are now Jay County Patriots.

The Lawrence Central Bear

Brook, near Kentland, was the home of author George Ade. His house is still there on the east side of town, and worth seeing. When Brook High School was still in operation, their teams were the Aces. Brookston High School fielded the Bombers. I don't know if the Brook Aces ever played the Brookston Bombers, but if they did it must have been quite an aerial dogfight! The purple-and-gold-clad Aces did win 12 Sectional championships in their 58-year history, including 5 in a row from 1929–33. They are now part of North Newton, the Spartans. The Brookston Bombers also won their fair share of Sectionals, nabbing 13 in their 59-year history as well as Regionals in 1949 and 1951 both at Logansport. In 1949 they knocked Peru out by 2 points, then defeated Camden by 13; in 1951 both of their wins were by the margin of a single basket, over the host Berries and Winamac. (Since Winamac had also won over Delphi by 2 points, that was quite a day in Logansport!). The Bombers also had a 17-3 season in 1964, 2 years before they were consolidated into Frontier Falcons.

Brook High School,   *the North Newton Spartan,*   *the Frontier Falcon*

Cory was famous for its apple orchards. These orchards covered some 280 acres, and in good years the locals harvested as much as 60,000 bushels of 37 varieties of apples. The Cory teams were called the Apple Boys, which is echoed by a team in the town of Cobden in southern Illinois, whose teams are called the Appleknockers!

The 1947 Apple Boys, coached by Richard Oglesby, were the Brazil Sectional champions. They squeaked by the Gosport Indians 41-40, the Spencer Cops 28-26, and the Brazil Red Devils 36-34, before handling Clay City rather easily 38-

The 1947 Cory team

25 in the title game. The Apple Boys wore orange and black. They became Clay City Eels.

Flint is located in Steuben County. Their team was called the Arrows, which I think is particularly good as they would have been the Flint Arrows, and flint is probably as good as it gets when it comes to arrows. They are now part of Prairie Heights High School in LaGrange, the Panthers, after passing through Orland as Tigers or Trojans.

Flint School

Cambridge City is located on the Whitewater River and gained considerable prominence when the National Road (Route 40) was built there along with the extension of the Whitewater Canal. This town is well preserved with many historic buildings.

There was originally some sentiment toward naming it Bridgeport, but Cambridge City won out, probably referring to the university town in England. The teams at the original high school there were called the Wampus Cats. I'm not sure what one looks like, but I'm told *The original Cambridge City High School and the Golden Eagle* by locals that a Wampus Cat knocks the opposition cattywampus. Today's Cambridge City Lincoln High School teams are called the Golden Eagles. The Wampus Cats enjoyed an undefeated regular season in 1952, going 20-1 under Coach Floyd Peters. only loss was a tough 2-pointer to Hagerstown in the Richmond Sectional, 47-45.

We'll have more about the Wampus Cats later.

One of my favorite snacks, introduced by Nabisco in 1912 or thereabouts, is those wonderful little round chocolate cookies with the sugar layer inside. Licking that sugar was always fun. Oreos. Would you believe that the original team name for Acton High School was exactly that, the Oreos? Regrettably, they soon moved to Redbirds and then Wildcats before they became part of the Flashes of Franklin Central.

The good people of Clay Township in Howard County had a well developed sense of humor. I don't think there were any brick houses there, but they still called their high school teams the Brickies. They are now part of Northwestern High School, the Tigers.

Clay Township High School, some adobe bricks, and the Tiger Paw

All of these teams, and every one that ever had 5 young men lace up a pair of sneakers extra tight, take a deep breath, and run onto the court for a shot at a Sectional championship win over a school 8 or 10 times their size, were looking for that "big moment." The Union Mills Millers' big moment, as recorded by Wendell Trogdon, has lasted over 50 years and remains vivid in the memory of Woody Jacobs, who played for the maroon-and-white-clad Millers when they won the 1950 Michigan City sectional, defeating the host school 54-44 in the final game. In 1948 the Millers won 20 games and lost 5 for Coach Charles Sanders, the same record they achieved for him in that Sectional championship year. The Union Mills gym was so small it was called the Cracker Box.

Union Mills High School

The Pittsboro Burros in Hendricks County won 7 Sectionals between 1922 and 1975 before being consolidated into Tri West. In 1935 L. M. Kitley's Burros had an undefeated regular season, finishing 25-1—and that was not a year they won a Sectional title! Max Gibbs led the Burros to a 22-2 mark in 1958, another non-Sectional-winning year for the Burros. However, 1975's 19-3 record for Bill Compton, the last year for the Red and White before consolidation, did result in their 7th Sectional title.

The Pittsboro Burros are now the Tri West Bruins.

Kingsbury, in LaPorte County, was settled by New Yorkers who named it after the town they had left behind. Kingsbury is near the 6,000-acre state fish and wildlife area. During World War II it was the site of an Army Ordnance plant that employed some 20,000 people. When they had their own high school, their teams were the Kingsbury Kings; their colors were black and gold.

The Kingsbury Kings

Not far from Kingsbury is Mill Creek, home of the Creekers (also called the Wildcats). The orange and blue Creekers/Wildcats won 20 of 23 games for Coach Robert Gray in 1953 and went 23-3 with Paul Godsey coaching in 1959. Neither school ever won a Sectional title, and both are now LaPorte Slicers.

Coal City is well named, as it is in the area of the extensive coal fields of western Indiana. These fields are so close to the surface that strip mining is used to extract the coal from the ground. As the mining areas are finished, they have been carefully restored to their pre-mining condition, well planted with grasses and trees, and provided with lakes and wetlands. The Coal City High School teams wore blue and white and were

Coal City High School

called the Colts (preceding the Indianapolis NFL team in those selections). The Coal City teams were also known as the Indians for a time. They are now consolidated into the Owen Valley Patriots.

The Midland Middies in Greene County are now the Shakamak Lakers. The Middies won their lone Sectional title at Lyons in 1924 with convincing victories over Odon, 42-10, and Scotland, 31-5, sandwiched around 16-13 and 17-13 wins over Bloomfield and the home team. Although Coach Lloyd Mitchell's 1950 team had a fine 21-2 record, they could not capture that 2nd Sectional, losing to Jasonville at Linton, 31-22.

Midland High School and the Shakamak Crest

The Middlebury Middies in Elkhart County enjoyed several excellent seasons. O. G. Kindy coached the 1932 and 1933 Middies to 16-7 and 17-4 records: Clarence Lubbers took over for 1 season, 17-8. He was succeeded by John Hazlitt, whose 1935 and 1936 squads finished 18-4 and 18-1. In 1944 Raymond Smith's Middies finished 21-3, and the next year Ed Overman brought the team home with a 20-2 record. Robert Biddle's 1951-54 teams won 68 and lost 21 and his 1957 team won 19 of 22 games. Since the next 2 years under Coach Jim Roush produced 21-2 and 18-4 marks that 3-year total came to an impressive 58 and 11. Irv Pratt's 1965 Middies turned in an 18-5 season record. They are now Northridge Raiders.

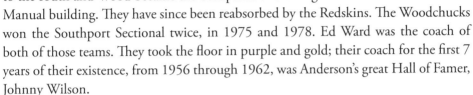

The Indianapolis Wood Woodchucks were created when the Manual Redskins built their new building several blocks to the south and Wood became the occupants of the original Manual building. They have since been reabsorbed by the Redskins. The Woodchucks won the Southport Sectional twice, in 1975 and 1978. Ed Ward was the coach of both of those teams. They took the floor in purple and gold; their coach for the first 7 years of their existence, from 1956 through 1962, was Anderson's great Hall of Famer, Johnny Wilson.

The Sugar Creek (remember to say "Crick") Crickets were covered earlier. The Deer Creek teams were also the Crickets. Those red and white Crickets enjoyed at least one outstanding year, going undefeated in the 1937 regular season for Coach Arthur Cohee and finishing 19-1. That one loss came to Burlington's Polar Cubs, 29-24, in the Flora Sectional. They are now Carroll Cougars.

Deer Creek High School

Oil Township in Perry County had its own high school until 1966. Their teams wore green and white uniforms and were called the Oilers. For a brief 3 years there was also a school in Oriole and they also called their teams Oilers before the 2 merged. Oil Township had 2 praise-worthy seasons back to back in 1957 and 1958, 18-2 both years for Coach Owen Lynch. They are now Perry Central Commodores.

Oil Township Oilers, Commodore Perry, and the Perry Central logos

There were also Commodores representing Decatur Catholic in Adams County whose colors were green and gold. The Commodores had 3 outstanding seasons from 1925 through 1927 when they won 68 games and lost only 9 for France Conter. They also won the state Catholic championship in 1930 for Coach George Laurent, defeating Jasper Academy in the final game. Their lone Sectional title after joining the IHSAA came in 1966 at Bluffton with wins over Jackson Center, Lancaster Central, and Ossian for Coach Bob Boyle.

The Otter Creek Otters are now Terre Haute North Vigo Patriots. The purple and gold Otters finished 16-4 for Coach Darrell Weir in 1928 and 16-5 in 1948 for Coach Joe Short. In their last 2 years before becoming Terre Haute Garfield Purple Eagles, en route to North becoming Patriots, Paul Thomas' 1960 and 1961 teams finished 17-4 and 16-5.

Otter Creek High School, home of the Otters

Star City High School teams are now Winamac Warriors

Star City has always sounded to me like the kind of name the Russians would use for one of their cosmonaut bases ... or maybe an epithet for Hollywood. Anyway, it is a town in Pulaski County whose team turned in a 9-4 record as early as 1913 and a 15-9 season for Lloyd Harrell in 1950. The purple and white Star City Stars are now Winamac Warriors.

The Parker Panthers in Randolph County went 4-0 in 1907, 8-3 in 1908, 9-1 in 1909, and 12-1 in 1920: 32 wins and 5 losses! Later they were for an extended period what Bill May refers to as "a tournament team" in his article in the Fall 2007 issue of *Indiana Basketball History*. That they truly were. A school that never had as many as 100 students enrolled in any year somehow managed to win 12 Sectional titles in 26 years, from 1938 through 1963, the first 2 under the coaching leadership of Cecil Moncreif. The 1940 team won 18 games for Coach Terry Bolander, losing 9. During that span their best records came in 1956 when Jim Poteet's team won 20 of 23 games, in 1959 when Jim Coulter's charges finished 25-2, and the next year with Coach Dennis Lewis at the helm. In 1962 when Coach Don Noblitt's Panthers won 18 and lost 4. Over the 7-year span beginning in 1956 Parker won 138 games and lost only 33. Several coaches, and yet the Sectional titles kept coming, even during years when the regular season records would

Parker High School

not have predicted another title postseason. Yes, the Parker Panthers were indeed a tournament team. They are now Monroe Central Golden Bears.

The Milltown Millers are now part of the Crawford County Wolfpack. In 1926 the blue and white Millers finished 18-5 for Coach Earl Young. Milltown won Paoli Sectional championships twice, in 1970 and 1976 for long-time coach Ron Ferguson,

The Milltown Millers and Milltown High School

who led the Millers from 1958 until their last year, 1976. That 1970 team finished 21-5, after 2 years of 19-3 and 18-3—which comes to 58 wins and 11 losses over a 3-year stretch. In 1970 they also won the Regional at Huntingburg, defeating Jeffersonville and North Harrison before losing to Seymour's Owls in the 1st round of the Sweet Sixteen, 68-60.

The Millersburg Millers in Elkhart County are now Fairfield Eagles. The black and gold Millersburg Millers won 17 and lost 7 for coach J. J. Kent in 1927 and were 18-6 with Carl Byerly coaching in 1930. They also had 2 fine seasons for Coach Bill Robinson, 20-4 in 1956 and 18-3 the next year.

The Millersburg Mill and School

In LaPorte County it was not common to pronounce the word "creek" as "crick." Thus the Mill Creek teams were called the Creekers. The Creekers (later called the Wildcats) wore orange and blue and won 20 of 23 games for Robert Gray in 1953 as well as 23 of 26 games for Paul Godsey in 1959. They have since become LaPorte Slicers.

Chapter 20

Our Agricultural Heritage: Landing Haymakers, Wearing Blue Jeans

Agriculture was and is extremely important to Indiana life. Corn and tomatoes, wheat and soybeans grow abundantly from Lake Michigan to the Ohio River. Once covered by the hardwood forests of oak, maple, walnut, sycamore and ash, the rich soil was uncovered and the sunlight let through by years of arduous cutting. When the original National Road was first opened, the trip across Indiana was a dark one, the road being thoroughly shaded by the thick, tall growth of trees. Now except where it passes through cities it is open, displaying unbroken views to the horizon of rolling land and beautiful farms and orchards. Several of our schools paid tribute to our agricultural heritage in their choice of team names.

Hayden is a farming community in Jennings County. The town was originally called Hardenberg, but when it became evident that the land around it was particularly well suited to the growing of forage crops, the name was changed to Hayden. When the high school was still open and unconsolidated, their teams were known as the Haymakers, partly because that is what they did on their farms and partly because that was what they laid on their opponents! Former Indiana governor Ed Whitcomb came from Hayden and took the court as a Haymaker himself. They are now Jennings County Panthers.

Hayden Haymaker and Jennings County Panther

Monroe City in Knox County was the home of a real "down home" politician named James Douglas Williams. A farmer for most of his adult life, he was elected governor of Indiana in 1876. Because he chose to wear suits made of the denim cloth he had grown used to wearing as a youth even as the elected head of state, he earned the nickname "Blue Jeans" Williams. Williams is credited with raising the funds required for Purdue University, primarily an agricultural school at the outset. He was also a champion of women's rights long before it became fashionable for male politicians to take such a stance. The Monroe City High School teams were called the Blue Jeans in his honor. They are now South Knox Spartans, and the high school building is now the Blue Jeans Center.

James D. "Blue Jeans" Williams and the Blue Jeans Center in the old Monroe City High School building. Blue Jeans Williams Museum

My wife and I stopped at the Blue Jeans Center and found an amazing amount of memorabilia of the various now-closed area schools as well as some friendly and knowledgeable volunteers whose efforts keep this important slice of Indiana history available. We were touched by the following reminiscences of Monroe City High School graduate Marlis Day in the February issue of the "Blue Jeans Community Center Newsletter" (team mascots added):

> *Looking back at my memories of attending school in Monroe City, I decided that one of my favorite memories was the basketball sectional each February....Whether the Monroe City Blue Jeans played or not, we went to the games and cheered...The [Adams] gym was divided into sections for Monroe City, Fritchton [Eagles], Wheatland [Jeeps], Bruceville [Hilltoppers], Oaktown [Oaks], Freelandville [Fighting Dutchmen], Decker [Aces], Decker Chapel [Panthers], Central Catholic [Vincennes] Rivet [Patriots], Sandborn [Blue Jays], Edwardsport [Powers], and Vincennes [Lincoln Alices]...It didn't matter who we played, we always cheered for any team playing Vincennes. It wasn't because they usually won, or because they were the biggest school and made the most noise, but because they were always allowed into the gym first and got all the chair seats...As the cheers went on, Vincennes fans always tried to make us feel small by poking fun at our country ways. What they didn't re - alize was that our smallness and our farming community were what we were most proud of. We were so proud of our team and our little school; we wouldn't have traded them places for anything.*

What they were most proud of was their small but mighty status and the wholesomeness of their farming communities. This says a very great deal, and I think would apply to hundreds and hundreds of our schools and towns. The Blue Jeans won 3 Sectional championships, in 1949, 1953, and 1961. The 1949 title came at Vincennes with wins over Wheatland, Oaktown, Fritchton, and the Alices. Maurice Sakel's squad then edged Loogootee, 35-34, before being nipped by Jasper, 57-55, also at Vincennes, to finish their season 27-4. But that's not the end of the story: Jasper went on to win the state championship. The Blue Jeans were 2 points from the title!

Four years later Monroe City won their 2nd Sectional crown, again at Vincennes, with victories over Bruceville, Freelandville, Wheatland, and Sandborn, for Coach Ray Evans, Jr., losing in the 1st round of the Regionals to Washington to finish 20-5.

Their final Sectional title was won in 1961, also at Vincennes. That year Jack Barry's Blue Jeans defeated Bruceville, Edwardsport, the home team Alices, and Decker Chapel. Their 2nd loss in a 29-game schedule came in the final game of the Huntingburg Regional, after Monroe City had snuck by North Central, 53-51, to old nemesis Jasper by a single point, 76-75.

Two Versions of the Fritchton Eagles and the Wheatland Jeeps. Courtesy Blue Jeans Williams Museum

A young man who would one day rise to be circuit court judge in Indianapolis, John Niblack, played on the Wheatland team in 1912 and 1913. He was one of 11 boys in the whole school.

Shawswick in Lawrence County, opened its first school in 1925 to 300 students and 13 teachers. There were 12 rooms for the 12 grades and the first graduating class in 1926 was composed of 3 students. This figure grew to 21 students in 1929, the 1st class that had

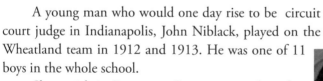

attended all 4 years of high school there. One story about how the school's basketball team received its name, the Farmers, is that coach John Armstrong once said around 1928 that his team was "shooting like a bunch of farmers."

I prefer to think that the town amidst the limestone quarries but still in good farming territory, named their teams with what they were proudest of—farming. The Farmers enjoyed several fine seasons between 1925 and 1974. In 1929 and 1930 they were 18-4 and 17-5, for Coach Fred George, but their best years came for Hall of Famer Knofel Fortner who led the Farmers for 14 seasons and captured Sectional crowns in 1952 and 1959 with records of 21-5 and 22-4. They also won 21 of 24 games for him in 1953. They are now Bedford Stars.

Knofel Fortner
Huron High School, 1933

23 yrs in Greene & Lawrence Co. schools... With a record of 340-161..four 20 victory seasons and two Bedford sectional championships (while at Shawswick) ... started coaching at Marco in 1936-37, then went to Scotland, Williams & Midland before going 14-7 and 18 - 3 in two years at Oolitic, winning the Lawrence Co. tournament each yr. ...in 1946-47, he began a 13 yr. tenure at Shawswick ...his teams went 207-82, winning the 1952-53-55 County Tourney championships & the 1952 & 1959 Bedford sectionals ... after coaching, spent 20 yrs. as a school supt. 18 yr. as the first supt. of the West Washington Schools elected two terms on both the IHSAA Athletic council and the Board of Control

Farmersburg in Sullivan County called their teams the Plowboys. The Plowboys won 34 games and lost 11 in 1956 and 1957 under Coach Paul Strain. They are now Thunderbirds at North Central High School.

Shawswick High School

The Farmersburg Plowboys, Farmersburg High School, and the North Central Thunderbird

The town of Wheatfield is in Jasper County, and you have to enjoy their selection: the Shockers, a name which, again, spoke to what they did most for their livelihood and also to what they expected to do to opponents on the athletic fields. The Shockers were 19-6 in 1957, 19-4 in 1958, 17-6 in 1959, and 17-5 in 1968 under Coach Fred Jones. The Shockers won Sectionals in 1950, 1965, and 1967. They are now Kankakee Valley Kougars.

Wheatfield High School and the Kankakee Valley Kougars

Dana, a small town in Vermillion County, is in the far western part of the state near the Illinois line. It is just about a long city block north of Route 36, which was once advertised as the most direct route from Indianapolis to Denver. It is on the great prairie, marvelous farming land, the thick black topsoil being measured in feet rather than inches. The train ran through the south side of Dana, and the feed mills and storage bins are still in evidence. The high school's teams were known very appropriately as the Aggies.

Dana, however, is also known for something far more important in my scheme of things. It was the birthplace of Ernie Pyle. He was born on a farm close to Dana. That farmhouse has been moved into the town. It is filled with the Pyle family furniture and other possessions and was until recently open to the public. Visitors could also enter the World War II Quonset huts at the rear of the property. The Purdue-educated guide who took us through was himself a veteran, very accommodating, and obviously proud of what he had to show us. In the huts is an impressive collection of memorabilia covering all of Ernie's too-short life as a journalist and war correspondent. There are his uniforms, typewriter, and some of the other possessions he had with him at the front. There is the jeep, or one like it, in which he was riding when the Japanese sniper cut him down on the tiny isle of Iwo Shima on April 18th, Paul Revere Day, in 1945. There are photos of his plain grave on that small atoll in the South Pacific. And there is much more. What made the greatest impression on me was the animated, life-size image of Ernie with his own voice reciting the magnificent words of perhaps his greatest column, which certainly contributed mightily to his Pulitzer Prize. It was a column about the soldiers in Captain Henry Waskow's company paying their final respects to their fallen leader on the mountainside in Italy near San Pietro after the captain's body had been brought down on the back of a mule. One by one the men went to their captain, knelt, paused, perhaps prayed. One young private spoke aloud: "I'm sure sorry, sir," he said. I hope this can be again made available to the public sometime soon.

The Aggies wore purple and white uniforms, and they won Sectional championships at Clinton in 1936, 1937, 1941, and 1948. They are now South Vermillion High School Wildcats.

The South Vermillion crest and Wildcat, Ernie Pyle, and mural in Dana

Mills were also important to Indiana from our earliest days. Gristmills, lumber mills, rolling mills, and windmills were constructed all over the state and were significant in the development of many towns. This significance was often reflected in the names those towns gave to their high school teams.

Noblesville was platted in 1823 by William Conner and Josiah Polk. It was either named for Lavinia Noble, or for United States Senator James Noble, or perhaps for both. The area is replete with interesting history. Conner originally had established a trading post in 1802 and married the daughter of the Lenape Chief Anderson, for whom the city of Anderson itself is named. It was in Conner's cabin that a meeting was held to select a final site for the new state capital near the center of the state to replace Corydon to the far south. Their selection is the reason Indianapolis is located where it is, rather than at Strawtown, the other contender.

After his Indian wife left him to go west with her tribe, Conner married Elizabeth Chapman. The home he constructed for her was the 1st brick house built in the area and is still a noteworthy site to visit in Conner Prairie Farm in nearby Fishers.

Originally surrounded by farmland and then well served by railroads, Noblesville became a natural milling site, and the high school teams have long been called the Millers. Recently the Indianapolis suburbs have reached out to Noblesville and made it one of their own. It is still the Hamilton County seat with an impressive courthouse and square, and many attractive homes, churches, and parks.

Noblesville Millers

The Millers got off to a slow start in basketball with only one winning season between 1915 and 1925, a span that included 2 winless years and 3 with but a single victory. Things started to turn around by 1933, when the Millers won 19 and lost 8. They were 15-8 the next year and in 1935 Coach Maurice Kennedy's charges put together a praiseworthy 26-2 record. They also had back-to-back 18-2 records under Coach Glen Harper in 1962 and 1963. The undefeated regular season, 24-1 in 1984, was followed by 22-2 and 23-3 seasons under the guidance of Coach Dave Nicholson. Dave McCullough coached the Millers to 22-5 and 20-4 records in 1997 and 1998. Tom Coverdale, who was to play such an instrumental role in the Indiana Hoosiers' run to the final game in the 2002 NCAA championship, led the Millers in those last 2 years. Overall the Millers have racked up 21 Sectional titles, 3 Regionals, and the 1957 Ft. Wayne Semi-state where they defeated the Marion Giants before losing to the eventual State Champion South Bend Central Bears.

There were also Millers in Milltown in Crawford County. This from the town's history on the internet:

> *Milltown has always been very strong in many sports. Milltown High School played its first basketball game during the 1916–17 season. Milltown's Millers first teams practiced on an outdoor court. Later the teams played their home games in an old lime shed which was considered one of the better gymnasiums in the area! The first girls basketball team was formed during the 1919-20 season.*

The Millers won Sectional titles in 1970 with a 21-5 record and in 1976, both at Paoli, and the Huntingburg Regional championship in 1970, won by defeating Jeffersonville, 72-69, and North Harrison, 70-66. Ron Ferguson coached the Millers from 1958 until their final year in 1976, and his 1968 and 1969 Miller teams finished 19-3 and 18-3 respectively. *Milltown High School, home of the Millers*

There are Millersburgs in both Warrick and Elkhart counties, but the school in the former called their teams the Wildcats. Those Wildcats did have a great season in 1941, 21-3 for Tom Goldsberry. They are now Knights at Castle. The Elkhart County Millersburg Millers were covered earlier.

Windmills throughout the state provided water for livestock and other farming needs. Between the 1870s and the 1930s there were, in fact, 76 companies within a 50-mile radius of Kendallville in northeastern Indiana producing windmills. Today this heritage is commemorated in the fascinating Mid-America Windmill Museum. This museum is located on 16 acres east of Kendallville and displays more than 100 windmills, the nation's largest collection. Butler, also east of Kendallville, fielded the Windmills as their team name. Opponents were thus placed in the unenviable position of having to joust with windmills whenever they played Butler High School. Cervantes would have been proud!

Butler High School

The poet Arthur Franklin Mapes was born in Butler. His poem "Indiana" is the official poem for our state. It begins

God crowned her hills with beauty
Gave her lakes and winding streams

And ends

Where the dreamy Wabash River
Wanders on through paradise.

Butler Windmills are
now Eastside Blazers

The Butler Windmills had strong seasons, in 1935 at 19-5, in 1942 at 18-4, and in 1943 at 18-3, the 1st when coached by John Moore and the latter 2 by Claus Jenkins. However, their finest seasons were under Coach George Cherry, when they strung together 3 good years beginning in 1953, 16-5, building to 19-5 the next year, and culminating in 20-3 in 1955. They then went 19-6 in 1957. The green and gold Windmills gained their Sectional title at Auburn in 1942. They are now part of DeKalb County's Eastside High School, the Blazers, keeping their colors if not their team name.

In Elkhart County is one of our state's best remaining mills, the Bonneyville Mill in Bristol. A visit to Bristol in the summer will reward the traveler with views of beautiful dahlias in flower, thanks to the Indiana Dahlia Society.

The Bristol Pirates are now Elkhart Blazers. The Pirates actually had an undefeated season: 7-0 in 1914 under Coach K. M. Snapp. They did not, however, compete in our state's 4th state championship tournament. They also did well in 1926 with a 15-3 record under Coach Bob McConnell, who had double-digit win totals in every one of his 5 years at the helm. In 1942 Coach Robert Irvin, in his only season at the school, led the team to 17 victories in 23 games, Benton Graham's 1954 Pirates came in at 16-5, and Dave Martin's 1960 team won 16 and lost 6.

Bristol High and the Bonneyville Mill

There are at least 3 other wonderful mills in Indiana, each with a covered bridge nearby and each with an interesting history. All are well preserved and worth a visit. Two are on Big Raccoon Creek, in Parke County. Both the Mansfield Mill and the Bridgeton Mill were built in the 1920s. The Bridgeton High School teams were the Raccoons. (Big Raccoons, no doubt.) Before consolidating into Riverton Parke, they first joined with the Rosedale Hot Shots. As Bridgeton they won their lone Sectional title at Clinton in 1944 with wins over Bloomington, Montezuma, Marshall, and Mecca for Tom Goldsberry.

The Mansfield Mill and Bridgeton School

The 4th not-to-be-missed mill is on Wildcat Creek in Carroll County, the Adams Mill, built in 1845. This park-like setting is a wonderful spot for a picnic and a taste of 19th-century Indiana. The tiny settlement around it was called Bolivar, but when the railroad came to nearby Cutler, the latter became the commercial center of the area. The high school is gone, but, when there was one, the teams were named for the creek: the Wildcats. Way back in 1912 Cutler finished with 8 wins and only one loss. The Wildcats were included in the Finals at Indiana University in 1913, when they were edged by Clinton's Wildcats in a catfight 30-28. Back again in 1914 Cutler's team gave a very serious lesson in the game of basketball to Jasper in the 1st round at Bloomington, 77-4. They lost the next game, a slightly more competitive one, to Franklin 11-5. Cutler won a Sectional championship at Logansport in 1922, also becoming one of the 8 winners of the Purdue University Regional by defeating Rochester 45-11 before losing to Vincennes in the Sweet Sixteen in Indianapolis. More recently, the Wildcats enjoyed a 13-5 season in 1940 under Coach Virgil Gwinn, capturing the Delphi Sectional with wins over Camden, the home team Oracles, and Burlington. They themselves became Burlington Polar Cubs before their final consolidation into Carroll High School as Cougars. From Wildcats to Polar Cubs to Cougars, quite a romp through the animal kingdom.

The Adams Mill and Cutler High School

Just north of Muncie was a rolling mill, and it was quite natural for the town that grew up around it to be called Roll. It was equally natural for the name selected for the high school teams there to be the Rollers. They intended to flatten their opposition and had pretty good success at it, too. For the 5 years between 1947 and 1951, the Rollers won 81 of 108 games for Coach Cletus Johnson with 19-2 and 19-3 seasons during that period. They also had a fine 17-5 season for Coach Raymond Cox in 1957. (Some report that the Roll teams were called the Red Rollers, which may well be the case. However, their banner at the Indiana Basketball Hall of Fame is navy blue and white. I am told that a possible reason for that is the fact that it used to be the practice of each senior class to select their own colors, and perhaps the class that provided the banner to the Hall had selected navy and white as theirs.) The Rollers won their only Sectional at Hartford City in 1951 defeating Jefferson, 42-38, Hartford City, 49-47; and Montpelier, 40-38. The Rollers were good at winning the close ones that year.

Roll High School, home of the Rollers, and the 1929 13-6 team

Pike County's Otwell is another example of a town that grew up around a mill. The Otwell Millers are now Pike Central Chargers. At the other end of the state, the Union Mills Millers are now a part of South Central High School in LaPorte County, the Satellites. Otwell's Blue and White won 19 games and lost only 4 as early as 1917 and 1918. They captured their Sectional crown in 1969 at Washington. To do so Coach Harold Anderson's squad had to beat the vaunted Hatchets in the 1st round, which they did by the convincing score of 82-66. They then defeated Barr Reeve, 54-39, and North Daviess, 80-77. Union Mills got theirs at Michigan City in 1950 when Coach Charles Sanders' maroon-and-white-clad team won 20 games and lost just 5, the same record his 1948 Millers had achieved. In the Sectional they eliminated Rolling Prairie, 60-39; Stilwell, 52-49; Wanatah, 61-31; and Michigan City, 54-44. In the Regional the Millers lost to the Vincennes Alices, a Final Four team.

The Otwell School and their Miller and the Union Mills School

Chapter 21

Our Current Most Popular Animals: Panthers, Tigers...and a Zebra?

Τhe Rochester Zebras," as Phil Smith of the *Warsaw Times Union* put it, "were one of the first small school powerhouses in Indiana high school basketball, despite never winning a state title. The stage was set early on for Rochester's 13 regional championships by 1943. Three years before the 1st IHSAA state tournament, Guy Barr of Rochester scored a record 97 points in one game during a 139-9 blowout of Bremen. The game was played Dec. 11, 1908."

Jerry Oliver, who coached the Indianapolis Washington Continentals to the state championship, attended Rochester High School in the lake district of northern Indiana. He confirms that the reason the Rochester teams are the Zebras had nothing to do with the African veldt or local zoos. It had everything to do with the vertical striped black and white uniforms worn by their early basketball teams.

Rochester's record over the years is a very impressive one, including an undefeated regular season at 21-1 in 1974 under Coach Galen Smith. That loss was a tough one to take, too, coming as it did in the final game of the Warsaw Sectional to Akron, 91-89, in overtime. Earlier the Zebras appeared in the Sweet Sixteen 6 times in the period from 1911 through 1919. They made it all the way to the Final Four in 1914 and 1917, losing in the semi-finals each year, to Anderson and to Gary Emerson. From 1918-21 the Zebras under Coach R. C. Johnson won 83 games and lost 21; in 1924 and 1925 Charles Ivey led the Zebras to wins in 45 of the 55 games they played. They were 20-5 in 1935, 26-3 in 1937, and 22-4 in 1938, all for Coach Clyde Lyle, losing in the semi-finals to eventual State Champion Anderson in 1937. Lyle's 1943 Sectional champions went 21-3, and the 1971 Zebras won 20 while losing only 4, capturing another Sectional crown under Jim Powers. All told Rochester has won 32 Sectionals, 6 Regionals (the 13 mentioned above includes Sweet Sixteen appearances prior to actual Regional tournaments), and the 1937 Logansport Semi-state.

The Lady Zebras have also had several memorable years, including 1979's undefeated regular season, 18-1. In 2000 the Scott Mills-led Lady Zebras finished 21-2 and Tony Stesiak's team went 20-2 record the next year. His 2003 team won 22 of 25 games, but it was 2004 that Rochester fans will remember for a long time. That year the girls brought home the Class 2A State Championship when they defeated Heritage Christian 50-41 to finish 25-3.

A Rochester Zebra— Pre-Jerry Oliver! And the Zebra

Zebras may have always been a relatively rare sight in Indiana, but the animal kingdom has been a very frequent source of inspiration when it came to the selection of mascots for our high school athletic teams. The IHSAA reports that there are currently 19 high schools with Panthers as their team name, the most popular choice in our state. We have covered Corydon Central and Knightstown elsewhere, but here are their fierce logos:

The Corydon Central and Knightstown Panthers

The two schools closest to my home in Indianapolis are both represented by Panthers: North Central, my daughter's alma mater and Park Tudor, my sons'. North Central finally presented us with a state championship in 1999, the 2nd year of class basketball. Not only did they win the Class 4A title, but they also won the short-lived Tournament of Champions, an event I attended and enjoyed. The other champions that the Panthers defeated gave excellent accounts of themselves and provided even more fuel for those who believe that class basketball in Indiana is a mistake. Clearly, there are strong arguments on both sides of that issue. Jason Gardner led North Central and was Indiana's Mr. Basketball that year before going on to star at the University of Arizona on several of Lute Olsen's fine teams. Gardner was the 1st of 3 Panthers to be named Mr. Basketball, followed in 2004 by A. J Ratliff and in 2007 by Eric Gordon. All were taught by North Central's excellent coach, Doug Mitchell. All told, the Panthers have won 11 Sectionals, 3 Regionals, and 2 Semi-state championships. The latter was in 2007, when Gordon's efforts for North Central fell just short as E'Twaun Moore led his East Chicago Central Cardinals, coached by Pete Trgovich, to the championship. The Panthers finished runner-up in an exciting, well played 87-83 game.

The North Central Panther

North Central's Amber Harris-led Lady Panthers won consecutive girls Class 4A titles in 2004 and 2005, coached, as previously mentioned by Alan Vickerey. The Lady Panthers have won 15 Sectionals, 5 Regionals and 3 Semi-state titles to go with those 2 state championships. Amber Harris was Indiana Miss Basketball in 2006.

Park Tudor has won many state championships in both boys and girls tennis, but none yet in basketball. My younger son played on one of those tennis teams that came close but could not get past North Central. He also played on the 1st basketball team coached by Todd Lickliter, son of Arlen Lickliter who coached many fine teams at North Central including 1968's 20-4 squad and 1979's 22-7 Regional champions. Todd's considerable success at Butler led to his selection as Steve Alford's replacement at Iowa. That son, by the way, was Park Tudor's high scorer in their Southport Sectional game his senior year. (My other son was a member of the Park Tudor soccer team that came oh-so-close to a state title, losing in a shoot-out—what a miserable solution that is to determining how to break a tie—to eventual champion North Central.)

Park Tudor basketball teams have won 2 Sectionals, the 2001 Class A at Clinton Central and the 2007 Class 2A at Triton Central. They also captured the 2001 South Newton Regional when Coach Ed Kelley's squad finished 19-5. Marc Lickliter coached the Lady Panthers to Sectional titles in 1999 and 2002 as well as the Regional crown in 1999.

Originally known as Park School prior to their merger with the Tudor Hall School for girls, the Panthers had fielded some very impressive teams. Although not yet in the IHSAA, their schedule often included many schools who were, as well as several private schools all over the Midwest. The 1948 team was led by Chuck DeVoe who would captain Princeton University's team 4 years later, leading the Tigers to an Ivy League championship and an NCAA berth. Brother John followed Chuck at Park School. In his senior year, 1952, John scored an amazing 73 points in one-game against an obviously outmanned Ohio Military Academy in Cincinnati. Brother Steve, a year younger, recalls the game with a chuckle: "We were feeding John and he just kept scoring until he seemed to get embarrassed about it and stopped shooting." Steve managed to chip in 27 points himself that day. When else have 2 brothers ever combined to score 100 points in a single game?

That season the Panthers finished 16-4. Fifteen of those 20 games were against IHSAA member schools in which John scored 429 of his season total of 612 points, eclipsing Hallie Bryant's 404 points scored in 20 games for Crispus Attucks. He also went to Princeton and captained their basketball team in 1956 with brother Steve again his teammate. From Panthers to Tigers, those DeVoe brothers made quite an impressive threesome. John, sadly, was taken from us much too early, suffering a fatal heart attack at an Indiana Pacers game, while I was with him, along with both of his brothers and his wife, Jane. I have missed his friendship and ready smile ever since.

The Bloomington South Panthers have amassed 40 Sectional championships (including the time when they were simply Bloomington High School) and 17 Regionals. Until 2009 their only Semi-state title was in 1960 when they ran into the Muncie Central Bearcat team that showcased the talents of Jim Davis, Ron Bonham, and John Dampier in the 1st game of the finals. They lost a rather one-sided contest to the eventual runners up. It was still a fine 16-2 season for Coach Keith Rhoads and his Panthers. They also had several other excellent years beginning as early as 1918 through 1921, when Cliff Wells coached those 4 teams to records of 25-4, 23-3, 19-12, and 21-8. That's 88 wins and 27 losses and includes 1919's state championship. Between 1913 and 1922 the Panthers made 5 other trips to the Sweet Sixteen, the 1918 and 1922 squads getting all the way to the Final Four. Bill Frohliger's 1967 Panther team finished 19-6 as did his 1970 squad, both bested by his 1971 team's record of 21-6.

It was in 1973 that the Panthers became Bloomington South. (Cougar was the mascot choice for Bloomington North.) Bill Springer coached the 1977 and 1978 Panthers to impressive 18-3 and 23-3 marks. J. R. Holmes took the reins in 1983, and 26 years later he is still at it, still doing well. In 1985 his team won 23 of 26 outings folowed by 19-6, 23-5 and 18-7 seasons, a 4-year span of 83 wins and just 21 losses. The Holmes-coached Panthers put together another commendable 4 years beginning in 1998: 17-5, 25-2, 194, and 19-3. This comes to 80 wins and only 17 lossses. Finally in 2009 Coach Holmes' team broke through, capping an undefeated 29-0 season by winning the Class 4A State Championship final game 69-62 over Ft. Wayne Snider in a battle of snarling Panthers before 17,681 fans at Conseco Fieldhouse. Shortly thereafter *USA Today*'s final ranking of high school teams placed the Panthers 3rd in the country behind only 2 residential prep schols who bring in players from all over the country, many of whom are on a post-graduate year. The paper

The Bloomington South Panther

also selected J. R. Holmes National Coach of the Year, 2009.Coach Larry Winters led the Lady Panthers to an undefeated regular season in 2002, finishing 23-1. Since 1976 they have compiled 5 Sectional titles and 2 Regionals.

In Grant County the 1998 Eastbrook Panthers won 17 games for Coach Jim Erwin and lost 6. They won their 2nd Sectional crown that year, in Class 2A to go with their 1979 open class title. The Lady Panthers had undefeated regular season in 1983 21-1 with John Drook coaching, and the next year 25-1 with Jim Etherington in charge. In the latter year they won one of their 5 Sectional championships as well as their lone Regional and Semi-state titles. In their Final Four appearance they lost to Crown Point, dropping a

The Eastbrook Panther

6-point decision to the Lady Bulldogs in the semifinals.

The Evansville Reitz Panthers coached by Clarence Riggs lost a heartbreaker in the 1951 state championship game to Muncie Central, 60-58. Their 1968 team under the coaching of Jim Barnett finished 23-5, losing another hard to take Regional final to Vincennes, 71-70. All told, the Panthers have won 10 of those tough Evansville Sectional championships (actually in 2008 it was held at Castle) and 3 Regionals to go with their 1951 Semi-state and state championship runner-up trophies. The Lady Panthers won Sectionals in 1976, 1981, and 1990. Their Regional title came at Gibson Southern in 1981, when they went on to capture the Bedford North Lawrence Semi-state and the Indiana state championship as well, finishing a marvelous 26-1 for Coach Louise Owen.

Ft. Wayne Snider's Panthers were coached by Roy Kline from 1965 through 1979. His best year was a fine 20-5 mark in 1967. All told, they have won 5 Sectionals. The Lady Panthers have enjoyed many successful seasons for Coach LaMar Kilmer, beginning with a 24-3 mark in 1984. In 1988 they won the state championship with an outstanding 27-1 mark, edging the Noblesville Lady Millers in the exciting final game by a 60-58 count. They finished with a 25-3 record and the State Runner-up trophy in 2001, losing to the 27-2 Ben Davis Lady Giants in the final game at Conseco Fieldhouse. Two years earlier they had also finished runner-up, that time to the 26-0 New Albany's Lady Bulldogs by 5 points, finishing 25-3. For the 3 years from 1991 through 1993, they won 53 games and lost only 10, beating even that impressive mark substantially during the period 1998 through 2000 when they rang up 72 wins while again losing only 10. Through the years they have taken 8 Sectional, 6 Regional, and 3 Semi-state nets for their crowded trophy case.

Northwood's Lady Panthers have an even more impressive story to tell. Coached for the last 31 seasons by Steve Neff, who is still on the bench in Nappanee, the Northwood girls have accumulated 19 Sectional titles, 10 Regionals, 2 Semi-states, and the 1999 Class 3A State Championship, defeating Linda Bamrick's previously unbeaten Indianapolis Cathedral Fighting Irish in a thriller, 72-71. Northwood finished that year 24-3, Cathedral 27-1. In addition, Northwood put together some other outstanding season marks: 24-1 in 1981; 21-3 in 1988; 18-1 in 1992. That year began an 8-year string during which the Lady Panthers won 169 games while losing only 20! Three undefeated regular seasons were included in that string, 1992, of course, 1995, 22-1 and 1997, 25-1.

Northwood's boys teams have won 3 Sectionals and 1 Regional, in 2007. In 1982 Tom Firestone coached the Panthers to an 18-4 mark. Dan Gunn coached the Panthers for 15 seasons beginning in 1993 with records of 19-6 in 1995, 18-6 in 2001, and 19-8 in 2007. Both teams play their home games in the Panther Pit.

The Snider and Northwood Panthers

SNIDER

In Royal Center Pioneer High School's Panthers won the Logansport Sectional in 1964 and the Caston Class A Sectional in 2002. In the school's 1st year, 1964, Berlin Rowe led the team to a 23-2 record. Don Andrews' 1974 team finished 20-3, followed the next year by Howard Leedy's 19-3 Panther team. The Lady Panthers have also garnered 2 Sectional crowns, both at Cass, in 1980 and 1981 for Coach Duane Hamilton. In Montezuma the Riverton Parke Panthers have also won 2 Class A Sectionals, both at North Vermillion, in 2003 and 2006. The Lady Panthers picked off their only Sectional title at West Vigo in 1992. In North Vernon the Jennings County Panthers have won 3 Sectionals and the 1998 Class 4A Jeffersonville Regional. Don Schroeder's 1972 and 1973 squads won 42 of 47 games, including the 1st of the school's 10 Sectional crowns. Joe Null's 1987 Panthers finished 21-2, and Kendall Wildey led the 1996 and 1998 teams to 21-4 records, including the school's only Regional title. The Lady Panthers have brought home 10 Sectional championships and 3 Regionals. Their best records were 19-3 in 1988, 18-5 in 1990, 18-4 in 1995, and 18-2 in 1996, all for Coach Bob Howe, and 19-3 for Joe Granecki in 2002.

The Pioneer, Riverton Parke, and Jennings County Panthers

The Gary Roosevelt Panthers have had an illustrious history since their commissioning as a high school in 1930, the first and only high school in Gary exclusively for African-American students. Louis Mallard took over as coach in 1954 and immediately led his first team to a 21-5 record. As an encore the 1955 Panthers did even better, 27-3, runner-up for the state championship to the Attucks Tigers in that memorable year. Hall-of-Famer Mallard's record at Roosevelt was truly remarkable. In 15 years at the Gary school, his teams won 325 games and lost just 62, an average of 22 wins and 4 losses every year for the entire period. In addition to his runner-up finish in 1955, Mallard got that coveted state championship in 1968 over Indianapolis Shortridge. Ron Heflin's Roosevelt record is also impressive. He held the job from 1977 through 1997. His teams turned in a 20-5 mark in 1981 followed by a 22-6 state runner-up finish the next year and a 20-3 record in 1984. In 1987 the Panthers won 24 of 27 games. Two years after they went 20-3 and followed that with a 23-3 record. Then in 1991, with Glenn Robinson as the driving force, the Roosevelt Panthers again climbed the heights of Indiana basketball, winning the final game against Alan Henderson's Brebeuf Braves at the Hoosier Dome to finish 30-1. More recently, Ron Broome led the 2003 Panthers to an excellent 23-2 mark. All told in addition to those 2 state titles and 2 runner-up trophies, the Panthers have won 24 Sectional, 12 Regional, and 6 Semi-state crowns.

The Lady Panthers have added 10 Sectional nets to the school's trophy case and enjoyed an undefeated regular season for Carl Horton in 1988, finishing 24-1.

The Western Panthers of Russiaville won 2 open class Sectionals, in 1983 and 1990, both at Kokomo, as well as 4 Class 3A Sectionals, all at Frankfort. Their only Regional title was in 2004 at Plymouth, Andy Weaver's team finishing 22-3. Western's Lady Panthers have added 4 Sectional nets to the school trophy case, 3 in a row for Mary Kay Alysworth 1979-1981. Griffith's Panthers won their Sectional crowns at Crown Point in 1967, Mack Harold's squad turning in a 20-4 mark, and at Calumet in 1973 with a 16-7 record for Bob Heady. In 1947 the Griffith Panthers won 19 of 23 games for Coach Vin Oliver, and in 2003 Jack Gabor's team finished 18-4. The Griffith Lady Panthers also have 2 Sectional titles, both Class 3A, both won at Calumet, in 1998 and 2000. In the latter year they also won the New Prairie Regional. Elwood turned in a brilliant undefeated regular season in 1923 for Coach Raleigh Phillips, finishing 26 and 1. In the Anderson Sectional the Panthers trounced Markleville 57-4 before losing to the host Indians 41-10. Anderson made it to the Final Four that year, dropping a 2-point decision to eventual State Champion Vincennes Lincoln in the semi-finals at the old Coliseum in Indianapolis. Elwood's Panthers did pick up Sectional titles in

The Western, Griffith, and Elwood Panthers and the Lakewood Park Panther Paw

1957 and 1960, both for Carl McNulty, with records of 19-7 and 17-7. Their girls teams have also won 3 Sectionals, the latter 2 with a 20-4 record for Shelly Taylor in 2005 and an 18-6 mark for (now) Shelley Renbarger, in 2007. Panthers are also the choice of a relatively new school, Lakewood Park Christian, in Auburn.

There are also 17 Tigers (Yorktown being a green Tiger). We have covered Lebanon, Peru, Alexandria, and Princeton elsewhere.

A word here about the Warsaw Lady Tigers. They won the 1st OFFICIAL Indiana State Championship in 1976. It is a fact that basketball for women seemed to die after the 1930s. Warsaw and other girls teams helped redeem that loss. The Lady Tigers were led by Judi Warren, Indiana's 1st Miss Basketball, who has been such an excellent spokesperson for the game and for our state ever since. This is how the Hall of Fame presents this outstanding achiever:

Warsaw bad cat

Judi Warren

Holds a special historical role in women's basketball in Indiana, being Indiana's 1st Miss Basketball and a member of the first IHSAA Girl's Basketball Championship Team in 1976 coached by Hall of Fame inductee Jan Soyez ... hit five free throws in the final sixty-four seconds to ice a 57-52 triumph over Bloomfield before a crowd of 7,362 ... chosen as the first recipient of the Mental Attitude Award ... after graduating from Franklin College she coached at South Dearborn, Maconaquah and Carmel High Schools ... while at Carmel she guided the Greyhounds to a state runner-up finish in 1995.

Not only did those Warsaw Lady Tigers win the 1st IHSAA Girls State Championship, they did it undefeated, 22-0. And they did it again 2 years later, again undefeated. The coach of those teams, Janice Soyez, is also a Hall of Famer:

The 1976 Warsaw Lady Tigers

Janice Soyez
Coached girl's basketball at Warsaw Community High School from 1968 to 1978 ... won-loss record 117-15 ... coach of the first IHSAA Girl's Basketball State Tournament Championship team in 1976 and won the third tournament in 1978 ...undefeated seasons both years (22-0) ... named Ball State University Alumnus Coach of the Year in 1976 and 1978 ... honored by the Indiana Coaches of Girls Sports Association in 1976 and 1978.

Interestingly, all 4 of our 1st girls state champions finished undefeated. The other 2 were East Chicago Roosevelt's Lady Rough Riders in 1977, 24-0, and 1979, 23-0, coached both years by Roberta DeKemper, whose first 4 teams never lost a regular season game, winning 91 and losing 2! Not only that, but the 4 runner-up schools were also undefeated entering the championship game: Bloomfield's Lady Cardinals, coached by Nancy Woodward, 20-1; Mount Vernon's (Fortville) Lady Marauders, coached by Carolyn Oldfather, 16-1; Jac-Cen-Del's Lady Eagles coached by Mary Jo McClelland, 22-1; and Anderson Madison Heights' Lady Argylls, coached by Billie Bienhart, 24-1.

Hall of Fame citations for Roberta DeKemper and LaTaunya Pollard (now Romanazzi) of East Chicago Roosevelt:

Roberta DeKemper
Coached for 17 years in East Chicago ... 11 Years as the head coach at East Chicago Roosevelt ... 4 years at East Chicago Central High School ... coaching record of 263-56 ... from 1976-1979 her teams won 91 of 93 games and captured two state championships ... conducted basketball clinics in Chad and Zaire ... coached national team in Cameroon in 1986 ... coach of the year awards in 1977, 1978, and 1987 ... inducted into East Chicago Sports Hall of Fame in 1991.

LaTaunya Pollard
Miss Basketball 1979 ... averaged 23 points and 8 rebounds per game during high school career at East Chicago Roosevelt ... high school team won the state championship in 1977 and 1979 ... named to McDonald's All Star team and won the MVP award ... holds 7 basketball records at California State Long Beach ... scored a total of 3,001 career points and averaging 23.4 ... member of the Kodak All-American squad for 3 years ... USA Basketball Athlete of the Year in 1982 ... Wade Trophy Winner senior year ... took her game to Women's Professional League in Europe ... 1983 averaged 39.5 ppg., which is still the all-time record in Italy ... from 1990-95 she averaged 36.6 points for the Sidis Aneona team Italy ... inducted into California State Long Beach Hall of Fame 1988 ... 2001 inducted into the Women's Collegiate Basketball Hall of Fame in Tennessee ... 2004 Silver Anniversary Team.

Back to the Warsaw Lady Tigers, whose first 2 state titles only begin to tell the whole story. In 1980 Mary Hurley coached the Warsaw girls to a 21-1 mark. Will Wienhorst took over as coach in 1987, a job he held through 2004, turning in season marks of 21-2 in 1988, 22-1 in 1989, and 21-1 in 1990. That's a 3-year mark of 64-4! What to do for an encore? How about 22-4 in 1991? That team lost the state championship final game to an undefeated Bedford North Lawrence Lady Stars team that finished 29-0 for Coach Pete Pritchett. Wienhorst's Warsaw team also finished 21-2 in 2003, and his last team won 26 and lost only 3. They were beaten in the 2004 Class 4A state final by Indianapolis North Central's Lady Panthers, led by Amber Harris and coached by Alan Vickery. In total the Lady Tigers have won 15 Sectionals, 12 Regionals, and 4 Semi-states to go with their 2 state titles.

The Warsaw Tigers boys teams have nothing to be ashamed of, either. As early as 1910 they turned in an undefeated season: 6-0. In 1920 they won 20 of 23 games for C. J. Roberts. The 1st of 36 Sectional and 12 Regional crowns came for Coach Frank Cash in 1923 with the Tigers turning in another 20-3 mark, a record his squad improved on the next year to 22-3. George Fisher coached the Tigers from 1927 through 1941, his best records coming in 1935, 20-4; 1936, 23-8; and 1938, 20-3. His successor was Wendell Walker, whose first two Tiger squads won 49 games and lost only 7. Fisher then returned for one more year, guiding the 1944 team to a 20-5 season. Boag Johnson coached the 1965 through 1967 teams to 60 wins and 7 losses and the 1969 team to a 22-5 finish. It was Al Rhodes, however, who led the Tigers to their greatest glory during his 22 years as head coach. His 1st squad, in 1981, won 22 and lost 5, capturing the Tigers' 1st of 4 Semi-state crowns. In their Final Four appearances, all under Rhodes, the Tigers were beaten by the Anderson Indians in the afternoon game in 1981; won the championship over the Vincennes Alices in 1984, with a 26-2 final record; again lost the afternoon game in 1992, this time to Lafayette Jeff's Bronchos and again finishing 26-2; and were beaten by New Albany's Bulldogs in yet a 3rd afternoon game of the finals in 1996 to end a 25-3 season.

The Warsaw Tiger and the Bloomfield Cardinal squared off in our 1st official girls state championship in 1976

Fishers was originally called Mudsock because of the mud in the streets and roads that caused horses to develop what appeared to be mud socks. When the railroad came, the name was changed to Fishers Switch, later shortened to Fishers. It was a small town when it had its own high school—their mascot was the Tiger. When some of the small schools in Hamilton County were consolidated into Hamilton Southeastern, the Tiger was temporarily lost in favor of the team name Royals represented by a Lion. However, with the explosive growth of Hamilton County (Fishers had a population of 350 in 1963, 2,000 in 1980 and 65,382 in 2007!) a new school was needed, and it was named Fishers High School. The old mascot was revived, and the Fishers Tigers again took the field and the court representing their new school. Now Hamilton Southeastern and Fishers annually compete for the Mudsock Trophy.

Fishers is another on any list of must-see Indiana locales, if only for the presence of Conner Prairie, an extensive and outstanding outdoor museum with period-costumed staff whose speech and actions always remain consistent with the era they are depicting. I have been told by knowledgeable persons all over the country that it is a model of what a historical park should be. The original Conner homestead is in the park, the importance of which to Indiana history was covered previously.

Early Fishers High School and today's Fishers Tiger

The original Fishers Tigers had a marvelous year for Coach Horace Love in 1947, winning 20 of 22 games. They did not win the Sectional that year, however, their lone such title at Kokomo in 1922, the year they also won the Purdue Regional. In the state tournament they beat the Goshen Redskins in the 1st round before losing to Terre Haute Garfield's Purple Eagles.

Yorktown's green-and-white-clad Tigers have had an illustrious history on the Indiana hardwood. Leslie Reeves led his 1931 team to an 18-3 mark. Then Art Beckner's 1933 through 1935 Tigers won 61 games while losing only 16, with 1934's squad turning in a 26 and 2 mark. Ken Sigler's 1939 team finished 20-5, and 11 years later Ed May's Tigers turned in a 22-4 record. From 1953 through 1955 Earl Snider's teams won 60 games and lost only 12, going 22-2 in the last year of that string. In 1966 the Tigers finished 20-5 with Dan Thornburg at the helm. Six years later Don Rogers' team finished 21-4. That year the Tigers beat

The Yorktown Green Tiger

Muncie Central to take the Sectional, then knocked out the Kent Benson-led New Castle Trojans before losing the Regional final to yet another NCC power, Richmond. In 1998 Joe Bradford's Tiger team came closest to their ultimate goal, getting all the way to the Class 3A State Championship game only to lose to the Cathedral Irish, finishing 24-4. The Tigers have won 4 Sectionals and the 1998 Regional and Semi-state crowns. The Lady Tigers have won 6 Sectionals and 1 Regional. Connie Lyons' charges had a terrific 4-year string from 1996 through 1999, winning 78 games while losing only 12.

The Northwestern Tigers in Howard County won the Class 2A State Championship in 2007 defeating the Winchester Golden Falcons in one of the most exciting finals ever, 78-74, double overtime. Jim Gish was the Tiger coach, and the team achieved a 25-2 mark, then a fine 22-3 record the next year. Earlier Tom Dean's 1951 team won 20 of 23 games, and in 1975 Steve David coached the Tigers to an undefeated regular season, 21-1. Allen Wayne's 1981 and 1982 teams each won 20 games, lost 4, and won a Sectional crown. Jim Yeakel's 1998 team registered a 22-4 year, and took the 1st Regional title. The next year was a 21-3 season. In total, the Tigers have won 8 Sectionals and 2 Regionals. The Lady Tigers have taken 4 Sectional championships. From 2001 through 2003, the 1st 2 years under Jeff Hoover and the last under Mike McKoskey, they won 64 games and lost only 8.

LaCrosse is one of the smallest public high schools in the state, with 110 students. Still their Tigers have taken 3 Sectionals. The 1st was in 1977, Steve Leonard's team winning 18 and losing 8. The 2nd was in 1989 with a sterling 23-3 mark under Bill Berger, and the 3rd was 2 years later, with Berger still coaching, when the Tigers finished 21-3. In 2008 Todd Miller coached the Lady Tigers to an undefeated regular season and a memorable 23-1 final record.

 *The Northwestern and LaCrosse Tigers*

When you go to Bluffton to play basketball you do so in the Tigers' Den. I suppose that can be intimidating, but what Indiana high school venue isn't? Anyway, the Bluffton Tigers have amassed 30 Sectional titles and 5 Regional crowns. Their lone trip to the state finals came in 2002 when they finished runner-up to the Class 2A State Champion Speedway Sparkplugs. The Tigers that year ended with a 24-4 mark, Wayne Barker coaching. The Lady Tigers also made it to the final game of the state championship once, too, Ron DeWitt's 21-6 1998 team losing to Southridge in the Class 2A title game.

The Lawrenceburg Tigers in their orange and black uniforms won 26 games for Coach George Bateman in 1947, losing only 2. In 1971 they won 20 of 24 starts with Marvin Pitcock at the helm. Jim Pugh coached the 1981 and 1982 squads to 19-5 and 20-4 records, and his teams had a good stretch from 1991 through 1993, finishing 18-5, 22-4, and 17-5. All told, the Tiger have run up 28 Sectional titles and 5 Regionals. The Lady Tigers have won 2 Sectional crowns.

Lawrenceburg High School and Tiger

The Hagerstown Tigers began playing basketball at least as early as 1909 when Charles Woolard coached the team to a 7-1 record. W. J. Stahr held the coaching reins from 1917–1925 and his 1920 and 1921 teams both finished 20-6. His 1924 Tigers were 20-8. Both the 1928 and 1929 teams won Sectional crowns, the former, coached by Willis Dorsett, finished 18-8 and the latter under Malfield Cain's direction, won 21 and lost 6. Cain's 1938 Tigers won 20 of 24 games, losing the Sectional final to Richmond's Red Devils. Two other Sectional titles are in the Hagerstown trophy case, from 1959 and 1965. The Lady Tigers had an undefeated regular season, 20-1, in 1993 under Coach Mike Beeson to win the 1st of their 3 consecutive Sectional titles.

Evansville Reitz Memorial High School's Web site includes the phrase "Through the eye of the Tiger." Rich Risemas coached the Memorial Tigers to Regional titles in 1986, 1987, and 1989 with records of 20-7, 25-2, and 20-7. Memorial earlier won Regional crowns under Ron Wannemueler in 1966 and 1970. Rick Wilgus coached the Tigers to their 8th Sectional crown with a 21-2 record in 2008. The Lady Tigers have added another 11 Sectional crowns and 2 Regional titles to the school's trophy case. Bruce Dockery's 23-5 Lady Tigers earned a runner-up trophy, losing to Ft. Wayne Bishop Luers in the 2006 Class 3A tournament, 65-54. Other 20-victory seasons for the lady Tigers came in 1987 for Coach Dan Edwards, and for Dockery's 1998 through 2006 teams, with the exception of 2002, when those 8 teams amassed 170 wins and only lost 34.

Crothersville's 1st basketball team was organized in 1908, 14 years before they were to have their first gymnasium. They, too, are the Tigers; their logo shows clearly that they also have the eye of the Tiger in Jackson County. Crothersville's Tigers turned in records of 17-6 for Coach Bill Lyskowinski in 1936, 16-6 for Fred Breckenridge in 1951, and 17-7, followed by 19-6, for Bill Peden in 1955 and 1956. In 1959 Ervin Cohen's Tiger squad finished 17-5; Jerry Owen's teams went 18-5 and 17-5 in 1980 and 1981.

Triton Central is in Shelby County, where both the Tigers and the Lady Tigers have won 5 Sectionals and 1 Regional. Marv Tudor's Tigers had a 20-3 season in 1964, followed by an undefeated regular season, 21-1, the next year. Hank West's team captured the school's 1st Sectional with a 20-3 mark in 1983. His 1989 squad brought home that one Regional crown. Jay Payne's 1997 Tigers won 21 and lost just 3. Larry Pringle has coached the Lady Tigers for 25 years, beginning in 1984. His 1996 team was undefeated in the regular season, finishing 20-1 and beginning a 7-year string when the Lady Tigers won 138 games while losing only 24.

Two new Tiger entries come from new charter schools in Indianapolis: Tindley Academy, made possible by the leadership of concerned citizens such as John Neighbors and the recently opened Indiana Math and Science Academy.

Let's close with 1 more panther.

South Bend Washington's Panthers won their 1st Sectional championship in 1938 for Coach John How. Their 2nd and 3rd both came under the leadership of Stubby Nowicki with very impressive 20-5 and 20-2 records in 1965 and 1977. The 1965 team also won the school's only Regional title. Milt Cooper's 1997 and 2002 Panthers added 2 more Sectional nets to the school's trophy case, finishing 17-8 and 22-4.

It has been the Lady Panthers, however, who have really put their mark on Indiana, and, indeed, national girls basketball. Marilyn Coddens has coached her girls to 137 wins while suffering only 14 defeats from 2003 through 2008. Included in that amazing run was the 2007 state championship with a 28-1 record and state runner-up finishes in 2006 and 2008. We have also just learned that the Lady Panthers again were runner-up for the state title in 2009, losing a 71-69 last second thriller to the Ben Davis Lady Giants who have been crowned by *USA Today* as national high school champions! Salving their wounds a bit, it has also just been announced in the same paper that "South Bend Washington senior Skylar Diggins has been named the Gatorade National Girls' Basketball Player of the Year for 2008-2009." Their 26-1 record in 2009 brings Washington's record for the 2003-09 period to a remarkable 163 wins and 15 defeats.

South Bend Washington Panthers

Our Panthers (19) and Tigers (17), plus 1 Zebra equal 37 of our current schools, or just over 9 percent.

Chapter 22

Bulldogs, Wildcats, and Cougars: Grrr, Yowl, and Purr

After Panthers and Tigers our next most popular animal teams names are our 14 Bulldogs, 12 Cougars, and 10 Wildcats.

Bulldog, Bulldog, Bow-wow-wow: Two versions of the New Haven Bulldogs, but not Yale

The Bulldog total includes the Columbus North Bull Dogs, 2 words, not one, a mistake I will not soon make again, at least when I am anywhere near people from that wonderful town. It is a national treasure of distinctive architecture and a true Indiana gem.

The Columbus Bull Dogs had back-to-back undefeated regular seasons in 1963 and 1964 and made it to the Final Four twice, in 1964 and 1975. They were coached by Hall of Famer Bill Stearman, whose citation follows:

Bill Stearman
MVP 3 of 4 varsity years at Columbus...all-conference...at Indiana University, concentrated on baseball...team won Big 10 in '48...Balfour Award winner as a junior that season...played for Cummins Engine's state AAU championship team in '48...coached at Waldron High School '49-52, with 48-18 record...took over Columbus reins in '52...concluded career with 653-318 record...22 sectional titles, 11 regional championships . . . 2 semi-state titles, earning his team Final Four berths in '64 and '75 . . . .coached Columbus to back-to-back unbeaten regular seasons in '63 & '64.

All told, as Columbus and North, the Bull Dogs have won 49 Sectional championships, 17 Regionals and 3 Semi-states. In 1918 they won their own Sectional, beating Aurora 31-13 in the final game. At Indiana University Fred Busenberg's team apparently received a forfeit from Franklin their 1st-round opponent. Anyway, the score was 2-0. The Bull Dogs lost their next game to Montmorenci, 16-13. They turned in their 1st 20-win season for Busenberg in 1919, finishing 22-3 and making it to the final eight by beating South Bend 24-3 and Rochester 11-5 before dropping a 20-16 decision to Thorntown. In 1921 Everett Case led the Bull Dogs to a 21-10 mark. Cliff Wells coached the next year's team to a 24-6 record, and in 1923 William Dobbins led the team to a 22-9 season. Three seasons, 3 coaches, 67 wins. Frank Newsom's teams also won 67 games in a 3-year stretch: 22-5 in 1929, 24-4 in 1929, and 21-2 in 1930. His 1932 squad won 23 of 28 games. Boots George turned in a 22-9 record in 1938, and Noel Genth's 1946 Dogs went 21-5. It was Stearman, though, who truly led Columbus High School to its greatest glory. He coached there from 1953 until 1972, when the school became North, and turned in 21-6 and 21-5 marks in his 2nd and 3rd year on the job. It is the period from 1963 through 1965 that really stands out. Those 3 years Stearman's teams had 2 undefeated regular seasons, 25-1 in 1963 and 27-1 in 1964, followed by 22-4 for a total of 74 wins and only 6 losses. The Bull Dog's lone defeat in 1964 was by 4 points to Huntington in the morning game of the state finals at Butler Fieldhouse, and Huntington would drop the night game to Lafayette Jeff by just 3 points. In 1963 the only loss of the season had also come in Indianapolis, to Muncie Central, eventual state champion, in the Semi-state tournament. So close, twice. In 1968 the Bull Dogs won 23 and lost 3, that 3rd loss coming to eventual runner-up Indianapolis Shortridge, also at (the recently renamed) Hinkle Fieldhouse.

Columbus North Bull Dogs

Stearman would coach North for another 24 seasons, making a total of 44 years at the same school! His 1975 team again made the Final Four with a 23-5 record, losing the afternoon game at Market Square Arena to Jack Butcher's Loogootee team. That game certainly pitted 2 of our state's greatest coaches across the court from one another.

The Columbus North girls have added 13 Sectional championships to the school's illustrious record.

Brownsburg strikes my fancy because all of the street signs in town are in the school's purple and white colors with the Bulldog mascot on them. Brownsburg has won 16 Sectionals and 6 Regionals. Their 1st Semi-state and state championship came in 2008 as they beat 4 of the top 4A schools in the rankings, North Central, Carmel, New Albany, and Marion, in the process. This run culminated in the last second shot by Gordon Heyward, snatching the victory from the Marion Giants that they had strived so hard to get. Earlier, the Bulldogs were coached for 26 years, 1916 through

1941 by John Symonds, winning their 1st and 2nd Sectional titles under his direction in 1927 and 1938. Glen Steele's 1946 Bulldogs won 22 games and lost only 3, and in 1959 Lucas Cevert led his team to a 25-4 mark and another Sectional crown. Steve Brunes enjoyed a highly successful tenure as Brownsburg's coach from 1988 through 1998, his squads gathering nets from Sectionals 7 times and Regionals 5 . Their best records were 24-3 in 1992 and 1994 and 20-5 in 1995. The Lady Bulldogs have added 11 Sectional titles, 2 Regionals, and the 1991 Semi-state to the school's trophy case. That 1991

The Brownsburg Bulldog

team had an undefeated regular season for Coach Mike Griffin, finishing 25-1, their only loss coming in the semi-finals of the championship 63-54 to Warsaw at Market Square Arena. Griffin coached the Lady Dogs for 18 years. His 1989 team won 20 of 25 games, and his 2000 and 2001 squads won 41 games and lost only 8.

We touched on the Lapel Bulldogs earlier, including their Class A State Championship season, 25-3, for Coach Jim Howell in 2005. As early as 1918 the Bulldogs turned in a 20-4 record and from 1930 through 1932 Lane Scott's teams won 59 of 70 games with 1932's 21-2 season heading the list. Paul Myer's 1925 team won the school's 1st Sectional. Fifteen years later Herman Hinshaw's squad won 22 games, lost 7, and won the Anderson Semi-state, defeating North Vernon 42-25 to earn the right to go to Indianapolis. There, at the Butler Fieldhouse, the Bulldogs dropped a nerve-wracking 38-36 decision to eventual State Champion Hammond Tech in the morning game. Dallas Hunter's 1974 squad finished an excellent 20-3 but could not get by the host Indians in the Anderson Sectional final game. The Lady Bulldogs have won 2 Sectional tournaments, in 2000 and

Lapel Bulldogs

2001 and the 2001 Regional for Kevin Brattain, whose 2006 and 2008 Lapel girls teams also turned in excellent 22-5 and 22-3 records.

The Batesville Bulldogs also had many memorable seasons. They won 22 of 26 games for Coach Paul Wenke in 1963 and were 24-2 with Kirby Overman holding the reins in 1971. Steve Cochrane led Batesville to a 22-2 record in 1983. Melvin Seifert-led Bulldog teams went 20-5 in 1994, 23-2 two years later and 26-2 in 1997. They also enjoyed 21-6 marks in 2001 and 2006. Over the course of years, the Batesville Bulldogs have won 28 Sectionals, 8 Regionals, and 2 Semi-states. The Lady Bulldogs have also fielded many good teams including consecutive undefeated regular seasons in 1989 and 1990 for Art Brebberman, 23-1, and 25-1, and his 1985 squad finished 21-4. In total they have won 12 Sectional and 2 Regional championships.

The Batesville Bulldogs

The Clinton Central Bulldogs won 21 games and lost only 3 for Ray Craft in 1966. With John Sloggett coaching they went 19-6 and 20-2 in 1980 and 1981 and 19-3 in 1995. Clinton's Dogs have won 5 Sectionals and the 1980 Frankfort Regional, downing Plainfield 53-43 and North Montgomery 46-44 in overtime. In addition, the Lady Bulldogs enjoyed a 20-3 season with Linda Barnett coaching in 1985 and an undefeated regular season at 19-1 in 1988. They have brought 9 Sectional and 2 Regional crowns back to their Michigantown home.

The Cannelton Bulldogs have won 6 Sectional championships. Although the Lady Bulldogs have not yet won a championship, they had a 16-3 record in 1984 for Coach Connie Russell. The Centerville Bulldogs have garnered 4 Sectionals as well as the 2004 Alexandria Class 2A Regional crown. Several past Centerville teams have run up very nice records as well. Ernest Mahan coached the 1926 team to an 18-6 mark, and Vernon Warner's 1929 squad did almost as well, finishing 17-6. Malcolm Ruby's 1937 team was 17-4, and his 1941 Bulldogs were 20-4. In 1957 with Cliff Swim coaching Centerville finished 19-4. Although the Lady Bulldogs have never won a Sectional, they had a good year in 1984 for Brenda Wolski, 16-4, and another for Dick Lawler, 16-5, in 2006.

In the town of Crown Point the Bulldogs won 18 of 23 games in 1953 with Dean Snider as their coach. Henry Allison's 1964 team did even better, finishing 20-4, and his 1967 outfit came in at 18-4, followed by 17-6 and 21-3 marks the next 2 years. That 3-year span was a stellar 56-13. Between 1966 and 2008 6 Sectional championships were won by Bulldog teams as well as the 1998 East Chicago Regional.

The Crown Point Bulldog

The Lady Bulldogs have amassed 17 Sectional crowns, 7 Regionals, and 4 Semi-states. They were coached by Tom May for 27 years, from 1981 through 2007. During that time they won 15 of their total of 17 Sectional titles, all 6 of their Regional crowns, and 3 Semi-states. They made it to the final game of the state tournament 3 years in a row, from 1983 through 1985. The 1st time Coach May's team lost to the powerhouse that was Bedford North Lawrence by 5 points, but the next 2 years his Lady Bulldogs won it all, going undefeated in 1984, 26-0, and 25-4 the next year. Three years, 2 state championships, a runner-up finish, 73 games won, and just 9 lost. Quite a record! Their 4th trip to the final game came in 1997, when they lost to Jan Conner's Martinsville Lady Artesians, 66-59, finishing their season with a 22-5 record.

Then there are the Evansville Benjamin Bosse Bulldogs. Theirs is an illustrious history. Since their 1st Sectional win in 1922, Bosse teams have won 25. They have also won 14 Regional crowns and 6 Semi-states. The Bulldogs 1st trip to the Final Four was in 1932 when they lost the afternoon game at Butler Fieldhouse by 4 points to Winamac. Back in 1939 the Bulldogs lost again at Butler, again by 4 points, this time to the eventual champion Frankfort Hot Dogs. In 1944 and 1945 they won back-to-back state championships, defeating fierce felines each year. First it was Kokomo's Wildkats and then it was South Bend Riley's Wildcats. The Bulldogs finished with 19-7 and 25-2 marks for coach Herman Keller. Bosse fans had to wait 17 years for their next trip to Indianapolis, but, again, they made the most of it, winning their 3rd state championship by 3 points over the East Chicago Washington Senators to finish 26-2 in Jim Myers' 1st year of a 19-year tenure as Bosse's head coach. After another long hiatus, this one of 20 years duration, Bosse was back to the final round in 1982, now under the guidance of Joe Mullan.

In one of the most stirring, closely contested days in the history of Indiana basketball, Bosse lost their only game of 28 by a single point to Gary Roosevelt after Plymouth had edged Indianapolis Cathedral by 3 points in the semi-finals. Plymouth's Pilgrims then upended the Roosevelt Panthers by 1 point in double overtime behind Scott Skiles' amazing 39-point performance. An unforgettable day, indeed. Mullan's Bulldogs would put together a 2nd straight undefeated regular season in 1983, 23-1. That's 50 wins and 2 losses in those 2 years. His 1990 team also did quite well, winning 24 of 27 games. The Bosse Bulldogs made their final appearance to date in Indianapolis in 2007, losing to Plymouth, this time in the Class 3A Championship game, Coach Jeff Hein's Bulldogs completing a 22-5 season.

Bosse's Lady Bulldogs have also done well, winning a total of 10 Sectionals, 7 Regionals, and the 1984 Seymour Semi-state. Jerry Canterbury coached the latter team to a 24-2 record and a trip to Market Square Arena, where his team lost to Indianapolis Warren Central in the semi-finals. Angie Oliver's 1997 Lady Bulldogs won 20 of 24 games followed the next year by a 21-2 mark and her 2007 squad finished 22-4.

Monrovia's Bulldogs, wearing green and white, had quite a streak going from 1923 through 1926. Herb Curtis was the coach; his team finished 19-6, 25-3, 24-3, and 23-3. The last 3 years of that string amounted to 72 wins and 9 losses. In 1959, with Dick Branham coaching, the Bulldogs won 18 and lost 5. Chris Sampson coached the 1999 and 2000 teams to 23-3 and 24-3 marks, winning the school's only Regional championships in the process. John Standeford, a name familiar to Purdue fans for his exploits as a wide receiver on some 1st-rate Boilermaker football teams, left his mark as Monrovia's all-time leading scorer with 1,899 points. All told, the Bulldogs have also won 6 Sectional titles, and the Lady Bulldogs have added 4. Monrovia has another notable alum named Branch McCracken.

Branch McCracken
His Indiana University Hoosiers won 3 Big 10 titles, 1 co-championship and 8 runner-up spots ... IU won national championships in 1940 and 1953 ... distinguished coaching career followed an equally luminous playing career, during which he set a Big 10 scoring record at IU and was an all-Big 10 selection ... played professionally in Indianapolis; Fort Wayne; Dea, Ohio; and Oshkosh, Wis. ... as a student at Monrovia High School, twice led school with only 32 male students to the championship of the Tri-State Tourney, a 74 team event at Cincinnati ... MVP of that tourney those years, 1925-26 ... coached 8 years at Ball State University before succeeding the legendary Everett Dean at IU.

Finally, the New Albany Bulldogs also have put together a most impressive record, amassing 46 Sectional, 16 Regional, and 8 Semi-state championships. Their 1st trip to Indianapolis came in 1950, when they lost the 2nd semi-final game in overtime to Lafayette Jeff. Hall of Famer Ed Siegel was a member of that team.

Two years later they were edged by eventual champion Muncie Central by a single point. Again in 1955 the Bulldogs ran into an eventual state champion in the semi-finals, the Tigers of Indianapolis Attucks this time. Kokomo would nip the Bulldogs in another semi-final game, another overtime loss, in 1959. Finally, in 1973 the Bulldogs achieved their dream as Kirby Overman's 21-7 team won the state championship by 5 points over the South Bend Adams Eagles. Seven years later Jack Ford's undefeated New Albany team again made it to the final game, beating the Fighting Niners of Andrean before losing to Bill Smith's 29-2 Indianapolis Broad Ripple Rockets, finishing 27-1. Back again in 1994 and 1996 the Bulldogs came oh-so-close yet 2 more times. In 1994 Jim Miller's team lost only their 2nd game of 27 to South Bend Clay by the slim margin of 61-57. Clay won the title that night in an exciting all-north final over Valparaiso, 93-88 in overtime. In 1996, Don Unruh's

24-4 squad made it all the way to the final game before losing an intense, could-have-gone-either-way, hard-fought, entertaining, 3-point, double overtime decision to Steve Witty's Ben Davis Giants.

The Bulldogs had made quite a record for themselves as early as 1914 when Edwin Hubble's team went 11-1, losing their only game in our 4th state tournament

The New Albany Bulldog and Crest

finals at Indiana University, 13-10 to Clinton. In 1936 Charles McConnell's Dogs won 25 games and lost only 4. Two years later his charges had a 21-5 season.

Gordon Raney's 1948 through 1952 teams put together an eye-catching 5-year string during which they won 117 games and lost only 18. Jim Miller's 1992 through 1997 teams performed a similar feat, winning 135 games while losing just 21 over a 6 year period. Most recently, Jim Shannon's 2008 team finished undefeated in the regular season with a 26-1 record.

The Lady Bulldogs have also been impressive. Angie Hinton's 1999 team won the Class 4A State Championship, undefeated, 26-0, with a 46-41 win over Ft. Wayne Snider. Her 1996 through 2000 teams won 109 games and lost only 11! This was followed by her own 2001 team's 19-3 record. Dave Rarick's 2002 team's 20-4 mark came next. Seven years, 148 wins, 18 defeats. All told, the Lady Bulldogs have won 12 Sectionals and 5 Regionals to go with their 1999 Semi-state and state titles. When you go to New Albany to play, you're in the Dog House.

Greenwood Christian Cougar

There are also 14 Cougars and 10 Wildcats in the list of our top 10 school mascot choices.

Bloomington North began operation in 1972, as Bloomington High School's purple and white Panthers became Bloomington South and Bloomington University's Univees were consolidated into North. They dropped their red and gold for the newly formed maroon and gold Cougars. George Fielding was their 1st boys basketball coach, a job he held 8 years. His 1974 team won 17 and lost 5 games and his 1979 squad went 19-5. Tom McKinney was the North coach beginning in 1988, and he put some real powerhouses on the floor. The Cougars were 19-6 in 1991, 17-5 in 1995, and 18-4 in 1996. But it was the next year that things really began to fall into place for McKinney and his Cougars: 28-1 that year was followed by 20-4, 17-4, 25-1, and 2 straight 22-3 seasons. Over that 6-year span the Cougars won 134 games and lost only 16! All told, the Cougars have won 15 Sectionals, 5 Regionals. and 2 Semi-states and the 1997 state championship. The Lady Cougars have added 3 Sectional and 2 Regional crowns, their most impressive season being 23-3 in 2003 for Steve Goddard.

The North Harrison, Central Noble, and North Daviess Cougars

The North Harrison Cougars have had some very good years. Their 1st successful season came in 1969 with John McKay coaching the Cougars to a 23-2 mark. In 1979 Bob Wood's team won 20 of 22 games. Jerry Hanger was at the helm in 1987 and 1988 when they went 22-4 followed by 21-4. In 1989 Phil Pace coached another good season with a record of 20-4. That's 73 wins and only 12 losses for that 3-year period. In total the Cougars have won 9 Sectionals and 1 Regional, in 1987 at Washington with victories over Southridge and Mitchell. The Lady Cougars have also excelled. They had 20-2 seasons in 1991 and 1992 as well as a 19-4 mark for Coach Larry Martin. They have added 10 Sectionals and 1 Regional title, the latter for Coach Missy Voyles, whose 2003 team had an undefeated regular season, finishing 25-1 and brought home the nets from Jasper to Ramsey.

The Central Noble Cougars won their 1st Sectional title at Columbia City in 1977. They were coached that year by Roger Schnepp and finished with a record of 18-7. More recently the Albion-based Cougars have won 3 Class 2A Sectionals and the 2001 Glenn Regional.

The North Daviess Cougars from Elnora won 18 games and lost 5 in their 1st season, 1969, coached by Bill Slaton. They won Class A Sectional crowns in 2001 at White River Valley and 2006 at Loogootee. Brent Dalrymple's 2008 squad finished 20-3. The North Daviess Lady Cougars have won 4 Sectional titles. New Prairie's Cougars won the 2003 Northwood Sectional, while the Lady Cougars have won 3 Sectionals as well. In Flora the Carroll Cougars won 18 of 21 games in 1992 for Coach Ed Geheb. They also won the Fountain Central Class 2A Sectional. The Lady Cougars won 3 Sectionals for the school in New Carlisle.

New Prairie and Carroll (Flora) Cougars

The Gary West Side Cougars have won 11 Sectionals and 5 Regionals and 2 Semi-states, in 1972 and 2002. In 1972 they defeated the Anderson Madison Heights Pirates to get to the state finals game, which they lost to the Connersville Spartans.

That year Coach Larry Brown's team finished 26-3 and his 1974 squad went 23-3. In 2002 the Cougars' dreams finally came true when the John Boyd-coached Cougars, 23-4, defeated Larry Bullington's Indianapolis Pike squad 58-55 to claim the Class 4A State Championship.

The Gary West Side Lady Cougars have snagged 14 Sectionals, 3 Regionals, and the 2005 Class 4A Semi-state. In the state final game Coach Rodney Fisher's five ran into Alan Vickrey's defending champion North Central Panthers and Indiana Miss Basketball Amber Harris and lost a hard-fought 57-54 decision, finishing with a 23-5 record. Fisher has coached the Lady Cougars for at least 24 years. His teams put together an amazing 3-year streak of undefeated regular seasons from 1991 through 1993, amassing 67 victories in 70 games! His 1998 through 2005 teams also won an impressive 167 games while losing only 34.

Gary West Side Cougars crest

The Greenfield Tigers became the Greenfield Central Cougars via the consolidation route. As Tigers they had won 13 Sectionals and the 1943 Anderson Regional. As Central Cougars they have won 7 Sectionals. The Tigers had their best records in 1943, 22-4 for Charles Englehardt, and in their final year, 21-4 for Joe Stanley in 1969. As Cougars their best record came in 1998, 20-4 for John Hamilton. The Lady Cougars have added 8 Sectional nets and 4 Regionals to the school's trophy case. Their best records were 20-4 in 1982 for Bob Caldwell and 21-4 for Terry Fox in 1987.

The North Putnam Cougars opened their doors in 1969 and immediately ran off 2 consecutive 20-4 seasons for Coach Dwight Tallman. Jim Sharp's 1975 Cougars also went 20-4 and followed that with another 20-win season. Eight Sectionals were won, including 1970 and 1971. The Lady Cougars, with Jim Spencer coaching, also put together a 20-4 season in 2001 and swept 4 straight Class 2A Sectional crowns from 2000 through 2003, adding Speedway Regional titles in the latter 2 years of that streak. The school is located near Roachdale.

The South Decatur Cougars take the floor in maroon and white uniforms. Davis Porter coached the 1989 team to a 17-4 mark, and 2-years later, with Will Mulroney coaching, the Cougars finished 21-3. His 1996 squad won 17 and lost 4. Four Sectional crowns have been brought back to the south side of Greensburg by the Cougars. The Lady Cougars enjoyed a nice streak for Coach Andy Honeycutt, starting in 1988 and ending in 1993, winning 94 games while losing only 24 during those 6 seasons, with the best mark, 17-2, coming in 1992. Kelly Fox coached the 1999 Lady Cougars to an 18-7 mark and the next year the team finished 17-5. During that period they won 4 Sectional titles.

Two recent additions to the scene have been the Cougars of Indianapolis Colonial Christian and South Bend Community Baptist.

The Greenfield Central, North Putnam, South Decatur, and Colonial Christian Cougars

The Whitko Wildcats came into existence in South Whitley in 1971, and were coached by Bill Patrick for 24 years. During that time his teams won 400 games and lost only 144.   The Wildcats won 21 of 23 games in 1979 and had an undefeated regular season at 21-1 the next year, followed by a 21-3 season in 1981. Three years, 64 wins, 6 losses! In 1987 they were 20-4, in 1989 20-7, and in 1990 21-4. Over the years the Whitko Wildcats *The Whitko Crest and Logo*

won 13 Sectionals, 2 Regionals and the 1991 South Bend Washington Semi-state. That year the Wildcats lost, in a catfight, I cannot resist saying, to the eventual State Champion Gary Roosevelt Panthers, in the afternoon game of the Final Four.

The Evansville Mater Dei Wildcats have won 9 Sectionals and 5 Regionals as well as the 2001 and 2004 Class 3A Semi-states. In 2001 Roger Sills' 26-2 team lost a white-knuckler in the final game of the state tournament to the Rebels of Muncie Southside by an 81-78 score in double overtime. Back again in 2004, with John Goebel now coaching, the Tigers were not to be denied, winning their 1st state championship by beating the Bellmont Braves 63-45 at Conseco Fieldhouse to finish 21-6. The Lady Wildcats have won 3 Sectional crowns. Their best record was 19-3 in 1991 for Coach Barb Orpurt.

In Brookville the Franklin County Wildcats have won 8 Sectionals and the 1965 Connersville Regional. Unfortunately, they ran into the eventual State Champion Indianapolis Washington's Continentals in the 1st round of the Sweet Sixteen, suffering their only defeat in a 24-1 season. In 2005 Tom Scheinbein's Wildcats turned in a 20-3 record. Hanover Central's Wildcats of Cedar Lake bagged their lone Sectional title in 1986 at Kankakee Valley, going 20-6 for Coach Terry Strawbridge. The Lady Wildcats have won 2 Sectionals as well as one Regional, in 1999, Dennis Foster's squad winning 21 of 26 games. The South Vermillion Wildcats won their only Sectional in the same year as Hanover Central, with a 16 and 6 record for Tim Wolf. Tim Terry has coached the Lady Wildcats for 28 years, winning 5 Sectionals in the process.

The Franklin County, Hanover Central, and South Vermillion Wildcats

Mt. Vernon is an historic town on the Ohio River in Posey County. From its earliest days barrel-making (cooperage) for the river trade was an important occupation. Hoop-poles were used in the process of making the barrels and the area became known to all on the river as "Hoop Pole Township." The Mt. Vernon Wildcats lost only 1 game in 1912 for Coach Arlyn Williams, but then they only played 5. In 1972 they won 22 of 24 games for Chuck Vallier, capturing the Princeton Sectional, one of their 6 such crowns and losing a tough 2-point decision to Tell City in the Evansville Regional. Their yearbook is called the *Hoop Pole,* or at least it was in 1929 when these team pictures appeared.

The 1929 Mt. Vernon High School boys and girls varsity basketball teams

Although the teams are known as the Wildcats today, at least the girls teams may have been called the Redbirds in 1929 because the *Hoop Pole* had the following comment: "Fourteen Redbirds received letters this season."

Hammond's Wildcats have amassed 32 Sectional championships and 9 Regionals as well as the 1938 Lafayette Semi-state. They would lose a hard-fought final game to the State Champion Ft. Wayne South Side Archers by a single basket, 34-32. Twenty-win seasons came in 1931, 22-7 for Paul Church; 1939, 20-8 for Chet Kessler; 20-5 in 1950 for Bob King; 20-5 for Orlando Wyman in 1966; 23-2 for Dick Barr in 1974; and 20-4 for George Green in 1997. The Lady Wildcats have won 3 Sectionals and the 1991 Hammond Regional.

The Mt. Vernon Wildcat

The Wildcats from South Bend Riley have put 13 Sectional nets in their trophy case as well as 5 Regionals and the 1945 Lafayette Semi-state. That year Wayne Wakefield's team beat Hammond, the Logansport Berries, and Huntington's Vikings to get to the final game, only to lose to Evansville Bosse. Bob Berger's 1990 and 1991

Wildcats won 44 games while losing only 8, and Mark Johnson led his 2003 and 2008 teams to 22-4 and 22-6 marks. The Lady Wildcats have won 5 Sectionals and 3

 The Hammond and Riley Wildcats  Regionals and were runners-up to Terre Haute South in the 4A state championship game of 2002 with a 24-4 record, followed the next year by a 23-4 season, both for

Coach Mike Megyesi.

The Lawrence North Wildcats have had only 1 head boys basketball coach in the history of the school, the legendary Jack Keefer.

Give Jack a good big man like, say, Eric Montross or Greg Oden, and a fast guard, preferably one who can shoot like Todd Leary or drive and feed like Michael Connoly, and he will deliver a state champion, and in the process not only set a state record for consecutive victories but amass over 600 wins for his school while he is at it. And his teams will, win or lose, do so with dignity, respect for the opposition, and love for the game. The Wildcats have won 15 Sectionals and 6 Regionals as well as 4 state championships: 1989, 1994, 2005, and 2006. The Wildcats were undefeated in 2006, 29-0, and Greg Oden was Indiana's Mr. Basketball that season. In 1989 and 1990 Keefer's Wildcats won 47 games and lost 10; they were 24-3 in 1992, 24-2 in 1998 and from 2003 through 2006 they won a remarkable 103 games while losing only 7 against the highest level of competition in the state. During their run they also broke the record for consecutive victories, previously held by Crispus Atuucks at 45, as the Wildcats racked by an even 50 straight.

Jody Whittaker's Lady Wildcats have done very well, too. Although they have won only 2 Sectionals, they have records of 20-2 in 2002, 21-5 in 2007, and 20-4 in 2008, also against some very stiff opposition.

The Lawrence North Wildcat

These top 5 4-legged animal team names covered here and in the previous chapter come to 72. You can add to this the variations on a theme, such as the Kokomo WildKats, the Greencastle Tiger Cubs, the Kankakee Valley Kougars of Wheatfield and the Howe Cadet Wildcats, getting to a total of 76 in this category, or just under 19 percent of our current list of 406 IHSA member schools with athletic team names.

The Kankakee Valley Kougars' 1st season was an impressive 17-5 for Coach Rich McEwan in 1971. Better yet were 1980 and 1981's 22-2 and 24-2 marks for Coach Bruce Hardy and the 1999 record of 19-4 under Jack Gabor's direction. The Kougars have won 12 Sectional titles and the 1981 Lafayette Jefferson Regional crown. The Lady Kougars did their school proud in 1995, winning 20 of 22 games for Coach Frank Ginzer. They have also won 12 Sectionals but have yet to capture their 1st Regional.

We have discussed Greencastle previously and will try to do justice to Kokomo later!

Jasper's Championship 1949 team with a "wildcat" mascot

Chapter 23

More Four-Legged Friends:
The Leo Lions, the Lady Bruins

In the last 2 chapters we examined our animal mascots in the Top Ten popularity-wise among our current schools. Not in the Top Ten, but still quite popular, are the 10 schools with Lions as their choice.

A pride of Hoosier Lions: Leo, Salem, Loogootee, Bremen, Rushville, Restoration Christian (Sellersburg, orig. Rock Creek Christian Academy), Lakeview Christian (Marion), and Richmond Academy. Our other Lions represent Anderson Liberty Christian, DuPont Baptist Academy, Indianapolis Horizon Christian High School Lions and Bloomington Lighthouse Christian Lions.

Several of these schools have been covered earlier, and some are too recent to have significant basketball histories. Leo and Rushville, however, both have very impressive stories to tell. The Leo Lions won 19 of 21 games for Coach Hubert Davis (not the former Tarheel star) in 1936 and 20-3 in 1940. In 1945 they enjoyed an undefeated season, winning 22 and losing 1 under Coach Sam Garman. That loss was to South Side, 30-26 in the Ft. Wayne Sectional after the Lions had defeated Huntertown in the first round. They were 19-4 under Waldemar Heller in 1957, and Will Doehrman's teams had back-to-back 20-4 and 21-3 records in 1960 and 1961. Harlen Frick's Lions won 23 and lost 2 in 1971 and followed that with a 22-2 mark the next year. Richard Butt was the coach in 1976 when the team went 19-6 and again in 1994 when the Lions had another undefeated regular season, finishing 23-1. Over the years the Leo Lions have cut down the Sectional nets 6 times. The Lady Lions have added 7 Sectional and 2 Regional nets to the school's collection. Mike Hay coached the Leo girls for 26 seasons. His 1988 team went 21-2 and from 1996 through 1998 his Lady Lions won 68 games and lost only 7.

The Rushville Lions had a bang-up season in 1922, when Arlie Suttton coached the Pride to a 29-4 mark. Three years after they racked up a 22-6 record for John Swain to improve upon the prior year mark under his guidance, 19-6. Robert Hinshaw coached the Lions from 1930 until 1943, and his teams of 1934, 20-7; and 1940, 21-5, were among the school's best ever. Paul Weaver's 1955 team won 21 and lost 6, a record Les Ray's 1960 team just fell short of matching at 20-6. Ray's next 2 squads finished 19-7 and 21-5. Jack Brown was coaching in 1963 and 1964 when the Lions went 17-6 followed by 23-4. Ken Pennington had the coaching job in 1971 and led that year's team to an 18-6 finish. However, it was Larry Angle's 1975 and 1976 boys who really pounced on the competition, running up 23-4 and 26-2 marks. Over the years the Lions have amassed 48 Sectional championships and 19 Regionals. Their lone Semi-state title came in 1976, when the Larry Angle-coached, Brad Miley-led Lions almost garnered the top prize. They lost the state championship game to the Marion Giants by 6 points. Rushville's Lady Lions had 2 undefeated regular seasons in 1978 and 1979 with identical 17-1 records for Larry Merica. They have won 5 Sectional titles and the 1981 Regional crown.

Several schools root for horses in various forms, such as the Pendleton Heights Arabians, and the 3 Chargers (including the North Montgomery Chargin' Chargers, covered previously) that are truly horses. West Noble and Ft. Wayne Carroll are clearly electricity-related Chargers, and Pike Central's is a medieval knight.

The West Noble and Ft. Wayne Carroll Chargers are not horses, but lightning bolts; and the Pike Central Charger is a Knight.

The Elkhart Memorial Chargers have won 6 Sectionals and 2 Regionals. The North Decatur Chargers have won 4 Sectionals. Twenty-win seasons came in 1974 20-6 for Jim Powers, and 1981, 1982, and 2002, (20-4, 20-5, and 20-3) for Steve Johnson. The Lady Chargers have won 9 Sectional titles and 1 Regional and turned in 20-5 and 22-5 records for Larry Fielstra in 2006 and 2008.

The North Decatur Chargers have won 3 Sectionals. The Lady Chargers had 2 fine seasons in a row for Coach Dennis Crowe, winning 17 of 20 games in 1992 and 18 of 22 the next year. They have won 2 Sectionals and the 2000 2A Austin Regional.

Elkhart Memorial and North Decatur Chargers

We also have 5 Mustangs (at Kouts the girls teams are the Fillies, and the middle school teams are the Ponies).

Our free-running Mustangs: Edgewood, Fountain Central, Munster, New Washington, and Kouts

The Edgewood Mustangs wear red and black. They won 19 of 23 games for Joe Null in 1980 and went 16-5, followed by 17-6 in 1988 and 1989 with Ron Hecklinski holding the reins. Jeff Bertsch's Mustangs had 15-6 and 18-7 seasons in 1992 and 1993 and 5 Sectional crowns. The girls teams had 4 excellent seasons in a row for coach Bill Atkinson beginning in 1988: 19-2, 20-3, 20-3, and 20-5, or 79 wins and only 13 losses! The Lady Mustangs have added 7 Sectional plaques to their trophy case at Elletsville as well as the 1986 and 1990 Greencastle Regional championships.

The Fountain Central Mustangs in their blue and gold uniforms got off to a great start for Coach Al Harden, going 17-4 and 19-2 in their 1st 2 years of existence, 1966 and 1967. Bryan Hughes' teams did even better in 1990 and 1991, finishing 21-4 and 23-1. That sole loss was a heart-breaking 57-56 decision to Twin Lakes in the Lafayette Sectional. They have brought 7 Sectional trophies home to Veedersburg. The Lady Mustangs had 17-5 and 21-4 seasons in 2000 and 2001 for Coach Phil Rash. They have won 2 Sectionals and the 2001 Class 2A Regional.

The red-and-white-clad Munster Mustangs won 18 games and lost 5 for Coach Dave Knish in 2000. They have won 5 Sectionals. The Lady Mustangs had a fine 16-3 season in 1980 for Coach Bob Maicher, and from 1998 through 2000, with Greg Luksich in the saddle, they won 52 games and lost 14. They have won 2 Sectionals.

Kouts has had an interesting degree of longevity in their boys basketball coaches, beginning with Luis French, who held the job from 1941-1953. His 1945 Mustang team was undefeated in the regular season, with an impressive 24 wins with only the 1 defeat, to Emerson in the final game of the Gary Sectional. Robert Gray coached the Mustangs from 1954 until 1969. Marty Gaff took over in 1984 and is still at the helm after 25 seasons, including 22-2 and 20-4 marks in 1995 and 1996. The Mustangs have won 6 Sectionals and 2 Regionals, and the Fillies have taken down the nets at the end of 10 Sectionals and 3 Regionals.

The Mustangs of New Washington have captured 4 Sectional titles and the 2001 Class A Northeast DuBois Regional. The Lady Mustangs have brought home the nets from 5 Sectionals as well as 4 straight Regionals from 1998 through 2001. In 1999 they also won the Loogootee Semi-state, losing the state title at Market Square Arena to Clinton Prairie, 50-42, to finish a fine season with 22 wins and 5 losses for Coach Terry White.

The Daleville Broncos enjoyed an excellent 20-7 season in 1933 under Ralph Heath and had to wait 50 years for another season of

singular success, when Everett Gates' squad won 19 and lost only 3. The wait was only 2 years for another Gates-led team to turn in a fine mark, 19-4 in 1985, the year they won their only non-class Sectional championship. They also won a 2008 Class A Sectional. We'll discuss the Lafayette Jefferson Bronchos later.

A compromise was made when Pendleton Heights High School was formed out of the merger of Pendleton and Markleville. The compromise allowed the new school to keep the green and white colors of Pendleton's Irish in exchange for the Marklesville Arabians losing their purple and white. A fair trade, I'd say. By the way, those Markleville Arabians won a Sectional crown in 1933, and the Pendleton Heights Arabians won 3 straight between 1994 and 1996. All told, the Arabians have won 6 Sectionals and 2 Regionals. As Pendleton Irish they also won 2 Sectional titles. From 1917 through 1919, under 3 different coaches, the Irish won 66 games and lost 22. The Bob Johnson-coached teams of 1936 and 1937 won 42 of 50 games. As Pendleton Heights, some good records were put together in 1988, when Rick Baumgartner's team won 19 of 22 games and in 1993, when his charges went 18-5, although Joe Buck's 1994 and 1995 squads each finished close behind, with 17-6 marks. Dick Dickey is a Pendleton Hall of Famer.

Dick Dickey

3 year starter at Pendleton, on All-Sectional team in 1944 ... played for Hall of Famer Everett Case at North Carolina State ... 1947 (26-5) 378 points - 3rd in NIT, 1948 (29-3) 451 points - 6th in NIT, (25-8) 355 points, 1950 (27-6) 460 points ... North Carolina State was 1st in Southern Conference all 4 years ... still 8th highest scorer in school history ... NCAA Final 4 in 1950 ... 1948 - Helms 1st Team All American, 1949 AP Honorable Mention ... 1950 AP 2nd team, Helms 3rd team, All NCAA Regional East Team, All NCAA Final Team ... played in East-West College All-Star game ... voted one of the five most valuable North Carolina State players of all time and number retired in February, 1999 ... only player in North Carolina State history to be All-Conference for 4 years .... one year with Anderson Packers in 50-51 and one year with Boston Celtics in 1951-52 ... 29 years with Farm Bureau Insurance.

The Lady Arabians have won 3 Sectionals, all for Wallace Dennis, all in a row, from 1994 through 1996, winning 54 games and losing only 13 in the process. Shari Doud's 2004 and 2005 teams also did well, winning 39 of 46 games.

The Pendleton Heights Arabians

Next in popularity among our current schools are the bears, in various subsets adding up to 12: the Evansville Central (see Chapter 22) and Lawrence Central Bears, the Monroe Central and Shelbyville Golden Bears, the Franklin Grizzlie Cubs, the Madison Cubs, the Muncie Central and Wheeler Bearcats, and 4 Bruins.

The Lawrence Central Bears have won 4 Sectional and 3 Regional titles. Curiously, in their 1st 2 Semi-state visits separated by 35 years, they drew Aurora in the 1st round each time. In 1942 Fred Keesling's Bears edged the Red Devils by 2 points; in 1977 the Red Devils returned the favor, edging Jerry Petty's team by 2 points, this time in overtime. Neither team made it past the next round, however. Back to the Semi-state in 1998, Lawrence Central found there were no Aurora Red Devils left for them to play and, no, they did not play South Dearborn either. They played the Jennings County Panthers in the 1st round of the Bloomington 4A tournament and won that one, but then they did run into another group of Red Devils, these from Indianapolis Pike, who beat the Bears en route to their own state championship. The Lady Bears have won 1 Sectional. Before there was a Lawrence Central on the east side of Marion County, there was a Lawrence High School, whose teams were the Lions.

The Lawrence Central Bears, three versions

The Monroe Central Golden Bears had an 18-4 season for Charles Moulton in 1977, followed by another 18-4 and a 17-4 mark for Steve Reed's 1979 and 1980 teams. They have won 6 Sectionals, the latter 4 at the Class A level. The Lady Bears have brought an additional 4 Sectional nets home to Parker, all won prior to the advent of class basketball.

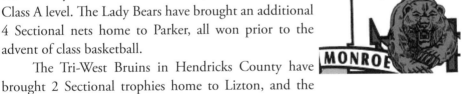

The Tri-West Bruins in Hendricks County have brought 2 Sectional trophies home to Lizton, and the Lady Bruins added 4 more. They won a pair of Class 2A Regional titles, in 1998 at Fountain Central and the next year at Danville. The Blackford Bruins have had fine seasons, beginning with 1971 and 1972, when Jon Stroup's teams won 20 and 22 games while losing 4 each year. Stroup's 1976 team won 20 of 25 games for a total of 10 Sectionals. The Lady Bruins went 18-3 for Marty Daniel in 1983. They brought Sectional nets back home to Hartford City from Eastbrook in 1995 and 1997.

Our other Bruins are found at Bethany Christian and Ft. Wayne Northrop. Northrop has had many exemplary seasons. Bob Dille coached the Bruins to 23-4 and 28-1 (!) in 1973 and 1974, the 2nd and 3rd years of the school's existence. A. C. Eldridge had 4 straight outstanding seasons beginning in 1984: 21-4, 25-2, 24-4, and 21-6. That's 91 wins and 16 losses in those 4 years. In total 9 Sectionals have been won by the Bruins as well as the 1974 Regional. Making the most of their opportunity, the Bruins initially defeated Logansport, 55-53, then Anderson, 67-52 to win the Semi-state. The Finals were at Bloomington, and Northrop won their opening game against Lafayette Jefferson by a 63-49 count and then captured their 1st and only state championship (so far) with a 59-56 victory over Jeffersonville.

The Lady Bruins have done very well, also. Dave Riley's state championship team in 1986 won 29 games and lost none, and the next year his Lady Bruins put together a 28-1 season, their only loss coming in the afternoon game of the state finals in Market Square Arena to Anderson Highland, 55-49, after 57 straight victories over 2 seasons. This was followed by 2 straight 21-4 years: 99 wins and 9 losses over those 4 years. In 1991 the Lady Bruins won 21 of 24 games, and the next year they went 24-2, then 25-1 in '93, and 21-5 in 1994, and 18-3 in 1995. From 1991 through 1995, that comes to 109 wins and 14 losses in those 5 years. They have won ten Sectionals and eight Regionals and that never-to-be-forgotten, undefeated, state championship in 1986 when they topped Scottsburg's Warriorettes, 58-53.

The Tri-West, Blackford, and Ft. Wayne Northrop Bruins

The Wheeler Bearcats have 1 set of Sectional nets in their trophy case, from their own 2A tournament in 2007. The Lady Bearcats have added 3 more. We'll discuss Muncie Central's Bearcats in some detail later.

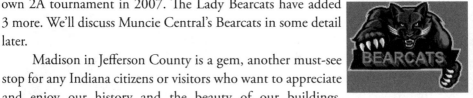

Madison in Jefferson County is a gem, another must-see stop for any Indiana citizens or visitors who want to appreciate and enjoy our history and the beauty of our buildings, fountains, and natural surroundings. Madison is on the Ohio River adjacent to the attractions of Clifty Falls State Park and the campus of Hanover College, another of our nation's excellent small liberal arts colleges with an exceptionally beautiful campus. An important port in the early days of our state, Madison has many historic homes. One of the most impressive homes in the entire Midwest is the Lanier Mansion, but there are many other fine examples of 18th and 19th century architecture throughout. Madison was the location used in the film of the James Jones novel *Some*

Came Running starring Shirley MacLaine, Frank Sinatra, and Dean Martin. The first Indiana regiment to serve in the Civil War, called by President Abraham Lincoln to send a force requested by the city of Louisville to save that city from the advancing Confederate army, was the Fifth Indiana, mustered in Madison. No one should miss this wonderfully preserved, historic town.

Before Milan's famous victory over Muncie Central, the Madison Cubs were the successful small school team of their day. (For a more complete treatment of this phase of our sport's history see Bill Cole's article "Age of the Giant Killers" in the Summer 2006 issue of *Indiana Basketball History* magazine.) In 1950 Madison's student body numbered 287, only 60 of whom were seniors. Indianapolis Tech was the largest school in the state, one of the largest in the country, with an enrollment of around 6,000 students. They were led by a wonderful athlete, Joe Sexson, who would later star at Purdue. Ray Eddy, soon also to have a close association and fine career at Purdue, coached the Cubs, whose tallest player was their 6′4″ center, Spence Schnaitter. In the Semi-state final game Madison bested the Tech Titans by a score of 55-46. The Final Four would have 3 of the state's largest schools: New Albany's Bulldogs with some 2,500 students, Lafayette Jefferson's Broncos with about 3,000, and the Marion Giants of similar size. In the early games it was Madison by a single point over Marion and Jeff by a basket over New Albany in overtime. What a great pair of games that must have been! At night the Cubs beat the Broncos soundly, 67-44, to claim their 1st and only state title. Spence Schnaitter was a standout star:

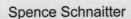
Spence Schnaitter
3-yr player for Hall of Fame coach Ray Eddy... led Cubs to state finals in each of last two seasons... team's top rebounder and second leading scorer behind Mr. Basketball Dee Monroe in 1949 when Cubs lost state title game by single point to Jasper...captain as senior, averaged 15.9 points per game for the year as the Cubs topped Marion and Lafayette Jeff for title, completing 2-yr run in which Madison went 51-6...named to Indiana All-Star team...earned 4th baseball letter and pitched 3 no-hitters...3-yr starter at Yale...team MVP as jr, captain as sr, and twice All-Ivy League...led Elis in rebounding two years and scoring once. He was later a practicing attorney and served ten years in the state legislature.

In total the Madison Cubs have run up an impressive 38 Sectionals and 12 Regionals. They also won Semi-state titles in 1941, 1949, and 1962 as well as that charmed year of 1950. On their 1st trip to the finals in Indianapolis, Ray Eddy's team was runner-up to the Washington Hatchets, dropping a 6-point decision, 39-33. In 1949 they again made it to the championship game and, in an all-southern-Indiana final, again finished runner-up, this time in a heart-stopper, 62-61, to those pesky Jasper Wildcats. Their last trip to the Butler Fieldhouse was in 1962, and once again the Cubs were a force to be reckoned with, losing a 4-pointer to Evansville Bosse's eventual state champion Bulldogs in the morning game. Madison's 1st 20-win season came in 1929, 21-4 for Charles Beer. Ray Eddy's 1941 and 1942 squads won 48 games and lost only 5, and from 1946 through 1950 his Cubs teams won 109 games and lost only 20. Julius "Bud" Ritter's Madison teams from 1959 through 1962 put 95 wins on the board and only lost 5 times! Included in this was the impressive string of 3 straight undefeated regular seasons, 25-1 in 1960, 23-1 in 1961, and 25-1 in 1962. Few schools can match that. Finally, Larry Bullington's 1994 Cubs won 21 of 24 games, his 1998 team went 20-5, and Jim Matthews' 2007 squad finished 21-4. The Lady Cubs have won 8 Sectionals and 3 Regionals.

In the next chapter the story of Evansville Central's Golden Bears boys teams will be told, so here I should mention the outstanding undefeated season turned in by the Lady Bears, coached by Gretchen Eisenhauer, in 1989, 22-1, bringing them their only Sectional title as well.

In this chapter (and the next) we have completed coverage of our current 10 lions, 11 horses (including Lafayette Jefferson's Bronchos whom we will cover later) of various kinds, and 12 bears in a variety of forms adding 33 four-legged animals to our compilation of today's schools' team names. This brings our total to 110, or just over 27 percent of our current schools.

Chapter 24

Evansville Central:
So Close and Yet So Far

There is some difference of opinion about which Indiana high school is the oldest in the state. Various schools laying claim to that include New Albany, Vincennes, Indianapolis Shortridge, and Evansville Central. Part of the reason for the different claims is definitional. Some are claiming to be the first founded, others the first free public school, or the first free public high school, or the first in continuous operation as a free public high school, etc. With all of that taken into account, it seems to me that Evansville Central has as strong a claim as any. This from their Web site, by Ira Harris:

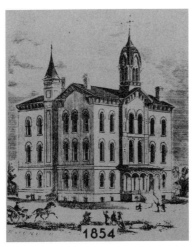

The 1st building, Evansville High School

CENTRAL HIGH SCHOOL is the oldest free public high school in continuous operation west of the Allegheny Mountains. It was established in 1854 as EVANSVILLE HIGH SCHOOL (and) opened on September 4, 1854 with an enrollment of 17 students—8 boys and 9 girls.

The school started on a quarter system with new students entering the high school in January of 1855. The report at the end of the year states that the high school had a year-end enrollment of about 30. In 1918 the name was changed to CENTRAL HIGH SCHOOL when another high school (Reitz) was built.

Evansville Central High School from 1868–1970

GOLD and BROWN, Central's colors, were chosen some years before 1908. There is a tradition that the combination was suggested by Helen Click, teacher at the school from 1895 to 1905, because they were the colors of her sorority (Meyer, *Central High School, Its First Hundred Years*)

"The Rouser" originated in 1917. Ada Bicking, music supervisor, suggested the tune of the University of Minnesota rouser, and a girl of the class of 1918 wrote the words. It first appears in the SAGAS of 1918 beginning, "Evansville High School, hats off to thee!" The change to "Central High School, hats off to thee!" the following year greatly improved the rhythm.

The Evansville Central Bear and crest

The mascot chosen for Central was the Bear, sometimes referred to as the Golden Bear because of the school's colors. Over the years the Bears have had an illustrious history in Indiana basketball. Twenty-win seasons have been earned 14 times, beginning with 1920s 20-4 mark. From 1946 through 1948 Central's teams won 75 games while losing only 8, the high-water mark being 1947, 26-2, for Coach Glen Bretz. The Bears have won 37 tough Evansville Sectionals and 20 Regionals.

Semi-state victories came in 1936, 1946, and 1948. In 1936 the Bears lost to the Ft. Wayne Central Tigers in the morning game of the state finals by 5 points. In 1946 they again lost the morning game of the state finals, this time by 3 points to the eventual Champion Anderson Indians, led by the great Johnny Wilson. Back again 2 years later, with perhaps their best chance to win the title, the Bears made it all the way to the final game. Unfortunately, star player Lee Hamilton, who would go on to become an esteemed member of Congress and highly respected foreign policy expert, injured his knee in the semi-final game, a victory over the Muncie Central Bearcats. The injury severely hampered Hamilton, who nonetheless finished as one of the Sweet Sixteen's top scorers with 56 points. He achieved this feat in spite of the fact that he only scored 3 in the final game loss to Lafayette Jefferson's Bronchos (a team they had beaten during the regular season). In fact, as Bill May points out in his book *Tourney Time*, "Unless I have overlooked something, Evansville Central is the school that has beaten eventual state champions most during the regular season but has never won a championship itself." They have done so 8 times in 7 different seasons. Hamilton was joined by teammate Gene Southwood on that year's *Indianapolis News* All-State team. Lee Hamilton's Hall of Fame citation:

Lee Hamilton
A 2-year starter for Evansville Central High School ... All-State as a senior ... led his team that year to Final Four ... scored 16 points in afternoon victory, but a fourth-quarter leg injury knocked him out of championship game ... named Trester Award winner, but his injury was so severe that presentation was made in locker room ... 4-year starter at DePauw ... named DePauw's outstanding senior in '52 ... continued his education in Germany and IU School of Law ... first elected to U. S. House of Representatives from Indiana's 9th Congressional District in 1965.

Although Central never captured that elusive state title, Bears fans are left with a series of might-have-beens to ponder. Three trips to the Final Four, with 1 runner-up finish when the star player is hurt, might be enough. Beyond these, however, were several other close calls in the 18 seasons from 1936 to 1953. We'll start with the 1936 Bears who lost that 5-pointer in the morning game at the Butler Fieldhouse. The very next year Central again lost to the eventual state runner-up by 5 points, this time to Huntingburg's Happy Hunters in the opening round of the Sweet Sixteen. In 1938 the Bears again made it to the Sweet Sixteen, losing a 1st-round game to another Final Four team, the Bedford Stonecutters. In 1939 Central lost to Bosse in the Evansville Sectional by 6 points. Bosse went on to be the runner-up to State Champion Frankfort, the Bulldogs losing to the Hot Dogs by 4 points in the morning game at the Butler Fieldhouse.

In 1942 Central lost to the Washington Hatchets in the 1st round of the Sweet Sixteen. By 2 points. And Washington won the state championship. For Central fans it was again "so close yet so far." Back to the Sweet Sixteen in 1943, the Bears again ran into the Stonecutters in the 1st round and lost to yet another Final Four team. Bosse pretty much dominated the Evansville scene for the next 2 years as the Bulldogs won their consecutive state championships.

After that came Central's 1946 close call to Anderson. In 1947 the Bears turned the tables on Bedford, winning a 1st-round Sweet Sixteen game before being bumped out by eventual state runner-up Terre Haute Garfield's Purple Eagles and Clyde Lovellette. Then came the heartbreak of 1948, but the Bears were back again to the Sweet Sixteen in 1949, losing to Bloomington's Panthers in the 1st round. The Panthers would be edged by Jasper's state champion Wildcats by a single point. In 1952 Central won their 1st-round Sweet Sixteen game over Terre Haute Garfield—in a 4-overtime sudden-death classic—before being edged by 2 points by the New Albany Bulldogs. Could that 1st game have simply exhausted the Golden Bears? Perhaps, but that's the way of state tournaments with a 2-games-in-1-day format sometimes and no one from Central is making excuses. At any rate, those same Bulldogs would lose to the eventual State Champion Muncie Central Bearcats by 1 point in the afternoon game of the state finals at Butler Fieldhouse. Evansville Central's Golden Bears were a mere 3 points off the title!

Hopes were high that 1953 might finally produce that elusive and coveted state title. Central put a strong, deep, experienced team on the court that year with 4 starters back from 1952's team. At one forward was John Harrawood, who would be named to the All-State 1st team by season's end; the center was 6'8" Jerry Clayton, a 2nd team All-State selection; the other forward was tough, scrappy Bob Wessel; and the guards were 2-year starter Clarence Doninger and the only newcomer to the starting five, football quarterback Charlie Martin. The 1st man off the bench was usually Herschel Pleiss.

The season started as anticipated with 12 straight victories, including wins over New Castle, Lafayette Jefferson, Indianapolis Attucks, city rivals Lincoln, Bosse and Memorial, the Vincennes Alices, the Washington Hatchets, and the Seymour Owls. Then came that (almost) inevitable 1st loss, at Bloomington, followed by a win over Jasper and a 2nd loss, this to Reitz, 70-63. Huntingburg and Bedford were defeated before a 3rd loss was incurred, by a single point, 66-65, to the New Albany Bulldogs. The regular season ended with a 16-3 record when the Ft. Branch Twigs were dispatched with relative ease.

The Sectional tournament was also captured with relative ease, wins over Memorial and Mt. Vernon and a revenge win over Reitz setting up the final against the Lincoln Tigers. The Tigers had dispatched Poseyville and Cynthiana after receiving a 1st-round bye. The title game was won by a convincing 19 points. Regional wins were even more impressive: over Owensville and Tell City, the closest margin being 28 points. Could this finally be the year?

Then the injury bug struck again. Bob Wessel broke his hand in practice the week between the Regionals and the Semi-state. Memories of 1948 flooded back, unbidden, to Central fans. Doninger's memory is that Wessel didn't play much, if at all, against the Washington Hatchets, a game the Bears won by 9. In the night game against Terre Haute Gerstmeyer's Black Cats with Arley, Harley and Uncle Harold Andrews, Hall of Famers all, the Bears built up a 16-point lead. Again, Doninger recalls Wessel gamely trying to play, the ball flying off his injured hand and out of bounds. Gradually the lead slipped away and turned into a depressing 7-point defeat. In Indianapolis the next week, Garfield would be edged by a single point in the state championship game by those other Bears, from South Bend Central. Eight points away that year.

An interesting line for me on the stat sheet shows that the best record for field goal percentage for that year's Sweet Sixteen carries the name of Clarence Doninger, former Indiana University athletic director. He was also president of the Evansville Senior class in 1953, as was his brother in the school's centennial year, 1954.

Following is the record for the Golden Bears in 1953:

Evansville Central	59	Boonville	53
Evansville Central	63	Bicknell	43
Evansville Central	77	New Castle	50
Evansville Central	58	Evansville Lincoln	47
Evansville Central	76	Lafayette Jefferson	52
Evansville Central	72	Evansville Bosse	52
Evansville Central	54	Winslow	44

HOLIDAY TOURNAMENT

Evansville Central	79	Seymour	49
Evansville Central	74	Crispus Attucks	67
Evansville Central	54	Evansville Memorial	38
Evansville Central	55	Washington	54
Evansville Central	67	Vincennes Lincoln	57
Evansville Central	40	Bloomington	55 L
Evansville Central	69	Jasper	64
Evansville Central	63	Evansville Reitz*	70 L

Evansville Central	62	Huntingburg	52
Evansville Central	77	Bedford	56
Evansville Central	65	New Albany	66 L
Evansville Central	66	Ft. Branch	42

EVANSVILLE SECTIONAL TOURNAMENT

Evansville Central	79	Evansville Memorial	36
Evansville Central	87	Mt. Vernon	61
Evansville Central	74	Evansville Reitz	61
Evansville Central	59	Evansville Lincoln	40

EVANSVILLE REGIONAL TOURNAMENT

| Evansville Central | 80 | Owensville | 37 |
| Evansville Central | 82 | Tell City | 54 |

BLOOMINGTON SEMI-STATE TOURNAMENT

| Evansville Central | 56 | Washington | 45 |
| Evansville Central | 71 | Gerstmeyer | 78 L |

Final record: 23 wins, 4 losses
Coach Walter Riggs

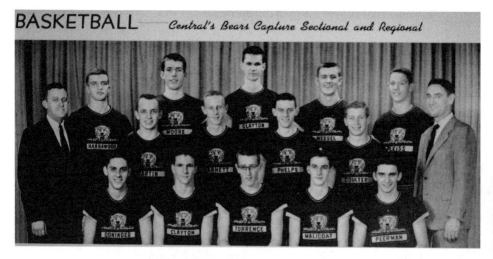

The 1953 Evansville Central Golden Bears

Pride—Hoosier pride and love of basketball—shown on a water tower in Perry county, a barn in Jefferson County, the Monroe City champ ball in the Blue Jeans Williams Museum, and the logos of (top) Spring Valley Black Hawks, River Forest Ingots, Valpo Vikings, Haubstadt Elites, Bloomfield Cardinals and Aurora Red Devils.

On a golden autumn afternoon country roads still lead to the many towns which no longer field teams. Boys and girls still practice on nets hung on barns such as the brown wood one in Bartholomew County. Indiana school identity is enhanced with logos: Beech Grove Hornets, Kokomo WildKats, Shelbyville Golden Bears, Fort Wayne South Side Archers, and Union Rockets.

THE
Monticello Herald's
Ninth Annual White County

BASKETBALL YEAR BOOK

Sectional Basketball
Tournament

THURSDAY
-FRIDAY-
SATURDAY

Monticello's New Gym

MARCH
2-3-4
1939

FREE DISTRIBUTION OF THIS
BOOK IS MADE POSSIBLE BY
THE ADVERTISERS

Round Grove
Burnettsville
Monticello
Brookston
Chalmers
Reynolds
Wolcott
Idaville
Buffalo
Monon

*One season, one region, one mad enthusiasm for a week. The Monticello Sectional, 1939.
Basketball yearbooks sponsored by ads from funeral homes and auto dealerships caught the
moment: teams posing, cheerleaders sizing each other up, kids getting autographs, people from out-
county pouring in. Then a frenzy of soaring shots and sagging spirits played out under the lights.
All too soon it is over; those lights dim in the gym and one bright star goes on to the Regionals.*

Lapel and Frankton jump for the ball while loyal fans cheer in the background with high hopes, but the scoreboard tells the final story.

Chapter 25

How 'bout Them Dawgs...
and Other Animals, Small and Large

In addition to our 14 Bulldogs from the canine world, we have the Frankfort Hot Dogs, Carmel Greyhounds, a pair of Huskies, and another pair of Wolves, plus the Crawford County Wolfpack and the White River Valley Wolverines. We have discussed Frankfort elsewhere, and the reason for their choice is pretty obvious. When I asked how Carmel got their mascot, I was told it came about years ago when Carmel was a small town, much more rural than suburban, and competing with other Hamilton County schools of similar size such as the Walnut Grove Wolves, the Arcadia Dragons, the Fishers Tigers (as we have seen, the recently re-established Fishers High School had the good historic sense to bring back the original mascot), the Atlanta Cardinals, and the Cicero Red Devils. The Carmel team was short, scrappy, and extremely fast. The opposing team's fans took to loudly saying something along the lines of "those Carmel kids run like greyhounds," and the name stuck. No one is positive what team Carmel was playing that night, but the most popular recollection is that it was Arcadia.

"Old North"...original Carmel High School, and the Carmel High School basketball team, 1918

Carmel has changed dramatically in the last few decades. Once a rural town with grain elevators, a railway depot, and a small single-screen theater on Rangeline Road, the community has grown enormously and is now one of the prettiest and most well-designed suburbs anywhere, with pioneering roundabouts, tree-lined boulevards, and a creative arts center. It is also home to one of the largest high schools in the state.

Basketball started early on in Carmel. From the school's Web site:

> *The start of Greyhound Athletics can be found in 1904 when Carmel played Atlanta in the first basketball game played in Hamilton County. Carmel won 4 to 2 and was led by future Principal and Superintendent Oliver Earl Hinshaw. The basketball program later went to the Sweet 16 in 1926, but would have to wait until 1966 for the next sectional championship.* [And 1970 for the next Regional title, also accompanied by a Semi-state crown with a 25-4 record.]

It was actually 1925 when the Greyhounds made it to the Sweet Sixteen according to the IHSAA and confirmed by Bill May. In those days there were 8 Regionals, 2 teams from each getting to make the trip to the State Fairgrounds Exhibition Building in Indianapolis. Carmel made it by defeating Stoney Creek and New Castle to join Muncie as the 2 representatives from Anderson. The Greyhounds were defeated by the Washington Hatchets in the 1st round of the state finals. In 1929 the Greyhounds, under Coach Edgar Cotton, went 17-5, followed by 16-5 the next year and for 4 years beginning in 1938, 18-4, 18-6, 17-7, and 16-6. Estel Hiatt was the coach for those last 2 seasons. In 1950 Marshall Koontz coached the team to a 22-2 record. But it was when Bill Shepherd arrived on the scene that Carmel, by then the larger school we know today playing big time competition, began to take its place with the powers of the state. In 1967 his team won 18 and lost 6, followed by 21-3, 24-1, and 25-4 seasons: a 3-year span of 70 wins and 8 losses, a 4-year span of 88 wins and 14 losses.

The Greyhounds had arrived on the scene and were there to stay. Eric Clark took over in 1971 and led the team to a 3-year mark of 56 wins and 18 losses. In 1976 and 1977 his teams had records of 17-7 and 22-7. Larry Angle took over in 1978 and led the team to 19-7, 21-3, and 18-7 records in his 1st 3 years. Bob Heady's 1993 Greyhounds won 21 of 27 games. As already mentioned, Carmel had won its 1st Sectional title, as a small school, at Noblesville in 1925. Then they went 41 years before getting their next, as a large school. In total they have won 22 Sectionals and 5 Regionals. In 1970 Shepherd's team was runner-up for the state championship, losing a 10-point decision to East Chicago Roosevelt at Hinkle Fieldhouse, in spite of son Bill's 40-point output in the final game. Seven years later the Greyhounds got that state championship, in a thriller 52-51 over John Molodet's East Chicago Washington Senators at Market Square Arena, Carmel was led by footballers Mark Herrman and Bart Burrell, who each scored 16 points in the final game.

The Lady Greyhounds have won 12 Sectionals themselves as well as 3 Regionals. They also made it to the state final game before winning their state championship. They were runner-up in 1995 to the Lady Vikings of Huntington North, as Judi Warren's team lost by 4 points to the 28-1 victors to finish 19-8 themselves. In 2008, however, the Lady Greyhounds, coached by Scott Bowen, did win the 4A title, defeating South Bend Washington 84-72 to finish 23-4.

The 'Hounds running rampant

Billy Shepherd played for his father and gained fame:

Bill Shepherd
Playing for his father and Hall of Famer Bill Shepherd, Sr., Billy scored 2,465 points in four years of competition. He ranked fourth in all-time scoring in Indiana and was a two-time All-State selection. After averaging 32 points per game his junior and senior years, he was selected Mr. Basketball in 1968. He and his dad were the first father-son combination selected for the Indiana All-Stars. He scored 70 points in a single game. He went on to play three years for Hall of Famer Tony Hinkle at Butler University. He's Butler's all-time leading scorer with over 1700 points.

The White River Valley Wolverines only came into existence in 1990, but they have certainly made their mark. In their first 3 years, coached by Dave Clark, they won an amazing 73 games while losing only 9. Joe Pigg coached the Wolverines to an undefeated regular season in 2000, finishing 25-1, followed the next year by a 22-6 finish. They have won 6 Sectionals and 4 Regionals. The Lady Wolverines have also done well, winning 5 Sectionals, 2 Regionals and the 2001 Loogootee Class A Semi-state. That year, with Joe Pigg coaching, the team finished 22-6, runner-up to the State Champion Triton Trojans, coached by Mark Heeter.

So, we still have Wolverines in Switz City at White River Valley High School. And isn't Butler thankful that the Graves family sent their fine young men to play outstanding basketball for Butler at Hinkle Fieldhouse. I had a chance to ask Matt Graves where the name Wolverines came from. He wasn't sure but remembered having a school student body vote for the final selection.

The Hamilton Heights Huskies have brought home 2 Sectional championships to Arcadia. The school was formed in 1965, joining the old Arcadia, Atlanta, Cicero, and Walnut Grove rivals together. The 1967 team, coached by Dean Small, finished 18-4. Their 1st Sectional title was won in 1975 when Jim Petty's Huskies completed an 18-6 season. Their 2nd Class 3A, came in 2003 under 16-year coach Bill Bowen, with a 17-7 mark. They have added 1 Sectional title, that also coming in 2003, also Class 3A.

The Huskies of Evansville North have captured 4 Sectionals and 2 Regionals. They made the most of their 1st trip to Indianapolis in 1967.

The Hamilton Heights and Evansville North Huskies

The Bob Ford-led (27 points in the final game) North team defeated Marion Crawley's 26-3 Lafayette Jefferson Bronchos in a memorable final, 60-58, to finish 27-2 for Coach Jim Rausch. The Lady Huskies started strong, with 63 wins and 16 losses in their 1st 5 seasons and have added 2 Sectional titles to the school's trophy case. Bob Ford's Hall of Fame citation:

Bob Ford
Played in the ABA...A Four-year varsity player, Robert was a member of the 1967 State Championship team. He was named a high school All-American and to All-City, All-State, and All-conference teams in 1968 before being named a member of the Indiana All Stars. He lettered for three years at Purdue and was a member of the World University Team in 1970 as well as a member of the Pan-American Team in 1971. He was named to both the All-Big Ten team and the Academic All-American team in 1972. He also played in the NBA. At the time he was included in the 1993 Silver Anniversary Team.

The Michigan City High School teams are now called the Wolves. Earlier they were the Red Devils, a name carried over to Elston when there were two public high schools in the city, the Rogers Raiders being the other. Each of these schools is covered elsewhere. Michigan City's Vernon Payne is a Hall of Famer:

The Michigan City Wolves

Vernon Payne
All-Conference, All-Sectional, All-Regional, led Northern Indiana Conference in scoring, held single season career scoring and assists records for Michigan City, Coached by Hall of Famer Doug Adams .. IU ranked 9th in all time scoring and 1000 point scorers for players restricted to 3 years ... MVP, All-Big Ten, 2 Balfour Awards, Naismith All-American ... National East-West All-Star Game ... Indiana-Kentucky All-Star Game ... coached college basketball for 18 years at 5 universities ... head basketball coach at Wayne State University 1977-1982 and Western Michigan University 1982-1989.

The Boone Grove Wolves won 19 of 24 games for Earl Greiger in 1959, followed by 19-4 and 17-5 seasons for a 3-year mark of 55 and 13. John Hinkey coached the Wolves for 17 years beginning in 1976, and his teams turned in marks of 22-2 in 1977, 20-4 in 1979, 19-3 in 1980, and 21-4 in 1981. That's 3 years, 60 wins, 11 losses. He followed this with 18-6 records in both 1983 and 1985. Matt McKay led the Wolves to another nice span, 5 years this time, from 1996 through 2000, of 91 wins and 30 losses. The Wolves

have notched 9 Sectional titles, and the Lady Wolves have added 3 Sectionals as well as the 2003 Class 2A Regional at Triton.

The Crawford County Wolfpack, down by Marengo, is just about as far away from Michigan City as you can get and still be in Indiana. Terry Enlow coached the Pack to 25-2 and 21-4 seasons in 1980 and 1981. Bill Breeden's 1990 squad turned in a 19-3 record. They have won 8 Sectionals and 2 Regionals. The Lady Wolfpack have added 3 Sectionals to the trophy case in Marengo.

Crawford County wolf

We have a few more of our 4-legged friends to mention: the Oregon-Davis Bobcats, the Benton Central Bison, the McCutcheon Mavericks, the Clinton Prairie Gophers, and the Paoli Rams.

The Clinton Prairie Gophers have won 2 Sectionals, both at Frankfort, in 1964 and 1982. The girls have added 9 Sectional trophies to the school's cache, just outside of Frankfort, as well as 4 Regionals. In 1999 they brought home the Class A State Championship as Connie Garret's 25-2 Lady Gophers defeated New Washington 50-42.

The word "maverick" either refers to a person of independent thought or action, or to an animal without an owner's mark on it. McCutcheon's Mavericks are raging bulls. The Mavericks have won 11 Sectionals and 4 Regionals. The Lady Mavericks have also won 11 Sectionals, to which they have added 6 Regionals and the 1993

The Clinton Prairie Gophers and McCutcheon Mavericks

Lafayette Jefferson Semi-state. In the state championship game that year they were beaten 70-60 by the 27-1 Lady WildKats of Kokomo, Don Burton's squad finishing 22-5.

The Paoli Rams have had several very strong seasons in recent years. Mike Brown became the Rams coach in 1989 and led the team to a 20-6 record, which was followed up with 19-3 and 19-5 marks the next 2 years. These were a prelude to 1992's 24-2 record, 1993's 21-5, and 1994's 24-4 mark. Six years, 127 wins, 25 losses! After 2 lean seasons Brown's Paoli Rams also turned in 19-6 and 22-5 records in 1998 and 1999. All told, Paoli teams have won 24 Sectionals, 7 Regionals, and the 1999 2A Southridge Semi-state. In an oddity the Rams defeated Bedford in 3 overtimes, 32-31, at the Mitchell Regional in 1936. What was odd about it was that the game was decided by free throws! Thank goodness that rule was a short-lived one. The Lady Rams have captured one Sectional title, in 1980.

The Paoli Rams now have charging company in the Indianapolis Baptist Academy Chargers

Benton Central High School, now the sole high school in Benton County, was formed in 1964 and completed by 1968 with the consolidation of the 10 previously independent high schools in the area, each with its own proud heritage and mascot: the Ambia Wildcats, Boswell Blackhawks, Earl Park Cardinals, Freeland Park Rockets, Fowler Bulldogs, Montmorenci Tigers, Otterbein Red Devils, Oxford Blue Devils, Pine Township Eagles, and Wadena Indians all became Benton Central Bison. Kirby Overman coached the boys teams to 16 wins and 5 losses in 1967. Dave Nicholson's 1973 and 1974 editions won 34 and lost 10. The Bison were coached by Pat Skaggs from 1996 until 2004, winning 152 games while losing 60 over that 9-year swing, with only 1 losing

season. The best records were 19-5 in 1998, 19-4 in 1999, 20-5 in 2001, and 22-4 in 2002. On the girls side Hall of Famer Jan Conner's teams won 12 of the school's Sectional titles and all 8 of their Regional crowns during her impressive 15 seasons as coach of the Lady Bison. Undefeated regular season were turned in in 1978, 18-1; in 1984, 22-1; and in 1985, 22-1. Her 1990 team was runner-up to Donna Cheatham's State Championship Scottsburg Wariorettes (26-1) in one of the most exciting State Finals ever, 74-72, overtime, to finish the year 24-3. Conner's overall record at her alma mater was 295 wins and only 43 losses. Including her 3 years at Warren Central and her 6 at Martinsville, where she won 2 state championships, her overall record was 434 wins and 71 losses! She was followed as coach by Sharon Versyp, the Mishawaka native who was the 1st Indiana Miss Basketball to play at Purdue and is now the Boilermakers' head women's basketball coach. Jeff Guenther's 2006 Lady Bisons enjoyed a fine 22-4 season.

The Oregon-Davis Bobcats have brought home 9 Sectional championships to their Hamlet campus as well as the 2006 and 2007 Triton Regionals. They play their home games in the Bobcat's Den. In 2007 they won the state championship with a 63-52 victory over the Barr-Reeve Vikings, to finish with a sterling 27-1 record for Coach Travis Hannah. The Lady Bobcats have won 5 Sectionals themselves as well as the 2007 Class A Culver Community Regional. That year Coach Terry Minix and her Lady Bobcats made it possible for the boys team to join them in accomplishing something that had never been done before in Indiana. They defeated Oakland City Wood 54-46 to finish 25-3 and win the state championship. When the Bobcats did the same a month or so later, it marked the 1st time in what is now the 34 years when it was possible to do it to have the same school win the boys and the girls official Indiana state basketball championships in the same year. Congratulations again to the Oregon Davis Lady Bobcats and Bobcats!

The Oregon-Davis Bobcats and the school crest

These 12 bring our 4-legged animal friends who have provided the inspiration for our current school team names to 120 (or is it 120 and a half? Logansport teams are, after all, both the Berries and Felix the Cat), or 30 percent of our total schools. Make that 121: the Indianapolis Metropolitan High School, just opened, is calling their teams the Pumas.

Chapter 26

The Top Two Animals in Our Closed Schools: Tigers and Bulldogs

Interestingly enough, of the approximately 800 schools that no longer exist in Indiana, about 350 or 44 percent took their team name from the animal kingdom, not at all a different proportion than that of schools today. The mix, however has changed somewhat. The top choices of our departed schools were the Tigers, followed by the Bulldogs, Wildcats, and Panthers. These 4 team names alone accounted for 128 schools, or just over 15 percent of the now-closed schools. We'll get to the 2 other big cats in the next chapter.

The Scipio, Sunman, Mays, South Bend Andrew Jackson, and Lima Tigers. Pennant Houck photo from exhibit courtesy IBHOF

The Scipio Tigers (now an elementary school whose logo is shown) won their only Sectional at Greensburg in 1928. Coach R. G. Millholland's Green and White defeated Clarksburg, Butlerville, and Burney to do so. They are now Jennings County Panthers after a spell as North Vernon Blue Devils. From big cat to the underworld and back.

Sunman snagged 2 Sectionals, their first at Batesville in 1938 for Jacob Lewis and then at Milan in 1966 for Ken Dieselberg, with a 20-5 record followed immediately by a 20-4 record in 1967. South Bend Jackson, wearing navy blue and white uniforms during their short existence (1965–75) got their Sectional title at LaVille in 1972.

Sunman and Scipio schools

Tigers were also at Green Township in Randolph County. These green-and-white-clad Tigers had a 15-5 season in 1950, Willie Satkamp coaching. They became Parker Panthers before finally becoming Monroe Central Bears. Quite a romp through the animal kingdom!

The blue-and-gold uni-formed Bippus Tigers (also known as the Yellow Jackets) started play in 1909, and in 1922 they won 16 of 18 games for Coach Harley Stech. The next year they were coached by a man whose last name, phonetically at least, has become familiar

in Indiana and *Green Township High School,* throughout *home of the Tigers* the country, Lamoine Shinkel. Chris Schenkel, the noted sportscaster, often mentioned his Bippus roots on the air. It was in 1952, with Paul Harwood coaching, that the Tigers had another fine

Bippus High School

season, finishing 20-4. Bippus was consolidated into Clear Creek, becoming Bulldogs before becoming Vikings at Huntington North.

The Mays Tigers wore black and gold, as several Tiger teams did, of course. In 1966, with Arlen King coaching they won 17 games while losing 6. Regrettably, they never captured that elusive Sectional.

In Decatur County the Jackson Township Tigers also wore black and gold and put together many fine seasons. How about their 3-year string for Coach Gerald Carter beginning with 1937's undefeated regular season, 24-1, followed by 22-3 *Mays High School* and 20-3 records. That's 66 wins and 7 losses! They also went 15-3 for David Hastings in 1942, 18-5 for William Howe in 1948, and 18-4 in 1951 with Wilbur Meyer coaching. Jess White coached the 1955 team to 16 wins in 20 outings, followed by a 21-2 record the next year and 19-6 in 1957 with Robert Lautenslager now at the helm. Glen Whitacre took the reins for the next 11 years until the school was consolidated into South Decatur. His best years were 16-5 in 1958, 17-6 in 1962, 18-6 in 1963, 18-5 in 1965, and 16-5 in 1967. Incredibly, through all of those good seasons, that one Sectional crown remained impossible to achieve.

The Jefferson Center Tigers in Whitley County were also known as the All Stars, and their colors were red and blue. Charles Bacon coached the Tigers/All Stars to a 17-4 mark in 1927. Levi Thompson's squad finished 15-4 in 1930 and 16-3 in 1932. The next year, Richard Ringham's Tigers won 17 and lost just twice. Roger Zwaer coached the Tigers to a 17-5 season in 1955.

Jefferson Center High School

The Jefferson Township Tigers were in Elkhart County. Wayne Lambright coached the 1966 team to a 15-7 mark, followed by 16-6 the next year. In 1950 the Orange Tigers from Fayette County, who again, and why not? wore orange and black uniforms, finished 20-2 under the guidance of Coach Byron Smith.

Those Switz City Central Tigers had a great year in 1955 when Coach Channing Vosloh's team won 29, lost only 3, were Wabash Valley Tournament Champions, and won 1 of their 4 Sectional crowns plus their only Regional. They made it to the Sweet Sixteen by defeating Terre Haute Garfield and Brazil at Bloomington. They then lost to the New Albany Bulldogs in the 1st round of the Sweet Sixteen. They became Wolverines at White River Valley in 1990.

Switz City Central Tigers 1955

The Wayne Township Tigers in Randolph County finished 17-5 in 1952, followed by a sterling 20-3 mark the next year for Coach Tracy Turner. They captured their lone Sectional crown at Winchester in 1937, upending Union City 33-29 in the final game.

The Ft. Wayne Central Tigers, once the only high school team in the city, won 20 Sectionals between 1925 and 1970 and also picked off 11 Regionals and 5 Semi-state crowns. In 1936 they made it all the way to the final game, losing to the Frankfort Hot Dogs. The next year they lost to the Huntington Vikings in the 2nd semi-final game by a 30-28 margin. In 1943 the Tigers captured the state championship at the Indianapolis Coliseum, beating another group of Tigers from Lebanon 45-40 to finish an outstanding 27-1 season for Coach Murray Mendenhall.

In 1946 Ft. Wayne Central again made it to the final game, this time losing a 67-53 decision to the Anderson Indians. On their last trip to the state finals in 1960, the Tigers dropped a heartbreaker, 62-61, in the 2nd semi-final game

Ft. Wayne Central High School, home of the Tigers

to the eventual champion East Chicago Washington Senators.

Hammond Tech teams were also the Tigers. Tech teams won 3 Sectionals and 1 Regional, the latter in 1940. The Brown and Gold made the most of their only trip to

the Sweet Sixteen, however, defeating the Mitchell Blue Jackets 33-21 to win their only state championship with a 25-6 record championship. The Helmsburg Tigers in their Blue and White had 2 good years for Coach Roscoe Baber, going 16-5 in 1948 and 20-5 the next year when they also won the Franklin Sectional. The Hopewell Tigers

Houck photo of pennant from exhibit courtesy IBHOF

also won their one and only Sectional at Franklin, way back in 1916. That was enough to put the Blue and Gold into the state finals at Indiana University, where they lost their opening game to eventual state champion Lafayette, finishing 15-4 for Coach Hugh Vandivier. Three years later they went 15-1.

First Hammond Tech Building

The Laketon Tigers in Wabash County wore black and gold uniforms. M. R. Burnsorth was the coach in 1924 when they completed an 18-2 season. Two years later they had an undefeated regular season for James Ward, finishing 24-1. Their only loss was to North Manchester in the 3rd round of the Sectional after the Tigers had defeated Linlawn and Roann. In 1941 Zera Blickenstaff's Tigers finished 19-3, and in 1960 Dick Piper coached his team to an 18-4 mark. They captured their lone Sectional in 1926

Laketon School

at North Manchester, getting revenge over the home team in the final game 24-15. In the Kokomo Regional Laketon lost to the Marion Giants, who went on to win the state championship.

There were also Tigers in blue and white representing North Central High School in Harrison County from 1955 through 1969. Ken Howard coached their 1966 team to a Sectional Title. Later they defeated New Albany 71-68 in the 1st round of the Jeffersonville Regional. They are now North Harrison Cougars.

The North Madison Tigers in their royal blue and white won 19 of 23 games for Ben Hassfurder in their penultimate year, 1952. The Talma Tigers in Fulton County had 2 of their best years for Dean Day in 1962 and 1963, their last years before becoming Akron Flyers and eventually Tippecanoe Valley Vikings. Our other Tigers (about whom we know very little) were found at Tefft, Tipton Township (Cass

County), Stilesville, and Adams Township (White County), who apparently had a female coach, Janice Blackwell, in 1929. We have covered the Montmorenci, Hamlet, Lima, and Tennyson Tigers earlier.

In LaPorte County those Rolling Prairie Bulldogs had their moments. In 1940 Coach Cleo Isom's team won 18 of 20 games, and with Coach Harlen Clark at the helm they won 22 and lost only 4 in 1951. Four years later Bob Leroy was the coach and the Bulldogs went 18-4. Finally, in 1962 they had another excellent season, 21-3, with Jack Gray coaching. The Bulldogs cut down the nets twice as Sectional champions, both at LaPorte, in 1940 and 1951, each time defeating Michigan City. They are now New Prairie Cougars.

The Greene Township and Wolcottville Bulldogs and Wolcottville High School

The Greene Township Bulldogs in St. Joseph County unfortunately never captured a Sectional title in their 42 years of existence from 1930 until 1971. Neither did the Wolcottville Bulldogs in LaGrange County, sorry to say. The former school was dispersed to various South Bend schools and to Glenn, and the latter's teams are now Lakeland Lakers.

Pennville's black and gold Bulldogs enjoyed several very successful seasons, including a 13-2 mark in 1920 for Ray Brubaker and a 27-5 season 1 year later for Harold Brubaker. In 1941 and 1942 Herb Yentes led the Bulldogs to 20-4 and 22-6 marks. In 1947 Lee Glentzer's Pennville team turned in a 19-5 season, and Jim Mallers' 1962 squad finished 20-5. The

Pennville High School, home of the Bulldogs

Bulldogs won 4 Sectional crowns between 1924 and 1962, at Portland and Hartford City. They were unable to translate those successes into Sweet Sixteen appearances, however.

Bicknell High School and the Bulldogs' Gym

Bicknell's old gold and black Bulldogs also won the Vincennes Sectional in 1942 for Pat Malaska and in 1945 for Harold Goodwin and were also unable to make it to the Sweet Sixteen either year, being elimated by Jasper each time. The West Township Bulldogs growled and barked in Marshall County. Although the Purple and Gold never captured a Sectional title, they did turn in a 14-6 record in 1952 before becoming Plymouth Pilgrims in 1965.

The Dillsboro Bulldogs, who wore blue and gold, won the Rising Sun Sectional in 1961 with an 18-6 record. They were coached by Arlan Hooker. Gaston's blue and white Bulldog teams enjoyed several successful seasons. Clarence Christopher was the coach there from 1936 through 1942, a 7-year stretch that saw his teams win 132 games while losing only 41. The best records came the first year, 21-3, and the last two, 21-6 and 21-4. Phil Hodson led the 1956 Bulldog Five to a 19-4 mark, immediately followed by 19-3. In 1965 and 1966, just prior to consolidation into Wes-Del, Leonard Burns' teams replicated that, again turning in 19-4 and 19-3 finishes. Fulton's Bulldogs won 19 games and lost 5 for Coach Bob Williams in 1951. They captured their lone Sectional title at Winamac in 1942. Jack Spencer coached the maroon and white Fowler Bulldogs to an excellent 19-2 mark in 1944. Duane Klueh's 1954 tean went 19-3, and Herschell Mallory's 1963 squad turned in a 22-2 mark. Fowler won 14 Sectionals between 1932 and 1967.

Gaston, Fulton, and Fowler High Schools

Hanover's navy blue and white Bulldogs won their only major Sectional in 1923 for their coach John Gable. Floyd Stillhammer's 1952 Dogs had an excellent 20-4 record. They lost a tough 46-43 sectional final game to Madison. Lynn's Bulldogs wore red and white and also won just 1 Sectional, that in 1950 at Farmland with a 22-5 record topping the previous year's 18-5. John Reid was the coach. Nappanee's Bulldogs have had many successful years on the hardwood court, beginning with Lloyd Hoover's

An early Nappanee school building

1919 team with its 19-2 record. John Longfellow was the coach in 1926 when the Bulldogs racked up a 21-4 mark. Herman Schulers' squads of 1932, 1934, and 1935 put together 22-4, 19-5, and 20-6 seasons; Guy Conrad's 1955 team finished 20-4, as did Keith Dougherty's in 1967. Seven Sectional nets were in the Nappanee trophy case. Regional championships were won by the Red and Blue in 1926 and 1935,

San Pierre High School

and on both of their Sweet Sixteen ventures, the Nappanee Bulldogs were ousted by the eventual State Champion: Marion's Giants in the 1st round in 1926 and Anderson's Indians, after the Bulldogs had defeated the Tipton Blue Devils, in 1935.

San Pierre's purple and white Bulldogs finished 19-3 for George Miller in 1952. They had a strong run in their final years before consolidation under Coach Max Eby: 17-4 in 1962, followed by 18-6 the next year and an undefeated regular season, 21-1, in 1964. That's 56-11, not half bad in any league. The Bulldogs' only loss in 1964 was a heartbreaking 48-47 decision to Oregon-Davis in the Knox Sectional. Interestingly, that Sectional title was won by North Judson, coached by John Bunnell, who finished 18-6. The next year the 2 schools became one.

South Whitley's Bulldogs finished 20-8 for Coach Don Sickafoose in 1929. Twenty-five years later they won 18 of 23 games and in 1956 were 19-5 for Coach Charles Beck. In 1963 and 1964 Paul Schoeff's charges finished 17-6 and 20-9. Bill Patrick's Bulldogs went 17-3 and 18-5 in 1969 and 1970. All told the Blue and White won 3 Sectional titles, at Fort Wayne in 1922, Columbia City in 1925, and Manchester in 1963. Sharpsville's Bulldogs also captured 3 Sectionals, in 1927 at Tipton, 1928 at Kokomo, and 1948 at Sheridan. They also won the Anderson Sectional in 1927, losing to Muncie's Bearcats in the 1st round of the Semi-state by 7 points. The Wilkinson Bulldogs won their 2 Sectionals at Greenfield in 1931 and 1955. Williams fielded black-and-white-clad Bulldogs, who won 19 of 24 games, Ed Boyer coaching, in 1957. Regrettably, they never got the opportunity to cut down the nets at a Sectional.

The Clear Creek Bulldogs had bang-up years in 1927

1963 Clear Creek Bulldogs

and 1928 for Coach Herman Shultz, winning an impressive 26 of 28 games followed by a fine 20-3 mark. Herdis Kolb led the 1940 and 1941 Bulldogs to successive 17-5 and 18-6 seasons. Cletus Lahr's 1945 team finished 17-6, and Phillip Lahr's 1956 five turned in a 23-3 mark. Two years later his team won 18 of 23 games, and in 1966 Charles Ridgeway's team was 18-6. The Bulldogs won the Warren Sectional in 1927 and the Huntington Sectionals in 1937 and 1956. In 1927 the Red and Black won the 1st round of the Logansport Regional, 26-24 over North Manchester before being eliminated by the hometown Berries, who in turn lost to eventual State Champion Martinsville in Indianapolis. In 1937 the Bulldogs also made it to the Regional final with a 28-20 win over Berne before being upended by Ft. Wayne Central at Huntington. In 1956 after a stirring 78-76 Sectional final win over the home team at

Huntington, the Bulldogs won another thriller over Bluffton in overtime, 76-71, before again losing the Regional final, this one to Marion's Giants in their own gym.

Dugger's black and gold Bulldogs won 20 of 25 games for Coach Tom Leaman in 1939 and turned in 17-8 and 17-4 marks for him the next 2 years. Two years later his squad won

Dugger Union Bulldog.   18 and lost 6. As Dugger Union, Joe Hart's charges had a nice run of 16-6, 18-6, 20-2, and 18-5 from 1984 through 1987. His 1989 and 1990 teams did even better, 22-3 followed by 21-2, and his 1997 team was 21-4. All told, they have won 13 Sectionals and 2 Regionals, 1930 at Vincennes and 2000 Class A at White River Valley. Although that 1930 team lost its 1st-round game against the Franklin Grizzlie Cubs, the 2000 team got all the way to the state championship game, where the 23-5, Chad Dunwoody-coached Lafayette Central Catholic Knights defeated Joe Hart's 24-4 Bulldogs, 82-70.

Bulldogs also played at Odon in Daviess County. Founded in 1835 and originally called Clarksburg after Colonel George Rogers Clark who camped near there in 1779, the current town adopted its present name in 1881, although the post office was called Clark's Prairie. After the Civil War the citizenry desired a new name, and the 2 men who led that charge were Dun Laughlin and Alex O'Dell. Somehow, the combination of their 2 names came out Odon, not to be confused with the Norse god or the Illinois town with his name, Odin. The first high school

An Early Odon high school

in Odon was begun in 1892, and until it was completed classes were held in the opera house. The class of 1902 was the first to graduate from Odon High School as a 4-year, commissioned institution and its student body consisted of 8 students. By 1925 there were 108 students enrolled and the gym was opened with the first game played there on February 25. A new gym was dedicated on February 13, 1951. (Thanks to Ursula

Darlington, the Odon Web site, and *The History of Odon and Clarksburg* by James E. Garten for these facts. They additionally report, on September 6, 1951, "Band wins State Championship at State Fair," their 2nd in 3 years!)

Anyway, the Odon Bulldogs enjoyed several fine seasons, beginning with an impressive 4-year streak from 1928–31 when they won 88 games for Coach O. T. Kent while losing only 18. Ken Johnson's 1935 and 1936 Bulldogs went 14-4 and 15-3. They also had a wonderful year for Coach Floyd Henson in 1959, when they won 26 games and lost only 3. The Bulldogs won the Washington Sectional and the Huntingburg Regional that year as well as winning the 1st-round of the Sweet Sixteen by beating the Brazil Red Devils. Then they dropped a double overtime, sudden-death heartbreaker to another pack of Bulldogs, these from New Albany, in the Semi-state championship. The *Odon Journal* reported as follows:

> *March 6, 1959*
> *Odon Wins Basketball Sectional*
> *The Odon Bulldogs had to win four games before they were the sectional champs. Elnora was their first victim by the score of 60-42. Washington Catholic took their loss with the final score being 58-34. Shoals was the next on the list for the Bulldogs and when the game was over the score was Odon 52-Shoals 38. The Bulldogs had a much more difficult time with the Hatchets of Washington but the outcome was the same with the Bulldogs winning the game by a score of 59-56. A three mile string of cars formed a parade to Odon from Washington. The team was escorted by the state police cars, fire trucks and many a local fan. A bonfire had been prepared at the school and a celebration was held in the gym. Within twenty-four hours a banquet had been planned with 1000 pounds of beef bar-b-qued, and 500 pounds of potatoes made into salad. A good time was had by all.*

> *March 13, 1959*
> *Odon Wins Basketball Regional*
> *The Odon Bulldogs had to face two very tough teams in the Regional. The first game was with Vincennes and was fought to the last second, when the score was tied 61 all. A last second shot winning the game by the score of 63-61. The evening game against Huntingburg, much the same story, had the Bulldogs on top by the score of 60-58. Again the team arrived home to a caravan of cars, fire trucks and police cars. Another bonfire and other celebrations in the gymnasium.*

March 20, 1959

Odon is Runner up in Semi State

The Odon Bulldogs met Brazil in the first game of the semi-state and the Bulldogs had little trouble pulling ahead to become the winner in the afternoon game. Score 78-65.

The evening game was a different story. At the end of regulation playing time the score was tied which sent the game into an overtime. At the end of the overtime the score was again tied. This brought about another overtime. This overtime was something special since the first team to score a basket would be

the winner of the game. Odon had the first chance of scoring and missed. New Albany got the rebound and preceded (sic) down the floor and made the shot which won them the game. Score: Odon 68, New Albany 70.

Not at all bad for a school of the size of Odon. What fun for the entire town! Perhaps they were helped by nearby Raglesville, whose teams were the Rockets before consolidation into

The last Odon High School

Odon in 1940. That combination added Plainville to become North Daviess Cougars in 1968.

In Kosciusko County the Mentone Bulldogs wore black and orange uniforms at some times and green and white at others. Whatever colors they wore, they had several superb seasons, beginning in 1935 with a 28-2 record for Coach Hardy Singer, winning a trip to the Sweet Sixteen in Indianapolis only to be ousted by Michigan City. Abe Hoogenboom led the 1954 Bulldogs to a 25-2 mark; Paul Bateman's 1960 squad won 20 of 25 games, and his 1962 and 1963 teams won 47 games and lost only 4. All told, Mentone won 5 Sectionals and that 1935 Regional before becoming Tippecanoe Valley Vikings.

Royal Center's black and gold Bulldogs won 4 Sectionals before they were consolidated into Pioneer. All 4 were accomplished at Logansport, 3 over the host school in the Berry Bowl. The 1963 Bulldogs also snared the Logansport Regional. In their Sweet Sixteen apperance they defeated Greencastle handily, 67-46 before losing the Semi-state final to Jefferson at Lafayette. Jeff was just edged by Muncie Central a week later in the Final Four, 73-71, as the Bearcats went on to claim the state championship that night. Coach Berlin Rowe's Royal Center Bulldogs had truly given their fans a season to remember.

Although the Patricksburg Bulldogs in Owen County never won a Sectional title, the Red and White had an excellent 22-2 season for George Bradfield in 1950. Neither Putnamville, Round Grove (White County) Scott (LaGrange County, whose colors were blue and red), Scott Center (Steuben County, blue and white), nor Needham's (Johnson County, purple and gold) Bulldogs ever won a Sectional title.

Chapter 27

The Next Two Most Popular Animals in Our Closed Schools:
Growl... Big Cats on the Prowl

After the Tigers and Bulldogs the most prevalent choices of our former schools were Wildcats and Panthers. We'll take them in that order.

Newburgh is an attractive, historic town on the Ohio River. The Wildcats won all 3 of their Sectional titles in the 50s: at Lynnville in 1955 and 1958 and at Boonville in 1959. Their colors were dark blue and gold for a time, then red, white, and blue. In 1958 they defeated Boonville 52-51 in the Sectional final and picked off a victory over Patoka in the Evansville Regional before losing to Reitz. In 1958 they defeated Tennyson and the next year Elberfeld to win those Sectionals. They are now Castle Knights.

Albany's Wildcats in Delaware County wore red and white (they were also called Redbirds at one time). George Yeager coached the Albany Wildcats to a 17-4 season in 1941 and Paul Armstrong's 5 won 19 of 25 games the next year. In 1959 John Bright led the Wildcats to an 18-3 mark. They are now Delta Eagles.

Newburgh and Albany Wildcats

The Ambia Wildcats in Benton County wore blue and gold uniforms and had an 8-2 season as early as 1918. They won Fowler Sectionals in 1956 and 1961, beating the home team in the final game each year.

The red and white Butlerville Wildcats got their lone Sectional win at Versailles in 1926. They defeated the host Lions, Batesville and Osgood, each by the same margin of 2 points! Ben Hassfurder coached the green and white Central Wildcats in Jefferson County to an 18-4 record in 1954. They also picked up their only Sectional win for Ray Staples at Madison in 1936 with wins over North Madison, Saluda, and the home team Cubs.

The Clinton Wildcats, wearing gold and black, had several impressive seasons, beginning as early as 1911 with an 8-2 record. They made it to the Final Thirteen the next year, losing to Franklin 16-14 in what was then called the Indianapolis District Tournament, held at the YMCA. They won their 1st-round game in the Sweet Sixteen in 1913 in a battle of Wildcats, defeating Cutler, 30-28. In 1914 the Wildcats were members of a fairly large company that assembled at Indiana University and the Armory to settle the issue of which school would be crowned the king of Hoosier basketball. Clinton defeated Bloomington 18-17; Brookville, 20-12; and New Albany, 14-9, before they lost to the champions-to-be Wingate by

Clinton High School

a 17-13 margin. And, remember, Wingate's score in the final game over Anderson was 36-8. Two years later, back at IU in yet another Sweet Sixteen, the Wildcats were ousted from the tournament by runner-up-to-be, Crawfordsville in the 1st round. Quite an auspicious beginning.

Paul Kelly's teams won 19 of 25 games in 1925, then followed that up with 20-7 the next year and 19-7 in 1927. That's 58 and 20 over that 3-year span. His charges did even better in 1930, winning 24 and losing 5. In 1935 Maurice Frump coached the Wildcats to a 21-7 mark. Bob Burton was coaching Clinton when they went 20-8 in 1955 and an even better 22-8 the next year. In 1968 Bob Collins brought the Wildcats home with another 20-win season, losing just 5. All told, the Clinton Wildcats amassed 22 Sectional and 4 Regional titles. In 1928 they edged the Ft. Wayne Central Tigers before losing the Semi-state finals to the Bedford Stonecutters. In their other 3 more recent ventures into the Sweet Sixteen, the Wildcats lost their 1st-round games, to the Greenfield Tigers in 1943, to the eventual State Champion Shelbyville Golden Bears in 1947 and to the Rushville Lions in 1950.

The Hillsboro Wildcats in Fountain County wore black and gold uniforms. Hardy Songer coached the Wildcats to a 20-7 mark in 1925, followed the next year by an 18-9 record and the 1st of the school's 5 Sectional titles. Ward Herman's 1933 team won 23 of 26 games; Frank Bogel led the 1955 team to 20 wins and 5 losses.

Hillsboro High School

The Brighton Wildcats won their lone Sectional crown in 1959 at Kendallville with wins over Wolcottville, LaGrange, and Howe Military Academy. Their uniforms were black and gold, and they were coached by Bob Halford. Chrisney wore orange and black uniforms. Their Wildcats won 2 Sectionals, in 1965 for Delphus Henke and in 1969 for Henry Ayres. Everton's purple and gold Wildcats had a terrific, undefeated regular season in 1946, 24-1 for Charlie Masters. Their only loss came to the home team in the Connersville Sectional. Revenge was sweet the next year when Everton edged the Spartans 27-24 en route to winning their only Sectional crown with a 28-24 victory over Liberty.

In Randolph County the blue and white Wildcats of Farmland have had several memorable seasons. Sectional crowns were taken in 1935 at Lynn in a 22-21 squeaker over Union City; in 1946 at home in another heart-stopper, 39-38 (overtime) over Parker; and in 1955 over Union 62-51 for coaches Vickery

Farmland High School

Higgins, Howard Rust and Fred Powell. Another excellent season for the Wildcats came in 1951 when Harvey Davidson's squad won 20 of 24 games including the 1st rounds of their own Sectional over Modoc and Union City before dropping a hard-fought 30-36 decision to Winchester. The Wildcats have since morphed into Monroe Central Bears.

The Hoagland Wildcats won 19 of 23 games for Dan Perry in 1942 and enjoyed back-to-back 17-4 seasons with Jim Chestnut coaching in 1951 and 1952. Paul Harwood's Hoagland Wildcats won 19 and lost only 3 in 1958. There are 2

Millersburgs in Indiana. One fielded the green and gold Wildcats in Warrick County who won 23 of 26 games for Tom Goldsberry in

Hoagland High School, which fielded the Wildcats

1941. (The other fielded the Millers in Elkhart County, covered earlier.) The Washington Center Wildcats in Whitley County wore red and white uniforms. They won their only Sectional title in 1916 for G. R. Hamilton at Logansport, defeating the powerful home team Berries 29-16 in the championship game. In 1938 Washington Center had a 16-4 record for Everett Juillerat. They are now Columbia City Eagles.

The Huntertown Wildcats had a marvelous 22-2 season in 1952 with Terry Coonan at the helm, and his 1954 five turned in an 18-3 mark. George Cherry was coaching in 1959 as his black and gold Wildcats finished 20-4. Richland Center put together a pair of outstanding seasons with Paul Rockwell coaching, 27-1 and 20-3 in 1950 and 1951. Rockwell's 1953 squad racked up 23 wins in 25 games and followed that up with 18-7, 20-2, and 19-4 records, or a 4-year span of 80 wins and 6 losses. The 1948, 1950, and 1957 teams won Sectional crowns. In 1950 they also won the Logansport Regional, losing their 1st-round Semi-state game to the South Bend Central Bears.

The Wolcott Wildcats in White County have cut down Sectional nets 4 times: in 1923 for Robert Lambert with a 21-7 record; in 1953 and 1954 with Ken Seiber coaching; and in 1959, Ted Dunn coaching the Cats to a 15 and 6 season plus a rare tie game.

Wolcott High School

Sidney, in Kosciusko County, enjoyed an excellent 22-4 season for Coach Maurice Medsker in 1942. The orange and black Wildcats were defeated by Warsaw in the Sectional championship game, after wins over North Webster, Mentone, and Etna Green. They are now Whitko, still Wildcats.

Sidney High School

Annaliese Krauter, though born in New York, spent the wartime years in Germany and met her American husband-to-be when he was stationed at Frankfort. She returned with him to live near his hometown of Sidney in the early 50s. In her fascinating book *From the Heart's Closet* she gives this account of her introduction to our favorite sport:

> It was at this time that I learned about the Hoosier phenomenon called Indiana High School basketball. As sparsely populated as Kosciusko County seemed to be during the week, on Friday nights everyone came out of the woodwork and converged on their respective high schools. Crowding into small, at times less-than-regulation-size gymnasiums, they enjoyed the spectacle known as Hoosier Hysteria.

> Sidney High School, [her husband] Joe's alma mater had the smallest gym in the county. It was referred to as the Cigar Box. There was one set of bleachers, three rows high on each side…At the far end was a stage where cheerleaders could boost themselves up…

> It all seemed very organized until tip-off time when the madness began. I thought my eardrums would burst. I had never heard such yelling, screaming and carrying on…

> Everybody knew Joe. For four years he had been one of the stars of the Sidney High School basketball team… That's when I heard names such as Stub Franz, Turkey Heater, Shorty Rector, Doity Riggs and 2 sisters named Pansy Plant and Leafy Plant…

Our sport, caught with fresh eyes and so well described.

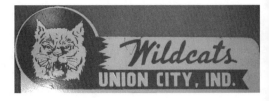

Union City High School, where the Wildcats fought. Houck photo of Wildcats sign from exhibit courtesy IBHOF

Then there is Union City. This unique city straddling the Indiana-Ohio line has had an interesting history. In the 1850s it was selected as the site for the convergence of 5 major railroad lines, making Union City a very important railroad hub in Indiana and one of the most important in the country. If there were no signs one would perhaps not know when Union City, Indiana, was left and Union City, Ohio, was entered, and vice versa.

The Indiana students are now in the consolidated Union City Community High School, the Indians. They were once, however, the Union City Wildcats. Charles McCullough coached the Wildcats for 15 years, with records of 23-4 in 1927 and 18-4 in 1941. Coach Harry Allison's 1954 team finished 22-3.

Our other Wildcats were found roaming around Gilead, Gilboa, New Waverly (also called the Scarlets), Van Buren Township (Brown County, also called the Bearcats), Gings, Selvin, and Monroe Township (Washington County), as well as at Cutler and New Salisbury, covered elsewhere. The Grass Creek Panthers in Fulton County never won a Sectional, but they did produce Hall of Famer Phil Wills:

The 1926 New Waverly Wildcats.

Phil Wills

From a Fulton Co. school of 63 students long since swallowed up in consolidation, Wills assures the Panthers a permanent basketball niche because he scored points like no one else in Indiana's high school history ... averaged 42.2 points as a senior ... more than 40 years later still the state record...one-game high was 60, in an 82-70 victory over Medaryville, he had 53 against ...at Purdue, Wills lettered 3 yrs. with a single-game high of 20 points...served 6 yrs. in the Army, earning 2 Bronze Stars & a Purple Heart for Vietnam duty and a Presidential Citation.

Grass Creek High School

The Panthers of Hanna (also known for a period of time as the Fishermen) never won a Sectional but deserve mention if for no other good reason than Hanna is my wife's maiden name. Though she is a Shortridge Blue Devil, or Felix the Cat, according to how she feels at the time, a certain portion of her mind feels considerable empathy for the town of Hanna and its high school. Hanna is now a part of South Central (Union Mills), the Satellites. The year 2008 was the 150th anniversary of the founding of Hanna, an occasion marked by the addition of the school's bell to the memorial above. They also remember 1948 in Hanna, the year Harlan Siegesmund's Panthers/Fishermen finished 18-4.

Hanna High School and its Memorial

The Chester Township Panthers in Wabash County, wearing blue and white uniforms, had several excellent seasons. Lamar Radamacher's 1943 team went 18-4; the next year Gerald Faudree's 1st Panther team turned in a 21-2 mark while capturing the school's initial Sectional. Faudree remained as head coach until the school consolidated into Manchester in 1957. His 1946 squad finished 20-4. The school's 2nd Sectional title came along with the Regional crown in 1948 and followed an undefeated regular season, a very impressive 27-1. The only loss was incurred to Portland in a battle of Panthers in the 1st round of the Semi-state after Chester had conquered North Central Conference powerhouses Kokomo and Marion in the Marion Regional. No Chester Township fan is likely to forget that season any time soon.

The Hancock Central Panthers prowled from 1956 through 1969 when they, along with Greenfield's Tigers, became Greenfield Central Cougars. It was a big cat lover's dream in Hancock County. The Panthers won their only Sectional in their 1st year, defeating Fortville, New Palestine, and Charlottesville, Coach Paul Bradford's squad winning 25 of 27 games. In the final game of the Indianapolis Regional tournament, the Panthers ran into another big cat in the form of Oscar Robertson's Crispus Attucks Tigers, ending their dream.

The Bright Panthers in Dearborn County wore (bright) blue and white uniforms, and in 1936 Coach Ed Driver's team won 18 of 21 games. In 1946 and 1947 Steve Goddard's "bright" boys won 34 games and lost only 9. The New Marion Panthers in Ripley County, wearing black and gold, won their only Sectional title at Milan in 1961, 54-51 over Sunman. They then beat Morristown in the 1st round of the Connersville Regional before losing the final game to the home team Spartans.

The Shelburn Panthers won 4 Sullivan Sectionals in the 1940s, their 1st in 1941 before they managed a 3-peat from 1947 through 1949. They also captured the 1947 Vincennes Regional with wins over Washington Catholic, 42-36, and Vincennes, 40-34, before dropping their only Sweet Sixteen appearance to state runner-up Terre Haute Garfield.

The Shelburn Panther and the Paragon Panther Paw

In Morgan County the Paragon Panthers, who are now Martinsville Artesians, never won that elusive Sectional title. The Green and White, however, had a wonderful season in 1936 when they notched 26 wins in 28 outings for Ray Fleenor. That 2nd loss came at the hands of Martinsville, after the Panthers had ousted the home team Panthers, the Eminence Eels, and the Smithville Skibos, in the final game of the Bloomington Sectional. Paragon fans remember that season well and fondly to this day.

Boggstown (l) and Burney High Schools

Boggstown used to be a fun place to go for a great meal and some good old-fashioned group singing. The high school there also fielded the Panthers. Coach Roger Ratliff's Blue and Gold clad Panthers went 17-6 in 1947, and John Hawkins' teams were 16-4 in 1954 and 16-5 the next year. The Burney Panthers won 18 of 22 games for Coach Clyde Bickley in 1947 and were 17-5 under John Miesel in 1950. They are still big cats as Triton Cental Tigers.

Clifford's Purple and White Panthers won 18 of 21 games for Marion Link, followed by 19-2 the next year. In 1938 they won 14, lost 4 and, in one of those rarities, tied one. That's 51-9-1 for those 3 years. Harlie Callon coached the 1945 team to a 15-4 mark. Max Liechty's Panthers went 16-5 in 1948, followed by a 15-5 season under Bob Brown the next year and 15-5 for Clyde Hayes in 1950. They are now Hauser Jets.

Corydon was our 1st state capital and the building there is a must-see for anyone touring our beautiful state. It is also home to the oldest county fair in Indiana. Both Corydon High School and the consolidated Corydon Central teams are called the Panthers and both are black and gold. In 1961 and 1964, Gene Cato coaching, the

The 1932 Corydon Panthers

Panthers finished 20-5 each year. Three years later John Wood's team finished 20-3. In 1993 and 1994 Bob Pels coached the Panthers to 18-4 and 19-4 marks. As Corydon, the Panthers won 7 Sectionals, and as Corydon Central, they have added 5 more at the 3A level. Corydon also won the 1961 Jeffersonville Regional by defeating Seymour 59-56 and Silver Creek 75-62. Central won 2 more, both 3A, in 2001 and 2003. In the latter year, after winning the Washington Regional by defeating Heritage Hills, 58-56, the Panthers were knocked out of the tournament by the eventual State Champion Indianapolis Chatard Trojans.

The Lady Panthers have done quite well themselves. In 1985 they finished 19-3 for coach Tom Preston, who led the team from 1979 through 1995. Michael Uhl took over and held the position until 2006. During his 11-year tenure, his teams won 208 games and lost only 48, an average of just under 20 wins per season and just over 4 losses. Top years were 24-3 in 2005 and 22-2 the next year. In 2005 the Lady Panthers finished runner-up in Class 3A of the state tournament, losing the final game to South Bend St. Joseph's Lady Indians. All told the Lady Panthers have won 16 Sectionals and 2 Regionals.

The purple and white Portland Panthers in Jay County also got after things rather early, winning 11 of 15 games for George Clayton in 1912. This placed them in the Final Thirteen, as we have been calling it. In the Muncie District Tournament Portland had the misfortune of drawing eventual State Champion Lebanon whose Tiger claws were a bit too much for those of the Panthers, 42-14. Their 1st 20-win season came in 1941, when they also lost 8 for Coach Paul Todd. Regional crowns were won in 1946 and 1948 for Harold Wallace. His 1946 squad won at Huntington with victories over Petroleum and Berne. They then lost to Gas City in the Muncie Semi-state to finish a bang-up year 24-3. Two years later they again won at Huntington, this time eliminating Chester Center and Hartford City before being sidelined themselves by the Bearcats at the Muncie Regional, finishing an even better 25-3. Harold Schultz led the 1972 and 1973 Panthers to 37 wins and 5 losses. Twelve Sectional and 2 Regional nets were in the Portland trophy case when they became Jay County Patriots in 1975.

The purple-and-gold-clad DeSoto Panthers won 22 of 25 games for their coach Burton Brinkerhoff in 1945. The red and white Panthers of Laurel finished 16-4 for Coach Lynn Sheets in 1975 and 17-5 under Jeff Siebert's guidance in 1983. Whitestown's Panthers have been covered previously. The Deputy Panthers in Jefferson

DeSoto and Laurel High Schools

County won their only Sectional title at Madison in 1925, defeating Saluda, Vevay, Madison, and Scottsburg. The Red and White were coached by Ernest Cashman. Our other Panthers were found at Belle Union (also called Bulldogs), Chandler, Decker Chapel, and Madison Township (St. Joseph County).

In the last two chapters we have covered the top 4 mascot choices for our now closed schools: Tigers, Bulldogs, Wildcats and Panthers, accounting for 124 of those approximately 800 schools, or 15 percent. Next chapter we'll examine as many of the rest as we can.

Chapter 28

Horses, Bears, and More:
Were the Bearcats Named for a Car?

We have discussed the 4 most popular animal mascots in our now-closed schools in the last 2 chapters. Next in frequency came our several choices from the ursine and equine world…and something called a bearcat, which seems to be a mixture of ursine and feline. And, I have not forgotten about our Zebras, either.

We once had 11 Bears, including 2 of the Golden variety. Of our 4 lost Cubs, we have covered New Paris elsewhere, leaving 3, and we have also dealt with the Cuzco Bear Cubs, the Chile Polar Bears, and the Burlington Polar Cubs. All of this comes to 18 ursines. We have also had a love affair with Bearcats, 10 having disappeared (including Monroe's Bearkatz).

Regarding the Bearcats, I have long harbored a theory that, since many of these team names were adopted in the twenties when the Stutz Bearcat, produced right here in Indiana, was one of the snazziest cars in the world, that perhaps the car itself had something to do with those choices. This theory, I have to admit, I have been totally unable to substantiate. However, it may be better than the one that emerges from my American Heritage Dictionary. Looking up "Bearcat" there one is referred to something called a "binturong" which turns out to be a "civet," which in its turn is described as "a carnivorous catlike mammal." OK, Go civets! Personally, I'll take the car.

The Stutz logo and 1919 Bearcat

Before turning our attention to Bearcats, though, we need to discuss the Bears themselves.

The South Bend Central Bears played a very significant role in the history of Indiana high school basketball, and not only because the incomparable John Wooden once coached there. Between 1931 and 1966 they won 19 Sectional championships, 10 Regionals, and 4 Semi-states. In their 1st Final Four appearance the Bears lost to the Madison Cubs in the morning game. That night Madison would lose a thriller, by 1 point, to Jasper's Wildcats. They took home the prize on their next trip to Indianapolis in 1953, winning a thriller of their own by 1 point over Terre Haute Gerstmeyer's Black Cats. Their 3rd trip came in 1957 when they reached the final game against 2-time defending champion Indianapolis Attucks. It was not to be for the Tigers, as the undefeated Bears emerged with their 2nd title, 67-55. In 1963 the Bears again made it to the final game, losing the championship to the Bearcats of Muncie Central by 4 points. Hall of Fame citations for Sylvester Coalmon, Jim Powers, and Mike Warren follow:

Sylvester Coalmon

Played for Hall of Famers Elmer McCall and Jim Powers at South Bend Central...1957 state championship team was the second to finish season unbeaten...four-year starter with scoring averages that steadily rose from 11.1 as a freshman to 17.3 as a senior...scored 1,169 points despite playing only 10 games as a junior because of a knee injury...enrolled at Northwestern and transferred to Fordham where his brother was a star. Air Force duty interrupted college career and finished at Tennessee Tech, where a recurrence of the knee injury ended playing career...went on to a 33-year teaching career at South Bend

Jim Powers

2-yr starting forward for Coach Wooden at Central in 1942 and '43 ...reached semi-state finals as junior... captain and leading scorer for state's #1 team as a senior but upset by Elkhart in regional...following military service rejoined Wooden at Indiana State...played on NAIA national runners-up in 1947 and champs in 1950...an asst coach for S.B. Central's state title teams in '53 and '57, assumed head role in '58... coached Bears to state finals in '63 with all-American guard Mike Warren ...174-94 in 11 years at Central.

Mike Warren

Twice an all-stater at South Bend Central...graduated in 1964 as Bears' career, season, and single-game scoring leader...set Elkhart regional record with 43-pt game as a senior...moved on to UCLA, where he was Bruins' floor general on two straight national championship squads...only player to ever captain 2 John Wooden coached teams...All-American as senior...started every game in his varsity career...academic All-American as a sophomore... inducted into the UCLA Hall of Fame and South Bend's Hall of Fame...entered into acting career, earning Emmy nomination in 1983 for his performances in "Hill Street Blues" on NBC. He won the NAACP's Image Award in 1983 as best actor ... very active in volunteer work, most notably with Special Olympics, Children's Hospital, the Sunshine Foundation and the March of Dimes

The South Bend Central Bears

The Lewisville Bears, coached by Beryl Bostwick for 25 years beginning in 1930, wore purple and white. His 1945 team won 15 of 17 games, including the New Castle Sectional. Bob Scott took over from 1955 through 1969. For the 5-year period beginning in 1957, Scott's teams, blessed with the presence of the state's most prolific scorer up to that time, Hall of Famer Marion Pierce, won 102 games while losing only 16. Even before Pierce's arrival (Marion's that is—Dale Pierce starred on the 1957 team) the Bears were undefeated in the regular season of 1957, their only loss coming in overtime to

Lewisville Bears are now Tri-High Trojans.

the home team in the final game of the New Castle Sectional. In 1961 Lewisville won its 2nd Sectional crown, turning the tables on the Trojans 56-49. In the Regional tournament the Bears were eliminated in the final game by Muncie Central's Bearcats, 50-41. Central went on to lose a 2-pointer to Indianapolis Manual in the semi-final game of the state finals the next week. Marion is honored in the Hall of Fame.

Marion Pierce
"Henry County Hurricane" scored 3,019 points in a 4-yr career at Lewisville, a record that stood for 29 years before it was broken by Damon Bailey just days before Pierce's induction into the Hall of Fame... 32.4 point career scoring average still unapproached...led Lewisville with just 81 students to 1 sectional crown ... named to 1961 Indiana all-star team...averaging 32 points a game, gained junior college All-American honors at Lindsey Wilson College.

In LaGrange County the Topeka Bears wore old gold and purple uniforms. They are now Westview Warriors, still located in Topeka, but we have precious little other data about them. There were also Bears at Westland in Hancock County, wearing red and white. Westland won the Greenfield Sectional by beating the host Tigers 23-21 in 1932. They became Greenfield Tigers in 1948 prior to becoming Greenfield Central Cougars. Another romp through the wild kingdom.

The Whitewater Bears in their green and white uniforms in Wayne County won the Fountain City Sectional in 1927 for Coach O. C. Johnson, defeating the mighty Richmond Red Devils, 29-18. They also had a fine 18-4 season for Ben Rhoades in 1958, 5 years before becoming Northeastern Knights.

The Ossian Bears in red and white chalked up a number of good seasons before becoming Norwell Knights. Harold Ferguson's 1927 Bears won 18 and lost 4. In 1934 Everett Renner's team went 21-4 and captured the school's 1st Sectional title. Clare Holly coached the 1937–39 Ossian teams to 67 wins and 16 losses over those 3 years, including a 26-4 season in 1939 that included another Sectional title. Two years later Ron Tresh led the 1941 team to another Sectional crown with a 22-4 record. In 1953 Ossian had an undefeated regular season, 24-1, with Harry Andes coaching the team to yet another Sectional title. Their 5th came in 1959, when Merlin Clinkenbeard's team won 20 of 26 games. Art Windmiller took over the next year and coached the Bears until their consolidation in 1967. His best years were 1961, 19-4; 1965, 22-3, and a final Sectional championship; 1966, 21-3; and 1967, 17-4.

Glendale's Golden Bears merged with Montgomery in 1948, becoming Vikings, a name they were proud to keep with the ultimate consolidation into Barr-Reeve in Daviess County. Our other Golden Bears were at Terre Haute Schulte, covered earlier.

The Marco Bears wore black and gold and enjoyed a 10-1 season as early as 1912. They joined with Lyons to become L&M, the Braves, before finally consolidating into White River Valley as Wolverines, covered previously. Before doing any of that, however, the Bears won the Linton Sectional in 1950, defeating Worthington 57-32, edging Solsberry, 37-36; and ousting Bloomfield, 46-31.

Houck photo from exhibit courtesy IBHOF

The delightfully named town of Etna Green with its New England and old English roots, fielded the Cubs. Their colors were purple and white. They put together two terrific seasons for their coach Jim Robbins in 1957 and 1958, finishing 23-2 and 26-1. That latter year they also won their lone Sectional crown at Syracuse with wins over Beaver Dam, the home team, Claypool, and North Webster. They are now Triton Trojans.

Etna Green School

The Pierceton Cubs were in Kosciusko County and put together several excellent seasons, beginning with 1941's 26 and 2 record for Bill Bryan. That year saw the Cubs capture their school's 2nd Sectional title at Warsaw with wins over Mentone, the home team Tigers, Sidney, and Atwood. They also won their 1st game in the Ft. Wayne Regional, 28-26, over Avilla, before being eliminated by North Side in the final game. Their 1st Sectional title came in 1928, also at Warsaw, with wins over Beaver Dam, Leesburg, Syracuse, and Silver Lake for Pete Hall. The Cubs' 3rd and final Sectional crown was won in 1957 at Syracuse. Burt Niles' squad defeated Sidney, Mentone, Silver Lake, and Etna Green en route to a 21-7 season. This was on the heels of the previous year's 20 and 4 mark, also for Niles, equaling Mark Heaton's 1952 squad's record.

Monroeville's Cubs wore black and white and had a 17-3 record as early as 1923 for Asa Brouwer. It was the 3-year period from 1947 through 1949 that stands out in their history, however. Bill Miller's 1947 Cubs finished 18-4, a precursor to 1948's breakout year when Monroeville not only won their only Sectional but their only Regional as well. The latter came at Ft. Wayne with wins over Milford and Garrett. The next year Harry Ginn took over the coaching reins and led the Cubs to an undefeated regular season, 24-1. Their only loss was by 7 points to Ft. Wayne Central in the semi-finals of the Sectional.

And now to our perhaps Stutz-inspired Bearcats. (We have discussed the Oolitic, Coal Creek, and Napoleon Bears earlier.)

The Georgetown Bearcats wore green and white. R. M. Plaskett coached the 1937 team to an undefeated regular season, finishing 20-1. Their only loss was to the host Bulldogs in the semi-finals of the New Albany Sectional. Lawrence Moore was on the bench when the Bearcats went 20-4 in 1948 and Wilbur Richard's 1953 team

Georgetown High School, home of the Bearcats

won 19 and lost 4. Joe Pezzulo coached the 1962 edition to an 18-4 record. They are now Floyd Central Highlanders.

Several of our former Bearcats took intriguing journeys through the mascot world on their path to consolidation. Unfortunately, we have very little other definitive history on these schools, and we hope this book will prompt the discovery of some of their stories.

The blue-and-white uniformed Whitewater-Fountain Central Bearcats, a merger of Little Giants and Bears in Wayne County, existed for only 4 years before becoming Northeastern Knights. In Decatur County the red and white Letts Bearcats joined Sand Creek Township in 1940, becoming blue and white Indians before becoming South Decatur Cougars. In Jennings County the Bearcats of San Jacinto wore Purdue's colors, old gold and black. They joined North Vernon in 1941, becoming Blue Devils before finally becoming Jennings County Panthers. In Brown County, the Van Buren Township black and red uniformed teams were called both the Wildcats and the Bearcats. In 1958 they became Nashville Hornets before finally becoming Brown County Eagles.

The Huntington Township Bearcats wore purple and gold and won 19 games in 1936, losing just 4, for the coach at that time, Wilbur Brookover. Their 1st sectional title came in 1944, Lloyd Hostetler coaching the Bearcats to a 17-7 mark. Robert Hendricks was coach

Whitewater-Fountain Central High School

in 1955, when the team's outstanding 25-2 record included their 2nd Sectional championship. Their 3rd and last came in 1958 for Paul Schoeff, with a 21-5 performance, and his 1961 squad won 20 games and lost only 4. They are now Huntington North Vikings. Our other Bearcats were at Hardinsburg. They wore old gold

Hardinsburg High School

and green uniforms and are now West Washington Senators.

The blue-and-white-clad Monroe Bearkatz under Coach Clyde Hendricks had a 20-4 record in 1921 and an even better 26-4 mark in 1922. Then again in 1942 and 1943, with Herman Neuenschwander at the helm, Monroe went 21-3 and 24-3, winning the Decatur Sectional and the Huntington Regional the latter year, defeating Bluffton 39-38 and Andrews 37-34 to do so. That 3rd loss came at the

hands of the Ft. Wayne Central Tigers in the Muncie Semi-state. What else did the Tigers accomplish? They only won the state championship the next week at the new Coliseum in Indianapolis with a 27-1 record. The Bearkatz also won a Sectional crown in 1947, Myron Knauff then coaching, losing to Portland, 36-33, in the 1st round of the Huntington

The 1918 Monroe Team

Regional. A bit later they became Adams Central Jets.

Monroe High School　　We had several members of the equine family representing our schools at one time. One was in Owen County, the Coal City Colts, whose blue and white colors preceded those of another Colts team held so dear. Then, in Ripley County, were Holton's Warhorses, who had an undefeated regular season in

1929, finishing 19-1 with James Petty coaching. That one loss was to Franklin 20-16 in the Columbus Regional after the Warhorses had won the Versailles Sectional. Holton teams won 3 Sectional crowns over the years. The Medaryville Black Horses in Pulaski County had an 11-3 record as early as 1915, then went 18-8 for Ralph Harris in 1927, 18-5 for Jack Stewart in 1951, 19-5 for Leslie Alt the next year, and 16-4 for Bill Wilson in 1963.

Coal City High School

In Howard County the West Middleton Broncos pranced, having wonderful 24-3 and 21-6 seasons for Ralph Phillips in 1924 and 1927. We have previously covered the Pittsboro Burros, Wainwright Mustangs, Montpelier Pacers, and the Markleville Arabians, and will do so for Nashville whose teams were occasionally called Broncos, but were usually called Hornets or Yellow Jackets. That gives us 9, or perhaps 9 and a half horses.

The Holton Warhorses and the Pittsboro Burro. (The Burro is the present elementary school logo.) Houck photo of Warhorse sign from exhibit courtesy IBHOF

Our next 4-legged entry no longer in use belongs to Shelbyville. Before they became the Golden Bears they were the Shelbyville Camels. (Or was it the kind of Camel that flew so famously in World War I, made by Sopwith? Apparently not.) Discussions with Karen and Charlene in the Shelbyville Public Library reveal that for years the teams were referred to merely as "the Black and Gold" with the coach's

name often being used, as in "the Mackmen." Don Chambers, a member of the 1947 state championship team, suggests that the name came from Thomas Campbell, who coached the Shelbyville basketball team from at least 1920 through 1927. Campbell's teams won 4 consecutive Sectional crowns and the 1924 Regional with a 23-4 record. I think that is almost certainly the genesis of the term. (Somewhat similarly, the Campbell University teams in North Carolina are the Fighting Camels.)

Although the use of the word "Camels" has been verified by long time residents of the city, no one I have been able to reach seems sure of the exact years it was used. It may well have ceased to be used when the coach left in 1928. Karen, however, pointed out that the Golden Bears team name came into common usage sometime in the 30s and was based upon a book written by resident Charles B. Major entitled *The Bears of Blue River*, published in 1901. (The Little Blue River merges into the Big Blue River on the north side of town on its way to Flat Rock.) There is a school in Shelbyville named for Major as well.

Under whatever name the Shelbyville teams have enjoyed great success. They have amassed 39 Sectional crowns, 12 Regionals, and 2 semi-States. As mentioned, in 1924 Thomas Campbell coached the Bears to a 23-4 season, including the school's 1st Regional title. H. T. McCullogh's 1930 and 1931 squads won 43

The Charles B. Major School

games and lost 12. Paul Lostutter's 1935 team had a 19-7 mark but got hot at the right time. They won the Columbus Regional and in the Sweet Sixteen defeated Logansport and Berne before being edged by the eventual state champion, Anderson, 30-28 in overtime. That's a close call!

Frank Barnes' teams had back-to-back 20-win seasons in 1941 and 1942, 20-7 and 21-5. His 1947 Golden Bears, led by Bill Garrett and Emerson Johnson, won the state championship, defeating Clyde Lovellette and the Terre Haute Garfield Purple Eagles in the final game, 68-58, at Butler Fieldhouse to finish with a 25-5 record. Barnes' 1952 team also finished 20-8. Carl Hughes led the Bears to a great 3-year streak beginning in 1967, 20-4, 21-4, and 20-5 for a total of 81 wins and 13 losses. From 1977 through 1980, Pat Rady's teams won 58 games, lost 22, and notched 2 more Regional titles. In 1986 the Bears again made it to the Final Four, again came up against Anderson, and again lost in overtime. This was by 1 point, 70-69; Anderson lost that night to Marion. The Lady Bears have won 4 Sectionals and one Regional. John Fair's 2002 team won 21 of 25 games. Bill Garrett's Hall of Fame citation:

Bill Garrett
Few men left as big a mark on Hoosier Hysteria ... 3-sport stand-out at Shelbyville High School ... led Bears to 1947 state title ... Mr. Basketball that year ... at Indiana Univ. became first black to play regularly in the Big 10 ... 2-time all-Big 10 ... All-American ... 3-yr performer with the Harlem Globetrotters ... returned to Indiana to coach Crispus Attucks ... led the Tigers to the state championship in '59 ... Indiana coach of the year ... after 10 years as coach and 2 as athletic director, moved to college ranks, including stint as assistant dean at IUPUI . . . beloved not only at Attucks, but at his hometown of Shelbyville where the gymnasium is named in his memory . . . died of a heart attack at age 45.

William L. Garrett Gymnasium, Shelbyville High School

Under Coach Harry Larrabee, the SHS Golden Bears secured an undefeated regular 21-0 record and won the HHC Championship in the 2005-06 season. Shelbyville finished 5th in the 4A AP poll. Unfortunately the team lost in a nail-biter of a game in the final round of the Sectionals to longtime rival, Columbus North High School.

So you thought I'd forgotten about our Zebras? No chance. We once had 3 more. Here they are: Francesville to the north, Rockport to the far south, and Jonesboro in the middle. The Francesville Zebras won their only Sectional title at Rochester in 1955.

Houck photos from exhibit courtesy IBHOF

Rockport

Francesville

At Rockport High School, shown below in the snow, there were basketball goals outdoors at an early date. The gym was not added until 1924. The trees are beautiful beeches, and the school annual was called *Beech Leaves.*

Rockport High School circa 1900 and 1938.

The Rockport Zebras won their 1st and only Sectional in 1954. Their school fight song was to the tune of "Boomer Sooner." But why were they called the Zebras? From the Rockport High School history Web site we get the answer: "In 1927, the zebra was adopted as the mascot of the school. The newspaper article said 'When you have seen them in their new suits they will easily show the reason for Zebra.'"

Jonesboro, first called Jonesborough, was originally laid out by a man named Obediah Jones, whose cabin was recently discovered under the siding of a home that was being remodeled. It is being restored by the Jonesboro Historical Society. The town is directly across the Mississinewa River from Gas City in Grant County. The Jonesboro Zebras put together an excellent string between 1932 and 1934: 23-5 and 25-1, Lawrence Gotschall coaching. This stellar performance was followed by 21-5 with D. V. Singer coaching. However, even with the undefeated regular season, even with the experience of 3 20-game win seasons, unfortunately the Jonesboro Zebras never won that elusive Sectional crown.

Jonesboro High School

Chapter 29

The Birds:
(Ours, Not Hitchcock's)

We can now turn our attention to other representatives of the animal kingdom in our current schools, beginning with our avian friends. The most popular of these, appropriately so in this country I think, is the Eagle, selected by 21 schools if you include our 3 Golden Eagles and the Fighting Eagles of Lake Station Edison.

As you approach many towns in our wonderful state you often find signs welcoming you to "The Home of the Braves...or the Lions..." or whatever the local high school mascot is. That is indicative of the importance still placed, even in this sophisticated, media-deluged 21st century, on their local high school, and the pride they have in it. One of my favorite such signs, though, is the one that greets you when you arrive in Austin, perhaps on US 31 coming from Crothersville, or from any other direction. Those signs read "Welcome to Austin, Where Eagles Soar."

Those Austin Eagles truly soared several times. From 1927  through 1930 they won 80 games and lost only 19, including 1928's 28-3 mark and the school's 1st Sectional championship. In 1957 and 1958 Coach Ray Green's Eagles won 37 of the 48 games they played. Then, in 1999, Jeff Embrey's charges won 22 of 25, and 3 years later under Scott Mathews they won 20 while dropping 5. In 2005, Ron Hahn now coaching, the Austin Eagles soared to a 20-6 record, including their 6th Sectional and 3rd Regional titles.

The Lady Eagles have also done well. Rick Rigel's 1980 team completed an undefeated regular season, finishing 16-1, starting a string of 18-2, 21-2, 19-2, 24-1, and 24-4 seasons, or 122 wins and only 12 losses! This included 3 Sectional and Regional titles and the Seymour Semi-state championship in 1985. In 1999 Dan Deaton led the Lady Eagles to the final game of the Class 2A State Championship, losing by a 59-48 count to Ft. Wayne Bishop Luers. A 5th Regional title was earned by the Lady Eagles under Jared Peterson in 2008 with another 24-4 record.

Columbia City also calls its teams the Eagles. They have fielded boys basketball teams from at least 1910 and girls teams from at least 1925.

1925 Columbia City girls team

For 18 years beginning in 1927 the boys teams were coached by Abe DeVol. His Eagles won 22 games and lost only 5 in 1932 and were 22-2 two years later. In 1950 with Roy Kilby at the helm they finished with a 22-3 mark. Mark Hammel led his Eagle squads to a 21-4 and 21-2 records in 1959 and 1966. Over the years the Columbia City Eagles boys teams have won 28 Sectionals, 5 Regionals, and 1 Semi-state championship. This latter came in 2004 when Chris Benedict's squad won 25 games, lost only 4, and finished runner-up to Jack Keefer's Lawrence North team in the 4A state final game, the 1st of 3 straight for the Wildcats in Greg Oden and Michael Connely's sophomore year.

The Columbia City Eagle

The Lady Eagles won their first Sectional in 1976 with a 14-4 record. They were coached for that year and the next by Lisa Hart. Hall of Famer Wayne Kreiger took the reins in 1978 and was still in charge in 2008, during which time his teams won 16 more Sectional crowns and 8 Regional titles. Twenty-victory seasons came in 1981, 20-3; 1982, 24-1; 1987, 20-5; 1989, 23-3; 1998, 20-5; and 2000, 20-6. In his 31 years as head coach Wayne Kreiger's Columbia girls teams had 29 winning seasons.

Wayne Kreiger

Participated in baseball, basketball and track in high school and basketball in college…third winningest coach in Indiana girls' basketball (471 wins)…began coaching at Columbia City in 1977…was an assistant coach for the Indiana All-Star Team and coach for the Jr. All-Star Team…West Noble Schools 1964 65…Huntington County Community Schools 1965-70…Columbia City HS 1970-present…assistant coach two years and boys varsity basketball coach for two years before taking over the girls program in 1977…received the Claude Wolfe Coach of the Year Award from Manchester College in 2005…won 16 sectionals, 8 regionals, one semi-state, one state runner-up.

We have discussed how Frankton's Eagle mascot came about in an earlier chapter, but mention needs to be made of their several excellent seasons on the Indiana hardwood. In 1928 with Richard Beck coaching, the Eagles won 17 and lost only 3. Twenty-five years later Muff Davis coached the 1953 team to a 14-4 mark. His 1962 Eagles won 14 and lost 5, followed by a 13-6 record the next year. In 1983 Calvin Bayley coached the eagles to a 17-5

The Frankton Eagle

season, followed by 18-3. In 1991 Rex Bauchert's Eagle team won 17 of 23 games. The Frankton girls team won back-to-back 2A Sectional and Regional titles in 1999 and 2000.

The Eagles of Fremont have won 5 Sectional championships, beginning with the Angola crown in 1925. The Lady Eagles have also captured 5 Sectionals as well as the 1999 Muncie Central Class A Regional.

The South Bend Adams Eagles have won 9 Sectional championships and 1 Regional, in 1973. They also won the Semi-state that year and in a high-scoring game in Indianapolis defeated the Anderson Indians 99-95 before losing the State Finals championship game by 5 points to the Bulldogs of New Albany.

Brown County High School in the charming town of Nashville was formed in 1961, taking the name Eagles. Their 1st season, under Coach Ted Shisler, was an excellent one, 20-3. Max Perry's Eagle squads from 1967 through 1969 won 52 games while losing 16. The next 2 years with Rudy Crabtree at the helm resulted in 18-5 and 16-5 records. Sectional titles were won in 1972, 1976, and 2003 (3A). The Columbus Regional championship was also theirs in 1976, and a thrilling tournament it was, indeed. In the 1st game Franklin beat Bloomington North in overtime. In the 2nd game it was Brown County by a single basket over Center Grove, and the finals saw the Eagles defeat the Grizzlie Cubs, 72-70 in DOUBLE overtime. I think the fans got their money's worth that day!

Mike Harmon coached the Lady Eagles to a 19-3 mark in 2005. His team joined Lynda Butler's 2002 team as 3A Sectional winners.

As early as 1932 the Lanesville Eagles put up a 22-4 record for coach Claude Turley. They were coached by Jerry Reinhardt for 29 years,

The South Bend Adams and Brown County Eagles

beginning in 1969. His best records were 18-5 in 1972 and 1994, along with 17-4 in 1975 and 17-5 in 1983. Mike Miller led the Eagles to consecutive Class A Sectional titles in 2006 and 2007 with records of 20-4 and 23-4. In 2007 they also won their only Regional title. The Lady Eagles enjoyed a 17-7 season in 2006 for Tim Coomer.

The Zionsville Eagles had a commendable 23-4 record in 1919, and with Guy Anderson coaching they finished 19-4 in 1934. In 1936 Paul Caldwell's Eagles went 23-2. Al Rosenstihl took over in 1945 and immediately rang up a 22-3 season, followed up by 21-3 in 1947 and 24-2 in 1949. Al Rosenstihl, as covered earlier in discussing the Lebanon Tigers, led the Eagles to a 20-6 mark in 1953, 21-5 in 1955, and 20-5 in 1956. All told, 12 Sectional nets are in the Zionsville trophy case along with those of the 1953 Lafayette Regional. The Lady Eagles have won 4 Sectionals.

The Eagles of South Putnam came into being in 1969. In their first season they won 17 games and lost only 3 for Coach Tom Goldsberry, whose 1974 team finished at 19-4. William Merkle's 1986 team won 18 of 24 starts. Keith Puckett's 1991

The Lanesville and Zionsville Eagles

team finished 17-6. They have won 8 Sectionals. The Lady Eagles enjoyed a good 18-4 season in 1982 and won their 1st Sectional title with Aubrey Satterbloom coaching. Debbie Steffy's 2004 Sectional champs went 20-4 and her 2005 squad finished the regular season undefeated, winning the 3rd of the school's Sectional crowns with a gaudy 24-1 mark.

Long-time Jac-Cen-Del Eagles coach Dave Porter turned in records of 22-4 in 1967; 24-3 in 1969; 19-4 in 1971; 19-6 in 1972; 19-4 in 1973; and 17-4 in 1977. Dave Carrington's 1985 squad was another 19-4 team, and Dave Bradshaw's 1992 and 1993 teams finished 24-2 and 21-2. In 2009 the state championship nets were added to their collection when the Eagles captured the Class A title with a 66-55 victory over

Triton at Conseco Fieldhouse. The Lady Eagles have amassed 13 Sectionals, 4 Regionals, and the 1978 Seymour Semi-state, losing the State Final game to Warsaw's Lady Tigers, Mary McClelland's girls only loss in a 22-1 season. Scott Smith's 2006-2008 Lady Eagles ran up 57 victories against only 12 defeats.

Delta's Eagles have won 8 Sectionals and 2 Regionals. They made the most of both Sweet Sixteen opportunities, capturing

The Jac-Cen-Del Eagles the 1997 Indianapolis and 2002 (3A) Semi-states. In 1997 Paul Keller's 24-5 Eagles finished runner-up to the 28-1 Bloomington North Cougars. However, in 2002, Delta won the Class 3A State Championship with a 22-6 record, Keller's Eagles besting Harding's in a battle of raptors, 65-54. The Delta Lady Eagles have won 5 Sectionals. Churubusco's Eagles turned in 12-1 and 11-1 seasons as early as 1911 and 1912. They have also had several strong seasons since, including 1935's 18-5 mark for Coach Willard Phillips and 1939's 18-8 mark for Arthur Rhoads. Robert Bussard led his old Gold and Black 1949 and 1950 Eagles to successive season

marks of 19-4 and 19-3. Dennis Hoff coached the 1988 team to a 17-4 finish.

The Churubusco Eagles   Oak Hill was formed in 1960 and immediately had a 22-4 season for Coach Phil McCarter, who followed it up with a succession of good years: 19-5, 20-6, 15-7, and 20-4. That's 96 wins and 26 losses in 5 years. Not bad, and, as an encore, his team won 18 of 24 games played in 1966. Galen Smith was coaching in 1970 and 1971 when the Eagles went 18-5 and 23-4. Jack Keefer got his prized 600 wins-plus record

The Delta Eagle mascot in full feather

started at Oak Hill, leading his 1973 through 1976 Eagles to 62 wins and 25 losses. Glenn Heaton's 1980 team won 17 and lost 5, and 3 years later his Eagles finished 19-3. Kevin Pearson's 1985 squad was 18-3. Six Sectional nets are in the Oak Hill trophy case in Converse as well as 2 from Regionals. The Lady Eagles won back-to-back 2A Sectional and Regional crowns in 2007 and 2008 as well as the 2008 Semi-state. That year Todd Law's team suffered their only loss of their 27-game season in the State Final game to Heritage Christian's 27-1 Eagles. That final was between 2 truly outstanding teams. More on this in a bit!

The Oak Hill Golden Eagles play their home games in the Eagles' Nest

Cambridge City Lincoln teams are also the Golden Eagles. Howard Sharp's 1967 team won 17 games while losing 6; John Bright's 1978 edition went 18-3. Mike Miller led the 1999 team to a 17-4 mark. The Lady Eagles won 3 Sectionals. Their only non-class Sectional was won in 1983, and they won 2A titles in 2004 and 2005.

The Cambridge City Lincoln Golden Eagle

Evansville Day has been a member of the IHSAA since 1980. Their best record during that time was 19-4 for their coach Kelly *The basketball-playing* Ballard in 1999. They have *Eagle of Evansville* yet to win their 1st Sectional title. *Day*

The Heritage Christian Eagles have won 3 Sectionals and 1 Regional. And the Lady Eagles have recently been dominant in Class 2A, winners of 6 Sectionals, 4 Regionals, and 4 Semi-state titles in the last 5 years. In their 1st final game, in 2004, Heritage Christian, coached by Dr. Mark Richards, lost to Rochester's 25-2 Lady Zebras, 50-41, finishing 21-6. After skipping the finals in 2005, the Lady Eagles have run off 3 straight state championships for Coach Rick Risinger. In 2006 they defeated Westview in the finals by a 46-34 score to finish 25-3. The next year it was a 62-44 win over Jimtown that enabled the Lady Eagles to finish 26-3 and take home the Conseco nets. In 2008 Heritage Christian, with 26 wins and 1 loss, met Oak Hill with their 26-0 record in a final game of Eagles versus Eagles. The Indianapolis 5 won by a large 53-31 margin to complete their 3-peat. They made it 4 in a row in 2009, again beating Oak Hill in a thrilling 60-58 overtime final game. They have recently been rated as high

as number 6 in the entire country by *USA Today*. And 2 of the teams rated higher were also from Indiana!

The Heritage Christian Eagle

Culver Academy with its beautiful campus, also fields the Eagles as do 5 new schools that have adopted the Eagle for their mascot: Thea Bowman Academy in Gary, Elkhart Christian Academy, Martinsville Tabernacle Christian, Ft. Wayne Keystone, Lafayette Faith Christian, and St. Theodore Guerin High School in Noblesville, the Golden Eagles. Although the Culver Academy Eagles have yet to win their 1st Sectional title, Lady Eagles have won 5, including 1963's 19-3 record for their coach Ronnie Smith.

The Elkhart Christian, Bowman, Culver Academy, and Martinsville Tabernacle Eagles and the Guerin Catholic Golden Eagles

GOLDEN EAGLES   Our state bird, the cardinal, is chosen by another 5 schools, and we have 6 Falcons including the Golden Falcons of Winchester.

Finally, we have 3 Hawks, 2 Owls, 2 Thunderbirds, a North Judson-San Pierre Blue Jay, and an Avon Oriole. Forty-one from the skies, if I am allowed by you purists to include the Thunderbirds.

Bloomfield's Cardinals have put together a number of excellent seasons in Greene County. Ralph Young coached the 1949 and 1950 Cardinals to 20-4 and 19-8 marks. Guy Glover took over the coaching reins in 1954, a job he held and held well until 1977. Over that span he put teams on the floor in 1955 that won 20 of 24 outings, 20-2 in 1956, 23-7 in 1959, 27-2 in 1960, 27-3 in 1961—that's a 3-year run of 77 wins and 12 losses!—20-5 in 1963, 20-4 in 1964, 22-4 in 1965—another 3 year string of 62-13! His Cardinals also won 34 of 47 games in 1971 and 1972 and enjoyed a 19-4 record in 1975. Steve Brett took over in 1978 and coached the Cardinals for 16 years himself. In 1984 and 1985 his teams won 34 of 45 games followed by a 23-2 mark in 1986 and 23-2 in 1988. Ron McBride has coached Bloomfield for the last 15 years—that's only 3 coaches in 55 seasons, some kind of mark for loyalty, I should think. McBride's Cardinals went 19-7 in 1994, 18-7 in 1999, and 19-6 in 2004. Overall, the Cardinals have amassed 29 Sectionals and 6 Regionals.

The Lady Cardinals started off with a bang, 20-1 and 19-1 in 1976 and 1977, Nancy Woodward coaching. They had another outstanding 2-year stint for Paula Fettig, winning 20 of 21 games in 1997 and 26 of 28 the next year. They have won 12 Sectionals, 4 Regionals, and 3 Semi-states. They finished runner-up to Judi Warren's Warsaw Lady Tigers in the inaugural official IHSAA state championship in 1976, losing 57-52; the next year they were again beaten by the state champion, this time in the semi-final game by East Chicago Roosevelt's

The Bloomfield Cardinal

Lady Panthers. In 1998, however, everything fell into place, and the Class A State Championship went back to Greene County with the Bloomfield Lady Cardinals and Coach Fertig, who could celebrate their 90-58 triumph over Morgan Township.

The Washington Catholic Cardinals won 19 of 22 games played for Coach Dave Worland in 1984 and followed that up with a 19-5 mark the next year. Two years later, with Ken Schultheis coaching, the Cardinals won 19 and lost only 4. Their best year was 1991, Mike Adams in the coaching box, when the Cardinals finished undefeated in the regular season, won 1 of their 5 Sectional titles, and their lone Regional crown, and finished with a sterling 24-1 record for the season. The Lady Cardinals had a wonderful 22-4 year in 2004 for Jim Mackey. They won their 4th Sectional and 3rd Regional, finishing runner-up for the Class A state title.

Southport's Cardinals have won 21 Sectionals and 2 Regionals in 1957 at Columbus and 1990 at Lawrence North. In 1957 the Cardinals beat Muncie Central before running into the Attucks Tigers, who would finish runner-up to South Bend Central that year, and in 1990 the Cardinals lost to the Damon Bailey led Bedford North Lawrence Stars by 3 points, the same margin by which BNL would defeat the Concord Minutemen that night. They play their games in the Bird Cage. Louie Dampier, Southport grad in 1963, also played on the Cardinals' 26-2 1962 squad, a team sometimes referred to as the best ever not to make the Final Four. Six members of that squad received scholarships to play college basketball. Bill Springer's 1990 Cardinals did make the Final Four and were the middle year of a 3-season string of 62 wins and 20 losses.

Louie Dampier

A 24 ppg scorer for Coach Blackie Braden's 1963 county and sectional champs... set sectional scoring record for game (40) and tourney (114)... two-time class president...member of Indiana All-Stars...played for Adolph Rupp at Kentucky... 3-time All-Conference, All-American and academic All-American in 1967... reached NCAA title game in 1966... in 10 seasons with the ABA's Kentucky Colonels, he set league all-time records for total points, 3-pointers, assists and minutes played . . . then played three seasons with the NBA's San Antonio Spurs.

The Southport Lady Cardinals have added another 9 Sectional titles to their school's trophy case as well as three Regionals and the 1980 State Championship, Coach Marilyn Ramsey's 25-2 squad, led by Amy Metheny, defeating Columbus East 67-73 in an overtime thriller.

East Chicago Central's Cardinals have won 13 Sectionals and 5 Regionals in their relatively short existence. They won the Class 4A State Championship in 2007 in a terrific final game featuring 2 of the finest high school stars in the country, the Cardinal's E'Twaun Moore and Indianapolis North Central's Eric Gordon. The Moore-led Cardinals won an 87-83 contest over the Gordon-led Panthers, finishing 23-3. The Lady Cardinals have added 8 Sectional titles and the 1987 Calumet Regional crown to the school's trophy case.

The East Chicago Central Cardinal

Our final Cardinal represents Seton Catholic High School in Richmond. Named for the first American born Saint, Elizabeth Ann Seton, the school just opened in 2002.

The Seton shield

233

The Winchester Golden Falcons have enjoyed many a fine season over the years. In 1929, with Maurice Kennedy coaching, they finished 23-5. In 1942, Lester Gant coached the Golden Falcons to a 21-6 mark, and the next year Tony Sharp's team went 21-2. Charles Shumaker's 1947-49 squads won 56 and lost only 16 games, the best season being the last at 21 and 4. Vince Guenther took over the next year and led his teams to 15-4 and 18-5 records. Pat Rady was the Winchester coach in 1973 and 1974 with records of 18-6 and 20-3. Tom Zell's team won 18 games and lost 6 in 1980.

In 1993 Al Williams coached the team to an 18-5 mark, but the Golden Age for the Golden Falcons was the period from 1998 through 2003. Chip Mahaffey was the Winchester coach for that entire period. His teams won 121 games over those 6 seasons and lost only 23. The best mark was 23-2 in 1998. All told the Golden Falcons have cut down the nets at the end of 21 Sectionals, 4 Regionals, and 2 Semi-states. They also taken home the state runner-up trophy twice, including a heart-breaking double-overtime loss to Northwestern in the 2007 2A final game 78-74.

The Lady Falcons have added the nets from 7 Sectionals to the school's trophy case. Coach Gary Homer's 2001 team went 22-5, his 2004 squad went 20-2, and his 2008 girls were 20-5.

The Frontier Falcons got underway in Chalmers in 1966 by rolling out a 20-3 mark for their coach Tom Spear. Spear coached 1 more year and was replaced by

The Winchester Golden Falcons

Norris Nierste, who held the position for the next 13 years. His Falcons went 17-7 in his 1st year; 19-7 in 1973; and 18-4 four years later. Bruce Haynes led Falcon teams of 1989 and 1990 to 18-6 and 17-6 marks. After a considerable struggle getting the Lady Falcons started (the girls won only 2 games of 86 during their 1st 6 years), they put together 17-3 and 16-4 seasons in 1996 and 2000 for coaches Bob Smock and Chad

Geheb, respectively. I think they should take considerable pride in those accomplishments following such a rough beginning. All told the Falcons have won 7 Sectionals, and the Lady Falcons continue to strive for their first.   *The Frontier Falcon*

The North Vermillion Falcons in royal blue and white got off to a fine start in their first season, Orville Bose coaching, when they finished 20-5 in 1965. James Calvin was coaching in 1969 when the Falcons won 24 and lost only 3. They have won 4 Sectionals and the 1969 Lafayette Regional. The Lady Falcons won 16 and lost 3 in 1995 for Coach James Puckett, won 19 and lost 5 in 1998 went 19-2 the next year for Chris Ross, and finished an impressive 20-4 in 2001 with Ken Gentrup in charge. They have won 10 Sectionals, 2 Regionals, and the 2002 and 2003 Southridge Class A Semi-states. In 2002 they brought the championship trophy home to Cayuga when they defeated Hebron 45-42 to finish a 25-1 season for Ken Gentrup. The next year his Lady Falcons suffered their only loss of the season in the final game, losing a heartbreaking 57-55 decision to Kathie Layden's Tri-Central Trojans to finish at 26-1.

North Vermillion

Perry Meridian's Falcons flew high in their 3rd and 4th years for Coach Dave Bertram, 21-6 in 1976 followed by 20-5. In 1984 Bob Hynds team won 22 and lost 6, and in 2003 Mark Barnhizer's Falcons went 22-5. Five Sectional nets are in the school's trophy case as well as those from Regionals won in 1976 and 1984. The 1984 team lost to New Castle in overtime, 74-73, and the Trojans in turn were beaten by the state championship Warsaw Tigers by only 4 points.

Roz Murphey coached the Lady Falcons to an undefeated regular season in 1981, 20-1, as did Mark Armstrong in 1997, 26-1. This came in the middle of a 3-year period when Armstrong's teams ran up 68 wins and only 10 losses. His 2003 team was state runner-up, losing to Kokomo's undefeated Lady Wildkats in the 4A final game, 44-42, to finish 24-5. The Lady Falcons have won 6 Sectionals and 3 Regionals.

The John Glenn Falcons have also achieved several 20-win seasons, beginning with a 21-3 mark in 1973, followed 2 years later by 20-4, both for Coach John Hans. Gordon Mosson coached the Walkerton-based Falcons from 1983 through 2007, and his teams won 20 or more games 5 times, including 2005's 20-7 Class 2A team, which won the school's 4th Sectional and only Regional (2A) crowns. Don Hutton's 2000 Lady Falcons finished 20-6 and won the school's 7th girls Sectional and 1st and only Regional crown to date. They play basketball in their well-named home gym: the Aerie.

Fairfield's Falcons finished 20-3 for Coach Terry Rickard in 1970 and 20-4 in 1981 for John Wysong. In 1995 Larry Lael's Falcons won 20 of 23 games. Fairfield has won 7 Sectional titles and the 2007 North Judson 2A Regional. Steve Proctor's 2005 Lady Falcons had an 18-5 season. The Decatur Central Hawks have won 5 Sectionals, the 1st in 1941 for Burke Anderson at Indianapolis with wins over Tech, Manual, Shortridge, and Ben Davis. Assigned to the Anderson Regional, the Hawks defeated Pittsboro before being eliminated by the host Indians. The Lady Hawks have picked off one, in 1982 for Russ Sarfaty, with an 18-8 record.

The Perry Meridian, John Glenn, and Fairfield Falcons

Harding's Hawks had a 4-year string for Coach Harlan Frick beginning in 1979 going 19-6, 17-8, 18-5, and 19-7, or 73 and 26 for the period, followed by 16-6 and 19-7 in 1984 and 1985. Frick's last year at Harding was 1989, when the Hawks finished 18-4. They have won 11 Sectionals, 8 Regionals, and 5 Semi-states, the latter all between 2001 and 2008. The Hawks won the 2A State championship in 2001, 73-70 over the Batesville Bulldogs, Al Gooden's squad closing out the year 23-5. The next year they were Class 3A runners-up to Delta's Eagles, finishing 23-5 again. In 2005 Gooden's team lost the final game, again in 2A to the Forest Park Rangers from Ferdinand by a 68-63 count and finished with a less impressive 16-10 record. The next year the Rangers did-in Gooden's 17-10 Hawks again in the 2A final, 61-55 this time. Finally, in 2008, Harding and Al Gooden had to settle for yet a 4th runner-up trophy, this time back in Class 3A, to the Washington Hatchets and Tyler Zeller's 43-point outburst, the Hawks closing out their year at 22-4. The Lady Hawks have added 6 Sectional titles and the 2006 South Adams Regional to the school's trophy case.

The Decatur Central and Harding Hawks

The Hebron Hawks fly in Porter County in their red and white uniforms. John Bastin's 1953 team won 18 and lost 7, and the next year the team won 22 games, and lost just 3. Both teams won the Sectional. Don Broughton coached the 1963 Hawks to a 20-3 record and followed that with 17-4 and 18-5 seasons, for a 3-year total of 55 wins and 12 losses. Paul

Schroeder came to Hebron in 1969, and that year's team finished 17-7. The next year they brought home a 21-2 mark. In 1978 Mike Lord's Hawks finished 20-5, and Gary DeSmet's 1982 squad came in at 21-2. In 1986 Hebron won 20 of 24 games with Kevin Leising coaching. Denny Foster coached the Hawks from 1987 through 1998 and turned in 2 memorable seasons, 24-1 in 1990 and 23-2 in 1994. The Hawks took home the nets from 8 Sectionals. The Lady Hawks added 3 more Sectional titles and 2 Regionals as well as the 2002 Class

Hebron Hawks

A Semi-state to the school's trophy case. They almost brought home the top prize from Indianapolis that year but lost a thriller by 3 points to the 25-1 North Vermillion Lady Falcons in another battle of raptors, Coach Jerry Bechtold's 25-3 team settling for the runner-up trophy.

At first blush I thought all 4 of our Blackhawks were related to the Sauk Indian chief, but, of course, 2 were not: Springs Valley and Sheridan. Springs Valley was formed by the combination of 2 former rivals that we have discussed elsewhere, the West Baden Sprudels and the French Lick Red Devils. For a fascinating in-depth look at the first season those schools became Springs Valley, see "Living a Dream" by the coach who lived it, Rex Wells, Indiana Coach of the Year 1958, in the Summer 2008 issue of the *Indiana Basketball History* magazine. Suffice it here to say that 1958, a truly historic season in the Valley, resulted in 25 victories and only 1 defeat for that 1st-ever Blackhawk team. Never before had a school posted an undefeated season in its very 1st year. That 1 defeat came at Butler Fieldhouse in the state finals to the state champions. It came about in the morning game when Ft. Wayne South Side, with an enrollment of close to 1,900 students and a team featuring 7-foot center Mike McCoy, would finally end the dream of the new school with 354 students and no starter over 6 feet 1 inch tall before just under 15,000 fans in the state capital. It is a fascinating story, well told by the man who lived it.

The basketball-twirling Blackhawk of Springs Valley

The Blackhawks have never repeated that undefeated regular season, nor have they returned to the state finals, but they have had their moments. Larry Bird, of course, led the 1973 and 1974 teams to 40 wins and only 7 losses and went on to be one of the greatest Hoosiers ever to play the game. Another Regional crown was won in 1964. Twelve Sectional nets are in the school's trophy case, and the Lady Blackhawks put together a 19-4 season in 2005, but that magical 1st season in 1958 will never be forgotten in the Valley. Nor should it be.

Our other current Blackhawks with a bird as their motif are in Sheridan. As early as 1913 the Sheridan Blackhawks also finished undefeated. . .but they played only two games! Their 1st of 13 Sectional titles came in 1926 when Coach Will Kingsolver's team finished 18-6. The glory years, however, came in the 30s under Fred Shanklin

and in the 50s under Larry Hobbs. Shanklin's 1936 Blackhawks won 20 of 23 games, and his 1938 through 1940 teams won 65 games and lost only 15, nabbing the Marion Regional crown in 1938. Hobbs' teams won 7 straight Sectionals beginning in 1949, and 2 Regionals, both at Kokomo, in 1950 and 1955.

The Sheridan Blackhawk His Blackhawk teams turned in 5 straight 20-victory seasons from 1950 through 1954, winning a total of 111 games while losing only 21. The Lady Blackhawks have yet to win a Sectional title.

North Judson was originally called Brantwood but took the name of Adrian Judson, a promoter of the railroad that was so important to the economic success of the community. Later, to avoid confusion with the southern Indiana town of Judson, "North" was added to the name. Nearby San Pierre was first called Culvertown and later changed its name to that of a local French Canadian saloon owner. The Monon and New York Central Railroads crossed in San Pierre, and the town was thus on the route of Abraham Lincoln's funeral train.

North Judson-San Pierre fields the Blue Jays, having kept the name of the pre-cosolidation North Judson teams. All 3 of the schools involved, the 2 pre-consolidation and the 1 combination, have enjoyed considerable success on the

The North Judson High School in 1921 and the Blue Jay Logo

hardwood. From 1951 through 1955 Coach Virgil Little's North Judson teams won 88 games and lost only 23. Coach Little's 1958 and 1959 teams did even better, finishing 22-4 and 23-2. In 1970 Jerry Hoover's Blue Jays won 19 of 23 games and 3 years later Bob Fuller's squad finished 18-4. Stew Hammel took over for the next 3 years and led the Blue Jays to 59 wins while losing only 13! Dave McCollough's 1986 team won 18 and lost 6 games, his 1990 edition went 19-5 followed by 4 years during which his Blue Jays won 68 games and lost just 27. Mark Vicor took over in 1995 and led the Blue Jays to an outstanding 25-2 mark, followed by a 19-4 season the next year. Over the years the Blue Jays have won 18 Sectionals and 3 Regionals.

The Lady Blue Jays have also had considerable success, winning 14 Sectionals, 6 Regionals and the 2005 Plymouth Semi-state. In that year they lost the 2A State

Championship final game to the Shenandoah Lady Raiders by 5 points, finishing at 22-4 for their coach John Hampton.

The Avon Orioles were covered earlier. Our 2 Owls are at Muncie Burris, also covered elsewhere, and at Seymour. The Seymour Owls have had a very illustrious history, fielding their first recorded team in 1911. Their 1st 20-win season came in 1927, when coach J. R. Mitchell's Owls finished 21-3. Bud Surface led the 1939 Owls to a 23-5 season and Jim Deputy's 1955 and 1956 teams went 20- 4 and 23-3. Hall of Famer Barney Scott coached the Owls from 1962 through 1974, finishing 21-6 in his 1st year on the job, 23-4 in 1964, 25-1 in

The Seymour Owls

1970, 23-2 in 1971, and 20-3 in 1972—that's 68-6 for those 3 seasons! That 1971 team lived dangerously in the tournament. In their own Sectional the Owls nipped Scottsburg, 80-79, and Jennings County, 84-83. Whew, but still undefeated. Things went a good deal more easily for the Owls in the Bloomington Regional. There they dispatched Brazil, 74-51 and the home team, 90-64. At the Evansville Semi-state Seymour won the 1st round, defeating Milltown 68-60 before the bubble burst and Loogootee's Lions dealt the Owls their only loss of a great season, 80-78. Scott's teams also went 21-4 in 1974 and 21-6 the next year. Nor did he leave the cupboard bare for his successor, Norman Beck, as the 1975 Owls also won 21 games, losing 6. All told the Owls have snagged 44 Sectional titles and 8 Regionals.

The Lady Owls were coached by Hall of Famer Donna Sullivan from 1976 through 2001. Her teams finished 20-5 in 1981, 23-3 in 1986, 22-4 in 1987, and 20-4, including the school's only Regional championship in 1991. For the 4 years beginning in 1986, Sullivan's Lady Owls won 82 games and lost only 16.

The Eastern Greene Thunderbirds also flew high several times. Coach Randy Snodgrass led his charges to an 18-4 mark in 1983 followed by an 18-5 mark one year later. A strong run began in 1994 with a 19-4 record for Coach Mark Barnhizer, followed by 19-3 records in each of the next 2 seasons. Andy Igel took over in 1997, and the Thunderbirds went 18-4 under his leadership that year, bringing their 4-year mark to an impressive 75 and 14. Igel's 2001 team did even better, finishing at an outstanding 23 and 2. That team captured the North Knox Class 2A Sectional and the Crawford County Regional before being eliminated by Batesville in the Southridge Semi-state. The Lady Thunderbirds have added 3 Sectional nets to the school's Bloomfield trophy case, in 1984, 1985, and 2008.

The North Central (Farmersburg) Thunderbirds in Sullivan County have won 3 Sectionals, in 1961, 1966, and 1967, all for Paul Weekley. The best record was 1967's

19-5. Roxanne Brown led the Lady Thunderbirds to a 14-2 mark and the 2nd of the school's 5 Sectional titles in 1978. Her 1980 team had an undefeated regular season, 14-1, and the next year her squad finished 16-4. Trent Olson's 2002 team picked up a Sectional crown with their 17-6 record, and his next year's squad won 18 of 22 games. When you come to play, you do so in the Thunderdome.

Our two Thunderbirds, North Central (Farmersburg) and Eastern Greene

Adding our newly named Indianapolis Irvington Ravens to our other 41 current birds brings our total today to just over 10 percent of our schools.

Chapter 30

Away They Flew:
Both the Schools and Their Mascots, Gone
With the Wind

The mix in the skies has changed a good deal. The most popular bird among the consolidated or closed schools was our state bird. There once were 25 Cardinals and Redbirds in Indiana. We also had 14 Eagles (including the Cortland and Bellmore Golden Eagles), 5 Owls, 4 Hawks, 3 Bluebirds (well, Nineveh's teams were Bluebirds and then Eagles), and 2 Blue Jays. We also had the New Goshen Falcons, the Patoka Wrens, those male geese, the Michigantown Ganders (covered elsewhere), and a pair of Penguins chosen by schools no longer in existence.

In Rush County the Milroy Cardinals had their share of glory. The 1920 Cardinals won 27 games for Coach H. T. McCullogh and lost only 3, winning the Rushville Sectional in the process. From 1938 through 1941 Roger Anderson's charges won 74 and lost only 18, including 1941's 23-2 mark. In 1946 Coach Bob Downey's Cardinals went 20-4, again winning the Rushville Sectional, and the next year, with the team then coached by Alex Boalby, the record was 20-3. Twenty years later, with Warren Stephens holding the reins, the 1966 Cardinals finished with a 20-4 record. The Milroy Cardinals are now Rushville Lions.

Milroy High School and their Cardinal

The Atlanta Cardinals flew in Hamilton County and will be covered in the last chapter. The Andrews teams were known as both the Red Devils and the Cardinals. They began playing interscholastic basketball at least as early as 1911, when they won 4 games and lost 3, and in 1918 they were 9 and 1. They put together a fine 18-5 season in 1924 for their coach LeRoy Schmalzried. Dean Snider's 1943 team turned in an outstanding record, undefeated in the regular season, 23-1, and winning the school's only Sectional crown, at Huntington, 29-23 over the home team. Their lone defeat came in the Regional finals, to Monroe, 37-34. In 1949 James Hughes

coached his Cardinals to an 18-4 record. His 1951 Cardinals were 17-4. Sanford Bruckheimer's 1959 squad registered a 19-2 mark, followed by 18-5 the next year and the same record again in 1963. The Andrews Cardinals are now Huntington North Vikings.

Although Galveston's red-and-blue-clad Cardinals never won a Sectional, they did have their moments. In 1953 Coach Ralph Rich led his team to a 20 and 3 mark with that 3rd loss being a real tough one, 44-43, to Royal Center in the Logansport Sectional. In 1958 Max Quirk's team also put together a good season, 18 and 5. They are now Lewis Cass Kings.

In Delaware County Royerton's Redbirds in their red and black uniforms had many excellent seasons. In 1932 Bob Hobbs' team won 18 games and lost 7, followed by 21-5 the next year and 16-4 in 1934. Hershel Brown's 1948 Redbirds finished 22-2. Myron Dickerson's 1961 squad was undefeated in the regular season, finishing 24-1 with their only loss to Burris in the Muncie Sectional, 80-74. Dickerson's next 4 teams all won 20 games, losing 4, 5, 4, then 3: 104 wins and 17 losses in 5 years. His

outstanding performance for basketball is recognized in the Hall of Fame.

Galveston High School and their Cardinal

Royerton High School

Springfield Township's Cardinals wore red and white before they were first consolidated into Whitewater Township, becoming Elkhorns, and then into Franklin County, becoming Wildcats. Les Korchok's 1959 squad won 17 of 21 games. Spurgeon's Cardinals in Pike County won the 1928 Petersburg Sectional, with wins over Birdseye, Huntingburg, Holland, and the home team Indians. They also won the Jasper Sectional the next year, where the Cardinals defeated Milltown, Marengo, Petersburg, and Holland. Cecil Couts coached both of those teams. Spurgeon also had an undefeated regular season for Delphus Henke, 21-1 in 1948. That defeat was a heartbreaker, 51-49, to the home team in the final game of the Jasper Sectionals.

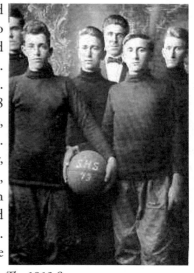

The 1913 Spurgeon team

The Clayton Cardinals won the Pittsboro Sectional in 1924 and the Danville Sectional in 1925 for Mark McCullough, triumphing in 35 games and losing 15 over those 2 years. In 1924 the Cardinals won by 1 point over Jeffersonville before losing by 2 to Connersville at the Richmond Regional, held at Earlham College.

Clayton High School

The next year Clayton beat Advance in the 1st round of the Frankfort Regional before losing the final game to the home team Hot Dogs. And how far did Frankfort get that year? They won their 1st state championship, is all. In 1941 Jean Franklin's Cardinals won 20 of 24 games. Clayton won their 3rd Sectional at Danville in 1947 for Bob Gossman. The Cardinals are now Cascade Cadets.

The Chalmers Cardinals snared the Monticello Sectional in 1933 for Clarence Kelly with wins over the home team, Wolcott, and the Monon Railroaders. The Earl Park Cardinals won 4 Sectional championships, 1933 at Fowler for Clyde Clodfelter, 1935 at Oxford, 1936 again at Fowler for Cleon Reynolds, and 1952 at Boswell for Bob Straight. Their best Regional result came in their 4th try, winning round one over Lebanon, 56-53, before being eliminated by Jeff, 50-45. This was hardly a disgrace, as Jeff was a state finalist that year.

The Fillmore Cardinals also won 4 Sectionals. Theirs came in 1949 and 1951 for J. W. Craig and in 1954 and 1955 for Sherrill Alexander, all at Greencastle. The 1954 team finished 24-1, their only loss coming at the hands of Montezuma, 55-52, in the Greencastle Regional. The Aztecs moved on to Indianapolis where they lost to . . . guess who? None but the Milan Indians in their historic season.

Fillmore High School

In Clinton County the Jackson Township Cardinals won their 1st Sectional title at Frankfort in 1941. Ray Hause coached the Cardinals to a 3-year mark of 57 wins and 9 losses from 1940 through 1942. Jackson's 2nd Sectional crown also came at Frankfort for George Bradfield in 1956, when they lost to Lafayette Jefferson in the final game of the Regional after dispatching Ambia 71-38.

Vallonia in Jackson County is a town with a fascinating history. It was first settled and named by Frenchmen. The name means "of or in the valley." The nicely restored fort in town and the adjacent museum make the town well worth a visit. The fort was built under the direction of William Henry Harrison in 1811 to protect area settlers from Indian raids. Two years later, under a large tree on the west side of town that became known as the Treaty Elm, hostilities were ended when several tribes signed a peace treaty with the Indiana territorial government. Some time later a vote was held on whether to move the state capital from Corydon to Vallonia, Vallonia losing by one vote.

Pre-consolidation into Brownstown Central, the Vallonia teams were the Redbirds. In 1946 Coach Ray Geyer's team had an excellent 18-3 record, followed by 14 and 4 the next year and a 20-3 mark in 1948. In 1950, with Hubert Bastin coaching, the Redbirds won 20 of 25 games including the Seymour Sectional title, their only one, with wins over Cortland, Seymour, and Brownstown. Two years later his team was 17-6, and in 1961 the Vallonia team won 17 games and lost 5 for Coach Charles Denbo.

Vallonia High School and the Fort Vallonia Sign

Vallonia High School 1959 graduate Dave Nicholson is in the Hall of Fame.

Dave Nicholson
Record 402–171...coached four undefeated teams at Darlington & Noblesville...averaged 16 wins per yr....coached and Indiana All Star & NBA player ... Past Pres. of Indiana Basketball Coaches Assoc....won conf. championships in 5 different conferences....IBCA Dist II Coach Of The Yr. three times...won 11 sectionals....rec. 16 Coach of The Yr. Award

Huntsville's Redbirds (or, according to some sources, Redmen—perhaps both at different times) won 13 games while losing 5 for Coach Robert Jones in 1943. They were an early consolidation into Union (Modoc), becoming Rockets in 1952. It is reported that Emison near Vincennes had Cardinals in early years.

Huntsville High School

In Shelby County the Flat Rock Cardinals wore red and white uniforms and won 19 games and lost only 4 for Coach Roger Whitcomb in 1934. They are now Southwestern Spartans. Further north, in Steuben County, the Salem Center Cardinals under Stewart Davis won 16 and lost only 3 in 1950. They are now Prairie Heights Panthers. Neither school won a Sectional title, and both wore red and white uniforms.

Flat Rock and Salem Center High Schools

The Harrison Township Cardinals in Delaware County had a 16-6 season for Francis Kiger in 1932 and went 17-6 for Charles Marcus in 1951. They are now Wes-Del Warriors. The Albany Redbirds (also called Wildcats) had an excellent 18-3 season in 1959 for John Bright. They are now Delta Eagles. The Economy Cardinals in Wayne County, who also wore red and white, won 16 games and lost 6 for Bill Townsend in 1954. They are now Hagerstown Tigers. Our other Redbirds were in Jay County at Gray where Ray Brubaker coached the 1947 squad to a 15-4 record. They are now Patriots.

Albany and Gray High Schools

We have covered the New Richmond and Salem Center Cardinals earlier. Other Cardinals were at Coalmont in Clay County, and Carrolton in Carroll County, 2 schools we would certainly like to know more about.

Carrollton High School

Cortland High School teams were the Golden Eagles with colors of black and gold. The Jackson County school posted a 15-3 mark for Coach Omar Ken in 1924 and a 17-8 record in 1927 for Coach Charles McBride. In 1957 Coach Sam Wiley led the Golden Eagles to 19 wins and 4 losses. Cortland had outstanding years in 1959, 22-3, and in 1962, 18-2 for Coach Sanford Singleton. They were consolidated into Seymour in 1975, thus the Golden Eagles became Owls. Our other Golden Eagles were at Bellmore (Union Township) in Parke County, whose colors were also black and gold. They, unfortunately, never won a Sectional title before becoming Rockville Rox in 1959.

Loogootee St. Johns, wearing green and white, were called the Eagles. They had a marvelous season in their last year, 21-1, in 1969 with Lloyd Gee coaching. That one loss came to Odon in the first round of the Washington Sectional, 76-68.

Eagles soared in scarlet and blue at New Salem High School. The school was in existence from 1910 until it was consolidated into Rushville in 1969. From 1929 through their last season in 1968, the Eagles had only 2 basketball head coaches. Emerson Headley held the job from 1929 until 1950, with Richard Dunn succeeding him from 1951 until 1968. Each coach led his teams to several fine seasons.

Loogootee St. Johns High School

Coach Headley's best marks were a pair of 19-6 records in his 1st 2 years followed by 19-8 in 1931 and 20-7 in 1934. His 1944 team won 18 and lost 5, followed by a 16 and 7 mark the next year. In 1948 the Eagles won 16 of their 20 games and in 1949 they were 17-7. Coach Dunn's charges won 19 and lost 4 in 1952 and were 17-7 in 1954. Their most impressive years were 1961 through 1965, winning 92 and losing only 25 over that 5-year span, finishing with their best mark, 21-3 in 1965. The Eagles are now Lions—from the king of the skies to the king of the jungle.

The Eagles also played for Charlottesville in Hancock County. These high flyers, who wore blue and white, won the Greenfield Sectional twice, in 1953 with wins over McCordsville, New Palestine, and Fortville; and in 1958 with wins over Greenfield, Fortville (in overtime), and Hancock Central. The 1953 team was coached by Dick Cummins and the 1958 team by Ellsworth McCleery. Earlier the 1940 team coached by Herman Smith finished 20-3, losing the Greenfield Sectional final to the home team.

Charlottesville High School

Harve Haggard coached the Monmouth Eagles in Adams County to a season win total of 16 of 20 games in 1932. The Black and Gold were 17-6 under Ernest Curtis in 1938. Myron Lehman's 1950 Eagles won 18 and lost only 4. Charles Holt's teams from 1953 through 1956 put together a 4-year string during which the Eagles won 80 games and lost only 22, including a 24-3 mark in 1956. Sectionals were won in each of those 4 years from 1953 through 1956. The 1956 team won the 1st round of the Ft. Wayne Regional before losing to South Side, 66-59. In 1963 Don Elder led the team to a 22-2 record, the 2nd loss coming to Adams Central in the 2nd round of the Sectional by 3 points.

The Perrysville Eagles wore maroon and gold. They won 20 games and lost only 7 in 1923, including the Kokomo Sectional and Purdue University Regional championships. The state finals were held in Indianapolis at the Old Coliseum, where Perrysville lost to Franklin in the 1st round. From 1949 through 1951 the Eagles won 58 games and lost only 9, with Fred Cates coaching the 1st year and John Gerrard the next 2. In 1960 Richard Kirkpatrick's team won 18 and lost 3.

The Ellettsville Eagles and the Terre Haute Garfield Purple Eagles have been covered elsewhere. Eagles also represented Markle, which fielded a team as early as 1907 (they were 1-0!) and had a 7-1 record in 1913. In 1937 they played a rare tie game. The orange and blue Markle teams gave way to the red and black of the Rock Creek Aces and then Huntington North Vikings, who added white to the color mix.

The Ervin Township (Howard County) Eagles were relatively short-lived, from 1927 until 1948, when they became Northwestern Tigers. The Folsomville Eagles became Boonville Pioneers. There were also Eagles at Jackson Center in Hamilton County, which will be covered in the last chapter, and, briefly (1930–33) at Central East Gary there were Fighting Eagles.

As early as 1914 the Harlan Hawks had an outstanding season, with 24 wins and only 3 losses for Frank Goldsmith. Apparently they did not enter the state tournament. In 1955 John Petrick's Hawks won 20 and lost only 2. The school was split when consolidated, some becoming Leo Lions, others Woodlan Warriors.

Harlan High School, home of the Hawks, has split into Leo Lions and Woodlan Warriors, Moral Township logo..

Hawks filled the skies over Moral Township (Shelby County), Burket, and Roachdale. The Moral Hawks won 17 games and lost 6 in 1935 with Earl Schaeffer coaching, a mark that his next team followed with a 15-5 record. William McNamara was the coach in 1940 and 1941, when his Hawk teams went 17-6 and 22-5. Art Cook's 1952–1954 squads won 62 games and lost only 8! Two years later they finished 17-4 under his leadership. Somehow, they never won a Sectional. Neither did the Hawks of Burket who were consolidated into Milford Trojans on their way to finally becoming Wawasee Warriors. In Putnam County the Roachdale Hawks came through to win Sectional championships at Greencastle in 1929 and 1935. They also won the Attica Regional in 1935 only to be edged 24-22 by the Berne Bears in their only Sweet Sixteen appearance. Cliff Davis coached that team to a 21-6 finish.

The Patoka Wrens in their red and white uniforms had a terrific season for Herman Sollman in 1955 winning 21 of 24 games. They won the Owensville Sectional championship, too. The Wrens had to go overtime to oust the Owensville Kickapoos in the 1st round, 49-47, followed by games with Oakland City, 67-51, and Princeton 60-50. This came 2 years after

Patoka High School Wrens are now a part of Princeton Community Tigers.

a 17-3 season. The Wrens also won 17 games and lost 2 for Coach Wilson Everett in 1963. After a period as White River Rapids they are now Gibson Southern Titans.

Patoka's teams were also the Wrens, and on January 31, 1958 all of their available 8 players fouled out in a game against Mackey that the Aces managed to win 70-56.

No record of all of any other team's players fouling out of any game has come to my attention.

Stewartsville, in Posey County, called their teams the Owls. Their yearbook was called *The Echo*, and it shows evidence that the school fielded both boys and girls teams as early as 1920, however, we have very litle other information to go on.

1920 Stewartsville boys basketball team

1920 Stewartsville girls basketball team

In Gibson County Francisco also fielded the Owls, as did Algiers, a short-lived-school (1922–26) in Pike County about which little is known, and 2 schools covered elsewhere: Elnora and Manilla. About all I could discover on Francisco is their team name, their colors, blue and white, and the fact that they fielded a basketball team at least as early as 1918 when Orb Hyslop was listed as their coach. The school was housed in a substantial building.

Francisco High School

Our 6th and final Owl entry is from Bryant in Jay County. Bryant was once surrounded by marshland, made famous in the novels of Gene Stratton Porter, who wrote about the Loblolly (Stinking Water, in a Miami dialect) and Limberlost marshes of Jay and Adams County. Her words:

When I arrived, there were miles of unbroken forest. . . streams of running water, the road around the edges corduroy made by felling and sinking large trees in the muck. Then the Winter Swamp had all the lacy exquisite beauty of such locations when snow and frost draped, while from May until October it was practically tropical jungle.–Gene Stratton Porter *The Moths of the Limberlost,* 1912

These were favorite nesting and hunting places for owls. The blue-and-white-clad Bryant Owls won the Hartford City Sectional twice in 1958 and 1963. In 1941 Lee Glentzer's Bryant team won 20 games and lost only 4, and in 1952 and 1953 Orville Wiebusch's teams went 18-5 and 18-4. Two years later William Fisher led the Owls to a 19-5 mark, and in 1958 Jack Nichols' squad finished 18-6. Wallace Dennis was coaching from 1966 through 1968, a 3-year string when the Owls won 54 and lost only 13. The following items are from the town's centennial publication, 1975:

The first game of basketball was played on Christmas Day (1900) on the school ground. Students and teachers had raised a fund and bought a ball. As no one knew how to play, although all had pored over the rulebook for many anxious hours and did learn enough to put up baskets, the principal invited… a Portland High School student to…bring a pick up team to show our boys how to play the game.

Worley Gierhart writes of the basketball team in 1907 [he lists the names of the other five players and the manager]… "Most of our games were played locally. I well remember a game we played with Pennville. We hired a bus from the Dan Montgomery Livery Stable. A lot of girls went along…who did the cheering for us…I believe that we lost the game but had a great time going and coming in the horse drawn bus."

Since that time our trophy case in the gym shows the result of student achievement in various sports, judging, etc. The basketball teams practiced and played games in Beck Hall until it was destroyed by fire in August 1924. The Portland Armory was then rented for practice and for games. In 1950 the new gym was under construction…the first game was played in the new gym on Feb. 8, 1951. Even though Ridgeville won the game, the community had reason to rejoice because it had been over 25 years since Bryant played on their own floor.

In the 75 years of the high school there have been 1221 graduates. The first graduating class was in 1901 with 2 graduates and the 1975 class has 36.

The Bryant Owls have every reason to be proud of their school, their community, and their accomplishments. They are now Jay County Patriots.

Rounding out our birds, we have previously discussed the Nineveh Bluebirds/ Eagles, the New Ross Blue Jays, the Selma Bluebirds, and the Sulfur Springs Blue Birds, leaving us with the Sandborn Blue Jays and the New Goshen Falcons. Sandborn won the 1957 Vincennes Sectional with an outstanding 26-3 record for Coach Jim Hannah. The Blue Jays beat Central Catholic 71-42, Monroe City 60-51, and the mighty Alices 65-59 to do so. In the Huntingburg Regional they defeated Sullivan 39-32 before Jasper ended their dream 47-37, in the final game. We know little else about New Goshen than their Falcon team name, their blue and gold colors, and that they were consolidated into West Terre Haute.

Finally, we need to remind ourselves of 3 other birds, all covered elsewhere, but necessary to be included in our total count. First, those charming tuxedoed birds, the penguins. One was found at Smithville, though the team name was the Skibos. The other belonged to a school still in existence, White's Institute in Wabash County. Now known as the Warriors, they were once called the Penguins. So, we once had 2 Penguins as well as the Ganders at Michigantown, bringing our total to 58 birds in our closed schools, or about 7 percent of the schools.

Chapter 31

Eels?...and Stingers:
Indiana Has a Unique Claim Here

We only have two fish, both Eels, a curiosity in that there are no other Eels in the country as far as I can ascertain, and yet we manage to have a double portion. We Hoosiers are an intriguing group.

Our two Eels, Clay City and Eminence

Those Clay City Eels have been a force to be reckoned with many times. In 1929 the Eels won 20 games and lost 7 for Coach Harold Miller. Fourteen years later, with Obert Piety at the helm, they won 21 of 26 games, and they enjoyed 18-5 and 17-4 marks for Coach Dick Liechty in 1952 and 1953.

The Golden Age for the Clay City Eels, however, was the stretch of 5 seasons beginning in 1972, a period in which that era's coach Ron Timberman's squads amassed 104 victories against only 19 defeats. In 1974, led by Bob Heaton, they had a 19-1 regular season and finished with a 24-2 mark. They won the 5th of the school's 7 Sectional titles and their only Regional crown, at Terre Haute. That 2nd loss came in the opening game of the Evansville Semi-state to Jeffersonville by a 62-56 count.

The next week in Indianapolis, Jeffersonville lost the state championship game by 3 little points to Ft. Wayne Northrop. It was a never-to-be-forgotten year for the Eels. The next year they finished an excellent 22-2. Three years, 65 wins, and 5 losses, maybe 9 points from a state title. A Golden Age . . . or maybe it was Platinum.

Our other Eels are at Eminence, where they invite their opponents to play in the Eel Tank. They won 3 Sectionals and 1 Regional. The latter was earned in 1962, when the Eels won at Martinsville by ousting Terre Haute Garfield 61-48 and Bloomfield 65-47. Coach Bill Gore's team finished 23-3, following up immediately with an undefeated regular season, 21-1 the next year. That single loss was a 4-pointer to Bloomington in the Martinsville Sectional. Two excellent years in a row for the Eels. In 1978 Jim Coon's squad won 22 of 25 games and the school's 2nd Sectional crown. The Lady Eels (can that really be right?) have done well, too. Jim Porter's 1995–1997 squads won 3 straight Sectional titles, and their records the 1st two years were a laudable 21-2 and 20-1. Terry Terhune led the girls to their only Regional title in 1999.

The question arises as to why these 2 schools selected Eels for their team names. In Clay City's case the map shows the Eel River circles the town on 3 sides. Eminence in Morgan County must have a different reason. There is no Eel River there, just Mill Creek. I need some help on this one. (Not an addition, but certainly a choice to be savored, is the mascot of the Columbus North swimming and diving teams: the Bull Frogs, also 2 words, you will note.)

We haven't forgotten our friends the bees, either, as we have 7 schools of our 406 whose teams are the Hornets as well as the Morristown Yellow Jackets. The animal kingdom, including those four-legged versions and the birds covered in previous chapters, accounts for about 42 percent of our current high school team names.

Rossville High School in Clinton County was founded in 1896 and rebuilt in 1967 after a devastating tornado. Their school crest says it all: the wheat shock for agriculture, the treble clef and mask for music and drama, the open book and torch for literary achievement and knowledge, and the star showing their location at the intersection of Highways 39 and 26.

The Rossville crest

Their teams are the Hornets, and the Hornets have enjoyed many outstanding seasons over the years, beginning with the 1937 team's 24-4 record for Coach Carl Adams. He also led the 1939 team to 20 wins in 24 outings. Larry Hobbs coached the Hornets to consecutive 21-3 marks in 1944 and 1945 and the undefeated regular season the next year, 26-1, as well as 1947's 24-3 record. Ninety-two wins and 10 losses in 4 years! Mike Jones-coached Rossville teams went 22-3 in 1969, 21-5 in 1970, and 24-3 in 1971 winning Sectional and Regional titles each year: 67-11 for the period. The 1971 squad defeated Jeff in the Lafayette Semi-state before losing to State Champion East Chicago Washington. Jones' 1975 Hornets finished 23-2. Bob Knapp, who played on that geat 19971 Rossvile team, coached the Hornets to 18 wins and 5 losses in 1988 and Jeff Henley's 1999 team was 19-4. The Hornets have won 16 Sectionals and 5 Regionals as well as the 2002 Class A State Championship, when the 23-4 Hensley-led Hornets defeated the Barr-Reeve Vikings 79-68. Rossville's Jennifer Jacoby, who scored 2,344 points for the Lady Hornets prior to an outstanding career at Purdue, was Miss Indiana's Basketball in 1991.

The Rossville Hornet

The Angola Hornets have stung several opponents over the years, as already covered. The Beech Grove Hornets had excellent seasons for Coach Steve Coffman in 1974 and 1975, 18-4 and 19-5, and for Bob Harris in 1995 18-5. They have won 3 Sectionals, at Southport in 1966, at Shelbyville in 1992, and the 2008 3A title at home. The Lady Hornets won the Class 3A State Championship in 2003 led by

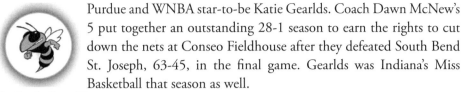

Purdue and WNBA star-to-be Katie Gearlds. Coach Dawn McNew's 5 put together an outstanding 28-1 season to earn the rights to cut down the nets at Conseo Fieldhouse after they defeated South Bend St. Joseph, 63-45, in the final game. Gearlds was Indiana's Miss Basketball that season as well.

The Beech Grove Hornets

Henryville's Hornets have also left their stingers in a few foes over the years. Under Coach Herman Furnish they enjoyed back-to-back undefeated regular seasons in 1945 and 1946 with 20-1 and 18-1 records respectively. His teams also had successful seasons in 1947, 17-6; in 1948, 18-5; and in 1951, 18-4. Jim Huter's team went 19-3 in 1963; the Hornets were 17-4 with Dennis Holt at the helm in 1981. The Henryville Web site contains the following interesting facts:

> The early history of Henryville Basketball is incomplete and document-ed information is hard to find. It is believed that intramural basketball was played as early as the 1913-14 school year. At least 2 games (both losses) were played against outside competition during the 1919-20 school year.
>
> Henryville first participated in Indiana High School Athletic Association tournament play on February 29, 1924 defeating Saluda 15-8 in the Hanover Sectional. Henryville lost their second round game to Vevay 4-46. On January 5, 1929, a new gym was dedicated with a 21-11 win over Silver Creek.
>
> In 1933-34, Henryville was known as the Blue Devils and wore blue and white uniforms. By the 1942-43 season, Henryville was known as the Hornets and wore black and gold uniforms.
>
> From February 4, 1944 through November 8, 1946, Henryville won 41 consecutive regular season games. This included two consecutive undefeated regular seasons in 1944-45 (19-0) and 1945-46 (17-0). Henryville is one of only a few schools in the history of the IHSAA to accomplish this feat.
>
> From February 4, 1944 through February 13, 1948, Henryville won 37 consecutive home games.

In the process the Hornets cut down the nets as Clark County champions 4 times, won 5 invitational tournaments, 4 conference titles and 2 Sectionals. Not a bad trophy case! The Lady Hornets added the 1994 Silver Creek Sectional to that case.

The Henryville (Lady) Hornets

The Gary Lew Wallace Hornets have won 7 Sectionals, and proving how tough the Gary Sectional is, 6 Regionals as well. In their Sweet Sixteen contests they have often been knocked out by the eventual state champion or runner-up. In 1943, after beating the Peru Tigers, Wallace lost to Lebanon, the runner-up that year; in 1953 the Hornets upended the Zionsville Eagles then lost to the eventual State Champion South Central Bears. In 1983 and 1986, after defeating the Benton Central Bisons and the Plainfield Quakers respectively, Wallace lost to the state runner-up Anderson Indians both times.

The Gary Lew Wallace and Indianapolis Howe Academy Hornets

The Indianapolis Howe Hornets, after a brief hiatus as a middle school, are back as Howe Academy. Between 1944 and 1986 the Hornets won 8 Sectionals, and after reopening at the secondary level they won the 2007 Whiteland 3A Sectional. They also won Indianapolis Regionals in 1964 and 1981. The Lady Hornets have added 2 Sectionals to the school's collection as well as the 1983 Center Grove Regional and the Ben Davis Semi-state.

Medora's stinger has also been felt by several opponents over the years. The Hornets won 20 of 24 games in 1942 for Coach Arthur Odle, Jr., and enjoyed

Medora High School, Home of the Hornets

19-3 and 17-6 seasons in 1951 and 1952 with Ray Hawley at the helm. In 1955 Olin Weddel's team won 17 and lost only 5, in 1959 Seaborn Hillis coached the Hornets to an 18-5 mark, and Troy Ingram's charges finished at 20-4 the next year. With so many of their former opponents now consolidated, winning has become more difficult for the Medora Hornets, one of the smaller schools still left in the region.

The Morristown Yellow Jackets have a rich basketball heritage, starting with a 3-year string under Coach Noel Genth from 1936 through 1938 when they won 65 games and lost only 8, including 1937's undefeated regular season mark of 23-1. That one loss came in the finals of the Shelbyville Sectional to Columbus, after wins over Fairland and Mt. Auburn.

In 1946 and 1947, with Gerl Furr coaching, the Jackets went 20-2 and 19-3. Larry Cline was at the helm in 1957 for a 23-2 mark, which he followed up with 18-5 in 1960. Morris Newman took the reins in 1961 and led the Jackets to consecutive seasons of 20-5, 15-9, 19-6, 17-4, 17-4 and 18-4: 6 years, 106 wins, 32 losses. Roger Bridge led the 1973 team to a 19-4 finish, and Dan Carmony's 1998 five won 22 of 24 games

played, including the school's only Regional title, Class A at Southwestern, 68-51 over the Rising Sun Shiners. Overall 9 Sectional crowns have been taken back to the hive by the Yellow Jackets. The Lady Yellow Jackets picked off 3 straight Southwestern Class A Sectionals beginning in 2001, when they also won their own Regional. Hall of Famer Marvin Wood is a Morristown graduate:

Marvin Wood
4-yr performer for Morristown. . . all-regional as a freshman . . . played 3 yrs for Butler University, where he says he just 'was very fortunate to be a part of the team' . . . 22-year coaching career was highlighted by fabled 1954 performance by his Milan team that struck a blow for small schools everywhere by beating mighty Muncie Central. . . made Final 4 the year before. . .Southeastern Ind. coach of yr 1953 and '54. . . named 1974 District 1 Coach of Year by Indiana Basketball Coaches Assn. . . . past pres. of Indiana High School Coaches Association.

Our closed schools were more attentive, proportionately, to our insect friends. We once had 14 Yellow Jackets (including the Blue variety found in Heltonville), 14 Hornets, and 4 Bees, and, as you have no doubt perceived, my personal favorite, the Honey Creek Honey Bees, covered previously. We also had the Spiceland Stingers. And we mustn't forget that we had a pair of Crickets and another of Gold Bugs, all covered elsewhere.

The Staunton Yellow Jacket, DuPont Hornet, and Waveland Hornet

The Staunton Yellow Jackets in Clay County wore blue and gold uniforms. They won 16 of 20 games for Coach Bill Peden in 1965 and had 19-5 and 20-4 seasons for Jim Buell in 1975 and 1977. Between 1951 and 1977 the Staunton Yellow Jackets won 5 Sectionals. They are now part of Northview, the Knights. The DuPont Hornets (their historic building is still an elementary school) wore gold and black uniforms for a time, then switched to red and black and are now Madison Cubs. Hall of Fame coach Donna Cheatham graduated from DuPont High School:

DONNA K. CHEATHAM

Donna Cheatham

Awarded 35 Coach of the Year Honors...coached the Reebok North/South Classic, East/West Indiana All-Star Classic...Hoosier Basketball Coaches Association... McDonald's All-Stars and the Indiana Girl's All-Star Team... coached two state championship teams, Scottsburg in 1989 and Southwestern at Hanover in 2002... 1986 Scottsburg team was the Indiana State Runner-Up... 1987 team won the Indiana Basketball Hall of Fame Classic Championship...during the summer of 1987, asked by the USIA to coach teams in Yauonde in Cameroon, Africa...44 players have earned college scholarships, while one player was named Miss Basketball...two players have received the Mental Attitude Award at the state finals and eight players have been named to the Indiana All-Star Team.

Waveland's Hornets have been covered earlier. There were also Hornets representing St. Berniece in Vermillion County. They wore red and black uniforms and had a 12-6 record in 1951 for Don Reel. They became Clinton Wildcats before becoming South Vermillion, still Wildcats.

Purple-and-gold-clad Yellow Jackets at Decatur had several seasons deserving of our attention. In 1920 and 1921 Coach Karl Grove's teams played a lot of games. Though they won 40 in those two years, they also lost 28. That 1921 edition played 37 games, going 19-18. Decatur also fielded a girls team at least as early as 1921.

The 1921 Decatur girls team

Anthony Moore took over as (boys) coach in 1922, and the Yellow Jackets again played over 30 games, winning 20 and losing 11. In 1925 they played a more normal 24-game slate for Coach Maurice Kennedy, winning 18 of their encounters. Herb Curtis was coach of the Yellow Jackets for a very impressive 5-year string that his Decatur teams put together from 1927 until 1931. Over that span his teams amassed 92 wins and lost only 20. Their best records came in 1927 when they were 22-5 and in 1931, when they finished at 22-3. Decatur won an impressive 11 Sectional championships beginning in 1952 and ending in 1959. In 1944 they also won the Huntington Regional. The Yellow Jackets have since become Bellmont Braves and Squaws.

Fairland's Hornets in Shelby County wore their scarlet and white uniforms. From 1942 through 1944 they won 56 games and lost only 12. The first 2 of those years Richard Willsey was the coach; the last year the job belonged to Ernest Bush. Max Bell coached the Hornets to another impressive 3-year string from 1948 through 1950, winning 63 games and losing only 8. This included 1949's undefeated regular season mark of 24-1. That loss came in the final game of the Greensburg Regional to Madison. Madison went on to be the runner-up to the state champion Jasper team in Indianapolis two weeks later. Quite a season for the Fairland Hornets! Their 2nd Sectional championship came in 1950, also at Shelbyville. The Hornets made it that year to the Regional final, where they again ran into those pesky Cubs from Madison. They lost again, but that was hardly a disgrace. In 1950 Madison won the state championship themselves. What an unforgettable 2 years for the Hornets!

Solsberry, Indiana, is not a cathedral town, nor is it a mis-spelling of one in England. It is in Greene County, near to one of the country's most impressive railroad trestles. The tracks run through the town, although I saw no train when I was there. A basketball goal is right near the track, along with a general store. The Solsberry Hornets, wearing purple and gold, experienced a bang-up season in 1953 for Coach Guy Glover. They finished at 25-2. Sectional championships were won in 1948 at Linton and at Switz City in 1957. In 1949 Solsberry defeated Brazil in the Martinsville Regional before losing to Bloomington in the final game there. In 1957 that 2nd loss came with a measure of revenge for Brazil, the Red Devils turning the tables on the Hornets in the 1st round of the Bloomington Regional. The 1953 team ousted Bloomfield in the Sectional final, then edged Staunton 54-52 in the 1st round of the Bloomington regional before being sidelined by Terre Haute Gerstmeyer.

1956 Solsberry Hornets

Recent scene in Solsberry

Russellville in Putnam County called their teams the Bees. As early as 1915 the Bees, who wore purple and white uniforms, won 7 of 10 games played. They won the 1921 Sectional at Greencastle. They also were 1 of the 8 winners of the Bloomington Regional that year, joining 8 teams from the West Lafayette Regional in the Sweet Sixteen at the Old Coliseum in Indianapolis. There they defeated Bloomington 27-22 in the 1st round before losing to Muncie 21-15. They are now North Putnam Cougars.

The Syracuse Yellow Jackets have been covered previously. Jasonville's Yellow Jackets in Greene County won 2 Sectionals, 1941 in Bloomfield with wins over Worthington, Solsberry, and Lyons, and 1952 in Linton, where they defeated Lyons and

Russellville High School

Solsberry rather easily before edging the home team 56-55. They are now Shakamak Lakers.

In Brown County the Nashville teams wore gold and black and were called both the Yellow Jackets and the Hornets. (Curiously, Nashville, Illinois, High School also calls their teams the Hornets.) The Yellow Jackets/Hornets won the Columbus Sectional in 1959 with a 21-2 record for Coach Ted Shishler, the only loss coming to Hagerstown in the Sectional by 2 points. They are now Brown County Eagles.

Nashville High School

Williamsburg's Yellow Jackets in Wayne County also wore blue and gold. As early as 1932 they enjoyed a 19-2 season. In 1955 they had that coveted undefeated regular season for Coach Vernon Warner, 24-1, their only loss coming in the final game of the Richmond Sectional to the home team Red Devils after wins over Economy, Fountain City, and Centerville. In 1962 and 1963 they won 18 and lost 4 followed by 16 and 5, Robert Stoker

NASHVILLE HORNETS

Richmond

Williamsburg High School

coaching. They merged with Webster, becoming Pirates, before being consolidated into Northeastern as Knights.

The green and white Hornets of Harrisburg stung their foes quite successfully during several seasons. Cecil Tague's 1953 team triumphed in 20 games and lost only 3. Paul Bateman's 1956 squad was 16-4 followed by an 18-6 record the next year. Those Hornets are now Connersville Spartans, after 1st

Emerson Houck photo from exhibit courtesy IBOF

becoming Fayette Central Chiefs for 8 years. The best record for the green-and-gold-clad Chiefs was 16-8 for Coach Robert Grove in 1960.

The Elberfeld Hornets were also called the Elites, and they were covered under that name earlier. The Howard Township Hornets won 18 and lost 9 in 1921 and had a 15-8 season for Dwight Singer in 1948. They wore black and gold and are now Northwestern (Howard County) Tigers. The Springville Hornets wore blue and white uniforms and won 17 of 22 games for Bill Luse in 1941. They became Oolitic Bearcats before both became Bedford North Lawrence Stars. There were also Hornets buzzing around Tangier, covered elsewhere.

The Burnettsville Bees only lost 2 games in 1914 . . . but they only played 8. The next year they won 16 and lost 8. Fred Gorman coached both of those teams. They had a 16-7 record for James Murphy in 1962, 2 years before becoming Twin Lakes Indians. Their colors were red and white.

Other Yellow Jackets were found at Alfordsville, Clinton Township (Putnam County), Fairview, Pulaski, and Macy. There were Hornets at Hanging Grove, but I don't know what was hanging there. Bees' nests? Bees were buzzing at Burns City in Martin County, and for a brief time there were Hornets doing the same at Metea in Cass County and at Brewersville in Jennings County. None of these, sad to say, ever won a Sectional. We hope there is considerably more information on all of these schools that will come to light in the near future.

So we now have about 51 percent of our current schools that have turned to the animal kingdom for inspiration for their team names.

For our closed schools we must remember to count a few other members of the animal kingdom that have been discussed, or will be, in various places. These include the following: 4 Beavers, 3 Zebras, 2 River Rats, 2 Otters, 2 Rams, and 1 each of Prairie Gophers, Polecats, Raccoons, Gorillas, Kangaroos, Woodchucks, and Bison (Bisons). Quite a menagerie. Oops, I almost forgot the scariest one of all: the Buck Creek Cobras! Riki-Tiki-Tavi, where are you?

All told, then, the animal kingdom provided the inspiration for about 55 percent of the mascots of our now-closed schools, not much different in total from that of today's schools.

What about the other remainder of our mascots? I promise we'll deal with those not discussed in other contexts later in some detail.

(Top) Waveland boys team and the Waveland girls team (below)

Chapter 32

Trojans and Royalty:
After Indians and Animals…What's Next?

Lions and Tigers and Bears. . .oh my. . .and Panthers, Wildcats, and so forth. Eagles, Cardinals, and Falcons. . .Hornets, Yellow Jackets, and Eels. Warriors and Braves. We have dealt with our Indian heritage and with the animal kingdom. In the process learning that those 2 categories account for the team names of about 52 percent of our high schools today and a somewhat higher percentage of our closed schools. Additionally, we have covered about another 10 percent of the schools with names that are truly unique, the Alices, Artesians, Oracles, Slicers, Shiners, Berries, and so forth of today and the Sprudels, Twigs, Stonecutters, Quarry Lads, Lightning Fives, Apple Boys, and the like from our consolidated schools. Now we can turn our attention to the variety of other choices that have been made for the team names of current schools. We will tackle those of the closed schools in the next chapter.

The leading 2 team names are historical and heroic: the Trojans (12) and the Knights (14), including the Indianapolis Arlington Golden Knights. The Tri-Central Trojans in Tipton County resulted from the consolidation of 3 schools, the Sharpsville Bulldogs, the Prairie Township Aces and the Windfall Dragons.

Tri-Central's crest utilizes 3 Olympic-style rings to represent the unity of these schools and the importance of sports and sportsmanship to their value system. The torch of learning is backed by the atomic symbol and reflects the values of science and academics. The clasped Trojan hands, running diagonally across the shield, finish the

The Tri-Central crest and Trojan

motif and represent the value of friendship between students.

The Tri-Central Trojans in Sharpsville have won 6 Sectionals, 3 Regionals, and the 2006 Class A Semi-state at Lafayette. They lost the last finals game to Hauser's Jets, finishing 23-4. In 1984 Cliff Hawkins led the Trojans to a 20-3 season, but it was from 2004 through 2006 that Tri-Central teams hit their stride, winning 68 games and losing only 9. This span included the undefeated regular season record of 23-1 in

2005 for Dave Diggs, who coached at the Tipton County school for 21 years and, of course, that state runner-up season for his replacement, Jeff Layden.

The Lady Trojans have won 4 Sectionals, 3 Regionals, and 3 Semi-states. Their 1st of 3 straight Class A State Championships, all coached by Kathie Layden, came in 2003, when Tri-Central gave North Vermillion's Lady Falcons their only loss in a 27-game season, 57-55, finishing 23-4 themselves. The next year they defeated the Washington Catholic Lady Cardinals, and in 2005 it was the Lady Jeeps of Northeast DuBois who were their final game victims. During that impressive period and through 2006, the Lady Trojans won 86 games and lost only 20.

West Central in Francesville seems to enjoy a great deal of influence from nearby Notre Dame. In fact, their fight song has the same tune as Notre Dame's. However, just to keep things balanced perhaps, the mascot is that of one of the Fighting Irish's fiercest football rivals: Southern California. The West Central Trojans have won 4 Sectional titles and the Lady Trojans have won 3.

The Triton Trojans in Marshall County enjoyed a 20-6 season in their 2nd year, under Coach Tony Newell, winning both Sectional and Regional championships in 1965. They defeated Cloverdale before running into a buzz saw disguised as Gary Roosevelt in the Semi-state final game. In 2008 everything came together for Jason Groves and his Trojan squad. They brought the state championship trophy back to Bourbon with a 25-2 record after defeating Indianapolis Lutheran 50-42 in the Class A final game. The Lady Trojans did the boys one better, winning back-to-back Class A State Championships for their coach Mark Heeter, defeating Rising Sun 57-54 in an overtime thriller in 2000 to finish 20-7 and White River Valley 55-38 the next year for a 23-3 mark.

West Central and Triton Trojans

The Covington Trojans have been playing basketball since at least 1912, when they split even in 10 games. In 1923, with Harry Mourer coaching, the Black and Gold had their first 20-win season, losing 9. Sox Sanford led the Trojans to records of 21-3 in 1928, 20-5 in 1930, and 20-4 in 1932. In 1940 Gene Rovenstine's team compiled a 22-3 mark, and in 1945 Howard Williams led his team to a 25-3 record. Don Reichert coached in 1947, when the team won 23 of 27 games; next year his record was 20-2. In 1954 Francis Goodnight's Trojans won 20 and lost 8. Bill Miller's 1960 squad achieved a 30-win season, losing only 4. They lost to State Champ East Chicago Washington in the final game of the Lafayette Semi-State 60-51, then went 22-4 the next year. In 1971 Dwayne Rater led the team to a 22-3 mark, and his 1974, 1977, and 1978 teams went 20-3, 22-2, and 22-1. The Trojans have won 18 Sectionals and 4 Regionals. The Lady Trojans have won 5 Sectionals, all for Coach Jack Hunter, who held the job for 23 years beginning in 1977. Their best record was 18-2 in 1982.

An early version of Covington High School

East Central's Trojans in St. Leon have captured 7 Sectionals. Steve Brunes' 1987 team won 23 of 25 games. After escaping with a 43-42 win over Jac-Cen-Del in the Sectional final, the Trojans' 2nd loss of the season came at the hands of Connersville in the 1st round of the Richmond Regional, 66-57. The Lady Trojans have added 4 Sectionals to the school trophy case. Pam Shively's 1992 squad won 18 of 21 games.

The Ft. Wayne Elmhurst Trojans have snared 6 Sectional crowns and 2 Regionals. In their 1st Sweet Sixteen appearance in 1984 they ran into eventual State Champion Warsaw, dropping an 83-75 1st-round decision to the Tigers. Back again in 2003, this time in Class 3A, they won the Lafayette Jeff Semi-state only to lose a Trojan vs. Trojan war to Indianapolis Chatard in the state championship final game. This they rectified in 2009 with a thrilling 3-point victory over Owen Valley in the 3A State Championship Final Game. Kevin Sweeney was their coach.

The Chatard Trojans have won 5 Sectionals and 2 Regionals to go with that much deserved 2003 state title. Their record that year was 22-2; the coach was Dan Archer. The Lady Trojans have added 3 Sectionals and the runner-up trophy in the 2008 Class 3A tournament, losing a heartbreaking 47-46 decision to Plymouth's Lady Pilgrims to finish 23-5.

Covington, East Central, Ft. Wayne Elmhurst, and Indianapolis Chatard: Trojans all

In Lake County, right on the Illinois line, is the home of the Highland Trojans. They have won 4 Sectionals, and the Lady Trojans have captured 6 as well as 4 Regionals. From 1999 through 2003 Coach Chris Huppenthal's Lady Trojans won an impressive 124 games, losing only 29. Included was the undefeated regular season mark of 26-1 in 2001.

Center Grove is in many ways similar to its north and west suburban Indianapolis counterparts Carmel and Brownsburg. Not too many years ago all were country towns and schools of considerably smaller proportions than is the case today. The Center Grove Trojans have been playing a good brand of basketball for many years. For example, from 1926 through 1928 the Trojans led by Coach Custer Baker won 56 games and lost only 11, including a 20-4 mark in 1926 and an undefeated regular season, 18-1, in 1927. Swede Chalmers coached the 1934 squad to a 24-2 mark, and Tom Jones' 1971 through 1975 teams compiled a 5-year mark of 90 wins and 27 losses. Over the years the Trojans have won 11 Sectionals and the 1972 Columbus Regional. That year, in a major upset, the Jones-coached Trojans edged an impressive Richmond Red Devil squad 62-61 in the Indianapolis Semi-state before losing to the eventual State Champion Connersville Spartans in the next game, finishing 21-6. The Lady Trojans have amassed 16 Sectional titles in the 33 seasons they have fielded a team. To this they have added 4 Regionals and the 1996 Southport Semi-state. That year they would go on to win the state championship with a 25-2 record, Joe Lentz's Lady Trojans defeating Valparaiso's Lady Vikings in the final game, 55-44. Over the 3-year period beginning in 1995, Lentz's teams ran up 67 victories in 74 games. Earlier, the Lady Trojans also had an undefeated season for Mike Swago, 20-1, in 1979.

The Highland and Center Grove Trojans

In Porter County the Chesterton Trojans were undefeated in 1924. . .but they played only 5 games. Their 1st 20-win season came for Walt Jones in 1938, 20-8, and they had a marvelous, undefeated regular season in 1955 for Evar Edquist, winning 24 games and their 1st of 3 Sectional crowns, at Valparaiso handily, over Kouts. Their lone loss was to Michigan City in the first round of the Hammond Regional. They also had 19-3 seasons for Virgil Little in 1962 and Tom Peller in 2008. In 1981 C. Hamilton's Lady Trojans had a terrific 26-2 season. In total they have won 6 Sectional crowns and 1 Regional, in 1985. The New Castle Trojans will be covered later along with their powerhouse fellow North Central Conference teams.

As mentioned, the name Knights was the most popular in this category with 14 schools selecting it, including the Golden Knights of Indianapolis Arlington. The Golden Knights have won 3 Sectionals and 1 Regional, in 1974, Coach Don Lostutter's team finishing 21-5. Eddie Ward's 1984 Knights won 20 of 26, and Larry Nicks' 1999 team won 20 and lost only 2. His 2005 squad finished undefeated in the regular season, racking up 23 victories against the 1 defeat. The Lady Golden Knights teams have added 2 Sectional crowns to the school's trophy case.

The Chesterton Shield

Two versions of the Arlington Golden Knight

The Castle Knights in Newburgh have won 6 Sectionals and the 2002 4A Seymour Regional, Steve Brune's squad winning 23 of 27 games. They were subsequently edged by Indianapolis Pike in the Semi-state, 57-55, and Pike would lose the state championship final game to Gary West, 58-55. That Castle team was right in the mix of the very best Indiana had to offer that year. Kenneth Nelson's 1962 team also had an outstanding record, 23-2. That 2nd loss came to Bosse in the final game of the Evansville Regional after Castle beat Tell City in the 1st round. The Lady Knights have amassed 14 Sectional and 3 Regional crowns. They also snared the 2006 4A Jeffersonville Semi-state and went on to win the state championship for Coach Wayne Allen, defeating South Bend Washington's Lady Panthers 83-72 to finish a very successful season at 25-3. From 2000 through 2007 the Ladies of the Castle turned in 165 games while losing only 35!

The Castle Knight and Crest

In Kendallville the East Noble Knights (and what else should noblemen be called but Knights?) have won 13 Sectionals and 2 Regionals. Jim Calvin's 1974 team won 21 of 24 games, as did Marty Johnson's 1989 squad, followed immediately by a 22-3 record. His 1993 team went 23-3, and in 1996 and 1997 they won 46 and lost only 7. Their Ladies have added 6 Sectional nets to the school trophy case, Bob Farmers' Ladies winning 35 of 43 games in 1984 and 1985. They draw cheering crowds in a gym cleverly named the Big Blue Pit.

In Brazil the Northview Knights take the floor in their dramatic black, silver, and maroon uniforms. They achieved Sectional championships in 1988 and 2004. From 2002 through 2004 the Knights put together an impressive total of 63 victories against only 11 defeats. John Crooks was the coach for the 1st year and Mitch Lancaster for the next 2. Although Jan Gambill's 1987 Lady Knights won 18 of 20 games, neither that team nor any other Lady Knights team has won a Sectional title.

The Mishawaka Marian Knights won 19 of 21 games for Coach Mike Lightfoot in 1983 and were 18-4 for Robb Berger in 1999. They won the LaVille Sectional in 1969 for Don Dubois. Their Ladies have yet to win a Sectional title.

The East Noble, Northview, and Mishawaka Marion Knights

In Ossian, Wells County, the Norwell Knights, coached by Jerry Lewis from 1969 through 1989, turned in several fine seasons under his leadership. They were 20-3 in 1973; 21-5 in 1978; 20-6 in 1980; and 24-4 in 1988. They won 9 Sectionals between 1972 and 1995 and the Marion Regionals in 1973 and 1988. In 1988 they defeated the Portage Indians before being edged by eventual state runner-up Concord, the Minutemen winning by a 65-60 final count. The Lady Knights have added 6 Sectional titles and the 1976 and 1977 Huntington North Regionals to the school's trophy case as well as the 1977 Fort Wayne Northrop Semi-state.

The Knights of Ft. Wayne Bishop Luers not only won their 1st Sectional title in 2009, they liked the experience so well that they made the absolute most of it that they could. They went all the way, capturing the 2A state finals game over Brownstown by an impressive 67-49 margin at Conseco Fieldhouse. Meanwhile, the Lady Knights have nailed down 7 Regionals and 6 Semi-States. Class 2A state championships were earned in 1999 when Gary Andrews' team finished 26-1 and defeated the Lady Eagles of Austin 59-48; the next year when the Andrews led Lady Knights defeated Forest Park in a scorcher, 62-60. The threepeat was achieved in 2001 when Andrews' squad turned in a sterling, undefeated 28-0 season by defeating Shenandoah's Lady Raiders 70-64. In 2002 Luers had moved up to 3A, but the juggernaut continued unabated. Teri Rosinski was now the coach and her team defeated the Gibson Southern Lady Titans to finish 21-5 with their 4th straight state championship. The streak ended in 2003 but in 2004 Luers was back in the title game, only to lose to Indianapolis Brebeuf Jesuit's 26-3 Braves in the 3A State Championship game. Two years later, however, Teri Rosinski's squad was back in the state final game and this time they were not to be denied, winning their 5th State Championship in 7 years, another 3A title, 65-54 over Evansville Memorial's Lady Tigers to finish 24-4. A very impressive run, to say the least. Lafayette Central Catholic Knights were covered elsewhere.

Recent additions are the Knights of Indianapolis Suburban Christian Academy, of Holy Cross in Vigo County, DeMotte Christian, Indianapolis Calvary Lutheran, and the Kings Academy in Jonesboro.

Norwell, Ft. Wayne Bishop Luers, Suburban Christian, and Kings Academy Knights

In Aurora the South Dearborn Knights finished 17-4 in their 1st season, 1979, under Coach Bob Finegan. In 1983 Bill Slayback led the Knights to a fine 20-3 mark, and Jim Shannon's 1990 team finished 18-5. All told the Knights have picked off 6 Sectionals. The Lady Knights finished 19-3 for Coach Henry Ahaus in 1982, and his next 2 squads finished undefeated in the regular season, 24-1 and 23-1. Not a bad 3-year stretch for the Lady Knights, 66-5! In 1987 Bill Snyder's team also finished undefeated in the regular season, turning in a 23-1 record. His 1993, 1994, and 1995 quintets turned in 20-4, 20-1, and 19-4 marks, another outstanding 3-year string, 59-9. The Lady Knights have won 11 Sectionals and 2 Regionals, in 1983 and 1984 at Columbus North. In Fountain City the Northeastern Knights hold sway. They have yet to win a Sectional, but turned in a very credible performance for Bob Stoker in 1968, 19-3. Their Ladies have come away winners of 4 Sectionals and 1 Regional, in 1998 with a 17-6 record for Krista Hendrickson. The Southwood Knights enter the lists in Wabash. They won the 2000 Class 2A Sectional for Steve McClure, whose 1999 team actually had a better won-lost record, 18-3. The Lady Knights have also achieved 1 Sectional crown, in 1979, for Mary McClelleand.

South Dearborn, Northeastern, and Southwood Knights

Although it is not obvious when you first hear the team name, when you see the depiction it is clear that the Pike Central Chargers in Petersburg belong in this section. The Chargers are quite evidently medieval knights. The Chargers won their only Sectional at Southridge in 1997, but they also brought the Southridge Regional championship plaque back to Petersburg as well with wins over Mitchell and Barr-Reeve. The Lady Chargers, however, have won 6 Sectionals in a row, all at Jasper, between 1990 and 1995. Not only did they accomplish that, but they put together the same string of Regional championships, all at Gibson Southern. Unfortunately, they were unable to turn any of those opportunities into further progression down the tournament trail.

Three of our Raiders belong here because they are clearly Knights: Northridge in Middlebury; Southern Wells in Poneto; and Southridge in Huntingburg. Northridge started with a bang in their 1st 3 years: Coach Irv Pratt's Raiders won 51 games while losing only 15. Their 1st Sectional crown came in *The Pike Central Chargers* 1975 with an 18-6 record. Five more Sectional titles have been brought home to Middlebury with the best record being Steve Austin's 1996 squad, 21-4. Southridge's proud heritage has been covered elsewhere, but mention will be made here of the impressive 1985 through 1987 record of 3 Sectional, 2 Regional, and 2 Semi-state championships under Coach Gary Duncan and a won-lost record of 66 and 14. The Lady Raiders have also had considerable success, with undefeated regular seasons in 1982, 1988, 1989, and 2005! The Lady Raiders have added 8 Sectional titles to the trophy case in Huntingburg to go with the 12 earned by the boys teams. Additionally, the Lady Raiders captured the 3A State Championship with a 22-6 record in 1998 for Coach Stan Roesner, beating Bluffton 62-57. They also turned in a 22-2 record for Greg Werner in 2007. Finally, the Southern Wells Raiders have won 3 Sectional titles and the 2000 Class A Regional held in their own gym, the Raiderdome. Jim Irwin's 1982 team finished with a 20 and 5 record. John Fouts led the Lady Raiders to 50 wins and 12 losses for the 3-year period beginning in 2004. His 2007 team won the school's only girls Sectional crown.

Northridge, Southridge, and Southern Wells Shields

Several schools have turned to further chivalry and royalty associations for their team names. Cass leads the way with the Kings, followed closely by the Kingsmen of Penn. The Cass Kings finished 18-3 in 1977 with Junior Mannies coaching. Roger Schnepp, who took over the next year, led that team to a 24-2 mark. In 1980 it was Dan Shahan in the coaching box, and the record was 21-2. Hall of Famer Basil Mawbey coached the 2001 Kings to a 22-2 record. All told, the Kings have won 8 Sectionals and the 2003 2A Blackford Regional and Warsaw Semi-state. That year Mawbey's quintet went on to claim the state championship, finishing undefeated, 26-0, by conquering the Forest Park Rangers 57-48 in the final game. The Lady Kings

(Queens?) finished 19-3 in 1994 for their coach Steve Ford, as well as 18-5 for him in 1998. His 2000 team finished 20-4. They have come home to Walton winners of an impressive 12 Sectionals. Mawbey's Hall of Fame Citation:

Basil Mawbey
Three-year letterman at Deedsville High School.... coaching career began at West Washington in 1971.... went on to coach Delta, Angola, Connersville, (state champions 1983) and Kokomo (state runner-up 1989) .... at time of induction is currently coaching at Lewis Cass High School and team is ranked number one in Class 2A....Coach of 1986 Indiana All-Star Team....noted for Basilball, as his teams are renowned for their defensive pressure....over 550 career victories.... Director and Founder of Longest Running Coaches Clinic in Indiana—23 years....guest speaker at over 150 camps and clinics, with eight in Australia.

The Kingsmen of Penn (reminiscent of Robert Penn Warren's stirring political novel *All the King's Men*) hold forth in Mishawaka and are perhaps more well known for their excellent football teams and marching bands than for basketball. As is fitting for royalty, they play their home games in the Palace. The Kingsmen have

Penn Kingsmen

put 14 Sectional championship nets in their school trophy case as well as those of 6 Regionals. In 1972 they defeated the Marion Giants in the Semi-state before losing to the Pirates of Anderson Madison Heights. Bob Miller coached that team to a 22-5 finish. In 1987 they again won the 1st round of the Sweet Sixteen, this time over Ft. Wayne Northrop's Bruins. Marion then extracted a measure of revenge by winning the final game of the Semi-state rather easily en route to their 3rd successive state championship. That Penn team was coached by Dann Gunn and ended with a 23-4 record. Their closest brush with a state title came in 2001, when the Kingsmen finished runner-up to Indianapolis Pike's Red Devils, Dean Foster's team finishing 23-3 in the 4A final in Indianapolis. Foster's 2006 and 2007 teams won 45 games and lost only 7. Earlier, Bob Brady's Kingsmen had back-to-back 20-4 seasons in 1963 and 1964. Their girls teams, the Lady Kingsmen, have won 11 Sectionals and 3 Regionals. Dennis Wood led the 1988 and 1989 girls teams to 44 wins in 49 games; his 1991 team finished 21-3. Dominic Ball's 1998 and 1999 squads won 41 of 49 games.

There are also 3 sets of Cavaliers: Culver, Tri-County, and Ft. Wayne Canterbury (the Lady Cavs, under Coach Scott Kreiger, won the 2008 Class A State championship with a 21-5 mark following their 23-2 record the year before); 2 Lancers, at Edinburgh and LaVille; and, in Pekin, the Muskateers of Eastern High School.

Paul Underwood coached the Culver Cavaliers from 1930 through 1945. His 1931 edition enjoyed an undefeated regular season, finishing 23-1, and his 1938 team won 23 of 28 games. His 1941 and 1942 teams won 23 and 24 games while losing 4 and then 2. His 1944 team again went undefeated, finishing 28-1, followed by a 22-5 record in his last year as coach. Underwood did not leave the cupboard bare, though, as his successor, Harold Serig, took his 1st team to a 22-6 mark. Serig's 1948 Cavaliers had an excellent 23-2 season and his 1953 quintet went 20-5. In total Culver teams have won 13 Sectionals and the 1944 and 1946 South Bend Regionals. In 1944, after defeating the Converse Bordermen in the 1st round of the Semi-state, the Cavaliers lost a heartbreaker, 24-23, to the LaPorte Slicers. The Slicers would lose to eventual State Champion Evansville Bosse by only 3 points in the afternoon game of the state finals. Twenty-eight wins. One loss. By 1 point. Four points away from the title. So close, and yet so far. Back to the Sweet Sixteen in 1946, Culver again won their 1st-round game, defeating East Chicago Washington's Senators, before losing another toughie, this to Flora's Badgers, 37-35. Culver Community's Lady Cavaliers have taken 4 Sectionals themselves.

Tri-County's 1st year was 1972. Rod Nesius' Cavaliers made it a good one, 19-4. In 1993 and 1994 Chris Keisling-led squads finished 18-5 and 18-3. Tom Bajzatt's 2007 team won 22 of 24 games. The Lady Cavaliers turned in a 17-3 record in 1982, followed by 15-5 and 19-2 seasons under Coach Don Erickson. All told, the boys teams have won 6 Sectionals and the girls have brought another 7 Sectional titles home to Wolcott.

Lancers represent LaVille in St. Joseph County, where the only Sectional championships came back-to-back in 1985, 19-6, and 1986, 18-7 under Coach Larry Radecki. The Lady Lancers have brought 5 Sectional crowns home to Lakeville, all under the coaching guidance of John Willoughby. Their best record was 1989's 19-4 mark. The Edinburgh Lancers were covered earlier.

Our Muskateers are in Pekin at Eastern High School. Bill White led the 1972 and 1973 Muskateers to consecutive 18-win seasons, including the 1st of the school's 3 Sectional championships. The Lady Muskateers snagged their only sectional title in 1996 under Sherry Wininger.

Eastern HS

(previous page) Culver and Tri-County Cavaliers, Edinburgh and LaVille Lancers and (above) the Eastern Muskateers

Rounding out our regal theme are 2 schools whose teams are the Royals: Hamilton Southeastern and Eastern Hancock. Both turn to the king of the jungle for their mascot.

The King of the Jungle represents Royals at Hamilton Southeastern and Eastern Hancock

The best records the Hamilton Southeastern Royals have put together came in 1970 for Norm Starkey, 17-5; 1990 for Stan Daugherty, 19-3; 1995 for Greg Habegger, 19-4; 2001 for Larry Bullington, 18-5; and 2003–04, when Brian Satterfield's Royals won 35 games and lost 10. That 1st Sectional title has continued to prove elusive. The Lady Royals have enjoyed a bit more success, beginning in 1989 when Barb Brouwer's squad won 17 of 21 games. However, it was the 4-year run beginning in 2004 that really shines. Haley Beauchamp coached the 1st two of those teams to consecutive 20-2 records, and Chris Huppenthal cranked that up to 22-4 and then the undefeated regular season of 2007, 25-1. His 1st team pulled down Sectional and Regional crowns and his 2nd did so for the Sectional alone. Those 4 years resulted in 87 wins and only 9 losses for the lady Royals.

In Charlottesville Eastern Hancock has had 3 20-win seasons, all with the exact same records. They were 20-6 for Tom Jones in 1968, the same record for Ron Bocken in 1974, and the same again for Aaron Spaulding in 2003. They have also won 3 Sectionals, but only overlapping 2 of the 20-win years. Their 1st Sectional title was earned at Rushville in 1968 with victories over New Salem, Morton Memorial, and Rushville. They proceeded to nip Connersville on the Spartan's own court 64-63 in the Regional before losing the final game to Jac-Cen-Del. Six years later the Royals grabbed the New Castle Sectional by overcoming Mount Vernon 56-55, eliminating Blue River Valley 82-64, and sneaking past the mighty Trojans in the fieldhouse, 63-62. Living dangerously again, Eastern won at Greenfield Central in 1981 by edging New Palestine, 48-47, and taking Mt. Vernon out in overtime. Whew. The Lady Royals, playing a somewhat abbreviated schedule in 1976 won 10 of 12 games for

Carolyn Jones. They also turned in a 16-4 mark for David Pfaff in 1985 and 16-8 for Pete Hubert in 2001. No Sectional titles yet, however, for the Lady Royals.

One other member of the aristocracy, covered elsewhere but not to be forgotten, is the DeKalb Baron.

Letter sweaters from the displays at the Indiana Basketball Hall of Fame in New Castle

Chapter 33

From Patriots to Saints:
And Below…Way Below

The next most popular team name remaining is, happily, as far as I am concerned, the Patriots, of whom we have 9. Heritage Hills, Terre Haute North, and Seeger Memorial have been covered elsewhere. In Allen County the red, white, and blue-clad Heritage Patriots coached by Gary Merrell won the Garrett 2A Sectional and Regional championships in 1998. Earlier Richard Westminster's 1980 Patriot team won 20 of 24 games. Their girls teams have been even more successful, capturing 9 Sectionals and 3 Regionals. They also won 3 Semi-state crowns, in 1978, 1982, and 1983 and Cheri Gilbert's 1982 team brought the state championship trophy back to Monroeville. Her 24-2 Lady Patriots defeated Valparaiso 52-45 that year. Gilbert's 4-year record from 1982 through 1985 was a remarkable 90 wins and only 9 defeats. Her 1983 team was undefeated in the regular season, finishing 25-1 in the school's attempt to repeat as state champions.

Heritage Patriots

Jay County became the Patriots when the 8 schools there consolidated: the Dunkirk Speedcats, Portland Panthers, Bryant Owls, Pennville Bulldogs, Redkey Wolves, Gray Redbirds, Madison Tomcats, and the Poling Yellow Jackets. The Patriots have won 18 Sectionals and the 2006 Blackford 3A Regional. They also won the Lafayette Jeff Semi-state crown and were runner-up to New Castle for the state title, with Coach Craig Teagle's squad losing 51-43 to finish a commendable 20-7 season. The Lady Patriots have taken 9 Sectionals themselves. Their best record came for John Engle's 1986 team, 20 wins and 3 losses.

The Jay County Patriot and the predecessor schools

The Owen Valley Patriots in Spencer also wear red, white, and blue uniforms. John Heckman coached the 1985 team to a 21-3 mark; Chitty Brink's 1995 squad won 17 and lost 4; and Trent Hickman's 2006 outfit finished 20-5. They notched Sectional crowns in 1971, 1985, and 2006 (3A). The Lady Patriots had a 16-4 season in 1986 for their coach Lew Scholl. Steve Redenbaugh coached the 1989 team to a 17-3 record, followed by 16-5, 16-4, 19-2, 18-4, and 23-3 seasons, or 109 wins and only 21 losses in 6 seasons. Not half bad, particularly for a school that had won only 4 games in 3 years just over a decade before. The Lady Patriots have won 6 Sectionals and the 1994 Ben Davis Regional.

In Union County another pair of red, white, and blue-clad Patriots headquarter in the aptly named town of Liberty. The boys team won the Connersville Sectional 3 times, in 1976, 1977, and 1979. Phil Snodgress' 1974 team had an undefeated regular season, 22-1, and 2 years later took home the school's 1st Sectional title with a 21-3 record. The girls team won the 2006 Class 2A Centerville Sectional.

The Union County Patriot

Vincennes Rivet High School is named for Father Jean Francis Rivet, who arrived in Vincennes in April 1795 with a commission from the War Department to be a missionary to the Indians of the area. Breaking our string of red, white, and blue uniforms, the Rivet Patriots wear purple and gold. In 1951 and 1952 Coach Henry Doll's teams won 42 games and lost only 10. Ralph Holscher's 1955 team won 21 games and lost 6. Although the Rivet Patriot's boys team has never won a Sectional title, the girls got theirs in Class A at North Daviess in 2008 with a 19-4 record for Tim Young. Rounding out our Patriots are 2 relatively new schools, Muncie Heritage Christian and Brownsburg Bethesda Christian. Neither one has a Sectional crown to their credit at this writing.

If we add our 8 Vikings to the Northfield Norsemen, we have another 9, of Scandinavian descent. Huntington North was just plain Huntington until 1967, but they have been Vikings the entire time. Their history is illustrious, beginning with 1918's 24-4 team, coached by M. C. Darnell, and their trip to the Sweet Sixteen at Indiana University. Wins over the Washington Hatchets and Vincennes Alices placed the Vikings in the Final Four. They were then defeated by Anderson, the Indians losing the championship game in overtime to Lebanon's Tigers. From 1920 through 1923 C. B. Stemen led the Vikings to 93 wins and 30 defeats. This included trips to the Sweet Sixteen in 1921 and 1923 in Indianapolis. The 1st trip saw the Vikings emerge victorious in their opening game over Syracuse before dropping a 1-pointer to Lafayette, but they lost the 1st-round game in 1923 to South Bend. Garland Crowe led the 1940 and 1941 teams to 20-6 marks and Harry Williams' 1945 squad won 20 and lost 9. His 1947 five finished 24-3. The 1945 squad beat Kokomo and Muncie

Central to win the Muncie Semi-state, losing the afternoon game at Butler Fieldhouse the next week to South Bend Riley. From 1962 through 1964 Hall of Famer Bob Straight's charges won 71 games and dropped only 12. Finally, Straight's Vikings had a memorable 5-year streak just before the consolidation of 1967, winning 108 games and losing 25. The best year was that 27-2 mark turned in by the 1964 team whose season ended with a tough 3-point loss to the Bronchos of Lafayette Jefferson, 58-55, at Butler Fieldhouse.

As North, the Vikings have continued their winning tradition. Marvin Tudor's 1973 and 1974 teams were victorious in 40 games and lost just 9, Glen Heaton's 1986 squad finished 20-5, and Eric Foster's team won 20 of 26 games in 1999. All told, the Vikings have won 58 Sectional and 10 Regional tournaments.

Meanwhile, the Lady Vikings were really lighting it up. From 1988 through 1990 Fred Fields' girls teams won 69 games, lost only 12, and captured the 1990 state championship with a 3 point victory over Bedford North Lawrence's vaunted Stars. His 1994–1996 fives did even better, snatching 74 wins in 80 games(!), including their 2nd state championship with a 28-1 record in 1995. They defeated Judi Warren's Carmel Greyhounds, 43-39, in the final game. The next year the Lady Vikings put together an undefeated regular season, 25-1, getting upended in the Semi-state. In total, the Lady Vikings have won 17 Sectional and 8 Regional championships.

Huntington High School and the Huntington North Viking

Barr-Reeve's Vikings in Daviess County won 20 of 22 games for Coach Hilbert Tooley in 1972. They turned in a 20-4 mark for Dave Omer in 1987 and a 19-5 record for him in 1992. Bryan Hughes took the reins the next year, and his 1997 quintet went 21-4. His 2002 team had a 24-5 record, and his 2006 squad finished at 19-5. Nine Sectionals and 2 Regionals have been won. The 2002 Vikings finished runner-up to Rossville's Hornets and the 2007 team, with a 23-4 mark, to the Oregon-Davis Bobcats in the Class A State Championships. The Lady Vikings turned in an 18-4 record for Jeff Sherfield in 1981, went 18-3 in 1992, and kept up that impressive pace with 16-4, 16-2 and 16-3 seasons under Dick Lemmon: 66-12 for those 4 years. They have triumphed in 5 Sectionals and also brought the 2000 Class A Oakland City Regional trophy home to Montgomery.

In their 1st year, 1965, the Blue River Valley Vikings had a terrific 22-1 season for Gene Hayes. In 1998 and 1999 Mike Wade led the Vikings to 22-4 and 22-3 seasons, and Barry Huckeby took over and led the next 2 years' teams to 21-3 and 22-6 marks: 2 coaches, 4 years, 87 wins, only 16 losses! They have won 7 Sectionals and 4 straight

Regionals. They finished runner-up to State Champion Attica's Ramblers in 2001, losing a hard fought final game by a 64-62 margin. Linda Poor's Lady Vikings went 18-4 in 1983 and 18-3 2 years later. The Lady Vikings have placed 4 Sectional nets in the school's trophy case in Mt. Summit.

North Posey's Vikings nabbed their only sectional at Princeton in 1966 with victories over New Harmony, Mt. Vernon, and Oakland City. The Lady Vikings, however, have knocked off 7 Sectionals and the 1987 Gibson Southern Regional.

The Barr-Reeve and Blue River Valley Vikings

North White's Vikings had a bang-up 1st year in 1964, Jack Woodruff coaching the team to a 20-6 record. Sectionals were won that year and in 1974 and 1984. That every 10-year sequence was almost kept alive by the Lady Vikings, who picked up their lone Sectional crown in 1993.

At Tippecanoe Valley in Akron the Vikings have won 8 Sectionals and the 2000 Class 3A West Lafayette Regional. Bill Patrick, whose impressive record at Whitko has been covered elsewhere, also coached the Vikings with consummate success, winning 180 games between 1999 and 2008 while losing only 47, capturing 3 Sectional titles in the process. Coach Patrick's overall record, including Sidney, Whitko, and Tippecanoe Valley, is 658 wins and 225 losses. Five Sectionals have also been captured by the Lady Vikings.

North Posey, North White, and Tippecanoe Valley, Vikings all

West Vigo's Vikings won 19 of 22 games played in 1996 with Steve DeGroote coaching. Their single Sectional title was earned in 1990 at South Vermillion. The Lady Vikings have won 3 Sectional titles. Our potent Valparaiso Vikings were covered earlier.

Now to our Norsemen, who sure look like Vikings to me. They are at Northfield in Wabash County, winners of 9 Sectionals and 2 Regionals. In 1990 the Norsemen defeated South Bend Riley in

The West Vigo Vikings

the Semi-state before dropping a tough 2-pointer to Concord's Minutemen. Concord ended up losing the state finals game to Damon Bailey and Bedford North Lawrence by a 3-point margin in that classic game. Five points from the championship: of such are dreams made. Tom Miller's Norsemen had a fine 22-2 season in 1970 and Steve McClure coached the Norsemen to 23-2 and 24-3 seasons in 1989 and 1990 and to a 22-3 mark in 1992. The Lady Norsemen had 18-2 and 18-3 seasons for Teresa Honeycutt in 1977 and 1978 and went 16-3 followed by 17-3 in 1986 and 1987, Steve Brubaker then in the coaching box. They have won 3 Sectionals and the 1978 Huntington North Regional.

In years past we have had such fun names as the Lightning Five. We now have the Franklin Central Flashes and the West Noble and Ft. Wayne Carroll Chargers.

The Northfield Norseman

An electrifying trio: the Franklin Central Flashes and the Chargers from West Noble and Carroll (Allen County)

The Franklin Central Flashes' name recalls the brilliant man who hung a key on the end of a kite string in a thunderstorm to prove that lightning was, in fact, electricity. Or did Ben Franklin actually ever do that? Whether or not, the Flashes have won 11 Sectionals. In their 2nd year the Flashes of 1961 won 20 of 24 games for Art Cook, a feat they replicated in both 1975 and 1976 under Coach Stanley Norman. James Mark, who has led the Flashes for at least 20 years, brought the 1993 squad to a 22-4 season, the 1996 and 1997 teams to 24-2 and 22-3 marks, and the 2007 edition to a 24-3 finish.

The Lady Flashes have won 9 Sectionals and the 1988 Center Grove Regional title. That year they defeated Bloomington North before losing the Semi-State to Noblesville by 5 points. Noblesville was runner-up that year to Ft. Wayne Snider, losing the final game by a single basket, placing Marv Knoop's Lady Flashes within 7 points of the best the state had to offer that year. More recently, Pam Taylor's 2005 team won 22 of 25 games.

The West Noble Chargers have yet to bring home a Sectional title to Ligonier, but they put together an excellent season in 1972 for Roger Tuggle, winning 21 and losing only twice. The Lady Chargers did win a Sectional title, in 1988 for their coach Dave Beckett in their own gym.

The Carroll Chargers registered an outstanding season in 1985 when Kent Lochmueller coached the team to a 23-3 mark. His 1992 team racked up 18 victories in 22 games and Rob Irwin's 2001 edition won 22 games while losing only 5. The Chargers have won 4 Sectionals and 2 Regionals. Lisa Miller coached the Lady Chargers to the 1st 3-quarters of a terrific 4-year string, beginning in 2001, when her teams won 58 games and lost only 11, followed by a 20-3 year for Lisa McBride's 2004 girls team, 78 wins and only 14 losses in 4 years. The Lady Chargers also have 5 Sectionals and the 1998 Class 3A New Haven Regional to their credit.

Similarly, we note the Blazers of East Side (Butler) and Michigan City Marquette and the Blue Blazers of Elkhart Central. Fire and lightning in evidence here, too.

Eastside, Michigan City Marquette, and Elkhart Central

The Eastside Blazers have picked up 3 Sectionals as have the Lady Blazers who have brought the 1979 Ft. Wayne Northrop Regional title to Butler. The 1st was at Angola in 1968 with wins over Hamilton in overtime, Fremont and Waterloo. The next was in 1993 at DeKalb where the Blazers beat Garrett and Fremont. The 3rd was a Class 2A crown in 2007, Scott Hudson's crew finishing with an 18-6 record. The Lady Blazers from Eastside won all 3 of their Sectionals in a row, beginning in 1977, the 1st two for Robert Brown and the 3rd for Valerie Gates with a 19-4 mark.

The Marquette Blazers won their lone Sectional in 2000, Class A. The Blue Blazers of Elkhart Central have a somewhat larger portfolio in Indiana high school basketball circles, having amassed 36 Sectional titles and 16 Regionals. They have made it to the Final Four on 6 occasions, the 1st in 1954, when they lost the morning game to Muncie Central to set up that memorable final game with Milan. Back again 2 years later, the Blue Blazers lost a tough 2-pointer to Lafayette Jeff, who would in turn be denied the title by a powerhouse Crispus Attucks Tiger 5. It would be 15 years before Central would make it back to the Final Four again, and this time they defeated New Castle's Trojans in a nail-biting triple overtime game before succumbing to East Chicago Washington in the state championship game that night. In 1978 the Blue Blazers were within 4 points of finally achieving their goal of a state title, losing by that margin to Muncie Central in the morning game of one of the most stirring Final Fours ever. That year, after the 89-85 1st game, Terre Haute South beat Merrillville by one point in overtime before losing another one-pointer in overtime in the finals. The Blue Blazers made their most recent trip to the finals in 1999, again being bested in a close game, this one by a 79-74 count to Indianapolis North Central.

Looking to the skies and beyond has brought inspiration for team names to several other schools as well. There are the Caston and Eastern (Howard County)

Comets; the Satellites from South Central (Union County); the Western Boone Stars (the Bedford North Lawrence Stars refer to the top artisan stonecutters, as noted previously), the South Adams Starfires, and our 3 Rockets, Indianapolis Broad Ripple, (covered elsewhere) Union (Modoc), and the Indiana School for the Blind and Visually Impaired. We might also put the Rising Sun Shiners in this category as well as the Indianapolis Northwest Space Pioneers, both covered elsewhere.

The Rensselaer Central Bombers only lost 1 game in 1913 . . . but they only played 6. In 1941 they enjoyed a 20-8 season for Coach William Baussman, winning the 4th of the school's 12 Sectional titles. Charles Franklin's 1946 Bombers finished 21-3, a precursor to next year's undefeated 24-1 season. That loss came at the hands of Gary Emerson, 47-43, in the Hammond Regional after Franklin's charges had defeated Morocco in the Sectional final. Larry McCrae's 1969 Bombers finished 20-3. The school's only Regional title was captured by Bill Zych's 1991 team with a 64-62 victory over Twin Lakes at Lafayette. The Lady Bombers have brought home the nets from 5 Sectionals and Jeff Marlow's 2006 team had an excellent 20-5 record.

The Eastern Comets got their only Sectional title at Kokomo in 1956. The Lady Comets, coached by Don Walker from 1987 through 2000, had winning seasons for 6 straight years beginning in 1987, winning 83 games and losing 33, with the best 2 years being 15-4 in 1988 and 1992. It was 1999, however, when they enjoyed a breakout season of 22 wins and only 4 defeats and brought not only the Sectional title but the Regional as well home to Greentown.

  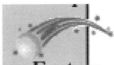

The Rensselaer Bombers and the Caston and Eastern Comets

The Caston team's name Comets came originally from both South Caston and North Caston, short-lived schools in Cass County, which were consolidated into Caston along with the Twelve Mile Milers, the Fulton Bulldogs, the Metea Hornets, and the Grass Creek Panthers. They nailed their lone Sectional title for Coach Dave Henson at Rochester in 1985. His Comets also won 18 of 21 games in 1986. Craig Teagle led the 1998 Comets to a 19-3 season. Doug Hicks' 2004 and 2005 teams each had bang-up 20-2 seasons. All told, the Comets have brought home 5 Sectionals championships to Fulton. The Lady Comets had a fine 3-year run for Floyd Henson from 1984 through 1986, winning 52 games while only losing 11. In 1996 Joel Martin's 5 enjoyed a 17-4 season.

In LaPorte County the South Central Satellites sport red, white, and blue uniforms. Opened in 1962, the school enjoyed 6 straight winning seasons at the outset. The best 2 years were 1967 and 1968, when Morrie Goodnight's charges went 21-3 followed by 19-3. They had another good 2-year spurt under Tom Lewis, winning 39 games and losing 7 in 1975 and 1976. They have brought 3 Sectional titles back home to Union Mills. The Lady Satellites have added the 2005 Class A Culver Sectional and Regional titles to the school's trophy case, Dan Huizenga's squad finishing 19-7. The next year his Lady Satellites had an even better record, 20-2, but no Sectional title to show for it.

Starfires, I guess, are pretty much like comets, or maybe meteorites, or even supernovas. In Indiana they represent South Adams High School. The South Adams Starfires' colors are black and gold, reminiscent of Purdue's. In 1992 and 1993 the Black and Gold had terrific years, 20-5 and 22-4, for John Hans. In the latter year they collected their 5th Sectional title and their 1st, and only to date, Regional crown. The Regional was won at Marion with a victory over Caston—how the skies over Grant County must have lit up that night—67-47, and the mighty Kokomo Wildkats, 59-52. The Lady Starfires have brought 2 Sectional nets back to Berne. South Adams home games take place in the wonderfully named Stardome.

The Union (Modoc) Rockets had 4 productive years for Keith Helms between 1953 and 1956, winning 68 games and losing only 25. In 1963 under Dan Waterfill the Jets rang up 22 wins in 24 games. That 2nd loss was to Parker in the final game of the Winchester Sectional, 73-67. In 1970 they turned in a 19-5 season for Larry Conklin. The Lady Jets have struggled a bit, but turned in an exemplary 16-4 mark in 1997 for Kirk Comer. They also won the 1998 Class A Sectional at Randolph Southern.

Union (Modoc) Rockets, South Adams Starfires, and South Central Satellites

I would place the charming town of Oldenburg in Franklin County on any list of places to see in Indiana. It was founded in the early 1800s by German settlers and is home to the Sisters of St. Francis of Oldenburg, The entire town has been placed on the National Register of Historic Places.

There are several ways to get there. You can go north on 229 from Batesville. From Hamburg you can take Rail Fence Road to Harvey Branch Road or from Penntown take St. Mary's Road to Hoff Road, then Five Points Road to Saw Mill Road passing Lovers Road enroute. Approaching the town one is impressed by the many church towers and spires that appear over the rolling hills of the countryside.

In town the German influence is evident in the place names, in the wonderful local cooking, the annual Freudenfest or Festival of Fun held each July. Unfortunately, like much of southern Indiana, the area is also in what is sometimes referred to as Tornado Alley. In the late afternoon of April 3, 1974, a dreadful tornado struck a bit south of Oldenburg on the campus of Hanover College. Perhaps in deference to such storms the Oldenburg Academy teams are the Twisters . . . no, Chubby Checkers, they are not named for you!

The Twisters girls teams won the school's only Sectional crown in 2006 for Coach Leslie Vertz. (Boys have been enrolled only since 2002.) There was also, fairly briefly, an Oldenburg School in town that did field teams at the high school level in the 30s, but I can find no record of what those teams were called or how they fared.

Similarly, the relatively new Anderson Indiana Christian Academy has selected Whirlwinds for the name of its teams, with the Bible for inspiration.

Looking perhaps the other direction there are our 6 schools whose teams are called the devils: 5 Red Devils (including West Lafayette, covered earlier) and 1 Blue (at Tipton, also covered earlier).

Indianapolis Pike has been a Red Devil squad to be reckoned with for many years. They have won 12 Sectionals, 6 Regionals, and 4 Semi-states. Their 1st State championship came in 1998, Class 4A, when Alan Darner's Devils defeated Marion's Giants in a thriller, 57-54, to finish with an outstanding 28-1 record. Their 2nd came in 2001, Darner's chargers defeating Penn's Kingsmen 56-42 to finish 26-3. One year later, with Larry Bullington now at the helm, Pike was defeated in the final game of the state tournament, 58-55, being edged by Gary West Side and finishing 24-4. Back in the 4A final game for the 3rd straight year, in 2003, Bullington's Red Devils turned in a magnificent 29-0 record, defeating the Barons of DeKalb, 65-52, for their

3rd State Championship in 6 years. Long-time Pike coach Ed Siegel was not able to garner one of those state titles before he retired, but his readily evident coaching skills and excellent record places him squarely in the Hall of Fame. Siegel won the school's 1st-ever Sectional and Regional titles in his 2nd year on the job in 1972. His 1976 team won 20 of 23 games and his 1987 squad finished 22-6, snagging Pike's 2nd Regional. In 1989 and 1990, Siegel's Devils won 45 games and lost only 8.

Ed Siegel
Coached over 30 years at Stillwell, Southwestern, Booneville and Pike High Schools...3-year letter winner in basketball, track and cross country...member of New Albany's first team to play in state finals (1950) ...four year letterman in basketball at Franklin College...coached over 30 years high school varsity level...won over 400 games at Stillwell, South-western, Boonville and Pike...coached 4 Indiana All-Stars . . . won over 450 games in his career, including six sectionals and 2 Regionals

The Lady Red Devils of Pike have won 4 Sectionals. They won 20 of 23 games for Amy Cherubinai in 2003 and finished 20 and 6 for Reggie White 3 years later.

The Lowell Red Devils have brought in 4 Sectionals. Steve Leonard's 1988 and 1989 teams won 38 games and lost only 9. The Lady Red Devils have added a pair of Sectional nets of their own as well the 2000 Class 4A Regional for Coach Patti McCormack.

Jeffersonville's Red Devils, from the opposite end of the state, have enjoyed considerably more success on the hardwood, annexing 34 Sectional titles and 15 Regionals. As early as 1921 C. C. Callahan coached the Jeffersonville team to a 23-2 season and in 1924 Emory Theiss led that year's team to a 22-3 mark. They have also scored 6 Semi-state victories. Before we had Semi-states, the 1934 Devils under Francis Hunk brought a gaudy 24-3 record with them to Butler Fieldhouse for their 1st Sweet Sixteen experience. There they won 2 games, over Wabash and Lebanon, before being eliminated by Arsenal Tech. In 1935 their record was even more impressive when they arrived at 49th and Boulevard Place: 28-0. The Devils dispatched Montgomery, Michigan City, and Richmond to reach the last game of the finals undefeated. Alas, they dropped a 23-17 encounter with Anderson, finishing 31-1. It would be 37 years before they would make it back, in spite of a 24-2 season in 1953 for William Johnson and a 23-3 season in 1958 for Cliff Barker. That next trip to Indianapolis came in 1972, when George Marshall's squad lost a nail-biting overtime game to Connersville in the afternoon session to finish 22-5. Since the Spartans won the state championship that night handily over Gary West, Red Devil fans headed south thinking what might have been but for a missed shot here or a favorable bounce there. Two years later the Devils were back, Marshall's team sporting an even better 25-1 record. Again they headed south with similar feelings as they were edged by 3 points in the state finals last game by Ft. Wayne Northrop. Two trips, 2 hard-fought games, 2 disappointments. Keeping with the every-other-year sequence, back came Jeffersonville with their large contingent of supporters in 1976. Perhaps 3 times would be the charm. But, no, it was not to be. This time it was the Marion Giants who did the Devils in, in the morning game at Market Square Arena, by 2 points. And Marion would win their 2nd title in a row that night by 6 over the Rushville Lions. Three trips. Five points separated the Red Devils from THREE state championships in the 70s alone. They must have begun to feel like Evansville Central!

It was to be 16 years before they would get back to Indianapolis, this time to the Hoosier Dome. New venue, new opportunity. New coach. Mike Broghton was now at the helm. His 1st Devil team the year before had finished 21-4, and this one came up I-65 sporting a 24-2 record. Surely this time would be different...but no, the results were eerily similar. Jeffersonville lost the morning game to another set of Red Devils, these from Richmond. By how many points? Two. In overtime, again. And who would ride the fire truck that night? Unfortunately for Jeffersonville, it was the wrong Red Devils, Richmond again winning an overtime game to edge Lafayette Jefferson's Bronchos. One of the most memorable days in Indiana basketball history was yet another black one for the Red Devil fans.

But the very next year Jeffersonville was back again. This team had an even more impressive season behind it, 27 wins and 2 losses. Could it finally happen? YES. The Red Devils and their coach Mike Broughton finished a 29-2 season with a 66-61 victory over Steve Witty's 27-2 Ben Davis Giants. A large cheer and, no doubt, an equally large sigh of relief for the Jeffersonville Red Devils and all of their fans. Two years later they would reappear at the Hoosier Dome, but, in a rematch with Ben Davis, they would lose to the eventual state champions by a score that left no room for the kinds of 2nd thoughts the Devils must have had so many times in the past.

Broughton's record since that magic season in 1993 continued to be a strong one. His teams turned in 22-3 and 23-5 marks in the next 2 years, bringing his 5-year record to a lofty 119 wins and 17 losses. In 1999 and 2000 his teams won another 42 games, dropping just 6. Jimmie Just also coached the 2006 Red Devils to a 23-2 mark.

The Jeffersonville Lady Red Devils have added 12 Sectional titles to the school's bulging trophy case as well as 2 Regionals. Rick Meyers' 1998 team won 21 of 24 games, and Chad Gilbert's 2002 through 2007 girls rang up 132 victories while losing just 20. Lou Watson is a Jeffersonville Hall of Famer.

Richmond, Jeffersonville, and Lowell Red Devils

Lou Watson
Coached at Huntington High School before returning to IU...asst coach, then 5 seasons as head coach, Started every game at Jeffersonville in 4-yr varsity career... 3-time all-sectional and all-regional... established scoring records... college career delayed by WW II...the only high school player on his service team, yet the leading scorer on unit ranked 3rd in nation...was 4-yr starter at Indiana Univ...MVP as junior and senior...all-Big 10 those years...broke IU's career and Big 10 scoring records...All-American third-teamer...2-time winner of coveted Balfour Award at IU.

At the other end of the spectrum are the Saints of Ft. Wayne Bishop Dwenger and Indianapolis Lutheran. The Bishop Dwenger Saints ran up 22 wins for their coach Ron Dietz in 1994, bringing home the school's 3rd Sectional and 2nd Regional titles. Two years later with Chris Johnson coaching, they turned in the same record, winning their 4th Sectional and 3rd Regional crowns. They added their 5th Sectional title

The Indianapolis Lutheran logo and Saints, as depicted at Ft. Wayne Bishop Dwenger

the next year. The Lady Saints have brought home 9 Sectional titles as well as the 1985 Regional championship, with a 20-3 record for long-time coach Dave Scudder. Scudder's 1990 team won 24 of 27 games, and his 1995 squad turned in a 24-3 mark. From 1985 through 1991 his Lady Saints racked up 124 victories and suffered only 26 defeats. Indianapolis Lutheran's Saints won 18 of 21 games for Coach Richard Block in 1988. Twenty years later, with Tom Finchum in the coach's box, the Saints won 22 games, losing only 5, including the Class A State Championship final game to Triton, 50-42. The Lady Saints, coached by Brett Andrews, won back-to-back Sectional titles with 19-6 and 19-4 records in 2005 and 2006. For the 3-year period beginning in 2004 they turned in 56 victories and just 15 defeats.

Chapter 34

We Begin with a Rebel Yell:
And How About Our Olympi-annes?

It seems as if a number of schools that are either on the south side of a particular city or county have decided they ought to be rebels. Not all have done so, of course, but we do have 7, and all have "south" somewhere in their school name except Roncalli, which is located on the south side of Indianapolis. What do they all rebel against? I'm not sure, but I am reminded of Marlon Brando's famous line in *The Wild One*. When asked, "What do you rebel against, Johnny?" his reply was: "Whatta ya got?"

We'll begin with the Hanover-based Southwestern Rebels where my friend John Collier's son Steve's tremendous performances led their teams in the early 70s. The following is from the school's Web site:

Steve Collier, son of legendary Hanover College coach John Collier, played for the Rebels in the years 1970-1974. During his career, the Rebels posted a record of 85 wins in 97 games. During Collier's junior and senior seasons, the team posted a record of 45-3, winning the school's first two sectionals. The team of 1974 still holds the school record for win percentage, finishing 23-1, a win percentage of 95.8. Selected as Indiana's Mr. Basketball in 1974.

In total the Rebels have picked off 6 Sectional titles and the 1998 Class 2A Regional in their own gym as well as the Indianapolis Semi-state that year, although they would lose the state championship to Alexandria by a 57-43 score. The Lady Rebels have won 7 Sectionals and 2 Regionals. They have also come away with Semi-states at Southport in 2002 and Southridge in 2003 at the 2A level. In 2002 the Lady Rebels brought the state championship trophy back to Hanover, Donna Cheatham's 5 defeating Shenandoah in the final game by a 70-64 score to finish 25-2. The next year Southwestern had to settle for the runner-up plaque, as Shenandoah extracted some measure of revenge by winning the rematch in a good old-fashioned barn burner, 52-51, Southwestern finishing another fine season at 21-8.

The Southwestern (Hanover) Rebel

The South Central Rebels have won 2 Sectionals, in 1974 at Floyd Central and the Class A at Springs Valley in 2002. The Lady Rebels have brought 5 Sectional championships home to Elizabeth as well, 2 Regional titles, and the 2006 Class A Southport Semi-state crown. That year they were runner-up to Lafayette Central Catholic by a score of 75-68, Randall Schoen's 5 finishing a fine season with 23 wins and 6 losses.

The Rebels of South Spencer had a 17-5 season for Coach Bob Collins in 1970 and rang up a 19-4 record 2 years later. Mitch Haskins was coaching in 1979 when the Rebels had a terrific undefeated regular season with 25 wins and only 1 loss, winning both the Boonville Sectional and the Evansville Regional. Reed Terry's 1990 squad won 18 of 23. In 1994 and 1995, Roger Guth's teams went 23-3 and 22-3. All told, the Rebels have won 8 Sectionals and 3 Regionals. In 1979 the Rebels lost in the 1st round of the Semi-state to Terre Haute South by 4 points. That was hardly a disgrace, as Terre Haute South lost in the Final Four to eventual State Champion Muncie Central in overtime. In 1993 the Rebels ran into the Jeffersonville Red Devils in the Evansville Semi-state, the year the Red Devils finally climbed the mountain and brought the title home with them. The next year Bloomfield ousted the Rebels in the 1st round of the Terre Haute Semi-state. The Lady Rebels have brought 4 Sectional nets home to Rockport.

South Central (Elizabeth) and South Spencer Rebels

The South Newton Rebels have won 7 Sectionals. The Lady Rebels have added 9 Sectionals to the school's trophy case in Kentland, as well as the 1980 and 1983 Valparaiso Regionals. The Randolph Southern Rebels had an impressive 4-year streak from 1971 through 1974, winning 77 games and losing only 13. Larry Conklin coached the 1st 3 of those years and Gary Drill the 4th. Gary Martin led the Rebels to another nice streak, this from 1980 through 1982, resulting in 58 wins and just 9 losses. The best seasons in these two series were 21-2 in both 1971 and 1982. Sectionals were brought home to Lynn in 1994 and 2001, Class A. Clark Rich coached the Lady Rebels to a commendable 20-4 record in 1992. They won their own Sectional that year and have also won 5 others.

Although Muncie Southside has been overshadowed by the tremendous success of Muncie Central, the Rebels in their shorter life have certainly achieved some memorable successes of their own. In 1964, Southside's 2nd season, Bob Heeter's teams had a 21-5 record, and 2 years later they improved on that to 22-3. John Robbins led the Rebels to a 22-5 in 1985 and Bill Hahn's 1991 team won 21 of 24 games. In 1995 Rick Baumgartner coached Southside to a 20-4 mark. He left after that season, but not because all of the talent was gone. Far from it. Jimmie Howell came in and achieved a 23-2 season in 1996 and 20-3 in 1997. The Rebels have won 16 Sectionals and 6 Regionals. In 1965, after defeating Columbus in the 1st round of the Semi-state, the Rebels were beaten by eventual State Champion Indianapolis Washington. In 1985 the Rebels defeated Lawrence North's Wildcats before losing to that year's state runner-up, Richmond. In 1989 Southside again won the 1st round of the Semi-state, this time over Connersville, before losing to Lawrence North, who would celebrate their 1st state championship, led by Eric Montross and Todd Leary. In 1999, at the 3A level, the Rebels were runner-up to the State Championship Plainfield Quakers, but 2 years later they finally broke through, winning their 1st state championship over Evansville Mater Dei in an overtime thriller, 81-78. Rick Baumgartner had come back to coach these 2 state finalist teams, his 1999 squad finishing 17-11, and the 2001 team coming in at 23-3.

The South Newton, Randolph Southern, and Muncie Southside Rebels

Seeing their logos leads me to believe that 2 of our Raiders belong here, too: South Ripley and Shenandoah. In their 4th year, 1970, South Ripley not only went undefeated in the regular season for Coach Dale Ricketts, they also won the 1st of the school's 6 Sectional titles and the 1st of their 2 Regional crowns. Their lone loss came in the Sweet Sixteen to Crispus Attucks. Ted Ahaus led the Raiders to their 2nd Regional title with a 21-5 record in 1981, and Randy Snodgrass coached his 1995 team to a 20-3 finish. The Lady Raiders have brought 2 Sectional plaques home to Versailles, as well as 1 for the 2001 Regional, with a 20-6 record for Coach Bill Snyder. His 2003 through 2005 quintets posted 54 wins and only 14 losses.

The Shenandoah Raiders opened their doors in 1968 and were coached for their 1st six years by Hall of Famer Ray Pavy:

Ray Pavy
3-sport standout at New Castle with all-North Central honors in both football and basketball ... twice all-sectional and all-regional ... helped write key chapter in Indiana basketball history when he matched up with Jimmy Rayl in the last regular season gamed played in New Castle's tiny Church St. gym ... Rayl scored 49 but Pavy hit 23 of 36 shots and 5 of 8 free throws for 51 points in a game forever known as the "Church Street Shootout" ... 1190 career points...captain of Indiana All-Star team... high school, all-sport starter at IU as sophomore before he was paralyzed in auto accident. Coached high school ball and is currently an assistant superintendent of New Castle Community Schools.

Pavy's 1970 Raiders won the school's 1st Sectional title and finished with a sparkling 25-2 record. Eleven years later Bob Heady led the team to a 25-3 finish including a Final Four berth. The Raiders lost the morning game at Market Square Arena to the eventual State Champion Vincennes Lincoln Alices. The Lady Raiders put together an extremely impressive 6-year string for Coach Todd Salkoski from 2000 through 2005. During that period they won 134 games and lost only 23, capturing Sectional and Regional crowns every year and 4 Semi-states. The 25-1 team in 2001 suffered its only loss in the 2A State Championship game to Ft. Wayne Bishop Luers; the 2002 team also finished runner-up to State Champion Southwestern Rebels, finishing 22-4. The next year the Lady Raiders were not to be denied, bringing the state championship trophy home to Middletown after turning the tables on Donna Cheatham's Southwestern team in a thriller, 52-51, finishing 24-5. After the 2004 season ended 22-2 in the Semi-state game, the 2005 Shenandoah girls did it again, winning their 2nd state championship over North Judson-San Pierre with a bit of room to spare, 54-49.

The South Ripley and
Shenandoah Raiders

Next on our list of popular names come 5 Spartans: Connersville, Homestead, North Newton, South Knox, and Southwestern (Shelby County). Noted for their skills at war and their abilities to live without many of life's amenities, the Greek city-state of Sparta has captured the imagination of many.

The Connersville Spartans were coached by Mose Pruitt for 19 years from 1924 through 1942. From 1925 through 1933, a 9-year period, the Spartans never won less than 18 games. Over that timespan they won 178 games and lost 79. Tops was 1930, when they won 24, losing 7. Obviously, they played a lot of games every year back then. More recently Myron Dickerson's Spartan teams of 1969 won 19 of 24

games and in 1972 won 26 and lost only 3. Hall of Fame coach Basil Mawbey had another great string of years, from 1980 through 1986, winning 143 games while dropping only 37 in that 7-year period. His banner year was 1983's state championship team, 26-2. Steve Dunnington coached for 1 year only, and his 1987 quintet won 20 and lost 4 games. All told, the Spartans have amassed 56 Sectional titles and 18 Regionals.

The Connersville Spartan

They have made it to Indianapolis twice, making the most of each trip by winning the state championship in 1972 as well as 1983. They did so on their first trip by beating Jeffersonville in overtime and then Gary West and in 1983 by beating Princeton by 5 points before edging Anderson by 1 in a stirring title game. The Lady Spartans have brought further glory to Connersville by winning 16 Sectionals and 4 Regionals. From 1997–99 Larry Millers teams ran up 67 wins against just 8 losses and in 2001 they won another 20, dropping just 5.

The Homestead Spartans reside in Allen County and have been at our favorite game for considerably less time than Connersville. They have certainly had their moments, however, going 24-3 and 22-2 for Coach Neal McKeeman in 1981 and 1982 as well as 18-5, followed by 20-6 for him in 1987 and 1988. They have won 5 Sectionals. The Homestead Lady Spartans have added 7 Sectionals and the 1997 Ft. Wayne Northrop Regional title to the school's trophy collection.

The North Newton Spartans have brought only 1 Sectional title back to Morocco, in 1978 from Kankakee Valley. The Lady Spartans, however, have won 5. The Southwestern (Shelbyville) Spartans had a fine 20-2 season in 1970 for coach George Marshall. They also finished 17-4 for Doug Curtis in 1991. They have won 2Class A sectionals as well as the 2003 White River Valley Regional. These Spartans also won the Semi-state that year and were runner-up to Lafayette Central Catholic for the state championship, dropping a 68-64 decision to finish 22-5 for Coach Stacy Meyer. The Lady Spartans have won 3 Sectionals and their own 2004 Class A Regional.

Some tough fighters; the Spartans from Homestead, North Newton, and Southwestern

While we're in Greece we should remember the already covered Crawfordsville Athenians and make mention of the Columbus East Olympians. Both Crawfordsville and Columbus are must-see towns in Indiana, the former with one of the loveliest small school campuses in America, Wabash College, and the latter with a collection of exquisite buildings designed by some of the world's greatest architects made possible by the foresight and generosity of J. Erwin Miller, former president and CEO of the Cummins Engine Corporation, whose elegant home and gardens are also open to the public there.

The Olympians were coached from their opening season in 1973 through 1980 by Lou Giovanni. For the last 5 seasons of that period, his teams won an even 100 games and lost only 26, with the premier year being 1979's 23-2 mark. They have won 8 Sectionals and 2 Regionals as well as the 1977 Indianapolis Hinkle Semi-state, losing to eventual champion Carmel in the 1st round of the Final Four.

One of my all-time favorite names for girls teams is that of the Olympi-Annes of Columbus East. In a memorable state championship game, 1980 at Market Square Arena, in spite of a heroic 42-point effort by Olympi-Anne Maria Stack, Columbus East lost in overtime to the Southport Lady Cardinals, led by Amy Metheny's 28 points, by a final score of 67-63. All told, the Olympi-Annes have won 11 Sectionals, 8 Regionals, and 4 Semi-states. They were also state runner-up in 2007, Class 4A, dropping the final game to South Bend Washington to finish 24-3 for Coach Danny Brown.

Crawfordsville Athenians and Columbus East Olympi-Annes: Houck photos from exhibits courtesy IBHOF

Not to be outdone by the Greek theme are our 3 schools with a Scottish flair. Though Anderson is actually a Scandinavian name, there are nevertheless Scots at Anderson Highland High School in Madison County. This name was selected by the students. The school paper is *The Tartan*, the yearbook is *The Higlander,* the literary magazine, *Echoles from the Glen.* The band, called the Marching Highlanders, features traditional kilts and plays mostly bagpipes. They march to "Scotland the Brave."

Though located in Fairmont, Madison-Grant High School serves portions of the 2 counties that comprise its name. Their teams are the Argylls. Our 3rd entry in the Scottish derby is the Floyd Central Highlanders from the evocatively named town of Floyds Knobs. Let's take them 1 at at time.

Anderson Highland was coached by Bob Fuller to a 20-2 mark in 1974, 25-1 in 1976, 18-4 in 1977 and 1979, and 23-1 in 1980 (along with Jerry Bomholz that latter year). In 1982 the Scots had another strong season, 22-3, with Butch Stafford coaching. The next 2 years Jerome Foley was in charge, and his teams turned in 19-4 and 18-4 seasons. That comes to a strong 59-11 for the 3 years. Alan Darner's 1988 team finished 18-3, and his 1990 through 1992 Scots went 18-5, 22-4, and 21-4, or 61 wins and 13 losses over those 3 years. Sectionals were won in 1976, 1980, and 1991 and Regionals in 1976 and 1991. In both of their Regional crown years the Scots were edged in the 1st round by the eventual state champion, Marion, by 2 points in 1976 and Gary Roosevelt by 1 point in 1991. Talk about bad luck! The Scots Lasses have also enjoyed some fine years, including 1993's 21-2, and have rung up 9 Sectional and 5 Regional titles. In 1987 they reached the state finals last game, losing to Noblesville's 27-0 Lady Millers to end a fine 22-6 season for Coach Bill Wilson. They won 20 games for Jim Teeters in 1980, losing only 2, and had a 21-2 season for Wilson in 1993.

Madison-Grant's Argylls won 19 games and lost 6 for Jack Ford in 1973. Terry Martin coached the Argylls for 15 years beginning in 1982. His 1989 team finished 17-5, his 1996 squad was 21-4, and his final quintet ended at 19-5. Sectionals were brought home to Fairmont in 1973, 1988, and 1996. The Lady Argylls have also won 3 Sectional crowns.

Floyd Central's green and gold Highlanders were coached for 31 years, many of which were outstanding, by Joe Hinton. From 1971 through 1975 the Highlanders won 103 games and lost only 17. In 1981 they went 21-5, 2 years later went 20-6 and in 1986, 20-8. In 1989 their record was 23-4. In total the Highlanders have won 14 Sectionals and 6 Regionals. Semi-state titles were earned in 1971 and 1989. In 1971 the Highlanders lost to eventual State Champion East Chicago Washington in the afternoon game at Hinkle Fieldhouse, and in 1989 it was runner-up Kokomo who ousted Floyd Central in the morning game by just 3 points at Market Square Arena. The Lady Highlanders (Lassies?) have cut down Sectional nets 5 times themselves.

Anderson Highland Scots, Madison Grant Argylls, and Floyd Central Highlanders

Seeing that Argyll logo reminds me of the 2 other toughest looking mascots, the Marauders of Mt. Vernon (Fortville) and the Cavemen of Mishawaka. The Marauders have captured 10 Sectionals and the 1987 and 1991 New Castle Regionals. In 1987 they beat Indianapolis Pike in the 1st round before being ousted by the eventual state runner-up Richmond Red Devils in the Semi-state final. In 1991 a similar result occurred when the Marauders got revenge on Richmond before losing to, again, the eventual state runner-up Indianapolis Brebeuf Jesuit Braves, led by Alan Henderson, in that Semi-state final. The Lady Marauders have won 11 Sectionals themselves, 6 Regionals, and the 1977 Ben Davis Semi-state. They finished runner-up to East Chicago Roosevelt, Carolyn Oldfather's team losing their only game of the 17 they played that year in the state finals at Hinkle Fieldhouse.

Mishawaka's Cavemen have won nine Sectionals and 2 Regionals. The first Regional title came in 1927, Coach Shelby Shake's Cavemen defeating New Paris 26-15 and Kewanna 38-15. This brought them to the state finals in Indianapolis, held at the Fairgrounds Exposition Building that year, where the Cavemen lost their opening-round game to Gary Emerson. Their next Regional title came in 1955 for John Longfellow. His 20-8 team nipped Nappanee 52-49 in overtime. The Cavemen beat Warsaw 63-52 at Elkhart, where they also defeated Hartford City 51-43, before losing to Ft. Wayne North Side, 54-48. After coaching Milan's state champions and the Indianapolis North Central Panthers, Marvin Wood had successful years at Mishawaka in 1974 and 1975, finishing 20-3 and 21-4. More recently, Robb Berger's 2005 squad won 20 games and lost only 3.

Wood also coached the Lady Cavemen (Cavewomen?) to a stellar 22-2 season in 1983, winning 1 of the 2 Regional crowns the girls have captured. The 2nd came the very next year with John Taylor coaching the Cave(wo)men to an undefeated regular season, 24-1. Mike Breske's girls teams won 3 straight Sectional crowns beginning in 1994, the 1st 2 teams taking 38 of 44 games. In total they have cut down Sectional nets 6 times. They play their home contests in what else but the Cave.

A mean pair, Marauders and Cavemen

Several schools have turned to government and the military for their team names, some honoring specific individuals, others generic. These include the Hammond Morton Governors, a team whose name honors our state's Civil War governor, a staunch supporter of Abraham Lincoln and remembered as a very able executive. After his tenure as governor, Morton served our state as a United States Senator. His home was in Centerville. The Governors won their lone Sectional in 1976, and the Lady Governors have snagged 4, the 1st 3 for Aletta Hicks in 1977 through 1979. *Hammond logo* The first 2 of those teams won 31 games and lost only 6.

West Washington and Washington Township teams are the Senators. The Washington Township Senators call Valparaiso home. Although the boys teams have yet to win a Sectional, the girls have won Class A Sectionals in 2002 and 2003 as well as the Caston Regional in 2003. The West Washington Senators are in Campbellsburg.

They won Sectionals at Paoli in 1990 with a thrilling 72-69 double overtime victory over Salem followed by a 71-68 conquest of Orleans; and 1996 with wins over Orleans, Mitchell, and Salem. The Lady Senators have also won two Sectionals, both Class A, and both at home, in 1998 and 1999.

GO SENATORS!

Washington Township Senators, Two Ways

The Perry Central teams are the Commodores. There are 2 famous Commodores Perry in our nation's history. The 1st, Oliver Hazard Perry, gained fame from his victory at the Battle of Erie during the War of 1812 when his stirring words "We have met the enemy and he is ours," caught the fancy of a nation, as did his battle flag, "Don't Give Up the Ship." His brother, Matthew, also a commodore, gained fame for sailing into the port of Edo (later renamed Tokyo), opening the reclusive Empire of Japan to trade with the West. The Commodores of Perry Central (not to be confused with the Midgets of Perry Central formerly in Boone County!) have won 2 Sectionals, at Southridge in 1978 with victories over Northeast Dubois, 59-53, and a close one over Jasper, 56-55; and at Crawford County in 1997, where they defeated Corydon, Tell City, and North Harrison. The Lady Commodores brought the Class A Sectional trophy home to Leopold from Oakland City in 2001.

George Rogers Clark, the hero of the battles of Kaskaskia, Illinois, and Vincennes, was given a land grant near the Falls of the Ohio, where he lived for a period when his brother William and Meriwether Lewis set off on their fabled exploration of the Louisiana Purchase. The Clarksville teams are the Generals, and they have won three Sectionals, all at Jeffersonville, in 1978, 1979, and 1988. The Lady Generals have

Commodore Oliver Hazard Perry's battle flag

also won 3 Sectionals, theirs all at Floyd Central, in 1984, 1986, and 1987.

Anthony Wayne, sometimes called "Mad Anthony," was not only a Revolutionary War hero but also the hero of the Battle of Fallen Timbers. Not only is the fort in northeastern Indiana named for him (which later became the state's 2nd largest city of Ft. Wayne), but so, too, is Wayne County on the Ohio border due east of Indianapolis. Ft. Wayne Wayne teams are also the Generals. The Generals were coached by Will Doehrman from 1973 through 1995. In 1981 they enjoyed a 20-7 season and in 1994 they won 20 and lost 6. Murray Mendenhall III coached the Generals to 18-6, 19-4, and 17-6 records in 1997, 1998, and 2000 respectively. They won 4 Sectionals and the 1981 Ft. Wayne Regional. The Lady Generals have won 1 Sectional in 1979 at Harding.

We also have three Lakers in Indiana. Shakamak, in Jasonville, uses an Indian logo, as we have seen and covered earlier. LaPorte La

The Clarksville and Ft. Wayne Wayne Generals

Lumiere, whose list of graduates includes the current chief justice of the United States Supreme Court, the Honorable John Roberts, does not have a symbol that I have been able to find, which in no way diminishes the value of the fine education they provide. Their beautiful campus surrounds a spring-fed lake, and their school's name suggests the Lamp of Knowledge. In 1979 Chris Balawender's Lakers won 15 games while losing only 4.

The La Lumiere Crest

Lakeland, in LaGrange, also fields the Lakers, and they use a lighthouse as a symbol. They have won 10 Sectionals. In their 1st year, 1965, they finished 20-3 for Richard Butt. In 1978 they turned in an outstanding 26-2 record for Bill Leiter. They won the East Noble Sectional with victories over Westview, 68-46; Fairfield, 73-55; and the home team, 83-54. In the Ft. Wayne Regional the Lakers defeated Angola, 56-48, before losing the final to North Side in a squeaker, 47-43. The Lady Lakers (Ladies of the Lake?) had a marvelous 20-2 season for Gary Myers in 1984 and another, 21-4, in 1998 for Jerry Severson. They have had added 3 Sectional crowns to the school's collection.

The Lakeland Lakers Lighthouse

Chapter 35

Pirates, Dragons. . .
and—Call Out the Marines!

Three of our current schools call their teams the Pirates: Charlestown, Greensburg, and Merrillville. None is near any significant body of water, although Charlestown is the closest, separated from the Ohio River only by the Indiana Arsenal Military Reservation. Merrillville is not too far from Lake Michigan. But Greensburg? Pirates of the Sand River, I guess.

There are several iterations of the Charlestown Pirates, one jolly, one pensive, and one peg-legged and a bit menacing. Whichever one held sway in 1976, John Wood's team won 20 games and lost only 5. Allen Cundiff led the Pirates to 21-3 and 19-3 seasons in 1990 and 1991. Nine Sectional prizes have been seized by the Pirates. The Lady Pirates have also nabbed 9 Sectionals. They have brought home 4 Regional nets as well, including 3 in a row beginning in 1991. That year they beat Seymour before running into Bedford North Lawrence's juggernaught in the Semi-state final. The next year they defeated Jennings County before again losing to BNL in the Semi-state final. In 1993 they made it to Indianapolis only to run into another tough opponent, Kokomo's Lady Wildkats, who beat the Lady Pirates in the morning game and went on to win their second straight state title that night at Market Square Arena.

Three depictions of the Charlestown Pirates

Merrillville, Indiana, was an historical stopping point for wagons headed west. There is no doubt that piracy was a problem for those honest folk using any of the 16 different trails that crossed the spot now occupied by the town. The John Wood grain mill, still an attraction, was the 1st of its kind in Lake County. Another attraction is the majestic Constantine and Helen Greek Orthodox Cathedral, situated on 37 acres and featuring a 100-foot diameter dome. There are 2 high schools in town, essentially right around the corner from each other. Their teams are the Merrillville High School Pirates and the Andrean High School Fighting 59ers. Now, Pirates I understand, but 59ers seemed off by 10 years until I noticed Andrean's address: 5959 Broadway. But that's not all. I was also informed by a proud alumna that the school moved to that location in 1959! And, after all, there was gold to be found in 1859 as well as 1849.

The success of these 2 schools in our state tournament has been remarkably similar: the Merrillville Pirates have won 15 Sectionals; so have the Andrean 59ers; the Pirates have won 6 Regionals and 2 Semi-states, the 59ers 5 and 2; both schools have made it to the state championship final game once, and both have lost. Merrillville's loss came in a good, old-fashioned barn burner, 58-57, when Steve Witty's Ben Davis Giants with their 24-2 record bested Jim East's 27-2 Pirates in 1995. Andrean's loss was to Leo Klemm's 24-2 Brebeuf Jesuit Braves in the 2000 3A championship game. Andrean, coached by Clint Swan, finished at 24-3.

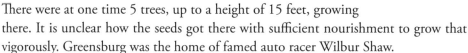

The Merrillville Pirate and the Andrean 59er

Greensburg is well known for the tree that grows out of the tower of the Decatur County Courthouse. It was first noted in 1870. There were at one time 5 trees, up to a height of 15 feet, growing there. It is unclear how the seeds got there with sufficient nourishment to grow that vigorously. Greensburg was the home of famed auto racer Wilbur Shaw.

The Pirates won 21 and lost 7 in 1931 with Frank Pruitt coaching. Harold Nugent was the coach in 1937 and 1938 when the teams went 21-6 and 20-5. Another 20-win season came in 1966 when Keith Greve was the coach. Phil Snodgrass led the Pirates to 19-5 and 21-3 marks in 1980 and 1993 respectively. All told the Pirates have amassed 34 Sectional and 5 Regional championships. The Lady Pirates won their lone Sectional at South Dearborn in 2008, Class 3A.

The Greensburg courthouse tree and the Pirate logo

The Indianapolis Cardinal Ritter Raiders also belong here, as was pointed out earlier. The Raiders have won 2 Sectional titles, Class 2A in 1999 and Class A 2004. The Lady Raiders have won 3, all for long-time coach Al MacDonald, the best record coming in 1991, 17-6.

Greensburg Lady Pirates

Who best to handle those Pirates and Raiders? My vote would be for the Marines. Our only Marines are those at Hamilton. Those marines have 4 Sectional championships and 1 Regional title in their trophy case. The Class A Regional title

 came in 2001 at Garrett, John Hohnstreiter's team besting Adams Central in a 2-overtime thriller. In the Kokomo Semi-state the Marines were edged by Kouts, 78-77. That year the Marines won 21 games and lost only 5. The Lady Marines have also won 1 Sectional. Semper Fi!

We have elsewhere covered our 4 schools that use Pioneers for their team names, as well as the Plainfield Quakers, and the Noblesville Millers. We also have 2 Giants, Indianapolis Ben Davis and Marion. (Marion will also be covered elsewhere.)

Our Giants, Marion and Indianapolis Ben Davis The Ben Davis Giants were coached by Marion Fine in 1958, when they ran up an excellent 22 wins and 3 losses, bracketed by 17-6 seasons before and after, a 3-year run of 56 and 15. His 1965 Giants won 19 of 26 games. In 1978 Jerry Hoover's team won 23 games and lost 5. Gayle Towles took over the Ben Davis reins from 1979 through 1988 and put together a terrific string of years from 1981 through 1986. During those 6 years Ben Davis teams won 125 games and lost only 23, topped by 1985's 25-4 record and 1984's 23-3. It was Steve Witty, however, whose tenure represented a true Golden Age for the Ben Davis Giants. His 1993 and 1994 teams each won 27 games and lost only 3, but his 1995 edition went an astonishing 32-1, followed immediately by 22-6 and 18-5 seasons. In 2001 the Giants, still coached by Witty, won 21 games and lost only 4, and the next year his quintet won 21 of 24 starts. All told the Giants have won 16 Sectionals, 7 Regionals, and 4 straight Semi-states, beginning in 1993. After finishing runner-up to Jeffersonville's 29-2 Red Devils in 1993, Ben Davis got that 1st state title in 1995 in one of the most exciting finals ever played, over that excellent 27-2 Merrillville Pirate squad we just discussed, 58-57. The repeat title over the Bulldogs of New Albany, 24-4, came in another scintillating final game, 57-54 in overtime, as Witty's charges finished an excellent season.

The Lady Giants also have done their school proud. Tammy Haley's 1981 team won 19 and lost 7. Stan Benge has been their coach from 1986 through at least 2009. His 1988 team went 18-6 and his 1990 through 1992 teams won 67 games and lost only 8, with a 23-3 record in 1990 and 24-3 in 1992. His teams had an even more impressive string from 1998 through 2004, during which time the Lady Giants won 168 games and lost only 20! Included in this was the banner year of 2000 with 28 games played and 28 games won. Twenty Sectional championships have been won by the Lady Giants as well as 10 Regionals, that last figure exceeded only by the Lady Kats of Kokomo (12) and the Lady Vikes of Valparaiso (11). Class 4A State Championships came back-to-back in 2000 and 2001: they won 55 games and lost

2 in the 3-year period. The 1st was a 56-53 final game win over the 25-2 Valpo Lady Vikes, and the 2nd was a 69-45 victory over a 25-3 Ft. Wayne Snider team to finish 27-2.

That the tradition is still strong in Wayne Township is attested to by the Super 25 Girls High School Baskeball Rankings in the March 11, 2009, edition of *USA Today*: Number 1 in the country, the Ben Davis Lady Giants, once again are crowned Class 4A Indiana State Champions, with a 30-0 record! Further proof that our Hoosier girls play an impressive brand of basketball is borne out by the rest of the paper's national rankings: Number 4 South Bend Washington's Lady Panthers, runner-up to Ben Davis in a closely contested, well-played final game in front of 13,449 fans, settled in the last 1.4 seconds 71-69 and their only loss in 27 games; and Number 12, Indianapolis Heritage Christian winners of their 4th straight Class 2A state title with a 26-1 record! To add to our healthy dose of Hoosier pride, Stan Benge was selected National Coach of the Year by *USA Today*, joining J. R. Holmes in giving Indiana both the boys and girls top coaching award for 2009 (see page 396).

Those games, and the Class A and 3A finals, were the 1st Indiana State Finals played at the new Lucas Oil Stadium. No one who attended those 4 games was disappointed in the quality of play or the competitiveness of the teams. As stated, the 4A game was a 2-pointer, settled in the last second. The 2A game was a 60-58 overtime victory by Heritage Christian over Oak Hill and the A game was an overtime thriller, Ft. Wayne Canterbury outlasting Vincennes Rivet. In the 3A game Ft. Wayne Elmhurst edged Owen Valley by 3 points.

Linton is smack in the middle of some of the nation's richest veins of coal right

Two different renderings of the Linton Miner

in west central Indiana. Since the veins were so close to the surface, no shafts were necessary to reach these veins, and strip-mining techniques were used to remove the coal. Once the topsoil was removed, the coal was exposed, and then it was removed by some truly giant equipment. Railroad lines were built right into the mines to haul the coal to the various points where it was needed. Many of Linton's men worked in those open-air pits. When the coal was exhausted the result was a pretty ugly scar on the surface of the beautiful rolling hills of the Indiana countryside. However, the topsoil was then carefully replaced, fields and trees were planted, and the result is a return to a more pristine state.

Linton's best-known citizen was the comedian Phil Harris. I used to love to hear his radio humor on a Sunday night, along with Jack Benny as we all gathered around our living room console, a piece of furniture about 3 feet high and veneered with attractive hardwoods. It was not until later that I realized how little of that whole space was used for the radio receiver and its speaker. The teams of Linton-Stockton High, proudly called the Miners, have won 16 Sectionals and the 1946 Martinsville Regional. At Martinsville Gar Ladson's Miners won 2 tight contests, 36-34 in overtime against the University Univees and 27-23 over the Honey Creek Honey Bees. The Lady Miners have added 3 Sectional nets to the school's trophy case.

The University of Notre Dame was founded in South Bend, Indiana, in 1842. With one of the most beautiful campuses anywhere, Notre Dame is known for the Golden Dome and an enviable record of athletic success, as well as for the high quality of its educational offerings. Cathedral High School, Indianapolis was founded in 1918 by Bishop Joseph Chartrand, and the Holy Cross Brothers of Notre Dame were engaged to serve as faculty. From the beginning, the school has had an extremely close relationship with the University of Notre Dame and has also enjoyed athletic and academic excellence. Cathedral teams have long been known as the Fighting Irish, perhaps even predating Notre Dame, known for many years only as the Irish, with a terrier, not the leprechaun, as their mascot. Cathedral uses the leprechaun mascot sparingly, as approved by Notre Dame, using the shamrock and the Celtic cross as symbols, as well as the shield of Bishop Chartrand with its Latin motto *Ipsa duce non fatigaris*—With her leading you shall not tire. (Thanks to Cathedral's Chris Kaufman

Celtic cross and Chartrand shield

for these insights.)

The Fighting Irish of Cathedral have an illustrious history, not only on the gridiron, but on the hardwood as well. Joe Dienhart coached the Irish team of 1928 to a 22-6 record, and his 1930 through 1933 squads won a splendid 83 games while losing only 23. In those days the Catholic schools in Indiana held their own state tournament which Cathedral's Irish won 4 times: 1928, 1929, 1933, and 1934.

Bill Frohliger's 1961 Irish squad finished 20-4; Gene Ancelet's 1972 and 1973 teams won 42 of 54 games. In 1982 Tom O'Brien led his team to a truly outstanding season, 27 wins and just 3 losses. After edging the Washington Continentals 62-61 to win the Indianapolis Regional that year, the Irish also beat Connersville and Muncie Central to win the Semi-state. Then the Irish ran into the Scott Skiles-led Plymouth Pilgrims. Cathedral lost a well-fought 62-59 game to the eventual state champions in the morning game at Market Square Arena. O'Brien's next year's squad also turned in a strong 20-3 record. They were ousted by an excellent Broad Ripple team 45-44, a team that would themselves be knocked out of the tournament in the Semi-state afternoon game when Steve Alford dropped his well-remembered 57-point bomb on the Rockets to help New Castle get to the final game. After Howard Renner's 1992 and 1995 teams won 21-4 and 23-3 games respectively, Cathedral's breakout year arrived: 1998, Peter Berg coaching. The 22-5 Irish won the Class 3A State Championship with a 72-47 trouncing of the Yorktown Tigers at the RCA Dome. In 2007 and 2008, Scott Hicks' teams won 44 games and lost only 5. In total Cathedral has won 8 Sectional and 4 Regional crowns.

The Lady Irish have also done their part to bring glory to the school's beautiful northeast side campus. Linda Bamrick has coached the girls teams there since 1992, and her first 20-win seasons came in 1996 and 1997, 20-4 and 21-3. From 1999 through 2001 her Lady Irish teams put together a remarkable record of 83 wins and 3 losses! One loss per year, 2 state championships, and 1 runner-up title! The Irish lost their only game of the 1999 season in the Class 3A final game to Northwood, a heartbreaking end to a great season, 72-71. The next year they put things right, again finishing 27-1, but winning the 3A title with a 1-point victory over Columbia City. To put icing on the cake, Bamrick's Lady Irish did it again in 2001, this time winning 29 games and losing just 1, defeating Plymouth by another 15-point margin. Her 2002 team won 21 of 24 games; her 2004 team was 20-4; and her 2005 team won 24 and lost just 2. In total, Bamrick's squads have won 12 Sectional and 3 Regional titles.

Indianapolis Scecina Memorial teams are the Crusaders. The Crusaders and the Lady Crusaders have won 2 Sectionals apiece. Perhaps their best all-time player was Tim McGinley, who went on to play at Purdue and has served his university so well as a multi-year trustee and chairman of the board of trustees. Tim is a Hall of Famer.

Tim McGinley
Led the city of Indianapolis in scoring in 1958, captain of Scecina team in 1958, setting all school scoring records ... coached by Hall of Famer Joe Sexson. . . 1958 Indiana All-Star ... three year starter at Purdue . . . second leading scorer during career to All-American Terry Dischinger ... defensive ace holding many top scorers below their average ... selected to several All Big Ten teams in 1961 and 1962 ... received Lambert Award for Purdue player with highest scholastic average ... played for Hall of Famer Ray Eddy ...1983 Silver Anniversary Team ... 1995 named male Big Ten Centennial Athletic Award Winner from Purdue University ... Distinguished Career Service Award Winner from the John Purdue Club.

The Scecina Memorial Shield

In Greek mythology the Titans were a race of deities eventually superseded by the Olympian pantheon of gods. In Indiana the Titans have emerged in several places and remain in 4: Indianapolis Arsenal Tech, Gibson Southern, Taylor, and Tri High schools.

Indianapolis Arsenal Technical High School occupies an historic campus that actually was home to a Union arsenal during the Civil War. Tech was the 3rd high school in Indianapolis, after Shortridge and Manual, and was for a fairly long time the school with the largest enrollment in the state. They were also, for a time, a member of the highly competitive North Central Conference, the only Indianapolis school ever to be included in that august group.

Tech's Titans (though they were simply known as the Greenclads at the time) came close to being the first Indianapolis school to win a state championship in 1929, when Tim Campbell's team lost the 1st of Tech's 4 state championship final games, this one to the Frankfort Hot Dogs by a 29-23 count. Beryl Black's Tech team had been in the Sweet Sixteen in 1920, when they defeated Kendallville before being eliminated by eventual runner-up Lafayette in the 2nd round. Campbell's 2nd state runner-up finish came in 1934 when the Titans dropped the final game to Logansport, 26-19. In 1952 it was Muncie Central who would beat Herman Hinshaw's Tech squad and star player Joe Sexson 68-49 in the final game, and Michigan City did the Titans in for the 4th time in a state title encounter, with Jack Bradford then in the coach's box, in 1966, 63-52. In total Tech's teams have won 19 Sectionals and 9 Regionals. Joe Sexson is featured in the Hall of Fame.

Joe Sexson
Mr. Basketball ... won Trester Award after leading Indianapolis Tech to runner-up spot to Muncie Central's state champions ... as a junior, Tech was ousted in semistate by eventual champion Madison ... four-sport high school athlete ... two-time MVP at Purdue University, where he averaged 16.6 points in 66 games to leave as schoolís leading career scorer ... coached at Southwestern and Scecina high schools before becoming assistant coach at Purdue ... became head coach at Butler Univ. where he was twice named Coach of the Year

The Lady Titans have added 14 Sectional nets to the school's trophy case as well as 4 Regionals, in 1976, 1977, 1978, and 1981. Their closest brush with a state championship came in 1976 when they dropped a tough 47-45 game to Bloomfield's

Lady Cardinals in the afternoon game of the finals in the first official girls state tournament. Their record that year was 20-5; Sue Jahnke was the coach. Ron Fyffe led the 1988 Lady Titans to a 20-3 record.

In Ft. Branch, Gibson Southern's Titans have nailed down 4 Sectionals and 2 Regionals. Their 1st season in 1975 resulted in 21 wins and only 5 losses with Chester Garrett coaching. Jerry O'Brien led the 1996 team to an 18-5 mark, the 1998 team to 18-6, and the 1999 team to a 22-3 finish. From 2001 through 2003 his squads racked up 65 wins and lost only 10. The Lady Titans, Jason Blackard coaching, won 18 of 21 games in 1997 followed by 21-1 and 18-5 seasons. They have won 8 Sectionals and the 2002 Jasper 3A Regional. That year they also nailed down the Semi-state and were runner-up to Ft. Wayne Luers in the State Final game, Blackard's charges finishing 24-5. They followed this with an undefeated regular season, 23 wins and only 1 loss. Blackard's 2006 Lady Titans put together a 22-5 season, and Mark Monroe's 2008 team finished 23-4.

Taylor's Titans have won 3 Sectionals, and 1 Regional, the 2000 2A, with Jeff Fisher's team finishing 21-4. The Lady Titans have captured 4 Sectionals and 2 Regionals. Dennis Bentzler's 2004 through 2006 teams had a splendid record of 62 wins and only 11 losses.

In Henry County Tri High's Titans were created from Spiceland's Stingers, Straughn's Indians, and Lewisville's Bears. They are located in Straughn. The school's teams have 2 Sectional nets in their trophy case (plus all of the hardware, basketballs, nets, and other memorabilia won by their 3 precursor schools) but have yet to capture their 1st Regional. Don Schwarzkopf's 1975 through 1979 teams won an impressive 102 games while losing only 21. The top 2 years were the New Castle Sectional championship ones, 22-2 in 1976, with wins over Union, Knightstown, and Eastern Hancock; and 24-2 the next year, when they defeated Mt. Vernon (Fortville), Eastern Hancock, and Knightstown in a squeaker, 52-51. Back to New Castle for the Regional the 1977 team ousted Jay County in another close one, 46-45, before the bubble burst against Richmond. The Lady Titans have won 3 Sectionals and the 1998 Class A Regional that was held in their own gym, Dave Bennett's team winning an impressive 23 of 25 games.

Jason's pursuit of the Golden Fleece is a well-known piece of mythology. Interestingly enough, it has recently been demonstrated that a stream with bits of gold flowing in it, usually panned in this country's experience, can be efficiently harvested

by placing a length of fleece into the stream. The gold becomes attached resulting in, voila, a golden fleece! Those ancient Greeks may have had something there after all. Anyway, Jason's famous ship was called the *Argo*, after the shipwright named Argus, who built it. Jason's men were called the Argonauts, and in one of their several adventures, Jason, who had some dragon's teeth made available to him, sowed those dragon's teeth and reaped a harvest of fully armed warriors. In Argos, Indiana, we have appropriately, the Dragons.

The Argos Dragons put together quite an impressive regular season win streak from 1979 through 1981: 3 straight seasons with only 1 loss, 76 straight regular season wins under Coach Phil Weybright who led the Dragons from 1974 through 1987. From 1977 through 1982 his teams won an impressive 132 games while losing only 16! This from a school with only 271 students.

Houck photos from exhibit courtesy IBHOF

Earlier Clyde Sims had coached the 1920 Dragons to a 20-5 mark, and Ray Henry's 1935 and 1936 teams went 19-6 and 19-5. In 1957 Bob Hileman led his Argos squad to a good 22-3 season. More recently Doug Snyder's 2003 quintet won 22 and lost only 2. The Dragons have won 6 Sectionals and the 1979 Elkhart Central Regional. That year they made it all the way to the Final Four by defeating Ft. Wayne Harding and Marion in the Semi-state before losing the morning game to eventual runner-up Anderson, their only loss against 28 wins. The Lady Dragons won 22 games and were outscored in only 5 for Coach Shelly Newell in 2006, winning Sectional and regional championships that year. The Dragon's Den may be a daunting place to play indeed.

The Silver Creek Dragons have also had several praiseworthy seasons in Sellersburg. In 1939 and 1940 Bruce Murr's teams won 23 and 24 games while losing only 2 each season. In 1954 and 1955 Ed Denton coached the Dragons to successive 19-3 and 19-5 marks, the former equaled by Joe Pezzullo's 1966 team. Ray Green led the 1969 Dragons to a 20-6 record, followed by 18-6 and 19-2 seasons, making his 3-year tenure at the school an effective 57-14. John Heaton was coaching Silver Creek in 1979 when they finished 21-3, and the next year when they went 18-5. Thomas Matthews' 1998 quintet finished 19-4. Over the years Silver Creek teams have won 11 Sectionals and 2 Regionals. Unfortunately for the Dragons their 1st venture into the Sweet Sixteen caused them to run into what is generally regarded as one of, if not the, finest high school teams ever to play basketball in Indiana, the 1969 Indianapolis Washington Continentals with George McGinnis and Steve Downing. Their other Regional title came in 2000, Class 2A. The Lady Dragons have won 4 Sectional crowns, all for Coach Lisa Cook, between 1986 and 1997.

Our third Dragons are found at New Palestine. The Dragons had an excellent 21-3 season for Coach Carl Hughes in 1989. They have won 4 Sectionals. The Lady Dragons had 19-3 seasons in 1990 and 1993, winning Sectionals each year for Al Cooper, whose 1992 team added the school's 3rd Sectional title.

Our trio of Dragons. St. George, Beware!

One of Silver Creek's finest Dragons was Hall of Famer Steve Green.

Steve Green
Spring of 1971 was Bob Knight's first IU recruit, after a 3 yr. playing career at Silver Creek under his father, Ray...scored 1,404 points on teams that went 58-14, then 1,265 on IU teams that went 76-12...he and John Laskowski were the Chicago Bulls' top 2 picks in the 1975 draft, but Green opted to sign with Utah in the ABA....played 5 pro. yrs., 4 with the Indiana Pacers, before returning to school to get a degree in Dentistry...was an Academic All-American & winner of an NCAA postgrad Scholarship.

The gryphon (elsewhere called a griffin) was another legendary creature with the head, talons, and wings of an eagle and the body of a lion. The Gryphon is the name for the teams from one of our state's newest arrivals on the scene, the International School of Indianapolis. Another mythical bird was the Phoenix. It would live for 500 years and then ignite its own nest, burn fiercely, and be reduced to ashes. However, from those ashes a new, young phoenix would emerge to live for another 500 years before repeating the process. Although not an IHSAA member, the Booker T. Washington High School in Terre Haute has the Phoenix for its mascot.

A rendering of a gryphon

Two of our schools have selected Cadets as their mascot: Ft. Wayne Concordia, where the ROTC program has a strong and significant emphasis, and Cascade, where I think alliteration won the day. The Cascade Cadets in Hendricks County have won 6 Sectionals, and the Lady Cadets have added 2 more to the trophy case in Clayton. In the school's 1st year, 1965, Jon Holmes coached the Cadets to a 20-win season with only 4 losses. Ft. Wayne Concordia's Cadets won 19 of 24 games for Coach Glen Parrish in 1963, and his 1980 team went 18-5. In 1989 Parrish's Cadets won 22 of 28 games. Parrish completed his 35th year(!) as Cadets coach, replaced by Tim Reinking in 1998. Reinking's 1999 team won 21 of 24 games. The Cadets have won 5 Sectionals and 2 Regionals, the latter in 1989 and 2000 (3A).

Ft. Wayne South Side teams are the Archers, and their logo makes it clear that the inspiration for that name came from England and Robin Hood.

The Archers under Coach Gilbert Ward won 20 games and lost 7 in 1924. They were 22-6 in 1929 for Coach J. McClure, whose 1932 and 1935 teams turned in 18-5 and 19-5 marks. Burl Friddle coached the 1937 Archers to an 18-5 record, not bad, but followed by 3 very strong seasons, 29-3, 25-3, and 25-4.

From 1938 through 1940 the Archers won 79 games and lost only 10! Scott Wayne coached a strong 5-year stretch from 1944 through 1948, during which his South Side teams won 94 games and lost only 18, the best year being 1947's 23-2 mark. Don Reichert also put together a nice string of years, beginning with 1956's 21-7, followed by 21-6, 28-2, and 22-5 seasons: 92 wins and 20 losses for those 4 years. Reichert's 1966 and 1967 teams finished 18-8 and 24-4.

Murray Mendenhall II led the Archers to 21-5, 19-5, and 22-5 marks in 1978, 1979, and 1981. Terry Flynn coached the 1993 team to a sterling 25-2 season. Greg Taylor was coaching for the 3 years from 1995 through 1997 when his teams turned in 23-4, 20-5, and 24-2 seasons. Greg Taylor's 1995—1997 Archers rang up 67 wins against 11 losses, and his 2000 team won 20 of 24 games. All told the Archers have won 28 Sectionals, 13 Regionals, and 4 Semi-states. On their 4 trips to Indianapolis they have won the state championship 34-32 over Hammond in 1938, lost by 3 points to Mitchell in the afternoon game, captured their 2nd state championship over Crawfordsville in 1958, and again lost in the afternoon game, this time to Lafayette Jeff, in 1967.

South Side Archer graduate Tom Bolyard is honored in the Hall of Fame:

Tom Bolyard
Signed by Baltimore Bullets...Asst Coach, Ft Wayne North, Asst Coach Indiana University...Graduated as South Side's All-time leading scorer ... also held single game scoring record .. two-time all-stater ... led South Side to '58 state championship ... Parade All-American that year ... most valuable player in Indiana-Ohio all-star game ... also a track standout, running on state championship mile relay team in '58 ... 3 year starter at Indiana University, ending career as Hoosier's 10th all-time scorer ... IU most valuable player and captain in '63 ... All-Big 10

The Lady Archers at South Side have recently had some marvelous years of their own. From 2006 through 2008 they have won 65 games and lost only 10 for their coach Andy Rang. This included their only Sectional title, 2007, with a 23-2 record.

Nine more of our schools have each uniquely chosen a human as their mascot. These are the Jimtown Jimmies, the Shawe Memorial Hilltoppers, the Greenwood Woodmen, the Gary Wirt Troopers, the University School Trailblazers, the Hammond Gavit Gladiators, the Manchester Squires (the Middle School teams were the Pages), and the brand new Fall Creek Academy in Indianapolis, the Engineers.

The Jimtown Jimmies have won 2 Sectionals and followed each with a regional title. In 2004 they brought the Class 2A State Championship home with a 63-59 victory over the Brownstown Central Braves. Randy DeShone's charges finished a 25-2 season by handing the runner-up team only their 2nd loss in 29 games. The girls team has added another 5 Sectional titles to the school's trophy case as well as the 2007 2A Rensselaer Central Regional crown. That year they brought home the runner-up trophy from Indianapolis, Gene Johnson's 5 ending a fine 24-3 season with a loss to Heritage Christian's powerhouse. Proving that Hoosiers can shoot free throws with the best of them, the Lady Jimmies set a new national record for free throw percentage in 2007 hitting at a rate of 79.4 percent.

The Gary Wirt Troopers have won 2 Sectionals. James MacDonald's 1989 Troopers did so by defeating West Side, 60-53, and then Roosevelt, in overtime, 51-49. In the East Chicago Regional the Troopers knocked out Munster before themselves being sidelined by Central. They won 18 of 23 games. The Lady Troopers enjoyed a 13-4 season in 1980 for Coach Rodney Fisher. The Gladiators of Hammond Gavit have won 3 Sectionals as have the Lady Gladiators who also won a Regional, in 2001,

Class 3A. With Tom Spiva coaching, the team won 21 of 25 games. Manchester's Squires were covered earlier.

The Jimtown Jimmies, Gary Wirt Troopers, and Gavit Gladiators

Greenwood's Woodmen have captured 12 Sectionals between 1940 and 2002. Once a small school they are now, as is true of so many of the Indianapolis suburban high schools, large 4A participants. In 1940, when Greenwood was still a small, rural school, Alvin Schumm coached the Woodman to an undefeated regular season and their 1st Sectional crown. They did this by defeating Whiteland, Union Township, Masonic Home, and the home team at Franklin. Their lone loss in 25 games also came at Franklin in the 1st round of the Regional tournament, to North Vernon by 3 points. Everett Swank's teams finished 21-3 and 20-8 the next 2 years, creating a 3-year run of 65 wins and only 12 losses. Jack Nay's 1963 and 1965 teams won 20 of 24 games and 22 of 27. The Woodmen take their opponents into the Woodshed when they come to Greenwood for a game.

Recently Fall Creek Academy in Indianapolis has opened, with their teams called the Engineers. Not far away on 16th Street in Indianapolis is the newly established Herron High School, occupying the building that once served as the city's art museum. The Herron teams are Achaeans, a historical and literary choice. The Achaeans were one of the 4 main tribes of old Greece. The name was used by Homer to refer to all Greeks in his epic works, the *Iliad* and the *Odyssey*.

Rockville is located in beautiful Parke County, which refers to itself as the Covered Bridge Capital of the World. Thousands of visitors come to the area every fall to enjoy the Covered Bridge Festival, and they are rewarded by more of these relics of a bygone age than exist in any other county in America. One of the most unusual names found anywhere is found in one of our oldest schools. Rockville traces its roots to 1876 and calls their teams the Rox. As early as 1914 Jesse Wood's Rockville team won 18 games, losing only 6, and in 1920 Joe Royce's squad turned in a 20-11 mark. In 1930 F. M. Klayer coached the Rox to a superb 23-4 finish, and Walt Dove's 1959 team won 21 of 27 games. Larry Liddle's 1962 and 1963 Rox did even better, 25-2, followed by 23-3, Sectional championships captured each year. As recently as 2008 Rockville had a marvelous season, 24-3 for Dave Mahurin, winning the school's 14th Sectional crown in the process.

The Lady Rox have cut down the nets after 5 Sectionals and the 1981 Greencastle regional. For the 3 years beginning in 1978, Larry Merica's teams won an imposing 52 games and lost only 4, including back-to-back undefeated regular seasons. The Rox and the Lady Rox play their home games in the raucous Rockadome.

The Westfield Shamrocks had a fine 18-4 season for Coach Robert Moore in 1954. That fourth defeat came at the hands of the Fishers Tigers by a single basket, 58-56, in the semifinals of the Sheridan Sectional. In 1992 Ed Baker's team won 17 games and lost just 5. The Lady Shamrocks have won three Sectional titles, the first in 1976 with a 9-2 mark for Vicki Thomas. In 1999 Don Renihan's team put together an excellent 23-3 and allowing the Westfield girls to also win their lone Regional crown at the 3A level. His next year's team also did well, finishing 18-4. His third sectional nets were cut down in 2010, this time at the 4A level.

Closing out this section, it is fun to note that we have both a Jug Rox and a Rox as well as a Clover and a Shamrock, and that the Westfield football teams are usually called the Rocks while the Plymouth football teams are the Rockies! We have covered the other 3 schools elsewhere.

Rockville Rox   *Shoals Jug Rox*   *Cloverdale Clovers*   *Westfield Shamrocks*

Ben Davis undefeated 2009 State Champions and USA Today *designated National Champions*

Chapter 36

Interesting Lost Names:
Hopping 'Roos, Hissing Cobras, and More

Over the years we have also lost a few intriguing names (and 3 of our 4 Zebras!). For example, we no longer have any Kangaroos. Or Cobras. Or Wampus Cats. Wampus Cats? Of course, right in Cambridge City, as mentioned before. But what does a Wampus Cat look like? We asked that question in a previous chapter. Now for a few more details. Well, there seems to be some debate about the origin of the odd name. Originally the wampus cat was a creature of Cherokee lore, chiefly in Tennessee, but it is also apparent in several other states. Some people have even claimed to have seen one, claiming that it's a cat-like beast that walks on its hind legs and has glowing, hypnotic eyes. As conceived by Conway (Arkansas) High School, the Wampus Cat has 6 legs: "4 to move with the speed of light, 2 to fight with all their might." More to our point, here is how the Cambridge City Wampus Cat looked on a cheerleader's sweater:

The Cambridge City Wampus Cats are now Cambridge City Lincoln High School Golden Eagles. Houck photo of Yell sweater from exhibit courtesy IBHOF

The Kangaroos once represented Kirkland Township High School in Adams County; the Cobras hissed their way around Buck Creek High School in Tippecanoe County. Interestingly, at least to me since I once lived in Australia, is the fact that Kirkland's colors were green and gold, the same as those of the Australian National Rugby Team Kangaroos. Now, there are plenty of kangaroos in Australia, but none roaming free in Indiana that I know of. So why were Kirkland's teams called Kangaroos? The best answer I have received is that one night they were playing one of their rivals and getting a high percentage of the rebounds. Somebody said, "Those Kirkland boys jump like kangaroos." And it stuck. The Kangaroos have been playing hoops since at least 1918, and in 1924 Charles Hoag's team won 15 of 21 games. They also had 18-6 marks in 1940 for Frank Harper and in their last year before consolidation into Adams Central, 1949, for Don Arnold. They won their lone Sectional at Decatur in 1928. Bill Bryan's 15-9 squad beat Berne, Hartford Township, and Geneva and also won their 1st-round game against Pierceton in the Ft. Wayne Regional.

Kirkland, where the Kanga-roos jumped

Hopefully, there never have been nor ever will be Cobras slithering around our fair state. Nevertheless that's the name chosen by Buck Creek. Probably some of the "Don't Tread on Me" philosophy of our forefathers. The Buck Creek Cobras were red and black and never got that coveted sectional title.

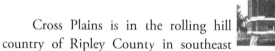

Buck Creek, where Cobras went to school

Cross Plains is in the rolling hill country of Ripley County in southeast Indiana, near the Ohio River and the point where Ohio, Indiana, and Kentucky meet. You can get to Cross Plains by driving through the wonderfully named towns of Friendship and Farmers Market or Pleasant (not to be confused with Pleasant Lake, Pleasant Ridge, Pleasant View, Pleasant Mills, Pleasantville, or Mt. Pleasant, either. As all Hoosiers know, Indiana is an extremely pleasant place!). When they had a high school, the Cross Plains Bobcats would have had some memorable games with their other neighbors, the Dillsboro Bulldogs. Perhaps they would have even gotten as far north as Kennard, where they would have encountered the Leopard Cats. The Cross Plains Bobcats won their lone Sectional at Batesville in 1942 by defeating Holton, Milan (in overtime), and Napoleon. The Dillsboro Bulldogs got theirs at Rising Sun in 1961. They eliminated North Dearborn, Lawrenceburg and the host Shiners before losing to the home team in the Connersville Regional tournament to finish 18-6 for Arlin Hooker. The Leopard Cats regrettably never captured that prized Sectional.

Kennard, home of the Leopard Cats, Houck photo of flag from exhibit courtesy IBHOF

Bobcats (sometimes called Bulldogs) also prowled at Marshall in Parke County wearing black and gold uniforms. They are now Turkey Run Warriors. I wish I knew more.

Mooreland's Bobcats in Henry County also favored black and gold. Is there a Purdue influence at work here? They won New Castle Sectional titles in 1923 and 1924, never an easy task. In 1924 Mooreland trounced Cadiz (a team that had won its 1st game by a 50-0 score over Sulphur Springs!), 43-19; doubled up Mt. Summit, 40-20; and edged the host Trojans, 24-21.They went on to win a game in the Ft. Wayne Regional, beating Shelbyville, 30-25, before being sent home to Henry County by South Bend. The next year the Bobcats trounced Lewisville 43-5, held the Trojans to 8 points while scoring 19 themselves, and closed it out with similar scores against Knightstown, 21-13, and Spiceland, 20-12. They also turned in an 18-5 season for Coach Dan Waterfill in 1961. They are now Blue River Valley Vikings.

The Moores Hill Bobcats, (or was it Bob Cats? I have to be careful here, remembering the Columbus North reaction to my faux pas about the Bull Dogs) wore purple and white uniforms before becoming South Dearborn Knights. Moores Hill has another special place in Indiana history. Moores Hill College was opened in 1885 with a building called Carnegie Hall after benefactor Andrew Carnegie. After the college was moved to Evansville in 1919 and renamed Evansville College (Evansville University in 1967), Carnegie Hall was utilized as Moores Hill High School. Unfortunately, they never came home from a Sectional with the top prize.

Moores Hill High School and Carnegie Hall

There were also black-and-gold uniformed Bobcats representing Forest in Clinton County. Herbert Brammell's 1934 Bobcats won 20 games and lost only 3. L. H. Victor's 1947 team won 19 and lost 3, and his 1950 through 1953 squads won a total of 52 games while losing 16, the best year being the last, 18-4. The school's last season before becoming Clinton Central Bulldogs was 1959 and Coach Mick Owens' Bobcats turned in a fine 20-5 record. In Vigo county the purple and gold Bobcats of West Terre Haute never won a Sectional title, but they did have at least 1 season to remember: 1956, when Dick Campbell's team won 16 of the 20 games played. We have previously reviewed the Lancaster Central Bobcats in Wells County.

There were Tomcats in Jay County at Madison Township High School and in Randolph County at Spartanburg. The latter Tomcats had several outstanding seasons, including 18-6 under Coach Harold Wakefield in 1942, 22-4 and 19-7 for

Tracy Turner 5 and 6 years later. Howard Rust took over as coach in 1948 and led his team to a 21-4 record but Lloyd Mitchell's charges topped that, 21-2 in 1954. Finally, Coach Phil Sprague's Tomcats had another excellent record in 1957, 20-3.

Spartanburg High SchooL

There were also Black Cats at Terre Haute Garfield and, for a while, Polecats in Poling, both covered elsewhere. We even had 2 River Rats, one representing Moscow and the other Newberry.

Newberry, home of the River Rats

The Redkey Wolves prowled the countryside in Jay County. Their 1st Sectional title came at Hartford City in 1939 with wins over Madison Township, the home team Airedales, and Portland for Coach Cleon Hutchison. At the Huntington Regional the Wolves dropped a 3-point decision to Ft. Wayne South Side to finish 21-5. Their 2nd Sectional title was earned in 1952, also at Hartford City, with wins over Poling, Gray, Bryant, and Portland. At the Marion Regional Redkey ousted Huntington before losing a heartbreaking 55-54 decision to the home team Giants. Marion would lose by 4 points to Muncie Central, that year's state champion. The Wolves were 5 points away from that title themselves!

The Redkey Wolf and Bridgeton School, home of the Raccoons

Still remembered in Hamilton County are the Wolves of Walnut Grove. Originally alive, the wolf that served as the school's mascot met a skilled taxidermist, and his stuffed body in its glass case occupied a place of honor in the school's main hallway and was always prominently displayed at home games. We'll discuss the Walnut Grove Wolves and their competition in more detail later.

Walnut Grove High School

The wolf and cheerleaders, circa 1952, courtesy of a former student of Walnut Grove High

We also once had Jaguars in Jackson Center (or Jackson Township, in Wells County) who won 13 of 17 games for Bill Hannah in 1949. The Otters in Otter Creek, the Bridgeton Raccoons, and the Morocco and Beaver Dam Beavers, are all covered elsewhere. In 1947–52, there were Otters at Jeffersonville Taylor.

Beavers tromped around at Huron in Lawrence County, where Beaver Creek winds its way through the town, and at Merom in Sullivan County. The Huron Beavers won 12 of 15 games for Vernon Crane in 1934, 16 of 21 and 15 of 20 for Robert Edwards in 1953 and 1955, and 13 of 17 for James Dunbar in 1960.

Of course, the king of the jungle was not forgotten, either. At least 14 of our now-closed schools chose Lions as their mascots, including Maxwell in Hancock County, which has become a Greenfield Central Cougar along with the Greenfield Tigers. Quite a catfight there. Maxwell did win 1 Sectional title, in 1941, for Bob Moore with wins over the Eden Flyers, 53-38; the New Palestine Dragons, 30-27; and the Mt. Comfort Buccaneers, 35-22.

The South Bend LaSalle and Maxwell Lion and the Greenfield Central Cougar

My favorites among the closed schools are the Lions of Lucerne and the Lyons Lions, covered earlier. The Liberty Center Lions, now Southern Wells Raiders, had many memorable seasons under a variety of coaches. As early as 1911 Sylvester Miller coached the Lions to a 9-4 mark. Herman Snyder's 1916 team won 21 of 25 games and played in the state finals at Indiana University, defeating Elkhart by 3 points before being eliminated by eventual State Champion Lafayette Jefferson in the next round rather decisively. In 1924 there were four 8-team Regional tournaments, each of which sent 4 single-game winners to the state finals at Indiana University. Austin Smith's Liberty Center team beat Bunker Hill at Ft. Wayne to get back to the State Finals, where they lost their 1st-round game to the eventual state champions, Martinsville. His next 2 teams won 21 and 17 games respectively while losing 5 each year. Ralph Strait's 1930 and 1931 squads went 18-3 and 16-2 and Elmer Hampton's 1936 edition went 19-4. Albert Harshbarger's 1940 team won 21 of 25 games, and Ernest Curtis coached the Lions to 22-4 and 21-4 seasons in 1942 and 1943. This was followed by Ira McBride's 1944 team with its 20-5 record. A 3-year mark of 63 and 13, 4 years out of 5 with 20 or more wins. Grrrowllll! The early 60s saw another fine 3-year run for Coach Richard Butt, 59-10 over that period with the best record being 21-3 in 1963. The Liberty Center Lions brought 8 Sectional titles to their consolidation with Southern Wells.

The Liberty Township Lions in Porter County wore blue and gold colors as they won 20 of 23 games in 1931 for Coach George Lowry, but they never won a Sectional title. South Bend LaSalle's Lions won 7 Sectionals and 3 Regionals. George Leonakis' 1971 and 1977 teams went 21-3 and 24-4. George Griffith's 1980-82 Lions won 62 games and lost only 15. Johnnie Johnson's Lady Lions went 21-4 in 1990 and they have won 3 sectionals and 2 Regionals.

The red and white LaGrange Lions ran off 4 straight Sectional titles from 1926 through 1929, all at home, and added the 1933 and 1954 Kendallville championships as well. Brownsville's red and black Lions won their only Sectional title in 1946 at

La Grange High School

Connersville with wins over Brookville, 31-27; Springfield, 34-33; the host Spartans, 34-28; and Harrisburg, 35-28, before being edged by Milroy in the 1st round of the Rushville Regional, 40-39.

Lawrence County was home to the blue and gold Fayetteville Lions. Although the Lions never won a Sectional championship, they did have some very good seasons. Orrin Flynn's 1940 squad won 18 of 21 games and Wendell Nikirk's 1967 and 1968 teams finished 17-4 and 20-3.

Clark Township in Johnson County is now a part of the Whiteland Warriors. Pre-consolidation these Lions also had several strong years. They were 19-7 for Coach

Harry Richey in 1929, and in 1945 and 1946 Coach Otto Hindman led his team to 17-4 and 16-4 marks. Then came an impressive 3-year streak beginning in 1951 when the Lions went 19-4, 20-4, and 17-5, the 1st 2 seasons coached by Bill Doig and the last one by Charles Ray. They also went 17-5 for Coach Ted Thompson in 1961. Their lone Sectional championship came in 1953 when the Lions defeated Whiteland, Nashville, and Greenwood at Franklin.

The black and gold Lions of Hazleton had an outstanding season in Gibson County in 1933, winning 27 games and losing only 2. They also won their only Sectional championship, at Owensville. The Lions defeated the Francisco Owls 20-12, got by the Elite from Haubstadt 18-14, and put the wood to Oakland City and Princeton. In the Evansville Regional they defeated Central 15-11 and Boonville 25-13. Their 2nd loss was a tough 2-pointer to Bedford, 26-24, in the 1st round of the Sweet Sixteen at Butler Fieldhouse. As Martinsville, that year's state champion, only beat Bedford by 4 points, Hazleton was clearly very competitive with the best the state had to offer that year. Their coach was Howard Decker. As covered elsewhere Hazleton and Patoka became the White River Rapids in 1963 and later became Princeton Tigers.

There were also red and white Lions at Lawrence High School in Marion County before they became Bears as Lawrence Central in 1942. The Saluda Lions in Jefferson County had a 15-6 season for Delbert King in 1953, but they never won a Sectional title. The Versailles Lions have been covered earlier.

Several different breeds of dogs were also evident in schools now closed as compared to the names in use now (although, as we have seen, Bulldogs were and are a popular choice). We had the Bainbridge Pointers, the Tippecanoe Police Dogs, and 2 variations of airedales (with imaginative spelling), the Mt. Ayr Ayrdales and the Hartford City Airedales. Those Bainbridge Pointers had several marvelous years. They were 18-4 for Coach Ebert Allen in 1917. This team had their 1st undefeated regular season in 1928 for Coach Frank Pruitt, going 20-1. That 1 loss was a 3-pointer to Greencastle in the Sectional. In 1959 they were 26-1 and made it to the Sweet Sixteen under Coach Ed Longfellow. To get there the Pointers beat Cloverdale by 25, Belle Union by 15, and Reelsville by 16 at Greencastle. In the Covington Regional they ousted Rockville by 13 and Crawfordsville by 12. They had yet to be seriously tested and were still undefeated. Sadly it was a different story in the Lafayette Semi-state. The Pointers ran into a strong Logansport team and lost by a 76-62 count to the Berries. The 1964 team won 21 of 24 games for Coach Kurt Grass. Hall of Fame coach Pat Rady's teams had back-to-back records of 23-3 in 1966 and 1967. (Close inspection of the Bainbridge banner at the Indiana Basketball Hall of Fame also reveals a fireman's helmet in the upper-left-hand corner. I have not yet had its relevance revealed to me. Were they once Dalmatians?)

Houck photo from exhibit courtesy IBHOF

Jeff Blue is Bainbridge's representatives in the Hall of Fame:

Jeff Blue

Still holds Putnam County career records for scoring (1,709 pts) and rebounding (953 rebounds)...27.6 ppg scoring average led Bainbridge to Lafayette Semi-state appearance...voted all-county, all-state, and member of Indiana All-star team...played for Tony Hinkle at Butler where he was all-conference three times and team MVP twice...established single-season and career rebounding records...led Butler to NCAA tourney with 22-6 regular season record...named Indiana Collegiate Conference's outstanding player after '64-'65 season...drafted by Boston Celtics.

The Mt. Ayr Ayrdales won their only Sectional at Monon in 1944 for Coach Herman Hall by defeating Rensselaer 35-14, Brook 27-23, DeMotte 18-15, and Goodland 38-24. They are now North Newton Spatans.

The Hartford City Airedales were coached by the great Wingate star Homer Stonebreaker for 2 years, his 1920 edition having a wonderful 27-5 season. They won the Hartford City Sectional by taking out Decatur 49-22, humbling Monroe 39-21, routing Bluffton 52-19, and lighting up Ossian 39-15. This qualified the Airedales for a trip to the finals at Bloomington where the competition was a bit stiffer. Still they acquitted themselves very well, defeating the Washington Hatchets, 23-19, and Milroy, 34-24, before losing to Lafayette Jefferson, 21-16, in the semi-finals. Not a bad season by any standard. Ten years later under Maurice Kennedy the Airedales won 23 of 26 games and another Sectional crown. Coach J. B. Good led the 1933 and 1934 teams to 21-5 and 24-2 marks, both years capturing Sectional titles. The 1934 team also picked off the tough Ft. Wayne Regional with wins over Ossian, 31-17, and Huntington, 32-23. In Indianapolis the drive continued with a 21-16 beating of the Princeton Tigers. In the next round they were in turn sent home by Logansport, 21-12. No disgrace, that, however: the Berries won their state championship the next day. Claude Weeks led the 1953 and 1995 Airedales to Regional crowns, and his 1957 five finished 23-2. How 'bout them dawgs!

Hartford City High School, a "dog house" for the Airedales, from a Houck photo from exhibit courtesy IBHOF

Monument City in Huntington County fielded the Greyhounds. The Purple and Gold had been playing basketball since at least 1908, and although they never brought the nets home from a Sectional, their 1946 team coached by Leslie Wilburn finished 18-4 and their last team in 1953 went 21-4 for Willard Barnes. At Boston in Wayne County there were Terriers in blue and gold uniforms. Although they never won a

Sectional, the Terriers put together a respectable 14-6 season in 1956 for Jim Hunt. They are now Richmond Red Devils.

In Franklin County the Brookville teams were called the Green Devils for a

Boston and Monument City High Schools

while, but then the team name was changed to the Greyhounds. Before returning to his alma mater, Hanover College, where he had such outstanding success, John Collier coached those Greyhounds. He was there from 1956 until 1966, a truly Golden Age for the Green and White; there was never a period like it before or after for the Greyhounds. Between 1958 and 1966 Collier's teams won 174 games and lost only 41. The 1958 team had an undefeated regular season, finishing 24-1. From 1961 through 1963 they were 18-4 followed by 19-2 and 17-6. The 1964 edition finished 20-5, and the next year Collier's team won 25 and lost only 2, making it to the Sweet Sixteen only to run into the Billy Keller-led State Champion Washington Continentals in the 1st round. In his last year at the helm in Brookville, Collier's team finished 22-3. A great run for a great man.

John Collier
Twice leading scorer and captain at Guilford H. S. ... 4-year letter-winner ... MVP as senior in 1944 ... at Hanover College started every game in his 4 years ... captain and MVP as junior ... helped Hanover win its first Hoosier Col. Conf. championship ... coached Vevay HS from 1951-56 and Brookville 1956-66 ... named coach of the year 3 times by Southeastern Indiana Coaches-Officials-Principals Assn... became Hanover basketball coach in 1966, athletic director 2 yrs later ... coached Panthers to five berths in the NAIA national tournament ... 3 times coach of the year in the Hoosier Collegiate Conference. His son, Steve, was Mr. Basketball in 1974.

Thanks again to Bob Chance, I recently learned an interesting fact about John, unrelated to basketball. When he was in the navy John played some baseball. He was a catcher. When he went to the Groton, Connecticut, submarine base, he replaced the catcher then on the team because of that man's impending transfer to another base. That catcher's name? Berra. Yogi Berra. How many catchers do you know who have displaced Yogi Berra from the line-up?

Collier's own Guilford High School sometimes called their teams the Quakers, sometimes the Wildcats. In 1942, with the coaching reins split between Curly Young and Garland Frazier, the team won 18 games and lost only 2. Earlier they won their lone Sectional title at Rising Sun in 1934. Their record that year was 15-7, and the coaching was done by Lewis Jacob. Guilford was 1st consolidated into North Dearborn, and then North Dearborn was consolidated into East Central.

The Brookville Greyhounds

From Wildcats/Quakers to Vikings to Trojans and for John Collier to Vevay Warriors, Brookville Greyhounds, and Hanover College Panthers. What a distinguished career!

Whitewater Township, also in Franklin County, fielded the Elkhorns, who won 21 and lost only 3 games for Coach Larry Riebsomer in 1962 and are now also Franklin County Wildcats.

Similarly, though Bison still roam in Benton County, there is something so appropriate about the Buffalo Bisons that once did roam in White County that I cannot leave them out at this point either. Those Bisons had pretty good years in 1945, 1946, and 1956, with records of 15-4, 16-5, and 17-6, the latter under Coach Jack Hart. They are now Vikings at North White High School.

The Franklin County Wildcat

Although we still have Rams in Paoli, we have lost 2 of these Ram teams, those at Grovertown in Starke County and Indianapolis Chartrand Rams. Groverton's teams were also called the Green Streaks with colors of green and gold. They had good seasons in 1942, 12-4 for Donald Wahl; the next year, 14-3 for Cal Kane, and 18-3 for B.R. Berkshire in 1950. They also had a nice string of 17-7, 16-9, 15-7, and 17-6 winning seasons for Larry Richey from 1957 through 1960. They were never able to win a Sectional title. They are now Oregon-Davis Bobcats. Chartrand, never Sectional champions either in their short, 6-year life, had a 14-5 season for Harold Schoen in 1967. The school is now part of Roncalli, the Rebels, along with the Sacred Heart and Kennedy Spartans.

The North White Viking

Finally, we also had Otters for a brief period at Jeffersonville Taylor. Opened only from 1947 until 1952, about all we know about Taylor is their intriguing mascot.

Chapter 37

Aces and Devils:
From the Top of the Deck to the Underworld

Now we can turn our attention to the other mascots adopted by closed schools. Here again, the mix of names is somewhat different from what we have now. We have already noticed how many of our pre-consolidation schools selected something related to basketball for their team names. In many cases this is because basketball was the only interscholastic sport played. These schools were small. As late as 1954 something close to 400 of the schools in our state tournament were smaller than Milan with its 161 students. These schools had been even smaller when they first took up the notion of playing other schools and attracting fans, and eventually vying for the championship not of a 7-or-8-team league, or even a 15-or-16-school county, but of the entire state of Indiana, trying to be the best among, at the peak time, almost 800 rivals. Basketball took only 5 starters and could be managed with a short bench if need be. Then perhaps baseball was added, football, even if only the 6-man variety, but for years it was basketball that was the life and death of the school, the community, the surrounding farms. No wonder we had many team names referring to our favorite pastime.

We have also seen that many of the team names chosen reflected where the town was located, what its main reason for being was, or what amused its citizens: the Stinesville Quarry Lads, the Monon Railroaders, the Elnora Owls, the Epsom Salts, the Cadiz Spaniards, the Morocco Beavers and so forth. We have looked at all of those schools that turned to the animal kingdom for their inspiration or to our Indian heritage. We have seen that those choices added up to some 80 percent of those 800 or so no longer with us. Here's the beginning of the story of the rest.

At one time we had 17 Aces. Now we have none. Perhaps my favorite would be the Decker Aces. Who wouldn't want to hold a deck o' aces? As it happened, those Decker Aces in their blue and gold uniforms were also called the Hilltoppers, and, under either name, they won 18 and lost 7 in 1941 and were 18-6 in 1944 for Coach Don Davis. They were also winners of 21 games while losing only 4 in 1951, Don Palmer then coaching. The Decker Aces won 2 Sectional championships before being consolidated into South Knox, becoming Spartans.

In Perry County the town of Bristow was originally called Slabtown. According to James H. Mosby in *A Living History of Perry County*, this was because the town was built on low ground and slabs from the local saw mill were used to make streets and roads. Bristow's colors were purple and gold and their teams were called the Purple Aces. They won 4 Sectionals between 1926 and 1934.

The green-and-white-clad Arcola Aces (also called the Greyhounds) in Allen County won 15 of 18 games for their coach Dwight Byerly in 1931 and experienced an outstanding undefeated season 10 years later under Coach Bennie Decker, finishing 20-1. That loss was to Elmhurst, 34-27, in the Ft. Wayne Sectonal. Charlie Sharp's team was 17-5 in 1948. They are now Carroll Chargers.

The Mackey Aces enjoyed a fine season in 1962 for Coach Howard Butler, finishing 18-4. They also captured the 1946 Princeton

Arcola High School

Sectional with wins over Mt. Olympus, Oakland City, Ft. Branch (in overtime) and Patoka. Their colors were blue and gold or blue and white, and they are now Wood Memorial Trojans. The Rock Creek Aces, who wore red and black, have been playing basketball since at least 1911. They won 15 of 20 games for Coach Burton Stephens in 1929 and 15 of 21 for Eddie Roth in 1955. They are now Huntington North Vikings. In Grant County the Van Buren Aces had terrific seasons way back in 1909 and 1910, 13-1 and 11-2. They were 18-5 in 1937 for Coach Clyde Miller and finished 19-5 under Jim Weddle 4 years later. In their last year before joining others to form Eastbrook Phil Jung's Aces won 15 of 20 games.

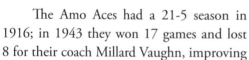

A trio of Aces: Van Buren, Rock Creek, and Mackey schools

The Amo Aces had a 21-5 season in 1916; in 1943 they won 17 games and lost 8 for their coach Millard Vaughn, improving on that the next year to finish 17-6 for Amos Shelton. In 1949 Wendell Scudder's Aces turned in a 19-5 record and Morris Pollard, who took over in 1950, led the Aces to a 19-4 mark that year and to a 20-5 record in 1953. Scudder returned to Amo in 1955 and led the Aces of 1958 through 1960 to 21-3, 19-3, and 17-3 finishes. Amo won 5

Sectionals between 1928 and 1958 before consolidating into Cascade. Unfortunately they ran into Martinsville in the 1st round of the Bloomington Regional in 1928 when the Artesians would be runner-up to state champion Muncie, losing the final game 13-12, and that was as close as they would come to advancing further. Nevertheless, a memorable season for all Amo Ace fans.

Amo High School and an Amo Aces Pennant Houck pennant photo from exhibit courtesy IBHOF

Ashley's Aces won 17 of 22 games for Dwight Graber, who was coaching in 1962. They also captured Sectional championships in 1946 at Auburn and in 1964 at Angola. In each of their Regional appearances, the Aces represented their school and town well, winning the 1st round in 1946 over Kendallville, 43-41, and over Adams Central 62-57 in 1964. Stendal is notable for, among other things, being a site for many ghost sightings. The Stendal Aces put some scare in their opponents when they captured 3 Sectionals: Petersburg in 1931, Jasper in 1932, and Huntingburg in 1939.

In Spencer County Dale fielded the Golden Aces, clad in gold and black. Their teams won 11 Sectionals between 1934 and 1968, including 4 in a row beginning in 1937 and 3 straight beginning in 1956. From 1963 through 1966, the Del Harris-coached Golden Aces won 71 games and lost just 19. Dale Hall of Famer

Ashley High, home of the Aces

Roger Kaiser's citation:

Roger Kaiser
Roger scored 1,649 career points at Dale High School as a 4-year varsity player. He was chosen as a member of the Indiana All-Star team in 1957. Following graduation he was a 3-year starter at Georgia Tech and was selected Most Valuable Player in the All-Southeast Conference for two years. He served his team as captain for two years and was named All American in 1960. He played ABA pro ball with Washington and Philadelphia.

The Rockport Democrat reported that Dale organized the school's 1st girls basketball team with Eugenia Strassell as coach on September 24, 1920. One other fact, of dubious relevance, is that Florence Henderson was born in Dale.

Dale High School

Our other Aces were at Brook and Freedom, both covered elsewhere, Greene Township (Parke County), Laconia, Prairie Township (Tipton County), and Quincy. The Laconia Aces won 18 of 21 games played in 1958 with Jerome Urich coaching. Their colors were Columbia blue and white. Eventually they were consolidated into South Central, becoming Rebels. Prairie Township's Aces in Tipton County wore purple and white and had consecutive seasons of 17-5 and 18-4 for Coach Felix Chambers in 1958 and 1959. They are now Tri-Central Trojans. Quincy's Aces wore old gold and blue and are now Cloverdale Clovers.

Kingman's teams were the Black Aces, who wore orange and black uniforms and won their only Sectional in 1936 at Attica. The Aces defeated Hillsboro, 32-24, West Lebanon, 37-24, and then edged the home team Ramblers, 27-25 in overtime, before claiming the crown with a 25-16 count over Veedersburg.

A Quincy letter sweater. Houck photo from exhibit, courtesy IBHOF

Curiously, there were also Black Aces (sometimes called the Indians as well) representing Newtown High School in Fountain County. Both schools are now Fountain Central Mustangs, Newtown having passed through Richland Township as Red Devils en route.

Kingman, Home of the Black Aces

Interestingly, the most popular team names of our consolidated schools were the 33 that involved the underworld. We had 17 Devils of the red variety, 11 more blue, 1 green, and 4 Demons, one of the blue persuasion. We have discussed the French Lick Red Devils (with the area's Pluto Water), as well as the Brazil, Auburn, and Hope Red Devils. The New Augusta Red Devils took that name with them when they were consolidated into Indianapolis Pike. The other Red Devils were found at Aurora, New Bethel (Wanamaker), Camden, Cicero, Otterbein, Jefferson, Judyville, Kendallville, Luce Township (Spencer County), Michigan City (Elston), Richland Township (Fountain County), and Wadesville (and for a part of the time at Andrews, also known as the Cardinals and covered elsewhere). We have also covered the Dover and Oxford Blue Devils elsewhere. The other 9 were fielded at Ashboro (for a time, also called the Shamrocks), Stoney Creek, Van Buren Township, North Salem, North Vernon, Kentland, Vernon, Indianapolis Shortridge, and Gary Froebel. The Green Devils were from Veedersburg, the Demons from Greens Fork and Fortville, and the Blue Demons represented Leesburg. For a brief period, from 1923 through 1934, we also had Demons at Deacon—which is reminiscent of the Demon Deacons of Wake

Forest University—in Cass County when that school was consolidated into Young America, going from Demons to Yankees.

The Aurora Red Devils in their red and white uniforms made it to the Sweet Sixteen in 1926 under Coach A. E. Abshire. The road to Indianapolis had run through Rushville, where the Devils upended 2 powerhouses of Indiana basketball, Richmond and Connersville, but they lost in the 1st round of the Sweet Sixteen against Frankfort.

Harold Ritter's 1954 and 1955 teams won 19 and 17 games, losing 2 and 4. Harold Hickman coached the 1957 Red Devils to a 22-4 mark. Carl Hughes led the 1966 team to a 21-5 finish, and Bill Slayback's 1976 and 1977 Devils each won 22 games, and lost 8. The 1977 team won the Connersville Regional by defeating Greensburg by 2 points and Union County by 4. At the Indianapolis Semi-state, the Devils edged Lawrence Central in overtime but Columbus East won the title by a 4-point margin. In total Aurora won 23 Sectional titles and 6 Regionals before they were consolidated into South Dearborn. The Lady Devils added 2 Sectional nets to the school's trophy case in the brief period between the beginning of official state tournament play and the 1979 consolidation.

Aurora Red Devils are now South Dearborn Knights. Houck photo from exhibit courtesy IBHOF

The Camden Red Devils, who were joined by the Rockfield Indians in 1949, won 3 Sectional titles: 1934 and 1935 at Delphi and 1949 at Flora. The 1934 team defeated Monroe Township, Carrollton and Cutler. They went on to win their 1st round game at the Logansport Regional, over Peru, 19-17. They lost their next game to the home team Berries. How did the Berries fare in Indianapolis? They won it all: their 1st and only state championship. Quite a year for Camden! Back at Logansport the next year the Devils dropped a toughie to Monticello, 24-22. The 1949 squad again won their 1st rounder at Logansport, 34-30, over Washington Township before the slipper fit Brookston instead in the final game. They also played a rare tie game as late as 1959. They are now Oracles at Delphi.

Losantville and Camden Schools

Losantville's Red Devils, coached by Russell Warren, won their only Sectional title at Union City in 1923 with a 38-11 trouncing of Winchester, almost doubling up on Spartanburg 29-16, slipping past Stoney Creek 24-20, and winning it all over Saratoga 32-20. They also had a very good 17-2 season for James Barker in 1927. They have become Union Rockets. From the underworld to the heavens!

Michigan City Elston's Red Devils won 11 Sectionals and 3 Regionals, including 1992's fine 23-6 season for Coach Dan Steinke. The Lady Devils have added 5 Sectionals and 1 Regional to the school's trophy case, putting together an undefeated regular season, 22-1, for Donnie Thomas in 1990.

Prior to becoming Elston in 1971, the Red Devils, who began play in 1910, had an illustrious history as well. They won 29 Sectional titles, 8 Regionals, and the 1966 state championship at the newly renamed Hinkle Fieldhouse in Indianapolis. Doug Adams' Devils defeated the Tech Titans 63-52 to finish 26-3. The Devils' first 20-win season came in 1935 for Coach T. A. Gill, 23-2. In 1954 Ishmael Osborne's squad won 22 of 25 games, and the next year Ralph Hooker's team went 20-6; his 1957 team

Two versions of the Michigan City and Elston Red Devils

won 20 and lost 5. Hall of Famer Doug Adams took the reins in 1958, a job he held into the Elston years, ending in 1977. His teams won Sectional crowns every year from 1958 through 1975. From 1958 through 1972 Adams-led Devil teams won 323 games and lost only 64! When Elston and Rogers (the Raiders, covered elsewhere) combined in 1996, the new, or recreated, Michigan City High School teams began to be called the Wolves (perhaps influenced by the University of Michigan Wolverines). The Lady Wolves won 22 of 24 games for Gary Collins in 2007 and followed that with 20-6 mark and a Sectional title in 2008. Doug Adams' Hall of Fame Citation:

Doug Adams
Devoted his high school (Hammond '43) and college (Ball State '49) energies to football, cross country and basketball. His junior varsity teams won 88 percent of their games over eight years. He was named Michigan City's varsity basketball coach in 1957. He owns 18 sectional crowns, 8 regionals and 1 semi-state. His 1966 team won the state championship. He garnered 12 conference championships in 17 of his 20 years. He was twice named Indiana Coach of the Year, once in 1966 by the media and again in 1972 by coaches.

Richland Township's Red Devils in Fountain County won 3 Sectional championships in their relatively brief 24-season existence. The 1st came for Coach Robert Brock in 1950 at Attica, where his teams conquered Wallace rather easily, before edging Attica by 3 points, and Covington by 1. His 1952 team got theirs at Covington in similar fashion. They won their 1st game easily, over Perrysville, then won a 3-pointer over Williamsport and beat the home team in an overtime thriller, 56-54. They went on to win their 1st-round game over the Rosedale Hot Shots before being sent home by Greencastle in the final game of the Lafayette Regional. Paul Moore's 1957 team brought home the school's 3rd Sectional title in similar fashion to the other 2. At Attica the Devils beat Williamsport Bingy Bombers and West Lebanon by 7 points each before claiming the title with a 75-73 win over Veedersburg. They won 15 games and lost 3.

The Otterbein Red Devils had an undefeated regular season, 24-1, in 1957 under Coach Dallas Sandifer, winning the Fowler Sectional with victories over Boswell, Ambia, Gilboa and Oxford. That 1 loss came at Lafayette in the Regional, by 7 points to Jeff, and Jeff went on to win the state championship. No one in Otterbein will soon forget how good their Devils were that year! The Devils also turned in a 20-3 mark for James Elbert in 1963, and finished 22-2 with Kirby Overman at the helm in 1965. Between 1924 and 1965 Otterbein won 9 Sectionals and the 1924 Regional at Purdue University when they beat Crawfordsville, 18-12, and Lebanon, 18-16. Otterbein's Dick Atha is a Hall of Famer:

Dick Atha

Dick was a 4-year varsity performer at Otterbein High School where he led the Red Devils in scoring his final 2 campaigns. He was named outstanding freshman scholar at Indiana State in 1950. For the next three seasons, "Iron Man" started every game for Coach John Longfellow's Sycamores. He was 3-time Indiana College Conference All-Star. After his sophomore year, he played on the U.S. team that won the gold in the 1951 Pan Am Games. He played professionally for the Knicks and then the Pistons before an injury ended his career. He returned to Benton County to coach Oxford for 10 years, then became principal of the new Benton Central school, later serving as athletic director.

Jefferson is located near Deerfield in Randolph County. Bob Reid coached 3 straight Jefferson Red Devil teams to records of 18-7, 19-8, and 17-7 between 1948 and 1950. They were known as the "gymless wonders," although they actually shared a gym with Saratoga and played their home games there. Jefferson's 1949 team won the

Hartford City Sectional defeating Dunkirk's Speedcats, 26-18; Portland's Panthers, 41-27; Pennville's Bulldogs, 42-28; and Roll's Rollers, 51-36. They then became the only county school to win a regional tournament, defeating Huntington Catholic 41-34 and Lancaster Central 36-33 at Huntington. Although the Red Devils lost to New Castle 49-43 in the Muncie Semi-state, they created memories for their school and community that have lasted a lifetime. Not bad for a school that only had 57 students in the upper 4 grades, just 22 of whom were boys! Cicero's Red Devils will be covered later.

Otterbein and Jefferson High Schools

The Gary Froebel Blue Devils won 10 Sectionals, 4 Regionals, and the 1941 Hammond Semi-state. As early as 1927 Froebel had an undefeated regular season, finishing 24-1 for Homer Osborn. That 1 loss was to Gary Emerson in the East Chicago Sectional and Emerson would go all the way to the State Finals before being ousted by the eventual State Champion Martinsville. In 1941 the Devils, under Hank Mantz, got all the way to the Final Four before losing to state runner-up Madison, 29-27. Mantz's 1950 and 1951 Devil teams won 50 games and lost only 4; Mickey Sofiak coached the 1962 Froebel squad to a 24-3 mark. His 1964 and 1965 squads won 42 games and lost 7.

In his book *The Origins of the Jump Shot*, John Christgau has this to say about one of those 1941 Froebel Blue Devil players:

> *His full name was* Davage "Dave" Minor, *but Gary, Indiana sportswriters called him "The Wheelhorse of Steel City." He began shooting the 1st jumpers seen around the Great Lakes in December of 1937 in his high school gym in Gary. By 1941, the shot was so unstoppable he used it to take the Froebel High School Blue Devils all the way to the Final Four of the Indiana State Tournament, the mother of them all. Eventually, he starred with the old Oakland Bittners of the AAU, and he was one of the 1st blacks signed in the NBA.*

Indianapolis Shortridge was the first high school in the city, begun in 1864 under the auspices of Dartmouth College graduate Caleb Mills, who was also a teacher and 1st principal of what was to become Wabash College. The school was first known as Indianapolis High School.

The Indianapolis Shortridge Blue Devils (also Felix the Cat, as all will recall, I'm sure) had long been active and often successful in sports, including basketball. As has been mentioned Shortridge claimed an unofficial Indiana state championship as early as 1905, a year in which they also defeated the purported champions of Iowa and

Illinois. They also played in the state tournament at Indiana University in 1913, losing to South Bend, and made the Sweet Sixteen in 1931 under new coach Ken Peterman, losing by 1 point to the Washington Hatchets.

The Blue Devils won 21 of 24 games in 1933 and again played in the state tournament, defeating Kokomo's Wildkats and the Vincennes Alices before losing in the quarterfinals to the Greencastle Tiger Cubs by 3 points. That Blue Devil team was led by Hall of Famer Bill Seward, whose citation follows:

Bill Seward
At 6-7, a towering high school center in 1932 and 1933 ... led Shortridge High School to Final Four in 1933 ... high scorer in state finals although only playing in 3 of 4 games ... All-State ... Gimbel Award winner ... received Shortridge's award as top scholar-athlete ... 3-year letter winner at Purdue University ... twice a Big-10 champion, playing with fellow Hall of Famers Norm Cottom and Jewell Young ... with a degree in mechanical engineering, he began a long and successful career in industry.

The 1933 Shortridge Blue Devils with Bill Seward easily identified

Ken Peterman coached Shortridge teams from 1931 until 1946, replaced by Jerry Steiner for 4 years and Cleon Reynolds, 1951 until 1963. During that time Shortridge and Crispus Attucks played memorable regular season, city, and state tournament games. Those Indianapolis Sectionals were shoot-outs at the Fieldhouse, with several teams struggling to get to the Regional and 15,000 rabid fans in attendance. In 1967, 1968, and 1969 George Theofanis was coaching when the Blue Devils won 23 games and lost 6, then won 25 and lost 5, and finally went 22 and 3. That's 70 wins and 14 losses against the best competition the state had to offer. Shortridge won 10 of those Indianapolis Sectionals between 1925 and 1969, the last 3 at the Coliseum. They also won 4 Regionals, beginning in 1931 at Anderson and ending in 1968 in Indianapolis, when they not only won their only Semi-state but finished runner-up to State Champion Gary Roosevelt by a 68-60 score. Oscar Evans, who was named 1st string All-State and an Indiana All-Star, led the Blue Devils in that final game loss with 23 points. Following are Hall of Fame citations for 1959 star player William "Bo" Crain, 1967 star George Pillow, and coaches Reynolds and Theofanis:

William "Bo" Crain

All-City team 1959, All-State team ... rebounding leader and 15.9 ppg ... coached by Hall of Famer Cleon Reynolds ... played 3 years for University of Utah ... All-Conference 1962 and 1963 ... 2nd team All-American ... 17.7 ppg for 3 years.

George Pillow

Leading scorer on Shortridge 1967 team... played for Hall of Fame Coach George Theofanis ... led team to the Indianapolis City Championship, sectional, regional, and to the final game of the semi-state....All-City Team, All-Sectional, All-Regional, All-Semi-State, All-State and Shortridge MVP in 1967....Indiana All-Star....played four years at Indiana State.... MVP 1971 and Converse All-American....All-Conference and Indiana College All-Star....1992 Hall of Fame Silver Anniversary Team....Game Director for the Circle City Classic....Indiana State University All-Decade Team....All-Century Team with Larry Bird.

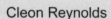

Cleon Reynolds

Over 500 victories in high school coaching, many during 13-yr tenure at Indpls Shortridge...3 of his best teams suffered narrow losses in sectional to legendary Crispus Attucks teams, all of which went on to win state championships...Blue Devils were regularly state ranked, including 3 number-ones...coached Indiana all-star team against Kentucky 3 years...moved on to 16 years at Marian College as basketball coach and athletic director...named to Hall of Fame Silver Anniversary team in 1975 and named Marion County Coach of the Year in 1977.

George Theofanis
As a senior at Washington selected to All-City and All-Sectional teams . . . began coaching career at Avon High School . . . also coached at Shortridge whose teams hold every all-time tournament record in its history . . . taking them to the 1968 state championship game and then was the man picked to succeed Tony Hinkle as Butler's coach . . . twice named Indiana Collegiate Conference Coach of the Year.

An early Shortridge High School

In Randolph County the royal blue-and-white-clad Stoney Creek Blue Devils finished 15-4 for Coach Paul Weaver in 1927 and turned in an 18-4 record in 1944 for Charles Miller and a 19-5 mark in 1952 for George Hiatt. Earlier they won 3 Sectionals, in 1922 at Union City with W. J. Morrison coaching, and in 1924 and 1925 at Winchester with Theodore Sedgwick at the helm. They became Farmland Wildcats before they became Monroe Central Golden Bears.

Van Buren Township's Blue Devils in Clay County had an outstanding season in 1959, winning 24 of 26 games for their coach Pete Chalos. In 1971 they won 19 while losing only 3 with Bill Murray coaching. Doug Price led the 1978 and 1979 teams to impressive 20-3 and 20-2 seasons. John Memmer's Blue Devil teams of the next 3 years won 50 games and lost just 17. All told, the Van Buren Blue Devils captured 4 Sectional titles. Since they did not consolidate into Northview until 1984, there were several years of girls teams at Van Buren, and they had 2 excellent seasons: 1977, 15-1, and the next year, 11-2, both for Jan Gambill.

Stoney Creek and Van Buren High Schools

The North Vernon Blue Devils won 23 games in 1926 for Coach Amos Mahon, also winning the first of the school's 13 Sectionals and 5 Regionals. That year they won the Rushville Regional with victories over Patriot, 51-23, and the home team Lions, 27-21. This earned them a trip to the Sweet Sixteen in Indianapolis at the Fairgrounds Exposition Building where they won their 1st-round game against Syracuse before being ousted by Bedford. Charles Englehardt coached the Devils from 1929 through 1938, and his 8 year record from 1930 through 1937 was an impressive 163 wins and 37 losses, topped by 1937's 24-3, record. They also won their 1st-round games in the Semi-states in 1937 over Greensburg and 1940 over Crawfordsville, attaining the Elite Eight for the 3rd time. The blue-and-white-clad

North Vernon High School

Blue Devils also had an outstanding season for Coach Dwight Graber in 1966, 22-5. They won their 5th Regional crown that year and their 4th Elite Eight berth with a win over Memorial at Evansville, proving once again that they truly belonged there.

Kentland's Blue Devils wore navy blue and white. Virgil Robbins coached the Devils to an impressive 4-year streak from 1951 through 1954, winning 85 games and losing only 15. In total they won 5 Sectionals between 1927 and 1965. North Salem's Blue Devils won 3 Sectionals: in 1930, 1957, and 1960. Vernon, though a gem of a town, never got to cut the nets down at the close of a Sectional tournament, although they did put 2 good years together for Ed Wells, winning 31 games and losing only 9 in 1952 and 1953.

Which brings us to an even scarier mascot, the lone Green Devils on our list from Veedersburg. Those Green Devils had 4 20-games-won-seasons between 1931 and 1942, each season led by a different coach. In 1931, under Lawrence Greeley, they won 22 and lost 5; in 1936 it was 20-6 under Eugene Wenz; in 1941 Clarence Lymon's team won 22 and lost 6; and the next year Ray Singer's team won 20 and lost 4. The Green Devils won 3 Sectionals. They also qualified for the 1920 state finals at Indiana University, but they lost their 1st-round game to Gary Emerson.

Fortville teams were simply called the Demons, and as early as 1918 they enjoyed a 20-3 season under Coach Carl Painter. The Demons were coached for 27 years by L. O. Brown beginning in 1931. Brown's teams won all 6 of the school's Sectional championships. His 1949 squad finished 20-5, defeating Amo in the 1st round of the Indianapolis Regional before losing to Summitville in the final game.

An early edition of Veedersburg School

Fortville High School

Greens Fork High School

The Greens Fork Demons won their only Sectional at Richmond in 1936 defeating the mighty Red Devils in the final game, 34-20. They also upended the Bearcats in the Muncie Regional before being sent home with heads held high by New Castle. Phyllis Beers comments on that in her *Ode to Our Alma Mater*:

From the looks of the trophies around and there's more we can't find—this school has produced some great athletes. I've stood many times in front of the trophy case and read and re-read the engraved names on the awards and beamed with pride as I read that '36 Sectional Team and related an occasion to someone that our basketball team won the sectional in 1936. You'd have thought I was there cheering them all the way but the real truth is I wasn't born for three more months.

Have you wondered or do you know why we were called "Demons?" I don't know the origin but I do know that to tackle those opposing us like "Little Giants, Bulldogs, Terriers, Bears and whatever a Wampus Cat is —to say nothing of Yellow Jackets, Cardinals, Tigers, Pirates, and the awful thought of those Red Devils well, we'd have to be some sort of spirit—So Demons were we!!

Sad to say, the Blue Demons of Leesburg were never able to capture a Sectional. That is to me a shame because every Indiana school I have ever encountered that has won only 1 Sectional title never seems to forget it. They can forget all of those losses, but the one triumph is a point of pride of place, of the value of striving against all odds. Did we lose that with the advent of class basketball? Or did consolidation take some of it away? Or is it just progress? If the latter, I may side with Will Rogers who once said "Progress may have been a good thing once, but it's been going on too long." Leesburg is now an elementary school, but they have not forgotten their Blue Demon heritage.

Our final entry is this section falls to Kendallville, also sometimes known as the Comets. The Comets/Red Devils had a fine string from 1919 through 1924, winning 111 games and losing only 41. The best marks came in 1922 and 1923 when they finished 21-5 and 20-5, Burton Eaton coaching the 1925 team and O. D. Guyman the 1926 squad. In 1927 John Swan's team went 19-6, and the next year Aubrey Stanley's team won 20 while losing 6. Two years later John Howe led the Comets to a 21-5 mark, which he followed up with 22-7 the next year. In 1939 and 1940 Charles Ivey's teams went 18-9 and 19-6. Harry Smith was coaching in 1946 and 1947 when even better records of 21-5 and 22-4 were turned in. Twenty-win seasons were also produced by Bob Igney's 1949 team, 21-3, and his 1951 and 1953 squads went 21-4 and 20-5 respectively. In all they have won 26 Sectionals and 5 Regionals. As Bob Gagen of the *Kendallvlle News-Sun* writes about the early years: "Finally with a gym of their own, KHS cagers went to Sweet Sixteen Four Years (1917-1920) in a Row." He continues:

> . . . *the following year (1917) under first-year coach W. S. Barnhart, enthusiasm and spirits were high as 30 boys showed up for tryouts. From this group an 11-man varsity was selected, with perhaps its most impressive member being Robert Gipson, who played on the 1915 Thorntown team which won the state championship. Other starters were freshman Robert Moses, Walter Kaiser, Ed Husselman and Captain Elmer Sawyer . . ..They would lose but three regular-season games, all on the road. The most vexing of these was a 43-34 loss to Albion in the county seat's opera house. According to the KHS yearbook, four lads were not accustomed to playing on a slippery dance floor ....*
>
> *The Crimson and Old Gold swept through the sectional played in their new gym, winning the championship game against Angola, 35-33, after which students snaked-danced down Main Street. Kendallville won its first-round game in the new Indiana University gym at Bloomington, but was crushed, 43-8, by Lebanon, the eventual state champion. Coach Leon J. Helmick, a 1915 Albion (Michigan) College graduate, took over the team for the 1918-19 school year. Its start was delayed for nine weeks because of worldwide influenza epidemic during which some 20 million people, including more than 500,000 Americans died . . .. The "Sweet 16" returned to Bloomington this year and KHS opened against Indianapolis Tech. Before the largest crowd that had ever witnessed a game in the IU gym, Tech won out 30-17. The 1920 team, led by four-year starter Bob Moses, went 18-8, registering the most wins in school history while playing a difficult schedule.*

Gertrude Fleisher, captain of the KHS 1921 team

Kendallville High School girls basketball team - 1921

Chapter 38

Trojans, Pirates and . . .
Years of Glory for More Closed Schools

After Aces and Devils the next popular team name for our closed high schools was Trojans with 20. In Noble County the Purple and White of Albion were playing basketball at least as early as 1912, when Alliman Heyman's team won 11 of 14 games, a feat they repeated 2 years later. The Trojans really hit their stride in 1960 under Coach Bob Macy, winning 20 and losing 8, which they followed up with 17-6, 18-7, and 19-6 seasons with Hi Platt doing the coaching. That's 72 wins and 27 losses in 4 years. Not half bad. In both 1960 and 1963 the Albion Trojans captured the Kendallville Sectional, defeating Berne in the 1st round of the Ft. Wayne Regional before losing to Central in the final game in 1963. They are now Central Noble Cougars.

Albion High School (l)

Larwill High School (r)

Rudolph Holycross coached the purple-and-gold-clad Larwill Trojans for 14 years, from 1934 until 1947. His 1941 team went 16-3, and his 1944 team did even better, 19-2. The next year's somewhat abbreviated schedule saw the Trojans again drop only 2 games, winning 13. They scored their only Sectional title at Columbia City in 1969 with wins over Churubusco, Manchester, and the home team. Roger Tuggle was the coach. In 1971 they became Whitko Wildcats.

For the following story we are indebted to *Indiana Basketball History* Magazine, Spring 2002.

The home of these particular Trojans is one of the most fascinating places in Indiana. As it happens, not only does the Indiana-Ohio state line pass through the middle of the town, it also passed through the middle of the high school as well. Ohio students entered at the eastern door, Indiana students the western door. Even the basketball court was bisected. Exactly. The state line ran through the center circle, half the floor in each state. A hot shooter could launch one from Indiana and score a basket in Ohio. Or vice versa, as at least 2 players, Randy Gilmer of visiting Lewisburg and Mike Simms of the home team, are reputed to have done. The Trojans, who wore red and gold uniforms, finished 26-2 for Coach Ed Osterman in 1951. Some,

College Corner High School

however, contend that the Trojans fielded their best team in 1969 when they were edged 57-56 by the Connersville Spartans in the Sectional, in something of a rerun of the Trojan Wars. Eventually the town's name was changed to West College Corner, the school was closed, and the Indiana students now attend Union High School in Liberty, the Patriots.

The Goodland Trojans in Newton County won 4 Sectional titles between 1928 and 1960. Hall of Famer Andy Zimmer was a Goodland Trojan who led the Gold and Blue to one of those Sectionals, in 1937. His team, coached by J. C. LaFollette, did so at Morocco with wins over Wheatfield, 37-15; Brook, 27-23; and Kentland, 36-4.

Goodland High School.

Andy Zimmer
A walk-on, the 6´ 5˝ Zimmer enrolled at Indiana...his sophomore year he started just two games and played as a backup when the 1940 Hoosiers won the NCAA title.. .was a recipient of the Balfour and Gimbel Awards. He retired as a Colonel in the Marines, where he received a Purple Heart and Bronze Star while serving in WWII and Korea.

The Milford Trojans captured 4 Sectional titles, all at Warsaw between 1925 and 1948. They also snagged the Fort Wayne Regional in 1925, losing to the Vincennes Alices 45-23 in the 1st round of their only Sweet Sixteen appearance. Their record that year was an impressive 28-3! Jeff Noble was the Milford coach, and his 1929 and 1930 Sectional titlists also rang up some nice records, 24-2 and 21-12. Bob Bushong's 1947 and

Milford High School

1948 Trojans were also 20-game-winners, 21-3 and 25-1. The latter, undefeated in the regular season, lost their only game in the 1st round of the Ft. Wayne Regional by

5 points to Monroeville. Finally, in 1961, Jerald Van Meter coached the Trojans to a 22-3 finish. They became Wawasee Warriors in 1968.

Hall of Famer Basil Mawbey was a Deedsville Trojan. Deedsville won their only Sectional at Peru in 1926 with wins over Peru, Amboy, and Clay Township. They lost by only 1 point to Flora in the Kokomo Regional. Patriot's red and white Trojans won their only Sectional at Madison the same year, defeating Hanover, Scottsburg, and Deputy. Lakeville's Blue-and-Gold took their only sectional crown 2 years earlier at South Bend. To do so they had to defeat Bremen, the home team, Culver, and Mishawaka. Ken Groff's 1957 team won 18 of 24 games.

North Webster in Kosciusko County was founded in 1834, and the 1st consolidated high school was opened in 1910. At the town's centennial it was recorded that the high school then had 48 students. The Trojans under Coach Sid Spencer won their lone Sectional in 1953 at Warsaw after an undefeated regular season. In the Regional final they lost the only game of the 28 they played to eventual State Champion South Bend Central. A truly memorable year for the Trojans and their fans. Don Butts also coached the Red and White to another great season in 1960, 21-4, losing the Sectional final to Columbia City.

Morgantown's purple and white Trojans had an undefeated regular season in 1931, with Loren Wilson's charges losing their only game to Monrovia in the Martinsville Sectional. In 1953 Keith Rhoades guided the Trojans to a 21-3 mark, and in 1956 Roger Adkins' charges won the school's only Sectional, at Bloomington, with wins over Ellettsville, Martinsville, Mooresville, and the home team, to finish 24-3. They were defeated by Terre Haute Gerstmeyer in the final game of the Martinsville Regional after beating Brazil in the 1st round.

Marion Bennett also fielded the Trojans, in blue and gold. Although they never won a Sectional championship, the Bennett Trojans had a strong year for Coach Steve Fitzgerald in 1962, finishing 20-3, and another 4 years later when Larry Wente's charges finished 20-2. In 1976 and 1977 Craig Plummer led the Trojans to 19-5 and 17-4 marks, and Rick Dessing's 1984 squad turned in a sound 18-3 record.

The Clinton Township Trojans in LaPorte County wore blue and gold and were coached to a 14-7 record by Howard Sharpe in 1941. Although they were never able to win a Sectional title, they did win 18 games for Noel King in 1949, losing 6. They are now South Central Satellites. The Orland Trojans in Steuben County wore gold and black uniforms and were also at one time called Tigers. They had a nice 3-year string beginning in 1951 when they won 44 games and lost only 22 for the coach, Don Arnold. They are now Prairie Heights Panthers.

The Manchester Trojans have been covered previously. Our other Trojans, neither of whom captured a Sectional crown, were Bentonville, whose uniforms were once black and gold and later red and white and Fairbanks, who wore purple and gold.

Bentonville is now part of the Connersville Spartans.

Fairbanks is now North Central (Sullivan) whose team is the Thunderbirds. East

Tipp, briefly part of the Trojans also, is now part of the Harrison Raiders.

Pirates (including Buccaneers) were the next most popular choice of our now-closed schools, with 11. In Miami County the purple and gold Amboy Pirates won 17 of 19 games in 1916. In 1940 they won the Peru Sectional with wins over Bunker Hill, Mexico, Clay Township, and Converse, 27-25 in overtime.

The Bristol Pirates also had their moments in Elkhart County. In fact, they were undefeated in 1914 for Coach K. M. Snapp, although they played only 7 games. In 1926, with Bob McConnell coaching, they won 15 games and lost only 3. Irvin Robert's 1942 Trojan squad finished 17-6. The blue-and-gold-clad Linlawn Pirates in Wabash County finished 18-4 in 1939. Roland DuBois was the coach. Absalom Wilsons' teams finished 16-5 in 1942 and 16-4 two years later.

Amboy and Bristol High Schools

In Vigo County the Glenn Pirates, in black and white uniforms as befits those who fly the Jolly Roger, not only won the Terre Haute Sectional in 1951 but also won the Bloomington Regional that year, defeating Linton and the home team in the process. In the Sweet Sixteen they lost a 1st round 56-46 encounter with Evansville Reitz. The powerful Panthers team would lose the state finals last game by just 2 points to the Bearcats of Muncie Central at Butler Fieldhouse 1 week later. The Reitz loss was the only one suffered by the Jack Williams-coached Pirates who finished 30-1. Quite a season!

The Anderson Madison Heights Pirates had an 18-4 record in 1959, followed by 19-5 the next year for Coach Paul Bradford. Phil Buck's 1975 Pirate squad finished 20-6, followed by 18-5 the next year. In 1980 the Pirates won 18 of 22 games, and the next year finished an excellent 23-2. The Pirates won 9 Sectionals, and 4 Regionals. Their lone Semi-state

Glenn High School

came at Ft. Wayne in 1972 when they defeated Garrett 83-71 and Penn 57-48. The Pirates lost to state runner-up Gary West in the morning game at Assembly Hall in Bloomington. The Lady Pirates won 26 games and lost only 1 in 1979 with Billie Bienert coaching. That was the year they won their only Sectional and Regional titles as well. After adding the Semi-state title with convincing wins over Northwood and

Bellmont, the Lady Pirates edged Indianapolis North Central 47-46 before losing the state final championship game to East Chicago Roosevelt by a margin that left little room for regrets, suffering their only defeat of the season.

In Hancock County the green-and-white-clad Bucccaneers of Mount Comfort, (whose school is now an elementary school) lost just 1 game in 1913…but they played only 4. They won 13 in 1918, losing 5; and went on to win 6 Sectional championships, all at Greenfield, in the 12 years beginning in 1923 and ending in 1934, 5 of which came under the guidance of Coach James Good. They are now Mt. Vernon Marauders, which may not be that much different from being Buccaneers after all.

The Mt. Comfort Buccaneer.

The Pirates at Noble Township in Wabash County wore blue and gold for their brief, 10-season life. They put together 3 excellent seasons in a row under Coach Robert Swihart from 1957 through 1959, 20-4, 18-4, and 20-5: 58 wins and 13 losses over that span but no Sectional championships. That changed in the school's last year when a 15-10 mark was good enough to triumph at Manchester in 1962 with wins over Lagro, the home team, and Wabash. They are now Southwood Knights.

The town of Elizabeth in Harrison County was named for the wife of Edward Veatch, who donated the land for the town in 1812. Around 1890 Clay Hill College began to provide seminary education, with the high school eventually occupying their building. The high school teams were the Pirates. They are now South Central Rebels.

Other Pirate teams were at Gentryville, whose green and white Pirates became Wildcats at Chrisney and Golden Aces at Dale before settling in at Heritage Hills as Patriots; Kempton, whose purple and gold teams became Yankees at Jefferson Township before becoming Tipton Blue Devils; Lafayette Central (Allen County), who wore red and black and are now Homestead Spartans; Tobinsport, who wore red and white and were also called Red Devils, now Bulldogs at Cannelton; Lovett, who wore black and orange and became Paris Crossing Lions/Pirates before becoming Jennings County Panthers; and Webster, black and orange, merged with Williamsburg for a brief period as Yellow Jackets before becoming Northeastern Knights; none of whom brought home a Sectional championship. Data is elusive on all of these schools. The Romney and Paris Crossing Pirates have been covered earlier.

One kind of selection that was popular once but has lost its allure has to do with school size, or maybe it was even player size. We once had 3 schools whose teams were the Midgets and 3 more who chose Little Giants for their mascots. The purple-and-gold-uniformed Perry Central Midgets from Boone County finished 17-4 under the direction of Coach Ken Reeher in 1951.

Mt. Comfort High School girls team in 1924

Wanatah (l) and Mt. Comfort schools

Houck photo of license plate for Perry Central Midgets from exhibit courtesy IBHOF

Plainville's Midgets have already been covered as have Jamestown's and Fountain City's Little Giants. Our other Midgets were found in LaPorte County at Wanatah. Their colors were red and white. Leonard Black's 1956 Wanatah Midgets won 17 games and lost 5. Our other Little Giants were found at New Point in Decatur County, who put together a 14-3 season for Norman Freeland in 1934.

We also had 4 Spartans, 6 Cossacks, and 3 Knights at one time. The Cossacks, a more popular team name in our earlier days than it is now, was a particularly understandable and appropriate choice for the red and white teams of Russiaville (in spite of the real source of that town's name, as we have seen previously). Although they were playing basketball in Russiaville as early as 1906, unfortunately they were never able to bring home a Sectional championship. They came closest in 1928, losing the final game of the Kokomo Sectional to the Sharpsville Bulldogs to finish a commendable 21-4 for Forest Roe.

The Ridgeville black-and-white-clad Cossacks won 5 Sectionals between 1920 and 1938. The 1920 victory placed them in the state finals at Indiana University, where they lost their 1st-round game to Milroy. The next year was the 1st year that the Regional tournament concept was introduced. The form was quite different than it is now. There were 2 16-team Regionals, at Purdue and IU, each sending 8 single-game winners to the state finals in Indianapolis. The Cossacks of Ralph Harris were one of

The 1920 Ridgeville Sectional Champions, IBHS

the IU winners, defeating Scottsburg 22-15 before being rather soundly dispatched by the Muncie (not yet Central) Bearcats, 39-4, in the Sweet Sixteen. Herman Beckley's 1938 Cossacks won 18 of 20 games, including the Hartford City Sectional, 39-29 over the home team in the final game, after getting by Dunkirk 25-24 in the semis. Their 2nd loss of the season came at the hands of South Side in the finals of the Ft. Wayne Regional, after the Cossacks had nipped Bluffton, 33-32 in overtime. They are now Winchester Golden Falcons.

The red and white Middletown Cossacks roamed the steppes of central Henry County. They had an undefeated regular season 23-1 for their coach Von Jameson in 1953, losing to the home team Trojans in the final game of the New Castle Sectional. His 1956 Cossacks were also undefeated prior to the state tournament, finishing 19-1. Their lone loss was to Muncie Central 60-54 in the final game of the Muncie Regional. Middletown teams won 6 New Castle Sectional titles between 1929 and 1962. They are now Shenandoah Raiders.

Russiaville and Middletown High Schools

The LaFontaine Cossacks (French Cossacks?) in Wabash County wore blue and white and were led to an undefeated regular season in 1938 by Coach Russell Walters. That 1 loss came in the opening round of the Wabash Sectional, to North Manchester. In 1954 Charles Steidel's Cossacks won 22 of 25 games. They were frustrated again in their attempts to win that 1 coveted Sectional crown, getting to the final game at Wabash this time only to be edged by the host Apaches, 52-50.

There were also briefly (1921–29) Cossacks at Rykers Ridge in Jefferson County. They became Jefferson Central Wildcats (who snagged their own lone Sectional title in 1936) before finally becoming Madison Cubs. Cossacks also represented Riley (Irish Cossacks?) in Vigo County, covered earlier.

The Pleasant Mills Spartans were in Adams County, coached to an impressive

22-5 mark in 1940 by Gerald Vizzard. They won the Decatur Sectional that year and again 2 years later with a much less spectacular record, finishing 12-13. Two other Spartans were at Jefferson Township (Huntington) and at Pleasant Lake. Neither of these teams, unfortunately, ever won a Sectional title. However, Pleasant Lake did

Pleasant Mills High School

achieve the Steuben County championship 3 times: in 1914, 1928, and 1944. They had 2 other memorable seasons: in 1941 when Coach Joseph Bohr's Spartans won 19 of 23 games and in 1918 when George Fairfield's squad finished 13-4. There were also Spartans representing the black-and-white-uniformed teams of Cromwell—now West Noble Chargers.

The Clarksburg Knights experienced an outstanding season in 1947, finishing 21 and 2 under the guidance of Coach Oliver Tippin. They also managed to capture the 1964 Greensburg Sectional crown with wins over St. Paul's Blasters, Burney's Panthers, and North Vernon's Blue Devils in a closely contested championship game, 74-72. The next week they were edged by Franklin's Grizzlie Cubs 69-67 at the Columbus Regional to finish 15-10 for their coach Dave Horn.

Noble Township, a short-lived school (1931–39) in Cass County, selected the team name Knights for an obvious good reason. Unfortunately not they nor our other Knights from Claypool in Kosciusco County ever snared that single elusive Sectional crown. Claypool, however, had some excellent seasons, including a 10-1 record for Frank Sanders in 1919. In their last 3 years before becoming Warsaw Tigers in 1966, Tom Miller's teams rang up 59 wins while absorbing only 10 defeats, with the best year being 1965, 22-2. That year in the Warsaw Sectional the Knights of Claypool nipped Leesburg 77-75 before having their final hopes for a Sectional title shattered by the home team in the next round.

Staying with our theme of noblemen, we had the Pekin Muskateers who, of course, retained that name when they joined with others to become Eastern (Washington County) High School. The Muskateers won 30 games and lost 12 for

Coach Lexie Mills in 1957 and 1958.

In Grant County we had the Upland Yeomen, who were also appropriately called the Highlanders. The Upland Yeomen had a 10-4 season as early as 1912 and a 15-7 record for Chuck Bragg in 1933. This was their penultimate season before consolidating into Jefferson Township, where they retained their team name. As Jefferson Township the Yeomen enjoyed fine 15-3 and 16-2 seasons for Don Oren in 1937 and 1938; Willard Orval's 1943 team won 18 and lost only 4, Larry Stockton's 1947 team went 18-7, and John Bragg's 1963 and 1964 squads finished 16-6. They are now Eastbrook Panthers.

Perhaps the most fitting team name involving royalty came from Rex Mundi High School in Evansville. Rex Mundi, King of the World, Monarchs. Makes good sense to me. The Monarchs won Evansville Sectionals and Regionals in both 1964 and 1969. In 1964 they

Upland High School

defeated the Martinsville Artesians and the Seymour Owls to capture the Semi-state crown before losing the afternoon game of the Final Four to eventual State Champion Lafayette Jefferson. In 1969 the Monarchs defeated the Bedford Stonecutters before losing to the Vincennes Lincoln Alices in the Semi-state finals. Equally fitting would be the Kingsbury Kings, covered elsewhere.

Moving away from royalty, Jac-Cen-Del High School in Ripley County is composed of the 3 townships there called Jackson, Center, and Delaware. Osgood was in Center Township, with their colors green and white, and their teams were the Cowboys. The Cowboys won their lone Sectional at Batesville in 1939 with wins over Milan, Sunman, and the home team, by 2 points, 29-27. They were in turn edged by the same margin at the Rushville Regional by

the host Lions, 36-34. There were also Cowboys at Kitchel in Union County. Curiously, they won back-to-back Sectionals at Connersville in 1942 and 1943 by defeating the home team in double overtime each year, 42-40 and 36-35! They also won 1st round games each year at the Rushville Regional.

An early Osgood school Building

We had Senators at East Chicago Washington, Presidents at McKinley and South Bend Wilson, and Rough Riders at East Chicago Roosevelt. Of the 3 the Senators had the most successful run under the guidance of Hall of Fame coach John Baratto (whose citation is elsewhere). All told, the Senators won 20 Sectionals, 12 Regionals, 8 Semi-states, and 2 state championships. Their 1st Sweet Sixteen appearance came in 1947, when they lost the afternoon game of the Final Four to the eventual champion Shelbyville Golden Bears and their star, Bill Garrett. Ray Ragelis, who would later lead the Big Ten in scoring as a star Northwestern Wildcat, led that Senator team. His Hall of Fame citation, as well as Vince Boryla's, who preceded him by a bit at Washington, follows:

Ray Ragelis
Leading scorer of East Chicago Washington in 1947, playing for Hall of Fame Coach Johnny Baratto ... a year later, as a senior, led Generals to semifinal championships ... leading scorer in East Chicago's loss to eventual state champion Shelbyville ... two-time all-Big 10 player at Northwestern ... Wildcats' most valuable player ... led Big 10 in scoring as a senior in 1951 ... played professionally two years with Rochester

Vince Boryla
Played with New York Knickerbockers 1949-54...Coached Knicks 1956-58 ... general manager of Knicks 1958-64 ... president and general manager of the ABA's Utah Stars...Consensus All-American in 1947-48 and member of 1948 U. S. Olympic basketball team, after graduating from East Chicago Washington ... played collegiately at Notre Dame and then Denver, earning distinction as AAU All-American 1946-47 and 47-48 .

Their next trip to the Final Four came in 1960, when the Senators, led by Phil Dawkins, beat Muncie Central 75-59, to win their 1st state title. Two years later, in spite of Bob Miles' 30-point performance in the final game, the Senators lost by 3 points to the Evansville Bosse Bulldogs, 84-81. In 1966 East Chicago Washington lost the morning semi-final game to Michigan City's Wolves, who would win the title that night. Five years later the Senators would win their 2nd state championship, undefeated 29-0, led by the trio of Ulysses (Junior) Bridgeman, Tim Stoddard, and Pete Trgovich, over the Blue Blazers of Elkhart, 70-60. Two of those 3 played leading roles on NCAA championship teams: Trgovich at UCLA, Stoddard at North Carolina State, and Bridgeman's Louisville team only lost by 1 point to UCLA in 1975!

In 1976 the Senators were back in the Final Four, losing to the runner-up Rushville Lions in the semi-finals. They got all the way to the final game the next year, dropping a heartbreaker by 1 point to the Carmel Greyhounds, 53-52. The Senators' final trip to the Final Four came in 1985 when they again lost in the semi-finals to the team that would finish runner-up that night, this time the Richmond Red Devils.

Houck photos of Senators from exhibits courtesy IBHOF

East Chicago Roosevelt took their inspiration, of course, from Theodore Roosevelt, not FDR, calling their teams the Rough Riders. They won 5 Sectionals and 1 Regional, but they sure made the most of that 1 opportunity in the Sweet Sixteen. That took place in 1970, and the Rough Riders defeated the Carmel Greyhounds, in spite of Dave Shepherd's 40-point outburst in the final game. Roosevelt was led by Jim Bradley, who scored 24 himself in that game as the Rough Riders finished their historic season 28-0 for Coach Bill Holzbach. Two years earlier, when Ray Walker was in the last year of his 26-year career with the school, he led the Rough Riders to a 21-1 record, their only loss coming at the hands of those pesky neighboring Senators in the Sectionals.

East Chicago Roosevelt Rough Riders, Houck photo of jersey from exhibit courtesy IBHOF

South Bend Wilson and Winchester McKinley are our 2 schools that had Presidents for their team name. Neither ever won a Sectional, unfortunately. McKinley, with William "Jack" Lee coaching, had a very solid season in 1941, finishing 17-4. Wilson turned in an outstanding undefeated regular season in 1945, 20-1, with John Jaworski coaching. Their lone loss was an overtime cliff-hanger to South Bend Adams, 40-38, in the Sectional semi-finals. A tough way for a great season to end.

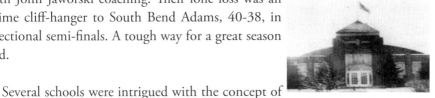

South Bend Woodrow Wilson

Several schools were intrigued with the concept of streaks and blazers. There were the Gary Edison Blazers and the Lizton (like Swayzee, the sign as you enter Lizton announces it is the only one so named in the world) Blue Blazers. There were Blue Streaks at both Center Township in Starke County and at Pleasantville in Sullivan County. In White County the Idaville teams were the Green Streaks; Terre Haute Wiley fielded the Red Streaks. Gary Edison got their 1 and only Sectional title in 1946 with wins over Kouts, Froebel, Horace Mann, and Lew Wallace. Lowell Sparks' team closed with an excellent 22-4 record after being sent home from the Hammond Regional by East Chicago Washington.

Lizton lost only 1 game in 1912...out of 5. They captured their only Sectional title way back in 1917 at Greencastle by handling Fillmore 39-5, dropping New Winchester 24-9, getting past Amo 20-16, and claiming the prize with a 17-11 victory over Plainfield. This earned them a trip to the state finals at Indiana University, but they lost the 1st-round game there to Muncie.

Of all of our Blazers and Streakers, Wiley shone the brightest. The Red Streaks

won 16 Sectionals between 1924 and 1970 as well as regional crowns in 1931, 1932, and 1942. Their 1st trip to the Sweet Sixteen was their most successful. The 1931 Wiley team defeated the Greensburg Pirates and the Rushville Lions before losing semi-final game 2 to the Greencastle Tiger Cubs, who would finish runner-up to the Muncie (not yet Central) Bearcats. In their other 2 Sweet Sixteen appearances, the Red Streaks lost their 1st

Terre Haute Wiley Gym, the home of the Red Streaks

game each time, to the Connersville Spartans in 1932 and the Bedford Stonecutters in 1942.

Converse Indiana's teams were the Bordermen. A glance at our state map shows why. Mostly in Miami County, the eastern edge of town spills into Grant County, and just to the south, no more than a mile away is Howard County. So Bordermen it was, for good reason. The 1928 Bordermen won 28 games, losing 8, but the 1944 team made most of their fans forget about 1928. In 1944, following an undefeated regular season, the Bordermen, coached by Dan Ballard not only won the 1st of their 3 Peru Sectional titles, they also captured the Logansport Regional with convincing

Converse High School, home of the Bordermen

wins over the home team Berries and the Oracles of Delphi. However, they lost in the 1st round of the Semi-state at Hammond to Culver's Cavaliers, 26-17, dashing all hopes for a state championship and ending the dream season at 27-1.

One of the more interesting team names belonged to a short-lived (1964 and 1965 only) school called White River. Close to both the Patoka and White Rivers, their teams were aptly called the Rapids. They were a

Hazleton (and White River) High School and Patoka High School

consolidation of the Patoka Wrens and the Hazleton Lions in Hazleton's School building. In 1966 White River, Mt. Olympus, Baldwin Heights, Lowell, Franklin and Princeton schools were all consolidated into North Gibson School Corporation, with the high schools becoming Princeton Community High School Tigers.

Margaret Johnson in the *Princeton Daily Clarion* July 22, 1971, had the following interesting comments about Patoka:

> *Patoka, the oldest town in Gibson County, was in existence before the organization of the county. In 1789 John Severns settled on the south bank of the Patoka River at a place now know as Severn's bridge.*
>
> *The 1st high school commencement was held in the Cumberland Presbyterian Church Friday, May 25, 1882. The graduates were* [four in number].

Patoka School 1875

One thing Indiana and northern Africa have in common is that we each have a White and a Blue River. However, to my knowledge, neither Egypt nor the Sudan have a Wabash River, but then neither do we have a Sphinx. With that rather dubious introduction, let us turn our attention to DePauw, in Harrison County.

The DePauw teams were the Blue River Echos. They were 1st consolidated into New Salisbury, becoming Tigers before finally becoming North Harrison Cougars. Both schools had more than one color combination for their uniforms: DePauw's were purple and gold and then blue and gold, and New Salisbury's colors were royal blue and white and then green and white. Neither DePauw nor New Salisbury ever won a Sectional, and we have precious little information about them.

DePauw and New Salisbury Schools

One of the largest electric power generating plants in southern Indiana is located in Edwardsport on the White River. Their teams were appropriately named the Powers, but, sadly, they were never powerful enough to gain a Sectional crown.

An early Edwardsport school building

433

Chapter 39

Other Often Quirky Names:
We Remember Them Fondly

Elsewhere mention has been made of the Pimento, Shadeland, and Wallace Peppers. And we have discussed the Mulberry Berries, the Logan(sport) Berries, the Poseyville Posies, the Shamrocks of Westfield, and the Clovers of Cloverdale, as well as the Young Sycamores in Terre Haute. We've cited the Hickories in Colfax, the Oakton and Oaklandon Oaks, and the Oakland City Acorns. Just to round out our teams with things that grow from the ground, there were 3 more Shamrocks at one time: these were at North Liberty, Somerset, and Ashboro (who were also called the Blue Devils, wearing blue and white at that time and green and white or green and gold as Shamrocks). Somerset enjoyed a memorable season in 1936, undefeated until the state tournament, finishing 24-1. John Hubbard coached the Shamrocks that year. His teams also went 16-6 and 16-4 in the 2 previous years, 54-11 over 3 years. Not bad in any league. The Shamrocks captured Sectional crowns at Wabash in 1932 and 1941. The latter, with Ray Bowser coaching, came with a 21-4 record earned by wins over Lagro, Chester Township, Laketon, and Roann.

The North Liberty Shamrocks also had an undefeated regular season. Theirs came in 1939. Larry Imhoff was the coach with a final record was 22-1, the lone defeat a 2-pointer to the host Cavemen in the Mishawaka Sectional. Joe Hamilton led North Liberty's Green and White to another excellent season in 1961, 22-2, and Bob Gowin's 1966 squad finished 20-3. That 2nd loss in 1961 again came at the hands of Mishawaka, and that 3rd loss in 1966 was dealt by LaVille.

The North Liberty Shamrocks and Somerset High School

Although Ashboro in Clay County never managed to take home a Sectional championship, they did graduate Hall of Famer Angus Nicoson:

Angus Nicoson
30-yr basketball coach, AD at Indiana Central University ... coached Indiana all-star team against Kentucky in 31 games, winning 19 ... at ICU, won more than 63 percent of games, retiring early due to ill health with 483-279 record ... named to Helms Foundation Basketball Hall of Fame ... served on board of dir. of US Olympic Committee, and Pan American and Olympic basketball selection committees ... past pres. of NAIA

Although the tulip tree is our official state tree, I do not think it enjoys as large a place in Hoosier hearts as does the sycamore, thanks in part to these haunting words and music written by Ballard MacDonald and James Hanley in 1917 and so ably sung by Jim Nabors before the start of so many of our Indy 500s:

> *Back home again in Indiana*
> *And it seems that I can see*
> *The gleaming candlelight, still shining bright,*
> *Through the sycamores for me.*
> *The new mown hay sends all its fragrance*
> *From the fields I used to roam.*
> *When I dream about the moonlight on the Wabash,*
> *Then I long for my Indiana home.*

(This is not our official state song, which is Paul Dresser's "On the Banks of the Wabash, Far Away," though the chorus evokes a similar mood and sentiment.) It was written first, before 1900.

> *Oh the moonlight's fair tonight along the Wabash*
> *From the fields there comes the breath of new mown hay.*
> *Through the sycamores the candle lights are gleaming.*
> *On the banks of the Wabash, far away.*

The Wabash flows by Terre Haute not far from the campus of Indiana State University, whose teams are the Sycamores. A laboratory school there fielded teams called the Young Sycamores. Coach Howard Bym led the Young Sycamores to a 7-4 mark in 1920 and a spot in the state tournament, which was held at Indiana University that year. The Normal school lost a 1st-round tussle with eventual State Champion Franklin and the great Fuzzy Vandivier. In 1922 and '23 the Young Sycamores turned in identical 20-9 records for Coach Bym. Paul Wolf took over as coach in 1933, a job he held for 15 seasons. His teams put together an impressive string from 1943 through 1946, winning 74 games and losing just 17. Wolf was replaced by Stan Smith, whose longevity was also impressive, coaching for 20 years with a sabbatical in 1957. The best seasons during his tenure were 23-5 in 1949: 18-6 in 1953, and 22-6 in 1954. The Young Sycamores won the Terre Haute Sectional title 3 times in 1944, 1949, and 1965.

Mauckport is on the Ohio River in Harrison County. It was originally platted in 1827 by Frederick Mauck and referred to as Mauck's Port. The citizens petitioned for a change in name to New Market, but there already was a New Market elsewhere in the state. As befits their port status, their teams were called the Pilots. (Perhaps the girls teams were the Co-Pilots, as is true of Cairo, Illinois.) Although they never managed to win a Sectional, we know they had cheerleaders and that their colors were black and gold. The school was consolidated into Corydon in 1959, becoming Panthers.

Mauckport High School and the Corydon Central Panther

Nina (Beanblossom) Faith in 1947, 3 years before the Mauckport High School closed, and (r) an earlier Mauckport cheerleader. Thanks to the excellent town ebsite and, again, to all the websites which made this book possible.

Dragons roared at Mongo in LaGrange County, at Arcadia in Hamilton County, and at Windfall in Tipton County, and there were Purple Dragons breathing, perhaps, purple fire at Pinnell in Boone County (covered earlier). The Mongo Dragons enjoyed a fine 19-3 season under Coach Carl Tingley in 1933, followed by an even better 20-2 mark the next year for that era's coach Ronald Treesh. The green and white Mongo

Dragons are now Prairie Heights Panthers.

Mongo High School

Windfall High School: The Dragon's Lair

The Windfall Dragons went undefeated in the regular season in 1957 for Coach Wilford Drake, finishing 23-1. That loss was a tough one, 58-54, to the home team Millers in the final game of the Noblesville Sectional. The Arcadia Dragons will be covered in the last chapter.

The only Titans among our closed schools were those found in the navy blue and red uniforms of Muncie North. In their 19-season history the Titans held up their end of the legend that is Muncie high school basketball. Myron Dickerson coached the Titans from 1973 through 1982; his teams turned in a record of 19-3 in his 1st year, followed immediately by 19-6, 23-3, 16-5, and 18-3 marks: 95 wins and 20 losses over 5 years. Sectionals were won in 1974 and 1975 as well as in 1984, when Coach Wayne Allen's team turned in a 9-5 record. The 1975 team also won the New Castle Regional. The Lady Titans under Carol Kegley won a Sectional title in 1981 and had a 19-3 season in 1984. We should mention the Giants at New Point in Decatur County. Or were they Little Giants, as some records seem to indicate? Either way they had good seasons in 1934 and 1935, going 14-3 for Coach Norman Freeland and then 15-5 for Coach Bertice Williams. They are now North Decatur Chargers.

The New Point school building

Rock Creek Center teams were the Dodgers, and according to some sources, were sometimes called the Does, as in female deer. Maybe. We need confirmation on this one. Either way, they won 15 games and lost 8 in 1927 for their coach Frank Day, the year they won their only Sectional crown at Bluffton with wins over Petroleum, Ossian, and in a 2-overtime thriller, Lancaster. The next week they lost a toughie, this time by 1 point, 20-19 to Columbia City. In 1944 the Dodgers won 15 of 17 games played. The blue and gold Dodgers 1st became Ossian Bears and are now Norwell Knights.

In Tippecanoe County the town of West Point, taking pride in the fact that their name was the same as the New York state home of the United States Military Academy, named their teams the Cadets. The Cadets had an undefeated regular season in 1925 for Harold Horn, their coach, reaching the elusive 30-victory mark, finishing 30-1. They did win the Sectional and the Regional that year and made it to the state finals in Indianapolis—their only loss, after defeating LaPorte in the 1st round, coming at the hands of Kokomo, the eventual state runners-up, by only 4 points, 33-29. They won a 2nd Sectional title as well the next year under Kenneth Hauk. Keeping the "H" theme going, their 3rd and last Sectional title came for Francis Hunk, whose Cadets finished 24-6 in 1929. Perhaps the Cadets sometimes played the Middies, who represented Middlebury and Midland, not Annapolis, both covered elsewhere.

West Point, home of the Cadets, and Midland, home of the Middies

Vikings and Norsemen have always seemed to capture the attention of Hoosiers selecting names for their teams. Eaton teams in Delaware County were the Norsemen. Vikings were found at Huntington (where they still reside as Huntington North), at LaPaz in St. Joseph County (both covered elsewhere), at Montgomery in Daviess County, and at Stillwell in LaPorte County. Neither Eaton nor Stillwell, both of whom wore purple and gold (did the Minnesota Vikings really copy the colors of our own purple and gold Vikings?), ever managed to snare that coveted Sectional title.

Eaton School, circa 1907 and (r)more recently

However, the Eaton Norsemen won 21 of 25 games for Shelley Caldwell in 1927. They were ousted from the state tournament by Yorktown in the Muncie Sectional. They also won 27 of 29 the next year for Bedford Butcher. That year in the Muncie Sectional they defeated Lincoln 95-2(!), Albany 40-13, and Gaston 43-18 before losing the final game to the host Bearcats 35-14. They also had a 22-4 season in 1956 for Cliff Barker and defeated Selma 57-44, edged Burris 64-61, and clobbered Harrison Township 68-35, before again running into those nasty Bearcats and dropping a 75-52 championship game.

The Montgomery (also known as Barr Township) Vikings, who wore black and white uniforms, won 21 of 25 games played for their coach Cabby O'Neil in 1935. Making this a year to be long remembered by this charming Daviess County community, the Vikings rolled through the Washington Sectional with wins over the vaunted Hatchets 20-18, Plainville 21-19, Odon 35-8, and Loogootee 29-19. The Regional was

Montgomery (or Barr Township) High School

also held at the Hatchet House, and the Vikings further thrilled their fans by defeating the powerful Alices from Vincennes, 22-17, and the Sullivan Golden Arrows, 29-23. This earned them a trip to Butler Fieldhouse, where the dream died with a 5-point loss to Jeffersonville's Red Devils. Since the Devils would be state runner-up to Anderson, losing to them was hardly a disgrace, and the Vikings were warmly welcomed on their return to Montgomery. In 1942 they turned in a 19-3 mark for Steve Craney. Craney's 1952 through 1955 teams also ran up 76 wins against just 17 losses. The best year came in 1952, 22-2, along with another Washington Sectional title with wins over Odon, Loogootee, and the home team. The Regional was at Vincennes, where the Vikings were eliminated in a barn-burner, 60-59, by Jasper. They kept the Viking name when they became Barr-Reeve in 1966.

In addition to those Attica Ramblers, covered elsewhere, there were also Ramblers at Huntington Catholic. A coach with the intriguing name of Cash Keller led the Ramblers to impressive marks of 19-9 in 1933, 25-4 in 1934, and 28-8 in 1935, as well as a 21-8 mark in 1937. Leo Crowe's 1941 team went 17-8. Ken Pegan-coached Rambler teams had a credible 3-year run of 15-6, 17-7, and 19-6, beginning in 1947. Dick Barr's 1960 squad finished 16-7, followed by 15-7 the next year and 18-5 in 1962. The latter 2 teams were coached by Richard Briggs. Sectionals were won in 1949 and 1959. That 1935 Rambler team won the Indiana State Catholic High School Tournament, which was held annually (except for 1934) from 1928 until 1942, beating Ft. Wayne Central Catholic's Fighting Irish in the final game. In 1941 they were runner-up to Evansville Memorial's Tigers in that tournament.

Ramblers was once a fairly popular team name. Perhaps this was because the "Muskrat Ramble" and other similar jazz tunes were also popular at about the time (the mid 20s) team names were being selected.

At any rate, there were Ramblers at Worthington in Greene County, at Silver Lake in Kosciusko County, and at Union Township in Johnson County. Union Township in blue and gold, won their lone Sectional at Franklin in 1952 with wins over Edinburgh 50-42, Whiteland 34-33, Clark Township 49-46, and Trafalgar 57-42.

Silver Lake rambled in blue and red and picked off their Sectional at Warsaw in 1947, defeating Burkett 50-26, Mentone 47-29, Pierceton 59-49, and the home team, 52-36. At the Ft. Wayne Regional they edged Kendallville, 35-34, before being eliminated by the South Side Archers.

The purple and white Worthington Ramblers nabbed their 1st Sectional in 1949 at Linton for Marvin Cave with a 19-6 record. The Ramblers began by sending Switz City home 57-42, then ousted the host Miners 39-34, and finished the job with a thrilling overtime victory over Bloomfield 47-45. Their 2nd Sectional title came in 1977 at Switz City for Floyd Carl. His team knocked out Linton, 67-62, and Bloomfield, 65-52. They are now White River Valley Wolverines. Raub, in Benton County, fielded teams sometimes called the Ramblers, other times called the Hornets. Under neither name were the Gold and Black able to win a Sectional before becoming Kentland Blue Devils en route to Rebelling at South Newton.

Worthington and Raub High Schools

Those Ft. Wayne Central Catholic Fighting Irish also had their moments, finishing 20-6 under Coach Leon Youngpeter in 1968. They won both the Sectional and Regional titles that year as well as their 2nd Sectional the next year. Additionally, they also captured 3 state Catholic high school tournaments in a 4-year period, in 1939, 1940, and 1942. In the latter year they defeated Indianapolis Cathedral in a battle of Fighting Irish teams, reversing the results of a similar meeting in 1929. The Irish wore purple and gold uniforms at times and green and white ones at other times.

Huntington Catholic and Ft. Wayne Central Catholic High Schools

Several schools selected Hilltoppers for their team names. Needmore (also called Marshall Township) in Lawrence County was one. They wore purple and gold and brought home their only Sectional title in 1964 at Bedford by sidelining Orleans, Oolitic, and Paoli. At Jeffersonville Russ Blackburn's Hilltoppers won the 1st round of the Regional 75-69 over Silver Creek before being eliminated by Seymour to finish 21-4. Blackburn's next 2 teams won 40 games and lost only 6, giving the Hilltoppers an outstanding 61-10 mark for those 3 years. Wallace Etcheson's 1948 squad also turned in an excellent 21-3 record.

Bruceville, one of the oldest schools in Knox County, was another. Those red-and-blue-clad Hilltoppers did themselves and their coach James Adams proud in 1926 and 1927, winning 21 of 24 games and following that up with 22 of 25. Not a bad 2-year run, 43-6! Decker Chapel teams, also in Knox County, were known both as the Hilltoppers and the Panthers (where they are covered). In Vermillion County the Hillsdale teams, in gold and blue, were also called Hilltoppers.

You have to want to go to Houston in Jackson County in the Hoosier National Forest because it is a bit away from any state road. Coming from the north on Route 135, which is a beautiful drive, particularly in the fall, you can get on the Christianburg Pike to Houston Road, which turns into the Buffalo Pike, and you're there. Or you can come more directly off 135 from the south, picking up Houston Road just north of Freetown. For a brief period there were also Hilltoppers at Houston, whose teams were also called Pirates. In 1935 they won 15 games, losing 7, Floyd Stark coaching. In 1939 they became Freetown Spartans, then Brownstown Central Braves.

Bruceville, Decker Chapel, and Houston schools

Mt. Summit in Henry County is not too far from the highest point in Indiana, which to be accurate is not exactly Edmund Hillary territory. They did call their teams the Highlanders, living as they did on the summit, then switched to Red Devils, or maybe used both names at once. Either way, they never won a Sectional but under Coach Gene Haynes, but did finish 16-4 in 1952 and 20-4 in 1964, their last year prior to consolidation into Blue River Valley, becoming Vikings.

Mt. Summit school

The Anderson St. Mary's teams remembered their Highland roots by calling their teams the Gaels. Although they were never able to win that tough Anderson Sectional,

Jack Tilley's 1964 team put together a commendable 18-4 record 3 years before the school dropped its high school program to concentrate on pre-school through 8th grade.

Anderson St. Mary's School

In Posey County the Griffin teams were called the Tornadoes. There is good reason for that. People still talk about the Great Tornado of March 18, 1925, that swept across Missouri, southern Illinois, and Posey, Gibson, and Pike counties in Indiana. Annapolis, Missouri, was 90 percent destroyed. Gorham, Illinois, and Griffin, where 150 homes were leveled, were both essentially wiped out. The tornado struck at 1:01 P.M. in Missouri and remained on the ground for 3 1/2 hours. More students and farm owners were killed than from any tornado to that time in United States history. The storm moved forward with a record speed of 73 mph, and for over 100 miles its path width held uniformly at about 3-quarters of a mile. The United Press reported the following:

> *One hundred persons were killed and 100 injured in Griffin, Indiana. This figure comprises two-thirds of the population.*

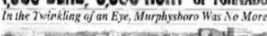

The good citizens of Griffin rebuilt their town and named their high school teams the Tornadoes. What better choice could they have made? In 1947 Marion Brooks coached the Tornadoes to a fine 22-4 finish, although they lost to Lincoln in the 1st round of the tough Evansville Sectional, 52-39.

Almost due north of Griffin were another collection of Tornadoes, these representing Gary Emerson. Noted for years for their football prowess, the Blue and Gray of Emerson also had some significant basketball success. The Tornadoes rang up a 21-5 season in 1927, Ralph Brasaemle coaching, and his 1937 through 1939 Tornado teams put together another 21-5 record. This was followed by 17-8 and 18-5 records. Bill Klug led the team to a 20-6 record in 1944, matched identically in 1947. The team posted a 19-6 mark the next year. In 1975 Earl Smith was coaching when the Emerson Tornadoes put together a 24 and 3 season. His 1978 and 1979 teams finished 19-4 and 18-6. Over the years Emerson teams won 5 Sectional championships and the 1975 Gary West Regional. However, before such things as Regionals existed, the Emerson Tornadoes made it all the way to the final game of the state tournament in 1917, losing an 8-point decision to the Lebanon Tigers. Back again to Indiana University, the next year Emerson lost to Anderson in the 1st round of the state finals. In 1919 the state finals were at Purdue University, and Emerson was again in the field, defeating Kendallville in the 1st round before losing by 3 points to a Lafayette team who would lose the championship game themselves by 3 points to Bloomington. The next year the finals were again at IU and Emerson was present again, dropping a 1st round encounter with Bedford.

Gary Emerson High School

In 1927 the venue for the state finals was the Coliseum at the state fairgrounds in Indianapolis. Once again Emerson was in the field, this year winning a 1st rounder over Mishawaka before being eliminated by the eventual state champion, Martinsville.

In White County the Rangers represented Reynolds. In the last 4 years of their existence, prior to being consolidated into the North White Vikings, the Rangers put together a very nice run. Jack Woodruff was the coach, and his 1960 team won 17 games and lost 5, followed by 20-3, 18-5, and 19-3 seasons. Four years, 74 wins, 16 losses. Not a bad finish, but sadly no Sectional crown to show for it. There were also Rangers representing Mt. Auburn in Shelby County, although they were also known as the Blackhawks at times. Baugo Township in Elkhart County, like Jimtown, fielded the Jimmies. They won their only Sectional at Elkhart in 1945, defeating Middlebury, Nappanee, and the hometown Blazers. At the South Bend Regional Baugo upended Culver before being eliminated by South Bend Riley. Since Riley would finish runner-up for the state championship in Indianapolis to Evansville Bosse, losing to them was hardly a disgrace for the red-and-black-uniformed Jimmies.

Morgan's Raiders made their way into Indiana and Ohio during the Civil War, led by Confederate Brigadier General John Hunt Morgan. The most important skirmish in Indiana took place in Harrison County and was known as the Battle of Corydon. Morgan Township teams in Harrison County were known as the Raiders. The Raiders won their 1st Sectional championship at Salem in 1962 for Bob Masterson with wins over Lanesville, Campbellsburg, North Central the town, and Corydon. Their 2nd came 3 years later, also at Salem with wins over Lanesville, Corydon, and Milltown. Each time they were eliminated from the tournament at Jeffersonville by Seymour. Masterson's 1959 through 1963 Raiders won an admirable 91 games and lost 28, with the high-water mark being 1963's 22-2 record.

The Masonic Home High School in Johnson County was open from 1925 through 1944. Their colors were scarlet and grey for a time, then blue and grey, and their teams were appropriately known as the Craftsmen, because every student, in addition to receiving a classical education, also learned a skilled trade. Although the

Masonic Home

Craftsmen never won a Sectional championship, they did put together an undefeated regular season in 1931, finishing 21-1 for Coach Dale Jamison, ending a 3-year period of 53 wins and just 9 losses.

Summitville teams were the Goblins. Several ghost sightings have occurred there, including a young man in a Confederate uniform seen in Beulah Park and a chained-up man drifting along Alexandria Creek. This kind of thing may or may not account for the mascot selection. At any rate, the Goblins did enjoy several excellent seasons before being consolidated into Madison Grant and becoming Argylls. In 1920 Paul

Summitville High School

Wooley coached the Goblins to a 27-win season, the team losing 6. Six years later John Moore was the coach, and the Black and Gold not only won 23 of 30 games but also captured the Anderson Sectional title with a resounding win over Elwood, 23-4; a close call with Pendleton, 20-19; and a 6-point victory over Alexandria. The Goblins went on to capture the Muncie Regional as well, winning 2 squeakers. They beat Indianapolis Shortridge, 20-18, and Noblesville, 12-10. In the state finals at the Fairgounds Exposition Building, the Goblins were spooked (sorry) by Martinsville in the 1st round. Martinsville, however, would be the state runner-up that year, so it was not at all a disgrace for Summitville to be eliminated by the Artesians. In 1931 Summitville won 19 games and lost 5 for Coach Earl Delph and in 1945 they finished 17-5 with Dale Prough coaching. Paul Bradford led the team to a 21-5 mark in 1949 when, again, the Goblins won both Sectional and Regional crowns. The Anderson Sectional resulted in wins over Alexandria, Pendleton, and Markleville, which qualified the Goblins for the Indianapolis Regional, won by defeating Tech and Fortville. In the Indianapolis Semi-state the Goblins were again eliminated by the school that would be the state runner-up. This time it was Madison's Cubs, and again the Goblins could return to Summitville with heads held high to an appreciative crowd.

Finally, there were the Comets at South Caston and North Caston, both short-lived schools, at Lagro, at Riverdale in DeKalb County and at Castleton, a school that lasted until 1941 in an area that is now a huge shopping center. The blue and grey Castleton Comets became Lawrence Central Bears. The South Caston Comets, who enjoyed a 16-5 record for Coach Ron Lebo in 1962, had their team name live on, adopted by Caston after consolidation. North Caston's blue-and-white clad Comets had 1 terrific season, 22-1 in 1962, followed by 2 good ones, 18-3 and 18-5, in their only years of existence, for Coach Shannon Jones. That's 58 wins and 9 losses, for an

Castleton School

87 percent winning percentage. Is there a school anywhere, or has there ever been one, with a better total record than that? That only loss in 1962 was in the semi-finals of the Peru Sectional, 59-56, to Clay Township, which would beat the home team to win the title. North Caston, too, took their name with them, joining their kindred souls from South Caston, and others, as Caston Comets.

The Lagro Comets streamed across the winter skies in Wabash County in their red and black uniforms. They fielded teams as early as 1912, when they recorded 6 victories in 9 games. Paul Bartholomew coached the Comets to 3 successful seasons in a row from 1930 through 1932, winning 50 games and losing only 14. His 1937 team did even better, winning 18 of 22 games. Although they never won a Sectional, Lagro came close in 1946 when John Huffman's squad put together an outstanding 20-3 season only to lose the final game of the Wabash Sectional to the home team Apaches after racking up wins over Chippewa, North Manchester and Linlawn. In 1957 Meredith Hanselman led the Comets to an 18-5 record, and in 1962 they consolidated into Southwood, becoming Knights.

The 1916 Lagro High School, home of the Comets

Lagro High School Comets

Chapter 40

The Large and the Small:
Good Times and Good Memories for All

Perhaps no single group of schools has created a record of performance at the highest levels of excellence in Indiana high school basketball to equal that of the fabled North Central Conference. First conceived of in 1926, the conference centered on basketball. It was initially the only sport. The 10 founding schools were:

Anderson*	Logansport*
Frankfort	Muncie*
Indianapolis Arsenal Tech	New Castle*
Kokomo*	Richmond*
Lebanon	Rochester
*Current Member	

Lafayette replaced Rochester in 1932 and Marion replaced Lebanon in 1934. Indianapolis Tech was forced to withdraw in 1961 when the school board required the Titans to play a full city schedule. At this point the NCC was a 9-member conference. In 1966 Frankfort withdrew because of their relatively small enrollment. In 1975 girls athletic programs were added to the conference schedules. In 2003 Lafayette Jeff left the conference and shortly thereafter Huntington North joined.

Today's North Central Conference: Anderson Indians, Huntington North Vikings, Kokomo WildKats, Marion Giants, Muncie Central Bearcats, New Castle Trojans, Logansport Berries (also Felix the Cat), and Richmond Red Devils

And, for the record, the former members:

Frankfort Hot Dogs, Indianapolis Arsenal Tech Titans, Lafayette Jefferson Bronchos, Lebanon Tigers, and Rochester Zebras

Prior to the emergence of class basketball tournaments, the dominance of the NCC was more evident. Of the 71 state championships contested from the 1st season of operation of the NCC until the last non-class state tournament, 27 of the crowned champions (38 percent) were in the NCC at the time of their final game victory and another 20 were runners-up. In 8 years the state finals final game was played between conference members.

Over the entire period of the official Indiana state tournament, 10 schools that were at least once NCC members have placed in the top 15 of all-time Sectional winners, led by Kokomo's 69. Marion has won 65, Lafayette Jefferson 61, Richmond 59, Muncie Central and New Castle 57 apiece, Logansport 56, Anderson and Lebanon 50, and Frankfort 46. Eight of the top 9 Regional winning schools come from this group, with only Evansville Central breaking into the line-up at number 7. Lafayette Jeff, Marion, Muncie Central, and Kokomo have all won more than 30 Regionals. At the Semi-state and state championship level similar rankings emerge, Marion having won 14 of the former followed by Muncie Central 13, Lafayette Jeff 12, and Anderson 11. Muncie Central has won 8 state championships, Marion 7, Frankfort 4, Anderson, Lebanon, and Lafayette Jeff 3 each, New Castle 2, and 1 apiece for Richmond and Logansport. The extent of this domination by these schools, who were all county seats and whose schools were generally much larger than any school they would meet in a Sectional, contributed in large manner to the desire for class basketball. Many of our 800 schools were proud to remember their one moment of glory when they finally claimed a Sectional crown. Many others never experienced that thrill, and

I am sure there was considerable resentment of the kind of success enjoyed by the NCC members, or, for that matter, by other big schools such as Vincennes Lincoln, Washington, and New Albany, who dominated their areas. That the emergence of class basketball came well after consolidation had dramatically reduced the size advantages held by such schools strikes me as paradoxical at best. Perhaps 2 classes would have made some sense; 4, to me, does not, particularly since we now have just over half as many schools as we did at the height of the state tournament's entrance lists.

This is not to marginalize the success of the NCC, or its contribution to our state's deserved recognition as an outstanding producer of high school basketball talent and the excitement surrounding the sport. Huge arenas were built on campuses, and for years they were filled with early-arriving and late-departing fans. Tickets were disputed in divorce cases and passed down in estates...or so I've heard. Whether or not this is true, it is incontrovertible that interest in Indiana high school basketball was immense. This interest provided Indiana with a kind of cohesiveness, a sense of statewide pride, a common culture that engulfed every part of the state, rural and urban, north and south. To a great extent that has not been lost even with the emergence of competing activities such as local professional sports teams and widespread television availability of sporting events. We are still all Hoosiers and we still love the sound a perfect shot makes when it hits only nylon or the thump, thump, thump of a round ball on a hardwood floor.

When one looks at the myriad of star players to have come out of the NCC: names such as Kent Benson, Steve Alford, Ray Pavy, Jimmy Rayl, Johnny Wilson, and many others, it is hard to know who to highlight, but here are a few Hall of Famers from several of the NCC schools:

Lamar Lundy, Richmond
Played 13 years with NFL Los Angeles Rams as member of legendary "Fearsome Foursome" ... All-State, 6-6 center played in Final Four for Hall of Famer Art Beckner . . . played on Indiana all-star team . . . was also All-State in football, and played in that sport in the high school all-star game . . . took his talents to Purdue, where he was MVP his senior year on both the basketball and football teams, the only Boilermaker to accomplish that feat ... lettered 3 years in both sports . . . played in the college all-star game at Chicago against NFL All Stars

David Colescott, Marion

During junior and senior seasons, he led the Marion High School Giants to consecutive state basketball championships in 1975 & 1976. . . .the team enjoyed 51 wins and six losses during these illustrious years under Hall of Fame Coach Bill Green. . . .after averaging 26.5 points per game during his senior year, he was named the Trester Award winner and Mr. Basketball for 1976. . . .the success continued at the University of North Carolina with Coach Dean Smith, as the team won 98 games and lost only 27 during the next four years. . . the collegiate highlights include an NCAA Runner-Up 1977, ACC Championship 1977, 78 & 79, free throw award 1979, All-ACC Tourney Team 1979 and Team Captain 1980.

Dalen Showalter, Logansport

Set North Central Conf scoring record in '56... also led NCC in scoring as junior...set Logansport single-game record with 41 points, single-season record with 585 points and career mark with 1,314 points...4-year varsity performer and 3-year starter...played in 4 regionals and 3 semistates...All-State as senior... named to Scholastic Coach All-American team that season... at U of Tenn, led freshman team in scoring...Southeastern Conf sophomore of the year...3-yr starter...captain in sr year...all-conf. as a junior and senior...led SEC in scoring as senior.

Bob Masters, Lafayette Jefferson

Marion Crawley called him the most coachable player he ever had. A Four-sport performer at Lafayette Jefferson ... Mr. Basketball in 1948, leading Bronchos to state championship . . . three-year starter at Indiana University ... All-American in '52 ... twice all-Big 10 ... won Big 10 Medal in '52 ... helped lead Hoosiers to second–and third–place finishes in conference ... went on to 20-year AAU career ... one of five players selected in '78 by National Association of Basketball Coaches for the "Silver Anniversary Award."

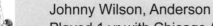

Johnny Wilson, Anderson

Played 1 yr with Chicago American Giants of Negro Baseball League...3 years with Harlem Globetrotters... Coached at Indianapolis Wood 8 yrs, then moved into collegiate ranks...basketball and baseball coach at Malcolm X Community College...Anderson High School's high-scoring legend...smashed 34-yr old record by scoring 30 points in 1946 state championship game, won by Anderson...Mr. Basketball...All-State...2-time all-North Central Conference...3-sport standout...moved to Anderson College to excel in 4 sports...2-time all-Hoosier Conf basketball player.

Jimmy Rayl, Kokomo

Mr. Basketball in 1959 ... led Kokomo to state runner-up spot ... his 114 points in final four games of 59 tourney broke Oscar Robertson's record ... 2-time All-State ... Trester Award winner ... 1,632 career points at Kokomo ... twice all-North Central Conference ... Star of Stars Award in '59 Indiana-Kentucky all-star game ... 2-time All-American at Indiana University ... 2 times all-Big 10 ... set IU single-game scoring record with 56, a feat he did twice ... school record 32-straight free throws . . .1,401 career points. . . member of World Cup championship team in '66. . .played on Goodyear's national AAU champions that same year. He played with the Indiana Pacers, with a high game of 32 points

Ron Bonham, Muncie Central

Member of two Boston Celtics teams that won NBA titles; played on first Indiana Pacers team...Twice a first-team all-stater at Muncie Central ... graduated in 1960 as Bearcats' all-time leading scorer with 2,023 points .. first-team all-state as junior and senior ... Mr. Basketball in 1960 ... led Muncie Central to state runner-up spot that year ... MVP of both Indiana-Kentucky all-star games ... helped University of Cincinnati to one national championship, and the runner-up spot the next season ... first team All-American as a junior, second team as a senior.

Jerry Ellis, New Castle

All Indiana All-Star, All-State, All-Semi-Final, All-Regional, All-Sectional, All-NCC ... 17th all-time scorer ... 16 varsity letters ... played basketball and football as a freshman at Indiana University ... 3 year starter on football team, leading rusher 1953 season and Balfour Award winner, captain ... 1954-81 US Air Force, retired as a Colonel ... flew over 400 combat missions, awarded Silver star, Distinguished Flying Cross, Bronze Star, 16 Combat Air medals, Vietnamese Cross of Gallantry with Palm, Legion of Merit ... 1975 Silver Anniversary Team.

Muncie Central was off and running by 1921. That year Maurice Murray's squad won 28 games and lost only 4, which began a streak of 20-game winning seasons for the Bearcats that would not be broken until 1935. Over that 14-year period Central teams would win 329 games and lose only 79, the last half of those years coached by Pete Jolly. His 1938 team would also win 26 of 30 games. From 1950 through 1955 the 'Cats turned in 143 wins while losing only 25 under the direction of Hall of Famers Art Beckner and Jay McCreary. A 3rd impressive string came from 1957 through 1963 as those 7 Central teams won 171 games and dropped 26. Included in that period was Hall of Fame coach John Longfellow's 1960 28-1 team. Their only loss was to East Chicago Washington in the final game of that year's state tournament. Also included is the 29-1 state championship team of 1963. Hall of Famer Bill Harrell's 1978 and 1979 teams won state titles with a combined record of 51 and 8, and his 1988 team won the state championship, his 3rd and the school's 8th, with a 28-1 mark. As recently as 2004 through 2007 the Bearcats have won 89 games and lost just 15. The Lady 'Cats have added 5 Sectional nets to the school's crowded trophy case.

Though Kokomo's 'Kats have only won that one state championship in 1961 with the incredible overtime victory over Indianapolis Manual and the Van Arsdale twins, it was certainly one of the most exciting final games of all time. Joe Platt's charges finished with a 28-1 mark. In 1917 the 'Kats finished 25-4 for Coach Mike Harrell and enjoyed a trip to the Sweet Sixteen. Chet Hill's 1926 team finished 20-4 and Alfred Campbell's Kokomo teams won 62 of 80 games from 1939 through 1941. Ralph King's charges turned in 21-8 and 22-4 seasons in 1944 and 1945 and Joe Platt led his 1952 team to a 25-3 mark. From 1958 through 1962 his teams amassed 123 victories against only 16 defeats! Basil Mawbey led the 1988 and 1989 Wildkats to 24-3, and 25-6 marks, and his 1995 through 1997 teams ran up a total of 69 wins and only 11 losses. The Lady Kats have added 3 state championships to the school's trophy case, 1992 and 1993 under Coach Mike McCroskey, with records of 26-1 and

27-1, and 2003 when Charlie Hall's team finished an undefeated season, 26-0. From 1990 through 1994 McCroskey's teams amassed 117 victories and lost only 10! His last team, in 1997, and Hall's first 2 teams went on to win 65 of 75 games played, and Charles Huppenthal's 2006 Lady 'Kats went 23-3. All told, the Kokomo girls have won 19 Sectionals, 10 Regionals, and 5 Semi-state crowns to go with those 3 state championships.

New Castle's 1st state championship came in 1932, when Coach Orville Hooker's Trojans won 28 of 31 games, including the final over Winamac 24-17 at Butler Fieldhouse. Their 2nd came 74 years later in 2006 at Conseco Fieldhouse with a 51-43 win over Jay County in the Class 3A final game to finish 21-6 for Coach Steve Bennet. The Trojans had been to the finals as early as 1914. That year George Bronson's team went to Indiana University and gave Vevay a serious hoops lesson, 34-0, before being sent home in the next round by New Augusta, 8-6. The Trojan's 1st 20-win season came in 1920, 20-10 for that era's coach Frank Allen. Their next came with 1932's magnificent team, followed by three 20-win seasons under Wilbur Allen: 21-7 in 1936, 22-7 in 1940, and 22-4 in 1944. Good seasons continued with 20-7 for Charles Stuckey in 1950 and 20-5 for Randall Lawson in 1959. In 1967 Cecil Teague took over the New Castle reins and immediately led the Trojans to a 25-3 mark, winning the Indianapolis Semi-state, 51-49 over Shortridge. It took State Champion Evansville North to send the Trojans back to New Castle in the 1st game of the state finals, 66-56. Between 1971 and 1973 Teague's teams won 61 games and lost only 16 against the toughest opposition the state had to offer. Sam Alford coached the Trojans from 1976 through 1995 and had several 20-victory seasons, starting with his 1st year, 21-7. His next came in 1983, 23-6, the year son Steve's unforgettable 57-point performance in the Indianapolis Semi-state morning game was enough to oust a very strong Broad Ripple team. Young Alford, however, could not lift the Trojans past eventual state champion Connersville that night. Coach Alford's next Trojan team finished 21-7 and won the Indianapolis Semi-state in heart-stopping fashion, 74-73 in overtime against Perry Meridian and 60-59 over Columbus North. Whew. Again, a state championship team would eliminate the Trojans in the 1st game of the finals. This time it was Warsaw's Tigers, 59-56. Alford also coached the 1990 and 1995 teams to 23-6 and 24-3 records. In 1997 Curt Bell's team finished a fine 24-2, and Steve Bennett's 2007 squad won 23 of 26 games. Bell's 2-year stint coaching the boys resulted in 43 wins and only 7 losses, but he had also coached the Lady Trojans to a 23-4 mark in 1993 and would later coach them to a strong 23-3 mark in 2007. In total the Lady Trojans have won 17 Sectional and 2 Regional crowns.

Logansport was led from 1923–45 by Hall of Fame coach Cliff Wells. From 1924 through 1931 his Berries put together an impressive series of 20-win seasons totaling 163 victories while suffering only 57 defeats and culminating in a Final Four appearance. They were beaten by fellow NCC member Muncie, 23-17, in the 1st semi-final game. Muncie went on to win the state title that night. From 1933 through

1935 Logansport's teams rang up 75 wins and lost just 14. Included was the school's lone state championship which came in 1934 with a 28-4 mark as they defeated Indianapolis Tech at the Butler Fieldhouse, 26-19. Wells' 1937 team finished 23-6, and his 1942 squad won 20 games while losing 9. Jim Jones coached the 1961 team to a 24-4 finish and his 1967 team won 20 of 26 games. Their last 20-win season came in 1976 under Jim Williams, 20-5. The Lady Berries have added 9 Sectional nets to the school's trophy case.

Marion's Giants won 15 of 19 games as early as 1910 and won the 1st of their 7 state championships in 1926, winning 27 of 29 games for Coach Eugene Thomas. The Giants began to hit their stride under Jack Colescott in 1965, winning 22 of 26 games. They amassed 70 victories and only 13 defeats from 1967 through 1969 when the 27-1 state runner-up team lost its only game to Indianapolis Washington's George McGiness-led, undefeated juggernaut, in a gut-wrenching 61-60 semi-final game at Hinkle Fieldhouse, one of the most exciting Final Fours ever played. Bill Green led the Giants to consecutive state championships in 1975 and 1976, finishing 28-1 and 23-5. Larry Liddle took over for the next 5 years and turned in an impressive record of 113 wins and only 22 losses. Green returned to the coach's box in 1982 and led the Giants to an amazing string of 6 years when they won 129 games and lost just 19. This culminated in 3 successive state championships (referred to in Marion as the "Purple Rein,") including 1985's undefeated 28-0 mark. Marion's most recent state championship came in 2000 when Moe Smedley's charges defeated Bloomington North 62-56 in the 4A final game to finish 28-1. Gordon Heyward's last-second shot gave Brownsburg the title over Marion in 2008, as Joe Luce's Giants finished 24-5. The Lady Giants had undefeated regular seasons in 1980 and 1981, finishing 23-1 and 25-1. Coach Sally Leyse's teams won Semi-state championships each year. In total they have won 14 Sectionals and 4 Regionals as well.

Anderson's Indians hit the ground running, making the Final Twelve in the first state tournament in 1911 and ending as state runners-up in 1914 and 1918. By 1919 they were winning 23 of 27 games and the next year hit the rarified atmosphere of a 30-win season, 32-3, for that era's coach Alva Staggs. Staggs' 1921 squad came in state runner-up for the school's 3rd time. Since this would happen 4 more times, that would amount to 7 major disappointments to go with the Indians 2 state championships, 1937 under Archie Chadd, 24-7, and 1946 under Charles Cummings, 22-7. Ray Estes' 1964–66 teams won 67 games and lost only 14. Norm Held's 1983 and 1984 teams ran up 48 victories against only 7 defeats; his 1992 and 1993 teams won 49 and lost just 5. More recently, Ron Hecklinski's Indians won 64 of 77 games from 1996 through 1998 and his 2006 squad finished 24-2. The Lady Indians have won 13 Sectionals, 9 Regionals and 2 Semi-states.

Lafayette Jefferson teams, the Bronchos, made the Final Eight in our 1st state tournament in 1911, followed by another Final Four appearance in 1913 with a 16-3 record. By 1916 the Bronchos had captured their 1st state championship with a 20-4 record for Coach C. F. Apking, defeating Crawfordsville 27-26 in overtime. State runner-up titles came in 1919 and 1920 for Broncho coach F. J. Grosshans, with records of 19-4 and 30-7, and the next year his team played 45(!) games, winning 34. An undefeated regular season was achieved in 1935 by the team for their coach A. B. Masters, 23-1. Marion Crawley took over in Lafayette in 1944, a job the Hall of Famer would hold until 1967 (except for 1965), during which time his Bronchos would win state championships in 1948 with a 27-3 record and in 1964 with a 28-1 mark, the school's 3rd and Crawley's 4th state titles. From 1946–48 Crawley's teams won 71 games and lost only 12. His 1956 through 1958 Bronchos won 67 games and lost 18, and his 1962 through 1964 squads went 73 and 11. In his last 2 years with Jeff, Crawley's teams won 45 of 54 games and were runners-up to the Bob Ford-led Evansville North squad in 1967, losing by a single basket. Crawley's Bronchos were also runner-up in 1950 to Ray Eddy's 27-1 Madison Cubs. The runner-up plaque also came to Jeff via Jim Hammel's 1992 team with a 28-3 record, losing an overtime game to Richmond's Red Devils in an all-NCC final. The Lady Bronchos have won 8 Sectionals and 5 Regionals, including a 22-2 record for Nick Cordell in 1983.

Richmond's Red Devils made it to the state finals in 1912, 1916, and 1917, the latter year with a 17-3 record for Coach Lyman Lyboult. Harold Wilson's 1923 team enjoyed an undefeated regular season, losing their lone game in the 2nd round of the finals at the old Coliseum to eventual state runner-up Muncie 33-30 to finish 28-1. Thirty years later Art Beckner's Red Devils turned in a 24-5 mark, but it was Dick Baumgartner's arrival on the scene in 1966 that began the new Golden Age of Richmond basketball. Baumgartner's record through 1977 was 218 wins and 63 losses playing in the upper echelon of the state's basketball powers. Still, that state championship remained elusive until George Griffith's 1992 team broke through with that thrilling overtime win over NCC rival Lafayette Jefferson to finish 24-5. This came after 2 frustrating runner-up finishes for Griffith's 1985 and 1987 Devils. They finished with records of 22-7 and 24-5. The Lady Red Devils have won 8 Sectionals and 1 Regional. Mel Young's 1991 team finished undefeated in the regular season with a final record of 20-1.

But the North Central Conference was far from the only place where Hoosiers were having fun watching high school basketball. Every county had its own tournament, every school had its own rivals. Conference championships were as coveted in many cases as were Sectional trophies. Towns with only 1 school associated that school's hardwood success with that of the town itself. Social engagements were planned around Friday and Saturday night games. Away games were attended en masse, the convoy stretching cross-country reminiscent of scenes from *Hoosiers*. Nowhere was this enjoyed more than by the citizens of Greene County.

Named for Revolutionary War hero General Nathaniel Greene of Rhode Island, Greene County gives you a real sense of the excitement and fun of Indiana high school basketball. The county is located a bit to the south of the west central portion of the

Greene County Courthouse, Bloomfield

state, bisected by the White River. The Eel River flows into the White in the county's northern part. There are no big cities in Greene County. There are farms, orchards, coal mines, and second growth forests. The total population of the county is 33,000. Bloomfield is the county seat.

In the 30s Linton was near the population center of the United States and has a marker to prove it (although Spencer, of course, in nearby Owen County was also once the center of population of the country and took that name for its teams, the Cops). It is the largest city in Greene County with a population of only 5,800. Yet, the Greene County tournament draws crowds of 3,000, selling out the Switz City gym even for the consolation game. The Eastern High School Thunderbirds gym in Bloomfield is routinely sold out for every home game, packing in 2,000 rabid boosters. According to one of the players in the Greene County tournament, there are several reasons for the continuing attraction of basketball to the area: no malls, no movie theaters, no miniature golf courses exist in the county. (They do, however, have a four-way bridge, which is unique.)

Before consolidation only one of the county's 12 high schools even fielded a football team, so basketball was truly king. In those days the tournament was strictly a county affair. There were the Linton Miners, the Worthington Ramblers, the Switz City Tigers, the Solsberry Hornets, and the Scotland Scotties. They would compete with their neighbors the Owensburg Indians, the Newberry River Rats, the Midland Middies, and the Jasonville Yellow Jackets. For a time there were also the Lyons Lions and the Marco Bears, but they became the L&M Braves, now further consolidated into the White River Valley High School Wolverines.

Jasonville, Lyons, and Scotland schools

Midland and Newberry Schools

Today there are only 4 high schools left in Greene County. Besides Eastern, Linton, and White River Valley, the Shakamak Lakers complete the line-up.

Eastern Thunderbirds, Linton Miners, WRV Wolverines and Shakamak Lakers

These 4 schools now invite 4 others from adjacent counties to fill the field for their annual tournament. A recent year's version included the Patriots from Rivet High School in Vincennes, the North Central High School Thunderbirds from Farmersburg (once represented by the Plowboys), the Dugger Union High School Bulldogs, and the championship team from Clay City, the Eels. You have to love the Greene County approach to basketball if you care at all about high school sports. (I am indebted to Steve Hanlon of *The Indianapolis Star* for his article of January 13, 2003, for much of this information.)

For years the teams in Greene County have battled for a special prize, known as the Keg. In 2008 the Keg was won by the Shakamak Lakers.

Porter County is another example of how small schools have a great deal of fun with our state sport. Consider the Porter County Conference. Schools currently in the conference are the South Central Satellites, the Hanover Central Wildcats, the Morgan Township Cherokees, the Boone Grove Wolves, the Kouts Mustangs and Fillies, the Washington Township Senators, the LaCrosse Tigers and the Hebron Hawks. The year 2008 marked the 50th anniversary of the conference; the future

The Greene County Keg

looks bright for another 50 years at least. The founding schools were current members Boone Grove, Hebron, Kouts and Morgan and Washington Townships as well as the Jackson Township Panthers, the Liberty Township Lions, and the Wheeler Bearcats, who have since moved elsewhere. The Westville Blackhawks were also members for a time.

Quiz yourself on which teams these fierce and funny logos represent

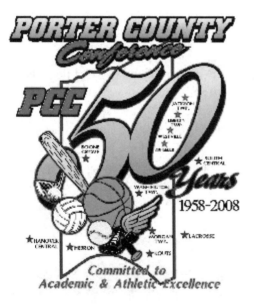

Enrollments of the current 8 schools range from Hanover's 686 students to LaCrosse with only 87. Average of the 8 current schools is only 348 students. The Porter County Boys Tournament predated the establishment of the conference and has been an annual event since 1924. Chesterton and Portage teams were included in the tournament until 1968, when they withdrew due to their growth. The girls tournament was added in 1973, 3 years before the IHSAA established the 1st official girls state championship tournament.

A Victory Keg travels around the conference as boys basketball games are won and lost. It is an old water keg that has circulated since November 16, 1967, and it's painted in the school colors of the team that holds it. It was first painted Wheeler green and white and is currently Morgan Township green and gold, although the latest picture I could get shows it in Kouts gold and black. Some serious records on the Keg are kept and are

available from the conference Web site.

Similarly, a Victory Kup was established for girls teams in 1975 in the conference with an equally competitive result. The Lady Senators of West Washington defeated Wheeler to win that first Kup. Here is the Kup, again in Kouts gold and black, as won at the time by the Fillies:

The 8 schools currently comprising the conference have won a total of 38 Sectional championships, of which 23 came prior to the advent of class basketball. The open era leaders are Hebron with 7 and Morgan Township with 6. Since 1998, Boone Grove has won 7 Class 2A Sectionals, bringing their grand total to 9. On the girls side of the ledger, current conference members have snared 26 Sectionals in total, 19 of which came in the era of class basketball.

The Victory Kup held by Fillie Juliette Keller

Just about every county in the state once had enough schools to have home and away schedules that did not require long bus or car trips, and enough schools for a meaningful county tournament. In Hamilton County they recently (well, 1990) had a nostalgia game between the Walnut Grove Wolves and the Jackson Central Eagles in the Hamilton Heights Gym. (Jackson Central was an early consolidation before the legislature made it a requirement state-wide, uniting the Atlanta Cardinals, the Arcadia Dragons, and the Cicero Red Devils in 1943.)

Players from the 50s and 60s from each school suited up and cheerleaders from each led the yells for the enthusiastic fans. In those days there were no Hamilton Heights Huskies, no Hamilton Southeastern Royals. The Fishers Tigers, Carmel Greyhounds, Westfield Shamrocks, Sheridan Blackhawks, and Noblesville Millers represented schools no larger than the aforementioned Wolves and Eagles. Gene Conrad, *Noblesville Daily Ledger* sports writer caught the spirit of those times perfectly in his column published Wednesday, February 14, 1990, entitled "The Ghosts of Walnut Grove and JC are Still Alive:"

[They] may have mixed a Wolf and an Eagle and come up with a Huskie...But they will never—as in never—erase those marvelous, whacko days of the 1950s and 1960s when it was an outrageous thrill to cram into the 600 seat Walnut Grove arena that had folding chairs on the stage and bodies jammed the foyers every weekend to see the Wolves take on the Eagles or Sheridan or Fishers or Westfield or whomever. Oh, sure the game has changed, new arenas take two seasons to build, forty years to pay for and a day's wages to get into...but they're still missing that incredibly grand atmosphere that made Saturday night a marvelous Mardi Gras and "Two bits, four bits six bits a dollar" the greatest basketball

love song ever written

...the Eagle arena [was] so small you had to stand sideways to take the ball out of bounds. and the longest road trip in those airy school buses in the dead of winter was to Markleville to play the Arabians...after the games the gang always headed to Scotty's Inn or Bill's Drive In where the specialty was a coke with a pretzel hanging on the straw.

The two schools combined [Walnut Grove and Jackson Central] didn't have 600 students which was perhaps the beauty of it all. Graduating classes would number anywhere from 30 to 50 and high school enrollments would have had to stretch to top 200. But there was something about being a Walnut Grove Wolf or a Jackson Central Eagle from rural mid-century Indiana that was special. There was no concern for Hinkle Fieldhouse or the AP poll...to be a Wolf or an Eagle meant you played just as hard, laughed just as often and learned just as much as the kids from the "city"...the Walnut Grove and Jackson Central good times were undiluted and Simon pure—the kind you always remember.

I don't think I've ever heard it put any better than that. Those memories permeate the atmosphere of Indiana, reaching every corner of the state and bringing us all together as Hoosiers.

For the record, the Atlanta Cardinals, in red and white uniforms, put together a 10 and 2 season as early as 1910—though in all probability those were not yet either their colors or their team name. In 1935 with Voss Hiatt as their coach the Cardinals won 16 games and lost 5. The Cardinals notched their lone Sectional title at Tipton in 1937 with wins over Carmel, Westfield, Sheridan, and Noblesville, also for Hiatt, finishing 16-8. They are now Hamilton Heights Huskies after a waystop as Jackson Central Eagles.

Further proof that basketball was being played in Central Indiana very early on comes from the fact that Arcadia enjoyed a 12-2 season in 1909. Eventually called the Dragons and wearing black and gold uniforms, Arcadia also won 11 of 14 games in 1915. Fred Anderson coached the Dragons to a 14-3 mark in 1921, and his 1924 team turned in a 21-8 mark. Wesley Abel's 1931 team won 15 of 18 games. Carl Bailiff's 1939 and 1942 teams finished 18-2 and 20-5 respectively. The Dragons' 1st Sectional title came at Kokomo in 1921 with wins over Russiaville, Tipton, Howard Township, and those other fearsome firebreathers, the Windfall Dragons. The 2nd came at Noblesville in 1924, Anderson's 21-8 Dragons beating Sheridan by 2 points, the home team by 10, and Carmel by 3.

The Cicero Red Devils had a terrific season in 1915 with Austin Landreth coaching, winning 20 and losing only 3. In 1930 they won 16 of 20 for Floyd Walter. Their colors were old gold and scarlet. Cicero picked up 3 Sectional titles: in 1916 at Anderson, in 1928 at Noblesville, and in 1932 at Sheridan. They also won the 1932 Marion Regional in a thriller by 1 point over the home team's mighty Giants, and a 10-point decision, 31-21, over Somerset. In the Sweet Sixteen at Butler Fieldhouse the Devils proceeded to edge the Vincennes Alices 17-15 before losing to New Castle in the next round. Losing to New Castle was no disgrace, however, as the Trojans were to be crowned state champions that year.

The original Fishers Tigers also wore red and white uniforms and experienced a memorable season in 1947, winning 20 and losing 2 for Coach Horace Love. In 1954 and 1955 William Reed's Tigers won 18 and then 16 while being defeated 6 times each year. Fishers won the Kokomo Sectional in 1922 with wins over Windfall, Noblesville, Greentown, and Howard Township. At the Indiana University Regional tournament the Tigers advanced to the state finals at the old Coliseum in Indianapolis, 2-0, when Wingate forfeited, or was disqualified. At the Coliseum Fishers won their 1st-round game against Goshen, 18-9, before being eliminated by eventual state runner-up Terre Haute Garfield.

The consolidated Eagles of Jackson Central inherited Carl Bailiff as their coach when they opened in 1943. His 2nd team there finished 19-4. Bailiff's Eagles won the school's one and only Sectional at Sheridan in 1945 with wins over Prairie Township, Walnut Grove and Tipton. In 1946 his team won 13 and lost just 3. Walter O'Brien coached the 1951 and 1952 teams to 15-7 and 17-6 marks.

Walnut Grove got started early, too, winning 8, losing 4, and tying 1 in 1910. They only lost 1 game in 1912 . . . but they only played 5! The purple-and-old-gold clad Wolves won 16 and lost 7 in 1941 for William Stults, enjoyed a 15 and 6 record in 1943 for Guy Bauchert, and won 19 while losing only 3 for Ray Rogers in 1957. Walnut Grove, regrettably, never managed to cut down the nets at a Sectional tournament.

Large and small, city and rural, east and west, north and south, it was basketball everywhere throughout our Hoosier State...and it still is!

Arcadia and Atlanta Schools

Cicero and Walnut Grove Schools

Basketball is about action, pure and simple. Young bodies, minds, and spirits in constant motion plotting strategies, taking chances, pushing limits and reaching higher than before, as in this photo of New Castle's Steve Alford in this 1983 *Indiana Basketball History* photo. The photos in this book, static as they are, cannot reflect the heart of the game, which is essentially kinesthetic. For that you must imagine all these young men and women away from the camera, in shorts or bloomers on the hardwood, rushing and panting, with 20 seconds to go. Or, better yet, on a Friday night to come, go down to the local gym and catch a game. Smell the sweat and popcorn, rise as one with the crowd. It's beter than Wii or the NBA on TV, even if you are only a spectator for one night.

Appendix

I. My favorite team names for current schools

II. My favorite team names for closed schools

III. A selection of gym names

IV. Our larger gyms

V. Undefeated State Champions

VI. Small school success stories

VII. Class basketball '50s style

VIII. Breaks High School

IX. Heltonville

APPENDIX I
MY FAVORITE INDIANA HIGH SCHOOL TEAM NAMES FOR CURRENT SCHOOLS

(Alphabetical by Team Name)

Vincennes Lincoln	Alices
Martinsville	Artesians
Crawfordsville	Athenians
DeKalb	Barons
Logansport	Berries & Felix the Cat
Mitchell	Blue Jackets
Hobart	Brickies
New Haven	Bulldogs
Cloverdale	Clovers
Perry Central	Commodores
Indianapolis Washington	Continentals
Indiana School for the Deaf	Deaf Hoosiers
Argos	Dragons
Clay City & Eminence	Eels
Indianapolis Cathedral	Fighting Irish
Andrean	Fighting 59ers
Ft. Wayne Wayne	Generals
International School of Indiana	Gryphons
Franklin Central	Flashes
Clinton Prairie	Gophers
Hammond Morton	Governors
Franklin	Grizzly Cubs
Washington	Hatchets
Frankfort	Hot Dogs
River Forest	Ingots
Hauser	Jets
Northeast Dubois	Jeeps
Shoals	Jug Rox
Castle, East Noble & Holy Cross	Knights
Leo	Lions
Tell City	Marksmen
Noblesville	Millers
Linton-Stockton	Miners
Concord	Minutemen
Whiting	Oilers
Columbus East	Olympi-Annes*
Delphi	Oracles

Heritage Hills

Plymouth

Plainfield

Garrett

New Harmony

Rockville

Anderson Highlands

Rising Sun

LaPorte

Speedway

Indianapolis Northwest

Manchester

Princeton

Greencastle

Oldenburg Academy

Kokomo

Greenwood

Rochester

Patriots

Pilgrims & Rockies

Quakers

Railroaders

Rappites

Rox

Scots

Shiners

Slicers

Sparkplugs

Space Pioneers

Squires

Tigers

Tiger Cubs

Twisters

Wildkats

Woodmen

Zebras

Honorable Mention: Columbus North Swim Team Bull Frogs

* Girls teams. Boys teams are the Olympians

APPENDIX II
MY FAVORITE TEAM NAMES FOR CLOSED INDIANA HIGH SCHOOLS
(Alphabetical by School Name)

For schools with more than one name, I have listed my favorite.

Acton	Oreos
Banquo	Ghosts
Battleground	Tomahawks
Beaver Dam	Beavers
Bedford	Stonecutters
Bloomingdale Academy	Immortals
Boston	Terriers
Bunker Hill & Lexington	Minutemen
Butler	Windmills
Cadiz	Spaniards
Cambridge City	Wampus Cats
Chili	Polar Bears
Clay Twp. (Howard County)	Brickies
Colfax	Hickories
Converse	Bordermen
Cory	Apple Boys
Decker	Aces
DePauw	Blue River Echoes
Deer Creek & Sugar Creek	Crickets
DuBois & Wheatland	Jeeps
Dunkirk	Speed Cats
Edwardsport	Powers
Epsom	Salts
Evansville Rex Mundi	Monarchs
Farmersburg	Plowboys
Flint	Arrows
Ft. Branch	Twigs
East Chicago Roosevelt	Roughriders
East Chicago Washington	Senators
Elnora	Owls
Fontanet	Beantowners
Goldsmith & Lincolnville	Gold Bugs
Griffin	Tornadoes
Haubstadt	Elites
Hayden	Haymakers
Holland	Flying Dutchmen
Honey Creek	Honey Bees

Huntingburg	Happy Hunters
Indianapolis Wood	Woodchucks
Indianapolis Shortridge	Felix the Cat
Ireland	Spuds
Jackson Twp. (Howard County) & Roanoke	Stonewalls
Kirklin	Travelers
Klondike	Nuggets
Knightstown	Knightengales
Ladoga	Canners
Lincoln	Railsplitters
Lynnville	Lyndies
Lyons	Lions
Lucerne	Lions
Marengo	Cavemen
Maukport	Pilots
McKinley & South Bend Wilson	Presidents
Mecca	Arabs
Michigantown	Ganders
Mill Creek	Creekers
Millersburg & Union Mills	Millers
Milton & Union Twp. (Huntington Co.)	Sharpshooters
Monitor	Commodores
Monon	Railroaders
Monroe City	Blue Jeans
Montezuma	Aztecs
Mt. Ayr	Ayrdales
Mt. Olympus	Mountaineers
Mulberry	Berries
Newberry and Moscow	River Rats
Nobel Twp. (Cass County)	Knights
Oil Twp. (Perry County)	Oilers
Otter Creek	Otters
Pimento	Peppers
Pine Village	Pineknots
Pittsboro	Burros
Poseyville	Posies
Raleigh	Sir Walters
Remington	Rifles
Roll	Red Rollers
Rome City	Romans
Rosedale	Hot Shots

Russiaville	Cossacks
St. Paul	Blasters
Scircleville	Ringers
Scotland	Scotties
Smithville	Skibos
Spencer	Cops
Spiceland	Stingers
Stinesville	Quarry Lads
Summitville	Goblins
Swayzee & Urbana	Speed Kings
Trinity Springs	Little Sulphurs
Twelve Mile	Milers
Wallace	Peppers
Warren	Lightning Five
Washington Twp. (Cass County)	Hatchets
West Baden Springs	Sprudels
West Point	Cadets
Wheatfield	Shockers
Williamsport	Bingy Bombers
Winslow	Eskimos

APPENDIX III
GYM NAMES

The names of some of Indiana's high school gyms are well worth recording—the big ones, the tiny little pits, and the ones with stages on one end. The last five pay homage to very special Indiana basketball names (as does Loogootee's alternate name).

Loogootee Lions	The Lion's Den*
Gary Roosevelt Panthers	The Panther's Den
LaCrosse Tigers	The Tiger's Den
Oregon-Davis Bobcats	The Bobcat's Den
Northwood Panthers	The Panther Pit
Penn Kingsmen	The Palace
Plymouth Pilgrims	The Rock
Westfield Shamrocks	The Rock
Lapel Bulldogs	The Dog House
New Albany Bulldogs	The Dog House
Logansport Berries	The Berry Bowl
Hobart Brickies	The Brick Yard
Mishawaka Cavemen	The Cave
East Noble	The Big Blue Pit
South Adams Starfires	The Stardome
Southern Wells Raiders	The Raiderdome
Argos Dragons	The Dragon's Den
Oak Hill Golden Eagles	The Eagles Nest
John Glenn High School Falcons	The Aerie
Connersville Spartans	The Spartan Bowl
Washington Hatchets	The Hatchet House
Washington Catholic Cardinals	The Bird Cage
Greenwood Woodmen	The Woodshed
Rockville Rox	The Rockadome
Eminence Eels	The Eels Tank
Alexandria Tigers	The Jungle
Eastern Green Thunderbirds	The Thunderdome
Vincennes Lincoln Alices	Alice Arena
Scottsburg Warriors	The Pressure Cooker
Noblesville Millers	The Mill
Anderson Indians	The Wigwam
Frankfort	Everett Case Arena
Monrovia	McCracken Gymnasium
Franklin	Vandivier Gymnasium
Shelbyville	Wm. L. Garrett Memorial Gym
Marion	Bill Green Arena

*Also known as Jack Butcher Sports Arena; (Avon's gym was called the Noise Box)

APPENDIX IV
GYM SIZES

Gyms in our schools are interestingly named in many cases. Another indication of the importance of Indiana high school basketball to all Hoosiers is the size of the gyms that have been built. Capacities in many cases exceed school student body size, others are even larger than the population of the town that built them. There are 34 with seating capacities of 5000 or more, according to the IBHOF.

New Castle	9314
Anderson	8996
East Chicago	8296
Seymour	8110
Richmond	8100
Elkhart Memorial	8000
Marion	7560
Elkhart Central	7373
Michigan City	7304
Gary West Side	7217
Lafayette Jefferson	7200
Southport	7124
Washington	7090
Columbus North	7071
Muncie Central	6547
Bedford North Lawrence	6347
Southridge	6092
Logansport	5875
Connersville	5847
Shelbyville	5832
Boonville	5650
Frankfort	5509
Center Grove	5500
Huntington North	5500
Martinsville	5500
Calumet	5480
Vincennes Lincoln	5466
Jeffersonville	5306
Greencastle	5280
Decatur Central	5200
Jasper	5200
Kokomo	5200
Greensburg	5041
Valparaiso	5000

APPENDIX V
UNDEFEATED STATE CHAMPIONS

School, year and class (If applicable)		Record	Coach

GIRLS

School	Year	Record	Coach
Warsaw	1976	22-0	Janice Soyez
East Chicago Roosevelt	1977	24-0	Roberta DeKemper
Warsaw	1978	22-0	Janice Soyez
East Chicago Roosevelt	1979	23-0	Roberta DeKemper
Crown Point	1984	26-0	Tom May
Ft. Wayne Northrop	1986	29-0	Dave Riley
Noblesville	1987	27-0	Ray Lyttle
Bedford North Lawrence	1991	29-0	Pete Pritchett
Martinsville	1998(4A)	29-0	Jan Conner
New Albany	1999(4A)	26-0	Angie Hinton
Ben Davis	2000(4A)	28-0	Stan Benge
Ft. Wayne Luers	2001(2A)	28-0	Gary Andrews
Kokomo	2003(4A)	26-0	Charlie Hall
Ben Davis	2009(4A)	30-0	Stan Benge
Ben Davis	2010	28-0	Stan Benge

BOYS

School	Year	Record	Coach
Indianapolis Crispus Attucks	1956	31-0	Ray Crowe
South Bend Central	1957	30-0	Elmer McCall
Indianapolis Washington	1969	31-0	Bill Green
East Chicago Roosevelt	1970	28-0	Bill Holzbach
East Chicago Washington	1971	29-0	John Molodet
Marion	1985	29-0	Bill Green
Indianapolis Pike	2003(4A)	29-0	Larry Bullington
Cass	2003(2A)	26-0	Basil Mawbey
Waldron	2004(1A)	27-0	Jason Delanry
Lawrence North	2006(4A)	29-0	Jack Keefer
Princeton	2009(3A)	29-0	Tom Weeks
Bloomington South	2009(4A)	26-0	J. R. Holmes

APPENDIX VI

From the beginning the small schools have been a force to be reckoned with in Indiana high school basketball. By 1970 most of the really small schools had followed the Legislature's orders and become consolidated. Here is a compilation of some of those schools Sweet Sixteen Appearances.

1911   Walton, Morristown, Oaktown
1912   Bicknell, Oaklandon, Wolf Lake
1913   Petroleum, Thorntown, Wingate
1914   Centerville, New Augusta, Marco, Rossville, Wingate
1915   Fairmount Academy, Westport, Thorntown, Montmorenci, Bloomingdale Academy, Bluffton
1916   Washington Center, Liberty Center, Hopewell, Cicero, Brookville
1917   Wingate, Trafalgar, Pendleton, Rockville
1918   Wingate, Montmorenci, Plainfield
1919   Spiceland Academy, Thorntown
1920   Milroy, Ridgeville, Spiceland Academy
1921   Walton, Ridgeville, Sandusky, Russelville
1922   Atwood, Cutler, Fishers
1923   Sullivan, Perrysville, Lyons
1924   North Manchester, Otterbein, Liberty Center
1925   Milford, West Point, Carmel
1926   Summitville, Hillsboro, Nappanee, Aurora, North Vernon
1927   Sharpsville, Waldron
1929   Dugger, Delphi
1932   Cicero, Delphi
1933   Wakarusa, Hazleton, Beaver Dam, Michigantown
1934   North Judson, Beaver Dam
1935   Mentone, Montgomery, Roachdale, Berne
1937   North Vernon
1938   Plainville, Delphi, SheridanSec1:
1939   Auburn, Ossian, Aurora
1940   Lynnville, Lapel, Garrett
1942   Wolf Lake, Aurora
1943   Monroe
1944   Decatur, Whiteland, Waynetown, Aurora, Converse
1945   Hope, Covington, Oxford, Auburn
1946   Lawrenceburg, Linton, Flora, Gas City
1947   Shelburn, Pendleton
1948   Chester Twp. (Wabash), Monroeville, Lawrenceburg

1949   Lawrenceburg, Summitville, Brookston, Auburn, Jefferson Twp. (Randolph), Attica

1950   Auburn, Richland Center, Elletsville, Winslow, Sheridan

1951   Winslow, Glenn, Edinburgh, Covington, Auburn, Brookston

1952   Auburn

1953   Zionsville, Attica, Milan

1954   Montezuma, Winslow, Milan, Mississinewa

1955   Switz City, Monticello, Sheridan

1956   New Ross, Princeton

1957   Monticello

1958   North Judson, Bluffton, Princeton, Springs Valley

1959   Bainbridge, Odon

1960   Carlisle, Covington, Bluffton

1961   New Ross, Corydon

1962   Knox, Eminence, Attica

1963   Royal Center, Ireland, Berne

1964   Garrett, Springs Valley

1965   Brookville, Princeton, Bloomfield, Cloverdale

1966   Bainbridge, Aurora, Cloverdale

1967   Liberty, Bainbridge

1968   Attica

1969   Silver Creek

1970   Milltown, Loogootee

Beaver Dam 1932-33 Regional Champions

APPENDIX VII
CLASS BASKETBALL, '50s STYLE

There has been speculation as to what Milan's basketball class would have been when its numbers were applied to today's four class system. Fountain Central grad ('82) and current IHSBHS secretary, Gary McGrady, has researched all 751 tournament participants from the 1954 IHSAA basketball tournament and determined just where all teams would stand. In 1954 Milan had an enrollment of 161 which would have put them in class 3A at that time. Other schools that might be considered surprising would be Carmel, which in 1954 had a paltry enrollment of 224, and Pike Township, with only 206. Both schools are now considered among the largest in the state classification.

APPENDIX VIII
BREAKS HIGH SCHOOL
by Bob Whalen

I believe that not too many people know that at one time Breaks had a high school, and they even had a basketball team in the early 1900s. Information on their basketball playing is very hard to find. I have found that they had a basketball team as early as the 1904–05 season. I read that they claimed to be the State High School Basketball Champion in 1905. I don't know why, or how, they had a claim. I do know that Crawfordsville had a poor season in 1904–05 as they were only 4 and 3.

I did find the Breaks schedule of games and scores for the 1907–08 season.

It was as follows:

28 All Stars (*) 18 Won
29 Elmdale H S 16 Won
31 Elmdale H S 20 Won
25 Yountsville H S 5 Won
15 New Richmond H S 13 Won
19 New Richmond H S 11 Won
 9 Newtown H S (+) 7 Lost

Breaks High School

Season Record Won 6–Lost 1—Coach Willam Stump

(*) I have no idea who this was

(+) All I found was N H S and I am only guessing it was Newtown.

I knew that both Elmdale and Yountsville had high schools in the early 1900s, but this was the first time I ever found any record of them playing basketball.

The players on the 1908 Breaks team were listed as: Edwards, Hammer, Herron, Tomlinson, and Tomlinson. NO FIRST NAMES were given. They also had a "Second Team" with seven players, no names, and a record of 4 and 2.

Breaks built a new school in 1906 that had grades 1 through 12. The Breaks basketball team never entered a sectional. I believe that the high school part of Breaks closed about the time of WW I. Crawfordsville played Breaks in basketball in the 1908-09 season and defeated them 20 to 4.

Wingate played them in the 1912–13 season and defeated them 51 to 21. Breaks is located a few miles northwest of Crawfordsville. After the high school closed they had a school with grades 1 through 8 until maybe the 1960s.

APPENDIX IX

A poem about Heltonville by Herman Ramsey written in 1919 captures the nature of small-town Indiana, in fact small-town America. It was brought to my attention by Wendell Trogdon, author of *Backroads of Indiana*. The poem is as follows:

> *Sort of scattered in the valley*
> *And a-stragglin' up the hill*
> *Is a little Hoosier village*
> *By the name of Heltonville.*

> *With this town of friendly neighbors*
> *It's your character that counts*
> *In establishin' your ratin'*
> *And not your bank accounts.*

> *They don't care about your money,*
> *Nor your job or motor car,*
> *It's the way you treat your neighbor*
> *That reveals just what you are.*

> *None of them are very wealthy,*
> *But none of them are poor;*
> *None of them would fail the needy;*
> *Turn the hungry from the door.*

> *They won't hold it much against you,*
> *If you dress up fit to kill,*
> *But your overalls are good enough*
> *For the folks in Heltonville.*

> *When there's sickness every member*
> *Of this faithful little band*
> *Stands beside you like a brother*
> *To put forth a helping hand.*

> *Why, your confidence is bolstered,*
> *And your patriotism thrills*
> *When you think our mighty nation*
> *Is made up of Heltonvilles.*

INDEX

A

Acton 218, 466
Adams Central 98, 309, 334, 367, 385, 398, 409
Adams Township 288
Advance 25, 171, 330
Akron 99, 100, 235, 287, 364
Alamo viii, 19, 20
Albany 294, 333, 438
Albion 212, 257, 420, 421
Alexandria 190, 191, 242, 253, 373, 444, 469
Alfordsville 52, 54, 347
Alquina 174
Ambia 169, 282, 294, 331, 413
Amboy 423, 424
Amo 49, 408, 409, 418, 431
Anderson iv, 14, 23, 31, 35, 64, 79, 80, 81, 124, 125, 131, 142, 147, 149, 160, 161, 162, 173, 187, 189, 190, 204, 213, 221, 229, 235, 241, 245, 252, 266, 273, 274, 278, 286, 290, 311, 316, 323, 328, 342, 362, 370, 377, 391, 415, 441, 443, 444, 447, 448, 451, 454, 460, 470
Anderson Christian Academy 150
Anderson Highland 268, 378, 379, 465, 477
Anderson Indiana Christian Academy 369
Anderson Liberty Christian 263
Anderson Madison Heights 243, 258, 357, 424, 477
Anderson St. Mary 441, 442
Andrean High School 384
Andrews 33, 62, 71, 240, 275, 309, 328, 329, 354, 372, 410, 471
Angola 141, 202, 315, 340, 357, 366, 382, 409, 420
Arcadia 172, 277, 280, 436, 437, 459, 460, 461
Argos 137, 391, 464, 469
Arlington 64, 349, 352, 353
Arsenal Technical 3, 72, 81, 125, 126, 127, 130, 159, 214, 269, 287, 304, 323, 370, 389, 409, 412, 420, 444, 447, 448, 454

Ashboro 410, 434, 435
Ashley 96, 167, 409
Atha, Dick 413
Atlanta 277, 278, 280, 328, 459, 460, 461
Attica 23, 51, 70, 71, 335, 364, 410, 413, 439
Atwood 307, 472
Auburn 31, 40, 67, 95, 96, 97, 105, 168, 195, 231, 242, 342, 409, 410, 443, 472, 473
Aurora 251, 267, 355, 410, 411, 472, 473
Austin 173, 264, 313, 354, 356
Avilla 169, 196, 307
Avon 173, 197, 198, 319, 326, 417, 469

B

Bainbridge 21, 403, 404, 473
Baldwin Heights 433
Banquo 32, 33, 44, 164, 466
Barr Reeve (also known as Montgomery) 234, 363
Barr Township 52, 439
Batesville 201, 204, 252, 284, 294, 323, 326, 369, 398, 429
Battle Ground 27, 28, 29, 171
Baugo Township 443
Beaver Dam 18, 40, 307, 401, 466, 472
Bedford 84, 85, 86, 166, 199, 226, 227, 274, 276, 282, 295, 403, 418, 429, 432, 436, 438, 440, 443, 466
Bedford North Lawrence 72, 85, 86, 109, 110, 158, 167, 239, 244, 253, 320, 347, 363, 365, 367, 383, 470, 471, 477
Beech Grove 161, 191, 261, 340, 341
Belle Union 302, 403
Bellmont xi, 151, 194, 259, 424
Bellmore 328, 333
Ben Davis 107, 125, 130, 147, 148, 192, 239, 249, 256, 320, 323, 342, 362, 371, 380, 384, 385, 386, 471
Benton Central 29, 102, 146, 160, 168, 169, 198, 281, 282, 342, 413
Berne 118, 177, 178, 179, 291, 301, 310, 311, 335, 368, 398, 421
Bethany Christian 268
Bicknell 144, 207, 275, 289, 472
Bippus 44, 285

Birdseye 189, 330
Blackford 65, 205, 206, 267, 268, 356, 361
Blackhawk 55, 88, 135, 151, 168, 324, 325
Bloomfield 31, 135, 168, 183, 220, 242, 243, 245, 307, 319, 320, 326, 339, 346, 374, 389, 440, 456
Bloomingdale 466
Bloomingdale Academy 29, 43, 66, 466
Bloomington 29, 41, 63, 81, 84, 143, 168, 174, 192, 193, 208, 232, 233, 238, 256, 267, 268, 274, 275, 286, 295, 300, 326, 339, 345, 346, 404, 409, 420, 423, 424, 443, 471
Bloomington North 174, 238, 256, 316, 317, 365, 454
Bloomington South 41, 238, 256
Bloomington University 129, 256
Blue River Valley 359, 363, 364, 399, 441
Bluffton 26, 29, 36, 49, 145, 159, 164, 173, 178, 190, 213, 222, 247, 291, 309, 356, 404, 427, 437
Boggstown 300
Boone Grove 140, 281, 457, 458, 459
Boonville 34, 108, 180, 275, 294, 370, 374, 403, 470
Borden 152
Boston 50, 57, 89, 110, 114, 266, 404, 405, 451, 466
Boswell 168, 169, 282, 330, 413
Bourbon 350
Bowers 20, 22
Bowling Green 108, 121
Brazil 43, 66, 107, 125, 193, 194, 217, 286, 292, 293, 326, 345, 353, 410, 423
Brebeuf Jesuit 148, 153, 241, 354, 380, 384
Bremen 190, 201, 202, 235, 263, 423
Brewersville 347
Bridgeton 232
Bright 299
Brighton 295
Bristol 167, 231, 232, 424
Bristow 34, 408
Broad Ripple 100, 101, 126, 127, 129, 130, 255, 367, 387, 453

Brook 192, 217, 410, 422
Brookston 99, 175, 196, 217, 411, 472
Brookville 80, 259, 295, 402, 405, 406, 473
Brownsburg 200, 251, 252, 454
Brownsburg Bethesda Christian 362
Brown County 298, 308, 316, 346
Brownstown 118, 119, 120, 151, 172, 196, 331, 354, 394
Brownsville 402
Bruceville 81, 186, 225, 226, 441
Bryant 99, 114, 116, 237, 336, 337, 361, 400
Buck Creek 28, 32, 348, 397, 398
Buddha 166
Buffalo 105, 406, 441
Bunker Hill 110, 152, 215, 402, 424, 466
Burket 335, 340
Burlington 68, 221, 233, 303
Burnettsville 347
Burney 284, 300, 428
Butcher 50, 51, 251, 438, 469
Butler 171, 212, 230, 231, 275, 366, 466
Butler Township 171
Butlerville 284, 294

C

Cadiz 181, 399, 407, 466
Cambridge City 218, 318, 397, 466
Cambridge City Lincoln 44, 117, 218, 318, 397
Camden 168, 217, 233, 410, 411
Campbellsburg 381, 443
Cannelton 69, 183, 253, 425
Carlisle 59, 63, 102, 157, 158, 163, 257, 473
Carmel 98, 242, 251, 277, 278, 351, 363, 378, 430, 431, 459, 460, 474
Carroll (and county) 68, 77, 213, 221, 232, 233, 258, 264, 333, 365, 408
Carrollton 77, 333, 411
Carthage 207
Cascade 330, 392, 393, 405
Cass County 15, 113, 117, 172, 176, 211, 215, 288, 347, 367, 411, 428, 467, 468
Castle 180, 239, 353, 464
Castleton 444, 445

Caston   144, 165, 211, 240, 367, 368, 381, 444, 445

Cayuga   164, 202, 322

Center (Delaware)   425

Center Grove   26, 192, 205, 316, 342, 351, 352, 365, 470

Center Township (Starke County)   431

Centerville   253, 346, 362, 381, 472

Central Catholic   30, 152, 187, 225, 291, 338, 354, 374, 377, 439, 440

Central Noble   212, 257, 421

Chalmers   321, 330

Chandler   34, 302

Charlestown   383

Charlottesville   299, 334, 359

Chatard   109, 301, 351, 406

Chester Center   164, 301

Chesterton   121, 144, 155, 159, 160, 352, 458

Chester Township   299, 434

Chili   47, 58, 193, 466

Chippewa   166, 445

Chrisney   295, 425

Churubusco   317, 421

Cicero   192, 277, 280, 410, 414, 459, 460, 461, 472

Clarksburg   164, 284, 291, 292, 428

Clarks Hill   28, 29

Clarksville   108, 381, 382

Clarksville Providence   108

Clay City   43, 193, 217, 339, 340, 457, 464

Claypool   307, 428

Clayton   173, 207, 274, 301, 330, 393

Clay Township   168, 219, 423, 424, 445

Clear Creek   285, 290

Clear Spring   119, 172

Clifford   5, 135, 300

Clinton (and county)   23, 43, 47, 58, 59, 60, 68, 182, 229, 232, 233, 253, 256, 295, 331, 340, 344, 347, 399, 464

Clinton Central   253

Clinton Prairie   281, 282

Clinton Township (LaPorte)   423

Cloverdale   166, 174, 193, 350, 396, 403, 410, 434, 464

Coal City   220, 309

Coal Creek   20, 21, 308

Coalmont   158, 333

Coesse   167

Colfax   59, 434, 466

College Corner   421

Colonial Christian   259

Columbia City   67, 167, 197, 208, 212, 257, 290, 296, 313, 314, 315, 388, 421, 423, 438

Columbus   25, 81, 131, 201, 309, 342, 375

Columbus East   xi, 378, 411, 464

Columbus North   152, 259, 251, 340, 355, 399, 453, 465, 470

Concannon   55, 158, 211, 212

Concord   109, 110, 111, 150, 320, 354, 365, 464

Connersville   25, 65, 78, 121, 129, 132, 152, 171, 174, 192, 200, 258, 259, 296, 300, 329, 330, 347, 351, 352, 357, 359, 362, 370, 375, 376, 377, 387, 398, 402, 411, 422, 423, 426, 432, 453, 469, 470

Converse   318, 358, 416, 424, 432, 466, 472

Cortland   118, 328, 331, 333

Cory   121, 217, 218, 466

Corydon   229, 236, 300, 301, 331, 381, 436, 443

Covenant Christian   150

Covington   21, 22, 23, 350, 351, 403, 413, 472, 473

Cowan   154, 155

Crawford County   138, 170, 171, 204, 223, 230, 277, 281, 326, 381, 436

Crawfordsville   13, 14, 18, 19, 20, 21, 22, 23, 46, 62, 64, 80, 99, 104, 123, 129, 172, 208, 295, 378, 393, 403, 418, 455, 464, 474

Crispus Attucks   v, 6, 56, 114, 115, 116, 119, 120, 123, 124, 125, 126, 127, 128, 129, 130, 131, 132, 133, 146, 237, 240, 255, 274, 275, 299, 304, 311, 320, 366, 375, 415, 416, 471

Cromwell   169, 428

Cross Plains   398

Crothersville   119, 173, 248, 313

Crown Point   92, 148, 160, 238, 241, 253, 471

Culver 102, 174, 196, 212, 213, 283, 319, 358, 359, 368, 423, 432, 443
Cutler 81, 233, 295, 298, 411, 472
Cuzco 193, 195, 303
Cynthiana 69, 208, 210, 275

D

Dale 34, 47, 104, 110, 117, 148, 192, 199, 214, 305, 375, 409, 410, 425, 444
Daleville 266
Dana 43, 228, 229
Danville 19, 49, 147, 148, 173, 200, 267, 330
Darlington 13, 20, 21, 22, 164, 292, 332
Dayton 25,30
Deacon 411
Decatur 83, 130, 152, 199, 285, 309, 344, 345, 384, 398, 404, 426, 428, 437, 470, 472
Decatur Catholic 221
Decatur Central 10, 205, 323
Decker 225, 407, 466
Decker Chapel 226, 302, 441
Deedsville 357, 423
Deer Creek 77, 221, 466
DeKalb (and county) 96, 97, 205, 231, 360, 366, 369, 464
Delphi 77, 78, 79, 100, 168, 194, 217, 233, 411, 432, 464
Delta 25, 52, 190, 294, 317, 323, 329, 332, 357, 426
DeMotte 166, 171
Denver 144, 228, 430
DePauw 93, 203, 273, 433, 466
Deputy 301, 326, 423
DeSoto 301, 302
Dillsboro 289, 398
Dover 25, 198, 410
DuBois (and county) 76, 195
Dugger 31, 81, 102, 158, 212, 291, 457, 472
Dunkirk 43, 361, 414, 427, 466
DuPont 122, 343
DuPont Baptist Academy 263
Dyer 165, 166

E

Earl Park 67, 198, 282, 330
Eastbrook 238, 268, 408, 429

East Central 351, 406
East Chicago 102, 104, 159, 170, 212, 253, 321, 394, 414, 430, 431, 466, 470, 471
East Chicago Roosevelt 243, 244, 278, 319, 380, 394, 425, 429, 431, 471
East Chicago Washington 212, 254, 287, 358, 366, 379, 429, 430, 452, 466, 470, 471
Eastern Greene 168, 326, 327
Eastern Hancock 359, 390
Eastern High School (Wahington County) 358, 456
Eastern (Howard) 118, 367
Eastern Randolph High School 298
East Noble 183, 196, 353, 354, 382, 464, 469
Eastside 231, 366
East Tipp 424
East Tippecanoe 28, 29
Eaton 16, 419, 438
Economy 332, 346
Eden 99, 100, 401
Edgewood 84, 265
Edinburgh 201, 205, 358, 359, 439, 472
Edwardsport 18, 225, 226, 433, 466
Elberfeld 66, 294, 347
Elizabeth 31, 203, 229, 321, 374, 425
Elkhart (and county) 53, 110, 141, 143, 156, 167, 177, 205, 214, 220, 223, 230, 231, 232, 286, 296, 304, 305, 366, 380, 391, 401, 424, 430, 443, 470
Elkhart Christian 319
Elkhart Memorial 264, 265, 470
Elletsville 83, 265, 334, 423, 472
Elnora 52, 53, 54, 257, 292, 336, 407, 466
Elwood 95, 241, 444
Eminence 174, 300, 339, 340, 464, 469
English 170
Epsom xi, 52, 53, 54, 71, 407, 466
Ervin Township 335
Etna Green 297, 307
Evansville vi, ix, 31, 34, 64, 69, 77, 80, 86, 101, 123, 156, 180, 185, 187, 193, 194, 200, 206, 207, 210, 214, 215, 260, 261, 267, 270, 271, 272, 273, 274, 275, 280, 294, 326, 339, 353, 371, 374, 399,

403, 442, 448

Evansville Bosse 51, 52, 70, 101, 109, 254, 261, 270, 358, 430, 443

Evansville Day 318

Evansville Harrison 145

Evansville Lincoln 117, 276

Evansville Mater Dei 151, 259, 375

Evansville Memorial 354, 439

Evansville North 63, 280, 453, 455

Evansville Reitz 208, 239, 248, 276, 424

Evansville Rex Mundi 429, 466

Everton 295, 296

F

Fairbanks 423, 424

Fairfield 80, 205, 223, 231, 323, 382, 428

Fairland 342, 345

Fairmount 29, 35, 36, 37, 472

Fair Oaks 137, 138, 171

Fall Creek Academy 394, 395

Farmersburg 102, 227, 326, 327, 457, 466

Fayette Central 65, 171, 347

Fayetteville 85, 402

Ferdinand 170, 184, 189, 323

Fillmore 182, 330, 331, 431

Fishers 141, 229, 245, 246, 277, 459, 461, 462, 472

Flat Rock 181

Flint 218, 466

Flora 68, 213, 221, 257, 358, 411, 423, 472

Floyd Central 200, 308, 374, 379, 380, 382

Fontanet 55, 57, 466

Folsomville 335

Forest 399

Forest Park 75, 189, 323, 354, 356

Fortville 243, 299, 334, 380, 390, 411, 418, 444

Fountain Central 31, 62, 64, 257, 265, 267, 308, 410, 474

Fountain City 121, 213, 306, 346, 355, 426

Fowler 102, 168, 169, 198, 282, 289, 294, 330, 413

Francesville 145, 312, 350

Francisco 336, 337, 403

Frankfort 6, 10, 21, 46, 47, 48, 49, 59, 62, 67, 71, 93, 107, 123, 135, 149, 155, 198, 213, 241, 253, 254, 274, 277, 281, 286, 297, 330, 331, 389, 411, 447, 448, 464, 469, 470

Franklin (and county) 14, 31, 45, 46, 78, 81, 92, 93, 102, 123, 142, 148, 193, 218, 233, 251, 259, 260, 267, 287, 291, 309, 316, 330, 334, 365, 368, 395, 403, 405, 406, 436, 439, 464, 469, 472

Frankton 6, 7, 190, 315

Fredonia 120

Freedom 118, 120, 121, 133, 410

Freeland Park 102, 120, 121, 198, 282

Freelandville ii, viii, 18, 80, 81, 121, 158, 185, 186, 225, 226

Freeman 14, 120

Freemont 120

Freetown viii, 118, 119, 120, 172, 441

French Lick 10, 86, 87, 88, 89, 324, 410

Friends Academy 107

Friendship 398

Fritchton 225, 226

Frontier 217, 321, 322

Ft. Branch 63, 66, 208, 274, 276, 390, 408, 466

Ft. Wayne 31, 34, 35, 36, 44, 97, 106, 123, 129, 149, 159, 197, 199, 213, 273, 286, 291, 382, 398, 399, 402, 404, 408, 421, 423, 424, 471

Ft. Wayne Bishop Dwenger 372

Ft. Wayne Bishop Luers 153, 191, 248, 313, 354, 376

Ft. Wayne Blackhawk Christian 135

Ft. Wayne Canterbury 358

Ft. Wayne Carroll 264, 365

Ft. Wayne Central 295, 307, 309, 435

Ft. Wayne Central Catholic 439, 440

Ft. Wayne Concordia 392, 393

Ft. Wayne Elmhurst 351

Ft. Wayne Harding 112, 194, 391

Ft. Wayne Keystone 319

Ft. Wayne North Side 45, 111, 138, 143, 173, 380

Ft. Wayne Northrop 268, 339, 354, 357, 366, 471, 371

Ft. Wayne Snider 147, 239, 256, 386

Ft. Wayne South Side 97, 125, 155, 212,

226, 263, 324, 334, 394, 400, 427, 440
Ft. Wayne Wayne 392
Fulton 174, 287, 289, 298, 367

G

Galveston 117, 329
Garrett 105, 106, 124, 149, 307, 311, 361, 366, 385, 390, 424, 429, 465, 469
Gary 102, 108, 133, 149, 156, 160, 319, 382
Gary Calumet 103, 104, 149, 160, 241, 321, 470
Gary East 335
Gary Edison 431
Gary Emerson 235, 380, 414, 418, 442, 443
Gary Froebel 133, 192, 410, 414, 431
Gary Horace Mann 62, 431
Gary Lew Wallace 194, 341, 342
Gary Roosevelt 80, 109, 123, 131, 132, 143, 144, 153, 240, 254, 259, 350, 379, 415, 469
Gary Tolleston High School 170
Gary West Side 25, 103, 104, 258, 329, 353, 369, 370, 377, 424, 426, 442, 470
Gary Wirt 394, 395
Gas City 35, 36, 159, 301, 312, 472
Gaston 148, 289, 438
Geneva 178, 179, 398
Gentryville 34, 425
Georgetown 308, 436
Gibson County 63, 65, 66, 207, 208, 336, 403, 433
Gibson Southern 66, 169, 239, 335, 336, 354, 355, 364, 389, 390
Gilboa 169, 298, 413
Gilead 298
Gill Township 102, 170
Gings 298
Glendale 307
Glenn 57, 168, 169, 257, 288, 322, 323, 469
Glenn (Vigo County) 424, 472
Glenwood 168
Goldsmith 39, 335, 466
Goodland 404, 422
Goshen 138, 140, 141, 205, 214, 246, 328, 338, 461
Gosport 168, 193, 217

Grandview 210, 211
Granville Wells 24, 26
Grass Creek 298, 299, 367
Gray 333, 361, 400
Graysville 81, 210, 211
Greencastle 23, 51, 62, 69, 93, 94, 104, 144, 166, 167, 192, 262, 265, 293, 330, 335, 346, 396, 403, 413, 415, 431, 432, 465, 470
Greentown 367, 461
Green Township 43, 285
Greene Township 288, 410
Greenfield 78, 99, 258, 259, 290, 295, 299, 306, 334, 359, 401, 425
Greensburg 63, 84, 135, 173, 258, 284, 345, 383, 384, 411, 418, 428, 432, 470
Greens Fork 121, 411, 419
Greenwood 394, 395, 403, 465, 469
Greenwood Christian 256
Griffin 252, 442, 466
Griffith 53, 241, 455
Grovertown 406
Guilford 203, 204, 405, 406

H

Hagerstown 97, 247, 332, 346
Hamilton (and county) 229, 245, 277, 278, 280, 328, 335, 359, 366, 384, 400, 436, 459, 460
Hamlet 33, 34, 197, 283, 288
Hammond 13, 52, 62, 102, 108, 123, 129, 132, 150, 160, 165, 194, 261, 352, 393, 412, 414, 431, 432
Hammond Clark 108
Hammond Gavit 394
Hammond Morton 380, 464
Hammond Tech 72, 159, 214, 252, 287
Hancock Central 299, 334
Hanging Grove 347
Harding 97, 112, 194, 317, 323, 382, 391
Hanna 299
Hanover 289, 373, 374, 423, 458
Hanover Central 255, 260, 457
Hardinsburg 308, 309, 436
Harlan 299, 323, 335
Harrisburg 347, 402
Harrison 28, 201
Hartford City 15, 32, 159, 233, 268, 288, 301, 337, 380, 400, 403, 404, 414,

427

Hartford Township 199, 398
Haubstadt 65, 403, 466
Hauser 98, 349, 367, 464
Hayden 32, 224, 466
Hazleton 208, 403, 432, 433, 472
Hebron 322, 323, 324, 457, 458, 459
Helmsburg 287
Heltonville 72, 343, 463, 476
Henryville 341
Heritage Christian (Indianapolis) 150, 236, 318
Heritage Christian (Muncie) 362
Heritage High School 58, 192, 361
Heritage Hills vi, 117, 150, 158, 192, 211, 224, 236, 301, 303, 318, 361, 362, 386, 394, 425, 464
Highland 160, 351, 352, 379, 441
Hillsboro 71, 295, 410, 472
Hillsdale 441
Hoagland 296
Hobart 104, 159, 464, 469
Holland 85, 184, 185, 188, 330, 466
Holton 32, 33, 309, 310, 398
Holy Cross 354, 387, 464
Homestead 376, 377, 378, 425
Honey Creek 52, 55, 168, 343, 387, 466
Hope 98, 173, 410, 472
Hopewell 287, 472
Houston 89, 118, 441
Howe 127, 128, 129, 195, 262, 295, 342
Huntertown 263, 296
Huntingburg 85, 102, 170, 184, 185, 186, 187, 188, 200, 208, 210, 223, 226, 230, 274, 276, 292, 330, 338, 356, 409, 466
Huntington (and county) 40, 118, 194, 197, 199, 208, 251, 261, 286, 291, 301, 308, 315, 328, 345, 372, 400, 404, 405, 428
Huntington Catholic 414, 440
Huntington North 33, 44, 118, 198, 279, 309, 329, 334, 354, 362, 363, 365, 408, 438, 447, 470
Huntington Township 308
Huntsville 169, 332
Huron 401
Hymera 53, 137, 138, 170, 211

I

Idaville 44, 175, 431
Indianapolis (for Broad Ripple, Howe, Pike, Shortridge, Tech, Warren Central, Washington etc., see individual school)
Indianapolis Baptist Academy 282
Indianapolis Calvary Lutheran 354
Indianapolis Cardinal Ritter 384
Indianapolis Cathedral 5, 50, 72, 83, 109, 129, 191, 239, 246, 254, 384, 387, 388, 440, 464
Indianapolis Chatard 109, 301, 351, 406
Indianapolis Heritage Christian 150, 236, 318, 362, 386, 394
Indianapolis Herron High 395
Indianapolis International School 392
Indianapolis Irvington 327
Indianapolis John Marshall 116
Indianapolis Lutheran 350, 372
Indianapolis Northwest 367, 465
Indianapolis Roncalli 373, 406
Indianapolis Suburban Christian Academy 354
Indianapolis Wood 221, 451, 467
Indiana School for the Blind and Visually Impaired 102, 367
Indiana School for the Deaf 2, 3
Indiana State Laboratory School 53
Indian Creek 152, 205, 209
Ireland 38, 187, 188, 467, 473
Irvington Community Charter School 39

J

Jac-Cen-Del 121, 204, 243, 317, 351, 359, 429
Jackson Center 222, 335, 401
Jackson Central 39, 459, 460, 461
Jackson Township 24, 30, 44, 84, 117, 118, 211, 285, 331, 401, 458
Jamestown 23, 24, 25, 147, 426
Jasonville 154, 220, 346, 382, 456
Jasper 63, 67, 69, 75, 97, 117, 166, 170, 184, 186, 187, 188, 200, 222, 225, 226, 228, 233, 257, 269, 270, 274, 275, 304, 330, 338, 345, 355, 381, 390, 409, 439, 470
Jay County 43, 216, 301, 332, 336, 337, 361, 390, 399, 400, 453
Jefferson 401, 404, 410, 413, 414, 448,

472
Jefferson Center   286
Jefferson Central   428
Jefferson Township   39, 110, 167, 171,
172, 286, 425, 428, 429
Jeffersonville   10, 25, 85, 161, 184, 223,
230, 240, 268, 287, 301, 329, 330, 339,
353, 370, 371, 372, 374, 377, 382, 385,
401, 406, 426, 436, 439, 440, 443, 470
Jennings County   173, 205, 224, 240,
267, 284, 308, 326, 347, 383, 425
Jimtown   151, 318, 394, 395, 443
Jonesboro   312, 354
Judyville   71, 410

K

Kankakee Valley   31, 166, 171, 228, 259,
262, 377
Kempton   39, 425
Kendallville   viii, 169, 170, 195, 197, 212,
230, 295, 353, 389, 402, 409, 419, 420,
421, 440, 443
Kennard   32, 33, 100, 398
Kentland   217, 374, 410, 418, 422, 440
Kewanna   165, 380
Kingman   410
Kings Academy   354, 355
Kingsbury   219, 220, 429
Kirkland Township   397
Kitchel   429
Kirklin   59, 467
Klondike   28, 58, 467
Knightstown   11, 12, 44, 64, 207, 236,
390, 399, 467
Knox   18, 76, 79, 121, 138, 139, 140,
144, 185, 186, 196, 202, 215, 224, 225,
290, 326, 376, 407, 441, 473
Kokomo   5, 35, 45, 78, 95, 97, 125, 141,
142, 159, 160, 177, 180, 193, 215, 241,
246, 254, 255, 260, 262, 282, 287, 290,
299, 322, 325, 334, 357, 362, 367, 368,
379, 383, 385, 415, 423, 427, 438, 447,
448, 451, 452, 453, 460, 461, 465, 470,
471
Kouts   265, 352, 385, 431, 457, 458, 459

L

Laconia   410, 436
LaCrosse   246, 247, 457, 458, 469
Ladoga   viii, 19, 20, 21, 178, 467

Lafayette   13, 24, 27, 29, 30, 31, 36, 52,
58, 59, 66, 79, 81, 97, 99, 104, 135, 144,
145, 152, 154, 155, 160, 170, 175, 187,
191, 194, 198, 213, 216, 245, 251, 254,
255, 261, 262, 265, 266, 268, 269, 270,
273, 274, 275, 280, 282, 287, 291, 293,
316, 322, 330, 331, 349, 351, 354, 361,
362, 363, 364, 366, 369, 371, 374, 377,
389, 393, 401, 403, 404, 413, 422, 429,
443, 447, 448, 450, 454, 455, 470
Lafayette Central   425, 440
Lafayette Central Catholic   152, 187, 291,
354, 374, 377
LaFontaine   33, 39, 428
LaGrange (and county)   150, 169, 194,
208, 212, 218, 288, 293, 295, 306, 382,
402, 436
Lagro   39, 196, 425, 434, 444, 445, 446
Lake Central   92, 159, 160, 165, 166
Lakeland   194, 195, 288, 382
Lake Station Edison   313
Laketon   196, 287, 434
Lakewood Park Christian   242
LaLumiere   382
Lancaster   44, 121, 122, 198, 199, 213,
222, 353, 399, 414, 438
Lanesville   316, 443
La Paz   193, 195
Lapel   7, 51, 252, 469
LaPorte   51, 52, 141, 156, 159, 168, 219,
220, 223, 234, 288, 358, 367, 382, 426,
438, 465
Lauramie Township   28, 30
Larwill   421
Laurel   301, 302, 309
LaVille   195, 284, 354, 358, 359, 434
Lawrence   440
Lawrenceburg   204, 247, 398, 472
Lawrence Central   216, 267, 403, 411,
444
Lawrence North   161, 175, 261, 314, 320,
375, 471
Leavenworth   137, 138, 170, 171
Lebanon   13, 14, 17, 18, 21, 22, 23, 25,
26, 27, 61, 67, 81, 91, 102, 123, 129, 145,
160, 193, 205, 207, 242, 286, 301, 316,
330, 342, 362, 370, 410, 413, 420, 443,
447, 448

Leesburg 307, 411, 419, 428
Leiters Ford 174
Leo 51, 52, 112, 153, 169, 185, 263, 264, 335, 384, 439, 464
Leopold 381
Letts 308
Lewis Cass 113, 117, 144, 329, 357
Lewisville 167, 305, 306, 390, 399
Lexington 110, 111, 116, 466
Liberty 41, 121, 362, 422
Liberty Center 41, 42, 118, 120, 121, 296, 362, 401, 402, 422, 434, 458, 472, 473
Liberty Township 121, 402, 458
Libertyville 121
Ligonier 40, 67, 170, 365
Lima 193, 194, 195, 284, 288
Lincoln ii, viii, 80, 117, 218, 397
Lincolnville 39, 196, 466
Linden 20, 22
Linlawn 287, 424, 445
Linton 55, 63, 193, 211, 220, 307, 345, 346, 386, 387, 424, 440, 456, 457, 472
Little York 199
Lizton 431,432
L&M 206, 456
Logansport 4, 5, 14, 15, 64, 67, 80, 135, 138, 140, 144, 172, 175, 194, 196, 197, 198, 211, 213, 215, 217, 233, 235, 240, 261, 268, 283, 291, 293, 296, 310, 311, 329, 389, 403, 404, 411, 432, 447, 448, 450, 453, 454, 464, 469, 470
Loogootee 50, 51, 52, 54, 207, 225, 251, 257, 263, 266, 279, 326, 333, 439, 469
Losantville 411
Lovett 425
Lowell 370, 371, 433
Lucerne 176, 177, 211, 401, 467
Luce Township 34, 410
Lynn 29, 171, 289, 296, 301, 374
Lynnville 34, 152, 213, 214, 294, 467, 472
Lyons 54, 81, 146, 206, 220, 246, 307, 346, 401, 456, 467, 472

M

Mackey 320, 408
Maconaquah 152, 168, 242
Macy 298, 347

Madison 31, 35, 49, 56, 67, 122, 123, 178, 190, 199, 201, 205, 258, 267, 268, 269, 270, 287, 294, 302, 304, 343, 345, 361, 379, 389, 399, 400, 414, 423, 428, 430, 444
Madison–Grant 35, 379, 444
Madison Township 399, 400
Manchester 196, 197, 287, 290, 291, 299, 315, 394, 395, 421, 423, 425, 428, 445, 465, 472
Manilla 209, 336
Manual 3, 4, 129, 130, 138, 141, 142, 143, 180, 221, 305, 323, 389, 452
Marco 206, 227, 307, 456, 472
Marengo 204, 281, 289, 330, 467
Marion (and county) 13, 26, 35, 36, 43, 44, 46, 51, 65, 85, 91, 123, 130, 132, 159, 185, 194, 197, 199, 215, 230, 252, 263, 264, 267, 269, 280, 287, 290, 291, 299, 311, 325, 354, 357, 368, 369, 371, 379, 385, 391, 400, 403, 416, 447, 448, 450, 454, 460, 470, 471
Marion Bennett 423
Marion Lakeview Christian 263
Markle 44, 334
Markleville 241, 266, 309, 444, 460
Marshall 40, 144, 232, 399, 440
Martinsville 6, 31, 54, 81, 85, 91, 92, 123, 128, 167, 192, 253, 282, 291, 300, 319, 402, 403, 409, 414, 423, 429, 443, 444, 464, 470, 471
Marquette 134, 366
Masonic Home 443
Matthews 110
Mauckport 436
Maumee Township 173
Maxwell 401
Mays 284, 285
McCordsville 334
McCutcheon 28, 29, 30, 281, 282
McKinley 429, 431, 467
Mecca 182, 232, 467
Medaryville 298, 309
Medora 342
Mellott 64, 65
Mentone 195, 293, 297, 307, 440, 472
Merom 102, 401
Merrillville 160, 366, 383, 384, 385

Metea 347, 367

Metz 55, 137, 138

Mexico 193, 195, 196, 424

Michigan City 67, 104, 129, 159, 168, 219, 234, 280, 281, 288, 293, 352, 366, 370, 389, 410, 412, 430, 470

Michigan City Rogers 116, 246, 280, 412

Michigan City Elston 280, 410, 412

Michigantown 67, 253, 327, 328, 467

Middlebury 155, 214, 215, 220, 356, 438, 443

Middletown 376, 427, 428

Midland 158, 220, 227, 438, 456, 457

Milan 8, 9, 10, 56, 72, 123, 125, 130, 158, 159, 182, 269, 284, 300, 330, 343, 366, 380, 398, 407, 429, 474

Milford 307, 335, 422, 472

Mill Creek 220, 223, 340, 467

Millersburg 223, 230, 231, 467

Milltown 223, 230, 326, 330, 443, 473

Milroy 77, 328, 402, 404, 427, 472

Milton 44, 121, 131, 467

Mishawaka 129, 141, 143, 145, 167, 283, 354, 357, 380, 423, 434, 443, 469

Mishawaka Marian 353

Mississinewa 36, 159

Mitchell 72, 73, 85, 88, 98, 128, 131, 200, 214, 220, 257, 282, 287, 326, 355, 381, 393, 464

Modoc 166, 296, 332, 367, 368

Mongo 436, 437

Monitor 28, 29, 467

Monmouth 334

Monon xi, 77, 100, 104, 105, 175, 325, 330, 407, 467

Monroe 41, 53, 73, 83, 98, 174, 199, 285, 296, 298, 303, 309, 328, 338, 390, 404, 411, 417, 472

Monroe Central 73, 222, 267, 285, 296, 417

Monroe City 186, 224, 225, 226, 351, 467

Monroe Township (Washington) 298, 411

Monroeville 307, 361, 423, 472

Monrovia 254, 255, 423, 469

Monterey 193, 195, 196

Montezuma 23, 43, 137, 182, 202, 232, 240, 330, 467, 473

Monticello 13, 66, 137, 138, 160, 174, 175, 181, 194, 330, 411, 473

Montmorenci 16, 17, 29, 35, 251, 282, 288, 472

Montpelier 65, 205, 206, 233, 309

Monument City 405

Mooreland 167, 399

Moores Hill 399

Mooresville 107

Moral 135, 335

Morgantown 174, 423

Morgan Township 135

Morocco 40, 67, 202, 377, 401, 407, 422

Morristown 121, 172, 300, 340, 342, 343, 472

Morton 175, 359, 380, 381, 464

Moscow 181, 182, 400

Mt. Auburn 168, 342, 443

Mt. Ayr 403, 404, 467

Mt. Comfort 401, 425

Mt. Olympus 207, 208

Mt. Summit 364, 399, 441

Mt. Vernon 63, 113, 156, 157, 260, 275, 276, 359, 364, 380, 390, 425

Mulberry 214, 434, 467

Muncie Burris v, ix, 39, 40, 44, 45, 46, 73, 155, 212, 326, 329, 439

Muncie Central 8, 9, 10, 24, 31, 44, 56, 91, 110, 130, 131, 132, 143, 146, 152, 159, 238, 251, 255, 267, 269, 273, 274, 293, 304, 305, 315, 320, 343, 366, 374, 375, 387, 389, 400, 424, 427, 430, 447, 448, 451, 452, 470

Muncie Heritage Christian 362

Muncie North Side 25, 329, 426

Muncie South Side 37, 259, 374, 375

Munster 265, 394

N

Napoleon 204, 308, 398

Nappanee 40, 53, 45, 239, 289, 290, 380, 443, 472

Needham 293

Needmore 440

New Albany 79, 83, 93, 100, 104, 131, 150, 180, 193, 199, 200, 204, 239, 245, 251, 255, 256, 269, 271, 274, 276, 286, 287, 292, 293, 295, 308, 316, 385, 436, 449, 469, 471

New Alsace 190, 203, 204
New Amsterdam 171
New Augusta 410, 453, 472
Newberry 400, 456, 457, 467
New Bethel 142, 410
New Bradford 104
Newburgh 294, 353
New Carlisle 257
New Castle iv, 5, 6, 45, 64, 76, 81, 89, 97, 121, 123, 124, 145, 161, 167, 274, 275, 278, 305, 322, 352, 359, 361, 366, 376, 380, 387, 390, 399, 414, 427, 428, 437, 447, 448, 452, 453, 461, 470
New Goshen 328, 338
New Harmony 31, 74, 75, 210, 364, 465
New Haven 194, 196, 250, 366
New Lebanon 102
New London 37, 38
New Marion 299
New Market 20, 22, 99, 436
New Palestine 299, 334, 359, 392, 401
New Paris 205, 303, 380
New Point 426, 437
Newport 43, 202
Newtown 410
New Prairie 241, 257, 288
New Providence 152
New Richmond 13, 15, 20, 21, 22, 333, 475
New Ross 10, 20, 21, 23, 182, 338, 473
New Salem 333, 359
New Salisbury 201, 298, 433
New Washington 265, 281
New Waverly 298
New Winchester 173
Nineveh 209, 328, 338
Noblesville 39, 229, 239, 278, 319, 332, 365, 379, 385, 437, 444, 459, 460, 461, 464, 471
Noble Township 425, 428
Normal 19, 436
North Caston 367, 444, 445
North Central (and conference) 5, 31, 97, 125, 150, 153, 159, 170, 226, 227, 236, 237, 244, 251, 258, 287, 299, 321, 326, 327, 352, 366, 376, 380, 389, 423, 424, 447, 450, 451, 452, 455, 457
North Central (Farmersburg) 443

North Daviess 52, 53, 54, 234, 257, 293, 362
North Decatur 164, 264, 265, 437
Northeast Dubois 75, 77, 195, 265, 350, 381, 464
Northeastern 121, 306, 308, 355, 425
Northfield 42, 118, 167, 362, 364, 365
North Harrison 201, 223, 230, 257, 287, 381, 433
North Judson-St. Pierre 145, 196, 290, 319, 323, 325, 376, 472, 473
North Knox 121, 144, 186, 202, 326
North Liberty 120, 434
North Madison 287, 294
North Manchester 196, 197, 287, 291, 428, 445, 472
North Miami 144, 145, 196
North Montgomery 21, 23, 253, 264
North Newton 217, 376, 377, 378
North Posey 63, 210, 364
North Putnam 258, 259, 346
North Salem 200, 410, 418
North Vermillion 240, 322, 324, 350
Northview 193, 194, 343, 353, 354, 417
North Vigo 56, 222
North Webster 297, 307, 423
Northridge 154, 214, 221, 356
Northwestern 190, 219, 246, 247, 304, 321, 335, 347, 429, 430
Northwest 100
Northwood 239
North Vernon 208, 240, 252, 284, 308, 410, 417, 428, 472
North White 105, 166, 364, 406, 443
Norwell 36, 159, 199, 213, 306, 354, 355, 438

O
Oak Hill 41, 42, 175, 317, 318, 386, 469
Oakland City 63, 64, 94, 208, 214, 283, 335, 363, 364, 381, 403, 408, 434
Oaklandon 63, 215, 216, 434, 472
Oaktown 63, 215, 216, 225
Odon viii, 54, 193, 220, 291, 292, 293, 333, 439, 473
Oil City 65, 205
Oil Township 221
Oldenburg 368, 369, 465
Onward 111

Oolitic 84, 85, 86, 184, 227, 308, 347, 440

Orange 65, 79, 286

Oregon-Davis 34, 159, 283

Oriole 2, 197, 221, 315, 326

Orland 218, 423

Orleans 80, 88, 142, 206, 207, 381, 440

Ossian 222, 306, 354, 404, 438, 472

Otterbein 169, 282, 410, 413, 414, 472

Otter Creek 57, 222, 401, 467

Otwell 234

Owensburg 168, 456

Owensville 34, 137, 138, 169, 207, 208, 275, 276, 335, 403

Owen Valley 63, 121, 168, 206, 220, 351, 362, 386

Owl Town 53

Oxford 198, 282, 330, 410, 413, 472

P

Paoli 150, 204, 223, 230, 281, 282, 381, 406, 436, 440

Paragon 300

Paris Crossing 205, 425

Parke County 66, 182, 232, 333, 395, 398, 410

Parker 171, 185, 222, 267, 285, 296, 368

Park (Tudor) School v, 237

Patoka 208, 294, 328, 335, 403, 408, 432, 433

Patricksburg 293

Pekin 88, 358, 428, 436

Pendleton (Pendleton Heights) 178, 264, 266, 267, 444, 472

Penn 356, 357, 365, 424, 469

Pennville 288, 337, 361, 414

Perry Central 24, 25, 170, 221, 329, 381, 425, 426, 464

Perry Meridian 322, 323, 435

Perrysville 334, 413, 472

Peru 110, 111, 193, 194, 195, 217, 242, 342, 411, 423, 424, 432, 445

Petersburg 167, 208, 330, 355, 409

Petroleum 35, 36, 301, 437, 472

Pierceton 307, 398, 440

Pike (and county) 69, 70, 167, 186, 234, 258, 264, 330, 336, 355, 356, 369, 442

Pike (Indianapolis township) 97, 206, 258, 267, 353, 357, 370, 410, 471

Pimento xi, 29, 52, 53, 434, 467

Pine Township 198, 282

Pine Village 71, 72, 467

Pinnell 25, 26, 436

Pioneer 176

Pittsboro 173, 219, 309, 310, 323, 330, 467

Plainfield 36, 37, 147, 342, 375, 385, 432, 465

Plainville 52, 54, 170, 211, 293, 426, 439, 472

Pleasant Lake 398, 428

Pleasant Mills 398, 428

Pleasantville 398, 431

Plymouth 108, 109, 112, 194, 197, 202, 241, 254, 325, 351, 387, 388, 396, 465, 469

Poling 216, 361, 400

Portage 159, 354, 458

Portland 35, 36, 288, 299, 301, 309, 337, 361, 400, 414

Poseyville 210, 275, 434

Prairie Creek 55, 57

Prairie Heights 200, 218

Prairie Township 349, 410, 461

Princeton v, 63, 65, 66, 80, 158, 180, 194, 207, 208, 237, 242, 335, 364, 377, 403, 404, 408, 432, 465, 471

Pulaski 145, 173, 195, 347

Putnamville 293

Q

Quincy 410

R

Raglesville 54, 293

Raleigh 38, 193, 241, 467

Randolph Southern 368, 374, 375

Raub 440

Redkey 32, 361, 400

Reelsville 166, 403

Remington 38

Rensselaer 166, 367, 394, 404

Restoration Christian 263

Reynolds 175, 443

Richland Center 296, 472

Richland Township 64, 410, 413

Richmond 13, 15, 20, 21, 22, 44, 121, 216, 218, 247, 306, 321, 330, 333, 346, 351, 352, 370, 371, 375, 380, 390, 405,

411, 430, 447, 448, 449, 455, 470, 475
Richmond Academy 263
Ridgeville 18, 337, 427, 472
Riley 55, 57, 78, 191, 428
Rising Sun 49, 289, 343, 350, 367, 398, 406, 465
Riverdale 444
River Forest (Hobart) 103
Riverton Parke 43, 182, 232, 240
Rivet 225, 362, 386, 457
Roachdale 72, 166, 177, 258, 335, 472
Roann 167, 287, 434
Roanoke 117, 118
Rochester 13, 65, 145, 165, 172, 233, 235, 236, 251, 312, 318, 367, 430, 447, 448, 465
Rock Creek 263, 334, 408, 437
Rock Creek Center 44, 437
Rock Creek Christian Academy 263
Rockfield 168, 411
Rockport 34, 211, 312, 374, 409
Rockville 13, 202, 333, 395, 396, 403, 465, 469
Roll 233, 234, 414, 467
Rolling Prairie 234, 288
Rome City 183, 467
Romney 25
Rosedale 43, 232, 413, 467
Rossville 59, 72, 340, 363, 472
Round Grove 293
Royal Center 138, 172, 175, 240, 293, 329, 473
Royerton 25, 329, 426
Rushville 38, 64, 145, 164, 168, 182, 204, 209, 263, 264, 295, 328, 333, 359, 371, 402, 411, 417, 429, 430, 432
Russellville 346
Russiaville viii, 181, 241, 427, 460, 467
Rykers Ridge 428

S

Sacred Heart 129, 406
Salem 88, 199, 263, 359, 381, 410, 418, 436, 443
Salem Center 200, 332, 333
Saluda 294, 302, 341, 403
Sandborn 186, 225, 226, 338
Sand Creek 173, 308
Sandusky 164, 472

San Jacinto 308
San Pierre 196, 290, 319, 325, 376
Saratoga 171, 412, 413
Scecina 388
Scipio 284, 285
Scircleville 58, 59, 468
Scotland 41, 183, 201, 220, 227, 456, 468
Scott Center 293
Scottsburg 146, 147, 268, 283, 302, 326, 344, 423, 427, 469
Seeger Memorial 62, 361
Sellersburg 263, 391
Selma 73, 154, 338, 439
Seton Catholic 321
Seymour 88, 112, 118, 146, 173, 200, 223, 254, 256, 274, 275, 301, 313, 317, 326, 331, 333, 353, 383, 429, 436, 441, 443, 470
Shadeland 29, 434
Shakamak 154, 220, 346, 382, 457
Sharpsville 290, 349, 427, 472
Shawe Memorial 394
Shawswick 226, 227
Shelburn 300, 472
Shelbyville 31, 57, 124, 135, 149, 177, 178, 204, 267, 295, 310, 311, 340, 342, 345, 377, 399, 429, 430, 469, 470
Shenandoah 181, 326, 354, 373, 375, 376, 428
Sheridan 39, 120, 126, 143, 154, 290, 324, 325, 459, 460, 461
Shipshewana 169
Shoals 50, 76, 89, 292, 396, 464
Shortridge ix, 3, 4, 13, 14, 80, 114, 123, 124, 125, 126, 127, 128, 129, 130, 131, 132, 241, 251, 271, 299, 323, 389, 410, 414, 415, 416, 417, 444, 453, 467
Sidney 297, 307, 364
Silver Creek 301, 341, 391, 392, 441
Silver Lake 307, 435, 440
Smithville 41, 300, 468
Somerset 434
Solsberry 307, 345, 346, 456
South Adams 171, 172, 177, 178, 179, 323, 367, 368, 469
South Bend Adams 255, 316, 431

South Bend Central 10, 14, 56, 91, 95, 141, 143, 159, 168, 194, 230, 251, 275, 288, 296, 303, 304, 305, 320, 350, 353, 358, 362, 387, 399, 415, 423, 443, 471
South Bend Clay 116, 192, 197, 256
South Bend Community Baptist 259
South Bend Jackson 284
South Bend LaSalle 401
South Bend Riley 101, 126, 153, 167, 254, 261, 363, 365, 443
South Bend St. Joseph 161, 301, 341
South Bend Washington 249, 279, 378, 386
South Bend Wilson 429, 431, 467
South Caston 367, 444, 445
South Central 31, 234, 299, 342, 367, 368, 374, 410, 423, 425, 457
South Dearborn 242, 267, 355, 384, 399, 411
South Decatur 258, 259, 285, 308
Southern Wells 36, 121, 154, 164, 356, 401, 402, 469
South Knox 225
Southmont 19, 23
South Newton 237, 374, 375, 440
Southport 129, 142, 173, 205, 221, 237, 320, 340, 352, 373, 374, 378, 470
South Putnam 316, 317
Southridge 75, 154, 184, 185, 188, 206, 247, 257, 282, 322, 326, 355, 356, 373, 381, 470
South Ripley High School 203
South Spencer 211, 374
South Vermillion 43, 229, 260, 344, 364
South Vigo 222
Southwestern 29, 30, 31, 168, 190, 191, 332, 343, 344, 370, 373, 374, 376, 377, 378, 389
South Whitley 259, 290
Southwood 39, 273, 355, 425, 445
Spartanburg 399, 400
Speedway 21, 48, 49, 247, 258, 465
Spencer 55, 63, 121, 183, 198, 210, 211, 217, 258, 289, 362, 374, 409, 410, 423, 456, 468
Spencerville 170
Spiceland 64, 343, 390, 399, 468, 472
Springfield Township 168, 330

Springs Valley 86, 87, 88, 89, 154, 187, 200, 207, 324, 374
Springville 347
Spurgeon 208, 330
Star City 145, 173, 222
Staunton 43, 343
Stendall 208
Stewartsville 210, 336
Stilesville 288
Stillwell 370, 438
Stinesville 83, 84, 407, 468
St. Berniece 344
St. John Township 165
St. Mary 369
Stockwell 30
Stonebraker, Homer 15
Stoney Creek 278, 410, 412, 417
St. Paul 83, 84, 87, 428, 468
Straughn 64, 167, 390
St. Theodore Guerin 319
Sugar Creek 59, 60, 221, 466
Sullivan (and county) 55, 81, 87, 102, 138, 147, 155, 156, 157, 158, 163, 166, 170, 180, 187, 195, 210, 211, 227, 300, 326, 338, 401, 423, 431, 439, 472
Sulphur Springs 64, 89, 399
Summitville 32, 418, 444, 472
Sunman 284, 285, 300, 429
Swayzee 32, 41, 42, 127, 159, 431, 468
Sweetser 175
Switz City 279, 286, 345, 440, 456, 473
Switzerland County High School 177
Syracuse High 208

T

Talma 287
Tampico 193, 195, 196
Tangier 202, 347
Taylor 389, 390, 406
Tecumseh 5, 27, 31, 66, 152, 213
Tefft 288
Tell City 34, 82, 138, 155, 163, 170, 179, 180, 183, 208, 275, 276, 353, 381, 464
Tennyson 33, 34, 288, 294
Terre Haute 8, 31, 32, 43, 51, 174, 180, 434
Terre Haute Booker T. Washington 392

Terre Haute Concannon 212

Terre Haute Garfield 102, 193, 222, 246, 274, 275, 286, 300, 311, 324, 400, 461

Terre Haute Gerstmeyer 53, 126, 276, 304, 345, 423

Terre Haute IS Lab School 53, 56, 435, 436

Terre Haute North 56, 361

Terre Haute Schulte 307

Terre Haute South Vigo 52, 55, 143, 152, 168, 206, 222, 366, 374

Terre Haute West Vigo 212, 338, 399

Terre Haute Wiley 55, 57, 333, 431, 432

Thea Bowman Academy 319

Thorntown 16, 17, 18, 25, 29, 59, 123, 137, 143, 155, 251, 420, 472

Tindley Academy 249

Tioga 137, 138, 174, 175

Tippecanoe 18, 27, 28, 29, 30, 32, 40, 41, 63, 154, 287, 293, 364, 397, 403, 438

Tipton 39, 40, 190, 288, 290, 349, 350, 369, 410, 425, 436, 460, 461

Tobinsport 425

Topeka 150, 169, 306

Trafalgar 152, 204, 205, 439, 472

TriCentral 77

Tri-County 38, 358, 359

Tri-High (Henry County) 64, 390

Trinity Lutheran 52, 89, 256, 468

Trinty Springs 89

Triton 49, 237, 248, 279, 281, 283, 307, 317, 350, 372

Triton Central 237, 248

Tri-West 200, 219, 267, 268

Troy 150, 183, 342

Tunnelton 166, 167

Turkey Run 21, 66, 144, 145, 202, 399

Twelve Mile 211, 367, 468

Twin Lakes 44, 159, 160, 175, 181, 347

Tyner Marshall County 169

U

Union (Dugger) 390, 412, 457, 467

Union Center 213

Union City 73, 161, 296, 298, 411, 417

Union County 121, 362, 367, 411

Union Mills 141, 219, 234, 299, 368, 467

Union (Modoc) 332

Union Township 44, 199, 333, 395, 439

Unionville 174

University 256, 387, 394

Upland 429

Urbana 42, 468

V

Vallonia 331

Valparaiso 116, 153, 159, 191, 193, 256, 352, 361, 364, 374, 381, 385, 470

Van Buren 41, 159, 193, 298, 308, 408, 410, 417

Veedersburg 64, 265, 410, 411, 413, 418

Vernon 63, 84, 173, 418

Versailles 202, 203, 204, 294, 375, 403

Vevay 176, 177, 302, 341, 405, 406, 453

Vincennes 41, 81, 143, 146, 160, 192, 193, 200, 206, 208, 225, 226, 233, 239, 292

Vincennes Lincoln frontispiece, viii, 2, 80, 81, 82, 117, 163, 164, 185, 234, 245, 271, 274, 275, 362, 376, 415, 422, 429, 435, 449, 461, 464, 469, 470

Vincennes Rivet 362, 386, 457

W

Wabash (and county) viii, 35, 39, 53, 54, 57, 135, 136, 137, 193, 299, 327, 355, 364, 370, 424, 425, 428, 434, 445, 472

Wadena 168, 282

Wadesville 410

Wainwright 28, 30, 309

Wakarusa 167, 472

Waldron 134, 135, 250, 471, 472

Walkerton 168, 196, 322

Wallace v, ix, 14, 44, 45, 71, 73, 267, 301, 323, 413, 431, 434, 441, 468

Walnut Grove viii, 39, 277, 280, 400, 459, 460, 461

Walton 172, 215, 357, 472

Wanatah 234, 426

Wapahani 73, 153, 154

Warren 33, 44, 291, 468

Warren Central (Indianapolis) 128, 148, 254, 283

Warrick (County) 33, 66, 230, 296

Warsaw viii, 40, 116, 135, 197, 235, 242, 243, 244, 245, 297, 307, 317, 319, 322, 351, 356, 380, 422, 423, 428, 440, 453, 471

Washington Catholic 300, 320, 469

Washington Center 296

Washington (Indianapolis Continentals) 65, 111, 125, 127, 129, 131, 143, 235, 301, 391, 405, 417, 470

Washington (Daviess County) 31, 34, 37, 45, 52, 54, 102, 109, 112, 113, 124, 156, 163, 185, 186, 187, 234, 270, 274, 275, 276, 323, 362, 404, 415, 439

Washington Mt. Vernon 113

Washington Township 113, 173, 381, 411, 457

Waterloo 96, 97, 204, 205, 366

Waveland 20, 22, 23, 343, 344

Wawaka 172

Wawasee 72, 148, 153, 208, 335, 423

Waynetown 20, 23, 32, 149, 472

Wayne Township 286, 332, 386

Wea 30

Webster 346, 425

Wes-Del 148, 289, 332

West Baden Springs x, 86, 87, 88, 89, 468

West Central 350

West College Corner 422

Western Boone 17, 26, 27, 198, 367

Western High School 37

Westfield 396, 434, 459, 460, 469

West Lafayette 13, 30, 31, 58, 79, 81, 154, 364, 369

Westland 306

West Lebanon 61, 410, 413

West Middleton 309

West Noble 172, 202, 264, 315, 365, 428

Westphalia 202

West Point 71, 438, 468, 472

Westport 173, 472

Westview 150, 169, 306, 318, 382

West Vigo 212, 240, 364

Westville 154, 155, 458

West Washington 207, 227, 309, 357, 381, 459

Wheatfield 228, 262, 422, 468

Wheatland 76, 225, 226, 466

Wheeler 119, 193, 267, 268, 458, 459

Whiteland 23, 115, 148, 149, 155, 342, 395, 403, 439, 472

White River Valley 63, 100, 187, 206, 257, 277, 279, 286, 291, 307, 335, 350, 377, 403, 432, 433, 440, 456, 457

White's Institute 150, 327

Whitestown 25, 26, 301

Whitewater 218, 306, 308, 330, 406

Whiting 31, 102, 103, 212, 464

Whitko 259, 297, 364, 421

Wilkinson 131, 290

Williams ix, 121, 125, 130, 131, 163, 224, 225, 226, 227, 289, 290, 321, 350, 362, 424, 437, 454

Williamsburg 346, 347, 413, 425

Williamsport 61, 62, 71, 468

Winamac 103, 145, 165, 167, 173, 196, 215, 217, 222, 254, 289, 453

Winchester 73, 150, 171, 173, 246, 286, 296, 319, 321, 368, 412, 417, 427, 431

Windfall 39, 349, 436, 437, 460, 461

Wingate 14, 15, 16, 18, 20, 21, 22, 59, 71, 123, 142, 295, 404, 461, 472, 475

Winslow viii, 68, 69, 70, 185, 186, 187, 206, 208, 275, 468, 472, 473

Whitko 197

Wolcott 297

Wolcottville 288, 295

Wolf Lake 102, 169, 212, 472

Woodburn 173

Woodlan 149, 173, 335

Wood Memorial 94

Worthington 10, 307, 346, 439, 440, 456

Wyandotte Woods 170

Y

Yankeetown 34, 215

Yorktown 242, 246, 388, 438

Young America 215, 411

Z

Zenas 173

Zionsville 21, 24, 25, 26, 27, 198, 316, 342

HALL OF FAMERS
(with citations in this book)
Adams, Doug 281, 412
Allen, Max 101
Altemeyer, Vern 146
Atha, Dick 413
Bailey, Damon 72, 85, 105, 110, 306, 326, 365
Baratto, Johnny 211, 212, 430
Blue, Jeff 404
Bolyard, Tom 82, 394
Bonham, Ron 238, 451
Boryla, Vince 425, 430
Cave, Marvin 10
Cheatham, Donna 12, 83, 146, 343, 344, 373
Coalmon, Sylvester 304
Colescott, David 450
Collier, John 203, 373, 405, 406
Crain, William "Bo" 132, 415, 416
Crowe, George 93
Crowe, Ray 93, 114, 115, 116, 119, 120, 125, 126, 128, 130, 132, 145, 471
Curtis, Glenn 91, 107
Dampier, Louie 320
DeJernett, Dave 112, 113, 124
DeKemper, Roberta 243, 471
Dickerson, Myron 24, 25, 329, 377, 437
Dickey, Dick 266
Dro, Bob 177, 178
Ford, Bob 64, 280, 455
Fortner, Knofel 84, 183, 227
Gardner, Earl "Red" 99
Garrett, Bill 124, 311, 429, 465
Hamilton, Lee 273
Jewell, Bob 114
Jones, Mike 71,72, 78, 340
Kaiser, Roger 409
Keefer, Jack 175, 261, 314, 317, 471, 492
Kreiger, Wayne 315
Kron, Tommy 180
Lochmueller, Bob 66
Lochmueller, Steve 180
Lundy, Lamar 449
Macy, Kyle 195
Masters, Bob 450
Mawbey, Basil 356, 357, 377, 423, 452, 471

McCaskey, Jake 21
McCracken, Branch 142, 255
McGinley, Tim 388
Memering, Jerry 80, 82
Milholland, John 149, 155
Nicholson, Dave 21, 230, 282, 332
Nicoson, Angus 435
Pavy, Ray 51, 85, 123, 376, 449
Payne, Vernon 281
Perigo, Bill 78
Pillow, George 415, 416
Pollard, LaTaunya 242, 244
Pollard, Morris 49, 408
Powers, Jim 235, 264, 304
Ragelis, Ray 429, 430
Rayl, Jimmy 5, 123, 376, 449, 451
Reynolds, Cleon 125, 126, 131, 132, 330, 415, 416
Robertson, Oscar 6, 114, 115, 116, 123, 125, 128, 130, 299
Schnaitter, Spence 265, 269
Seward, Bill 415
Sexson, Joe 388, 389
Shepherd, Bill 72, 98, 278, 279
Showalter, Dalen 450
Soyez, Janice 243, 471
Stearman, Bill 135, 250
Steiner, Jerome 178
Stonebraker, Homer 15
VanArsdale, Dick 142
VanArsdale, Tom 142
Vandivier, Fuzzy 31, 92, 93, 436
Wallace, Tom v, ix, 44, 45, 73
Warren, Judi 242
Warren, Mike 304, 305
Watson, Lou 82, 371, 372
Wheeler, Babe 193
Wills, Phil 298
Wilson, Johnny 124, 162, 221, 273, 449, 451
Wood, Marvin 8, 158, 159, 343, 380
Wooden, John 6, 91, 112, 303, 305
Wyman, Orlando "Gunner" 80, 82, 180
Zimmer, Andy 422

WHAT WE LEARNED

The following pages are all new, representing what we have discovered in the years following publication of the first edition of *Hoosiers All*. One thing is clear: whether it is friends getting together on the playground after work, or behind the barn on a brisk afternoon, or an important game being played before thousands and televised to many more, we love our "hoops." In forty-nine states it's just a game but in Indiana it's a love affair, and every March it's Hoosier Hysteria.

WHAT WE LEARNED

In writing the first edition of Hoosiers All, *I had two purposes in mind: one was to gather and make available in one place as much information as possible on the history and lore of Indiana high school basketball. The other was to encourage readers to add whatever they could to this history and lore. Here are some of the more interesting things that have been brought to my attention, or that I have discovered for myself, since* Hoosiers All *was first issued in August of 2009. My thanks to everyone who has made these contributions.*

Earliest Mascots

Although I referred to the selection of Felix the Cat as the mascot of both Indianapolis Shortridge and Logansport high schools in the mid 20s as perhaps the first official mascots in our state, and have acknowledged that the Vincennes Alices may well have a prior claim, I have since discovered that as early as 1908 the Hillsboro teams were called the Little Giants. Here is a photo that would lend credence to that:

The Hillsboro teams were later called the Wildcats. We are indebted to their excellent web site for the above picture as well as for the following information about their teams:

"In 1926 Hillsboro entered sectional play with an unimpressive regular season record of 10-8, including a loss at Monrovia whose star player was Branch McCracken. But the team caught fire in the sectional, winning their three games easily, then taking the regional in Greencastle by defeating Oxford and Monon. There were no semi-states in this era, so Hillsboro became the first Fountain County team to reach the "Sweet Sixteen." The state finals were held in the old exposition building (Cattle Barn) at the State Fairgrounds in Indianapolis that year. Hillsboro was by far the smallest school in the finals (six boys in the class of 1926), and played North Vernon in the first game in front of a crowd of 9,000. After leading at halftime the Wildcats finally went cold after a magical run and lost 34-23. Marion, led by Charles "Stretch" Murphy, went on to win the title over Martinsville with legendary John Wooden." *(Author's* note: One of the officials in the state tournament had the familiar name of Birch Bayh! Also in 1926 there were only 8 Regionals, with two winners from each going on to Indianapolis. The other winner at Greencastle was Frankfort. The Hillsboro coach was Hardy Songer.)

"In 1933 Hillsboro had perhaps their best all-time team, starting the season 15-0, beating the likes of Decatur Central, Crown Point, and Rockville. Their only regular season loss came at Brownsburg in a game scheduled late in the season as a battle of unbeatens. The team went on to win the school's third Sectional and finished the season with a loss to host Crawfordsville and Hall of Famer Pat Malaska in the Regional." (Author's note: That team won 23 games and was coached by Herman Ward).

Shortridge teams also soon adopted the name Blue Devils after a school-wide contest was won by David Burns, who remembered a group of French airmen from World War I with a similar name who had stayed at his home. Gregg Nowling, Media Specialist at Shortridge, has also shown me several pictures from his extensive school archives of Shortridge teams with the name Satans on their uniforms. Logansport teams are also called the Berries.

Shortridge Satans Oscar Evans and Leonard Taylor receive runner-up trophy after 1968 state championship game (Courtesy Indiana Historical Society)

Other contenders for earliest mascot honors:

Vincennes Lincoln: The team was known as the Pirates at a very early date as well as, of course, the Alices, which was made official in the 20s. From the school's website: *March 4, 1911—For first time team is referred to as "Alices" by Vincennes Commercial; Nov. 1924—Name "Alices" is officially used as nickname for Vincennes Lincoln High School Athletic Teams. Prior to that they were the "Pirates."*

LaPorte: Brian Avery, current athletic director at Speedway High School and alum of LaPorte points out that the name Slicers was adopted very early on by his high school. Wilhelm Van Berkel's original slicing machine came to LaPorte from Chicago in 1915. According to the Indiana State Museum a contest was held in 1917 to rename the high school's athletic teams, previously known as the Orange and Black. The name Slicers won.

Crawfordsville: Bill Boone has written that the Crawfordsville High School teams were originally referred to as the Gold and Blue or sometimes the Old Gold but the yearbook was called *The Athenian* as early as 1906. Until the mid twenties the school teams were often called the Midgets but from at least 1925 on they were the Athenians.

A Word About Culver

The Culver High School teams were called the Indians until 1967, when the name Cavaliers was adopted to coincide with their consolidation. I am also informed that the 1922 Culver team included two African American players. Locals feel this may have been the first integrated team in the state. I have found no one who disputes that as of this date.

New Market

The New Market Purple Flyers nailed down the first of their seven county championships in 1939 when Coach Jack Hester's team edged Ladoga in a thriller 29-28. This began a run of three straight titles and four out of five for the Purple and White.

Hester's 1940 edition snuck by New Ross 22-21, and the next year his Flyers trounced Darlington 35-19, finishing 17-5. Two years later Hester's Flyers defeated defending champion Bowers convincingly, 35-25, en route to a 14-6 record. Hall of Famer Earl "Red" Gardner was a 1941 New

Market graduate. It was to be 15 more years before a New Market team would cut down the championship nets again, doing so for Coach Larry Robinson, 63-55, over Waveland in 1958 on the way to a 19-3 record. Four years later Coach Bob Tandy led his team to the school's sixth crown in a close final game, 62-59, against New Ross. Crown number seven was won in 1966, Jack

The 1939 Purple Flyers

Hester once again at the helm, in a heart-stopping 74-72 game against defending champion Coal Creek. New Market squads won two Sectional titles, the first in 1950 when Coach Bill Melvin's five defeated the Crawfordsville Athenians in the final game by a 51-43 count, finishing the season with a 20-6 mark. The other Sectional title, generally referred to as the Miracle of New Market because after a 2-17 regular season record the Purple Flyers won at Crawfordsville by defeating Coal Creek 78-70, the home team Athenians 78-75, New Ross 81-63, and Waveland 57-50 for Coach Jim Petty in the final game.

How Beech Grove Became Hornets

Steve Nontell reports the following:

"I can share the as-yet unclear story on Beech Grove's own nickname (still needing further research). I have found early references by students and fans, in old *Indianapolis Star* basketball columns in which they called the team the Tomahawks, but that may have just been a personal reference to the aggressive success of the first decent teams the school fielded in the mid-1920s. The name seems to have become Yellowjackets by 1930, according to some old school publications, but their first major tourney title—the 1931 Marion County one—is credited by some to have inspired the name change to Horn-etts, as a tribute to their coach, Olin L. Van Horn (later the Principal). That less-than-macho form of the name soon became shortened to Hornets."

Indianapolis All-girl Catholic Schools
Also from Steve Nontell:

"Something worth adding might be the short-lived teams of Indianapolis's all-girls Catholic schools. They had the sad fate of joining in on the beginnings of IHSAA girls' sports at about the same time that dwindling finances and changing demographics brought about their closures. There were 3 of note originally—Ladywood, St. Agnes, and Our Lady Of Grace (this latter located on the north border of Beech Grove). By the first girls state tourney in 1976, Ladywood-St. Agnes had been formed from a merger, and had chosen an alliterative yet smart-alecky unique nickname—the Lizards! Our Lady Of Grace went with the gentler yet no less alliterative Gazelles." (Authors note: Ladywood-St. Agnes is now a proud part of Indianapolis Cathedral, the Fighting Irish. I am also informed that the St. Agnes girls were once referred to as the Stags).

Were Guilford Teams Ever Called Quakers?
Bob Chance states that Guilford teams were never the Quakers, although the IHSAA has that name listed along with Wildcats and Yellow Jackets. Bob says they were the Cyclones from 1926 to 1934, then the Yellow Jackets, and finally, not sure when, the Wildcats.

East Chicago Roosevelt
In the absence of other data, I have generally referred to girls teams as the Lady counterpart of their boys teams, as, for example the Warsaw Lady Tigers. East Chicago Roosevelt boys teams were the Rough Riders in honor of President Theodore Roosevelt and consistent with my approach I have referred to the girls teams on page 243 as the Lady Roughriders. Apparently they were called the Riderettes.

Some Interesting Gym Memories
Dan Carpenter has several memories to share:

"As best that I can recall, Hillsboro gym, Fountain County, had bleachers only on one side; the other three walls were brick. These walls were the out of bounds.

The line was painted at the bottom and adjacent to the wall; therefore, no driving fast break on either end. If so, it ended rather quickly since the backboard was hung on the brick wall.

"The Alamo gym, Montgomery County, was too short in length therefore had two ten second lines. When bringing the ball down the court a team had to pass over both lines then it could use the first one

as part of the playing court. I believe this gym is still standing and used for storage.

"The Wingate gym, Montgomery County, is also still standing. It had a large stove, I believe coal, in one corner for heat surrounded by, if my memory serves me right, woven wire fence to keep everyone away from it. The floor also had several dead spots throughout where the ball would not rebound from a dribble. The Wingate players knew where these were and avoided them while the visiting team had to find out the hard way.

"The Veedersburg gym, Fountain County, had bleachers on both sides, a stage on one end (which was very common) and two or three rows of bleachers on a balcony on the west end with the back board attached to it. Students could go up on the balcony and shake the basket when the visiting team had that end of the floor if they didn't get caught.

"In 1949–50, Richland won 18 scheduled games to 0 losses. First loss was to Attica 47 to 30 in the Wabash Tourney at Attica in the first game. (Attica never scheduled such a small school.) Then in the state tourney, we beat Attica 37 to 34. also at Attica, then beat Covington 32 to 31 for Richland's first Sectional title, then lost to Clinton 60 to 54 at Greencastle Regional.

"Attica, after getting beaten by Richland in the Sectional, wanted to come to Richland's gym for a pep deal. When we got out of class, our gym was almost full with very little room for us."

(Author's note: For more on Indiana high school gyms, see Kyle Neddenriep's fine new book, *Historic Hoosier Gyms*, also available from the Hall of Fame gift shop.)

Some Randolph County Information

From Paul, no last name provided:

"I would like to add a missed school. Randolph County had 18 schools prior to 1950. You covered 17 of the schools but missed the Jackson Township Bulldogs. Per Bill May, the school first played in a Sectional at Winchester in 1921. They reached the final Sectional game 2 times until the school was consolidated with Ward Township in 1957. Union City beat them 37 to 22 at the Lynn Sectional in 1933. Parker beat them

41 to 39 at Winchester in 1938. After joining Ward Township, which included the Jefferson school by then, Ward-Jackson won the 1961 Sectional at Winchester beating Parker 66 to 65. In 1962 Jackson became part of Union City school system. You had the information correct on the Jefferson school, which became the only Randolph County school to win a Regional prior to class basketball, in 1949. The school was located in Ward Township and that consolidated Saratoga and Jefferson schools in 1954. Thanks again for a book that provides so much information on the history of Indiana High School Basketball."

(Author's note: The Jackson Township teams in Randolph County were indeed omitted inadvertently from *Hoosiers All* and are now included in the paragraph on all of our Jackson Township teams that once existed in nine different Indiana counties.)

A Wealth of information from John Edgerly:

"I have recently read your 2009 *Hoosiers All* book on Indiana high-school nicknames and found it just as enjoyable as your *Go Huskies, Beat Felix The Cat* (which I located in the mid-summer of 2006 at New Castle's Indiana Basketball Hall of Fame—and had a blast poring through, while I chose to picnic in nearby Spiceland's lovely little town park near the old 1937 Stingers' gym). I'm originally from Logansport and grew up with seeing, in the company of my Uncle John, the "Berries" play at the old, 1926-constructed Berry Bowl at 13th and Market Streets. I still have a large collection of both Logansport and other schools' lore, featuring booster pins from over 100 Hoosier high schools. What I found intriguing about your book was that several of the pins photographed—such as the green and white, Ft. Wayne South Side Archers button in the color section—were among a collection of some 400 pins I donated in 1991 to the Basketball Hall of Fame, just after it was relocated to New Castle!

"What an enormous task it must have been to assemble all that information. I'd like to somehow be able to send you some of my own gatherings, including color shots of old, vanished mascots from schools in this part of the state (not depicted in your book): Deer Creek's "Crickets" on a maroon-and-white license-plate ornament at Betty's Stop and Shop in that small Carroll County village, the Kirklin Travelers (which used a gold and black greyhound-like mascot, which I snapped from an old t-shirt design on the wall of Fredy's Cafe, off State Road 29 and across from the Kirklin American Legion post), and a Macy Yellow Jackets license plate dating from the early 1950s, observed up at Nyona Lake in southeast Fulton County (where my family lived in the summertime with Macy the closest town and post office just over the line in northern Miami County).

"I guess there will always be inconsistencies in the team nicknames and mascots, and what I'm contributing for you isn't to sound like some annoying "know-it-all" but simply what I came across while following the Berries (I started going to the games in the mid-50s and graduated from LHS in 1967). I've long heard the story of the adoption of Felix the Cat as Logansport's mascot, but as long as I can remember, the team's always been referred to as the "Berries"; they don't call themselves—and never have—Felix the Cat. The actual nickname is obscured in local lore, and all I've been able to pick up is that the football field was reportedly first built in the middle of a berry patch (raspberries, blackberries, whatever—I'm not sure). This would make more sense, if football had been the big sport at Logansport (which it might have been in the distant days). But from my early interest through high school and beyond, basketball—and later baseball—have been the primary focal points of sporting interest. We typically placed a stuffed Felix the Cat doll (roughly, a yard tall) in the center of the Berry Bowl floor, and when tourney-time rolled around, LHS was drawn as Felix in the preview cartoons—probably because no one knew how to sketch a bunch of berries.

"The perpetually-powerful (at that time) North Central Conference was also labeled the Big Ten: Logansport, Kokomo, Frankfort, Lafayette Jeff, Indianapolis Tech, Marion, Anderson, Muncie Central, New Castle, and Richmond were the participants. All 10 schools' banners (with their respective colors and years of either conference or state titles) were suspended from the Berry Bowl rafters, 5 at each end.

"Logan's red and black banner dominated the south end of the Berry Bowl, just over the basket, with the ball-catching net behind that protected any loose balls from going down the entrance/exit ramp that descended all the way to Market Street. The Logansport, Frankfort, Richmond, Muncie Central, and Anderson banners were on the south end—while the north end had those from Kokomo, Lafayette Jeff, Marion, New Castle, and Indianapolis Tech. When I first started following the sport, I had trouble with connecting the "Technical Green Wave" banner (in shiny green with white lettering) with Tech, until my uncle explained it. And one puzzlement that I've found, even when reading of high school hoops events in the 1950s, is that Tech is referred to as the Titans, but they didn't adopt this name until after they dropped out of the NCC in 1961. (Logansport *Pharos-Tribune* editor John Strey verifies this in his 'Stray Slant on Sports' column, during 1957–59—which I've checked on microfilm, although they do use the alternate, off-the-cuff reference to Tech as the Greenclads, especially when Tech won the NCC in '58.) But Indy Tech was certainly the Green Wave when they played their last conference game at the Berry Bowl in 1961, won by the Berries in a 70-68 heart-killer! This was additionally the incredible 24-4 season, where Logan went all the way to the Final Four at Butler Fieldhouse (the last time, to date, that the Berries have advanced so far) and lost in the afternoon session—announced on what was then Indianapolis' Ch. 6, WFBM-TV by Tom Carnegie—to the eventual state champion (and conference arch-rival) Kokomo! (Boo—we cheered, in vain, for Indy Manual's Redskins and the Van Arsdale twins that night.)

"Ah, memories. Jean Paul Richter said it best in 1808: 'Remembrance is the only paradise out of which we cannot be driven.'"

(Author's note: Above are some examples from John Edgerly's collection. He has presented many to the Hall of Fame).

Little Jeff

Washington Township High School in Clinton County was located in the town of Jefferson. To differentiate the Warriors teams from those of Lafayette Jefferson they were often referred to as Little Jeff. Although they never won a Sectional title, the Warriors did win 18 games in 1924 for Maurice Kennedy. The school was consolidated into Clinton Prairie in 1961. The colors of the Clinton Central Bulldogs are green and white, (Dartmouth's colors and Yale's mascot?). Those colors were chosen "because they were the only good ones left" that had not been used by any of the five former rivals that consolidated to form the new school (Forest, gold and black; Kirklin, black and gold; Michigantown, red and white; Scircleville, red and white; Sugar Creek, blue and gold).

The Indiana Catholic Tournament

The Indiana State Catholic Basketball Tournament ran from 1928 until 1942, after which the Catholic schools joined the IHSAA and began participating in its state championship tournament. The tournament winners were: 1928 Indianapolis Cathedral; 1929 Indianapolis Cathedral; 1930 Decatur Catholic; 1931 Washington St.Simon; 1932 Indianapolis Cathedral; 1933 Indianapolis Cathedral; 1934 no tournament; 1935 Huntington Catholic; 1936 Anderson St. Mary; 1937 Anderson St Mary; 1938 Anderson St. Mary; 1939 Ft. Wayne Central Catholic; 1940 Ft. Wayne Central Catholic; 1941 Evansville Memorial; 1942 Ft. Wayne Central Catholic. The winners of the Indiana tournament qualified for the National Catholic Interscholastic Basketball Tournament that was held at Loyola University (Chicago). At Loyola Indianapolis Cathedral captured the National Championship in 1933, Ft. Wayne Central Catholic did so in 1939 and 1940 and Anderson St. Mary's took home the runner-up title in 1936.

Jay County

Dean Monroe sent the following observations:

"Poling High School—In your book you referred to Poling as the Polecats. My research indicates that they were never the Polecats, only Yellow Jackets. I think I know where you got that information. When Harley Sheets published his "Where In The World Is" booklets, it had Polecats listed as the nickname. I asked Harley where he got that information, and he said that he called the Jay County High School and some kid told him that was the nickname. So when I did my research, I double-checked with two of the earliest graduates of Poling, and they confirmed that Poling was only the Yellow Jackets and they never heard of them being the Polecats. The nickname of Yellow Jackets was suggested by Kenneth Skinner, a student and 1928 graduate, and approved by the school officials.

"As far as how the Jay County teams got their nicknames, there are not a lot of interesting stories. Pennville was the Bulldogs, a pretty common nickname. But they got the name because Oscar Jones used to attend all the games and take his pet bulldog to the games. The team adopted him as their mascot in 1924." (Author's note: another contender for first mascot in Indiana.)

"Legend has it that Bryant got their nickname, Owls, from a baseball game and not basketball. They were playing a game and it was getting pretty dark, but the umpires refused to call the game. At one point in the game, the pitcher faked pitching the ball and the catcher faked catching it and they fooled the umpire into calling a strike, even though no pitch was actually thrown. The game was called when the batter hit a pop-up and no one could find the ball. Someone remarked that only an owl could have seen and caught that ball. The next day, the ball was found on the infield, probably where it landed the night before.

"Gray ordered new uniforms around 1926 and instead of their past usual colors, blue and yellow, they got bright red ones. The students got together to vote on a nickname and the boys wanted Tigers or something more vicious. The girls wanted Redbirds. The girls won the debate, as they usually do.

"From what I could gather, the other schools, Madison, Portland, Redkey, Poling, and Dunkirk, it was simply a case where the students or team got together, gave suggestions and voted on the nickname, pending approval from the school administrators. I do know that the nickname of Speedcats was suggested by player Ralph Bantz. I suspect it was a derivation from the nickname Bearcats of nearby Muncie, but I do not know for sure."

Linden High School

From Tom Speaker, Head Coach Linden High School 1968–71:

"I know all the hard work that is put into [your book *Hoosiers All*] and I appreciate it. [However] there is a painful error [in it]. Probably the pain is only to Linden town and high school, which is now part of North Montgomery, and my kids, particularly seniors Daryl Warren, one of the best players ever to play in Montgomery County, Keith Airy, Mike Klinker, and Keith Winger.

"[You mention] our team with a record of 19-3, coached by Tom Speaker. However... at the end of the paragraph the sentence says 'Apparently neither Linden nor Waveland won (the Montgomery County Tournament) title . . .'

"Linden won the final Montgomery County Championship (1971) with the senior players mentioned above as well as other players. The next year the town of Linden lost their school to consolidation and their identity. The last county championship is one of the proud memories they still maintain."

Tom Speaker's gold-and-black uniformed Bulldogs won that 1971 championship with a 67-59 victory over the Waveland Hornets after an opening win over New Ross 80-71 and a tough 73-70 come-from-behind victory over a very good Darlington Indian five that had led by 9 at halftime. In his excellent book *The Last County Championship,* Tom and his co-author David White point out that consolidation came later to Montgomery County than it had to the others in the area, and thus their tournament was truly the last of many. The book chronicles that 1971 tournament from the perspective of everyone involved and evokes memories that should not soon be forgotten by any fan of Indiana high school basketball. (Author's Note: Tom now lives in West Lafayette and we met for lunch at Stookey's in Thorntown. He is a delightful man, just the sort whom I think we would all want to have coaching our own young men and women.)

Over the years Linden teams had also won five other county championships. Their first came in 1937 for Coach Cliff Davis, 37-20 over Bowers, in a year that saw the Bulldogs finish 21-6. The next was in 1948 with a 29-21 beating of Alamo for Coach Alex Cox en route to a fine 17-3 season record. In fact, for the three years

Montgomery County Tournament Traveling Trophy & keg

WE SALUTE THE 1971 COUNTY CHAMPS

BEST OF LUCK TO THE
LINDEN BULLDOGS
IN THE CRAWFORDSVILLE SECTIONAL

Linden's 1971 champions

beginning in 1947 Linden teams won 51 games while losing only 10. In 1952 Coach Ralph Bunton's team edged Ladoga by the margin of a single basket, 47-45 to win the school's third county championship. They would finish 19-4 that year. The 1960 championship came by a 52-49 count at the expense of New Ross for Coach Bill Springer, whose team put a 20-3 mark in the books. In 1964 a thrilling overtime contest saw Coach Marvin Arnold's 15-7 Linden team prevail in the final game of the Montgomery County Tournament, 68-67, again over those scrappy Ladoga Canners who seemed to lose a lot of close ones.

The First State Championship Tournament

For some time 1911 was not considered the first tournament, but it was eventually declared so in 1957. Thirteen schools were desired for that event, one from each Indiana congressional district, but the Indianapolis School Board would not allow Shortridge or Manual to attend, thus the field consisted of twelve schools. Some districts held playoffs to decide what school should represent them. In other cases the teams with the best records were invited. There were 222 IHSAA member schools in 1911. Here are the scores:

1911 Indiana State Basketball Championship
Bloomington (Indiana University) March 10-11

Crawfordsville	36	Anderson	16
Walton	21	Morristown	23
Bluffton	38	Evansville	22
Lafayette	34	Oaktown	14
Lebanon	23	Valparaiso	10
New Albany	19	Rochester	18
Crawfordsville	31	Walton	12
Bluffton	34	Lafayette	20
Lebanon	28	New Albany	10
Crawfordsville	42	Bluffton	16
Crawfordsville	24	Lebanon	17

In 1912 District Tournaments were held at Muncie, Vincennes, Indianapolis, and South Bend. Entering schools were Lebanon, Portland, Marion; Orleans, Evansville, Bicknell; Richmond, Oaklandon, Franklin, Clinton; Whiting, Wolf Lake, and Culver. The finals at Bloomington were Lebanon 28, Orleans 13; Franklin 29, Whiting 21; and Lebanon 51, Franklin 11. There were 244 IHSAA member schools in 1912.

Indiana University's first Assembly Hall, site of the first state tournament

The growth in number of participants in our tournament was nothing short of remarkable. Basketball truly became the Hoosier sport. By 1920 372 were entered, and two years later the figure was 488. In 1925 674 schools vied for the crown won by the Frankfort Hot Dogs. That was the year the inventor of the game, Dr. James Naismith, a Canadian by birth, visited our state finals game along with 15,000 other fans and was quoted as saying that while it was invented in Massachusetts, "basketball really had its origin in Indiana, which remains the center of the sport." One year later the entry list passed the 700 level for the first time, at 719. It would not drop below 700 until 1960, when the wave of consolidations that would hit the state was just beginning. The high water mark was 787 in 1938, when the Ft. Wayne South Side Archers were the champions. By 1970 the field was trimmed to only 443 entrants, falling slightly below 400 for most of the latter third of the 20th century. It is now right around the 400 level.

Alamo

I assumed the Alamo Warriors were so called to commemorate the famous 1836 stand of Jim Bowie et al at the Texas shrine in San Antonio. A visit to Marcheta's wonderful antique store in Crawfordsville proved that to be an erroneous assumption. Among the many pieces of Indiana basketball memorabilia that may be seen there was the clearly Indian chief on the cover of the Alamo Warrior yearbook on display.

Newtown High School and More

Bill Boone, retired English and Latin teacher at Crawfordsville High School, has been an extremely active collector and compiler of Indiana high school and Wabash College basketball history. He is a former Ladoga Canner and Wabash College Little Giant and is now part of a group that is working to restore and retain as much of Montgomery County's rich basketball heritage as possible. He has brought several errors in my book to my attention, including my misspelling of Homer Stonebraker's name, for which I am truly sorry. He says "your book…is the best I've ever looked at on Indiana basketball…Thanks for using my stuff on Charlie Bowerman. He was really fun to play with." Bill goes on to comment: "On page 410, you mention the nickname of Newtown High School as being the Aces or Indians. I don't think they ever had a nickname. I checked that out with the oldest graduate of Newtown HS and that was his recollection. That would have been Ira 'Zeke' Williams, a really fine basketball official from Newtown." (Author's note: Bill may well be right on this as is usually the case, but my others sources do have Newtown listed as having black and gold colors and Aces or Indians as their team name).

Wawasee Preparatory School

In 1925 the Spink family of Indianapolis built a luxurious hotel at Cedar Beach on Lake Wawasee. Around 1940 the hotel was closed and eventually sold to the Crosier Order of

Wawasee Preparatory School

the Roman Catholic Church which extensively remodeled the building and opened Our Lady of the Lake Seminary in 1948. In 1965 the seminary was closed and the facility was converted to a coeducational school called Wawasee Preparatory School which existed from 1968 through 1975. In 1972 Coach Rex Yentes led his Wawasee Prep squad to an impressive record of 20 wins in 21 games. They were not, however, IHSAA members until 1974, and then only briefly.

Paris Crossing

Niles Layman is a Paris Crossing alumnus and former player who has devoted a great deal of effort to preserving that school's basketball heritage as well as the history of some of their competitors. His work has been given to the libraries of both the Hall of Fame and the IHSAA. He has made the following points to me:

"On page 418 of your book, where you talk about the Vernon team coach—Ed Wells. I am not sure his name was Ed; everyone around here knew him as Art or Arthur. He was a 1937 graduate of Paris Crossing HS.

"Paris Crossing had a better team in 1954 [Author's note: I had included the 1955 team with its 17-5 record in my book]. That team went 16-2, losing to Madison in the Saturday afternoon game. The one game they lost during the season was to Dupont and Paris beat them later in the season, getting their revenge.

"The 1956 team went 12-7 (Author's note: my records show 14-7) and lost to Scottsburg Saturday afternoon. Losing to Scottsburg was hardly a disgrace. The Warriors won the Madison Sectional and the Columbus Regional that year, being ousted by undefeated state champion to be Crispus Attucks in the Indianapolis Semi-state. One common thread on all three of these teams was a player by the name of Charles Baker. He scored 35 points in two different Sectional games, once in 1955 and once again in 1956."

Girls Basketball in Parke County

Several writers have recently examined the history of girls basketball in Indiana and, although much remains to be learned and analyzed, important bits of information continue to arise.

Until a recent trip to Rockville where I met Roleen Pickard, a Marshall (Indiana) High School graduate and retired teacher and coach at Noblesville and Indianapolis North Central, I had subscribed to the generally held belief that although interscholastic girls high school basketball had seen significant play in Indiana beginning very shortly after the invention of the game by James Naismith in the final decade of the 19th Century it had stopped sometime in the early 30s.

On the back cover is a photo of the Indianapolis Shortridge girls team of 1905 claiming to be the state champions. Over the next 25–30 years several schools claimed state championships including Wabash and Sullivan, but there was no official tournament, as all Hoosiers know, until 1976, when Judy Warren's Warsaw Lady

Tigers thrilled the state and drew an impressive crowd to Market Square Arena. The Lady Tigers are pictured on page 242, and it is interesting to note the evolution of uniforms over the years right up to the 2009 Ben Davis Lady Giants on page 396. Roleen Pickard has added some very important new information to this with her revelation that the Marshall High School Lady Bobcats competed with at least four other west central Indiana schools in at least the years 1948 and 1949. Games were played between Marshall's Lady Bobcats, the Lady Aztecs of Montezuma, the Parke County Greene Township Lady Aces, the Kingman Lady Black Aces, and the Bellmore Lady Golden Eagles.

This begins to fill what has been a significant void in at least my own knowledge of Indiana girls basketball, and I write in hopes that we can generate more information on girls teams during the period prior to 1976 when our records have been kept in so much better detail.

Following are photos of the 1948 Marshall girls team and the 1920 Kingman Aces with Roleen's mother, Ruth Lindley, holding the ball. Roleen herself is also holding the ball in the 1947–48 Marshall picture. The records of the 1948 Marshall A and B teams are also shown. The Marshall coach was Phyllis Carlin.

1948 Marshall girls team

Kingman Black Aces Girls 1920. Roleeen Pickard's mother, then Ruth Lindley, is holding the basketball

Marshall Bobcats Girls A Team 1948 Record:

Marshall	37	Greene Township	39
Marshall	12	Kingman	21
Marshall	40	Montezuma	24
Marshall	33	Green Township	33
Marshall	18	Bellmore	18
Marshall	17	Kingman	29
Marshall	25	Montezuma	17
Marshall	21	Bellmore	31
Marshall	24	Tournament held at Bellmore, Opponent not named	

Marshall Bobcats Girls B Team 1948 Record:

Marshall	18	Greene Township	?

Marshall	7	Kingman	7
Marshall	17	Montezuma	13
Marshall	14	Greene Township	11
Marshall	15	Kingman	15
Marshall	29	Montezuma	23

Roncalli and Antecedents

Indianapolis Sacred Heart teams were called the Spartans and their colors were royal blue and gold. Although I have no information about their records during their existence from 1915 until 1966, I do know that they were coached by Hall of Famer Bill Green from 1959–64. After being renamed Kennedy High School, they along with St. Mary's and Chartrand, became part of the Roncali High School Rebels (see page 406).

I failed to do justice to Roncalli's basketball success in the body of *Hoosiers All*, another omission that I will try to correct now. The Rebels won their first Sectional and only regional crowns in 2005, at the 3A level for Michael Wantz with a 19-7 record. His next year's squad also captured a Sectional title, something his 2007 team was not able to do in spite of their outstanding record of 20 victories and only 2 losses. However, Sectional nets were again placed in the Roncalli trophy cabinet in 2009 and 2011. Since their first title in 1977, the Lady Rebels have cut down Sectional nets 13 times, also winning 5 Regional crowns and the 1986 Indianapolis Semi-state when they were led by Indiana All Star Diane Hoereth.

Eight of these titles were won for Coach Bob Kirkhoff between 1985 and 1995 when his teams put together some very impressive seasons, including 22-2 in 1985, 21-5 in 1987, 18-2 in 1988, and an undefeated regular season of 18-1 in 1989. Also, from 1994 through 1996, his teams amassed 66 wins while only losing 11! The best record was 24-3 in 1996, when they were led by Indiana All Star Sarah Hurrle. Kirkhoff's teams also won nine city championships and he was named Marion County Coach of the Year 3 times. Overall his Lady Rebel teams won 74 per cent of their games. More recently the Lady Rebels have added Sectional crowns in 2004 for Linda Niewedde and, under Sara Riedeman, whose latter team brought home a Regional championship as well.

And from Gary Armbruster:

"I am the Director of Corporate Relations at Roncalli High School and, of course, we are the Rebels now. We are named after Pope John XXIII whose name was Angelo Guiseppe Roncalli. He called Vatican II in the early 60s which ruffled a LOT of feathers in the Catholic Church and changed how the Catholic Mass was celebrated primarily changing the Mass from Latin to the vernacular of the people. Shaking up the Church, he was known in many circles as the Rebel Pope and thus, we became the Roncalli Rebels when our school was formed from the consolidation of Bishop Chartrand and Kennedy Memorial High Schools. Kennedy was known as Sacred

Heart Central from 1914–1966 but was renamed to honor the fallen President. Both schools, as you mention in the book, were known as the Spartans."

White River

In addition to the White River High School that existed in Gibson County from 1963–65, there was also a White River High School in Randolph County, similarly short-lived, from 1957–59. Their teams were called the Little Giants and neither White River school had a distinguished basketball record. The Little Giants were preceded by the McKinley Presidents and became Winchester Falcons along with the Lincoln Wolves, Ridgeville Cossacks, and Ward Jackson Flyers. The latter won their lone Sectional at Winchester in 1961 for Dennis Lewis by getting past Ridgeville 68-65, edging Farmland 60-58 and then sneaking by Parker 66-65. Whew! Earlier, as Ward Township, the Flyers won 49 games while only losing 17. The best year I could find for Lincoln was 1942, when they won 12 games and lost 7 for Merritt Beck. The McKinley Presidents wore red, white, and blue uniforms and put together a fine 17-4 season for Jack Lee in 1941.

Farmland

In Chapter 20 I discussed Indiana's proud agricultural heritage, but I omitted the Farmland Wildcats, also in Randolph County, now Monroe Central Golden Bears. The Wildcats won the first of their three Sectional championships in 1935 at Lynn by defeating Stoney Creek 20-17; Wayne 28-17; the home team 29-16; and Union City 22-21 for Vickrey Higgins. Their 2nd came in 1946 on their home court for Howard Rust when they defeated Winchester 33-30, McKinley 40-17, Union City 46-33, and then by edging Parker in an overtime thriller, 39-38. The Wildcats cut down their third and final Sectional nets in 1955, this time at Winchester by demolishing Green Township 51-19; defeating Ridgeville 70-50; besting Union City 56-50; and sending Union home, 62-51. Fred Powell coached that team to its 18-6 record. Although unable to win a Sectional, Harvey Davidson's 1951 team turned in an excellent 20-4 mark, that fourth defeat a tough three-point loss to Winchester in the semi-finals of the Farmland Sectional and Fred Smith's 1961 team also turned in a fine 18-5 mark.

Tomcats

Also in Randolph County were the purple-and-gold-clad Spartanburg Tomcats, who won their only Sectional title for Tracy Turner at Farmland in 1947 with a fine 22-4 mark by doubling up on Lincoln 52-26, defeating Farmland 50-45, and Parker 49-41, and winning a nail-biter in overtime over Winchester, 48-44. Although no more Sectional titles were forthcoming, Turner's 1948 team, which finished 19-4, and Howard Rust's 1949 squad, which came in at 21-4, put together a three-year record of 62 wins and only 12 losses! In 1954 Lloyd Mitchell coached the Tomcats to a sterling 21-2, mark, and Phil Sprague's 1957 team put together an excellent 20-3 season.

Our other Tomcats sported red, white, and blue uniforms and represented Madison Township in Jay County. Although never able to bring home a Sectional title, Madison Township enjoyed several fine seasons. In 1926 Harold Brubaker's team finished 22-2 with that second loss coming in the final game of the Portland Sectional to the home team Panthers. Four years later Brubaker's team won 21 of 25 games and from 1926 through 1935 Brubaker's teams rang up 177 wins against only 63 losses. In 1963 Leonard Burns led Madison Township to an 18-5 mark, followed by 18-3 for Art Habegger the next year.

Interlaken

The Interlaken Bulldogs, who wore red and white uniforms, only existed from about 1908 until 1919, when they were consolidated into Rolling Prairie. The only year for which we have a record was a very good one, 9-4 in 1917.

Switzerland County High School

In 1968 the Vevay Warriors and the Patriot Trojans consolidated to form the Switzerland County Pacers, located in the beautiful community of Vevay. The Pacers have a history of coming together at Sectional time. The best record of their six championship years was 15-8 for Scott Holdsworth in 1999, after his previous year's edition had managed to get a crown with a 9-15 record. The other titles were won by Bernie Burke's teams in 1975 (10-13) and 1988 (12-11), and David Todd's 2006 team (13-11). The Columbia blue-and-orange-clad Pacers enjoyed their best record in 1982 when Burke's team finished 18-5. The Lady Pacers have cut down Sectional nets five times, beginning in 1989 for Wayne Daugherty and including the 1991 (16-6), 1996 (11-10), 1997 (15-6), and 2004 (19-6) seasons, all coached by Wayne Ellegood.

They also won 15 of 18 games for Barbara Steffan in 1979 and 16 of 20 games in 1988. Prior to consolidation the Warriors won five Sectional titles, the first in 1927 for Harold Benedict at Scottsburg, edging the home team 15-14, beating Madison 31-21 and then sneaking by North Madison's Tigers, 20-19. In 1931 Benedict's squad won at Madison, topping the Cubs in the final game, 19-12, and six years later his team won again, this time at Aurora, 24-17 over the home team. Title number 4 was earned by John Collier's 1955 Warrior squad, with wins over Rising Sun, 63-52; Lawrenceburg 48-41, and the home team 44-42. Their fifth came for Dan Kile in 1958, this time at Dillsboro where they upended the Moores Hill Bobcats 49-44, the home team Bull Dogs 67-60, and the Rising Sun Shiners 57-47. At the Rushville Regional Vevay defeated Versailles 71-56 before the dream was ended by the home team Lions, 48-43. The Patriots captured their sole Sectional title for Coach DeHart in 1926 at Madison by defeating Hanover 18-13, Scottsburg 16-13, and Deputy 34-14.

Michigan City

Michigan City St. Mary's was founded in 1885 in St Mary's parish. In the fall of 1934 a boys basketball team was formed following the construction of a new gym. The school's name was changed to Marquette High School when it began to serve all of Michigan City rather than a single parish. The school building on 11th Street still reads St. Mary's. St Mary's teams were called the Indians, and their colors were red and white. They became Marquette Blue Blazers in 1968. Father Marquette was essentially the town founder. He began the first settlement in what was to become Michigan City, the gateway to Lake Michigan. We know St. Mary's never won a Sectional in their 26 years as IHSAA members (1942–68), but that is about all the data we do have on their basketball teams, unfortunately.

New Prairie

The New Prairie Tigers wore orange and black uniforms in LaPorte County. Although they never were crowned Sectional champions, their best records were 17-6 for Coach Bob Noel in 1962 and 15-3 under the direction of Harry Oglesby in 1943. That third loss came in the second round of the South Bend Sectional to the Riley Wildcats.

Lakeville

Lakeville teams were called the Trojans, and they wore blue and gold uniforms. They won their only Sectional championship at South Bend in 1924 by defeating Bremen 40-13, the home team 26-17, Culver 29-18, and Mishawaka 39-24. They finished the season for Coach Ken Goff with an 18-6 mark. They were consolidated into LaVille, becoming Lancers in 1965.

North Montgomery

The North Montgomery Chargin' Chargers have put toget her several fine seasons, capturing 11 Sectionals in the process. Their first came in 1974 under the direction of Chuck Kristen in the school's third year of existence, with a 19-5 record. In 1984, with Dwayne Rater at the helm, the Chargers went 19-4 and cut down the school's sixth set of Sectional nets. The 2006 and 2007 Sectional champs came for Coach Scott Radecker with 19-4 and 18-5 marks, and in 2009 North Montgomery won their 11th crown, this one at the 3A level. The Lady Chargers have added nine Sectional crowns to the school's trophy case, winning four in a row from 2004 through 2007, the latter year racking up a sparkling 21-3 mark for Coach Terry Bartell.

More Lions

Two Lions have been added to our list of basketball playing high schools in Indiana: Indianapolis Horizon Christian and Bloomington Lighthouse Christian.

Horizon Christian

Jefferson County Central

Jefferson County Central High School teams were the Wildcats. The Green and White snagged their only sectional title at Madison in 1936. To do so they defeated North Madison 36-21, Saluda 26-12, and the home team Cubs 24-21.

Bethany and Bethesda Christian

The Bethany Christian Bruins from Goshen fielded their first boys basketball team in 1966, and in 1988 Jim Butler's squad turned in an excellent 19-3 record. This followed on the previous season's 15-6 mark and was the highlight of a six-year stretch that saw the Bruins rack up 81 wins while losing only 30. In 1998 Butler's squad won the first of 4 Sectional titles and the first of 2 Regional crowns, finishing 17-7. The second Sectional was won two years later and the nets from their second Regional championship were cut down in 2002. Their fourth Sectional crown came in 2009, all at the Class A level. The Lady Bruins turned in back-to-back 16-3 seasons for Trish Yoder in 1988 and the next year for Dan Bodiker. Their lone Sectional title was won in 1998 for Randy Graber. Nineteen-eighty-eight and 1998 were fine years all around for the school.

Bethesda Christian is in Brownsburg, fielding their first boys team in 2004. They got off to a fine start winning 66 of the first 92 games played with the best record during that period being Todd Foster's 2007 squad, which finished 20-5. The Patriots captured a Class A Sectional title in 2009. The Lady Patriots have yet to earn a Sectional title.

Arcola

The Arcola Greyhounds wore green and white uniforms in Allen County until they became a part of Carroll High School in 1968. Although they never won a Sectional title, they had an outstanding undefeated regular season for Coach Bennie Decker in 1941, finishing 20-1, with their sole loss being to Elmhurst 34-27 in the Ft. Wayne Sectional. Earlier Dwight Byerley's Greyhounds had put together 40 wins in 54 games in the three seasons culminating with 1931's 15-3 mark. In 1948 Charlie Sharp's team won 17 and lost only 5.

Graceland Christian

Graceland Christian existed from 1981 until 2007 in Floyd County. Their teams were the Warriors, and their colors were blue, gold, and white. In 1984 Steve Marcum's Warriors enjoyed a fine season, finishing 18-3. Wes Porter's 1987 squad won 19 of 23 games, beginning a four-year streak during which the Warriors put 68 wins on the board while suffering just 18 losses. Chad Leach's teams put together back-to-back 19-4 seasons beginning in 1996. However, it was the next two years that Warrior fans remember most vividly. Ryan Davis's 1998 team won 25 games and lost only 5, garnering Sectional and Regional championships in the process. The

Warriors won the Henryville Class A Sectional by soundly defeating Borden 87-54 before nipping New Washington in a 74-73 overtime thriller. They proceeded to win the Springs Valley Regional by defeating the home team 97-58. After winning the first game at the Terre Haute Semi-state over Morristown 70-57, their splendid season ended one game away from the RCA Dome in Indianapolis when they were finally eliminated by Bloomfield 75-62. Ric Cadle took the reins and the next year again led the Warriors to a regional championship, this one at Southridge 67-56 over Orleans, finishing 17-6. The now-vacant Graceland Christian school building was used for some of the Henryville students whose school was destroyed in the horrific tornado of January 2012.

A Wealth of Jackson Townships

There were nine schools in different counties named Jackson Township. One was in Porter County, and their teams were Panthers with colors of maroon and white. Their best records were 17-5 in 1951 for Bob Schumaker and 16-7 for Calvin Dehlander in 1967. They have been consolidated into Chesterton. In Tippecanoe County the Jackson Township Spartans wore red and white. They were consolidated into Southwestern in 1956. In Wells County the Jackson Township teams were called Jaguars and they enjoyed a 16-6 season for Ken Ross in 1954 before being consolidated into Southern Wells in 1966. Unfortunately, we have no data on the Jackson Township teams that played in Steuben County and were consolidated into Orland in 1930. The Boone County Jackson Township teams were the Rockets and wore black and white uniforms. Before becoming part of Granville-Wells in 1955, the Rockets put together an excellent season for Coach Darrell Everhart, 17 wins and only 3 losses. The Clinton County Jackson Township teams were the Cardinals and their colors were red and tan. They won two Sectionals, the first for Ray Hause in 1941 with an 18-4 record, the central year of a three-year period that saw the Cardinals, win 57 games while losing only 9! Their second Sectional crown was earned in 1956 for George Bradfield, when they won the Frankfort Sectional by defeating Mulberry 42-37 in overtime. Decatur County's Jackson Township teams were the black and gold clad Tigers.

They also captured two Sectional titles, going 18-4 for Wilbur Meyer in 1951 and 19-6 for Bob Lautenslager in 1957. From 1937 until 1939 Gerald Carter led his Tiger teams to an incredible 66 (or perhaps 76) wins and just 7 losses! (Some listings show the 1939 team's record as 30-3 but it may have been only 20-3, as they did not win a Sectional title that year, and it is hard to play 33 games without getting deep into the state tournament. In the Greensburg Sectional they lost to Burney in the second game after defeating Sandusky in the first.) After the undefeated regular season of 1937 the Tigers were eliminated by the home team Pirates in the semi-finals of the Greensburg Sectional, finishing 24-1. They also had a fine season for Joe White in 1956, 21-2, before being consolidated into South Decatur in 1968. In Howard County the Jackson Township Stonewalls wore blue and white. The Stonewall Jackson namesakes put together their only Sectional crown by rolling over Clay Township 23-9, edging Greentown 22-20, and beating West Middleton 26-20 and Russiaville 13-8. At Marion they lost their first Regional game by a single basket, 22-20, to Somerset. They were consolidated into Eastern in 1951. Our ninth Jackson Township school was in Randolph County. They were the Bulldogs, and their colors were orange and black. (Princeton University's colors, Yale University's mascot. Quite classy.) Their best record was an impressive one, 22-4 for Coach Les Ray in 1952. After defeating Saratoga 57-43 in the first game of the Winchester Sectional, the Bulldogs were eliminated by Farmland, 42-37. After a brief period as the Ward-Jackson Flyers, the one time Bulldogs eventually became Winchester Falcons.

Kniman

Kniman in Jasper County, according to the Rensselaer Public Library, never had varsity teams because they only went from grades one to ten. The school existed from 1925 until either 1939 or 1943, according to various sources, and a gym with a stage was constructed for the school in 1938. However, Kniman did have coaches and had a reputation for sending good athletes to nearby schools, such as DeMotte and Wheatfield (where they were consolidated). Kniman is now considered by many to have a grill that produces outstanding pizza!

Morgan Township

In Harrison County the Morgan Township Raiders wore red, white, and blue uniforms. They won two Sectional titles, the first in 1962 for Coach Bob Masterson. That was accomplished at Salem with victories over Lanesville 66-39, Campbellsburg 51-41, 46-44 over North Central (Ramsey) and 54-51 over Corydon. The next year Masterson's Raiders put together a sterling 22-2 season, losing a heartbreaking 38-36 thriller to the home team in the final game of the Salem Sectional. Sectional title number two came in 1965 with Cecil Goff at the helm, again at Salem, 74-40 over Lanesville, 54-43 over Corydon, and 68-48 over Milltown. Consolidation into North Harrison came in 1969.

Middletown

Also in Harrison County there were the New Middletown Rangers (not to be confused with the Middletown Cossacks in Henry County), resplendent in black and gold or black and white uniforms. Coach Ed Schneider's 1951 and 1952 squads put together back-to-back 18-4 seasons, followed by 18-5 the next year. Although they never won a Sectional title (the Rangers won their first two games in the New Albany-Jeffersonville Sectional in 1951 before losing in the semi-finals to the Bulldogs who were an Elite Eight finisher that year), 54 wins and 13 losses in three years is a memorable run indeed. They were consolidated into Corydon in 1954.

North Dearborn

The North Dearborn Vikings were themselves a 1959 consolidation of the Bright Panthers and the Guilford Yellow Jackets/Wildcats (who had absorbed New Alsace in 1928). The Scarlet and Grey won four Sectional titles, the first in 1962 for Seaborn Hillis, winning the final game at Rising Sun over Lawrenceburg 64-56. Bill Slayback's Vikings captured the other three, going 18-6 in 1963, defeating the home team 77-60 at Rising Sun; defeating Dillsboro 56-46 at Rising Sun and finishing 21-3 in 1964; and routing Vevay at Lawrenceburg 76-41 in 1968, when their final record was 19-4. In 1973 they were combined with the Sunman Tigers from Ripley County to become the East Central Trojans.

Vernon and North Vernon

In discussing North Vernon I have referred to their teams as the Blue Devils. Niles Layman informs me that the North Vernon teams were actually called the Panthers, a mascot continued with the formation of Jennings County High School in 1968. Vernon is a charming and historic town just south of the considerably larger North Vernon, and it was their teams who were called the Blue Devils prior to joining North Vernon in 1964.

Munster

A bit more is needed to do justice to the Munster Mustangs than was done on page 265. Mike Hackett's teams in 2003 and 2004 put together excellent seasons, 21-2 and 20-2. The Munster record in 2005 was 20-4. His 2006 and 2007 teams did almost equally as well, 20-4 followed by 21-4.

Union Township (Johnson County)

Union Township in Johnson County enjoyed an excellent 23-3 season for O. J. Sloop in 1927. In the Franklin Sectional the Ramblers more than doubled up on Trafalgar, 28-13, and put a serious hurt on Whiteland, 47-9, before losing a heartbreaking 28-27 decision to the home team in the final game. Ten years later Sloop's Blue and Gold did even better in the regular season, entering the Franklin Sectional with a sterling 22-1 record. In the tournament they defeated Masonic Home 34-20, Trafalger 48-17, and Center Grove 25-17, before again losing the championship to the Grizzly Cubs, this time by a 34-27 count. Sloop's 1948 team finished 20-4, and his 1952 team finally won the school's only Sectional title, also at Franklin. This was accomplished by defeating Edinburgh 50-42, then squeaking past Whiteland 34-33 and Clark 49-46 before upending Trafalgar 52-47. At the Shelbyville Regional, Union won another nail-biter 49-48 over the North Vernon Panthers before being eliminated by the home team Golden Bears. It is worthy of note that O. J. Sloop's coaching career at Union Township in Johnson County lasted from 1926 through 1957 with the exception of three years during World War II over which span he led his teams to almost 400 victories.

Union Township (LaPorte County)

Union Township in LaPorte County fielded the blue and white clad Tigers. Although the Tigers never won a Sectional crown, they had some remarkably good years between 1954 and their consolidation into LaPorte, becoming Slicers in 1965. Coach William Yates' 1954 team went 17-4, followed by 16-7 the next year. But it was the 1956 and 1957 Tigers who really got their fans going with excellent 20-3 and 22-2 records, a two-year record of 42-5! In 1956 Union opened their Sectional quest at Michigan City by defeating Wanatah 73-66 before losing to LaPorte. The next year they edged Wanatah in overtime by a single point in a 70-69 thriller before again being sent to the sidelines by the Slicers, also at Michigan City. Yates' 1960 team went 21-4 beating St. Mary's and Clinton Township before being sent home by the home team at Michigan City. One year later the Tigers put together a tremendous undefeated regular season, suffering their only loss of the season in the final game to the home team again at Michigan City, nevertheless putting a 24-1 record in the books. One other undefeated regular season was accomplished in Union Township's last season for Jack Eller whose 1965 team finished 20-1, the sole loss by three points, 75-72, to Westville in the final game of the Michigan City Sectional.

The Mellott Derbies

There was a period when coaches were not permitted to talk to their players during a time out. The players stayed on the court and a cart with water and towels was brought out to them by one of the student managers. At Mellott the cart took on a very special form. As the Mellott teams were known as the Derbies the cart itself was constructed in the form of a derby. Dan Carpenter has discovered one of these carts in excellent shape and it will be donated to the Hall of Fame as a special form of memorabilia. As

The Mellott Derby Cart

mentioned on page 64, the Derbies won their lone sectional title at Veedersburg in 1928. Scott Edgar's team soundly defeated West Lebanon 33-10 and Newtown 31-18 before edging Attica in an 18-17 thriller in the semi-finals. The Red and Black then cut down the nets after dispatching Kingman 34-29.

Clinton Prairie

I included the Clinton Prairie Gophers in my list of favorite mascots for our current schools, but I failed to give them proper mention in the body of the book. For that, I apologize and will now try to correct that oversight. The Gophers came into existence when the Colfax Hickories, Jackson Township Cardinals, Mulberry Berries, and Washington Township Warriors were brought together in 1961, two years after

Clinton Central came into being.

The red-and-black-clad Gophers have cut down the nets at the conclusion of two Sectionals, the first in 1964 with a 16-8 record under Coach Dee Baker. The second came in 1982, when Bob Smith's team won 17 and lost 8. Moving on to the Frankfort Regional the Gophers edged Plainfield's Quakers 53-52 before being sidelined by Western Boone's Stars 27-24. It intrigues me that the Stars subsequently lost to Gary Roosevelt in the opening round of the Lafayette Semi-state by the margin of one basket, 38-36, before Roosevelt also edged Anderson Madison Height's Pirates by a bucket, 62-60. Then, in one of the closest, most hard fought state finals ever at Market Square in Indianapolis the Panthers snuck by Evansville Bosse 58-57 before dropping a thrilling double overtime final game to Scott Skiles and the Plymouth Pilgrims, 75-74. The Gophers were one basket behind Roosevelt who were one point behind Plymouth…in two overtimes. Puts Clinton Prairie mighty close to the title in my book.

The Lady Gophers did get that coveted state title with an outstanding 25-3 record for Connie Garrett in 1999, defeating New Washington 50-42 to bring home the Class A title to the countryside near Frankfort. Garrett coached the Lady Gophers for 36 seasons, from 1972 through 2007. Her teams also won four Regional crowns and nine Sectional titles. Garrett led the Lady Gophers to almost 400 wins during her impressive tenure at Clinton Prairie.

Cloverdale & Bainbridge

Jim Bindley, who played guard for Terre Haute Schulte more years ago than he cares to admit, points out that in 1966 something almost occurred that had only happened once before, when the tournament was much smaller. In Putnam County both Cloverdale and Bainbridge had outstanding seasons. The Clovers, under Hall of Fame coach Jim Miller, turned in a 27-2 record, winning the Evansville Semi-state by besting Vincennes 76-57 and North Vernon 73-66. Bainbridge, just up the road, also coached by a Hall of Famer, Pat Rady, ran up 23 wins and only 3 losses, Hall of Famer Larry Steele leading the charge. Because the Semi-state dividing line was Route 40, between the two schools, Cloverdale after winning the Terre Haute Regional was sent to Evansville while Bainbridge after winning the Covington Regional headed for the Lafayette Semi-state. At Lafayette the Pointers were sent home by East Chicago Washington's Senators, 78-74. Had Bainbridge won that Semi-state crown it would have marked the first time since 1913 that two schools from the same county (Wingate and Crawfordsville, Montgomery County) had qualified for the Final Four in any single class tournament. Both Cloverdale and Bainbridge were in the midst of some pretty impressive seasons: the Clovers from 1966 through 1969 won 94 games and lost only 9! The Pointers won 46 and lost 6 in 1966 and 1967.

Winchester Community High School "Golden Falcons"

The following came from Dane Starbuck:

"Winchester received State attention when it knocked off Hammond High School 61-60 in the Huntington Holiday Tournament in December 1974. Hammond began the 1974 season first in the state polls and ended the regular season first in the polls, with the defeat to the Winchester Golden Falcons being their only regular season loss. Winchester went on to become ranked as high as 11th in the Associated Press, before losing to Muncie Northside High School, led by Indiana All-Star, Sammy Drummer, in the New Castle Regional. During the Falcon's 20-3 season, the team had a 15 game winning streak, won the Tri-Eastern Conference championship undefeated and, in addition to Hammond, defeated several larger schools including New Castle, Muncie Southside, and Huntington North."

(Author's note: Winchester teams enjoyed many successful seasons mentioned on page 321 but much more needs to be said about this fine and historic school. Winchester's teams were originally called the Yellow Jackets and they were practically charter members of the IHSAA, joining one year after that organization was founded in 1904.

Here are some interesting facts from the Randolph Central website: It was not until 1851 that Indiana made provision for public education. The first schools in Randolph County were conducted by the Society of Friends. These included Quaker schools at White River, east of Winchester, and Dunkirk, west of Winchester.... In 1842 the Randolph County Seminary opened on West Franklin Street in Winchester. It was one of the best-known schools of its kind in Indiana. By 1865 there were thirty-seven one-room schoolhouses serving the students of Franklin, Ward, and White River Townships.... Randolph County became widely known for its consolidation of one-room schools into rural high schools in the early twentieth century under the leadership of the County Superintendent of Schools, Lee L. Driver. Two consolidated schools were built in White River Township: Lincoln, West of Winchester, in 1908-09, and McKinley, east of Winchester, in 1911. Two consolidated schools also served Ward Township. Jefferson School, built in 1911, served the western part of the township, while Saratoga School served the eastern part. Franklin Township's pupils were consolidated into Ridgeville School in 1923. The School City of Winchester remained a separate entity.... In 1950 high school pupils from Lincoln High School were transported to McKinley High School. A new structure, White River High School, was built just west of McKinley in 1956-57.... Jefferson's high school students were sent to Saratoga in the fall of 1955, and Saratoga School became known as Ward High School.... In 1958 Ward (Saratoga) School became known as "Ward-Jackson School,".... In the fall of 1959 Winchester High School became Lee L. Driver

High School.... Ridgeville High School functioned until their students were sent to Winchester in the fall of 1966, and the name of Lee L. Driver High School was changed to Winchester Community High School.

Randolph County under the leadership of Dr. Driver was recognized by the Boston Journal of Education in 1933 as the greatest exponent of the movement toward consolidation of one-room schools into rural consolidated high schools in the nation.

The genealogy of the present Winchester Community High School is as follows:

Lincoln Wolves(1927-50)

White River Little Giants (1957-59)

McKinley Presidents (1921-57)

Ridgeville Cossacks (1913-14, 1919-66)

Ward-Jackson Flyers (1958-62)

Jackson Twp. Bulldogs (1919-58)

Ward Twp. Flyers (1955-58)

Jefferson Red Devils (1919-55)

Saratoga Warriors (1914-15, 1919-55)

Overall, the Winchester Yellow Jackets/Golden Falcons have won 25 Sectionals, 6 Regionals and 3 Semi-states. Twenty plus victory seasons, in addition to that of 1975 for Hall of Fame Coach Pat Rady, were accomplished in the following years:

1928 20-4 and 1929 23-5 for Maurice Kennedy

1932 21-4 for Bedford Butcher

1942 21-6 for Lester Gant

1943 21-2 for Tony Sharpe

1949 21-4 for Charles Shumaker

And then the magical run for Chip Mahaffey: 23-2 in 1998, 23-3 in 1999, and the first of three State Champion Class 2A runner-up finishes, losing 59-53 to Westview in 2000 to finish 22-6, capping a three year record of 68-11. In 2007 his Golden Falcons would again lose the state title game, this one a heartbreaking two overtime decision to Northwestern to finish 22-5 followed by another tough loss in the state title game in 2008, this by a single basket to Ft. Wayne Luers, 69-67, to finish 23-4, 45-9 for those two years. Mahaffey's Golden Falcons of 2009 won 21 of their 25 games and the next year they were 21-5, 42-9 for that two year span. Rick Owens took over in 2011 and led the team to a 22-3 mark, losing in the Regional final to the Yogi Ferrell-led Park Tudor State Champions. That's a 5-year mark of 109 wins and only 21 losses!

The Lady Golden Falcons have cut down Sectional nets 13 times including six straight from 2007-2012, the first two for Gary Horner. Horner's 2001 squad also finished 22-5, his 2004 team finished 20-2, and his 2007 and 2008 teams turned in 19-4 and 20-5 records respectively. But that was not the end of their run.

In 2009 with Dale Dodd now at the helm the Lady Golden Falcons rang up another 20 win season, losing just 4. Kirk Comer then became the coach and led his 2010 team to an undefeated regular season, 25-1, with the sole loss coming in the Semi-state to Austin's State Champion Lady Eagles. His 2011 team again made it to the Semi-state, losing to Brownstown Central and turning in a record of 21-5, bringing their 5 year total to 105 wins and only 19 losses, very comparable to that turned in by their male counterparts. What a great period to be a Golden Falcon fan.

My thanks to Principal Tom Osborne for providing me with some of this information.)

Russiaville

Although the painting of Russiaville High School by Mary Ellis is shown on page 181, I failed to do justice to the school's basketball heritage there. Although the Cossacks never were able to win a Sectional title, they did have some fine seasons to remember before being consolidated into Western High School. We have records of games played by Russiaville as early as 1906, and in 1910 they won three of the four games they played for Coach T. D. Hanson, followed by a 7-3 mark the next year and a 4-1 record for Ord Fortner in 1912: 14-5 for the three-year period. In 1928 Russiaville had a marvelous season, winning 21 games and losing only 4 for Forest Roe. The season ended in the final game of the Kokomo Sectional with a loss to the Sharpsville Bulldogs.

Monument City

The pronounced drought throughout much of Indiana during the summer of 2012 has resulted in the reemergence of Monument City, inundated in 1966 when the Salamonie Reservoir was created in Huntington County. Although Monument City was covered on page 405, new facts have come to my attention. In 1908 Pearl Huff coached the Purple and Gold to an undefeated season: 3-0! The next year with Harley Stech at the helm the team played a rare tie game, ending the season 4-3-1. From 1944–46 the Greyhounds won 52 games and lost just 13, Leslie

Monument City prior to being inundated

Wilbern coaching the first two years and Dale Decker the last. The school's last season was 1953 when they put together a fine 21-4 record for Willard Barnes. After a period as Lancaster Township Lancers, they became Huntington North Vikings.

More on the North Central Conference

As we have pointed out elsewhere, the powerful North Central Conference sent two teams to the Final Four several times, including placing both teams in the championship game EIGHT times:

1929   Frankfort   29   Indianapolis Tech   23

1934	Logansport	26	Indianapolis Tech	19
1952	Muncie Central	68	Indianapolis Tech	49
1979	Muncie Central	64	Anderson	60
1985	Marion	74	Richmond	67
1986	Marion	75	Anderson	56
1987	Marion	69	Richmond	56
1992	Richmond	77	Lafayette Jeff	73 (OT)

(Lebanon defeated Anderson 24-20 in overtime in 1918, 8 years before both became founding members of the NCC).

Additionally, in 1948 the NCC sent three teams to the final four, Muncie Central, Anderson and Lafayette Jefferson. That was not, however, one of the years when the conference won both the title and the runner-up awards as Evansville Central spoiled the party by defeating Muncie Central in the opening game before losing to Jeff that night.

Whitestown

From Ed Baker: "I did notice that you credited Robert Mills as the coach of the 1962 Whitestown Panthers who had a record of 18-6. Actually that team was coached by Frank Melson, who left after the season. Coach Mills was my coach and he coached only one year, 1962-63, after which Whitestown consolidated with Lebanon High School.

"An interesting fact about that Whitestown team was that 4 of the 6 losses were to Pinnell high School. They played twice during the season, home and home, and in the final game of both the Boone County tournament and the Zionsville sectional. Whitestown could not beat Pinnell that year." (Author's note: 1962, final game at Zionsville was Pinnell 61 Whitestown 50.)

Wolf Lake

Captain Cliff Pappe is a chaplain in the Indiana National Guard. He has done considerable research on the 1940–42 Wolf Lake Wolves (not Wolverines, he tells me, although that is what is listed in several generally reliable references I have seen). These teams were led by Cliff's maternal grandfather, 6´3˝ Art Keister, and his brother Paul one inch shorter. Graduating in 1942 along with other starters, Roger Stangland and Delbert Hartman, Wolf Lake compiled the remarkable record of 70 wins and only 5 losses

Wolf Lake's 1942 champions

including 3 straight Noble County championships and 50 straight regular season victories, all for coach John Reid. The 1940 squad lost its first game of the season to Avilla before running off 19 straight wins. In the Kendallville Sectional the Wolves defeated Topeka, Brighton, and LaGrange before being ousted by the home team Red Devils (or Comets) to finish with a 22-2 record. The next year saw Wolf Lake's team reel off 21 straight regular-season victories before losing their only game 26-24 in overtime to LaGrange in the first round of the Kendallville Sectional after a nasty flu bug had laid low most of the starting five.

In 1942 the Wolves captured the Kendallville Sectional by defeating Wolcottville 34-31, Shipshewana 35-24, the home team 28-13, and Albion 39-23. They then moved down to Ft. Wayne for the Regional, and after getting by the Butler Windmills 31-27 they accomplished a major upset by soundly trouncing the number-3 team in the state, Ft. Wayne Central, by a 39-24 count, finishing the Tigers' fine season with a 23-3 record. (Central would win the state championship the next year with their outstanding 27-1 record for Murray Mendenhall.) Thus were the Wolves one of the smallest schools ever to qualify for the Semi-state tournament from the northeast corner of Indiana in the years of one-class basketball. At Muncie the Wolves were sent home by the Burris Owls, who would go on to finish runner-up to the repeating State Champion Washington Hatchets at the Butler Fieldhouse. That season ended with an outstanding record of 27-2, with the only regular season loss coming at the hands of an alumni team, 29-27, in overtime at midseason! Cliff tells me that there are still many in Noble County who will swear that the flu-sidelined 1941 Wolves were actually even better than the 1942 regional champs.

The Lost Schools of Marion County

The IHSAA Membership History compiled by Ward and Gladys Brown and published in 1984 indicates that up until 1983 there had been 51 Marion County high schools with memberships in the association. Most fielded basketball teams, some for a short time, others for quite a few years. The Catholic schools that have closed have been covered elsewhere. Here is what we know about those lost public schools:

Acton, on the southeast side fielded teams from 1914-37. We know their teams were called Oreos, Redbirds, and finally Wildcats before consolidating into Franklin Central. Their last game was a 27-22 loss to Beech Grove in the first round of the 1937 Indianapolis Sectional.

Bunker Hill, near Acton, joined them in 1927 after 5 years of fielding their own teams.

Castleton, now an immense shopping mall on the far northeast side, fielded its teams called the Comets in blue and grey uniforms from 1916–41 prior to consolidating into Lawrence Central. In 1915 the Comets won 4 games and lost only 1. Their final game was a loss to New Augusta, 43-32, in the 1941 Indianapolis Sectional.

Cumberland, an historic town east of Indianapolis on the National Road, fielded teams from 1916–24. Their final game in the Indianapolis Sectional was a 20-14 loss to Arsenal Tech.

Although Fishers is generally and currently associated entirely with Hamilton County, apparently there was once also a Fishers High School in Marion County. Other than their membership in the IHSAA from 1917–21 I can find no data on them.

The Lawrence Lions roamed the northeast side of Marion County from 1914 until 1941, when they were merged with Castleton and Oaklandon to form Lawrence Central. Lawrence teams wore red and white uniforms and their final game was a loss to Shortridge in the 1941 Sectional.

New Augusta, northwest of the city, fielded the Red Devils from 1913 until being consolidated into Pike Township High School in 1944. In 1914, coached by Russell Hoffman, New Augusta made it to the finals at Indiana University where they upended Martinsville 22-18 and New Castle 8-6 before being sent home by the Rochester Zebras. In their final Sectional appearance, the Devils were assigned to Lebanon where they ousted Advance 56-40 before losing their last game to the home team Tigers, 31-27.

New Bethel, on the far southeast side of Indianapolis, also called their teams the Red Devils, and they fielded basketball teams from 1912 until 1937 when they, too, were consolidated into Franklin Central. Their colors were Purdue's, Old Gold and Black. In their final year at the Indianapolis Sectional New Bethel acquitted themselves quite well, defeating Castleton's Comets 36-17 before losing to Ben Davis, 42-25.

Oaklandon, on the east side, fielded teams called the Oaks. They played basketball from 1912 until 1940, when they were consolidated into Lawrence Central. In 1912 the Green and White made it to one of four district tournaments, the winners of which were designated to go to Bloomington for the Final Four of the state tournament. At the Indianapolis YMCA Oaklandon was defeated by Richmond 31-14. In their final sectional appearance in 1940 they were defeated by Warren Central 35-28.

Valley Mills teams, mascot unknown, wore blue and white and competed from 1915 until 1931 when they were consolidated into Warren Central. Their final Sectional appearance was a first round loss to Southport, 23-15 in 1931.

West Newton was a community in the southwest corner of Marion County that was founded by Quakers. We have no record of colors or mascots but do know they won 10 of 16 games in 1916. They were consolidated into Decatur Central in 1931 and in their final Sectional appearance they defeated Lawrence 17-16 before losing to Southport 28-22. West Newton did produce Hall of Famer Murray Mendenhall, whose citation is as follows:

Murray Mendenhall—High School: West Newton 1918

College: DePauw 1922 Inducted 1964
Won 418 and lost 153 during 23-year high
school coaching career ...coached 4 sports at Fort

Wayne Central, winning state basketball championship in 1943... won 10 sectionals, 8 regionals, and 4 semistate...coached Fort Wayne Zollner Pistons 2 yrs & Anderson Packers 3 yrs, winning National Basketball League title with that team in '48-'49...was named league's coach of the year the previous season...at De-Pauw University, starred 3 years for a team that lost only 8 games in the span, beating such teams as IU, Purdue & Notre Dame... named best college player in 1922...played semi-pro football & pro basketball.

Freelandville Follow-Up

The frontispiece shows a picture of the 1941 Freelandville team that won the Vincennes Sectional in 1941, marking the first time since 1921 that the Alices had not emerged as champions in their own gym. That team, representing a school with a total of 56 students (considerably fewer than Milan's enrollment of 161 in 1954), made it to the finals of the Washington Regional, losing to the home team in the Hatchet House, which was hardly a disgrace because Washington went on to win the Indiana state championship trophy that year.

We raised the question of what happened to those fine young men whose world was turned upside down just nine months later with the Japanese attack on Pearl Harbor. One of the players, Bob Jones, got in touch with me after reading *Hoosiers All* and provided me with the answers. We collaborated on an article published in the Fall 2012 issue of the *Indiana Basketball History Magazine,* with some more facts about the stirring season for the Fighting (not Flying, per Bob Jones, as I had written) Dutchmen and what had in fact happened to those young men. Only one died in the war, a pilot, lost in a training accident. Three were exempt, farmers in an essential industry. Most served in the army, Bob and his brother in Europe, where they were reunited shortly after Christmas 1944 in a foxhole in Germany near the Luxembourg border with shrapnel and bombs exploding above and around them, truly Hollywood-like. After the war all had successful lives. Bob, now 87, and his wife Vera, live in Edwardsport not far from where the Freelandville High School once stood. The memories of that 1941 basketball tournament continue to shine brightly.

BOB, left, and GEORGE JONES

A Further Word about the Mt. Vernon Marauders

Fortville is named for Cephas Fort, an early settler who was instrumental in bringing the New York Central Railroad to the Hancock County community located in Vernon Township. Mt. Vernon High School was formed in 1963 when the Mt. Comfort Buccaneers were merged with the Vernon Township Vikings, the latter a 1959 consolidation of the Fortville Demons and the McCordsville Pirates. The Mt. Vernon Marauders received some mention on page 379. Here's more: The Marauders were coached by Jimmy Howell (who would later lead Lapel to the Class A state championship in 2005) from 1982 through 1995. The odd years were very good ones for Howell's teams from 1983-87, 20-4, 21-7 and 22-4 with three Sectional titles and the 1987 New Castle Regional crown, that title won by defeating the Rushville Lions 77-54. They reached the finals of the Indianapolis Semi-state by ousting Pike 63-56 before losing to eventual state runner-up Richmond by a 77-67 count. From 1990-92 Howell's squads went 20-4, 22-6 and 22-3, a three year record of 64 wins and only 13 losses, cutting down three more sectional nets and the 1991 New Castle Regional nets, the latter with a 55-49 victory over North Decatur. After edging Richmond 75-73 at the Indianapolis Semi-state the Marauders again lost to state runner-up, this time being sent back to Fortville by the Alan Henderson-led Brebeuf Jesuit Braves. All told the boys teams have won 11 sectional crowns to go with their two regional championships.

The Lady Marauders were very strong in the first years of the Indiana girls official state championships, winning 71 games and losing only 8 from 1976-78. Coached by Carolyn Oldfather and led by Hall of Famer Barbara Skinner they turned in successive undefeated regular seasons of 29-1 in 1977 and 20-1 the next year. Sectional titles were won every year from 1976 through 1979 with Regional crowns in 1977 and 1978 and the program's sole Semi-state title in 1977. Tom Earlywine was the Lady Marauder coach from 1980-1991 and his last 3 teams ran up 20-4, 18-4 and 20-3 records, 58-11, with two Regional crowns in the three year period. More recently Julie Shelton's 2000 team turned in an excellent 22-2 season with her 2005 edition bringing home both Regional and Sectional titles. In total the girls teams have won 13 sectionals, 7 Regionals and 2 Semi-states, the latter in 2012 at the 3A level. In the state championship game Coach Shelton's team was edged 42-39 by Ft. Wayne Concordia and finished the season 23-6.

Barbara Skinner
Led Mt. Vernon High School, Fortville to a four year mark of 71-8 ... named to the Indiana All-Star team ... at Butler University earned 8 varsity letters, scored 1,448 points and averaged 14.5 points, 509 career assists ... held 16 individual records at Butler when she graduated ... 1983 MVP led her team to an 88-12 four year record with three national tournament appearances ... AIAW State Tournament "All-Tournament Team" twice ... Barbara and sister, Liz, were first females inducted into Butler University Hall of Fame 1998 ...

Our New Champions

Since the publication of the first edition of *Hoosiers All* in August of 2009 we have crowned 12 Indiana Boys State Champions and 12 Indiana Girls State Champions. Twenty-four teams have likewise captured runner-up trophies and there have been 48 Semi-state winners, 96 Regional champs, and 384 Sectional titlists. Such are the mathematics of two four-class basketball tournaments per year. It has not been possible for us to update all of these numbers in the text, so the figures there still apply as of the end of the 2009 season. However, it is notable that Park Tudor not only won their first ever boys basketball state championship, but they won two, back to back in 2011 and 2012, 2A titles after coming oh, so close in 2010. The Panthers, led by Indiana All Star and IU recruit Yogi Farrell and coached by Ed Schilling, were a team with at least four Division I recruits whom many knowledgeable observers have said might well have given 4A champions Carmel a very good game, thus adding grist to the single class basketball enthusiasts in our state. Our champions, runners-up and the final game scores in the past three seasons are as follows:

Boys:

2010	4A Indianapolis North Central	95	Warsaw	74
	3A Washington	65	Gary Lew Wallace	62 (ot)
	2A Wheeler	41	Park Tudor	38
	A Bowman Academy	74	Barr-Reeve	52
2011	4A Bloomington South	56	Kokomo	42
	3A Washington	61	Culver Academies	46
	2A Park Tudor	43	Hammond Bishop Noll	42
	A Indianapolis Metropolitan	59	Triton	55
2012	4A Carmel	80	Indianapolis Pike	67
	3A Guerin Catholic	64	Norwell	48
	2A Park Tudor	79	Bowman Academy	57
	A Loogootee	55	Rockville	52

Girls:

2010	4A Ben Davis	99	Merrillville	52
	3A Ft. Wayne Concordia	59	Rushville	48
	2A Austin	70	Ft. Wayne Bishop Luers	65 (ot)
	A Ft. Wayne Canterbury	69	Vincennes Rivet	65
2011	4A Jeffersonville	43	Penn	29
	3A Evansville Memorial	58	Benton Central	50 (ot)
	2A Ft. Wayne Bishop Luers	59	Brownstown Central	46
	A Vincennes Rivet	49	Turkey Run	40
2012	4A Indianapolis North Central	50	Columbus North	48 (ot)
	3A Ft. Wayne Concordia	42	Mt. Vernon (Fortville)	39
	2A Evansville Mater Dei	56	Ft. Wayne Luers	52 (ot)
	A Ft. Wayne Canterbury	64	Northeast Dubois	54

The Washington Hatchets also won two state titles over this three-year period, adding to their already bulging trophy case, thanks in large part to the contributions of the third member of the Zeller family, current IU star Cody. In addition to Park Tudor as first-time champions were long time contenders the Wheeler Bearcats and the Loogootee Lions as well as newer schools the Bowman Academy Eagles, the Indianapolis Metropolitan Pumas, and the Guerin Catholic Golden Eagles.

On the girls side, the Ft. Wayne Canterbury Lady Cavaliers won two more state titles (three of the last four state championship nets now reside in their trophy case) as did their neighbors the Concordia Lutheran Lady Cadets. First time champions were the Evansville Mater Dei Lady Wildcats, Jeffersonville Lady Red Devils, Austin Lady Eagles, and Vincennes Rivet Lady Patriots.

It should also be noted that when Stan Benge's Ben Davis team won the 2010 championship with a 28-0 record it represented consecutive undefeated seasons, going with their previous mark of 30-0. The Lady Giants went on to win the first 23 games of the next season before losing their only game, to Carmel 65-62, in the Regional final. This brought their undefeated streak to 81 and their undefeated regular season streak to 91.

It should be mentioned that several schools over this period also achieved significant milestones. The Frankton Eagles, coached by Brent Bobster won that school's first-ever Sectional crown as chronicled so well by Roger Dickinson's article in the Spring 2012 issue of the *Indiana Basketball History Magazine*.

A Word About Class Basketball

In the years from 1911 until the last one class tournament in 1997, we crowned 87 boys teams as state champions, representing only 47 different schools out of the 1200 or so who had tried. Many hundreds of those who tried never even were able to win a Sectional title. The IHSAA lists 157 schools that won just one Sectional crown. In the 15 years since the inception of class basketball, the IHSAA has already awarded state championship plaques to 60 teams representing 45 different schools, 6 of which were champions during the single class era, providing first-time trophies to 39 schools.

On the girls side, we crowned 22 official state champions between 1976 and 1997, coming from only 17 schools. Since 1998 there have also been 60 girls teams that have won the title of state champion, representing 37 schools with only one repeat from non-class days. Clearly, class basketball has spread the wealth and perhaps that was one of the desired goals. At the same time it has to some extent reduced the value of the title "Indiana State Champion." Is the trade off worth it? Who knows, but I have yet to hear any player from any winning team complain about their state championship!

Would a return to single-class tournaments bring back the crowds of well over 1,000,000 fans who attended the boys tournament in earlier years or put 41,046 in the seats as occurred when Damon Bailey's Bedford North Lawrence stars won their title in 1990 over the previously undefeated Concord Minutemen in the Hoosier Dome? Or 16,622 for a girls finals in Market Square Arena like that of 1989 when Renee Westmoreland led her Scottsburg Lady Warriors to a thrilling overtime victory over an excellent Benton Central Lady Bison team?

Those are records other states only dream about, and they may well never be attained again here, either. Wendell Trogdon has detailed the many reasons for this other than class basketball in his book *Who Killed Hoosier Hysteria?* Society is different now. To me, though, our tournaments remain a high point in any athletic year and they are still the envy of many other states. Are there any better days of high school basketball anywhere than our present Final Fours, when eight of our top boys and girls teams strive to win their own class championship? It will take some convincing to get me to believe that there is.

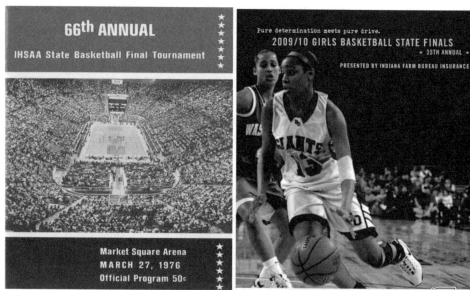

A Final Word About the Title of My Book

One of the goals of writing *Hoosiers All* was to preserve in one place the many team names that have existed and still exist for all of the schools that ever played basketball in Indiana. Some schools as far as we have been able to discover, never did select a special team name for their hardwood heroes, but most did, especially after it became the common thing to do sometime in the mid-20s probably. But my theory was and is that whatever we call ourselves, from Alices to Zebras, at the end of the day we're all Hoosiers. I have to chuckle, though, when I remind myself of a conversation I had about this book with Ralph Taylor, former Washington Continental and Purdue Boilermaker great. Ralph, I have discovered as I have grown to know him, is a sensitive, intelligent, engaging man whom anyone would be proud to count among their friends. He was then president of the Hall of Fame, and he came up to me and told me he enjoyed my book, but he wished I had called it *Boilers All* instead of *Hoosiers All*. I replied that even Boilers were Hoosiers, and he agreed with a smile. So, Hoosiers all we are, and I, for one, am proud of it…but I still love the Boilers equally well!

Ralph Taylor and Billy Kelly with the 1965 state championship trophy, Indianapolis Washington 64, Ft. Wayne Northside 57.

What We Still Don't Know

There are still several schools about which we have very little or no data. We encourage anyone who does to pass the information on to the Hall of Fame in New Castle.

Algiers Pike County Owls consolidated Otwell 1926
Allen Township Miami County Yellow Jackets consolidated Macy 1933
Bentonville Fayette County Trojans black & gold consolidated Connersville 1953
Boxley Hamilton County black & orange consolidated Sheridan 1932 (4-2 in 1912)
Bringhurst Caroll County consolidated Flora 1928 (8-3 in 1916)
Cates Fountain County possibly Clippers blue & white consolidated Kingman 1925
Clark Township Johnson County Lions blue & white consolidated Whiteland 1965
Concord Township DeKalb County Tigers orange & black consolidated Riverdale 1953
Clinton Township Putnam County Yellow Jackets consolidated Bainbridge 1947
Deedsville Warriors black & gold consolidated Oil Twp/Tell City 1937
Evansville Douglass 1926–29 consolidated into Evansville Lincoln
Granger St. Joseph County consolidated Mishawaka 1931
Marion Township Jennings County Panthers red & white consolidated Paris Crossing 1940
Marion St. Paul (1942–54) succeeded by Marion Bennet until 1993
Needham Township Johnson County purple & white consolidated Franklin 1939
Osceola St. Joseph County consolidated Penn 1924
South Bend Catholic (1942–53) consolidated South Bend St. Joseph's
South Bend Central Catholic (1942–52) consolidated South Bend St. Joseph's
South Bend St. Mary's (1974–76) consolidated South Bend St. Joseph's
Springfield Township Indians consolidated Michigan City Elston 1950
Teegarden Marshall County consolidated Walkerton (St. Joseph County) 1925
Union Township LaPorte County Tigers blue & gold consolidated LaPorte 1965
Union Township Perry County green & white consolidated Oil Twp/Tell City 1938
Valley Mills Marion County (1913–31) blue and white Comets consolidated Warren Central
Warren Township (1932-37) St. Joseph County students spread to New Carlisle,
    South Bend Washington, South Bend Wilson
Waterloo Fayette County consolidated Alquina/Connersville 1920

ALL TIME INDIANA GIRLS ALL STARS

Here is my all time Indiana Girls All Star Team. I'll announce my starting lineup at game time. What's yours?
Top Row: LaTaunya Pollard, Gary Roosevelt; Amber Harris, Indianapolis North Central; Amy Metheny, MD, Southport. Second Row: Bria Goss, Ben Davis; Sharon Versyp, Mishawaka; Katie Gearlds, Beech Grove; Judi Warren, Warsaw; Shanna Zollman, Wawasee. Third Row: Shyra Ely, Ben Davis; Skylar Diggins, South Bend Washington/Clay; Stephanie White, Seeger; Tonya Burns, Leo; Ta'Shia Phillips, Brebeuf Jesuit. Fourth Row: Carol Blauvelt, Heritage; Teri Rosinski, Norwell; Katie Douglas, Perry Meridian; Jodi Whitaker, Austin (I have selected only girls who played from 1976 on for this team).

INDIANA ALL TIME ALL STAR BOYS TEAM

Here is my all time Indiana boys basketball All Star team. I'll disclose my starting lineup at game time. What's yours?

Top Row: Clyde Lovellette, Terre Haute Garfield; Damon Bailey, Bedford North Lawrence; Oscar Robertson, Indianapolis Crispus Attucks; Greg Oden, Lawrence North. Second Row: George McGinnis, Indianapolis Washington; Scott Skiles, Plymouth; Eric Gordon, Indianapolis North Central; Don Schlundt, South Bend Washington/Clay; Charles "Stretch" Murphy, Marion. Third Row: Terry Dischinger, Terre Haute Garfield; Ray Pavy, New Castle; Johnny Wooden, Martinsville; Larry Bird, Springs Valley; Steve Alford, New Castle; Homer Stonebraker, Wingate. Fourth Row: Robert "Fuzzy" Vandivier, Franklin; Rick Mount, Lebanon; Glenn Robinson, Gary Roosevelt; Calbert Cheaney, Evansville Harrison.